Understanding Art

ARS 100

Lois Fichner-Rathus

CENGAGE
Learning™

Australia • Brazil • Japan • Korea • Mexico • Singapore • Spain • United Kingdom • United States

Understanding Art: ARS 100

UNDERSTANDING ART, NINTH EDITION
Lois Fichner-Rathus

Executive Editors:
 Maureen Staudt
 Michael Stranz

Senior Project Development Manager:
 Linda deStefano

Marketing Specialist:
 Courtney Sheldon

Senior Production/Manufacturing Manager:
 Donna M. Brown

PreMedia Manager:
 Joel Brennecke

Sr. Rights Acquisition Account Manager:
 Todd Osborne

Cover Image:
Getty Images*

*Unless otherwise noted, all cover images used by Custom Solutions, a part of Cengage Learning, have been supplied courtesy of Getty Images with the exception of the Earthview cover image, which has been supplied by the National Aeronautics and Space Administration (NASA).

For product information and technology assistance, contact us at
Cengage Learning Customer & Sales Support, 1-800-354-9706

For permission to use material from this text or product, submit all requests online at **cengage.com/permissions**
Further permissions questions can be emailed to
permissionrequest@cengage.com

This book contains select works from existing Cengage Learning resources and was produced by Cengage Learning Custom Solutions for collegiate use. As such, those adopting and/or contributing to this work are responsible for editorial content accuracy, continuity and completeness.

Compilation © 2010 Cengage Learning
ISBN-13: 978-1-111-77430-1

ISBN-10: 1-111-77430-7

Cengage Learning
5191 Natorp Boulevard
Mason, Ohio 45040
USA
Cengage Learning is a leading provider of customized learning solutions with office locations around the globe, including Singapore, the United Kingdom, Australia, Mexico, Brazil, and Japan. Locate your local office at:
international.cengage.com/region.

Cengage Learning products are represented in Canada by Nelson Education, Ltd.
For your lifelong learning solutions, visit **www.cengage.com/custom.**
Visit our corporate website at **www.cengage.com.**

Printed in the United States of America

Table of Contents

(*Note – this is a "custom" textbook that has been designed specifically for this course in a joint effort between your instructor and the publisher. Please note that some chapters have been removed intentionally and some pages may be black & white as dictated by the changes.)

PREFACE

■
—

Everyone wants to understand art. Why not try to understand the song of a bird?
Why does one love the night, flowers, everything around one without trying
to understand them? But in the case of a painting, people have to understand.
— Pablo Picasso

There is a note of frustration in Picasso's statement, reflecting perhaps the burden of having to explain his paintings to viewers who were trying desperately to understand them. Perhaps he was concerned that some of the "indescribable" in art—that which mesmerizes, enchants, frightens, and delights—would be, quite literally, lost in translation. Maybe he was guarding against affixing meaning to his work that he as the artist never intended. Picasso seems to suggest, in this quote, that mystery enhances experience and that too much knowledge will compromise the authenticity of the relationship between art and the viewer. Do you think Picasso was right?

Here we are, together, embarking on the study of art and art history between the covers of a book called *Understanding Art*. Maybe we can declare Picasso's view half right, and it can serve as our cue for how to confront what we are about to see. A textbook on art is not like a textbook in other academic disciplines. Yes, there is a special vocabulary of art. Yes, this vocabulary is woven into a language that, once learned, enables us to better verbalize the visual. But the most important aspect of an art book is its images, because a student's journey toward understanding art ought to always begin with looking.

Think of this art appreciation textbook as your "*i*-book"—it begins with looking at *i*mages. Having said that, *learning to look* is equally important for art appreciation, and that's where some other "*i*-words" play an important role: *i*nformation, *i*nsight, and *i*nterpretation. We gather information about how a work of art is conceived and constructed using elements, design principles, composition, content, style, and symbolism. We explore the motives of artists and the historical, social, political, and even personal contexts in which a work of art came into existence. These investigations will lend insight into the complex factors contributing to the creation of works of art. And as we gather confidence in our knowledge and insights, we will turn more comfortably to the dimension of interpretation—your dimension. It is here where the "I" really counts, for we all bring the weight of our own experience to our interpretations, our unique perceptions to our likes or dislikes of a work of art.

Picasso said, in the same interview, "People who try to explain pictures are usually barking up the wrong tree." The words *explain* and *understand,* though, have very different meanings. One can argue that only artists can *explain* their work, can make intelligible something that is not known or not understood. But *understanding* is defined as full awareness or knowledge that is arrived at through an intellectual or emotional process—including the ability to extract meaning or to interpret. The ability to *appreciate,* or to perceive the value or worth of something from a discriminating perspective, then, is the consummate reward of understanding.

What's New in This Edition

The ninth edition of *Understanding Art* contains two new chapters, one on Site-Specific Art (Chapter 10), the other on Art in the Twenty-First Century: A Global Perspective (Chapter 22). Site-specific art is typically produced in or for a single location and is not intended to be relocated. Chapter 10 shows how such works range from the ephemeral, as in small sculptures of rapidly melting ice, to large enduring works, such as stone walls and jetties. Chapter 22 illustrates how artists across the globe are informed by their cultural and national traditions, their artistic training, their knowledge of the political world at large, and their awareness of the art world around them—past and present. We see how globalization has struck the world of art, widening artists' perspectives, yet how artists have also managed to hold fast to many local ideas and ideals.

As you peruse the pages, you will also notice a new pedagogical tool: Works are accompanied by scales that provide an immediate sense of the size of the art.

The ninth edition also has many new works of art. In many cases, improved prints or photographs of works shown in earlier editions were obtained. There are also, as we shall see, a number of new A Closer Look and Compare and Contrast features.

The Approach of *Understanding Art*

The ninth edition of *Understanding Art,* as earlier editions, remains a textbook that is intended to work for both students and professors. *Understanding Art* continues to serve as a tool to help organize and enlighten this demanding, often whirlwind-like course. My goal has been to write a book that would do it all: edify and inform students and, at the same time, keep them engaged, animated, and inspired while meeting the desire of instructors for comprehensive exposition. All in all, *Understanding Art* contains a fully balanced approach to appreciating art. The understanding and appreciation of art are enhanced by familiarity with three areas of art: the language of art (visual elements, principles of design, and style), the nature of the media used in art, and the history of art.

Features

The ninth edition of *Understanding Art* contains unique features that stimulate student interest, emphasize key points in art fundamentals and art history, highlight contemporary events in art, and reflect the ways in which professors teach.

Compare + Contrast   These features show two or more works of art side by side and phrase questions that help students focus on stylistic and technical similarities and differences. They parallel the time-honored pedagogical technique of presenting slides in class for comparison and contrast. For example, "Compare and Contrast Wood's *American Gothic* with Rosenthal's *He Said . . . She Said*" in Chapter 4 shows how artists may use different styles to illustrate themes about similar subjects.

Exercises on ArtExperince Online include interactive exercises directly linked to all the Compare + Contrast features.

A Closer Look   These features offer insights into artists' personalities and delve into various topics in greater depth. In Chapter 5, "Life, Death, and Dwelling in the Deep South" highlights an African American artist's portrayal of the organic relationship between a woman and her home in South Carolina. In Chapter 19, "Why Did van Gogh Cut Off His Ear?" offers a number of explanations, including psychodynamic hypotheses, for why the Postimpressionist mutilated himself. Visit the Storm King Art Center, a 500-acre sculpture garden in New York in Chapter 9.

A Closer Look is also expanded upon further through ArtExperience Online.

ArtTour   The ninth edition includes eight ArtTours on the cities of New York, Washington D.C., Jerusalem, Rome, Dallas/Fort Worth, Florence, London, and Paris. Each ArtTour is rich in photographs and works of art. The ArtTours are no mere lists of works and sites and museums in these cities. Instead, the tours literally walk students through the cities, providing them with routes they can take to benefit from the cultural riches that are available. The ArtTours in New York, Washington, D.C., and Dallas/Fort Worth will help many students appreciate the art and architecture that are situated close to home.

The companion ArtExperience Online expands on the ArtTours with helpful "travel-guide" information, such as additional photos, maps, restaurant guides, and links to useful web pages. The tours are meant to encourage students to travel as well as to guide them once they have reached their destinations.

Quotations   Quotations at the top of pages by artists, critics, and others allow students to "get into the minds" of artists and others in the art world. For example, Chapter 22, Art in the Twenty-First Century, includes quotations by Damien Hirst, Zhang Huan, and Kara Walker.

Glossary   Key terms are boldfaced in the text and defined in a glossary at the end of the textbook. A "Talking Glossary" also appears on the companion website.

The Contents of the Ninth Edition of *Understanding Art*

The ninth edition of *Understanding Art* contains many new artists and their works including Prajakta Palav Aher, Alexandre Arrechea, Alice Aycock, Gustave Caillebotte, Enrique Chagoya, Nathan Coley, John Singleton Copley, Walter de Maria, Jean Ulrick Désert, Rineke Dijkstra, Peter Eisenman, Viola Frey, Thomas Gainsborough, Andy Goldsworthy, Wang Gongxin, Rody Graumans, Walter Gropius, Cai Guo-Qiang, Palmer Hayden, Michael Heizer, Herzog & De Meuron, Zhang Huan, Ali Muhammad Kashigar Isfahani, Emily Jacir, Adil Jain, Wu Jide, Inigo Jones, Menashe Kadishman, Anish Kapoor, Gitte Kath, Liz Magic Laser, Alexander Liberman, Fang Lijun, Hew Locke, Martina López, The Luo Brothers, Mariko Mori, Vik Muniz, Takashi Murakmi, Emily Mary Osborn, Pipilotti Rist, Kay

Sage, Paula Scher, Yinka Shonibare, Charles Simonds, Philippe Starck, Emma Stebbins, Friedrich St. Florian, Mart Di Suvero, Betty Woodman, Zhang Xiaogang, and Akira Yamaguchi.

The book is organized into the following parts:

I. Introduction   The first chapter of the text, "What Is Art?" helps the student arrive at a definition of art by discussing the things that art does, from enhancing our environment to protesting injustice and raising social consciousness.

II. The Language of Art   Chapters 2–4 provide comprehensive discussion of the visual elements of art, principles of design, and style, form, and content. The language of art is then applied throughout the remainder of the text in discussions of media and surveys of art through the ages and throughout the world.

III. Two-Dimensional Media   Chapters 5–8—on drawing, painting, printmaking, and imaging—explain how artists combine the visual elements of art to create two-dimensional compositions. The media discussed are as traditional as drawing a pencil across a sheet of paper and as innovative as spray painting color fields and clicking a mouse to access a menu of electronic techniques and design elements.

IV. Three-Dimensional Media   Chapters 9–12 discuss the opportunities and issues provided by three-dimensional art forms, including sculpture, a new chapter on site-specific art, architecture, and craft and design.

V. Art Through the Ages   Chapters 13–18 contain a solid core of art history on the development of art from ancient times to the dawn of the modern era. Chapter 18, "Art Beyond the West," introduces students to art forms Beyond the Western tradition, for example, the art of Africa, the South Pacific, and the Americas; the Islamic art of the Near, Middle, and Far East; Indian art; and the art of China and Japan. The chapter offers a broadening experience, as students learn that much of this art cannot be appreciated by means of the same concepts and standards that are applied to Western Art.

VI. Art in Modern and Postmodern Times   Chapters 19–21 examine the great changes that have occurred in the world of art since the late eighteenth century. These chapters attempt to answer the question, "Just what is modern about modern art?" Whereas some artists have rejected the flatness of the canvas and moved art into innumerable new directions, some have maintained traditional paths. Controversy and conflict are part of the modern history of art. But movements such as Postmodern art and Deconstructivist architecture also make it possible to speak of the "modern world and beyond." Although nobody can say exactly where art is going, these chapters discuss the various movements and works that appear to be most vital at the current moment.

Art in the Twenty-First Century: A Global Perspective

New Chapter 22 shows how the phenomenon of globalization has created a new art world in which cultures are no longer distant from one another and people and places are no longer separate as they once were. As a result, we have trends such as hybridity, appropriation, high art and low culture, and post-colonialism in the arts. We see how these trends are expressed today within—and without—various cultural traditions around the world.

Student Resources

ArtExperience Online

New platform, new design, the ArtExperience Online provides access to additional resources through the **flashcards** of images in the text. Use flashcards to study for exams, and learn more about each work through links to quizzing, related video, audio, websites, interactive tutorials and exercises, and ArtTours. Videos include demonstrations of various studio art techniques, YouTube clips, topical video podcasts, and three dimensional panoramic views of architecture.

Companion Website

The companion site contains chapter-based study tools including: critical thinking questions, crossword puzzles, essay quizzes, internet exercises, tutorial quizzing, flashcards, and glossaries.

Thinking and Writing about Art

Thinking and Writing about Art, also written by Lois Fichner-Rathus, enhances students' critical thinking and interpretive skills.

SlideGuide

The SlideGuide is a student lecture companion that allows students to take notes alongside representations of the art images shown in class. It features reproductions of the images from the book with full captions, page numbers, and space for note-taking.

Instructor Resources

PowerLecture with Digital Image Library and JoinIn

This lecture and class preparation tool makes it easy for you to assemble, edit, and present customized lectures using Microsoft PowerPoint. Use these presentations as they are or edit them, adding your own notes and images to personalize your presentation. The PowerLecture also includes a Resource Integration Guide, an electronic Instructor's Manual, and a Test Bank with multiple-choice, matching, short-answer, and essay questions in ExamView® computerized format. Use JoinIn on Turning Point® software for classroom personal response systems ("clickers").

Bring **digital images** into the classroom with this class presentation tool that makes it easy to assemble, edit, and present customized lectures for your course using Microsoft® PowerPoint®. Available on DVD, PowerLecture with Digital Image Library provides high-resolution images (maps, diagrams, and the fine art images from the text) for lecture presentations, either in an easy-to-use PowerPoint presentation format, or in individual file formats compatible with other image-viewing software. A zoom feature allows you to magnify selected portions of an image for more detailed display in class or you can display images side by side for comparison and contrast. You can easily customize your classroom presentation by adding your own images to those from the text.

WebTutor™ on Blackboard and WebCT

WebTutor on WebCT and Blackboard is easy and efficient to use, combining course management with textbook content in a flexible format that enables you to assign pre-formatted, text-specific content that is available as soon as you log on or customize its environment in any way you choose—from uploading images and other resources, to adding Web links, to creating your own practice materials.

Acknowledgments

I consider myself fortunate to have studied with a fine group of artists, art historians, and art professionals who helped shape my love of art and my thinking about art throughout my career. *Understanding Art* would not have taken its present form and might not have come into being without the broad knowledge, skills, and dedication of James S. Ackerman, Stanford Anderson, Wayne V. Anderson, Whitney Chadwick, Michael Graves, George

Heard Hamilton, Ann Sutherland Harris, Julius S. Held, Sam Hunter, Henry A. Millon, Konrad Oberhuber, John C. Overbeck, Michael Rinehart, Andrew C. Ritchie, Mark W. Roskill, Theodore Roszak, Miriam Schapiro, Bernice Steinbaum, and Jack Tworkov.

I wish to thank those reviewers who helped in revising this edition: William P. Andrews, Mississippi State University; Laura Antonow, University of Mississippi; Kristine Beadle, Calhoun Community College; Roger J. Crum, University of Dayton; Clifford Davis, Rivier College; Beverly Dennis, Jones County Junior College; Carolyn Fox-Hearne, Kilgore College; Rosemary Goodell, Baton Rouge Community College; Stephen B. Henderson, Quinnipiac University; Sherri Hill, Manatee Community College; and Hideki Kihata, Saginaw Valley State University.

The ninth edition of *Understanding Art* is also indebted to the support and expertise of a fine group of Wadsworth publishing professionals. Let me begin by acknowledging the support of Sean Wakely, executive vice president, Cengage Arts and Sciences; Clark Baxter, Publisher; Sharon Adams Poore, Senior Development Editor; Wendy Constantine, senior media editor; Lianne Ames, senior content project manager; Kimberly Apfelbaum, assistant editor; Nell Pepper, editorial assistant; Cate Rikard Barr, senior art director; and Diane Wenckebach, senior marketing manager. I would also like to thank Sarah Evertson, Joy Westberg, Annie Beck, and Shawn Girsberger.

Lois Fichner-Rathus

About the Author

Lois Fichner-Rathus is Professor of Art in the Art Department of The College of New Jersey. She holds a combined undergraduate degree in fine arts and art history, an M.A. from the Williams College Graduate Program in the History of Art, and a Ph.D. in the History, Theory, and Criticism of Art from the Massachusetts Institute of Technology. Her areas of specialization include contemporary art, feminist art history and criticism, and modern art and architecture. She has authored grants, contributed to books, curated exhibitions, published articles in professional journals, and exhibited her large-format photographic prints. She resides in New York.

1

WHAT IS ART?

■

Everyone wants to understand art. Why not try to understand the song of a bird?
Why does one love the night, flowers, everything around one without trying to understand them?
But in the case of a painting, people have to understand.
—Pablo Picasso

Beauty, truth, immortality, order, harmony—these concepts and ideals have occupied us since the dawn of history. They enrich our lives and encourage us to extend ourselves beyond the limits of flesh and blood. Without them, life would be but a mean struggle for survival, and the value of survival would be unclear.

In the sciences and the arts, we strive to weave our experiences into coherent bodies of knowledge and to communicate them. Many of us are more comfortable with the sciences than with the arts. Science teaches us that the universe is not ruled purely by chance. The sciences provide ways of observing the world and experimenting so that we can learn what forces determine the courses of atoms and galaxies. Even those of us who do not consider ourselves "scientific" recognize that the scientific method permits us to predict and control many important events on a grand scale.

The arts are more elusive to define, more difficult to gather into a conceptual net. We would probably all agree that the arts enhance daily experience; some of us would contend that they are linked to the very quality of life. Art has touched everyone, and art is all around us. Crayon drawings, paper cutouts, and the like are part of the daily lives of our children—an integral function of both magnet and refrigerator door. We all look for art to brighten our dormitory rooms, enhance our interior decor, beautify our cities, and embellish our places of worship. We are certain that we do not want to be without the arts, yet we are hard-pressed to define them and sometimes even to understand them.

> *The beautiful is in nature, and it is encountered in the most diverse forms of reality.*
> *Once it is found, it belongs to art, or, rather, to the artist who discovers it.*
>
> —GUSTAVE COURBET

In fact, the very word *art* encompasses many meanings, including ability, process, and product. As ability, art is the human capacity to make things of beauty and things that stir us; it is creativity. As process, art encompasses acts such as drawing, painting, sculpting, designing buildings, and using the camera to create memorable works. This definition is ever expanding, as materials and methods are employed in innovative ways to bring forth a creative product. As product, art is the completed work—an etching, a sculpture, a structure, a tapestry. If as individuals we do not understand science, we are at least comforted by the thought that others do. With art, however, the experience of a work is unique. Reactions to a work will vary according to the nature of the individual, time period, place, and culture. And although we may find ourselves standing before a work of art that has us befuddled, saying, "I hate it! I don't understand it!", we suspect that there is something about the nature of art that transcends understanding.

This book is about the visual arts. Despite their often enigmatic nature, we shall try to share something of what is known about them so that understanding may begin. We do not aim to force our aesthetic preferences on you; if in the end you dislike a work as much as you did to start, that is completely acceptable. But we will aim to heighten awareness of what we respond to in a work of art and try to communicate why what an artist has done is important. In this way, you can counter with, "I hate it, but at least I understand it."

As in many areas of study—languages, computers, the sciences—amassing a basic vocabulary is intrinsic to understanding the material. You will want to be able to describe the attributes of a work of art and be able to express your reactions to it. The language or vocabulary of art includes the visual elements, principles of design, style, form, and content. We shall see how the visual elements of art, such as line, shape, and color, are composed according to principles of design into works of art with certain styles and content. We shall examine many media, including drawing, painting, printmaking, the camera and computer arts, sculpture, architecture, ceramics, and fiber arts.

When asked why we should study history, the historian answers that we must know about the past in order to have a sense of where we are and where we may be going. This argument also holds true for the arts; there is more to art history than memorizing dates! Examining a work in its historical, social, and political context will enable you to have a more meaningful dialogue with that work. You will be amazed and entertained by the ways in which the creative process has been intertwined with world events and individual personalities. We shall follow the journey of art, therefore, from the wall paintings of our Stone Age ancestors through the graffiti art of today's subway station. The media, the forms, the styles, and the subjects may evolve and change from millennium to millennium, from day to day, but uniting threads lie in the persistent quest for beauty or for truth or for self-expression.

Many philosophers have argued that art serves no function, that it exists for its own sake. Some have asserted that the essence of art transcends the human occupation with usefulness. Others have held that in trying to analyze art too closely, one loses sight of its beauty and wonderment.

These may be valid points of view. Nevertheless, our understanding and appreciation of art often can be enhanced by asking the questions "Why was this created?" and "What is its purpose?" In this section, we shall see that works of art come into existence for a host of reasons that are as varied as the human condition. Perhaps we will not arrive at a single definition of art, but we can come to understand art by considering our relationship to it.

ART AND BEAUTY

Art and beauty have been long intertwined. At times, the artist has looked to nature as the standard of beauty and has thus imitated it. At other times, the artist has thought to improve upon nature, developing an alternative standard—an idealized form. Standards of beauty in and of themselves are by no means universal. The Classical Greeks were obsessed with their idea of beauty and fashioned mathematical formulas for rendering the human body in sculpture so that it would achieve a majesty and perfection unknown in nature. The sixteenth-century artist Leonardo da Vinci, in what is perhaps the most famous painting in the history of Western art, enchants generations of viewers with the eternal beauty and mysteriousness of the smiling *Mona*

1-1 LEONARDO DA VINCI.

Mona Lisa (c. 1503–1505).

Oil on wood panel. 30¼" × 21".

Louvre Museum, Paris/©Réunion des
Musées Nationaux/Art Resource, NY

1 in.

1-2 Kenyan woman, Masai tribe.

Standards for beauty can differ from culture to culture.

©Jim Zuckerman/CORBIS.

Lisa (Fig. **1-1**). But appreciation of the stately repose and refined features of this Italian woman is tied to a Western concept of beauty. Elsewhere in the world, these features might seem alien, unattractive, or undesirable. On the other hand, the standard of beauty in some non-Western societies that hold scarification, body painting, tattooing, and adornment (Fig. **1-2**) both beautiful and sacred may seem odd and unattractive to someone from the Western world. One art form need not be seen as intrinsically superior to the other; in these works, quite simply, beauty is in the eye of the society's beholder.

ART AND OUR ENVIRONMENT

We have all decided at one time or another to change the color of our bedrooms. We have hung a poster or painting here rather than there, and we have arranged a vase of flowers or placed a potted plant in just the right spot in the room. We may not have created works of art, but we did manage to delight our senses and turn our otherwise ordinary environments into more pleasurable havens.

A Portrait in the Flesh

FOR CENTURIES, ARTISTS have devoted their full resources, their lives, to their work. Orlan has also offered her pound of flesh—to the surgeon's scalpel. Orlan (Fig. **1-3**) is a French multimedia performance artist who has been undergoing a series of cosmetic operations to create, in herself, a composite sketch of what Western art has long set forth as the pinnacle of human beauty: the facial features that we find in classic works such as Botticelli's *The Birth of Venus* (Fig. **1-4**), Leonardo's *Mona Lisa* (Fig. 1-1), and Boucher's *Europa,* or, more specifically, Venus's chin, the Mona Lisa's forehead, and Europa's mouth.

Most people undergo cosmetic surgery in private, but not Orlan. Several of her operations have been performances or media events. Her first series of operations were carried out in France and Belgium. The operating rooms were filled with symbols of flowering womanhood in a form compatible with medicine: sterilized plastic fruit.

There were huge photos of Orlan, and the surgeons and their assistants were decked out not in surgical greens but in costumes created by celebrated couturiers. A recent operation was performed in the New York office of a cosmetic surgeon and transmitted via satellite to the Sandra Gering Gallery in the city's famed SoHo district. Orlan did not lie unconscious in a hospital gown. Rather, she lay awake in a long, black dress and read from a work on psychoanalysis while the surgeon implanted silicone in her face to imitate the protruding forehead of *Mona Lisa.*

When will it all end? Orlan says that "I will stop my work when it is as close as possible to the computer composite,'" as the lips of Europa split into a smile. ∎

* Margalit Fox, "A Portrait in Skin and Bone," *New York Times*, November 21, 1993, V8.

1-3 French performance artist Orlan, who has dedicated herself to embodying Western classic beauty as found in the works of Leonardo, Botticelli, and Boucher through multiple plastic surgeries. Here Orlan is being "prepped" for one in a series of operations.
©2009 Orlan/Artists Rights Society (ARS), New York/ADAGP, Paris.

1-4 Detail from *The Birth of Venus*, 1486 by Sandro Botticelli.
Detail. Tempera on canvas. 5'8⅞" × 9'1½".
Uffizi Gallery, Florence.
©Scala/Art Resource, NY

1-5 JOYCE KOZLOFF.
Galla Placidia in Philadelphia
(1985).
Mosaic installation. 13' × 16'.
Penn Center Suburban Station, Philadelphia.
Courtesy of Henri Gross, Penn Associates,
Philadelphia.

1 ft.

Works of art have been used to create pleasing environments for centuries. From tapestries that adorned and insulated the cold stone walls of medieval castles to elaborate sculpted fountains that provided focal points for manicured, palatial gardens, whatever other functions they may serve, many works of art are also decorative. Joyce Kozloff's *Galla Placidia in Philadelphia* (Fig. **1-5**), a mosaic for the Penn Center Suburban Station in that city, elevates decorative patterns to the level of fine art and raises the art-historical consciousness of the casual commuter. The original Mausoleum of Galla Placidia is the fifth-century chapel and burial place of a Byzantine empress, a landmark monument known for its complex and colorful mosaics. Kozloff's own intricate and diverse designs dazzle the eye and stimulate the intellect, providing an oasis of color in an otherwise humdrum city scene.

Glass sculptor Dale Chihuly's *Fiori di Como* (Fig. **1-6**) is a 70-foot-long ceiling installation suspended above the reception area of the Bellagio Hotel in Las Vegas. Even in a city of neon and assorted trappings of excess, Chihuly's piece dazzles with its colors and textures. Reminiscent of the undulating shapes and brilliant palette of Venice's renowned murano glass, it is another set piece in the hotel's interior decor that is intended to transport its guests to that famed small town of Bellagio on the shore of Italy's spectacular Lake Como.

1-6 DALE CHIHULY.
Fiori di Como (1998).
70' × 30' × 12'.
Bellagio Hotel, Las Vegas, NV. Courtesy of Dale Chihuly, Seattle, WA.

It is the glory and good of Art,
That Art remains the one way possible
Of speaking truths, to mouths like mine at least.

—ROBERT BROWNING

ART AND TRUTH

What does it mean for art to "speak a truth"? The concept of truth in art is subjective; it can mean many and different things to each viewer. Does it mean true to nature, true to human experience, true to materials? The answer is yes to all of these and more. Art can be used to replicate nature, or reality, in the finest detail. Renaissance painters came up with techniques and devices to create a convincing illusion of three-dimensionality on two-dimensional surfaces. Artists throughout history have used their rendering skills to trick the eye into perceiving truth in imitation. Sometimes the tales of their virtuosic exploits survive the work, as in anecdotes recorded on the subject of the ancient Greek painter Apelles. In one such story, we are told that the artist, fearful that other painters might be judged more superior at realistic representation, demanded that real horses be brought before paintings of horses that were entered into a competition. When the horses began to neigh in front of Apelles' work, he received the recognition he deserved.

Artists have sought to extract universal truths by expressing their own experiences. Sometimes their pursuit has led them to beauty, at other times to shame and outrage. The "ugly truth," just like the beautiful truth, provides a valid commentary on the human condition.

In her self-portraits, the Mexican painter Frida Kahlo used her tragic life as an emblem for human suffering. At the age of 18, she was injured when a streetcar slammed into a bus on which she was a passenger. The accident left her with many serious wounds, including a fractured pelvis and vertebrae, and chronic pain. Kahlo's marriage to the painter Diego Rivera was also painful. She once told a friend, "I have suffered two serious accidents in my life, one in which a streetcar ran over me. . . . The other accident was Diego."[1] As in *Diego in My Thoughts* (Fig. **1-7**), her face is always painted with extreme realism and set within a compressed space, requiring the viewer to confront the "true" Frida. When asked why she painted herself so often, she replied, "Porque estoy muy sola" (Because I am all alone). Those who knew Kahlo conjecture

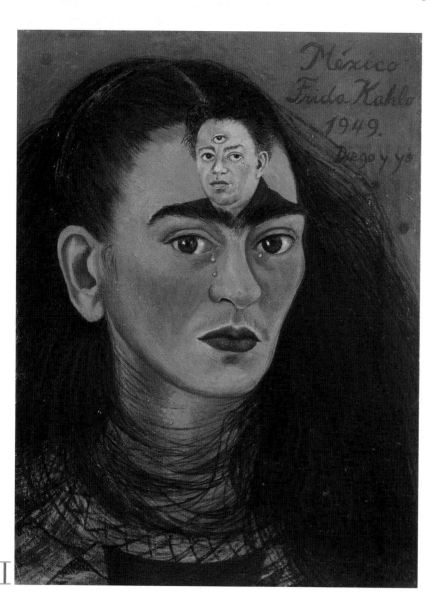

1 Martha Zamora, *Frida Kahlo: The Brush of Anguish* (San Francisco: Chronicle Books, 1990), 37.

1-7 FRIDA KAHLO.
Diego in My Thoughts (Diego y yo) (1949).
Oil on canvas, mounted on Masonite. 24" × 36".
©2008 Banco de México Diego Rivera & Frida Kahlo Museums Trust. Av. Cinco de Mayo No. 2, Col. Centro, Del. Cuauhtémoc 06059, México, D.F.

*All passes. Art alone
Enduring stays to us;
The Bust outlasts the throne,
The coin, Tiberius.*

—HENRY AUSTIN DOBSON

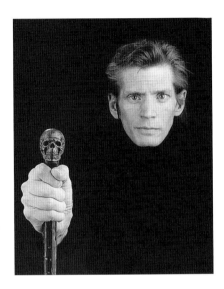

1-8 ROBERT MAPPLETHORPE.
Self-Portrait (1988).
Gelatin silver print.
©The Robert Mapplethorpe Foundation.
Courtesy of Art and Commerce.

ART AND IMMORTALITY

In the face of certain death, an artist such as Robert Mapplethorpe can defy mortality by creating a work that will keep his talents and his tragedy in the public's consciousness for decades. Human beings are the only species conscious of death, and for millennia, they have used art to overleap the limits of this life.

In *Four Marilyns* (Fig. **1-9**), Pop artist Andy Warhol participated in the cultural immortalization of a film icon of the 1960s by reproducing a well-known photograph of Monroe on canvas. Proclaimed a "sex symbol" of the

that she painted self-portraits in order to "survive, to endure, to conquer death."

Another haunting portrayal of unvarnished truth can be seen in Robert Mapplethorpe's *Self-Portrait* (Fig. **1-8**). The veracity of the photographic medium is inescapable; the viewer is forced to confront the artist's troublesome gaze. But the portrait also discloses the truth about Mapplethorpe's battle with AIDS, and perhaps suggests an attempt to reconcile his inevitable death. The artist's skeletal head slips into a background haze, while his tightly clenched fist grips a cane with a skull atop it and juts forward into sharp focus. The anger and defiance of Mapplethorpe's whitened knuckles contrast with the soft, almost pained expression of the artist's face.

Modern artists who discarded the practice of manipulating materials and techniques to create illusionistic surfaces built their compositions instead on the principle of "truth to materials." Paint retained its identity as paint, rather than pretending that it was cloth or glass or leaves. Modern architects also championed truth to materials by making visible the raw, structural elements of a building and arguing their aesthetic validity.

1 in.

1-9 ANDY WARHOL.
Four Marilyns (1962).
Synthetic polymer paint and silkscreen ink on canvas. 30" × 23⅞".
Image ©The Andy Warhol Foundation, Inc./Art Resource, NY. ©2009 Andy Warhol
Foundation for the Visual Arts, Inc/Artists Rights Society (ARS), New York.

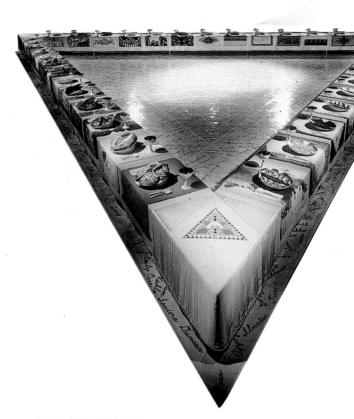

1-10 JUDY CHICAGO.
The Dinner Party (1974–1979).
Painted porcelain and needlework. 48' × 48' × 48' × 3'.
©2009 Judy Chicago/Artists Rights Society (ARS), New York.

work, which was constructed to honor and immortalize history's notable women, revolves around a fantastic dinner party, where the guests of honor meet before place settings designed to reflect their personalities and accomplishments. Chicago and numerous other women artists have invested much energy in alerting the public to the significant role of women in the arts and society.

ART AND GLORY

The desire to immortalize often goes hand in hand with the desire to glorify. Some of art history's wealthiest patrons, from the Caesars of ancient Rome and the Vatican's Popes to emperors around the world, commissioned artists to create works that glorified their reigns and accomplishments. The Roman Emperor Trajan's tomb (Fig. **1-11**), 128 feet high, is covered with a continuous spiral relief that recounts his victories in military campaigns in great detail. Centuries later, the French would adapt this design for a column erected to glorify the victories of the Emperor Napoleon Bonaparte.

In China during the early third century BCE, the First Emperor of Qin prepared a tomb (Fig. **1-12**) for himself that was not only filled with treasure, but also with facsimiles of more than 6,000 soldiers and horses, along with

silver screen, she rapidly rose to fame and shocked her fans by taking her own life at an early age. In the decades since Monroe's death, her image is still found on posters and calendars, books and songs are still written about her, and the public's appetite for information about her early years and romances remains insatiable. In other renderings, Warhol arranged multiple images of the star as if lined up on supermarket shelves, commenting, perhaps, on the ways in which contemporary flesh peddlers have packaged and sold her—in death as well as in life.

The lines between life and death, between place and time, are temporarily dissolved in the renowned installation *The Dinner Party* (Fig. **1-10**) by feminist artist Judy Chicago. The idea for this multimedia

1-11 Column of Trajan, Forum of Trajan, Rome, dedicated 112.
128 feet high.
Courtesy of Joost van Dongen

1-12 Terra Cotta Warriors.
Pit No. 1 (Han Dynasty c. 210 BCE)
Museum of the First Emperor Qin, Shaanxi Province, China.
akg-images/Laurent Lecat

render the unseen. Often the physical attributes granted to their gods were a reflection of humans. It has been said, for example, that the Greeks made their men into gods and their gods into men. In other societies, deities were often represented as powerful and mysterious animals, or composite men-beasts. Ritual and ceremony grew alongside the establishment of religions and the representation of deities, in actual or symbolic form. Until modern times, one could probably study the history of art in terms of works expressing religious values alone.

Art has been used to express hopes for fertility, to propitiate the gods, to symbolize great religious events and values, and to commend heavenward the souls of the departed. Inuit artist Jessie Oonark, who lived in the Canadian Arctic, created the image *A Shaman's Helping Spirits* (Fig. **1-13**) as a

1 ft.

1-13 JESSIE OONARK.
A Shaman's Helping Spirits (1971).
Stonecut and stencil. 37⅛" × 25⅛".
Art Gallery of Ontario, Toronto, ON. Gift of the Klamer family, 1978.
©2003 Jessie Oonark

bronze chariots. The site, which is still being excavated, was probably intended to recreate the Emperor's lavish palace. The sheer manpower that was necessary to create the imperial funerary monument—literally thousands of workers and artists—is a testimony to the Emperor's wealth, power, and ambition.

ART AND RELIGION

The quest for immortality is the bedrock of organized religion. From the cradle of civilization to the contemporary era, from Asia to the Americas, and from the Crimea to the Cameroon, human beings across time and cultures have sought answers to the unanswerable and have salved their souls with belief in life after death. It is not surprising that in the absence of physical embodiments for the deities they fashioned, humans developed art forms to visually

symbol of the healing rituals associated with the medicine men of her culture. Shamanism is a religion based on a belief in good and evil spirits that can be controlled and influenced only by the power of the shaman, a kind of priest. The strong, flat shapes and bright colors lend a directness and vitality to her expression.

Another artist of color, Aaron Douglas, translated a biblical story into a work that speaks to the African American sensibility. In his *Noah's Ark* (Fig. **1-14**), one of seven paintings based on James Weldon Johnson's book *God's Trombones: Seven Negro Sermons in Verse*, Douglas expressed a powerful vision of the great flood. Animals enter the ark in pairs as lightning flashes about them, and the sky turns a hazy gray purple with the impending storm. African men, rendered in rough-hewn profile, ready the ark and direct the action in a dynamically choreographed composition

that takes possession of and personalizes the biblical event for Douglas's race and culture.

The spectacular Hagia Sophia (Fig. **1-15**) was built as a Christian church in 532–537 CE. After the Ottoman conquest of 1453, it was converted to an Islamic mosque. In contemporary Istanbul, the building serves as a museum. The dome of the ancient church is a wonder. Although it is made of stone, it seems to float on the light that streams through the windows encircling its base like diamonds in a necklace. Light sparkles in the mosaic tiles and is reflected by glistening marble surfaces and ceremonial objects. Intellectually, the visitor may ponder how that monstrous weight is supported and how the dome can have survived century upon century of earthquakes and human assaults. But emotionally, it seems as if paradise is beckoning outside the dome.

1 ft.

1-14 AARON DOUGLAS.
Noah's Ark (c. 1927).
Oil on masonite. 48" × 36".
The Carl Van Vechten Gallery of Fine Arts, Fisk University, Nashville, TN.

1-15 ANTHEMIUS OF TRALLES AND ISIDORUS OF MILETUS.
Hagia Sophia, Constantinople (modern-day Istanbul), Turkey (532–537 CE).
Interior view.
©Lawrence Manning/CORBIS.

1-16 SUZANNE VALADON.
Adam and Eve (1909).
Oil on canvas. 16.2 cm × 13.1 cm.
Musee National d'Art Moderne,
Centre Georges Pompidou, Paris, France.

1 in.

general) was responsible for humankind's fall from grace and loss of paradise. For hundreds of years, Christianity perpetuated a negative view of women based on this ideological position. In the twentieth century, Suzanne Valadon subverted the traditional assignment of blame and guilt in a new version of the story of Eden in which Adam appears to lead Eve's hand toward the apple (Fig. **1-16**). His body parts are covered in shame by a strategically placed vine, not hers.

ART AND IDEOLOGY

Throughout history, works of art have been used to create or reinforce ideology. Defined as an organized collection of ideas, ideologies articulate the way societies look at things. These ideas spring from commonly held beliefs or are imposed on members of society by ruling or dominant classes. The degree to which an ideology is perpetuated depends on the degree to which members of a society subscribe to it.

When it comes to ideology, sometimes images speak louder than words. Think of representations of Adam and Eve. Every time you see Eve tempting Adam with an apple, you are witnessing the representation of an ideology in art, in this case that Eve (and, by extension, women in

ART AND FANTASY

Art also serves as a vehicle by which artists can express their innermost fantasies. Whereas some have labored to reconstruct reality and commemorate actual experiences, others have used art to give vent to their imaginary inner lives. There are many types of fantasies, such as those found in dreams and daydreams or simply the objects and landscapes that are conceived in the imagination. The French painter Odilon Redon once said that there is "a kind of drawing which the imagination has liberated from any concern with the details of reality in order to allow it to serve freely for the representation of things conceived" in the mind. In an attempt to capture the inner self, many twentieth-century artists looked to the psychoanalytic writings of Sigmund Freud and Carl Jung, who suggested that primeval forces are at work in the unconscious reaches of the mind. These artists sought to use their art as an outlet for these unconscious forces, as we shall see in Chapters 19 and 20.

Marc Chagall's self-portrait, *I and the Village* (Fig. **1-17**), provides a fragmented image of the artist among fantasized objects that seem to float in and out of one another. Fleeting memories of life in his Russian village are assembled like so many pieces of a dreamlike puzzle, reflecting the fragmentary nature of memory. Chagall's world is a happy, though private, one; the strange juxtaposition of images is reconciled only in the artist's own mind.

A similar process of fragmentation and juxtaposition was employed by German artist Max Beckmann in *The Dream* (Fig. **1-18**), but with a very different effect. The suggestion of space and atmosphere in Chagall's painting has given way to a claustrophobic room in which figures are compressed into a zigzag group. The soft, rolling hills and curving lines that gave the village painting its pleasant, dreamy quality have been forfeited for harsh, angular shapes and deformations. Horror hides in every nook and cranny, from the amputated and bandaged hands of

the man in red stripes to the blinded street musician and maimed harlequin. Are these marionettes from some dark comedy or human puppets locked in a world of manipulation and hopelessness?

1-17 MARC CHAGALL.

I and the Village (1911).

Oil on canvas. 6'3⅝" × 4'11⅝".

1-18 MAX BECKMANN.

The Dream (1921).

Oil on canvas. 73⅛" × 35".

ART, INTELLECT, AND EMOTION

Art has the power to make us think profoundly, to make us feel deeply. Beautiful or controversial works of all media can trigger many associations for us. Whether we gaze upon a landscape painting that reminds us of a vacation past, an abstract work that challenges our grasp of geometry, or a quilt that evokes family ties and traditions, it is almost impossible to truly confront a work and remain unaffected. We may think about what the subjects are doing, thinking, and feeling. We may reflect on the purposes of the artist. We may seek to trace the sources of our own emotional response or advance our self-knowledge and our knowledge of the outside world.

Consider Jenny Holzer's installation of **conceptual art** illuminating the interior spiral of New York's Solomon R. Guggenheim Museum (Fig. **1-19**). Conceptual art does not necessarily represent only external objects. It also challenges the traditional view of the artist as creative visionary, skilled craftsperson, and master of one's media. The "art" lies in the artist's conception. **Wordworks** such as this seem to comment on the impersonal information systems of modern times, while posing a challenge to the formal premises of art and stirring an intellectual response in the viewer. Holzer's wordworks compel readers to stop and think, sometimes through the presentation of piercing feminist declarations. This particular piece urges readers to reconsider the rules by which they live and warns that sometimes we do not rethink our lives until we are faced with disaster.

At its most extreme, the conceptual art product may exist solely in the mind of the artist, with or without a physical embodiment. Consider this wordwork by Robert Barry:

ALL THE THINGS I KNOW
BUT OF WHICH I AM NOT
AT THE MOMENT THINKING—
1:36 PM; JUNE 15, 1969

or a concept by artist Lawrence Weiner, sold to a patron, who installed the work himself: "A two-inch wide, one-inch deep trench, cut across a standard one-car driveway."

1-19 JENNY HOLZER.
Untitled (1989–1990).
Selection from "Truism: Inflammatory Essays, The Living Series, The Survival Series, Under a Rock, Laments, and Mother and Child Text."
LED electronic display signboard installation. 11" × 162' × 44" (27.9 cm × 49.4 m × 111.8 cm).

Art is harmony.

—GEORGES SEURAT

*I try not to have things look as if chance had brought them together,
but as if they had a necessary bond between them.*

—JEAN-FRANÇOIS MILLET

ART, ORDER, AND HARMONY

Artists and scientists have been intrigued by, and have ventured to discover and describe, the underlying order of nature. The Classical Greeks fine-polished the rough edges of nature by applying mathematical formulas to the human figure to perfect it; the nineteenth-century painter Paul Cézanne once remarked that all of nature could be reduced to the cylinder, the sphere, and the cone.

One of the most perfect expressions of order and harmony is found in the fragile Japanese sand garden (Fig. **1-20**). These medieval gardens are frequently part of a pavilion complex and are tended by the practitioners of **Zen**, a Buddhist sect that seeks inner harmony through introspection and meditation. The gentle, raked pattern of the sand symbolizes water and rocks, mountains reaching heavenward. Such gardens do not invite the observer to mill about; their perfection precludes walking. They are microcosms, really—universes unto themselves.

When can order pose a threat to harmony and psychological well-being? Perhaps this is the question that Laurie Simmons set out to answer in her color photograph called *Red Library #2* (Fig. **1-21**). Here, in a compulsively organized library, where nothing is a hair out of place, a robotlike woman assesses her job well done. She has become one with her task; even her dress, hair, and skin match the decor.

1-20 Ryoanji Zen Temple, Japanese sand garden, Kyoto, Japan.
©2005 Topham/The Image Works.

1-21 LAURIE SIMMONS.
Red Library #2 (1983).
Color photograph. 48½" × 38¼".
Collection of the artist.
Courtesy of Sperone Westwater, NY

The *Piano Lesson*(s) by Matisse and Bearden

FREQUENTLY AN ARTIST WILL USE COMPOSITION, or the arrangement of elements, to impose order. In Henri Matisse's *Piano Lesson* (Fig. **1-22**), every object, every color, every line seems to be placed to lead the eye around the canvas. The pea green wedge of drapery at the window is repeated in the shape of the metronome atop the piano, the wrought-iron grillwork at the window is complemented by the curvilinear lines of the music desk, and the enigmatic figure in the upper-right background finds her counterpart in a small sculpture placed diagonally across the canvas. Through contrast and repetition, unity within the diversity is achieved. The painting exudes solitude, resulting from the regularity of the compositional elements more than the atmosphere in the room. The boy's face appears quite tense, in fact, under the watchful eye of the seated woman behind him.

With Matisse's painting in mind, does Romare Bearden's *Piano Lesson* (Fig. **1-23**) appear then to be an example of disharmony, of disorder? Certainly it is a cacophony of shapes, lines, and unpredictable vantage points. But as in Matisse's

1 ft.

1-23 ROMARE BEARDEN.
Piano Lesson (1983).
Oil with collage. 29" × 22".
The Walter O. Evans Collection/SCAD Museum of Art. Art ©Romare Bearden Foundation/Licensed by VAGA, New York, NY

1 ft.

1-22 HENRI MATISSE.
Piano Lesson (1916).
Oil on canvas. 8'½" × 6'11¾".
Museum of Modern Art, New York. Mrs. Simon Guggenheim Fund.
Digital Image ©The Museum of Modern Art/Licensed by SCALA/Art Resource, NY.
©2009 Succession H. Matisse, Paris/Artists Rights Society (ARS), New York.

painting, color repetition draws the composition's disparate parts together—the red of background is balanced by the touches of red in the costumes of the figures up front; an undulating green strip on the piano is echoed in the billowing green drapes beyond. Ironically, there seems to be a more genuine feeling of serenity, despite the jumbled atmosphere. Is it because Matisse's seated woman—not touching? not feeling?—has a more flesh-and-blood counterpart in Bearden's work—a teacher? a mother?—who guides the young girl with the loving placement of a hand on her shoulder? When seen side by side, these paintings convey two different experiences. Matisse's piano student seems a product of his surroundings, a child of privilege partaking in an obligatory cultural ritual. Bearden's student, an African American girl in an apartment decorated catch-as-catch-can, seems to be breaking the bonds of her surroundings through the transcendence of music. ■

ART AND CHAOS

Just as beauty has its dark side and the intellect is balanced by the emotion, so, too, do order and harmony presume the existence of chaos. Artists have portrayed chaos in many ways throughout the history of art, seeking analogies in apocalyptic events such as war, famine, or natural catastrophe. But chaos can be suggested even in the absence of specific content. In *Eclipse* (Fig. **1-24**), without reference to nature or reality, Native American artist Jaune Quick-to-See Smith creates an agitated, chaotic atmosphere of color, line, shape, and movement. The artist grew up on the Flathead Indian reservation in Montana and uses a full vocabulary of Native American geometric motifs and organic images from the rich pictorial culture of her ancestors.

1 ft.

1-25 LOUISA CHASE.
Storm (1981).
Oil on canvas. 90" × 120".
Purchased with funds from National Endowment for the Arts and Alliance for Contemporary Art, 1982.53. Photograph ©Denver Art Museum.

1 ft.

1-24 JAUNE QUICK-TO-SEE SMITH.
Eclipse (1987).
Oil on canvas. 60" × 60".
©2007 Jaune Quick-to-See Smith and Flomenhaft Gallery

ART, EXPERIENCE, AND MEMORY

From humanity's earliest days, art has served to record and communicate experiences and events. From prehistoric cave paintings—thought to record significant events in the history of Paleolithic societies—to a work such as the Vietnam Memorial in Washington, D.C.—installed in honor of American service personnel who died during this country's involvement in that war—art has been used to inform future generations of what and who have gone before them. Art also conveys the personal experiences of an artist in ways that words cannot.

American painter Louisa Chase was inspired to paint nature's unbridled power as revealed in waves, waterfalls, and thunderstorms, although the intensity of her subjects is often tempered by her own presence in the piece. In *Storm* (Fig. **1-25**), a cluster of thick, black clouds lets go a torrent of rain, which, in league with the decorative **palette** of pinks and purples, turns an artificial blue. The highly charged images on the left side of the canvas are balanced on the right by the most delicate of ferns, spiraling upward, nourished by the downpour. Beneath the sprig, the artist's hand cups the raindrops, becoming part of the painting and part of nature's event as well. Chase said of a similar storm painting, "During the [marking] process I do become the storm—lost—yet not lost. An amazing feeling of losing myself yet remaining totally conscious."[2]

The photographer Alfred Stieglitz, who recognized the medium as a fine art as well as a tool for recording events, happened upon the striking composition of *The Steerage* (Fig. **1-26**) on an Atlantic crossing aboard the *Kaiser Wilhelm II*. He rushed to his cabin for his camera, hoping that the upper and lower masses of humanity would maintain their balanced relationships to one another, to the drawbridge that divides the scene, to the stairway, the funnel, and the horizontal beam of the mast. The "steerage" of a ship was the least expensive accommodation. Here the "huddled masses" seem suspended in limbo by machinery and by symbolic as well as actual bridges. Yet the tenacious human spirit may best be symbolized by the jaunty patch of light that strikes the straw hat of one passenger on the upper deck. Stieglitz was utterly fascinated and moved by what he saw.

More than 80 years after Stieglitz captured the great hope of immigrants entering New York harbor, African American artist Faith Ringgold tells the story of life and dreams on a tar-covered rooftop. *Tar Beach* (Fig. **1-27**) is a

2 Louisa Chase, journal entry for February 20, 1984, in *Louisa Chase* (New York: Robert Miller Gallery, 1984).

1-26 ALFRED STIEGLITZ.

The Steerage (1907).

Photograph.

Image ©NMeM/Royal Photographic Society Collection/SSPL/The Image Works. ©2009 Georgia O'Keeffe Museum/Artists Rights Society (ARS), New York.

1-27 FAITH RINGGOLD.

Tar Beach (1988).

Acrylic paint on canvas and pieced fabric. 74" × 68½".

Collection of the Solomon R. Guggenheim Museum, New York. Gift, Mr. and Mrs. Gus and Judith Lieber, 1988, 88.3620. ©Faith Ringgold 1988

painted patchwork quilt that stitches together the artist's memories of family, friends, and feelings while growing up in Harlem. Ringgold is noted for her use of materials and techniques associated with women's traditions as well as her use of narrative or storytelling, a strong tradition in African American families. A large, painted square with images of Faith, her brother, her parents, and neighbors dominates the quilt and is framed with brightly patterned pieces of fabric. Along the top and bottom are inserts crowded with Ringgold's written description of her experiences. This wonderfully innocent and joyful monologue begins:

> I will always remember when the stars fell down around me and lifted me up above the George Washington Bridge . . .

ART IN THE SOCIAL AND CULTURAL CONTEXT

Faith Ringgold's *Tar Beach* tells us the story of a young girl growing up in Harlem. Her experiences take place within a specific social and cultural context. In recording experience, artists frequently record the activities and objects of their times and places, reflecting contemporary fashions and beliefs, as well as the states of the crafts and sciences.

The architecture, the hairstyles, hats, and shoulder pads, even the price of cigars (only five cents), all set Edward Hopper's *Nighthawks* (Fig. **1-28**) unmistakably in an American city during the late 1930s or 1940s. The subject is commonplace and uneventful, though somewhat eerie. There is a tension between the desolate spaces of the vacant street and the corner diner. Familiar objects become distant. The warm patch of artificial light seems precious, even precarious, as if night and all its troubled symbols are threatening to break in on disordered lives. Hopper uses a specific sociocultural context to communicate an unsettling, introspective mood of aloneness, of being outside the mainstream of experience.

In Richard Hamilton's *Just What Is It That Makes Today's Homes So Different, So Appealing?* (Fig. **1-29**), the aims are identical, but the result is self-mocking, upbeat, and altogether fun. This little collage functions as a veritable time capsule for the 1950s, a decade during which the speedy advance of technology finds everyone buying pieces of the American dream. What is that dream? Comic books, TVs, movies, and tape recorders; canned hams and TV dinners; enviable physiques, Tootsie Pops, vacuum cleaners that finally let the "lady of the house" clean all the stairs at once.

1-28 EDWARD HOPPER.
Nighthawks (1942).
Oil on canvas. 30" × 60".
Friends of American Art Collection, 1942.51, The Art Institute of Chicago. Photography ©The Art Institute of Chicago.

1 ft.

Hamilton's piece serves as a memento of the time and the place and the values of the decade for future generations.

We more commonly think of visual art (painting and sculpture, for example) when we consider the connection between art and social or cultural context, but art history is full of examples of architecture that reflect or embody the ideas or beliefs of a people at a point in time. Think of the Parthenon in Classical Athens or Chartres Cathedral in the Middle Ages. Symbolism is often disguised in architecture, but sometimes it is the essence of its design. Zaha Hadid's Sheikh Zayed Bridge (Fig. 1-30), connecting Abu Dhabi island to the mainland, is composed of sweeping, irregular rhythms of arches. Hadid has acknowledged the influence of Arabic calligraphy on the flowing forms of her structures, but in this work, the arches—each different from one another in height and span—reflect the dunes of the nearby topography, thus connecting it (metaphorically and literally) to a specific place and time.

1 in.

1-29 RICHARD HAMILTON.
Just What Is It That Makes Today's Homes So Different, So Appealing? (1956).
Collage. 10¼" × 9¾".
Kunsthalle Tubingen, Germany. Collection of G. F. Zundel. © Richard Hamilton. All Rights Reserved, DACS 2008

1-30 ZAHA HADID.
Sheikh Zayed Bridge, Abu Dhabi, 2006.
Courtesy Zaha Hadid Architects

ART AND SOCIAL CONSCIOUSNESS

As other people have, artists have taken on bitter struggles against the injustices of their times and have tried to persuade others to join them in their causes, and it has been natural for them to use their creative skills to do so.

The nineteenth-century Spanish painter Francisco Goya used his art to satirize the political foibles of his day and to condemn the horrors of war (see Fig. 19-6). In the twentieth century another Spanish painter, Pablo Picasso, would condemn war in his masterpiece *Guernica* (see Fig. 20-9).

Goya's French contemporary Eugène Delacroix painted the familiar image of *Liberty Leading the People* (Fig. **1-31**)

in order to keep the spirit of the French Revolution alive in 1830. In this painting, people of all classes are united in rising up against injustice, led onward by an allegorical figure of liberty. Rifles, swords, a flag—even pistols—join in an upward rhythm, underscoring the pyramid shape of the composition.

Suzanne Lacy and Leslie Labowitz's performance, *In Mourning and in Rage* (Fig. **1-32**), was a carefully orchestrated media event reminiscent of ancient public rituals. Members of feminist groups donned black robes to commemorate women who had been victims of rape-murders and to protest the shoddy media coverage usually given to such tragedies.

Millions of us have grown up with a benevolent, maternal Aunt Jemima. She has graced packages of pancake mix

1-31 EUGÈNE DELACROIX.
Liberty Leading the People (1830).
Oil on canvas. 8' 6" × 10' 10".
Louvre Museum, Paris.
©Réunion des Musées Nationaux/Art Resource, NY

Art has always been employed by the different social classes who hold the balance of power as one instrument of domination—hence, a political instrument. One can analyze epoch after epoch—from the Stone Age to our own day—and see that there is no form of art which does not also play an essential political role.

— DIEGO RIVERA

1-32 SUZANNE LACY AND LESLIE LABOWITZ.
In Mourning and in Rage (1977).
Performance at Los Angeles City Hall.
Photograph courtesy of Suzanne Lacy and Leslie Labowitz.

1-33 BETYE SAAR.
The Liberation of Aunt Jemima (1972).
Mixed media. 11¾" × 8" × 2¾".
University of California, Berkeley Art Museum; purchased with the aid of funds from the National Endowment for the Arts (selected by The Committee for the Acquisition of Afro-American Art). Courtesy of Michael Rosenfeld Gallery, LLC, New York, NY.

and bottles of maple syrup for generations. How many of us have really thought about what she symbolizes? Artists such as African American artist Betye Saar have been doubly offended by Aunt Jemima's state of servitude, which harks not only to the days of slavery but also to the suffocating traditional domestic role of the female. Sharon F. Patton notes:

> *The Liberation of Aunt Jemima* subverts the black mammy stereotype of the black American woman: a heavy, dark-skinned maternal figure, of smiling demeanor. This stereotype, started in the nineteenth century, was still popular culture's favorite representation of the African-American woman. She features in Hollywood films and notably as the advertising and packaging image for Pillsbury's "Aunt Jemima's Pancake Mix."[3]

The Aunt Jemima in Betye Saar's *The Liberation of Aunt Jemima* (Fig. **1-33**) is revised to reflect the quest for liberation from servitude and the stereotype. She holds a broomstick in one hand but a rifle in the other. Before her stands a portrait with a small white child violated by a clenched black fist representing the symbol of Black Power. The image of the liberated Aunt Jemima confronts viewers and compels them to cast off the stereotypes that lead to intolerance.

1 in.

3 Sharon F. Patton, *African-American Art* (New York: Oxford University Press, 1998), 201.

1-34 MIRIAM SCHAPIRO.
Wonderland (1983).
Acrylic and fabric collage on canvas. 90" × 144" (framed).
©Smithsonian American Art Museum, Washington, DC/Art Resource, NY.
©2007 Miriam Schapiro and Flomenhaft Gallery

ART AND POPULAR CULTURE

Have you come across embroidered dish towels or aprons with the words *God Bless Our Happy Home* or *I Hate Housework*? Miriam Schapiro's *Wonderland* (Fig. **1-34**) is a collage that reflects her "femmage" aesthetic—her interest in depicting women's domestic culture. The work contains ordinary doilies, needlework, crocheted aprons, handkerchiefs, and quilt blocks, all anchored to a geometric patterned background that is augmented with brushstrokes of paint. In the center is the most commonplace of the commonplace: an embroidered image of a housewife who curtsies beneath the legend "Welcome to Our Home."

Some of the more interesting elevations of the commonplace to the realm of art are found in the **readymades** and **assemblages** of twentieth-century artists. Marcel Duchamp's *Fountain* (Fig. **1-35**) is a urinal, turned upside down and labeled. Pablo Picasso's *Bull's Head* (see Fig. 9-15) is fashioned from the seat and handlebars of an old bicycle. In **Pop Art**, the dependence on commonplace objects and visual clichés reaches a peak. Prepared foods, soup and beer cans, media images of beautiful women and automobile accidents became the subject matter of Pop Art. As we saw in Figures 1-9 and 1-29, Pop Art impels us to cast a more critical eye on the symbols and objects with which we surround ourselves.

ART AND THE NEEDS OF THE ARTIST

Artists may have special talents and perceptive qualities, but they are also people with needs and the motivation to meet those needs. Psychologists speak of the need for "self-actualization"— that is, the need to fulfill one's unique potential. Self-actualizing people have needs for novelty, exploration, and understanding; and they have aesthetic needs for art, beauty, and order. Under perfect circumstances, art permits the individual to meet needs for achievement or self-actualization and, at the same time, to earn a living.

Murals such as José Clemente Orozco's *Epic of American Civilization: Hispano-America* (Fig. **1-36**) were created for a branch of the Works Progress Administration (WPA), a federal work-relief program intended to help people in

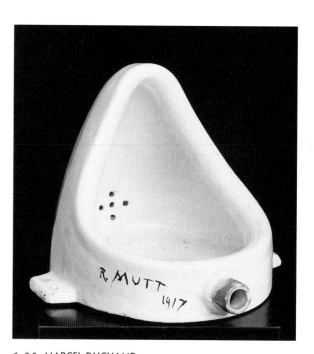

1-35 MARCEL DUCHAMP.
Fountain (1917). 1951 version after lost original.
Porcelain urinal. H: 24".
©2009 Artists Rights Society (ARS), New York/ADAGP, Paris/
Succession Marcel Duchamp.

1 ft.

discussion of the meanings and purposes of art is meant to facilitate the individual endeavor to understand art but is not intended to be exhaustive. Some people will feel that we have omitted several important meanings and purposes of art; others will think we have included too many. But these considerations hint at the richness and elusiveness of the concept of art.

In Chapters 2, 3, and 4, we expand our discussion of the meanings and purposes of art to include the "language" of art. These chapters will not provide us with a precise definition of art either, but they will afford us insight into the ways in which artists use elements of art, such as line, shape, and color, to create compositions of a certain style and content. Even though art has always been with us, the understanding of art is in its infancy.

the United States, including artists, survive the Great Depression. The WPA made it possible for many artists to meet basic survival needs while continuing to work, and be paid, as artists. Scores of public buildings were decorated with murals or canvas paintings by artists in the Fine Arts Program (FAP) of the WPA. Some of them were among the best known of their generation. Orozco's epic also met another, personal need—the need to call attention to and express his outrage at what he believed to be financial and military injustices imposed on the Mexican peasants.

Creating works of art that are accepted by one's audience can lead to an artist's social acceptance and recognition. But sometimes art really is created only to meet the needs of the artist and nothing beyond—with no thought to a sale, or exhibition, or review, or recognition. Such is the story of *outsider art*, a catchall category that has been used for works by untrained artists; self-taught artists who have been incarcerated for committing crimes and who use the circumstances of their isolation as a motive for creating; people who are psychologically compromised and sometimes institutionalized for conditions ranging from autism (Fig. **1-37**) to schizophrenia. Works of art by these individuals and others like them are almost always *not* intended to be seen. Thus, in the purest sense, they come into existence to meet some essential emotional or psychological need of the artist and the artist alone.

As we noted at the outset, the question "What is art?" has no single answer and raises many other questions. Our

1 in.

1-37 MATTHEW I. SMITH.
Untitled (n.d.).
Graphite on paper. 8½" × 11".
Photo Courtesy of Ricco/Maresca Gallery

VISUAL ELEMENTS OF ART

*I found I could say things with color and shapes that I couldn't say
in any other way—things I had no words for.*
—Georgia O'Keeffe

Color and shape are but two of the visual elements of art. The language of art is the language of our visual and tactile experiences in the world, and the words or vocabulary of this language consist of the visual elements of *line, shape, light, value, color, texture, space, time,* and *motion.* Line can define shape; light can reveal it. Color can describe the world we see around us and reveal the psychological worlds within us; we are blue with sorrow, red with rage. Texture is linked with all the emotion of touching, with the cold sharpness of rock or the yielding sensations of flesh. We exist in space; we occupy space and space envelops us. Time allows us to develop into what we are capable of being; time ultimately takes from us what we have been. We are all in motion through space, in a solar system that is traversing the rim of our galaxy at thousands of miles per second, or rotating on the surface of our own globe at a thousand miles per hour. Yet it is the smaller motion—the motion of lifting an arm or of riding through a field—that we are more likely to sense and hence to represent in art.

FRANK GEHRY, Guggenheim Museum, Bilbao, Spain. (1997). Façade.
©Guenter Rossenbach/zefa/Corbis.

This vocabulary—*line, shape, light, value, color, texture, space, time,* and *motion*—comprises what we call the **visual elements** or **plastic elements** of art. Artists select from a variety of mediums, including, but by no means limited to, drawing, painting, sculpture, architecture, photography, textiles, and ceramics. They then employ the visual elements of art to express themselves in the chosen medium. In their self-expression, they use these elements to design compositions of a certain style, form, and content.

Visual elements, design, style, form, and content—these make up the language of art. Languages such as English and French have symbols—words—that are combined according to rules of grammar to create a message. The visual arts have a "vocabulary" of visual elements that are combined according to the "grammar" of art, or principles of design. These principles include unity, balance, rhythm, scale, and proportion, among others. The composition of the elements creates the style, form, and content of the work—even if this content is an abstract image and not a natural subject, such as a human figure or a landscape. In this chapter, we explore the basic vocabulary or visual elements in the language of art.

LINE

Line is at once the simplest and most complex of the elements of art. It serves as a basic building block around which an art form is constructed and, by itself, has the capacity to evoke thought and emotion. In geometry, we learn that line is made up of an infinite number of points and that the shortest distance between two points is a straight line. In art, a line is more commonly defined as a moving dot.

Characteristics of Line

Measure of Line

The **measure** of a line is its length and its width. If we conceptualize line as a moving dot, the dots that compose it can be of any size, creating a line of lesser or greater width, and of any number, creating a shorter or a longer line.

Some works of art, such as Sol LeWitt's *Lines from Four Corners to Points on a Grid* (Fig. **2-1**), have lines whose measures are carefully devised. LeWitt's lines are so precise

and mathematical that he was acutely conscious of their measure. The act of measuring to create exact mathematical relationships seems to be intrinsic to the work—or is the work. LeWitt's installations are temporary; their "ownership" means possession of a set of instructions for reproducing them. The Whitney Museum of American Art owns the work (the instructions), but once placed it (the instructions) "on loan" to the Museum of Modern Art.

By contrast, the notion of measuring the lengths of line that are both the subject and the process of Jackson Pollock's *Number 14: Gray* (Fig. **2-2**) seems ludicrous and incomprehensible. Pollock's lines weave and overlap and swell and pinch, creating a sense of infinite flow and freedom from constraint (where constraint is defined as logical and mathematical measurement). LeWitt's lines are precise; Pollock's are gestural, fluid, and loose. The effects of the LeWitt and the Pollock are very different. The LeWitt is static; the Pollock expands and contracts, shoots forward and recedes.

Expressive Qualities of Line

The works by LeWitt and Pollock also reveal the expressive characteristics of line. Lines may be perceived as delicate, tentative, elegant, assertive, forceful, or even brutal. The lines in the LeWitt installation are assertive but cold. The emotional human element is missing. The work seems to express the human capacity to detach the intellect from emotional response, and perhaps to program computers (and other people) to carry out precise instructions. The lines in the Pollock work combine the apparently incongruous expressive qualities of delicacy and force. They are well rounded and human, combining intellect with passion. The LeWitt suggests the presence of a plan. The Pollock suggests the presence of a human being weaving elegantly through the complexities of thought and life.

Types of Line

The variety of line would seem to be as infinite as the number of points that, we are told, determine it. Lines can be straight or curved. They can be vertical, horizontal, or diagonal. A curved line can be circular or oval. It can run full circle to join itself where it began, thereby creating a complete shape. Curved lines can also be segments or arcs—parts of circles or ovals. As a line proceeds, it can change direction abruptly: A straight line that stops

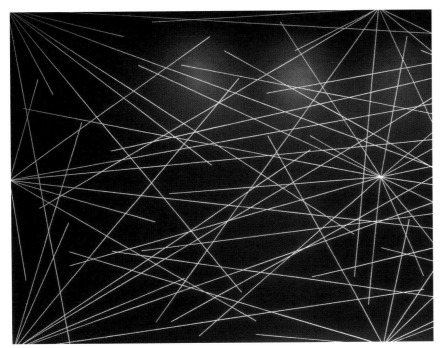

2-1 SOL LEWITT.

Lines from Four Corners to Points on a Grid (1976), detail.

A 6-inch (15 cm) grid covering each of four black walls. White lines to points on grids. First wall: 24 lines from the center; second wall: 12 lines from the midpoint of each of the sides; third wall: 12 lines from each corner; fourth wall: 24 lines from the center; 12 lines from the midpoint of each of the sides, 12 lines from each corner. White crayon lines and black crayon grid on black walls. Dimensions variable.

Whitney Museum of American Art, purchase, with funds from the Gillman Foundation, Inc. (78.1.-4). ©2009 The LeWitt Estate/Artists Rights Society (ARS), New York.

1 in.

2-2 JACKSON POLLOCK.

Number 14: Gray (1948).

Enamel and gesso on paper. 22¾" × 31".

Image ©Yale University Art Gallery/Art Resource, NY. ©2009 The Pollock-Krasner Foundation/ Artists Rights Society (ARS), New York.

1 in.

2-3 EDWARD WESTON.

Knees (1927).

Gelatin silver print. 6¼" × 9³⁄₁₆".

Image: San Francisco Museum of Modern Art, San Francisco, CA. Alan M. Bender Collection.
Bequest of Alan M. Bender. ©1981 Center for Creative Photography, Arizona Board of Regents

into space. Edges are perceived because the objects differ from the backgrounds in value (lighter versus darker), texture, or color. If you hold up your arm so that you perceive it against the wall (or, if you are outside, the sky), you will discriminate its edge—its contour line—because the wall is lighter or darker, because it differs from the wall in color, and because the texture of flesh differs from the wallboard or plaster or wood or brick of the wall.

Edward Weston's photograph *Knees* (Fig. **2-3**) highlights the aesthetic possibilities of contour lines. Weston was drawn to the sculptural forms of the human figure, plant life, and natural inanimate objects such as rocks. In *Knees*, the contour lines (edges) of the legs are created by the subtle differences in value (light and dark) and texture between the legs and the wall and the floor. The legs take on the abstract quality of an exercise to demonstrate how contour lines define the human form and how shading creates or *models* roundness.

Actual line can be distinguished from *implied line*. The points in **actual line** are connected and continuous. The LeWitt (Fig. 2-1) and Pollock (Fig. 2-2) are examples of works with actual line. Works with **implied line** are completed by the viewer. An implied line can be a discontinuous line that the viewer reads as continuous because of the overall context of the image. Implied lines can be suggested by a series of points or dots, as in Part B of Figure **2-4**. They

and changes course becomes a zigzag. A curved line that forms an arc and then reverses direction becomes wavy. Circular and oval lines that turn ever inward on themselves create vertiginous spirals. Art's most basic element is a tool of infinite variety.

Contour lines are created by the edges of things. They are perceived when three-dimensional shapes curve back

2-4 A, B, and C Actual line (A) versus two kinds of implied lines, one formed by dots (B) and the other formed by psychologically connecting the edges of a series of straight lines (C).

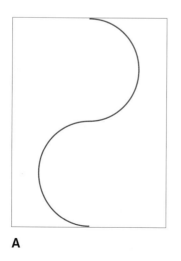

A

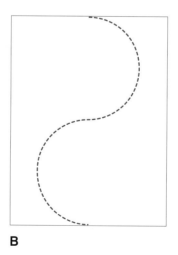

B

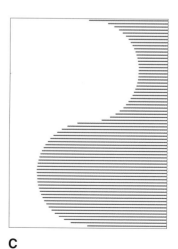

C

1 ft.

2-5 LEONARDO DA VINCI.
Madonna of the Rocks (1483).
Oil on panel, transferred to canvas. 78½" × 48".
Louvre Museum, Paris
©Réunion des Musées Nationaux/Art Resource, NY

2-6 The pyramidal structure of the *Madonna of the Rocks*.
©Réunion des Musées Nationaux/Art Resource, NY

can be suggested by the nearby endpoints of series of parallel or nearly parallel lines of different lengths, as in Part C of Figure **2-4**. The movements and glances of the figures in a composition also imply lines.

One of the hallmarks of Renaissance paintings is the use of implied lines to create or echo the structure of the composition. Geometric shapes such as triangles and circles are suggested through the use of linear patterns created by the position and physical gestures of the participants and, often, glances between them. These shapes often serve as the central focus and the main organizational device of the compositions. In the *Madonna of the Rocks* (Fig. **2-5**), Leonardo da Vinci places the head of the Virgin Mary at the apex of a rather broad, stable pyramid formed not by actual lines but by the extension of her arms and the direction of her glance. The base of the pyramid is suggested by an implied line that joins the "endpoints" of the baby Jesus and the infant John the Baptist. Figure **2-6** highlights the pyramidal structure of the composition.

A mental or perceptual connection can create a **psychological line**. If a character in a painting points to an object, or if one figure gazes directly toward another—as in Emily

1 ft.

Mary Osborn's *Nameless and Friendless* (Fig. **2-7**)—we perceive the connection between the two as a psychological line, even though the artist has not created an actual or implied line. In Osborn's painting, which represents the plight of the woman artist, a small boy (her brother?) stares directly at the condescending art dealer as he feigns serious consideration of her work. The boy's unflinching glance and the dealer's face are visually connected with a psychological line. Another psychological line connects the downward face of the impoverished woman with the tip of her shoe, which emerges from the bottom of her long, black skirt. She stands in judgment, fidgeting with the fringe of her shawl, not quite knowing where to look. Gestures and glances such as those in Osborn's work lead the viewer's eye around the composition. As such, psychological lines are also called compositional lines.

Functions of Line

The line, as an element of art, is alive with possibilities. Artists use line to outline shapes, to evoke forms and movement, to imply solid mass, or for its own sake. In groupings, lines can create shadows and even visual illusions.

To Outline and Shape

When you make or observe an outline, you are describing or suggesting the edge of a form or a shape. Line defines a shape or form as separate from its surrounding space; line gives birth to shape or form. Line grants them substance.

In addition to defining shape, line can also function as form itself. *Madonna and Child* (Fig. **2-8**) by Rimma Gerlovina and Valeriy Gerlovin is a revision of one of the most popular religious themes of the Renaissance. Taking their cue from works by artists such as Raphael, the Gerlovins use their signature combination of the body and braided hair to embroider a contemporary image of the Virgin Mary and the infant Jesus. The Gerlovins are the principal subjects of their work, and in this piece Gerlovina serves as the model for the Virgin. Braid extensions of her own sandy brown hair cascade from a sculptural head whose three-dimensionality stands in marked contrast to the flatness of the rippling braids. These braids flow into the

contours of the Christ-child's body, nested in the palm of a sculpted hand.

To Create Depth and Texture

The face of Elizabeth Catlett's sturdy *Sharecropper* (Fig. **2-9**) is etched by a series of short, vigorous lines that are echoed in the atmosphere that surrounds her. The lines give the woman's features a gaunt, hollowed-out look and are also used to create a harsh texture in a turbulent environment. The textures of her garment, hair, and hat are also represented by series of lines.

1 in.

2-9 ELIZABETH CATLETT.
Sharecropper (1968).
Color linocut. 26" × 22".
Hampton University Museum, Hampton, VA. Art ©Elizabeth Catlett/Licensed by VAGA, New York, NY.

2-10 Illusion of three-dimensionality.

Dots and lines can be used to create the illusion of three-dimensionality through shading. Part A shows the method of stippling, in which shading is represented by a pattern of dots that thickens and thins. Part B represents shading by means of hatching—that is, using a series of closely spaced parallel lines. Part C shows the method of cross-hatching, in which the series of lines intersects another series of lines. Part D shows how directional changes in hatching can define contours.

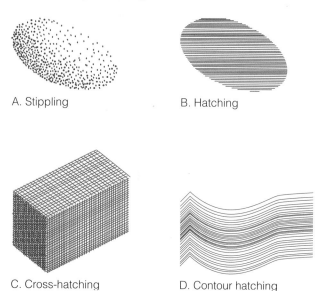

A. Stippling

B. Hatching

C. Cross-hatching

D. Contour hatching

Modeling on a two-dimensional surface is the creation of the illusion of roundness or three dimensions through the use of light and shadow. As shown in Figure **2-10**, shadows can be created by the use of dots and lines. Part A shows the method of **stippling**, of using a pattern of dots that thickens and thins. Areas where the dots are thicker are darker and create the illusion of being more shaded. Part B shows the technique of **hatching**, or using a series of closely spaced parallel lines to achieve a similar effect. Areas in which lines are closer together appear to be more shaded. **Cross-hatching**, shown in Part C, is similar to hatching, but as the name implies, a series of lines run in different directions and cross one another.

Contours can be created when hatching changes direction, as in Part D. Notice how the sharecropper's face is carved by hatching that alters direction to give shape to the wells of the eyes, the nose, the lips, and the chin. Directional changes in hatching also define the prominent anatomic features of the sharecropper's neck.

To Suggest Direction and Movement

Renaissance artist Sandro Botticelli's *The Birth of Venus* (Fig. **2-11**) shows how line can be used to outline forms and evoke movement. In this painting, firm lines carve out the figures from the rigid horizontal of the horizon and

2-11 SANDRO BOTTICELLI.
The Birth of Venus (c. 1482).
Oil on canvas. 5'8⅞" × 9'1⅞".
©Scala/Art Resource, NY

1 ft.

1 in.

2-12 JACOB LAWRENCE.
Harriet Tubman Series, No. 4 (1939–1940).
Casein tempera on gessoed hardboard. 12″ × 17⅞″.
Hampton University Museum, Hampton, VA. ©2009 The Jacob and Gwendolyn
Lawrence Foundation, Seattle/Artists Rights Society (ARS), New York

the verticals of the trees. Straight lines carry the breath of
the Zephyr from the left, and the curved lines of the drapery imply the movement of the Zephyrs and of the nymph
to the right. Implied compositional lines give this work an
overall triangular structure.

Horizontal lines, like horizon lines, suggest stability.
Vertical lines, like the sweeping verticals in skyscrapers,
defy gravity and suggest assertiveness. Diagonal lines
are often used to imply movement and directionality,
as in the directionality and movement of the breath of
the Zephyr in *The Birth of Venus*. African American artist
Jacob Lawrence used assertive sticklike diagonals to give
the slave children in his painting *Harriet Tubman Series,
No. 4* (Fig. **2-12**) a powerful sense of movement and directionality. While the horizon line provides a somewhat
stable world, the brightly clad children perform acrobatic
leaps, their branchlike limbs akin to the wood above. The
enduring world implied by the horizon is shattered by the
agitated back and forth of the brushed lines that define
ground and sky. Such turmoil presumably awaits the children once they mature and realize their lot in life.

SHAPE, VOLUME, AND MASS

The word *shape* has many meanings. Parents or teachers
may tell you to "shape up" when they are concerned about
your behavior. When you started arranging things in your
dorm room or apartment, you may have had thoughts
as things began to "take shape." Such expressions suggest "definition"—that is, pulling things together within
defined boundaries to distinguish them from what surrounds them. We say our bodies are "out of shape" when
they violate our preferred physical contours. In works of
art, **shapes** are defined as the areas within a composition
that have boundaries that separate them from what surrounds them; shapes make these areas distinct.

Shapes are formed when intersecting or connected lines
enclose space. In Botticelli's *The Birth of Venus* and in the
Lawrence painting, for example, shape is clearly communicated by lines that enclose specific areas of the painting.
Shape can also be communicated through patches of color
or texture. In three-dimensional works, such as sculpture
and architecture, shape is discerned when the work is

viewed against its environment. The edges, colors, and textures of the work give it shape against the background. Piet Mondrian's *Composition with Red, Blue, and Yellow* (Fig. **2-13**) features colorful geometric shapes—rectangles of various dimensions—that are created when vertical and horizontal black lines slice through the canvas space and intersect to define areas distinct from the rest of the surface.

The word **form** is often used to speak about shape in sculpture or architecture— three-dimensional works of art. Helene Brandt's *Mondrian Variations, Construction No. 3B with Four Red Squares and Two Planes* (Fig. **2-14**) is a translation of Mondrian's composition into three dimensions. Therefore, some artists and people who write about art might

2-14 HELENE BRANDT.

Mondrian Variations, Construction No. 3B with Four Red Squares and Two Planes (1996).
Welded steel, wood, paint. 22" × 19" × 17".
Courtesy of the artist.

2-13 PIET MONDRIAN.

Composition with Red, Blue, and Yellow (1930).
Oil on canvas. 18⅛" × 18⅛".
©2008 Mondrian/Holtzman Trust c/o HCR International, Warrenton, VA. USA

prefer to speak of the *form* of the Brandt sculpture rather than its shape. Others use the word *shape* to apply to both two-dimensional and three-dimensional works of art. We will use the terms interchangeably.

The word **volume** refers to the mass or bulk of a three-dimensional work. The volume of a work is the amount of space it contains. In geometry, the volume of a rectangular solid is computed as its length times its width times its height. But one might use the concept more loosely to say that a structure has a great *volume* as a way of generally describing its enormity. Gerrit Rietveldt's Schroeder House in Utrecht (Fig. **2-15**) seems to be a volumetric translation of Mondrian's geometric shapes. Here is an example of the usefulness of the term *volume* as it conveys a sense of containment.

Mass

Like volume, the term *mass* also has a spe-cific meaning in science. In physics, the mass of an object reflects the amount of force it would require to move it. Objects that have more mass are harder to budge. In three-dimensional art, the **mass** of an object refers to its bulk. A solid work made of steel with the same dimensions as Helene Brandt's sculpture would have more mass.

We would be hard-pressed to conjure a better exemplar of mass than Rachel Whi-teread's Holocaust Memorial in Vienna (Fig. **2-16**). It possesses the gravity of a stone pyramid and evokes the simplicity and serenity of a mausoleum. Built of con-crete and weighing 250 tons, the memorial is designed as an inverted library—the "books" protrude on the outside—in recognition of the significance of study to the Jewish people,

2-16 RACHEL WHITEREAD.
Holocaust Memorial, Vienna (2000).
©Reuters/CORBIS.

1 ft.

2-17 MARK TANSEY.
Landscape (1994).
Oil on canvas. 181.6 cm × 365.8 cm.
©Mark Tansey. Courtesy Gagosian Gallery, New York.

"the people of the book." But the doors to this "library" are bolted, making the books inaccessible. In the wake of the destruction of the Austrian Jewish community, there is no longer any use for them. The names of the places to which the country's Jews were deported for annihilation are inscribed in alphabetical order around the exterior. There is murder, death, and loss here, and the massiveness of the memorial shapes a sense of gloom that cannot be lifted.

Actual Mass versus Implied Mass

The Whiteread Memorial has **actual mass**. It occupies three-dimensional space and has measurable volume and weight. Objects that are depicted as three-dimensional on a two-dimensional surface (such as a drawing or a painting) have what we call **implied mass**. That is, they create the illusion of possessing volume, having weight, and occupying three-dimensional space. Consider a two-dimensional work of art that features massive shapes, broken and fragmented and piled in a pyramidal shape, like so much fuel

for a funeral pyre of art's historical icons. In *Landscape* (Fig. **2-17**), Mark Tansey meticulously portrays the remnants of colossal sculptures amid the unending sands of a bleak desert. His realistic style gives the illusion of three dimensions on the two-dimensional canvas surface and implies the extraordinary mass of the oversized stone figures. In the painting, the shapes have implied mass, whereas the sculptures they reference, in reality, have actual mass.

Types of Shape

Shapes that are found in geometric figures such as rectangles and circles are called **geometric shapes**. Geometric shapes are regular and precise. They may be made up of straight (rectilinear) or curved (curvilinear) lines, but they have an unnatural, mathematical appearance. Shapes that resemble organisms found in nature—the forms of animals and plant life—are called **organic shapes** and have a natural appearance. Most of the organic shapes found in art are soft, curvilinear, and irregular, although some natural shapes, such as those found in the structure of crystals, are harsh and angular. Artists also work with *biomorphic* and *amorphous* shapes.

Geometric shapes can be **rectilinear** when straight lines intersect to form them. Geometric shapes can also be **curvilinear** when curving lines intersect to form them or when they circle back to join themselves and make up closed geometric figures. Geometric shapes frequently look crisp, or hard-edged. David Smith explored the relationships among diverse geometric shapes such as cylinders, cubes, and disks in works such as *Cubi XVIII* (Fig. **2-18**). His *Cubi* series represents nothing found in nature. Rather, they are abstract geometric concepts rendered in steel.

Frank Gehry, the architect of the Guggenheim Museum in Bilbao, Spain (Fig. **2-19**), refers to his work as a "metallic flower." Others have found the billowing, curvilinear shapes to be reminiscent of ships, linking the machine-tooled structure that is perched on the water's edge to the history of Bilbao as an international seaport. It is as if free-floating geometric shapes have collided on this site, and on another day, they might have assumed a different configuration.

1 ft.

2-18 DAVID SMITH.

Cubi XVIII (1964).

Polished stainless steel. 9' 7¾" × 5' × 1' 9¾".

Museum of Fine Arts, Boston. Gift of Susan W. and Stephen B. Paine, 68.280. Photograph ©2009 Museum of Fine Arts, Boston. Art ©Estate of David Smith/ Licensed by VAGA, New York, NY

2-19 FRANK GEHRY.

Guggenheim Museum, Bilbao, Spain (1997).

©E. Streichan/Zefa/CORBIS

Picasso's *Les Demoiselles d'Avignon* with Colescott's *Les Demoiselles d'Alabama: Vestidas*

IN THE YEAR 1907, A YOUNG PABLO PICASSO unveiled a painting that he had been secretly working on for a couple of years. A culmination of what was known as his Rose Period, this new work—*Les Demoiselles d'Avignon* (Fig. **2-20**)—would turn the tide of modern painting. Picasso had studied the work of African and Iberian artists in Parisian museums and galleries. He was struck by the universality of the masks, believing that their rough-hewn, simplified, and angular features crossed time and culture. This painting launched the movement called Cubism, which geometricizes organic forms. The contours of the body in *Demoiselles* are harsh and rectilinear, forming straighter lines than are found in nature. The women in the painting are expressionless and lack identity; some of them even have rectilinear masks in lieu of faces. The intellectual exercise of transforming the human form into geometric shapes takes precedence over any interest in expressing the plight of these women, who are prostitutes in the French underworld. The "figures" in the work transcend the period and culture in which the women lived and worked.

You have probably heard the expression "Clothing makes the man." In Robert Colescott's *Les Demoiselles*

2-21 ROBERT COLESCOTT.
Les Demoiselles d'Alabama: Vestidas (1985).
Acrylic on canvas. 96" × 92".
Collection of Hanford Yang, New York, courtesy Phyllis Kind Gallery

d'Alabama: Vestidas (Fig. **2-21**), it could be argued that clothing makes the woman. The women in Picasso's painting are dehumanized in part by their nudity. The subjects of Colescott's painting, executed some 80 years later, are given strong individuality by their choice of costume. Colescott's painting is one of the thousands of instances in which one artist transforms the work of another in a certain way to make a certain point. Picasso's nudes have a harsh and jagged quality that gives an overall splintered effect to his work; the movement of the women seems to be abrupt and choppy. By contrast, Colescott's women are well rounded (in the literal sense) and fleshy—they are natural, organic, "real" counterparts to Picasso's geometry. The flowing, curvilinear lines of the women cause them to undulate across the canvas with fluid movement.

Whereas Picasso's rectilinear women are timeless (and "placeless"), the curvilinear, clothed women of Colescott are very much tied to their time and place—an American South full of life and spontaneity and emotional expression. Whereas Picasso seemed to relish the intellectual transformation of the prostitutes into timeless figures, Colescott seems to revel in the tangibility and sensuality of his sexy subjects. ■

2-20 PABLO PICASSO.
Les Demoiselles d'Avignon (1907).
Oil on canvas. 8' × 7'8".
Museum of Modern Art, New York. Acquired through the Lillie P. Bliss Bequest.
Digital Image ©The Museum of Modern Art/Licensed by SCALA/Art Resource, NY
©2009 Estate of Pablo Picasso/Artists Rights Society (ARS), New York

Elizabeth Murray's *Tangled Fall* (Fig. **2-22**) is reminiscent of any number of bodily organs or underwater life—although no medical student or botanist could ever quite place it according to kingdom, phylum, and so on. The shape looks rawly excised from some creature. The interlacing tubes are reminiscent of veins and capillaries carrying who knows what (or who wants to know what). Such imagery is said to have a biomorphic shape—that is, it has the form (the Greek *morphē*) of biological entities. Rather than have strictly defined shapes, whose boundaries are unyielding, biomorphic shapes seem to ebb and flow, expand and contract, or metamorphose as directed by some inner life force.

Shapes need not be clearly defined or derived from nature or the laws of geometry. Many artists, such as the contemporary painter Helen Frankenthaler, create **amorphous** shapes. In *Bay Side* (Fig. **2-23**), Frankenthaler literally poured paint onto her canvas, creating a nebulous work that is dense in form and rich in texture. The "contents" of the loosely defined shapes spill beyond their boundaries, filling the canvas with irregularly shaped pools of poured paint.

1 ft.

2-22 ELIZABETH MURRAY.
Tangled Fall (1989–1990).
Oil on canvas. 83½" × 66" × 19".
©Elizabeth Murray, courtesy PaceWildenstein, New York

2-23 HELEN FRANKENTHALER.
Bay Side (1967).
Acrylic on canvas.
©2008 Helen Frankenthaler.

Time is not just a mental concept or a mathematical abstraction in the salt desert of Utah's great basin. It can also take on a physical presence.

—NANCY HOLT

2-24 BARBARA KRUGER.

Untitled (What Big Muscles You Have!) (1985).
Photograph. 60" × 80".

Image ©CNAC/MNAM/Reunion des Musees Nationaux/Art Resource, NY.
Courtesy Mary Boone Gallery

Positive and Negative Shapes

Viewers usually focus on the objects or figures represented in works of art. These are referred to as the **positive shapes**. Whatever is left over in the composition, whether empty space or space filled with other imagery, is termed the **negative shape** or shapes of the composition.

Positive and negative shapes in a work of art have a **figure–ground relationship**. The part or parts of the work that are seen as what the artist intended to depict are the figure, and the other parts are seen as the ground, or background. Barbara Kruger's *Untitled What Big Muscles You Have!* (Fig. **2-24**) illustrates that the figure and ground can be distinct even when the relationship between the two is not so clear-cut. Against a satirical running text of the mindless mantra of a hero-worshiper, Kruger sums up the litany with the proclamation "What big muscles you have!" The viewer identifies the larger type as figure and the smaller type of the running text as ground. Notice the visual tension between the large and small type. As we read the larger type, our eye shifts to the pattern and flow of the words behind, and vice versa. The smaller type serves as a kind of psychological wallpaper, signifying one of the horrors of an age of male supremacy that Kruger hopes we left behind in the last millennium.

For many sculptors, negative shapes, or open spaces, are part and parcel of their compositions. The positive shapes in Nancy Holt's *Sun Tunnels* (Fig. **2-25**) consist of the huge concrete pipes she placed in the Utah desert. But the views framed by looking through the interiors of these massive structures—the voids, or negative shapes—have as much or more meaning than the solids. The flow

2-25 NANCY HOLT.

Sun Tunnels (1973–1976).
Concrete. Great Basin Desert, UT.

Image ©Scott T. Smith/CORBIS. Art © Nancy Holt/
Licensed by VAGA, New York, NY

2-26 A Rubin vase.
Gestalt psychologists use this drawing to illustrate the fact that humans tend to perceive objects within their context. When we focus on the vase, it is the figure, and the white shapes to the sides are part of the ground. But when we focus on the "profiles of heads" suggested by the white shapes where they intersect with the sides of the vase, the vase becomes the ground. The drawing is ambiguous; that is, it can be perceived in different ways. As a result, the viewer may experience figure–ground reversals.

of air and light through the pipes—the "sun tunnels"—lends them a lightness of being that contrasts with their actual mass. The artist has, in effect, enlisted the sun as an element in her composition.

Gestalt psychologists have noted that shapes can be ambiguous, so as to encourage **figure–ground reversals** with viewers. Figure **2-26** shows a Rubin vase, which is a classic illustration of figure–ground reversals found in psychology textbooks. The central shape is that of a vase, and when the viewer focuses on it, it is the figure. But "carved" into the sides of the vase are the shapes of human profiles; when the viewer focuses on them, they become the figure and the vase becomes the ground. The point of the Gestalt psychologists is that we tend to perceive things *in context*. When we are focusing on the profiles, the vase is relegated to be perceived as ground, not figure.

The Rubin vase and other psychological illusions were favorite subjects for the contemporary artist Jasper Johns. His painting *Spring* (Fig. **2-27**) shows Rubin vases on a flat canvas with muted colors, among human figures and other fragments of the psychological mind. The askew vases are ambiguous, encouraging figure–ground reversals. The shadowed vase beneath them in the center right is given more prominence by its implied three-dimensionality, and therefore the viewer is not as encouraged to perceive profiles in the negative shapes to its sides. Psychology buffs will also find a well-known drawing of a younger/older woman in the purple space just below the shadowed vase. Can you see why this drawing is ambiguous and allows the viewer's perceptions to shift back and forth so that now one sees a younger woman and now an older woman?

1 ft.

2-27 JASPER JOHNS.
Spring (1986).
Encaustic on canvas, 75" × 50".
Digital Image ©The Museum of Modern Art, New York/ Art Resource, NY. Art ©Jasper Johns/Licences by VAGA, New York, NY

2-28 EDWARD STEICHEN.
Rodin with His Sculptures "Victor Hugo" and "The Thinker" (1902).
Carbon print, toned.
©Réunion des Musées Nationaux/ Art Resource, NY. Reprinted with permission of Joanna T. Steichen.

Edward Steichen's photograph of the sculptor Auguste Rodin silhouetted against his sculpted portrait of Victor Hugo (Fig. **2-28**) creates a visual limbo between figure and ground. The eye readily perceives the contours of the face of Rodin sitting opposite his bronze sculpture of *The Thinker*, also set against the Hugo sculpture. The viewer's sense of what is a positive shape and what is a negative shape undergoes reversals, as the white-clouded image of the background work seems to float toward the viewer. The spectrelike image of Hugo hovers between and above the dark images, filling the space between them and pushing them visually into the background.

Shape as Icon

Some shapes have entered our consciousness in such a way as to carry with them immediate associations. They are never mistaken for anything else. We could say that they have become cultural icons in the same way that an icon of an opening folder in the toolbar of a word-processing program signifies "Click here to view a list of your files." Some of these images have symbolic resonance that raises them above their actual configuration. Consider the Christian Cross, the Jewish Star of David, or the Chinese symbol of yin yang.

Based on what has been called the most famous photograph in the world, the stylized shape of the social activist and revolutionary, Che Guevarra (Fig. **2-29**), has become an icon associated with class struggle, guerilla warfare, and, in general, counterculture. Although many young people wear merchandise from wristwatches to tee shirts emblazoned with the bearded, beret-sporting Che, it is not necessarily because they are familiar with who he was and what he did (an Argentinian physician-turned-Marxist revolutionary who joined Fidel Castro's efforts to depose the U.S.-backed dictator, Fulgencio Battista). From Cuba, Che went on to inspire (or incite) revolutions in Africa and Latin America, where he was captured with the help of the U.S. Central Intelligence Agency (the CIA) and executed. For most young people, Che's instantly recognizable image is simply synonymous with rebellion against authority and idealistic struggle.

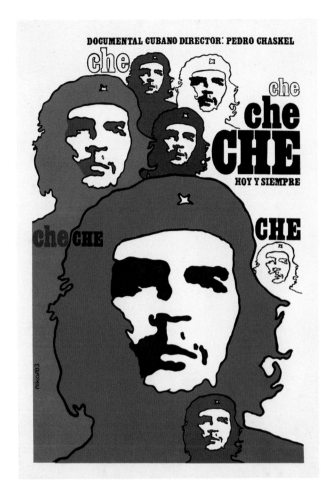

2-29 Che, Hoy y Siempre Movie Poster by Niko
©Swim Ink 2, LLC/CORBIS.

2-30 An Advertisement for the iPod™.
©Justin Sullivan/Getty Images

Similarly, the ad campaigns for the iPod MP3 players from Apple, Inc. have capitalized on shape—from the minimalist design of the iPods to the print ads featuring the silhouetted shapes of consumers using the product (Fig. **2-30**). The shapes of Apple products—iPods, Mac computers, and iPhones—have been so intrinsic to their appeal that financial commentators link the company's success to consumer identification with the products' shapes. Shape is a powerful visual element, and the representation of shape is a powerful design tool.

LIGHT AND VALUE

Light is fascinating stuff. It radiates. It illuminates. It dazzles. It glows. It beckons like a beacon. We speak of the "light of reason." We speak of genius as "brilliance." **Visible light** is part of the spectrum of electromagnetic energy that also includes radio waves and cosmic rays. It undulates wavelike throughout the universe. It bounces off objects and excites cells in our eyes, enabling us to see. Light is at the very core of the visual arts. Without light there is no art. Without light there is no life.

One of the lobes of the brain contains a theater for light. Somehow it distinguishes light from dark. Somehow it translates wavelengths of energy into colors. We perceive the colors of the visible spectrum, ranging from violet to red. Although red has the longest wavelength of the colors of the visible spectrum, these waves are measured in terms of *billionths* of a meter. And if our eyes were sensitive to light of a slightly longer wavelength, we would perceive infrared light waves. Sources of heat, such as our mates, would then literally glow in the dark. And our perceptions, and our visible arts, would be quite different.

Light makes it possible for us to see points, lines, shapes, and textures. All of these can be perceived as light against dark or, in the case of a pencil line on a sheet of paper, as dark against light. Light against dark, dark against light—in the language of art, these are said to be differences in *value*.

The value of a color of a surface is its lightness or darkness. The value is determined by the amount of light reflected by the surface: the greater the amount of light reflected, the lighter

2-31 FANG LIJUN.
No. 2 (1990–1991).
Oil on canvas. 31½" × 39⅓".
©Rheinisches Bildarchiv Koln. Courtesy of the artist.

1 ft.

the surface. More light is reflected by a white surface than by a gray surface, and gray reflects more than black. White, therefore, is lighter than gray, and gray is lighter than black.

Infinite shades of gray lie between black and white. Consider the variations in Fang Lijun's *No. 2* (Fig. **2-31**).

Figure **2-32** is a value scale of gray that contains seven shades of gray, varying between a gray that is almost black to the left and one that is slightly off-white to the right. When we describe works of art in terms of value, not only do we distinguish their range of grays, but we also characterize their *relative* lightness and darkness, that is, their value contrast. **Value contrast** refers to the degrees of difference between shades of gray. Look again at Figure 2-32. Note that there are circles within the squares. Each of them is exactly the same value (they are all equally dark). However, their value contrast with the squares that contain them differs. The circle and square in the center are of the same value, and therefore they have no value contrast. The circles at either end of the scale have high value contrast with the squares that contain them.

Drawing objects or figures with high value contrast makes them easy to see, or makes them "pop." Consider Figure **2-33**. Part A shows a gray sentence typed on gray paper that is nearly as dark; it is difficult to read. Part B shows nearly black type on off-white paper; it is easy to read. Part C shows light type that is "dropped out" of dark gray—it, too, pops out at the reader because of high value contrast.

We can discuss the relative lightness and darkness in a work regardless of whether it is a black-and-white or

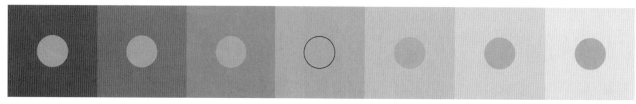

2-32 A value scale of grays.
Do the circles become darker as they move to the right, or do they only appear to do so? How does this value scale support the view of Gestalt psychologists that people make judgments about the objects they perceive that are based on the context of those objects?

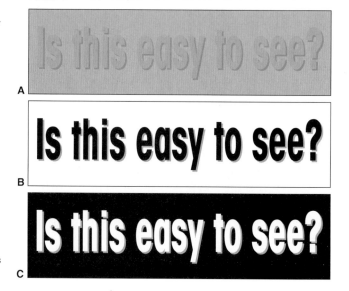

2-33 Value contrast.
Artists and designers know that figures with high value contrast are easier to see. They tend to "pop" out at the viewer. Why is Part A of this figure relatively difficult to read? Why are Parts B and C easier to read?

1 ft.

full-color composition. The term *value pattern* describes
the variation in light and dark within a work of art and
the ways in which they are arranged within a composition. Value patterns can be low-contrast or high-contrast.
A high-contrast value pattern can be seen on the left side
of David Salle's *Angel* (Fig. **2-34**), and a low-contrast value
pattern can be seen on the right side.

Chiaroscuro

Artists use many methods to create the illusion of three
dimensions in two-dimensional media, such as painting,
drawing, or printmaking. They frequently rely on a pattern
of values termed **chiaroscuro**, or the gradual shifting from
light to dark through a successive gradation of tones across
a curved surface. By use of many gradations of value, artists can give objects portrayed on a flat surface a rounded,
three-dimensional appearance.

In *La Source* (Fig. **2-35**), Pierre-Paul Prud'hon creates
the illusion of rounded surfaces on blue gray paper by
using black and white chalk to portray light gradually
dissolving into shade. His subtle modeling of the nude
is facilitated by the middle value of the paper and the
gradation of tones from light to dark through a series of
changing grays. Prud'hon's light source is not raking and
harsh, but diffuse and natural. The forms are not sharply
outlined; we must work to find outlining anywhere but
in the drapery and in the hair. The softly brushed edges

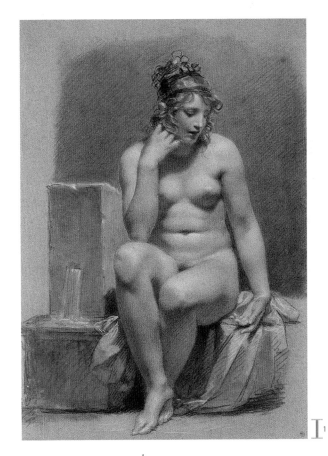

1 in.

2-35 PIERRE-PAUL PRUD'HON.
La Source (c. 1801).
Black and white chalk on blue gray paper. 21 3/16" × 15 5/16".
Sterling and Francine Clark Art Institute, Williamstown, MA.

1 in.

2-36 PABLO PICASSO.
Self-Portrait (1900).
Charcoal on paper. 8⅞" × 6½".
Museu Picasso, Barcelona. ©2009 Estate of Pablo Picasso/
Artists Rights Society (ARS), New York.

Descriptive and Expressive Properties of Value

Values—black, grays, white—may be used purely to describe objects, or they can be used to evoke emotional responses in the viewer.

Black and white may have expressive properties or symbolic associations. Consider the photograph of a performance piece by Lorraine O'Grady (Fig. **2-37**) staged in protest of the opening of an exhibit entitled "Personae," which featured the work of nine white artists and *no* artists of color. Labeling herself "Mlle Bourgeoisie Noire" (or Miss Middle-Class Black), O'Grady appeared in an evening gown constructed of 180 pairs of white gloves and shouted poems that lashed out against the racial politics of the art establishment. Clearly, the white gloves were both evocative and provocative. They were at once a symbol of high society and servitude, of the elegant attire of the exclusive dinner party and the vaudevillian costume of blackface and white-gloved hands.

2-37 LORRAINE O'GRADY.
Mlle Bourgeoise Noire Goes to the New Museum (1981).
Courtesy of the artist.

of the figure lead your eye to perceive three-dimensional form (continuing around into space) rather than flat, two-dimensional shape.

Picasso used chiaroscuro in his *Self-Portrait* (Fig. **2-36**), sketched at the age of 19. Although he restricted himself to the use of charcoal, he managed to effect a more subtle gradation of tone through shading that softly delineates his facial features. Sharp contrasts are eliminated by the choice of a buff-colored paper that provides a uniform flesh tone. In effect, the sides of the nose and cheek are built up through the use of soft shadows. The chin and jaw jut out above the neck through the use of sharper shadowing. The eyes achieve their intensity because they are a dark counterpoint to the evenly modeled flesh. There is a tension between the angularity of the lines in the drawing and the modeling. If you focus on the lines, the drawing may seem to be more angular and geometric than organic, but the use of chiaroscuro creates a more subtle and human rounding of the face.

Rothko's *Number 22* with Rothko's *Black on Grey*

THE AMERICAN ARTIST MARK ROTHKO (1903–1970) worked in many styles during his lifetime. His early work, like that of many twentieth-century artists, was largely in a realistic vein. By the time he was 40 years old, he showed an interest in **Surrealism**, which was imported from Europe. But within a few years, he was painting the **Abstract Expressionist** color-field paintings with which he is mainly associated.

He painted *Number 22* (Fig. **2-38**) in 1949, at about the time a critic remarked that his work tended to evoke the color patterns of French Impressionists and to create "lovely moods." The realistic images of his early days and the symbols of his Surrealistic days were replaced with large, abstract fields of color, which were more or less vertically stacked. Here Rothko uses a high key palette with intensely saturated color. The values in *Number 22* are bold, jaunty, hot, and abrasive. We observe the work of an innovative 46-year-old painter coming into his own—creating his mature style, being invited to teach in academies across the country, and receiving some critical acclaim. The light values seem to imbue the work with boisterous emotion and life. Rothko was developing his signature image of "floating" rectangles that continued to be his model throughout his life's work. The canvases consisted solely of these shapes,

stacked one atop the other, varied in width and height and hue, edges softened with feathered strokes that created the illusion of subtle vibration. By not referring to any specific visual experience, the high key values of these nonobjective works seem to suggest a divine, spiritual presence. The luminosity of *Number 22* is perhaps suggestive of the birth of the universe. The red band in the middle is reminiscent of a horizon line, but all is aglow and alive.

Compare *Number 22* to a work Rothko painted some 20 years later: *Black on Grey* (Fig. **2-39**). The painting reveals one of the most dramatic and resonant uses of black in the history of abstract painting. Toward the end of the 1960s, Rothko began to simplify his color fields, stretching his rectangles out to the very edges of the canvas and effectively dividing the surface into two simple fields. He also reduced his palette to low key values—particularly grays, browns, and black. In Rothko's last painting, *Black on Grey*, created just before he took his own life in his studio on February 25, 1970, black and gray merge at a horizon punctuated by a dull light. Darkness falls heavily on the mottled gray field; note that the title, *Black on Grey*, underscores the symbolism of the encroaching of death. It is as if he has brought his life, and his life's work, to a close. The spiritual presence has flickered out. ■

2-38 MARK ROTHKO.
Number 22 (1949).
Oil on canvas. 117" × 107⅛".

2-39 MARK ROTHKO.
Black on Grey (1970).
Acrylic on canvas, 80¼" × 69".

*It is only after years of preparation that the young artist should touch color—
not color used descriptively, that is, but as a means of personal expression.*

—HENRI MATISSE

COLOR

Color is a central element in our spoken language as well as in the language of art. The language connects emotion with color: we speak of being blue with sorrow, red with anger, green with envy.

The color in works of art can also trigger strong emotional responses in the observer, working hand in hand with line and shape to enrich the viewing experience. The Postimpressionist Vincent van Gogh often chose color more for its emotive qualities rather than for its fidelity

to nature. Likewise in some amorphous abstract works, such as *Bay Side* (Fig. 2-23), color seems to be much of the message being communicated by the artist.

What is color? You have no doubt seen a rainbow or observed how light sometimes separates into several colors when it is filtered through a window. Sir Isaac Newton discovered that sunlight, or white light, can be broken down into different colors by a triangular glass solid called a prism (Fig. **2-40**).

Psychological Dimensions of Color: Hue, Value, and Saturation

The wavelength of light determines its color, or **hue**. The visible spectrum consists of the colors red, orange, yellow, green, blue, indigo, and violet. The wavelength for red is longer than that for orange, and so on through violet.

The value of a color, like the value of any light, is its degree of lightness or darkness. If we wrap the colors of the spectrum around into a circle, we create a color wheel such as that shown in Figure **2-41**. (We must add some purples not found in the spectrum to complete the circle.) Yellow is the lightest of the colors on the wheel, and violet is the darkest. As we work our way around from yellow to violet, we encounter progressively darker colors. Blue–green is about equal in value to red–orange, but green is lighter than red.

The colors on the green–blue side of the color wheel are considered **cool** in "temperature," whereas the colors on the yellow–orange–red side are considered **warm**. Perhaps greens and blues suggest the coolness of the ocean or the sky, and hot things tend to burn red or orange. A room decorated in green or blue may appear more appealing on a hot day in July than a room decorated in red or orange. On a canvas, warm colors seem to advance toward the picture plane. Cool colors, on the other hand, seem to recede.

The **saturation** of a color is its pureness. Pure hues have the greatest intensity, or brightness. The saturation, and hence the intensity, decrease when another hue or black, gray, or white is added. Artists produce **shades** of a given hue by adding black, and **tints** by adding white.

2-40 Prism.

A prism breaks down white light into the colors of the visible spectrum.

Courtesy of Bausch & Lomb.

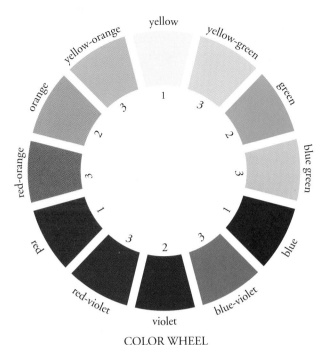

yellow

yellow-orange · · · · yellow-green

orange · · · green

red-orange · · · blue green

red · · · blue

red-violet · · · blue-violet

violet

COLOR WHEEL

2-41 A color wheel.
The color wheel bends the colors of the visible spectrum into a circle and adds a few missing hues to complete the circle.

Additive and Subtractive Colors

When all those years as a child you were mixing finger-paints together, or rubbing crayons across already colored surfaces, you probably thought you were adding colors to other colors. In a piece of irony in which science contradicts common sense, it turns out that you were actually subtracting colors from one another. **Additive colors** have to do with mixing *lights*, and **subtractive** colors have to do with mixing *pigments*.

Additive colors are rays of colored light, which, when overlapped or "mixed" with other rays of color, produce lighter colors and white (Fig. **2-42**). White light can be recreated by overlapping orange-red, blue-violet, and green. Because these colors cannot be derived from the mixing of other colored light, they are called **primary colors**. When they are overlapped, they form lighter colors known as **secondary colors**: the overlap of orange-red and green create yellow; the overlap of blue-violet and green create indigo (or cyan); and lights of blue-violet and orange-red "mix" to form magenta. White is at the center of the three-way overlap of these primary colors.

Subtractive color refers to the mixing of pigment rather than light, and is actually more relevant to the experience of the artist (Fig. **2-43**). When you apply a pigment to a surface, as in applying paint to a canvas, you are applying a substance that causes that surface to reflect every color of the visible spectrum *except for the color you see on the surface*.

Complementary versus Analogous Colors

With pigments, red, blue, and yellow are the primary colors, the ones that we cannot produce by mixing other

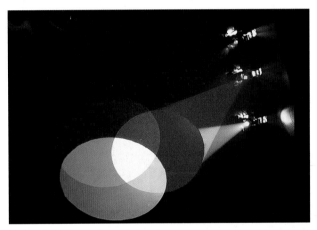

2-42 Additive color mixtures.
One adds colors by mixing lights.
©Fritz Goro, Time & Life Pictures/Getty Images.

2-43 Subtractive color mixtures.
One subtracts colors by mixing pigments.
©Fritz Goro, Time & Life Pictures/Getty Images.

2-44 ROMARE BEARDEN.

J Mood (c. 1985).

Collection of Wynton Marsalis. Art ©Romare Bearden Foundation/
Licensed by VAGA, New York, NY

hues. Mixing pigments of the primary colors creates secondary colors. The three secondary colors are orange (derived from mixing red and yellow), green (blue and yellow), and violet (red and blue), denoted by the number 2 on the color wheel. Tertiary colors are created by mixing pigments of primary and adjoining secondary colors and are denoted by a 3 on the color wheel.

Hues that lie next to one another on the color wheel are **analogous**. They form families of color, such as yellow and orange, orange and red, and green and blue. As we work our way around the wheel, the families intermarry, such as blue with violet and violet with red. Works that use closely related families of color seem harmonious, such as Romare Bearden's *J Mood* (Fig. **2-44**). Works that juxtapose **complementary** colors—colors that lie across from one another on the color wheel—will have the opposite effect. They will appear jarring and discordant rather than harmonious.

Victor Vasarely's *Orion* (Fig. **2-45**) is an assemblage of paper cutouts that take on different intensities depending on their backgrounds. Vasarely, an Op artist, sought to create optical illusions in many of his works. In *Orion*, the shifts from warm to cool hues cause elements of the arrangement to move toward or away from the viewer. The progressions of circles and ellipses within lighter and darker squares contribute to the pulsating sense of the piece.

Local versus Optical Color

Have you ever driven at night and wondered whether vague, wavy lines in the distance outlined the peaks of hills or the bases of clouds? Objects may take on different hues as a function of distance or lighting conditions. The greenness of the trees on a mountain may make a strong impression from the base of the mountain, but from

1 ft.

2-45 VICTOR VASARELY.

Orion (1956).

Paper on paper mounted on wood. 6' 10½" × 6' 6¾".

Hirshhorn Museum and Sculpture Garden, Smithsonian Institution,
Washington, DC. Gift of Joseph H. Hirshhorn, 1966, 66.5389.
©2009 Artists Rights Society (ARS), New York/ADGAP, Paris.

2-46 CLAUDE MONET.

Haystack at Sunset near Giverny (1891).

Oil on canvas. 28⅞" × 36½".

Museum of Fine Arts, Boston. Juliana Cheney Edwards Collection. Bequest of Robert J. Edwards in memory of his mother ©Museum of Fine Arts, Boston, Massachusetts, USA, Juliana Cheney Edwards Collection/The Bridgeman Art Library

1 ft.

a distant vantage point, the atmospheric scattering of light rays may dissolve the hue into a blue haze. Light-colored objects take on a dark appearance when lit strongly from behind. Hues fade as late afternoon wends its way to dusk and dusk to night. **Local color** is defined as the hue of an object as created by the colors its surface reflects under normal lighting conditions. **Optical color** is defined as our perceptions of color, which can vary markedly with lighting conditions.

Consider the *Haystack at Sunset near Giverny* (Fig. **2-46**) by the French Impressionist Claude Monet. Hay is light brown or straw-colored, but Monet's haystack takes on fiery hues, reflecting the angle of the light from the departing sun. The upper reach of the stack, especially, is given a forceful silhouette through flowing swaths of dark color. Surely the pigments of the surface of the haystack are no darker than the roofs of the houses that cling tenuously to an implied horizontal line across the center left of the picture. But the sun washes out their pigmentation. Nor can we with certainty interpret the horizontal above the roofs. Is it the top of a distant hill or the base of a cloud? Only in the visual sanctuary to the front of the haystack do a few possibly accurate greens and browns assert themselves. The amorphous shapes and pulsating color fields of *Haystack* lend the painting a powerful emotional impact.

In *The Night Café* (Fig. **2-47**), Vincent van Gogh used color expressively rather than realistically. A café is generally seen as a place to unwind and relax in the company of friends, yet the artist chose this harsh palette to tell the

2-47 VINCENT VAN GOGH.

The Night Café (1888).

Oil on canvas. 27½" × 35".

©Yale University Art Gallery/Art Resource, NY

1 ft.

angry or white when frightened), but they have in common their use of symbolism: Feelings and behavior are symbolized with color.

Abstract notions and ideas also have their symbolic color coordinates. For example, what does it mean if one is true to the red, white, and blue? If you are an American citizen, it means that you are loyal to your country—The United States of America—as symbolized by the red, white, and blue colors of the flag. But this would also be true if you were, say, a British student or a French student, because their national flags (the Union Jack or the Tri-Color) bear the same color combination, albeit with different designs.

In a subtle but chilling commentary on issues of equality, oppression, and difference, contemporary Nigerian British artist Yinka Shonibare reworked typical Victorian costume in fabrics expressing African identity, both constructed and adopted. In *Victorian Couple* (Fig. **2-48**) the profiles of the coat and bustle may seem familiar, but the colorful textiles and printed designs create a cultural disconnect with symbolic ramifications. Shonibare was born in London of Nigerian parents and spent most of his childhood in Nigeria. He returned to England to study at the University of London and has focused his art on issues of African identity and authenticity, in which the symbolism of color plays a central role.

This brings us to an important fact concerning color and symbolism: The symbols of colors, their meanings, are culture-specific. You may associate white with a bride in American culture, but in China, brides wear red. If you happen to spot a young Chinese American newlywed couple posing for their wedding portraits in a city park, you will likely notice that even though the bride is dressed in white, she wears a prominent red ribbon on her bodice—East meets West.

Texture is another element of art that can evoke a strong emotional response.

2-48 YINKA SHONIBARE.
Victorian Couple (1999).
Wax-printed cotton textile. Approx. 60" × 36" × 36" and 60" × 24" × 24".
Courtesy of Stephen Friedman Gallery, London

1 ft.

world that this is a place where one "can ruin oneself." The red of the walls and the green of the ceiling clash, yet the billiard table and the floor, which both contain reds and greens, marry the two. The agitated swirls of local color that surround the lamps create lights that never were—a psychological display of brilliance and agitation.

Color as Symbol

The connectedness between emotion and color often explains an artist's palette choices. We all link mood with color—we are green with envy, red with anger, blue with sorrow, white with fright. Some of these descriptions may be more accurate than others (faces really do turn red when

TEXTURE

The softness of skin and silk, the coarseness of rawhide and homespun cloth, the coolness of stone and tile, the warmth of wood—these are but a few of the **textures** that artists capture in their works. The word *texture* derives from the Latin for "weaving," and it is used to describe the surface character of woven fabrics and other materials as experienced primarily through the sense of touch.

The element of texture adds a significant dimension to art beyond representation. An artist may emphasize or even distort the textures of objects to evoke a powerful emotional response in the viewer. Consider the contrasting use of texture—and the differing emotional impact—of Leon Kossoff's *Portrait of Father, No. 2* (Fig. **2-49**) and Marie Laurencin's *Mother and Child* (Fig. **2-50**). The first

contains the harsh, gouged textures of **impasto**—that is, the thick buildup of paint on the surface of the canvas. The textures formed by the technique create an overall aggressive, confrontational feeling. If you try to imagine the image rendered with smoother, flatter strokes, some of the dysphoria might well be diminished. As it is, the texture might suggest to some the type of father/authority figure that the psychoanalyst Sigmund Freud believed young boys fear. In Freud's theory, fathers are dangerous rivals for the affections of their mothers.

Laurencin's *Mother and Child*, like Kossoff's *Portrait of Father, No. 2*, is an oil painting. But here the brushstrokes are shorter and flatter, and they gradually build up the imagery rather than "carve" it. The overall texture of *Mother and Child* is soft and seems comforting, reinforcing the feeling of tenderness between mother and child.

In these contrasting portraits, the role of texture surpasses the literal content of the works—that is, they are both portraits of people—to add an emotional dimension for the viewer. The father becomes an oppressive figure by virtue of the tension in the texture, and the mother

1 ft.

2-49 LEON KOSSOFF.
Portrait of Father, No. 2 (1972).
Oil on board. 60" × 36".
Courtesy of L. A. Louver, Venice, CA.

1 ft.

2-50 MARIE LAURENCIN.
Mother and Child (1928).
Oil on canvas. 32" × 25½" (81.3 cm × 63.8 cm).
City of Detroit Purchase, 28.99. Photograph ©1989 The Detroit Institute of Arts. ©2009 Artists Rights Society (ARS), New York/ADAGP, Paris.

becomes a symbol of nurturance by virtue of the tranquility in the texture. In both portraits, texture augments the meaning of the work.

Types of Texture

In three-dimensional media such as sculpture, crafts, and architecture, the materials have definable textures or *actual texture*. In a two-dimensional medium such as painting, we discuss texture in other terms. For example, the surface of a painting has an *actual* texture—it can be rough, smooth, or something in between. But we typically discuss the surface only when the texture is palpable or unusual, as when thick impasto is used or when an unusual material is added to the surface.

Actual Texture

Actual texture is *tactile*. When you touch an object, your fingertips register sensations of its actual texture—rough, smooth, sharp, hard, soft. Any work of art has actual texture—whether it is the hard, cold texture of marble or the rough texture of pigment on canvas. Vincent van Gogh's *Sunflowers* (Fig. **2-51**) is rendered with a great deal of surface texture. Van Gogh used impasto—the most common painting technique that yields actual texture—to define his forms, and he often deviated from realistic

colors and textures to heighten the emotional impact of his work. The surface texture of the painting goes beyond the real texture of the blossom to communicate an emotional intensity and passion for painting that is independent of the subject matter and more linked to the artistic process—that is, to the artist's method of using gestural brushstrokes to express his sensibilities.

Visual Texture

Simulated texture in a work of art is referred to as **visual texture**. Artists use line, color, and other elements of art to create the illusion of various textures in flat drawings and paintings. The surface of Rachel Ruysch's *Flower Still Life* (Fig. **2-52**) is smooth and glasslike; however, an abundance of textures is *simulated* by the painstaking detail of the flowers and leaves.

2-52 RACHEL RUYSCH.
Flower Still Life (after 1700).
Oil on canvas. 29¾" × 23⅞".
The Toledo Museum of Art, OH. Purchased with funds from the Libbey Endowment, Gift of Edward Drummond Libbey, 1956.57

2-51 VINCENT VAN GOGH.
Sunflowers (1887).
Oil on canvas. 43.2 cm × 61 cm.
The Metropolitan Museum of Art, N.Y. Rogers Fund
Image copyright ©The Metropolitan Museum of Art/Art Resource, NY

2-53 DAVID GILHOOLY.
Bowl of Chocolate Moose (1989).
Ceramic. 10" × 6" × 7" (25.4 cm × 15.2 cm × 17.8 cm).
Courtesy of the artist.

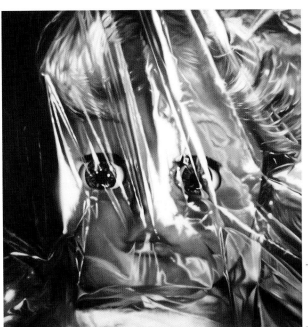

2-54 JAMES ROSENQUIST.
Gift Wrapped Doll #19 (1992).
Oil on canvas. 60" × 60" (152 cm × 152 cm).
Art ©James Rosenquist/Licensed by VAGA, New York, NY.

Artists employ a variety of materials to create visual texture, or the illusion of surfaces or textures far removed from their actual texture. Touch David Gilhooly's *Bowl of Chocolate Moose* (Fig. **2-53**), and, your eyes will tell you, your hand will come away covered with that sticky confection. The surface may appear to be warm and pliable, as if this chocolate moose were panting and melting away into an edible dessert. In fact, it is hard and cool to the touch. The actual texture of the ceramic from which it is made is completely contrary to the illusion that the artist has achieved. *Chocolate Moose* is an artistic pun of virtuoso technique that demonstrates how the visual texture of a work of art affects our response to it. What memories does it conjure up for you? Eating a chocolate bar on a warm summer day?

The success of the visual pun in Gilhooly's *Chocolate Moose* is wholly dependent on the artist's ability to fool the eye. Artists call this **trompe l'oeil**—the French phrase that literally means "trick the eye." Trompe l'oeil

has made its appearance throughout the history of art, from first-century BCE Roman wall painting to contemporary Photorealism.

In *Gift Wrapped Doll #19* (Fig. **2-54**), Pop artist James Rosenquist uses a common medium—oil on canvas—to simulate the texture of cellophane wrapped around the head of a wide-eyed porcelain doll. The folds of the transparent wrap reflect light, tearing across the innocent face like white-hot rods. We feel, as observers, that were we to poke at the cellophane, we would hear a crackling sound and the pattern of lightning-like stripes would change direction. The image of a doll is usually that of a cuddly companion, but Rosenquist's specimen is haunting and sinister. Perhaps it is a commentary on the ways in which the Western ideal of beauty—blue eyes, blond hair, and a "Cupid's bow" mouth—can suffocate the little girls who grow into women.

Subversive Texture

Textures are sometimes chosen or created by the artist to subvert or undermine our ideas about the objects they depict. **Subversive texture** compels the viewer to look again at an object and to think about it more deeply.

1 in.

You may take objects such as a cup, saucer, and spoon for granted, but not after viewing Meret Oppenheim's *Object* (Fig. **2-55**). Oppenheim uses subversive texture in lining a cup, saucer, and spoon with fur. Teacups are usually connected with civilized and refined settings and occasions. The coarse primal fur completely subverts these associations, rendering the thought of drinking from this particular cup repugnant. *Object* also shows how textures can simultaneously attract and repel us. Does Oppenheim want the viewer to ponder the violence that has enabled civilization to grow and endure?

SPACE

"No man is an island, entire of itself," wrote the poet John Donne. If Donne had been speaking of art, he might have written, "No subject exists in and of itself." A building has a site, a sculpture is surrounded by space, and even artists who work in two-dimensional media such as drawing and painting create figures that bear relationships to one another and to their grounds. Objects exist in three-dimensional space. Artists either carve out or model their works within three-dimensional space, or else somehow come to terms with three-dimensional space through two-dimensional art forms.

In Chapters 10 and 12, which discuss the three-dimensional art forms of sculpture and architecture, we explore ways in which artists situate their objects in space and envelop space. In Chapter 12, we chronicle the age-old attempt to enclose vast reaches of space that began with massive support systems and currently focuses on lightweight steel-cage and shell-like structures. In this section, we examine ways in which artists who work in two dimensions create the illusion of depth—that is, the third dimension.

Overlapping

When nearby objects are placed in front of more distant objects, they obscure part or all of the distant objects. Figure **2-56** shows two circles and two arcs, but our perceptual experiences encourage us to interpret the drawing as showing four circles, two in the foreground and two in back. Likewise, this perceptual phenomenon allows an artist to create the illusion of depth by overlapping objects,

2-56 Overlapping circles and arcs.

or apparently placing one in front of another. Many of the works in your textbook illustrate the technique of overlapping and its effect in suggesting space—whether deep, as in Church's *The Andes of Ecuador* (Fig. 2-68), or shallow, as in Orozco's *Epic of American Civilization* (Fig. 1-36).

Relative Size and Linear Perspective

The farther objects are from us, the smaller they appear to the eye. To recreate this visual phenomenon and to create the illusion of three-dimensionality on a two-dimensional surface, such as a canvas, artists employ a variety of techniques, among them **relative size** and **linear perspective**.

For example, things that are supposed to be closer to the viewer are larger, whereas things that are supposed to be more distant are smaller. This simple principle of relative size can do wonders to suggest spatial complexity in works such as *Heirs Come to Pass, 3* (Fig. **2-57**) by Martina López.

The space in the composition is divided into three principal areas—foreground, middle ground, and background. The stagelike setting consists of a broad and minimally defined landscape that fills most of the area of the piece, leaving just a small strip for a cloud-soaked sky. With no apparent design, figures (from old family photographs) are digitally patched into the print. They range from looming to barely visible, and their size relative to one another creates whatever illusion of space there is. For López, this "visual terrain" is open, not only to her own memories, but also to those of the viewer.

1 ft.

2-57 MARTINA LÓPEZ.
Heirs Come to Pass, 3 (1991).
Silver dye bleach print made from digitally assisted montage. 76.2 cm × 127 cm.
Smithsonian American Art Museum. Gift of the Consolidated Gas Company Foundation
Image ©Smithsonian American Art Museum, Washington, DC/Art Resource, NY. ©Martina López

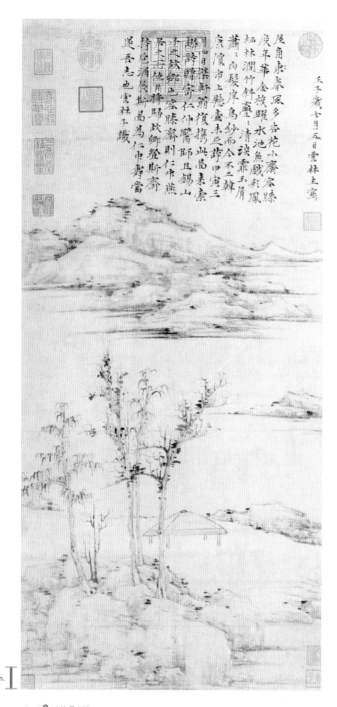

1 in.

2-58 NI ZAN.

Rongxi Studio (Late Yuan/Early Ming dynasty, 1372 CE).
Hanging scroll; ink on paper. H: 29¼".

Collection of the National Palace Museum, Taipei, Taiwan, Republic of China.

In the Chinese ink drawing shown in Figure **2-58**, the natural elements at the top and bottom of the scroll are shown at the same size, as if they were seen from the same distance. Yet the viewer—particularly the schooled viewer—tends to perceive the hills at the top as being

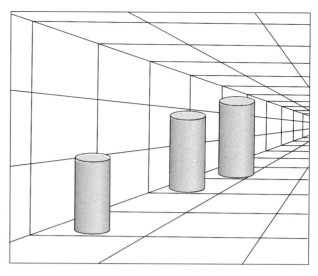

2-59 A visual illusion.

farther away. Objects depicted at the bottom of a work tend to be perceived as being closer to the viewer.

We see this again in Figure **2-59**. Note how the cylinders appear to grow larger toward the top of the composition. Why? For at least two reasons: (1) Objects at the bottom of a composition are usually perceived as being closer to the picture plane; and (2) the converging lines are perceived as being parallel, even when they are not. However, if they were parallel, then space would have to recede toward the center right of the composition, and the cylinder in that region would have to be farthest from the viewer. According to rules of perspective, a distant object that appears to be equal in size to a nearby object would have to be larger, so we perceive the cylinder to the right as the largest, although it is equal in size to the others.

Figures **2-60** through **2-63** show that the illusion of depth can be created in art by making parallel lines come together, or converge, at one or more **vanishing points** on an actual or implied **horizon**. The height of the horizon in the composition corresponds to the apparent location of the viewer's eyes, that is, the **vantage point** of the viewer. As we shall see in later chapters, the Greeks and Romans had some notion of linear perspective, but Renaissance artists such as Leonardo da Vinci refined perspective.

In **one-point perspective** (Fig. **2-60**), parallel lines converge at a single vanishing point on the horizon. Raphael's (1483–1520) Renaissance masterpiece *School of Athens* (Fig. **2-64**) is a monumental example of one-point perspective. Representing Philosophy, it was one of four matching frescos depicting the most valuable aspects of a pope's education. The painting is a virtual who's-who of intellectual shakers and movers from antiquity to the

2-60 One-point perspective.

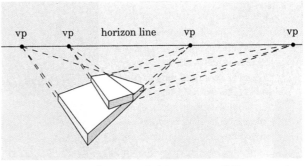

2-62 Perspective drawing of objects set at different angles.

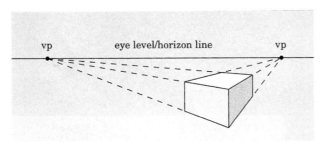

2-61 Two-point perspective.

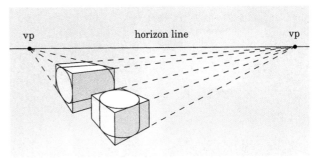

2-63 Curved objects drawn in perspective.

Renaissance. Plato (left) and Aristotle (right) occupy the center of the congregation, sharing the spotlight and representing divergent philosophical perspectives. The horizon line cuts through the center of their bodies, and the vanishing point sits squarely between them (Fig.

2-65). Converging on this point are orthogonals that can be traced from the patterns of the marble flooring below the horizon line and the horizontal entablatures sitting atop the piers that recede dramatically toward the rear of the arcade.

2-64 RAFFAELLO SANZIO (CALLED RAPHAEL).
Philosophy, or School of Athens (1509–1511).
Fresco. Approximately 26' × 18'.
©Scala/Art Resource, NY

2-65 Perspective in *School of Athens*.
Raphael's painting is a powerful example of one-point perspective.
©Scala/Art Resource, NY

In **two-point perspective** (Fig. 2-61), two sets of parallel lines converge at separate vanishing points on the horizon. You would be hard-pressed to find a clearer use of two-point perspective than in Gustave Caillebotte's *Paris Street: Rainy Day* (Fig. **2-66**). We see the building in the background from the eye level of the figures in the foreground. The sight lines follow the receding dual facades of the building toward two distinct vanishing points (Fig. **2-67**).

We can use additional sets of parallel lines to depict objects that are set at different angles, as shown in Figure 2-62. Figure 2-63 shows how curved objects may be "carved out" of rectangular solids.

Atmospheric Perspective

In atmospheric perspective (also called *aerial perspective*), the illusion of depth is created by techniques such as texture gradients, brightness gradients, color saturation, and the manipulation of warm and cool colors. A gradient is a progressive change. The effect of a **texture gradient** relies on the fact that closer objects are perceived as having rougher or more detailed surfaces. The effect of a **brightness gradient** is due to the lesser intensity of distant objects.

Frederic Edwin Church's masterpiece, *Andes of Ecuador* (Fig. **2-68**), relies in part on atmospheric perspective to create the illusion of deep vistas. The foreground of the picture contains great botanical detail. As the vista recedes into the distance, the plants and hills become less textured and the colors become less saturated. Church belonged to the Hudson River School of nineteenth-century American painting. The group's members used landscape as a vehicle for communicating the feeling of awe they experienced when they encountered the romantic, scientific, and religious ideas of the era—a world without limits.

The haunting painting *Schunnemunk Mountain* (Fig. **2-69**) reveals Sylvia Plimack Mangold's fascination with the transitional moments of the day. Here in the evening of the Hudson River Valley, brightness gradients employing purple, navy, and cobalt set the hills beneath the sky. The dark foreground is rendered more vacant by twinkling lights that suggest habitation in the valley beyond.

1 ft.

2-66 GUSTAVE CAILLEBOTTE.
Paris Street: Rainy Day (1877).
Oil on canvas. 83½" × 108¼".
Charles H. and Mary F. S. Worcester Collection, 1964.336, The Art Institute of Chicago.
Photography ©The Art Institute of Chicago.

2-67 Perspective in Caillebottoe's *Paris Street: Rainy Day*.
The use of two-point perspective in the Caillebotte painting is powerful and obvious. It draws our attention upward from the prominent figures in the foreground.
Charles H. and Mary F. S. Worcester Collection, 1964.336, The Art Institute of Chicago.
Photography ©The Art Institute of Chicago.

1 ft.

2-68 FREDERIC EDWIN CHURCH.

Andes of Ecuador (1855).

Oil on canvas. 48" × 75".

Original purchase from the Mary Reynolds Babcock Foundation, Z. Smith Reynolds Foundation, ARCA Foundation, and Anne Cannon Forsyth, 1966.2.9. Reynolda House, Museum of American Art, Winston-Salem, North Carolina

2-69 SYLVIA PLIMACK MANGOLD.

Schunnemunk Mountain (1979).

Oil on canvas. 60" × 80⅛".

Courtesy of Dallas Museum of Art, Dallas, TX.

1 ft.

I paint with shapes.

—ALEXANDER CALDER

TIME AND MOTION

Objects and figures exist and move not only through space but also through the dimension of time. In its inexorable forward flow, time provides us with the chance to develop and grasp the visions of our dreams. Time also creates the stark limits beyond which none of us may extend.

Artists through the ages have sought to represent three-dimensional space in two-dimensional art forms as well as to represent, or imply, movement and the passage of time. Only in modern times have art forms such as cinematography and video been developed that involve *actual* movement and *actual* time.

Actual Motion

Artists create or capture **actual motion** in various ways. **Kinetic art** (from the Greek *kinesis*, meaning "movement") and photography are two of them. Most works of art sit quietly on the wall or, perhaps, on a pedestal, but kinetic art is designed to move.

The **mobiles** of Alexander Calder are some of the most popular examples of kinetic art in the twentieth century. The colossal mobile that hangs in the interior of the East Building of the National Gallery of Art (Fig. **2-70**) is composed of winglike dashes and disks of different sizes that are cantilevered from metal rods such that they can rotate horizontally—in orbits—as currents of air press against them. However, the center of gravity remains stable, so the entire sculpture is hung from a single point. Unlike a painting, the mobile changes according to the movement of air above and the movement of the observer below, who might shift vantage points to create new compositions, new relationships among the shapes and lines.

With Liz Magic Laser's *The Thing #25* (Fig. **2-71**), the work of art is the record of a moment in time choreographed for the purposes of the photograph. Many of Laser's works examine the relationship between people and liquid; her subjects are typically immersed in it, spattered by it, or projecting it. What captivates the viewer, however, is the way in which time has stopped in this work, exaggerating the impact and ejection of a mysterious green goo.

2-70 ALEXANDER CALDER.

Untitled (1972).

East Building mobile.

National Gallery of Art, Washington, DC. Gift of the Collectors Committee, 1977. 76.1, Image ©2003 Board of Trustees, National Gallery of Art, Washington, DC, 1976. ©2009 Calder Foundation, New York/Artists Rights Society (ARS), New York.

1 ft.

Implied Motion and Time

The Thing #25 captured motion through the use of **stopped time**. Other works of art imply motion; that is, the viewer infers that motion is occurring or has occurred. **Implied motion** and **implied time** are found in Baroque sculptor Gianlorenzo Bernini's *Apollo and Daphne* (Fig. **2-72**) through the use of diagonal lines of force that help simulate movement from left to right. In the Greek myth, the wood nymph Daphne beseeches the gods to help her escape the overtures of Apollo. As Apollo gains on her, her prayer is answered in a most ironic manner because the gods choose to facilitate her "escape" by transforming her into a tree. In Bernini's sculpture, we see Daphne just at the point when bark begins to enfold her body, her toes begin to take root, and her fingertips are transformed into the branches of a laurel. The passage of time is implied as she is caught in the midst of her transformation.

In *Apollo and Daphne*, motion is implied in the fluid strides and seamless transfiguration of Daphne. Motion can also be implied through repetitive imagery. We are all familiar with the way in which comic strips suggest the motion of the characters by repetition of imagery that changes slightly from frame to frame. This technique spans time and culture.

In an illustration from the medieval Moutier-Grandval Bible (Fig. **2-73**), the entire story of Adam and Eve is told through the repetition of the characters in comic-strip fashion—in horizontal strips stacked one atop the other. Time passes from the Creation of Adam through the Temptation and the Expulsion from the Garden of Eden to the last segment, in which we find Eve having given birth and Adam toiling in the fields. The pictorial elements—such as the landscape—are kept to a minimum, focusing our attention on the principal characters and the narrative.

The Illusion of Motion

There is a difference between implied motion and the illusion of motion. Works such as *Apollo and Daphne* imply that motion has occurred or that time has passed. In other works, artists use techniques to suggest that motion is *in the process of occurring* rather than having occurred. We say that these works contain the illusion of motion.

Early experiments with photography provided an illusion of the figure in motion through the method of rapid multiple exposures. In his *Man Pole Vaulting* (Fig. **2-74**), Thomas Eakins—better known for his paintings—used photo sequences to study the movement of the human

1 in.

2-73 *Scenes from Genesis* (c. 840 CE).
Illustration in the Moutier-Grandval Bible. 20" × 14¾".
©The British Library/HIP/Art Resource, NY

2-74 THOMAS EAKINS.

Man Pole Vaulting (c. 1884).
Photograph.

Courtesy of the Metropolitan Museum of Art. Gift of Charles Bregler, 1941 (41.142.11). Copy photograph ©The Metropolitan Museum of Art, New York.

body. In the wake of these experiments, several artists created the illusion of motion by applying the visual results of multiple-exposure photography to their paintings.

Marcel Duchamp's *Nude Descending a Staircase #2* (Fig. **2-75**) in effect creates multiple exposures of a machine-tooled figure walking down a flight of stairs. The overlapping of shapes and the repetition of linear patterns blur the contours of the figure. Even though an unkind critic labeled the Duchamp painting "an explosion in a shingle factory," it symbolized the dynamism of the modern machine era.

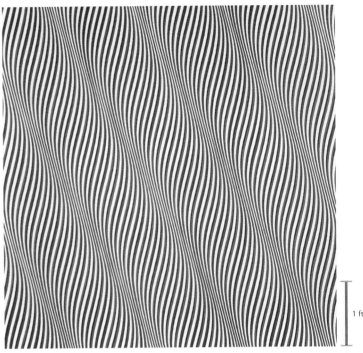

1 ft.

2-76 BRIDGET RILEY.
Gala (1974).
Acrylic on canvas. 5'2¾" square.

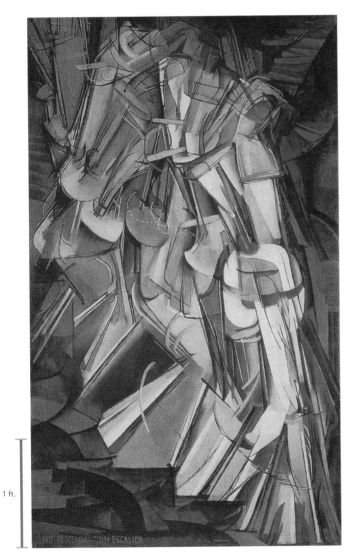

1 ft.

2-75 MARCEL DUCHAMP.
Nude Descending a Staircase #2 (1912).
Oil on canvas. 58" × 35".
Philadelphia Museum of Art, Louise and Walter Arensberg Collection.
Image ©The Philadelphia Museum of Art/Art Resource, NY.
©2009 Artist Rights Society (ARS), New York/ADAGP, Paris/
Succession Marcel Duchamp.

The movement of the 1960s and 1970s known as **Op Art** was based on creating optical sensations of movement through the repetition and manipulation of color, shape, and line. In kinetic sculpture, movement is real, whether activated by currents of air or motors. In Op Art, bold and apparently vibrating lines and colors create the illusion of movement. Bridget Riley's *Gala* (Fig. **2-76**) is composed of a series of curved lines that change in thickness and proximity to one another. These changes seem to suggest waves, but they also create a powerful illusion of rippling movement. Complementary red and green colors also contribute to the illusion of vibration. When we look at a color for an extended period of time, we tend to perceive its **afterimage**. Red is the afterimage of green, and vice versa. Therefore, there seems to be a pulsating in Riley's selection of color as well as in the tendency of the eye to perceive the lines as rippling.

If the visual elements are considered the basic vocabulary of art, principles of design might be viewed as the grammar of art. Artists use principles of design to combine the visual elements into compositions. In art, as in life, this "language" is idiosyncratic to the individual.

3

PRINCIPLES OF DESIGN

He searched disorder for its unifying principle.
—Brian O'Doherty on Stuart Davis

Unity is one of the principles of design, which, like visual elements, are part of the basic language of art. Just as people use principles of grammar to combine words into sentences, artists use principles of design to combine the visual elements of art into compositions that have a certain style, form, and content.

Design or **composition** is a process—the act of organizing the visual elements to effect a desired aesthetic in a work of art. Designs can occur at random, as exemplified by the old mathematical saw that an infinite number of monkeys pecking away at an infinite number of typewriters would eventually (though mindlessly) produce *Hamlet*. But when artists create compositions, they consciously draw upon design principles such as unity and variety, balance, emphasis and focal point, rhythm, scale, and proportion. This is not to say that all artists necessarily apply these principles, or even always recognize the extent of their presence in their work. In fact, some artists prefer to purposefully violate them.

UNITY AND VARIETY

Unity is oneness or wholeness. A work of art achieves unity when its parts seem necessary to the composition as a whole. Artists generally prefer to place some variety within a unified composition to add visual interest, but the principle of variety is most often subservient to the sense of oneness or overall unity in a work.

Ways to Achieve Unity and Variety within Unity

Andy Warhol built *Ethel Scull Thirty-Six Times* (Fig. **3-1**) on the principal of a grid—an extreme example of unity—drawing attention to the ubiquity of mass-produced consumables of any and all types, including human beings of celebrity. Reflecting his signature compositional arrangement, the work consists of the repetition of silk-screened photo-booth-type images, in this case of Ethel Scull, an important patron of the arts in the 1960s. An overall unity abides within the nine-by-four grid and repetitive color scheme, but the wide variety of expressions create a multidimensional view of Scull's appearance and personality. Warhol's multiportrait serves as an excellent illustration of variety within unity. The more you look at works of art, the better you will become at sensing the unity of compositions and at pinpointing the ways that artists achieve it. Sometimes the techniques will be obvious, and at other times they will be subtler.

Archibald Motley Jr.'s *Saturday Night* (Fig. **3-2**) offers the viewer a captivating array of characters—from the dining and drinking patrons and the waiters balancing

3-1 ANDY WARHOL.
Ethel Scull Thirty-Six Times (1963).
Synthetic polymer paint silkscreened on canvas. 79¾" × 143¼".

1 ft.

3-2 ARCHIBALD J. MOTLEY JR.

Saturday Night (1935).

Oil on canvas. 81.3 cm × 101.6 cm.

The Howard University Gallery of Art, Washington, D.C.

Courtesy Valerie Gerrard-Browne and Chicago History Museum

of unity in this work. Here the diversity of the players in this mythologized narrative of American history—the Spanish conquistador, the European colonizer, the Native American—are joined symbolically and pictorially by the echoing shapes and lines and rhythms that define and distinguish the figures and landscape elements. The emergence of a visual pattern of similar elements dominates the individual parts.

their orders on tottering trays to one particularly flamboyant woman in a flame red costume who seems lost in the expressive rhythms of her solo dance. Yet this cacophony of sights and sounds and movements achieves a sense of oneness through a unified color field. To be sure, there is also some variety in the color scheme: The eye leaps from patches of black to black and from white to white, mimicking the riot of movement in the nightclub. However, the overall composition is unified by the pulsating reds that seem to emanate from the center of the dance floor and bathe the atmosphere with emotion, energy, and an almost mystical glow.

Although color harmonies also contribute to a sense of oneness in Thomas Hart Benton's *Palisades* (Fig. **3-3**), the curvilinear rhythms of shape and line are the strongest purveyors

When working with the principles of variety and unity, an artist will often keep one or more aspects of the work constant so that despite the multiplicity of images or elements, the composition's overall unity will not be compromised. The device of continuity to effect unity is also seen

3-3 THOMAS HART BENTON.

Palisades, from the American Historical Epic series (1919–1924).

Oil on cotton duck on aluminum honeycomb panel. 66⅛" × 72".

Nelson-Atkins Museum of Art, Kansas City, MO. Bequest of the artist (F75-21/2). Art ©T. H. Benton and Rita R. Benton Testamentary Trusts/UMB Bank Trustee/Licensed by VAGA, New York, NY

in a work that is, literally, a world apart—Delilah Montoya's *Los Jovenes* (Youth) (Fig. **3-4**). It too features eight figures (and here a hovering image of the Virgin of Guadalupe), some interacting, some not; some confronting the viewer, some not the least bit interested in doing so. Continuity is reflected in the ages of the youths, their ethnicity, and a suggested bond of friendship. As in *Palisades*, our eye can travel from one side of the photograph to the other, picking out lights and darks, shifts in foreground and background, and the prominence of hand gestures and positions. The visual flow is effortless.

All of the works we have discussed have **visual unity**; most embrace the principle of variety within unity. There is, however, a way to achieve unity in a composition that does not rely on the consistency or repetition of the elements of art. Sometimes artists pursue, instead, a unity of ideas and impose a **conceptual unity** on their work. They will recognize that the strength of a composition lies in the diversity of elements and their juxtaposition. They reject visual harmonies in favor of discordant punctuations and focus on the relationships between the meanings and functions of the images. Emma Amos's *Measuring Measuring* (Fig. **3-5**) offers an example of conceptual unity. The "ideal" human form is represented by works of art from the Western canon flanking the seminude figure of an African woman. "Measuring" has at least a double meaning—the

3-5 EMMA AMOS.
Measuring Measuring (1995).
Acrylic on linen canvas, African fabric, laser-transfer photographs. 84" × 70".
Courtesy of the artist and Flomenhaft Gallery

3-4 DELILAH MONTOYA.
Los Jovenes (Youth) (1993).
Collotype. 23.3 cm × 25.4 cm.
Image ©Smithsonian American Art Museum, Washington, DC/ Art Resource, NY. ©Delilah Montoya

measure of the African standard of beauty against that of the Western tradition and the measure of black against white. The images are physically incongruous, and the elements of the composition do not encourage visual unity. What unites this composition is the concept behind the work: the challenge to address the standard and the canon.

Emphasis on Variety

When artists emphasize variety, they are usually exaggerating differences rather than similarities among their images. Palmer Hayden's painting called *The Subway* (Fig. **3-6**) is a demographic and ethnic cross section of the strap-hanging population of 1930s New York City. Even though they are unified by the common need to move efficiently from place to place beneath the streets of the metropolis, this fact is not the main theme of the work. Rather, the artist builds

3-6 PALMER HAYDEN.
The Subway (c. 1930).
Oil on canvas. 31" × 26½".
New York State Office of General Services, Adam Clayton Powell, Jr.,
State Office Building, New York, New York, USA

his painting around the individuality and diversity of the riders. Hayden's emphasis on variety is signified in the juxtaposition of the light and dark hands at the center of the painting. This snapshot of subway life hasn't changed much in three-quarters of a century. The underground in New York City remains a great equalizer, and as one surveys the contemporary scene, one finds an even greater human diversity, with even more emphasis on variety.

BALANCE

Most people prefer to have some stability in their lives, to have their lives on a "firm footing." In the same way, most people respond positively to some degree of balance in the visual arts. When we walk, run, or perform an athletic feat, balance refers to the way in which our weight is distributed, or shifts, so that we remain in control of our movements. **Balance** in art also refers to the distribution of the weight—of the actual or apparent weight of the elements of a composition. As the athlete uses balance to

control movement, so might the artist choose to use balance to control the distribution or emphasis of elements such as line or shape or color in a composition.

The Classical Greek artist Polykleitos was perhaps the first artist to observe the body's shifting of weight in order to achieve balance and to develop a set of rules to apply this observation to representations of the figure. In his *Doryphoros* (Fig. **3-7**), or Spear Bearer, Polykleitos featured his weight-shift principle. He observed that when the body is at rest, one leg bears the weight of the body and the other is relaxed. Further, in order for the body to balance itself, the upper torso shifts, as if corresponding to an S curve, so that the arm opposite the tensed leg is tensed, and the one opposite the relaxed leg is relaxed. Thus, with the weight-shift principle, tension and tension and relaxation and relaxation are read diagonally across the body. Overall figural balance is achieved.

3-7 POLYKLEITOS.
Doryphoros (c. 450–440 BCE).
Roman copy after bronze Greek original. Marble. 6' 6".
National Museum, Naples. ©Scala/Art Resource, NY

3-8 LYGIA CLARK.
Cabeça Coletiva (Collective Head) (1975).
Courtesy, Cultural Association, "The World of Lygia Clark." "Family Clark's Collection."

Actual Balance and Pictorial Balance

Sculptures such as *Doryphoros* have *actual weight* and may thus also have actual balance. Even though actual weight and **actual balance** are not typically at issue in two-dimensional works such as drawings, paintings, and prints, we nonetheless do speak of balance in these compositions. **Pictorial balance** refers to the distribution of the apparent or *visual weight* of the elements in works that are basically two-dimensional, and there are many ways to achieve it. Brazilian artist Lygia Clark's photograph of her performance piece *Cabeça Coletiva* (Collective Head) (Fig. **3-8**) possesses both actual and pictorial balance. She and her students filled a large hatlike object with fruit, shoes, love letters—even money—and walked amidst the public,

distributing the offerings. The photo reveals that the bearer of gifts is literally engaged in a balancing act while the visual weight of his figure is balanced to the left and right by the companions who guide him.

Symmetrical Balance

You can divide the human body in half vertically, and in the ideal, as in Leonardo da Vinci's most famous drawing, *Proportion of the Human Figure* (Fig. **3-9**), there will be an exact correspondence between the left and right sides. **Symmetry** refers to similarity of form or arrangement on either side of a dividing line or plane, or to correspondence of parts in size, shape, and position. When the correspondence is exact, as in Leonardo's drawing, we refer to it as *pure* or *formal symmetry*. In reality, nature is not as perfect as Leonardo would have had it.

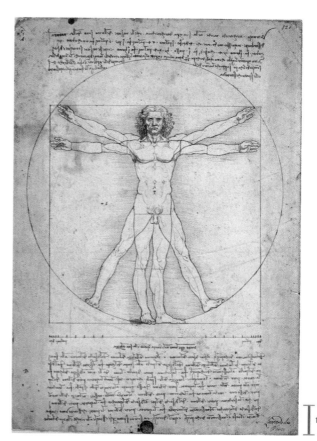

1 in.

3-9 LEONARDO DA VINCI.
Proportion of the Human Figure (after Vitruvius) (c. 1485–1490).
Pen and ink. 13½" × 9¾".
Academia, Venice, Italy. ©Scala/Art Resource, NY

3-10 The United States Capitol Building, Washington, D.C.
©Kenneth Garrett/Woodfin Camp Associates.

Examples of pure or formal symmetry appear no more frequently in art than in nature. More typically, **symmetrical balance** is created through *approximate* symmetry, in which the whole of the work has a symmetrical feeling, but slight variations provide more visual interest than would a mirror image. When the variations to the right and left side of the composition are *more* than slight, yet there remains an overall sense of balance, there is said to be **asymmetrical balance**.

In *pure* or *formal symmetry*, also known as **bilateral symmetry**, everything in a composition to either side of an actual or imaginary line is the same. The regularity and predictability of symmetry cannot help but conjure a sense of peace, calm, comfort, and order. The effect of repetition can be mesmerizing. In architectural works like the United States Capitol Building (Fig. **3-10**)—the house in which the laws of the land are created—repetition and symmetry can imply rationality and decorum, tying the structure of the building to a certain symbolic ideal. The design of the Capitol consists of a solid rectangular structure flanked by identical wings that extend from the central part of the building, project forward at right angles, and culminate in "temple fronts" that echo the main entrance beneath a hemispherical dome. An ordinary citizen of the republic takes pride in the architectural grandeur, feels secure in the balance of all of the parts, and—with the obvious references to Greek architecture of the Golden Age—feels a part of the history of democracy. It is no coincidence that, for the nation's Capitol, our founders adapted structures such as the Parthenon of Athens in the hope of associating the new republic with the ancient birthplace of democracy.

In many works of art, the symmetry is *approximate* rather than exact. For example, the overall impression of William Wegman's *Ethiopia* (Fig. **3-11**) is that of symmetry, primarily attributable to the echoing shapes of the Weimaraners' heads and the firm

1 ft.

3-11 WILLIAM WEGMAN.
Ethiopia (2006).
Pigment print. 36" × 44".
Collection of Lois Fichner-Rathus. ©William Wegman.

vertical line that bisects the composition. Yet there are elements that break the monotony of the symmetry, such as the juxtaposition of near-complementary shades of red and green, and the contrast of the clear, detailed face of the dog on the right with ghostlike iteration on the left.

Asymmetrical Balance

When your eyes are telling you that the elements of a composition are skewed but your brain is registering overall balance, chances are you are witnessing asymmetrical balance. There is probably a human tendency to effect balance at any cost. Sometimes the right and left sides of a composition bear visibly different shapes, colors, textures, or other elements, yet they are arranged or "weighted" in such a way that the impression, in total, is one of balance. In such cases, the artist has employed the design principle of *asymmetrical* or *informal balance*.

In Wu Jide's *River Dwellers* (Fig. **3-12**), patches of white and well-placed touches of color are responsible for the overall visual balance in an asymmetrical and essentially

1 in.

3-12 WU JIDE.
River Dwellers (1998).
Multiblock woodcut printed with
water-soluble ink. 42.9 cm × 34.6 cm.
Muban Foundation, London

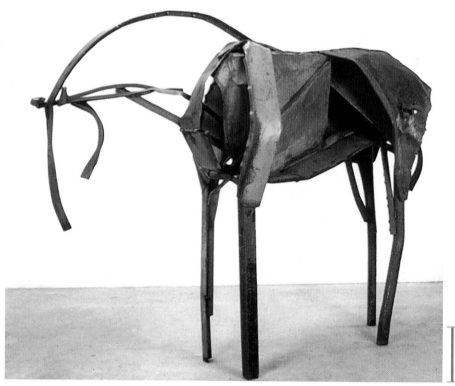

3-13 DEBORAH BUTTERFIELD.
Verde (1990).
Found steel. 79" × 108" × 31".
©1990 Deborah Butterfield, Bozeman, Montana

1 ft.

monochromatic composition. Like a movie within a movie, the large, square canvas sail of a small boat is printed with a scene of another boating party. The bright colors of the sail dominate the ochre atmosphere of the woodcut, as does the scale of the figures therein. Asymmetrical balance is achieved as the artist picks up the reds and yellows and blues of the sail and adds them as almost random touches to other parts of the composition. The stark white of the sail, which provides a luminous backdrop for the boating group, is echoed in scattered bits and pieces that float like large snowflakes or a torn love note, and tie the entire work together.

In Deborah Butterfield's *Verde* (Fig. **3-13**), the mane and head of the horse are defined by greenish strips of steel that enframe void space. (The title *Verde* calls our attention to the finish of the steel, a greenish coating referred to as *verdigris*.) The *actual weight* of this upper part of the horse is negligible. The body, on the other hand, is composed of heavy molded sheets of steel, approximating the volume of the animal's torso. Overall visual balance is achieved in this work because the outlines of the head and neck, silhouetted against the white wall, pop out at the viewer. They become so prominent that they carry enough *visual weight* to balance the more densely compacted sheet metal of the animal's body.

Horizontal, Vertical, Diagonal, and Radial Balance

In works of art with **horizontal balance**, the elements at the left and right sides of the composition seem to be about equal in number or visual emphasis. The United States Capitol Building (Fig. 3-10) has horizontal balance. So too does Gertrude Käsebier's delicately textured photograph *Blessed Art Thou among Women* (Fig. **3-14**). Notice how the dark value of the girl's dress is balanced both by the dark wall to the left and by the woman's hair. Similarly, the stark light value of the vertical shaft of the doorway to the left and the light values of the right side of the composition are in equilibrium.

3-14 GERTRUDE KÄSEBIER.
Blessed Art Thou among Women (c. 1898).
Photograph.
©NMPFT/Royal Photographic Society/SSPL/The Image Works

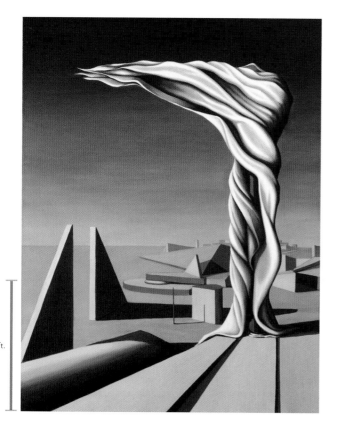

her backward glance facilitate the connection. The spray-painted image of a bride and groom echoes their figures, balancing the composition and creating a symbolic connection. The viewer's eye moves from the couple to their graffiti counterparts and back along the perceived diagonal.

In the case of **radial balance**, the design elements radiate from a center point. Radial balance is familiar to us because nature offers us so many examples. From the petals of a daisy and the filaments of a spider's web to the sun's powerful rays, lines or shapes radiate from a central point and lead the viewer's eye in a circular pattern around the source.

Radial balance is frequently a major principle of design in art forms such as ceramics, jewelry, basketry, stained glass, and other crafts. The decorative tabletop from nineteenth-century Iran (Fig. **3-17**) is a classic example of radial balance. At the center of the piece is a large, round, intricately painted tile surrounded by a circular garland of flowers, birds, and clusters of grapes.

With **vertical balance**, the elements at the top and bottom of the composition are in balance. In Kay Sage's *I Saw Three Cities* (Fig. **3-15**), a firm horizon line separates a bleak landscape from a bleaker sky. Most of the visual weight in the composition occurs in the lower half, where geometric shapes casting long shadows lead your eye from the picture plane toward a kind of desolate futuristic city. The hard-edged structures that litter the landscape, however, are balanced in the upper reaches of the sky by a flowing column of drapery that billows up from the ground and across to the left, floating toward the source of the light on a strange breeze that breaks the stagnant gray air.

Artists employ **diagonal balance** by establishing equal visual weight to either side of a pictorial space that is divided by means of a perceived diagonal. In Adil Jain's *Two Heads* (Fig. **3-16**), the photographer captures the juxtaposition of evocative images and, in the process, creates a striking compositional equilibrium. The elderly couple on a bench in the lower right are partially cut off by the frame of the camera's viewfinder. Yet they are pulled back into the work along an implied diagonal that visually connects them to the large blue square of the trash receptacle behind them. The diagonal positioning of the woman and

3-16 ADIL JAIN.

Two Heads from the series *London Portraits*.

© Adil Jain Photography in perpetuity.

3-17 ALI MUHAMMAD KASHIGAR ISFAHANI.
Iranian tabletop (1887).
Nine separate tiles. Table diameter, 136 cm.
©Victoria and Albert Museum, London/Art Resource, NY

Both the central tile and the garland
are enframed by narrow, decorative
bands; diagonals fan outward from
these bands toward the perimeter,
dividing the remaining space into
eight separate pictorial segments.
Like the spokes of a wheel, the narrow framing device directs the gaze of
the viewer both outward and inward and
provides order to the content. The tiles are
decorated with scenes inspired by the *Book
of Kings*, an Iranian epic.

1 ft.

Imbalance

Balance affords a certain level of comfort. The viewer will
usually try to impose balance on a work, even when there
is asymmetry. But not all art is about comfort; not all
art aims to be aesthetically pleasing. Some artists aim to
shock the viewer or to play into a viewer's discomfort by
creating works with **imbalance**.

Consider Robert Capa's photograph *Death of a Loyalist
Soldier* (Fig. **3-18**), which was taken during the Spanish Civil
War. The photographer has captured the soldier just as an
enemy rifleman shot him. By allowing the composition to
remain unbalanced, or weighted on the left, the drama of
the moment is intensified. The long black shadow behind

3-18 ROBERT CAPA.
Death of a Loyalist Soldier
(September 5, 1936).
Gelatin silver print.
©Magnum Photos, Inc./Robert Capa.

the soldier seems to pull the figure toward the ground, as he stumbles from the impact of the bullet. The photographer no doubt maintained the visual imbalance in the composition to correspond with the physical imbalance of the victim.

In Capa's photograph, there is a clear sense of movement. The soldier has been running down a grassy hill and suddenly falls backward. Imbalance in a work of art can be used to capture a sense of movement—the fourth dimension—in a two-dimensional or a three-dimensional work. Niki de Saint-Phalle's *Black Venus* (Fig. **3-19**) is a larger-than-life figure of a woman in a psychedelic bathing suit who is catching a beach ball. The placement of the legs and feet at the very least suggests a precariously balanced body. She seems to leap into the air to catch the ball, defying gravity and her own ponderousness. Despite, or because of, her mountainous appearance, the unbalanced position of her lower body gives the figure a contradictor y sense of weightlessness. Niki de Saint-Phalle challenges the ideal of feminine beauty in the Western tradition with figures such as *Black Venus*. How does this

3-19 NIKI DE SAINT-PHALLE.

Black Venus (1967).

Painted polyester. 110" × 35" × 24".

Whitney Museum of American Art, New York. Gift of Howard and Jean Lipman Foundation, Inc. (68.73). ©2009 Artists Rights Society (ARS), New York/ADAGP, Paris.

3-20 CHUCK CLOSE.

Lucas II (1987).

Oil on canvas. 36" × 30".

Collection of John and Mary Shirley. ©Chuck Close, courtesy of PaceWildenstein, New York

1 ft.

3-21 THE LUO BROTHERS.
Welcome the World Famous Brand (2000).
Collage and laquer on wood. 246 cm × 126 cm × 3 cm.
Courtesy Ray Hughes Gallery, Sydney, Australia.

EMPHASIS AND FOCAL POINT

For the most part, we do not view a work of art as we read a page of text. The eye does not start in the upper left corner and then systematically work its way to the right in rows. Rather, some feature of the work usually commands our attention. Artists use the design principle of **emphasis** to focus the viewer's attention on one or more parts of a composition by accentuating certain shapes, intensifying value or color, featuring directional lines, or strategically placing the objects and images. Emphasis can be used to create **focal points** or specific parts of the work that seize and hold the viewer's interest.

As if the overwhelming presence of the face—that is, the *content*—in Chuck Close's *Lucas II* (Fig. **3-20**) is not enough to focus the viewer's attention on the center of the composition, the artist emphasizes or draws our eye to a single point—the focal point—between the subject's eyes by creating a target-like pattern of concentric circles around it. The circles are intersected by broken lines of color that radiate from the center, causing a sense of simultaneous movement outward from the center point and back inward.

Emphasis on a particular area or image in a composition can be effected when several of its components direct the viewer's gaze toward a focal point. *Welcome the World Famous Brand* (Fig. **3-21**) by The Luo Brothers features their signature emphasis on the convergence of consumerism and globalism. Mimicking the garish packaging of Chinese merchandise, their compositions are often overcrowded, intensely colored, and exuberant in mood. There is so much energy bound up in the

spirited form stand apart from traditional Western nudes such as the *Venus of Urbino* (see Fig. 16-29)?

> *If today's arts love the machine, technology and organization, if they aspire to precision and reject anything vague and dreamy, this implies an instinctive repudiation of Chaos and a longing to find the form appropriate to our times.*
>
> —OSKAR SCHLEMMER

3-22 PABLO PICASSO.
Family of Saltimbanques (1905).
Oil on canvas. 83¾" × 90⅜".
Chester Dale Collection, 1963.10.190. Image ©2007 Board of Trustees, National Gallery of Art, Washington, DC. ©2009 Estate of Pablo Picasso/ Artists Rights Society (ARS), New York.

1 ft.

imagery that it is almost impossible for the eyes to stop and focus. Emphasis through placement is an important device in this work, and to achieve it, once again, The Luo Brothers use mimicry. The "enthroned" baby raising up a McDonald's sandwich in the center of the piece becomes the focal point. It is emphasized by the red and yellow bands of lines that look like divine rays emanating from behind the baby, who, in turn is bolstered on a floating rectangle by lesser, though no less jubilant, little ones. To the left and right are regimented stacks of burgers riding on chariots pulled by teams of lambs. Brightly colored peonies add to the outrageously festive atmosphere. This formula—enthroned central figure buoyed by devoted onlookers and flanked by symmetrical groups of regimented figures—is standard in religious altarpieces over centuries of art history. The Luo Brothers appropriate this formula to sharpen their statement about what we "worship" in contemporary society.

In Pablo Picasso's *Family of Saltimbanques* (Fig. **3-22**), we see how artists use the principle of emphasis by isolation, in which they separate one object or figure from the many. Amidst a rather desolate landscape, figures of circus performers stand silent, seemingly frozen in their sculptural poses. The patterns, colors, and costume variety of the main figural group are, interestingly, less visually significant than the more delicately rendered figure of the woman seated apart from them in the lower right. Picasso has emphasized her aloneness by pulling her from the group. Her solitude draws us into her private musings; her inner world becomes the focus of our attention.

In *Bauhaus Stairway* (Fig. **3-23**), Oskar Schlemmer used powerful directional lines and a bright area of color to create the focal point in his composition. The diagonal thrusts of the staircase railing would meet in the center of the composition and would by themselves create the focal point. However, the focal point is further reinforced by the orange-red of a woman's sweater, while it partially obscures the meeting of the diagonals and leaps out against a backdrop of quiet blues and off-whites. Content helps too. The people in the foreground are in the act of climbing the stairs and, in so doing, ascending toward the focal point of the composition.

The power of content can sometimes overwhelm the power of shape, texture, and other elements of art to the point that despite other devices used to create focal points, the image will have the tendency to negate or override

1 ft.

3-23 OSKAR SCHLEMMER.
Bauhaus Stairway (1932).
Oil on canvas. 63⅞" × 45".
The Museum of Modern Art, New York. Gift of Philip Johnson.
Digital Image ©The Museum of Modern Art/
Licensed by SCALA/Art Resource, NY.
©2009 The Oskar Schlemmer Estate and Archive, Secretariat:
IT-28824 Oggebbio (VB), Italia.

1 in.

3-24 EDGAR DEGAS. *Woman Leaning near a Vase of Flowers* (Mme Paul Valpinçon; erroneously called *Woman with Chrysanthemums*) (1865). Oil on canvas. 29" × 36½".

The Metropolitan Museum of Art, New York. H. O. Havemeyer Collection. Bequest of Mrs. H. O. Havemeyer, 1929 (29.100.128). Image copyright ©The Metropolitan Museum of Art/ Art Resource, NY.

them. In Edgar Degas's *Woman Leaning near a Vase of Flowers* (Fig. **3-24**), the centerpiece—quite literally—of the composition is an enormous bouquet of chrysanthemums. It has almost everything one could ask of a focal point—central position, brilliant color, dominant texture. And yet our eyes are drawn to the woman who sits off to the side of the vase, daydreaming, gazing beyond the borders of the canvas. A viewer's gaze is seduced by the sight of a human face.

If you look at Francisco Goya's *The Third of May, 1808* (Figure 19-6) , you will see one of the best historical examples of the design principle of emphasis. Goya uses multiple strategies to focus the viewer's eyes and sympathies on a Spanish peasant who is about to be executed by riflemen under the authority of the French Emperor Napoleon. The doomed man's bright white shirt, spotlighted by a cube-shaped lantern, immediately fixes our gaze. The bayonets read as strong, repeated, horizontal lines pointing directly at the victim; the soldiers lean determinedly into action

along diagonals that also direct our eyes toward the group. Can you name other ways in which Goya has used emphasis in this painting?

RHYTHM

The world would be a jumble of sights and sounds were it not for the **regular repetition** of sensory impressions. Natural **rhythms**, or orderly progressions, regulate events ranging from the orbits of the planets to the unfolding of the genetic code into flesh and blood. Artists can enhance or exaggerate individual elements in their compositions through minor and major variations in rhythm. And rhythm can move a viewer visually as well as emotionally. Repetitive patterns can be used to lead the eye over the landscape of the work and to evoke a psychological response in the viewer.

Rhythm can be present in a work of art even if there is a slight variation in repetition. Magdalena Abakanowicz's *Backs* (Fig. **3-25**), from a series of body works called *Alterations*, consists of 80 fiber sculptures representing human backs. Although the individual forms look like hunched-over figures, they are without heads, legs, or arms. Even the fronts of the torsos have been hollowed out, leaving an actual and symbolic human shell. In this work, the artist, whose mother was mutilated by the Nazis in World War II, seems to bring to her work the memory of the dehumanization she witnessed. The potency of this message is largely attributable to the repetition of forms that have lost their individuality.

Rhythms are also found in architecture. The ceiling of the mosque at Córdoba, Spain (Fig. **3-26**), is supported by a rhythmic progression of arches that span the distances between the columns. Mosques constructed with this design could be expanded in any direction by adding columns and arches as the congregation grew.

3-25 MAGDALENA ABAKANOWICZ.
Backs (1976–1982).
Burlap and glue. 80 pieces, 3 sizes: 61 cm × 50 cm × 55 cm; 69 cm × 56 cm × 66 cm; 72 cm × 59 cm × 69 cm.
©Magdalena Abakanowicz. Courtesy of the Marlborough Gallery, New York.

3-26 Sanctuary of the Mosque at Córdoba, Spain (Islamic) (786–987 CE).
Interior view.
©Adam Woolfitt/CORBIS.

Making art is about objectifying your experience of the world, transforming the flow of moments into something visual, or textual, or musical. Art creates a kind of commentary.

—BARBARA KRUGER

SCALE

Scale refers to size—small, big, or in between. Scale is the relative size of an object compared with others of its kind, its setting, or human dimensions. The Great Pyramids at Gizeh (see Fig. 13-12) and the skyscrapers of New York are imposing because of their scale; that is, their size compared with the size of other buildings, their sites, and people. Their overall size is essential to their impact.

Barbara Kruger's multimedia installation *Power Pleasure Desire Disgust* (Fig. **3-27**) combines steadily changing video images of talking heads and projections of the artist's signature phrases and text all over the gallery floors and walls. The overwhelming scale of the work envelops us so completely and the slogans bombard us so relentlessly that it may seem as though the thoughts expressed in the environment have somehow originated in our own minds—phrases we may have once used to hurt others or that have been used to hurt us, comments that may have cut to the quick. But interspersed with the bitter are flashes of wit, even flirtatiousness, as the work touches on communication across boundaries of gender and social

definition. Thoughts are compelling and haunting things, made all the more inescapable by the sheer size of their verbal and written articulation.

In the Count de Montizon's photograph *The Hippopotamus at the Zoological Gardens, Regent's Park* (Fig. **3-28**), we see how artists communicate the scale of objects in their works by comparing them with other objects. In this photograph, a specimen record of the zoo's prized tenant, the photographer used *relative* size to communicate size. We see that it takes nine people standing shoulder to shoulder to match the length of one animal lazing in the sun. The photographer used the relationship between the familiar (the observers) and the unfamiliar (the hippopotamus) to communicate the size of the hippo to those who weren't there to witness it firsthand. At the time the picture was taken, 1852, the hippopotamus was not yet a familiar denizen of zoos in Europe and the United States. A gift from the pasha of Egypt to Queen Victoria, this hippo was the main attraction at the London Zoo.

Nineteenth-century London's hippopotamus was exotic, its size dramatic. In relation to the scale of ordinary human beings, it was extraordinary. In viewing the photograph, a

3-27 BARBARA KRUGER. *Power Pleasure Desire Disgust* (1997). Multimedia installation. Courtesy of Deitch Projects, New York and the Mary Boone Gallery

person could pretty much grasp the magnitude of the animal. By contrast, in Magritte's *Personal Values* (Fig. **3-29**), it is impossible for the viewer to comprehend the dimensions of any of the objects within the work because their familiar size relationships are subverted. We don't know whether the objects—the comb and matchstick and glass—are blown out of proportion or whether the bed has shrunk. We cannot rely on our experience of actual dimension to make sense of the content of the work, so our tendency to understand size in relation to other things fails us.

Hierarchical Scaling

Standing "ten feet tall" is a familiar idiom. We use it to describe heroes or to communicate a certain pride we feel in our own accomplishments. It describes our feelings about a deed that sets others or ourselves above the rest, even if for one fleeting moment. In the visual arts, this metaphor, this idiom, finds its analogy in **hierarchical scaling**, or the use of relative size to indicate the relative importance of the objects or people being depicted. The method has been used for literally thousands of years. In ancient Egyptian art, members of royalty and nobility are sized consistently larger than the underlings surrounding them, making very clear their social positions. In medieval manuscript illumination, artists often had their celestial figures, such as angels and saints, tower over humans.

3-28 COUNT DE MONTIZON.
The Hippopotamus at the Zoological Gardens, Regent's Park (1852). Salted-paper print.
©NMPFT/RPS/SSPL/The Image Works

1 ft.

3-29 RENÉ MAGRITTE.
Personal Values (1952).
Oil on canvas. 31⅝" × 39½" (80 cm × 100 cm).
Image ©Banque d'Images, ADAGP/Art Resource, NY. ©2009
C. Herscovici, London/Artists Rights Society (ARS), New York

1 ft.

1 ft.

In Viola Frey's *Family Portrait* (Fig. **3-30**), we interpret the positioning and relatively large scale of the central male figure as an indicator of his status within the family. Frey includes only his head and shoulders, against which are measured the full-bodied figures of the other family members. The influence of the patriarch is sensed not only in his relative size, but also in the crowding of the group.

Distortion of Scale

Some artists distort or even subvert the realistic scale of objects to challenge the viewer to look at the familiar in a new way. Sometimes they are interested in providing a new perspective on the forms of things; sometimes on the relationships between things.

Altering the viewer's sense of scale partly creates the visual shock and sheer humor of Marisol's *Baby Girl* (Fig. **3-31**). A wooden doll with adjustable limbs and torso—the sort used for drawing exercises in art classes—sports a portrait of Marisol herself. It is perched on the stocky thigh of the baby, who neither looks at nor touches the "toy." The baby girl—by any other definition a subject that suggests delicacy and softness—is transformed into a cumbersome hunk of a figure. Only the shirring of her puffy sleeves and frilly gathers of her white dress soften the harshness of the overall form. Marisol's manipulation of scale and our perception of it are confirmed by the fact that in looking at the illustration of this work in your book (without sneaking a peek at the dimensions), you would have no real sense of how large or small the work actually is.

PROPORTION

"Everything is relative." That is, we tend to think of objects or of works of art as large or small according to their relationships to other things—often to ourselves. However, the objects depicted within works of art can also be large or small in relationship to one another and to the work as a whole. **Proportion**, then, is the comparative relationship, or ratio, of things to one another.

Artists through the ages have sought to determine the proper or most appealing ratios of parts of works to one another and the whole. They have used proportion to represent what they believed to be the ideal or the beautiful. They also have disregarded or subverted proportion to achieve special effects—often to compel viewers to take a new look at the familiar.

3-32 ALICE NEEL.
The Family (John Gruen, Jane Wilson and Julia) (1970).
Oil on canvas. 4'11⅞" × 5'.
©Estate of Alice Neel.

The Canon of Proportions

The ancient Greeks tied their vision of ideal beauty to what they considered the "proper" proportions of the human body. Polykleitos is credited with the derivation of a **canon of proportions**—a set of rules about body parts and their dimensions relative to one another that became the standard for creating the ideal figure. The physical manifestation of his canon was his *Doryphoros* (Fig. 3-7). Every part of the body is either a specific fraction or multiple of every other part. Ideally, for Polykleitos, the head is one-eighth of the total height of the body, and the width from shoulder to shoulder should not exceed one-fourth of the body's height.

Violating the Canon for Expressive Purposes

If the *Doryphoros* represents ideal form, Alice Neel's *The Family* (Fig. **3-32**) leaves the canon behind in what appears

to be the pursuit of unidealized form. The enlarged heads, elongated fingers and calves, and outsized feet are glaring obstacles to realistic representation. And yet, somehow, there is an overarching realism despite these artistic liberties that emanates from the relationships among the family members.

The Golden Mean

Just as the Greeks developed a canon of proportions for representing the human figure in the ideal, they developed the concept of the **golden mean** or the **golden section** in order to create ideal proportions in architecture. The golden mean requires that a small part of a work should relate to a larger part of the work as the larger part relates to the

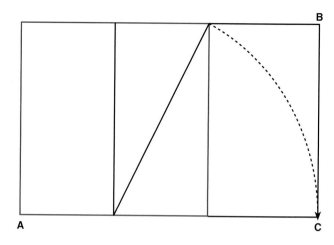

3-33 The golden mean.

To create the golden mean, a line is divided ("sectioned") so that the ratio of the shorter segment (AB) is to the larger segment (BC) as the larger segment (BC) is to the whole (AC). Line segment BC is 1.618 times the length of segment AB. Segment BC is the "mean" in the sense that its length lies between the smaller segment (AB) and the entire line (AC). The Greeks considered segment BC to be "golden" in that its use created what they considered to be ideal proportions in architecture.

whole. The line in Figure **3-33** is divided, or *sectioned*, at point B so that the ratio of the shorter segment (AB) is to the larger segment (BC), as the larger segment (BC) is to the whole line (AC). Segment BC is the golden mean.

The rectangle in Figure **3-34** is based on the golden mean and is termed a **golden rectangle**. Its width is 1.618 times its height. The golden rectangle was thought by the Greeks to be the most pleasing rectangle, and it became the basis for many temple designs.

A golden rectangle can be made either by measuring the lengths of the lines or by rotating the diagonal of the half square, as shown in Figure 3-34. We can also rotate the diagonal of the square in both directions, sort of like a windshield wiper. If we add the second smaller rectangle, we obtain a rectangle that is made up of a central square and two smaller rectangles (Fig. **3-35**). The entire rectangle is called a root five rectangle, because its length is 2.236 (the square root of 5) times its width.

The proportions of the root five rectangle have also served as the frame for various works of art and architecture. If you superimpose a diagram of a **root five rectangle** over a photograph of the east facade of the Parthenon (Fig. **3-36**), you can see the almost compulsive adherence to geometric order that the Greeks visited on their places of worship. The facade is constructed of eight columns. The four in the center fit within the central square of the root five rectangle. The portions of the facade occupying the flanking rectangles include the two end columns to either side as well as the outermost points defined by the steps leading to the temple platform.

Most viewers are unaware of the mathematical basis for the Parthenon's design, but they come away with an overall impression of harmony and order. The root five rectangle is also the foundation of some paintings that have harmonious compositions. Michelangelo's *The Fall of Man and the Expulsion from the Garden of Eden* (Fig.

3-34 The golden rectangle.

The width of this rectangle is exactly 1.618 times its height. The triangle can be created by rotating the diagonal of the half square on the left (outlined in red) to the base on the right (point C). This "ideal" rectangle became the basis for the floor plans of Greek temples and represented the artistic embodiment of the Greek maxim "Moderation in all things."

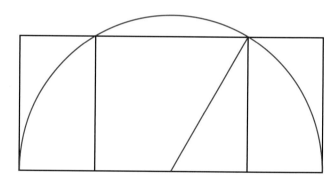

3-35 The root five rectangle.

One obtains a root five rectangle by rotating the diagonal of the square in Fig. 3.34 in both directions. The rectangle obtains its name from the fact that its length is 2.236 (the square root of the number 5) times its width. The root five rectangle has frequently been used to define the frame for works of art, including buildings (see Fig. 3.37) and paintings (see Fig. 3.38).

3-37), from the Sistine Chapel ceiling (see Figs. 16-21 and 16-22), maximizes the components of the root five rectangle. The central square contains the Tree of Knowledge from the book of *Genesis*, that all-important symbol of the temptation and fall of man. The Tree connects the imagery in the outer parts of the root five rectangle—the repetitive figures of Adam and Eve as separated by time and the serpent.

3-36 The east facade of the Parthenon, superimposed with a root five rectangle. When we do not consider the gable (which is absent in this photograph), the facade of the Parthenon is a root five rectangle.

©Borromeo/Art Resource, NY

3-37 MICHELANGELO.

The Fall of Man and the Expulsion from the Garden of Eden (1508–1512).

Portion of the Sistine Chapel ceiling. Fresco.

©Erich Lessing/Art Resource, NY

4

STYLE, FORM, AND CONTENT

The duty of an artist is to strain against the bonds of the existing style.
—Philip Johnson

Human languages combine words according to rules of grammar to express and communicate emotions and meanings. Artists use the language of art to combine the visual elements of art according to principles of design. The resultant works of art are said to have style and form and to express and communicate a certain content.

Despite individual differences—and despite wholesale revolutions!—through the ages several characteristic methods of expression have developed that we refer to as *style*. Works of art can also be said to have a certain *form*, which is the totality of what we see—the product of the composition of the visual elements according to (or in total violation of) principles of design. The *content* of a work includes not only its form but also its subject matter and its underlying meanings or themes. Some works of art can seem to be devoid of content other than the pencil marks or, perhaps, the swaths of paint we find on a sheet of paper or on a canvas (see left). But many are filled with levels of content, more of which are perceived by some viewers than by others. The content of a work varies with the amount of information available to the viewer. For example, viewers who are aware of the symbolism of a particular work of art will find more content in it. Awareness of style, form, and content helps viewers understand and appreciate the visual arts more fully.

NEW YORK, UNITED STATES–APRIL 1949: Contact sheet of artist Jackson Pollock dribbling sand on painting while working in his studio on Long Island.
©Martha Holmes/Time & Life Pictures/Getty Images.

STYLE

In the visual arts, **style** refers to a distinctive handling of elements and media associated with the work of an individual artist, a school or movement, or a specific culture or time period. Familiar subjects may come and go, but creativity, originality, and authenticity dwell in the style or unique handling of the artist.

One of the best ways to illustrate stylistic differences is to choose a group of works with a common theme (such as those illustrated in Figures 4-1 through 4-10) and challenge ourselves to articulate the similarities and differences among them. The first and seemingly obvious connection is that all of the works represent couples. Yet immediately we are struck by the differences among them, both in terms of the stories they imply and the styles in which they are rendered. To begin with, the images demand that we get beyond the conventional definition of "couple," for not all couples are composed of a male and a female. What is really striking, however, are the variations in *style*, sometimes linked to the use of different media and sometimes connected to diverse cultural contexts, but always indicative of the characteristic approach of the artist to the subject.

Art, Culture, and Context

The Mayan ceramic couple (Fig. **4-1**), for example, is an eighth- to tenth-century pre-Columbian sculpture, whose garments, hairstyles, and facial features link it to the life and times of the Yucatecan people before the onslaught of the Europeans. Similar telltale attributes connect Roy Lichtenstein's *Forget It! Forget Me!* (Fig. **4-2**) to the United

1 in.

4-1 *Amorous Couple* (Mayan, Late Classic, 700–900 CE). Polychromed ceramic. H: 9¾".

Founders Society Purchase, Katherine Margaret Kay Bequest Fund and New Endowment Fund, 77.49. Photograph ©1993 Detroit Institute of the Arts, Detroit, MI.

1 ft.

4-2 ROY LICHTENSTEIN.

Forget It! Forget Me! (1962). Magna and oil on canvas. 79⅞" × 68".

Rose Art Museum, Brandeis University, Waltham, MA. Gevirtz-Minuchin Purchase Fund 1962. ©Estate of Roy Lichtenstein.

4-3 HENRI DE TOULOUSE-LAUTREC.
The Two Girlfriends (1894).
Oil on cardboard. 48 cm × 4.5 cm.
Musée Toulouse-Lautrec, Albi.
©Francis G. Mayer/CORBIS

4-4 ROBERT MAPPLETHORPE.
Ken Moody and Robert Sherman (1984).
Photograph.
©The Estate of Robert Mapplethorpe. Courtesy Art and Commerce Anthology.

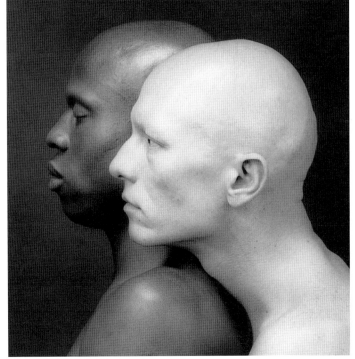

1 in.

States in the decade of the 1960s. Henri de Toulouse-Lautrec's *The Two Girlfriends* (Fig. **4-3**) transports us to the demimonde of turn-of-the-century Paris where, as we were told in the film *Moulin Rouge*, the greatest thing is to love and be loved in return. The weather-worn faces and postcard-perfect surroundings in Grant Wood's *American Gothic* (Fig. 4-9) suggest the duality of rural life in modern America—hardship and serenity—whereas contemporary photographer Robert Mapplethorpe (Fig. **4-4**) drew the world's attention to what it was like to be gay and living in America at the end of the millennium. The tumult of Germany in the years leading up to World War I can be felt in the dark palette, whirling brushstrokes, and existentialist expressions in Oskar Kokoschka's *The*

4-5 OSKAR KOKOSCHKA.

The Tempest (1914).

Oil on canvas. 71½" × 86½".

©Erich Lessing/Art Resource, NY. ©2009 Fondation Oskar Kokoschka/Artists Rights Society (ARS), New York/ProLitteris, Zürich.

1 ft.

1 ft.

4-6 CONSTANTIN BRANCUSI.

The Kiss (c. 1912).

Limestone. 23" × 13" × 10".

Philadelphia Museum of Art. Louise and Walter Arensberg Collection. Image ©The Philadelphia Museum of Art/Art Resource, NY. ©2009 Artists Rights Society (ARS), New York/ADAGP, Paris.

Tempest (Fig. **4-5**). Donna Rosenthal's *He Said . . . She Said* (Fig. 4-10) seems to tap into some sort of collective unconscious ballroom in its unique yet universal ruminations. Constantin Brancusi's *The Kiss* (Fig. **4-6**) could be said to transcend context in the simple accessibility or readability of its subject.

In their abstraction, Jackson Pollock's *Male and Female* (Fig. **4-7**) and Barbara Hepworth's *Two Figures* (Fig. **4-8**) are more difficult to decipher. Pollock's painting was created while he was undergoing psychoanalytic therapy and ought to be read in that context. It reveals a complex scheme of images that he believed were derived from his collective unconscious mind. Hepworth, by contrast, aims to disconnect her work from context by reducing her figures to their most common denominators—organic vertical shapes punctuated by softly modeled voids. Yet curiously, when we view *Two Figures* in the context of this grouping of "couples," it seems to belong, even if eyes may resist making a connection.

Context has a profound influence on style. We can see this in the similarities among artists of a specific era, regardless of their individual "signature." Claude Monet and Auguste Renoir, for example—both Impressionist

My aim in painting has always been the most exact transcription possible
of my most intimate impression of nature.

— EDWARD HOPPER

All the really good ideas I ever had came to me while I was milking a cow.

— GRANT WOOD

4-7 JACKSON POLLOCK.
Male and Female (1942).
Oil on canvas. 73⅓" × 49".
Philadelphia Museum of Art. Partial gift of Mrs. H. Gates Lloyd.
Image ©The Philadelphia Museum of Art/Art Resource, NY. ©2009 The Pollock-Krasner
Foundation/Artists Rights Society (ARS), New York.

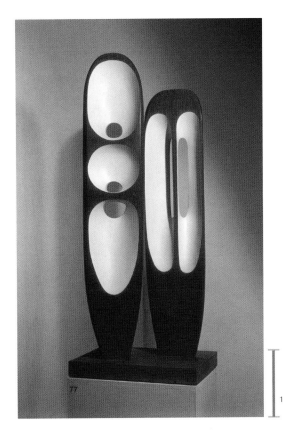

4-8 BARBARA HEPWORTH.
Two Figures (Menhirs) (1954–1955).
Teak. H: 54".
Image ©Art Institute of Chicago, IL/The Bridgeman Art Library.
©Bowness, Hepworth Estate.

artists working in nineteenth-century France—are recognized for their distinct styles, but they have more in common with each other than they do with, say, Rembrandt. And although you probably wouldn't mistake one for the other, the works of both artists are very much a product of their culture at a moment in time.

Styles in art are numerous, ever changing, and ever new. The vocabulary we use to discuss style, on the other hand, has been fairly standard for a long time.

Realistic Art

Realism refers to the portrayal of people and things as they are seen by the eye or really thought to be, without idealization, without distortion. Wood's painting (Fig. 4-9) is described as realistic in terms of style. The term, with a capital *R*, also defines a specific school of art that flowered during the mid-nineteenth century in France. Realism featured subjects culled from daily life and experience and developed a new respect for the real substance of the artist's materials.

Grant Wood's renowned *American Gothic* is a painstakingly realistic portrait of the staid virtues of the rural life in America. It is also one of our more commercialized works of art; images derived from it have adorned boxes of breakfast cereal, greeting cards, and numerous other products. Note the repetition of the pitchfork pattern in the man's shirtfront, the upper-story window of the house, and in the plant on the porch. He is very much tied to his environment. Were it not for the incongruously spry curl falling from the mistress's otherwise tucked-tight hairdo, we might view this composition—as well as the sitters therein—as solid, stolid, and monotonous.

We think of most photographs as realistic. The very nature of the technique—shooting, capturing, documenting—suggests candid truth, unadulterated reality. Although photographers in the twentieth century and beyond have pursued photography as an art form and strained against the bonds of representation, the impact of Mapplethorpe's photographs is largely a result of his unflinching realism (Fig. 4-4).

Realistic versus Representational Art

The Lichtenstein couple (Fig. 4-2) is portrayed in a style that departs from strict Realism, yet the observer clearly identifies the caricature-like renderings of the figures as that of a man and woman. This is representational art. It presents natural objects in recognizable, though not realistic, form. *Forget It! Forget Me!* is an example of Pop Art, which adopts the visual clichés of the comic strip. Donna Rosenthal's *He Said . . . She Said* (Fig. 4-10) also clearly depicts an interaction between a man and a woman, in this case capturing the verbal clichés of the human comedy. Both works can be described as representational.

The term *representational art*, often used synonymously with figurative art, is defined as art that portrays, however altered or distorted, things perceived in the visible world. The people in the Lichtenstein work may not be realistic, but they are clearly recognizable. The Mayan couple (Fig. 4-1) and Toulouse-Lautrec's *The Two Girlfriends* (Fig. 4-3) are similarly representational but not realistic.

Expressionistic Art

In expressionistic art, form and color are freely distorted by the artist in order to achieve a heightened emotional impact. Expressionism also refers to a modern art movement, but many earlier works are **expressionistic** in the broader sense of the term.

In *The Burial of Count Orgaz* (see Fig. 16-29), El Greco's expressionistic elongation of the heavenly figures seems to emphasize their ethereal spirituality. Postimpressionist Vincent van Gogh relied on both an expressionistic palette and brushwork to transfer emotion to his canvases. Kokoschka's expressionistic painting *The Tempest* (Fig. 4-5) is marked by frenzied brushstrokes that mirror the torment of his inner life as well as the impending darkness of war in Germany. Reclining figures occupy the center of a dark, imaginary landscape. Images of earth, water, and flesh merge in a common palette and bevy of strokes; little distinguishes one from another. All seem caught up in a churning sky, very much in danger of being swept away.

Abstract Art

The term **abstract** applies to art that departs significantly from the actual appearance of things. Such art may be completely **nonobjective**; that is, it may make no reference whatsoever to nature or reality. On the other hand, abstract art may be rooted in nature, even though the finished product bears little resemblance to the source that inspired it. Several aspects of the Brancusi sculpture (Fig. 4-6) are recognizable: One can discern an upper torso, arms, eyes, and hair. Yet the artist seems to have been more interested in the independent relationships of the shapes than in being true to the human form. For this reason, we would more likely characterize *The Kiss* as abstract rather than representational.

In *The Kiss*, the human torso is reduced to a simple block form. Twentieth-century proponents of **Cubism**, such as Pablo Picasso and Georges Braque (see Figs. 20-6 and 20-7) also transcribed natural forms into largely angular geometric equivalents. To some degree, despite their reduction to

Wood's *American Gothic* with Rosenthal's *He Said . . . She Said*

THE STYLE OF A WORK OF ART refers to the characteristic ways in which artists express themselves and the times in which they live. In our consideration of the theme of couples, we were able to assess the way in which a full range of media, methods, and styles contributes to the uniqueness of each work. If we add to these the historical and cultural contexts of the works, we gain insight into the ways in which art reflects its place and time.

Consider Grant Wood's *American Gothic* and Donna Rosenthal's *He Said . . . She Said*. On a trip to Europe in the 1920s, Wood was influenced by the realistic works of fifteenth-century German and Flemish painters. His initial goal in *American Gothic* (Fig. **4-9**) was to render realistically the rural Iowan house in the background of the painting. He enlisted a local dentist along with his own sister to pose as models for the farmer and his wife. The realism of their faces is so exacting and their expressions so intent that the viewer cannot but wonder what thoughts lie buried in their minds.

And then there is the expression "to wear one's heart on one's sleeve." In Rosenthal's *He Said . . . She Said* (Fig. **4-10**), thoughts and feelings are broadcast plainly, as the (implied) individuals quite literally wear their thoughts on their clothes—a suit and party dress made from the pages of discarded books and newspapers. We know exactly what's on their minds, verbalized through cultural stereotypes of the conflicting wishes of males and females—his reluctance to make a commitment, her hope that he will still remember her in the morning. Other works by Rosenthal express man's desire for sex and woman's desire for security. Stereotypes are by definition extreme; they represent conventional notions and not individual conceptions. Yet Rosenthal succeeds in her communication with the viewer in large part because we identify with these phrases.

As the physical couple is absent from the work, we are left with the notion that the clothes make the individual. This is conceptual art; that is, the ideas being expressed by the artist have greater meaning than their physical expression. ■

4-9 GRANT WOOD.
American Gothic (1930).
Oil on beaverboard. 29⅞" × 24⅞".
Friends of American Art Collection, 1930.934, The Art Institute of Chicago. Photography ©The Art Institute of Chicago. American Gothic, 1930 by Grant Wood. All rights reserved by the Estate of Nan Wood Graham/Licensed by VAGA, New York, NY

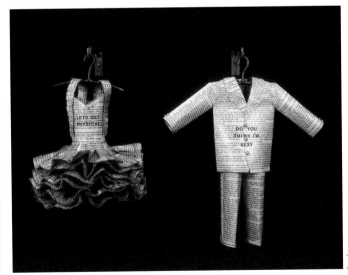

4-10 DONNA ROSENTHAL.
He Said . . . She Said: "*Let's get physical*"—
"*Do you think I'm sexy*" (1999).
Mixed media. Suit: 12" × 12" × 1½"; dress: 10" × 8" × 8".
Courtesy of Bernice Steinbaum Gallery, Miami, FL.

Copy nature and you infringe on the work of our Lord. Interpret nature and you are an artist.

— JACQUES LIPCHITZ

Abstract painting is abstract. It confronts you.

— JACKSON POLLOCK

essential geometric components and line–shape relationships, the figures of Picasso and Braque remain somewhat decipherable. In any event, both artists—despite some brief dabbling in nonobjectivity—abstracted from reality.

Jackson Pollock's *Male and Female* (Fig. 4-7) "figures" are a great deal more difficult to discern than Brancusi's, but the totemic shapes bear some visual cues that suggest gender differences. At the time of the painting, Pollock was undergoing psychoanalysis, and he was quite convinced that the unconscious played a major role in his art. Using a method called **psychic automatism**, Pollock attempted to clear his mind of purpose and concerns so that inner conflicts and ideas could find expression through his work. The result in *Male and Female* is abstraction.

Although much of Barbara Hepworth's sculpture has been inspired by nature, it is not always derived from nature. That is why we characterize work such as *Two Figures* (Fig. 4-8) as nonobjective; that is, it is not intended to make any reference to reality. On the other hand, entitling the piece *Two Figures* places viewers in a quandary. It sends us searching for details that might represent the human form, even gender differences. Is the taller "figure" the male? Could the concave shapes in the shorter figure suggest femininity? Here the connection to reality may be fully in the eye of the beholder. The truth is that nonobjective artists do this type of thing quite a lot. Sometimes they label their paintings and sculptures *Untitled* partially as a way to discourage Rorschach-like readings of their work. At other times, they assign titles to their nonobjective works based on some association that is triggered by the work itself.

A case in point is Judy Pfaff's *Voodoo* (Fig. **4-11**), a nonobjective painting in which highly saturated colors and jagged shapes comprise the content and spirit of the work. Though the elements and technique are the "subject" of the work, the title suggests the presence of mysterious figures undulating in a Caribbean jungle undergrowth. One of the issues that many viewers have with nonobjective art is that they want it to make sense. They want to connect it with something familiar—even if the familiar in this case is as abstruse as the title, *Voodoo*. But nonobjective art is just that—nonobjective—and viewers might come closer to the intention of the artist by allowing themselves to focus on what's there rather than to go on scavenger hunts for what probably isn't.

1 ft.

4-11 JUDY PFAFF.
Voodoo (1981).
Contact paper collage on Mylar. 98" × 60" (framed).
Albright-Knox Art Gallery, Buffalo, NY; Edmund Hayes Fund, 1983. Courtesy of the artist.

To give a body and a perfect form to your thought, this alone is what it is to be an artist.

— JACQUES-LOUIS DAVID

FORM

The form of a work refers to its totality as a work of art. Form includes the elements, design principles, and composition of a work of art. A work's *form* might include, for example, the colors that are used, the textures and shapes, the illusion of three dimensions, the balance, rhythm, or unity of design. **Formalist criticism**, by extension, is an approach to art criticism that concentrates primarily on the elements and design of works of art rather than on historical factors or the biography of the artist.

CONTENT

The **content** of a work of art is everything that is contained in it. The content of a work refers not only to its lines or forms but also to its subject matter and its underlying meanings or themes.

The Levels of Content

We may think of works of art as containing three levels of content: (1) subject matter, (2) elements and composition, and (3) underlying or symbolic meanings or themes.

Consider a comparison between the subject matter of two visually similar paintings as a way of exploring these levels. In 1793, just a few years after the taking of the Bastille and the start of the French Revolution, Jacques-Louis David painted *Death of Marat* (Fig. **4-12**), a memorial to a political martyr. Almost 200 years later, Sandow Birk appropriated David's image for *Death of Manuel* (Fig. **4-13**), his graphic deposition on urban violence.

4-12 JACQUES-LOUIS DAVID.
Death of Marat (1793).
Oil on canvas. 63¾" × 49⅛".
Musées Royaux des Beaux-Arts de Belgique, Brussels.
©Erich Lessing/Art Resource, NY

4-13 SANDOW BIRK.
Death of Manuel (1992).
Oil on canvas. 33" × 25".
Courtesy of Koplin Del Rio Gallery, Culver City CA

David's *The Oath of the Horatii* with Kruger's *Untitled (We Don't Need Another Hero)*

THE OATH OF THE HORATII (Fig. **4-14**), by Jacques-Louis David, is one of the most readily recognizable works of the nineteenth century—indeed, the whole of the history of art. It is a landmark composition—symbolically and pictorially. David worked for the king of France in the days before the French Revolution. Ironically, although the *Oath* was painted for Louis XVI, who along with his wife, Marie Antoinette, would lose his head to the guillotine, the painting became an almost instant symbol of the Revolution. The loyalty, courage, and sacrifice it portrayed were an inspiration to the downtrodden masses in their uprising against the French monarchy. David, because of his position, was imprisoned along with the members of the court and other French aristocracy, only to be—as it were—"bailed out" by another who could use his services as a painter. Thus David, court painter to the French king, would become painter to Napoleon Bonaparte, who would eventually crown himself emperor.

Pictorially, the work is also groundbreaking. It compresses space and forces us to concentrate on the meticulously rendered figures in the foreground. This treatment of space would open the door to the flattening of space in Modernist paintings. The tradition of treating the picture frame as a window frame through which one peers into the infinite distance would be abandoned by many artists in favor of the two-dimensionality of the canvas.

4-14 JACQUES-LOUIS DAVID.
The Oath of the Horatii (1784).
Oil on canvas.
11' × 14'.
Louvre Museum, Paris.
©Réunion des Musées Nationaux/Art Resource, NY

1 ft.

Knowing something of the historical circumstances under which *The Oath of the Horatii* was created, and understanding what is new about it in terms of style and composition, helps us appreciate its significance. But our full comprehension and appreciation of the work can only occur with our consideration and interpretation of the subject matter. The subject of David's *The Oath of the Horatii* is, on the face of things, fairly easy to read. Three brothers—the Horatii—swear their allegiance to Rome on swords held high by their father. They pledge to come back victorious or not come back at all. Their forward-thrusting and stable stances convey strength, commitment, and bravery. And there is something else—something that has been referred to by feminist critics and scholars as a *subtext*, or an additional level of content in the work. David's *Oath* is also a painting about the ideology of gender differences. The women in the painting collapse in the background, terrified at the prospect of the death of the brothers. To make matters worse, one of the Horatii sisters is engaged to be married to one of the enemy. She might lose her brother to the hands of her fiancé, or vice versa. The women's posture, in opposition to the men's, represents, according to historian Linda Nochlin, "the clear-cut opposition between masculine strength and feminine weakness offered by the ideological discourse of the period." Whatever else the content of this painting is about, it is also about the relationship of the sexes and gender-role stereotypes.

Several contemporary feminist artists have challenged the traditional discourse of gender ideology as damaging both to men and women. Barbara Kruger's *Untitled (We Don't Need Another Hero)* (Fig. **4-15**) can be interpreted as an "answer" to David's *Oath*. In appropriating a Norman Rockwell illustration to depict the "innocence" of gender ideology—in this case, the requisite fawning of a little girl over the budding muscles of her male counterpart—Kruger violates the innocuous vignette with a cautionary band blazing the words *We don't need another hero*. The representation of the opposition between strength and weakness—male and female—is confronted and replaced with the gender discourse of a more socially aware era.

The subject matter of these works is strangely related, oddly linked. Visually, the works could not be more dissimilar. In David's composition, the subtext of gender ideology exits simultaneously with the main narrative—that of the soldiers preparing for battle. In Kruger's work, by contrast, the main narrative *is* gender ideology—and how to counteract it. In both, however, the essential nature of evaluating the content, or subject matter of the works we view, is underscored. They are, after all, really about the same thing, aren't they? ■

4-15 BARBARA KRUGER. *Untitled (We Don't Need Another Hero)* (1987). Photographic silkscreen, vinyl. 109" × 210". Collection of Emily Fisher Landau, New York. Courtesy of Mary Boone Gallery, New York.

1 ft.

There is a macabre similarity between the two paintings in their elements and composition. David's Marat is found dead in his bath—murdered by a counterrevolutionary fanatic named Charlotte Corday. The artist brings the viewer face-to-face with the slaughtered hero, whose arm drops lifeless and whose sympathetic facial expression leans toward us yearningly. Birk's Manuel is rendered in the same pose, although Marat's bath has been replaced with a Chevy Impala, riddled with bullets. Marat's left hand holds a false letter requesting a visit from the would-be murderer; Manuel's left hand grasps the steering wheel of his car. Marat's head is wrapped in a turban; Manuel's, in a brightly printed bandana. In both paintings, the figure is set in the extreme foreground, and the backgrounds are monochromatic and nondescript. The spatial depth is severely limited. This dramatic silhouette effect, coupled with the strong linear style used to render the figures, creates the feeling of a sculptural frieze.

The underlying themes or symbolism in these works may not bear the same relationship as do the elements and composition. Yet the choice of the David prototype suggests ideas of revolution, heroism as it is defined within a group or culture, and the cold-blooded murder of the unsuspecting victim. The appropriation of the David image by Birk validates the historic significance of the eighteenth-century painting. Understanding the relationship between the two makes each more meaningful to the viewer.

Iconography

I prefer winter and fall, when you feel the bone structure in the landscape—the loneliness of it—the dread feeling of winter. Something waits beneath it—the whole story doesn't show.

— ANDREW WYETH

Winter is a perennial symbol of death and aloneness in the arts, and fall is a common symbol of either harvest or decline. Yet artists who paint the winter or the fall, or who write of them, may not directly speak of death or of the harvest. "The whole story" does not always show, but rather may lie beneath a work of art.

Iconography is the study of the themes and symbols in the visual arts—the figures and images that lend works their underlying meanings. Bronzino's sixteenth-century masterpiece *Venus, Cupid, Folly, and Time (The Exposure of Luxury)* (Fig. **4-16**) is a classic example of works in which there is much more than meets the eye. The painting weaves an intricate allegory, with many actors, many symbols. Venus, undraped by Time and spread in a languorous diagonal across the front plane, is fondled by her son Cupid. Folly prepares to cast roses on the couple, while Hatred and Inconstancy (with two left hands) lurk in the background. Masks, symbolizing falseness, and other objects, meanings known or unknown, complete the scene.

1 ft.

4-16 BRONZINO.
Venus, Cupid, Folly, and Time (The Exposure of Luxury)
(c. 1546).
Oil on wood. Approx. 61" × 56¾".
©National Gallery, London, UK/The Bridgeman Art Library

I would like to leave a will and testament to declare everything void at my death, and it's not unrealistic. I mean it, because only I know the work as it ought to be. All posthumous interpretations are less.

— DAN FLAVIN

Works such as these offer an intricate iconographic puzzle. Is Bronzino saying that love in an environment of hatred and inconstancy is foolish or doomed? Is something being suggested about incest? self-love? Can one fully appreciate Bronzino's painting without being aware of its iconography? Is it sufficient to respond to the elements and composition, to the figure of a woman being openly fondled before an unlikely array of onlookers? No simple answer is possible, and a Mannerist artist such as Bronzino would have intended this ambiguity. Certainly one could appreciate the composition and the subject matter for their own sake, but awareness of the symbolism enriches the viewing experience.

Whereas Bronzino's painting illustrates a complex allegory, the symbolism of which would seem relevant only to the initiated, Willie Bester's *Semekazi (Migrant Miseries)* (Fig. **4-17**) uses images and objects to communicate a tragic story to anyone who will listen. Bester is an artist who was classified as "colored" under South African apartheid rule and thus, as with most nonwhite artists, was deprived of opportunities for formal training in art. Collages such as *Semekazi* combine painting with found objects in a densely covered surface that seems, in its lack of space and air, to reflect the squalid living conditions among black Africans. The many images and objects serve as symbols of rampant oppression and deprivation affecting a whole people, while a single portrait of a worker in the center of the composition—peering from under bedsprings—serves as a single case study.

The paintings by Bronzino and Bester, as far apart in time, tenor, and experience as can be imagined, both supply the viewer with clear, familiar images intended to communicate certain underlying themes. But in some cases, the underlying themes may be at least in part the invention of the viewer. In Helen Frankenthaler's *Bay Side* (see Fig. 2-23), for example, we may interpret the juncture of the blue and tan fields as surf meeting sand. Did the artist intend this symbolism, however, or is it our own invention? Many of us love a puzzle and are willing to spend a great deal of time attempting to decipher the possible iconography of a work of art. In other cases, the subject matter of a work may be in the eye of the beholder.

Our exposition of the language of art is now complete. We have seen that artists use the visual elements of art

4-17 WILLIE BESTER.
Semekazi (Migrant Miseries) (1993).
Oil, enamel paint, and mixed media on board. 49¼" × 49¼".
By courtesy of Sotheby's Picture Library. ©2005 Willie Bester

in compositions that employ various principles of design. Their compositions are usually created within certain traditional and contemporary styles. The totality of the form of their works—everything that we see in them—also has certain subject matter or content, which may exist on several levels. Our understanding of these various levels of content helps us appreciate the works.

Several chapters follow that show how artists apply the language of art to works in two dimensions and three dimensions. Then we survey the history of art, where we see how artists through the ages and around the globe have spoken a similar language. Although it may take us adults years to become fluent in the spoken languages of other peoples in other times and other places, we may find ourselves capable of more readily understanding the language in their visual works.

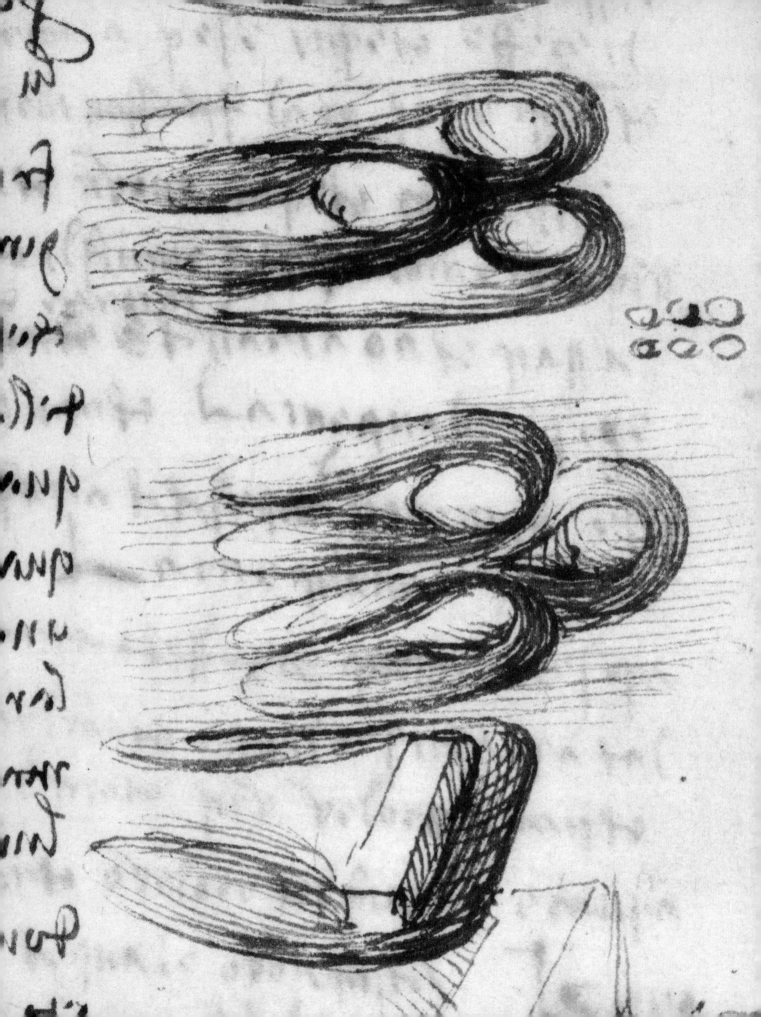

DRAWING

■
—

*Drawing . . . is the necessary beginning of everything in art,
and not having it, one has nothing.*
—Giorgio Vasari

The first sketch was probably an accident. Perhaps some Stone Age human idly ran a twig through soft clay and was astounded to find an impression of this gesture in the ground. Perhaps this individual then made such impressions as signs for family members (as in an arrow pointing "that way") and to record experiences, such as the hunt for a beast or a gathering around a fire. Similarly, a child may learn to trace a shell fragment through damp sand at the shore's edge. Soon the child is drawing sketches of geometric shapes, animals, toys, and people. Michelangelo was engaging in an essentially similar act when he sketched his models from life—albeit with a bit more skill and flair.

In this chapter, we discuss drawing, the most basic of the two-dimensional art forms. In the next two chapters, we discuss two other forms of two-dimensional art—painting and printmaking. We shall see how people over the centuries have used a variety of materials, frequently from surprising sources, to express themselves through two-dimensional art forms.

In its broadest definition, **drawing** is the result of an implement running over a surface and leaving some trace of the gesture. But as we shall discover, the art of drawing goes far beyond this simple description.

The surface, or **support**, onto which an image is sketched is usually, although not always, two dimensional. Most often the support is **monochromatic** paper or parchment, although drawings can be found on a variety of surfaces. The implements can range from charcoal (which is burnt wood) to bristle brushes dipped in ink. Most drawings, by virtue of the implements, consist of black and tones of gray. But many full-color drawings have also been created with colored chalks, pastels, and wax crayons.

Some drawings are predominantly **linear**; others are constructed solely by tonal contrasts. The quality of line and the nature of shading are affected by the texture of the support. We shall see how the artist capitalizes on the idiosyncratic characteristics of the implements and support to capture a desired expression in the drawing.

CATEGORIES OF DRAWING

Drawing is basic to the visual arts. For centuries, painters and sculptors have made countless preparatory sketches for their major projects, working out difficulties on paper before approaching the more permanent medium of paint or bronze. Architects proceed in the same fashion, outlining buildings in detail before breaking ground. Drawing has also served artists as a kind of shorthand method for recording ideas.

Artists carry sketchbooks everywhere, and perhaps there is no one better known for his "little book of leaves" than Leonardo da Vinci (see the sketch by Leonardo on page 104), who advised artists to note everything, and when the book was "full, [to] keep it to serve [their] future plans, and take another and carry on with it." Leonardo's

5-1 REMBRANDT VAN RIJN.
Copy of Leonardo da Vinci's
Last Supper.
Red chalk on paper. 14" × 18¼".
Image copyright ©The Metropolitan Museum of Art/Art Resource, NY

1 in.

own work also served as inspiration for generations of artists who, like Rembrandt (Fig. **5-1**), copied his masterpieces. Imitation has been said to be the sincerest form of flattery, and art-world luminaries and students alike have "gone to school on" the works of the masters. Copying permits the artist to, in a sense, retrace another artist's steps—from conception to completion. Far from being an exercise in mere duplication, the effort can lead to an understanding and feeling of form, rhythm, and design. Sometimes such copies give us a bit of insight into how an artist might have changed a composition, in the copying artist's view, for the better. Although Leonardo's setting for the *Last Supper* is quite spare, with a simple rectangular window behind the figure of Jesus, Rembrandt has added an elaborate draped canopy and more architectural detail, no doubt more befitting of the event in his eyes. Rembrandt copied Leonardo's famed fresco from an engraving that another artist made after the original. Many artists in history have traveled well beyond their cities of origin, however, to meet the works of the masters and to unlock their secrets through the scrutiny of copying.

But drawing does not serve only a utilitarian purpose. In most cases, drawing is the most direct way of bringing what is in the artist's mind to the artist's surface. Many artists enjoy the sheer spontaneity of drawing, tracing a pencil or piece of chalk across a sheet of paper to capture directly their thoughts or to record the slightest movement of their hand.

Many drawings, by contrast, stand as complete works of art. Gary Kelley's sensual and rhythmic pastel drawing (Fig. **5-2**) possesses all of the detail, all of the finish of a work of art in a medium that might be considered more permanent. Its powerful zigzag composition contributes to the sense of life and movement, as do the contrasts between the harsh angularity of the male singer's zoot suit and the sinuous curves of the woman who writhes in response to his music. Kelley's drawing was commissioned as a promotional piece for the Mississippi Delta Blues Festival and was no doubt purposefully reminiscent of the Harlem jazz age as depicted by 1930s African American artists such as Archibald J. Motley Jr. (see Fig. 3-2).

Drawings may thus be said to fall into at least three categories:

1. Sketches that record an idea or provide information about something the artist has seen
2. Plans or preparatory studies for other projects, such as buildings, sculptures, crafts, paintings, plays, and films
3. Fully developed and autonomous works of art

1 in.

5-2 GARY KELLEY.
Promotion for the Mississippi Delta Blues Festival (c. 1989).
Pastel. 24" × 14".
Courtesy of the artist and Richard Solomon.

DRAWING MATERIALS

Over the millennia, methods of drawing have become increasingly sophisticated and materials more varied and standardized. It would seem that we have come a long way from our prehistoric ancestors' use of twigs, hollow reeds, and lumps of clay. Drawing materials can be divided into two major groups: *dry media* and *fluid media*.

Drawing is the honesty of the art. There is no possibility of cheating. It is either good or bad.

—SALVADOR DALÍ

Dry Media

The **dry media** used in drawing include silverpoint, pencil, charcoal, chalk, pastel, and wax crayon.

Silverpoint

Silverpoint is one of the oldest drawing media. It was used widely from the late Middle Ages to the early 1500s. Silverpoint drawings are created by dragging a silver-tipped implement over a surface that has been coated with a **ground** of bone dust or chalk mixed with **gum**, water, and **pigment**. This ground is sufficiently coarse to allow small flecks of silver from the instrument to adhere to the prepared surface as it is drawn across. These bits of metal form the lines of the drawing; they are barely visible at the start but eventually oxidize, becoming tarnished or darkened and making the image visible. Each silverpoint line, a soft gray to begin with, mellows and darkens to a grayish brown hue. If the artist desires to make one area of the drawing appear darker than others, it is necessary to build up a series of close, parallel, or cross-hatched lines in that area to give the impression of deepened tone. Because they lack sharp tonal contrasts, the resultant drawings are often extremely delicate in appearance.

The technique of working in silverpoint is itself delicate. The medium allows for little or no correction. Thus, the artist is not in a position to experiment while working. The artist must have a fairly concrete notion of what the final product will look like, and the lines must be accurate and confidently drawn. The nineteenth-century *Head of a Man* (Fig. **5-3**) by the French artist Alphonse Legros illustrates the way in which the artist must use techniques of cross-hatching and clusters of small lines to model form with the silverpoint medium. The portrait is a dramatic record of the topography of a man's face, rendered with the utmost clarity and control. Legros concentrates his efforts—and the viewer's attention—on the intent gaze of the face; the hair and collar are only faintly suggested. Working in silverpoint has its rewards. The drawings, painstakingly rendered, are flawless in execution, their finish exquisite and polished. But the technique is not for the fainthearted. Students interested in working in silverpoint are encouraged to create detailed preliminary sketches in hard pencil before launching into the other, more permanent, and less forgiving medium.

1 in.

5-3 ALPHONSE LEGROS.
Head of a Man (19th century).
Silverpoint on white ground. 8¾" × 7".
The Metropolitan Museum of Art, New York. Gift of the Artist, 1892 (92.13.1). Image ©The Metropolitan Museum of Art.

Pencil

Silverpoint was largely replaced by the lead **pencil**, which came into use during the 1500s. Medieval monks, like the ancient Egyptians, ruled lines with metallic lead. Pencils as we know them began to be mass-produced in the late eighteenth century. A pencil is composed of a thin rod of **graphite** encased within wood or paper. The graphite is ground to dust and mixed with clay, and the mixture is baked to harden the clay. The relative hardness or softness of the implement depends on the quantity of clay in the mixture. The more clay, the harder the pencil.

Pencil is capable of producing a wide range of effects. Lines drawn with hard pencil can be thin and light in tone; those rendered in soft lead can be thick and dark. The sharp point of the pencil will create a firm, fine line suitable for meticulous detail. Softer areas of tone can be achieved through a buildup of parallel lines, smudging, or stroking the support with the side of the lead tip.

As seen in the contrasting works of Giorgio de Chirico and Alberto Giacometti, pencil can be manipulated to achieve dramatically different effects that complement the subject. Chirico's mannequin (Fig. **5-4**) is a controlled

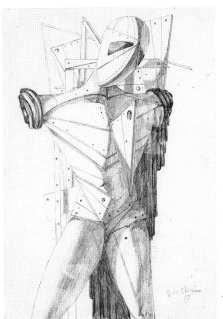

5-4 GIORGIO DE CHIRICO.

Condottiero (1917).

Pencil. 12⅜" × 8½".

Staatliche Graphische Sammlung, Munich.
©2009 Artists Rights Society (ARS), New
York/SIAE, Rome

5-5 ALBERTO
GIACOMETTI.

Head (1946).
Pencil. 5⅞" × 4¼".

©2009 Artists Rights
Society (ARS), New York/
ADAGP/FAAG. Paris

construction of wood pieces that have been fitted together to the likenesses of muscles, ligaments, and tendons. The precision of the construction is communicated through the fine lines of a hard pencil point.

Giacometti's drawing (Fig. **5-5**), on the other hand, is a free expression of energy or, perhaps, anxiety. The highly abstracted head seems bound up in a frozen psychological state, one of inner turmoil created by the artist's agitated scribbling and reworking of bold pencil strokes. The contrast of thick black lines against the harsh white paper seems to echo the expressive nature of the drawing rather than convey the features of the subject. Giacometti was clearly not interested in creating a portrait likeness. Rather, he used his medium to render the distorted impression of an agitated figure, perhaps projecting his own inner conflict onto his subject. Chirico, by contrast, used pencil in a more static and controlled manner to present us with a factual duplication of his bizarre inanimate object.

Drawing is perhaps the most traditional of media. The exercise of drawing from life has been integral to the art academy experience for hundreds of years, a method by which the human form might be painstakingly analyzed and recorded. Perhaps this is why, in part, Adrian Piper chose the medium of drawing to render her dramatic *Self-Portrait Exaggerating My Negroid Features* (Fig. **5-6**). With it, Piper invites the spectator to focus on those aspects of her physical genetic composition that reveal her mixed black and white parentage. The portrait gives us an unflinching record of Piper's countenance, but perhaps more important,

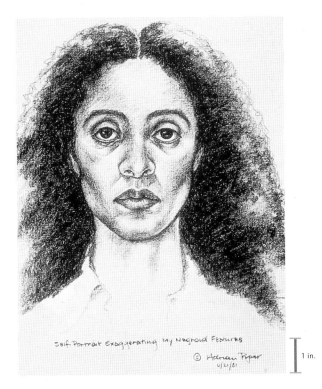

5-6 ADRIAN PIPER.

Self-Portrait Exaggerating My Negroid Features (1981).
Pencil on paper. 10" × 8".

©Adrian Piper Research Archive, Collection Eileen and Peter Norton.

the image challenges us to confront our prejudices about the physical differences between the races.

Adrian Piper has authored "calling cards" to hand out to people whom she overhears making racist remarks: "I regret any discomfort my presence is causing you, just as I am sure you regret the discomfort your racism is causing me."

Charcoal

Charcoal, like pencil, has a long history as a drawing implement. Used by our primitive ancestors to create images on cave walls, these initially crumbly pieces of burnt wood or bone now take the form of prepared sticks that are formed by the controlled charring of special hardwoods. Charcoal sticks are available in textures that vary from hard to soft. The sticks may be sharpened with sandpaper to form fine and clear lines or may be dragged flat across the surface to form diffuse areas of varied tone. Like pencil, charcoal may also be smudged or rubbed to create a hazy effect.

When charcoal is dragged across a surface, bits of the material adhere to that surface, just as in the case of silverpoint and pencil. But charcoal particles rub off more easily, and thus the completed drawings must be sprayed with a solution of thinned varnish to keep them affixed. Also, because of the way in which the charcoal is dispersed over a surface, the nature of the support is evident in each stroke. Coarsely textured paper will yield a grainy image, whereas smooth paper will provide a clear, almost pencil-like line.

A self-portrait of the German Expressionist Käthe Kollwitz (Fig. **5-7**) reveals one aspect of the character of the charcoal medium. Delicate lines of sharpened charcoal drawn over broader areas of subtle shading enunciate the

5-8 CLAUDIO BRAVO.
Package (1969).
Charcoal, pastel, and sanguine. 30⅞" × 22½".
©Christie's Images/CORBIS

two main points of interest: the artist's face and her hand. Between these two points—that of intellect and that of skill—runs a surge of energy described by aggressive, jagged strokes overlaying the lightly sketched contour of her forearm.

Values in the drawing range from hints of white at the artist's knuckles, cheekbone, and hair to the deepest blacks of the palm of her hand, eyes, and mouth. The finer lines override the texture of the paper, whereas the shaded areas, particularly around the neck and chest area, reveal the faint white lines and tiny flecks of pulp that are visual remnants of the papermaking process.

Charcoal can be expressive or descriptive, depending on its method of application. Claudio Bravo's *Package* (Fig. **5-8**) is a finely rendered, trompe l'oeil drawing that bears almost no trace of the artist's gesture and almost no indication of the "dusty" quality of the media—primarily charcoal and pastel. The illusion of the smooth sheen and crinkled indentations of the wrapping paper, attributed to painstaking gradations in value, is so convincing that the implied texture of the package completely overrides the actual texture of the

5-7 KÄTHE KOLLWITZ.
Self-Portrait (1924).
Charcoal. 18¾" × 25".
Rosenwald Collection, 1943.3.5217. Image ©2007 Board of Trustees, National Gallery of Art, Washington. DC. ©2009 Artists Rights Society (ARS), New York/VG Bild-Kunst, Bonn

drawing materials. The viewer is enticed to touch the forbidden surfaces, just to test whether they are real.

Chalk and Pastel

The effects of charcoal, **chalk**, and **pastel** as they are drawn against the paper surface are very similar, though the compositions of the media differ. Chalk and pastel consist of pigment and a **binder**, such as **gum arabic**, shaped into workable sticks.

Chalks are available in many colors, some of which occur in nature. **Ocher**, for example, derives its dark yellow tint from iron oxide in some clays. **Umber** acquires its characteristic yellowish or reddish brown color from earth containing oxides of manganese and iron. Other popular "organic" or "earth" colors include white, black, and a red called **sanguine**.

Michelangelo used red chalk in a sketch for the Sistine Chapel (see Chapter 15), in which he attempted to work out certain aspects of the figure of the Libyan Sibyl (Fig. 5-9). Quick, sketchy notations of the model's profile, feet, and toes lead to a detailed torso rendered with confident lines and precisely defined tonal areas built up from hatching. The exactness of muscular detail and emphasis on the edges of the body provide insight into the concerns of an artist whose forte was sculpture.

In contrast to Michelangelo's essentially linear approach to his medium, the *Portrait of a Woman* (Fig. 5-10) by the nineteenth-century French painter Jean-Baptiste Carpeaux appears to materialize from the background through subtle tonal contrasts. Whereas Michelangelo emphasized the edges of his model, Carpeaux was more interested in the subtle roundness of his model's form. Carpeaux capitalized on the effect of soft chalk drawn across a coarsely textured paper to create a hazy atmosphere that envelops the sitter.

Pastels consist of ground chalk mixed with powdered pigments and a binder. Whereas chalk drawings can be traced to prehistoric times, pastels did not come into wide use until the 1400s. They were introduced to France only in the 1700s, but within a century, pastels captured the imagination of many important painters. Their wide range of brilliant colors offered a painter's palette for use in the more spontaneous medium of drawing.

One of the masters of pastel drawing was the nineteenth-century French painter and sculptor Edgar Degas. The directness and spontaneity of the medium was well suited to some

1 in.

5-9 MICHELANGELO.
Studies for *The Libyan Sybil* (1510–1511).
Red chalk. 11⅜" × 8⅜".
The Metropolitan Museum of Art. Joseph Pulitzer Bequest, 1924 (24.197.2).
Image copyright ©The Metropolitan Museum of Art/Art Resource, NY

1 in.

5-10 JEAN-BAPTISTE CARPEAUX.
Portrait of a Woman (1874).
Black chalk heightened with white, on buff paper.
7⅞" × 5⅝".
Sterling and Francine Clark Art Institute, Williamstown, MA

Drawing Materials | **111**

If I could have had my own way, I would have confined myself entirely to black and white.

—EDGAR DEGAS

5-11 EDGAR DEGAS.

Woman at Her Toilette (1903).

Pastel on paper. 30" × 30½".

Mr. and Mrs. Martin A. Ryerson Collection, 1937.1033, The Art Institute of Chicago. Photograph ©The Art Institute of Chicago.

5-12 JAUNE QUICK-TO-SEE SMITH.

The Environment: Be a Shepherd (1989).

Charcoal, colored chalk, and pastel. 47" × 31¼".

©2007 Jaune Quick-to-See Smith and Flomenhaft Gallery. Collection of Lois Fichner-Rathus.

of his favorite subjects: ballet dancers in motion, horses racing toward a finish line, and women caught unaware in the midst of commonplace activities. Degas's *Woman at Her Toilette* (Fig. **5-11**) is a veritable explosion of glowing color. The pastels are manipulated in countless ways to create a host of different effects. The contours of the figure are boldly sketched, whereas the flesh is composed of more erratic lines that create a sense of roundness through a spectrum of color. Degas scratched the pastels over the surface to form sharp lines or dragged them flatly to create more free-flowing strokes. At times the colors were left pure and intense, and at other times subtle harmonies were rendered through blending or smudging.

Jaune Quick-to-See Smith's *The Environment: Be a Shepherd* (Fig. **5-12**) is an effective combination of drawing media: charcoal, colored chalk, and pastel. The earth tones of sepia, brown, greens, and grays evoke the desert Southwest and enhance the imagery of a Native American narrative. The upper right and lower left bear charcoal sketches of a horse and rural church; they are overworked, leaving ghostlike images of themselves reverberating in space. In the center, a shepherd's (priest's?) robe hovers with arms outstretched, like a spectre admonishing the abusers of the environment. Throughout the drawing, contrasting images that refer to intertwined cultural legacies are held together with tenuous, grasslike strokes. The media and the sketchy manner in which they are handled effectively creates the feeling of a "mental sketchbook"—fleeting memories sparked by incongruous objects.

Crayon

Strictly defined, the term **crayon** includes any drawing material in stick form. Thus, charcoal, chalk, and pastels are crayons, as are the wax implements you used on walls, floors, and occasionally coloring books when you were a child. One of the most popular commercially manufactured crayons for artists is the **conté crayon**. Its effects on paper are similar to those of chalk and pastel, although its harder texture makes a greater clarity possible.

Life, Death, and Dwelling in the Deep South

SOME YEARS AGO, AFRICAN AMERICAN SCULPTOR Beverly Buchanan came to know Ms. Mary Lou Furcron. They were both artists, one might say. Both the builders of structures. Both nurturing, creative, and colorful. Ever since this meeting, Buchanan's life and art have revolved around the art and life of the Southern shack dweller.

This way of living is an existence unto itself, as the photographs indicate (Fig. **5-13**). Ms. Furcron's shack reflects her life, and her life reflects the shack in which she lived. She devoted a part of each day to maintaining the structure, replacing rotted posts with new logs; using bark, lathing, and other odd materials to repair the siding. The shack stood as an organic and ever-evolving structure—an extension of Ms. Furcron herself. Because the shack required her constant attention for its survival, her move to a nursing home brought its rapid disrepair. Just one month after Ms. Furcron's departure, the shack was unrecognizable as its former self.

Buchanan's art, in sculpture, and especially in drawing, reflects a structural approach to the creation of the shack image. As Ms. Furcron built with the recycled remnants of nature and human existence, so does Beverly Buchanan.

Her mixed-media shacks are created from old pieces of wood, metal, and found objects, such as in *Hometown—Shotgun Shack* (Fig. **5-14**). Her oil pastel drawing *Henriette's Yard* (Fig. **5-15**) is vigorously and lovingly constructed of a myriad of vibrant strokes. These strokes at once serve as the building blocks of the shack image and the very stuff that reduces the structure to an almost indecipherable explosion of color. The precarious balance of the shacks in relation to one another and the uncertain ground on which they stand further symbolize the precious and fragile nature of the shack dwelling, and human existence. ■

5-14 **BEVERLY BUCHANAN.**
Hometown—Shotgun Shack (1992).
Wood, mixed media.
12" × 9¼" × 15".
Courtesy of Bernice Steinbaum Gallery, Miami, FL

5-15 **BEVERLY BUCHANAN.**
Henriette's Yard (1995).
Oil pastel on paper. 60" × 60".
Collection of Lois Fichner-Rathus. Courtesy of Bernice Steinbaum Gallery, Miami, FL

A

B

5-13 Photographs of Ms. Mary Lou Furcron's home.
Photo A shows the shack while Ms. Furcron was living in it and tending to it. Photo B shows the shack just one month after her placement in a nursing home.
Courtesy of Bernice Steinbaum Gallery, Miami, FL

1 ft.

1 ft.

5-16 CHUCK CLOSE.
Self-Portrait / Conté Crayon (1979).
Conté crayon on paper. 29½" × 22".
©Chuck Close, courtesy of PaceWildenstein, New York

In his *Self-Portrait / Conté Crayon* (Fig. **5-16**), Chuck Close seems less interested in clarity than in creating the illusion of a grainy and blurry photographic likeness. The artist superimposed a grid over his portrait and then transferred the "contents" of each of the squares of this grid to another, enlarged grid on a 29 1/2-inch-by-22-inch piece of drawing paper using conté crayon. By working square by square, Close could focus on the almost infinite tonal variations inherent in black-and-white photography and attempt to recreate them through scribbled, hatched, blurred, and smudged lines. The contrasts in value differentiate the details of the artist's portrait—from his bald head and eyeglasses to his mustache and beard. Many of the artist's unidealized portraits are based on this grid-transfer method, some featuring the vibrant colors of pastel and oil paint (see Fig. 3-20).

Wax crayons, like pastels, combine ground pigment with a binder—in this case, wax. Wax crayon moves easily over a support to form lines that have a characteristic sheen. These lines are less apt to smudge than charcoal, chalk, and pastels.

Fluid Media

The primary **fluid medium** used in drawing is ink, and the instruments used to carry the medium are pen and brush. Appearing in Egyptian **papyrus** drawings and ancient Chinese scrolls, ink has a history that stretches back thousands of years. Some ancient peoples made ink from the dyes of plants, squid, and octopus. By the second century CE, blue-black inks were being derived from galls found on oak trees. The oldest-known type of ink is India or China ink, which is used in oriental **calligraphy** to this day. It is a solution of carbon black and water, and it is permanent and rich black in color.

As with the dry media, dramatically different effects can be achieved with fluid media through a variety of techniques. For example, the artist may alter the composition of the medium by diluting it with water to achieve lighter tones, or may vary the widths of brushes and pen points to achieve lines of different character.

Pen and Ink

Pens also have been used since ancient times. The earliest ones were hollow reeds that were slit at the ends to allow a controlled flow of ink. **Quills** plucked from live birds became popular writing instruments during the Middle Ages. These were replaced in the nineteenth century by the mass-produced metal **nib**, which is slipped into a wooden **stylus**. Many artists use these pens today.

Pen and ink are used to create drawings that are essentially linear, although the nature of the line can vary considerably according to the type of instrument employed. A fine, rigid nib will provide a clear, precise line that is uniform in thickness. Lines created by a more flexible quill tip, by contrast, will vary in width according to the amount of pressure the artist's hand exerts.

Jean Dubuffet all but fills his *Garden* (Fig. **5-17**) with pen-and-ink scribbles of varying thicknesses outlining mostly organic shapes. Just as a garden's plant life may give the eye a variegated experience of texture as well as color, Dubuffet's lines vary in length and thickness, sometimes culminating in little pools of ink. Here and there more angular, even craggy shapes suggest a path or an outcropping of rock, but the artist's aim is not to realistically depict any garden you might have visited. Rather, the high horizon line and the endless intertwining create an overall sense of being ensnared within a sea of shapes and textures.

Drawing is like making an expressive gesture with the advantage of permanence.

—HENRI MATISSE

5-17 JEAN DUBUFFET.

Garden (1952).

Pen and carbon ink on glazed white wove paper. 18¾" × 23¾".

Harriott A. Fox Fund, 1952.1144, The Art Institute of Chicago. Photograph ©The Art Institute of Chicago. ©2009 Artists Rights Society (ARS), New York/ADAGP, Paris.

Pen and Wash

Fine, clear lines of pure ink are often combined in drawings with **wash**—diluted ink that is applied with a brush. Wash provides a tonal emphasis absent in pen-and-ink drawings. In Giovanni Battista Tiepolo's eighteenth-century drawing (Fig. **5-18**), the contours of the biblical figures are described in pen and ink, but their volume derives from a clever use of wash. An illusion of three-dimensionality is created by pulling the white of the untouched paper forward to function as form and enhancing it with contrasting areas of light and dark wash. The gestural vitality of the pen lines and the generous swaths of watery ink accentuate the composition's dynamic movement.

Brush and Ink

Brushes are extremely versatile drawing implements. They are available in a wide variety of materials, textures, and shapes that afford many different effects. The nature of a line in brush and ink will depend on whether the brush is bristle or nylon, thin or thick, pointed or flat tipped.

Likewise, characteristics of the support—texture, absorbency, and the like—will influence the character of the completed drawing. Brush and ink touched to silk leaves an impression quite different from that produced by brush and ink touched to paper.

Japanese artists are masters of the brush-and-ink medium. They have used it for centuries for every type of calligraphy, ranging from works of art to everyday writing. Their facility with the technique is most evident in seemingly casual sketches, such as those done in the late eighteenth and early nineteenth centuries by Japanese

5-18 GIOVANNI BATTISTA TIEPOLO.

Hagar and Ishmael in the Wilderness (c. 1725–1735).

Pen, brush and brown ink, and wash, over sketch in black chalk. 16½" × 11⅛".

Sterling and Francine Clark Art Institute, Williamstown, MA

5-19 KATSUSHIKA HOKUSAI.
Boy Playing Flute (c. 1800).
Ink and brush on paper. 4½" × 6¼".
Freer Gallery of Art, Smithsonian Institution, Washington, DC.

artist Katsushika Hokusai (Fig. **5-19**). Longer, flowing lines range from thick and dark to thin and faint, capturing, respectively, the heavy folds of the boy's clothing and the pale flesh of his youthful limbs. Short, brisk strokes humorously describe the similarity between the hemp of the woven basket and the youngster's disheveled hair. There is an extraordinary simplicity to the drawing attributable to the surety and ease with which Hokusai handles his medium.

Brush and Wash

The medium of brush and wash is even more versatile than that of brush and ink. Although it can duplicate the

5-20 LEONARDO DA VINCI.
Study of Drapery (c. 1473).
Brush, gray wash, heightened with white, on linen. 7⅜" × 9¼".
Louvre Museum, Paris.
©Réunion des Musées Nationaux/Art Resource, NY.

1 in.

5-21 CLAUDE LORRAIN.
Tiber above Rome (c. 1640).
Brush and wash. 18.5 cm × 26.8 cm
©British Museum/Art Resource, NY

linearity of brush-and-ink drawings, it can also be used to create images solely through tonal contrasts. The ink can be diluted to varying degrees to provide a wide tonal range. Different effects can be achieved either by adding water directly to the ink or by moistening the support before drawing.

It is again surprising to note how adaptable the drawing media can be to different artistic styles or subjects. Consider the drawings by the Italian Renaissance master Leonardo da Vinci (Fig. **5-20**) and the seventeenth-century French painter Claude Lorrain (Fig. **5-21**). Even upon close inspection, one would not guess that both works were created in the same medium, despite their tonal emphasis. Leonardo captured the intricacies of drapery as it falls over the human form, dramatically lit to provide harsh contrasts between surfaces and crevices. The voluminous folds are realized through a meticulous study of tonal contrasts.

The shape of Lorrain's landscape also relies on tonal variations rather than line, but here the similarity ends. Leonardo's drawing is descriptive, and almost photographic in its realism. Lorrain's work is suggestive—a quick rendition of the artist's visual impression of the landscape. Whereas Leonardo worked his wash over linen, Lorrain worked on damp paper. By touching a brush dipped in ink to the wet surface, Lorrain made his forms dissolve into the surrounding field and lose their distinct contours. Broadly brushed liquid formations constructed of varying tones yield the impression of groves of trees on the bank of a body of water that leads to distant mountains. These nondescript areas of diffuse wash were here and there given more definition through bolder lines and brushstrokes applied after the paper was dry. Leonardo used brush and wash to reveal form. Lorrain used it to define space.

5-22 HONORÉ DAUMIER.
Counsel for the Defense (the Advocate)
(1862-1865).
Pen and ink, charcoal, crayon, gouache,
and watercolor. 20⅜" × 23¾".
The Corcoran Gallery of Art. William A. Clark Collection.
©The Corcoran Gallery of Art/CORBIS.

1 in.

CARTOONS

The word **cartoon** derives from the Italian *cartone*, meaning "paper." Originally, cartoons were full-scale preliminary drawings done on paper for projects such as fresco paintings, stained glass, or tapestries. The meaning of cartoon was expanded to include humorous and satirical drawings when a parody of fresco cartoons submitted for decoration of the Houses of Parliament appeared in an English magazine in 1843. Regardless of their targets, all modern cartoons rely on carica-ture, the gross exaggeration and distortion of natural features to ridicule a social or political target.

Honoré Daumier is perhaps the only famous painter to devote so great a part of his production—some 4,000 works—to cartoons. Known for his riveting images of social and moral injustices in nineteenth-century France, he also created caricatures in which he displayed a sharp, sardonic wit. Daumier's *Counsel for the Defense (the Advocate)* (Fig. **5-22**) is a taunting illustration of the theatrics employed by a defense attorney to win sympathy for his client. The crocodile tears streaming down his face along with his melodramatic gestures are in stark contrast with the composure of the defendant. Yet her inscrutable smile suggests that she might not be quite as innocent as the lawyer pretends.

Cartoons have a long history of social commentary, consciousness raising, and political activism. We are all familiar with the children's books of Dr. Seuss, but few of us are aware of Theodor Seuss Geisel's political cartoons (Fig. **5-23**). For two years during World War II, Dr. Seuss was the chief editorial cartoonist for the New York tabloid newspaper *PM*. During that time, he drew more than 400 cartoons, many of which pertained to the war effort. It's fascinating to see Dr. Seuss's legendary, signature style (and creatures) called into service for an altogether different purpose.

5-23 DR. SEUSS.
Cages Cost Money!
Buy More U.S. Savings Bonds and Stamps!
From Dr. Seuss Collection, the Mandeville Special
Collections Library, University of California, San Diego.

Drawing is among the most personal things you can do. It doesn't have any rhetoric
or anything to tell. It's a dialogue between the art and yourself.

—SANTIAGO CALATRAVA, architect

NEW APPROACHES TO DRAWING

Drawings display endless versatility in terms of their intended purposes, their media, and their techniques. It is not unusual to find drawings that are not "drawn" at all on materials that are far removed from traditional paper. You'd be right to ask, "What *is* a drawing after all?"

Jackson Pollock, an American artist working in the 1940s and 1950s, dripped and whipped enamel paint onto paper surfaces. His spontaneous gestures read like an almost-but-not-quite-recognizable calligraphy (Fig. **5-24**). The expansive definition of drawing has led the medium from its traditional roots to one, like painting or printmaking, that is an end in itself. Galleries such as The Drawing Center in New York City feature exhibitions of drawings exclusively, concentrating on both historical and cutting-edge work (Fig. **5-25**).

5-24 JACKSON POLLOCK.
Untitled (1950).
Pencil, duco on paper. 22" × 59⅜".
Graphische Sammlung, Staatsgalerie, Stuttgart. ©2009 Pollack-Krasner Foundation/
Artists Rights Society (ARS), New York

1 ft.

5-25 MARGARET HONDA.
Exchange (2003–2004).
Vinyl on Mylar, 50 elements.
Dimensions variable.
Photo Cathy Carver/The Drawing Center, New York

6

PAINTING

Suddenly I realized that each brushstroke is a decision. . . . In the end I realize that whatever meaning that picture has is the accumulated meaning of ten thousand brushstrokes, each one being decided as it was painted.
—Robert Motherwell

The line between drawing and painting is sometimes blurred. The art historian will speak of linear aspects in painting or painterly qualities in drawing. At times, the materials used in the two media will overlap. **Painting** is generally defined as the application of pigment to a surface. Yet we have already seen the use of pigment in pastel drawings.

Paint can be applied to many surfaces. It has been used throughout history to decorate pottery, enhance sculpture, and embellish architecture. In this section, we explain the composition of paint and explore painting in works created on two-dimensional supports.

PAINT

To most of us, paint is synonymous with color. The color in a paint derives from its pigment. The pigment in powdered form is mixed with a binding agent, or **vehicle**, and a solvent, or **medium**, to form **paint**—the liquid material that imparts color to a surface. Pigments are available in a wide chromatic range. Their color is derived from chemicals and minerals found in plant and animal life, clay, soil, and sand.

Different vehicles are employed in different painting media. The main criterion for a successful vehicle is that it holds the pigments together. Lime plaster, wax, egg, oil, acrylic plastic, water, and gum arabic are commonly used vehicles. Unfortunately, most vehicles are subject to long-term problems, such as cracking, yellowing, or discoloration.

The task of a medium is to provide fluency to the paint so that the color may be readily dispersed over the surface. Water or turpentine is frequently used as a thinning agent for this purpose.

TYPES OF PAINTING

A variety of supports and tools have been used throughout the history of art to create paintings. We shall discuss the characteristics of several types of painting.

Fresco

Fresco is the art of painting on plaster. **Buon fresco**, or true fresco, is executed on damp, lime plaster; **fresco secco** is painting on dry plaster. In buon fresco, the pigments are mixed only with water, and the lime of the plaster wall acts as a binder. As the wall dries, the painted image on it

6-1 GIOTTO.

Lamentation (c. 1305).
Fresco. 7′7″ × 7′9″.

Scrovegni Chapel, Padua, Italy.
©Alinari/Art Resource, NY

1 ft.

*Remember that a picture—before being a horse, a nude, or some sort of anecdote—
is essentially a flat surface covered with colors assembled in a certain order.*

— MAURICE DENIS

becomes permanent. In fresco secco—a less popular and less permanent method—pigments are combined with a vehicle of glue that affixes the color to the dry wall.

Fresco painters encounter several problems: Because in true fresco the paint must be applied to fresh, damp plaster, the artist cannot bite off more than it is possible to chew—or paint—in one day. For this reason, large fresco paintings are composed of small sections, each of which has been painted in a day. The artist tries to arrange the sections so that the joints will not be obvious, but sometimes it is not possible to do so. In a fourteenth-century fresco painting by the Italian master Giotto (Fig. **6-1**), these joints are clearly evident, particularly in the sky, where the artist was not able to complete the vast expanse of blue all at once. It is not surprising that sixteenth-century art historian Giorgio Vasari wrote that of all the methods painters employ, fresco painting "is the most masterly and beautiful, because it consists in doing in a single day that which, in other methods, may be retouched day after day, over the work already done." Another problem is that although fresco paintings can be brilliant in color, some pigments will not form chemical bonds with lime. Thus, these pigments are not suitable for the medium. Artists in Giotto's era, for example, encountered a great deal of difficulty with the color blue. Such lime resistance limits the artist's palette and can make tonal transitions difficult.

Leonardo da Vinci, in his famous *The Last Supper* (see Fig. 16-17), attempted to meet these nuisances head-on, only to suffer disastrous consequences. The experimental materials and methods he employed to achieve superior results were unsuccessful. He lived to see his masterpiece disintegrate beyond repair.

Despite these problems, fresco painting enjoyed immense popularity from prehistoric times until its full flowering in the Renaissance. Although it fell out of favor for several centuries thereafter, Mexican muralists revived the art of fresco after World War I.

Encaustic

One of the earliest methods of applying color to a surface was **encaustic**. It consists of pigment in a wax vehicle that has been heated to a liquid state. The ancient Egyptians

6-2 Mummy portrait of a priest of Serapis, from Hawara, Egypt, ca 140–160.
(Egypto-Roman, Faiyum, c. 160–179 CE).
Encaustic on wood. 14" × 8".
©The Trustees of The British Museum, London

and Greeks tinted their sculptures with encaustic to grant them a lifelike appearance. The Romans applied encaustic to walls, using hot irons. Often, as in the Egyptian Mummy portrait of a priest of Serapis (Fig. **6-2**) dating back to the second century CE, the medium was applied to small, portable wooden panels covered with cloth. As evidenced by the startling realism and freshness of the portrait, encaustic is an extremely durable medium whose colors remain vibrant and whose surface maintains a hard luster. But encaustic is a difficult medium to manipulate: one must keep the molten wax at a constant temperature. For this reason, it has been used only by a handful of contemporary artists.

1 ft.

6-3 KAY WALKINGSTICK.
Solstice (1982).
Acrylic and wax on canvas. 48" × 48" × 3½".
Collection of the artist.

Native American painter Kay Walkingstick derives a certain plasticity from her very different use of acrylic and wax on canvas (Fig. **6-3**). In *Solstice,* two flattened arcs of sharply contrasting hues are about to merge in a viscous sea of mauve and purple. The canoelike image, although common to Native American symbolism, can also be viewed as an abstraction signifying the shifting of seasons from autumn to winter—a kind of quiet cosmological passage. Walkingstick builds her textural surface through successive layers of colored wax, gouging the field here and there with lines that reveal the palette of the lower layers. It is at once an image of power and of solitude.

Tempera

Tempera, like encaustic, was popular for centuries, but its traditional composition—ground pigments mixed with a vehicle of egg yolk or whole eggs thinned with water—is rarely used today. Tempera now describes a medium in which pigment can be mixed with an emulsion of milk, different types of glues or gums, and even the juices and saps of plants and trees. The use of tempera dates back to the Greeks and Romans. Tempera was the exclusive painting medium of artists during the Middle Ages. Not until

the invention of oil paint in northern Europe in the 1300s did tempera fall out of favor.

Tempera offered many advantages. It was an extremely durable medium if applied to a properly prepared surface. Pure and brilliant colors were attainable. Colors did not become compromised by gradual oxidation. Also, the consistency and fluidity of the mixture allowed for a great deal of precision. Tempera, unlike oil paint, however, dries quickly and is difficult to rework. Also, unlike oils, it cannot provide subtle gradations of tone.

Tempera can be applied to wood or canvas panels, although the latter did not come into wide use until the 1500s. Both types of supports were prepared by covering the surface with a ground. The ground was generally a combination of powdered chalk or plaster and animal glue called **gesso**. The gesso ground provided a smooth, glistening white surface on which to apply color.

All that is desirable in the tempera medium can be found in Figure **6-4**, the panel painting by the fifteenth-century Italian artist Gentile da Fabriano. Combined with the technique of **gilding**—the application of thinly hammered sheets of gold to the panel surface—the luminous reds and blues and pearly grays of the tempera paint provide a sumptuous display. The fine details of the ornate costumes testify to the precision made possible by **egg tempera**.

Several contemporary artists, such as the Swiss Photorealist painter Franz Gertsch, have also been enticed by the exactness and intricacies made possible by tempera. Suited to a methodical and painstaking approach to painting, this medium of the old masters yields unparalleled displays of contrasting textures and sharp-focused realism, as shown in Gertsch's large-scale portrait of *Silvia* (Fig. **6-5**).

Oil

The transition from egg tempera to **oil paint** was gradual. For many years following the introduction of the oil medium, artists used it only to apply a finishing coat of glazes to an underpainting of tempera. **Glazing**, or the application of multiple layers of transparent films of paint to a surface, afforded subtle tonal variations and imparted a warm atmosphere that was not possible to achieve with tempera alone. Oil paints have been in wide use since the fifteenth century. Oil paint consists of ground pigments combined with a linseed oil vehicle and turpentine medium or thinner. Oil paint is naturally slow in drying, but drying can be facilitated with various agents added to the basic mixture.

6-4 GENTILE DA FABRIANO.

Adoration of the Magi (1423).

Tempera on wood panel. 9' 10⅛" × 9' 3".

Uffizi Gallery, Florence.

©Scala/Art Resource, NY

6-5 FRANZ GERTSCH.

Silvia (1998).

Tempera on unprimed canvas. 9' 6½" × 9' 2¼".

museum franz gertsch, Burgdorf, Switzerland

A good painter is to paint two things, namely, man and the working of man's mind.

—LEONARDO DA VINCI

Oil painting's broad range of capabilities makes it a favorite among artists. It can be applied with any number of brushes or painting knives. Colors can be blended easily, offering a palette of almost limitless range. Slow drying facilitates the reworking of problem areas. When it is finely applied, oil paint can capture the most intricate detail. When it is broadly brushed, it can render diaphanous fields of pulsating color. Oil paint can be diluted to a barely tinted film to achieve subtle flesh tones, or it can be applied in thick impasto that physically constructs an image, as in *Head of St. Matthew* (Fig. **6-6**) by a follower of Rembrandt.

The first oil paintings were executed on wood panels, and then a gradual shift was made to canvas supports. Like wood panels, the canvas surface is covered with a gesso ground prior to painting. The pliability of fabric stretched over a wooden framework renders the working surface more

6-6 FOLLOWER OF
REMBRANDT VAN RIJN.
Head of St. Matthew (c. 1661).
Oil on wood. 9⅞" × 7¾".
Widener Collection, 1942.9.58. Image ©2007
Board of Trustees, National Gallery of Art,
Washington, DC.

1 in.

The *George Washingtons* of Stuart and Lichtenstein

6-7 GILBERT STUART.
George Washington (1796) (detail).
Oil on canvas. 39⅝" × 34½" (entire work).
©National Portrait Gallery, Smithsonian Institution/Art Resource, NY. William Francis
Warden Fund, John H. and Ernestine A. Payne Fund, Commonwealth Cultural Preservation
Trust. Jointly owned by the Museum of Fine Arts, Boston, and the National Portrait Gallery,
Washington D.C., 1980, 1980.1

THE VERSATILITY OF OIL PAINT is seen in portraits of
George Washington by two American artists who worked
centuries apart. Gilbert Stuart's familiar eighteenth-century
portrait (Fig. **6-7**) provides us with our stereotypical image
of Washington. The work was left unfinished; much of the
composition still reveals the reflective gesso ground. How
did Stuart create a realistic likeness with his brushwork and
modeling? The illusion of three-dimensionality is provided
by the graceful play of light across the surfaces of Washington's face. Some features are sharply defined, others cast into
shadow. Although this image is second nature to us, we can
still notice the sensitivity with which Stuart portrayed his
famous sitter. What do the delicate treatment of the pensive
eyes and the firm outline of the determined jaw tell us about
the personality traits of the wise and aging leader?

Roy Lichtenstein's contemporary portrait (Fig. **6-8**), by
contrast, is an image of glamour and success. What gives
us this impression? A younger, debonair Washington is
presented as if on a campaign poster, or as a comic-strip

hero with a chiseled profile akin to that of Dick Tracy.
The eyes are alert and enthralling; the chin is jaunty and
confident. How does Lichtenstein capitalize on oil paint's
clarity and precision? Sharp contrasts, crisp lines, and dot
patterning such as that found in comic strips deprive the
painting of any subtlety or atmosphere. The rich modeling
that imparted a sense of roundness to Stuart's figure is
replaced by stylized shadows that sit flatly on the canvas.
Lichtenstein forsakes the psychological portrait in favor
of billboard advertising. This is a Washington who has
suffered visual saturation by the contemporary media; the
physical characteristics tell us nothing of the human being
to whom they refer. ∎

6-8 ROY LICHTENSTEIN.
George Washington (1962).
Oil on canvas. 51" × 38".
©Estate of Roy Lichtenstein.

1 ft.

6-9 ED PASCHKE.
Anesthesio (1987).
Oil on linen. 68" × 80".
Phyllis Kind Gallery, Chicago and New York. Courtesy of the artist.

that need no special preparation. Acrylic paint is flexible and fast drying, and, as it is water soluble, it requires no flammable substances for use or cleanup.

One of the few effects of oil paint that cannot be duplicated in acrylic is delicate nuance of colors. Like oil, however, acrylic paint can be used thinly or thickly; it can be applied in transparent films or opaque impastos, as in Helen Oji's *Mount St. Helen's* (Fig. **6-10**). The artist fills the shaped canvas with an explosion of color and texture that simulates the unbridled power of one of the world's few active volcanoes. This image, which gave rise to a whole series on these natural wonders, serves, from another perspective, as "textile" ornamentation for a Japanese kimono. Canvases shaped in this garment design first preoccupied Oji in an earlier series, and here the reference to her Japanese heritage (her parents were interned during World War II, while she grew up in California) and the volcano image may symbolize a convergence of cultures from both sides of the Pacific.

receptive to the pressure of the artist's implement. The light weight of canvas also allows for larger compositions than were possible on wooden panels.

Contemporary artist Ed Paschke's oil painting of Abraham Lincoln (Fig. **6-9**) resurrects a hackneyed image by traversing it with abstract patches of neonlike color. The effect is not unlike that attained by a teenager who defaces a poster of a presidential candidate with spray paint, or it could almost be a face on a video screen with electronic color bleeding through irrelevantly on the image. In either case, environmental "noise" obscures the target. Ironically, the need to work to see through the obfuscating patches of color renders the image of the president more tantalizing.

Acrylic

Acrylic paint offers many of the advantages of oil paint, but "without the mess." Acrylic paint is a mixture of pigment and a plastic vehicle that can be thinned (and washed off brushes and hands) with water. Unlike linseed oil, the synthetic resin of the binder dries colorless and does not gradually compromise the brilliance of the colors. Also, unlike oil paint, acrylic can be used on a variety of surfaces

1 ft.

6-10 HELEN OJI.
Mount St. Helen's (1980).
Acrylic, Rhoplex, glitter on paper. 60" × 72".
Collection of Home Insurance Company, New York. Courtesy of the artist

Superheroes: East Meets West

THE ACRYLIC PAINTINGS OF JAPANESE American Roger Shimomura blend Western Pop Art with traditional Japanese imagery as found in *ukiyo-e* prints. As a child during World War II, Shimomura was interned with his parents and grandparents in Idaho. At the same time, ironically, his uncle served with the valiant 442nd division of Japanese Americans. Shimomura remembers statements made by white Americans about Japanese Americans during this deeply disturbing period. For example, Idaho's attorney general remarked, "We want to keep this a white man's country."

Shimomura's *Untitled* (Fig. **6-11**) is at first glance an amusing clash of American and Japanese pop cultures. American cartoon characters, Donald Duck, Pinocchio, Dick Tracy, and the combination Batman-Superman, vie for space on the crowded canvas with Japanese Samurai warriors and a contemporary Japanese. The battle of East and West imagery may reflect the tensions within the artist regarding his ancestral roots and his chosen country. This is succinctly symbolized in the inclusion of Shimomura's self-portrait-as-Statue-of-Liberty in the extreme upper left. In this painting, conflicts between people and cultures are safely if not satirically played out among their stereotypes and myths. ■

6-11 **ROGER SHIMOMURA.**
Untitled (1984).
Acrylic on canvas. 60" × 72".
Courtesy of the artist and Flomenhaft Gallery

1 ft.

Watercolor

The term **watercolor** originally defined any painting medium that employed water as a solvent. Thus, fresco and egg tempera have been called watercolor processes. But today watercolor refers to a specific technique called **aquarelle**, in which transparent films of paint are applied to a white, absorbent surface. Contemporary watercolors are composed of pigments and a gum arabic vehicle, thinned, of course, with a medium of water.

Variations of the watercolor medium have been employed for centuries. Ancient Egyptian artists used a form of watercolor in their paintings. Watercolor was also used extensively for manuscript illumination during the Middle Ages, as we shall see in Chapter 14. **Gouache**, or watercolor mixed with a high concentration of vehicle and an opaque ingredient such as chalk, was the principle painting medium during the Byzantine and Romanesque eras of Christian art. This variation has enjoyed popularity across time and a myriad of styles and is used to great effect by many contemporary artists, such as David Hockney (Fig. **6-12**).

Transparent watercolor, however, did not appear until the fifteenth century. It is a difficult medium to manipulate, despite its simple components. Tints are achieved by diluting the colors with various quantities of water. White, then, does not exist; white must be derived by allowing the white of the paper to "shine" through the color of the composition or by leaving areas of the paper exposed. To achieve the latter effect, all areas of whiteness must be mapped out with precision before the first stroke of color is applied.

With oil paint and acrylic, the artist sometimes overpaints areas of the canvas in order to make corrections or to blend colors. With transparent watercolors, overpainting obscures the underlying layers of color. For this reason, corrections are virtually impossible, so the artist must have the ability to plan ahead, as well as a sure hand and a stout heart. When used skillfully, watercolor has an unparalleled freshness and delicacy. The colors are pure and brilliant, and the range of effects surprisingly broad.

Contemporary painter Ralph Goings—one of the driving forces behind and consistent contributors to the school of Photorealism—uses transparent watercolor ingeniously. His virtuoso handling of the medium can be seen in works

6-12 DAVID HOCKNEY. *Punchinello with Block,* for "Parade Triple Bill" (1980). Gouache on paper. 14" × 17". Copyright ©David Hockney.

1 in.

1 in.

6-13 RALPH GOINGS.
Rock Ola (1992).
Watercolor on paper. 14" × 20¾".
Courtesy O. K. Harris Works of Art, New York, NY

1 in.

6-14 EMIL NOLDE.
Still Life, Tulips (c. 1930).
Watercolor on paper. 18½" × 13½".
Collection of the North Carolina Museum of Art, Raleigh.
Bequest of W. R. Valentiner. G.65.10.51. ©Nolde Stiftung Seebüll

such as *Rock Ola* (Fig. **6-13**), which belie the difficulties of the medium. Confident strokes of color precisely define the gleaming "retro" chrome surfaces of a diner interior—the classic backdrop for the countertop jukebox and standard "still life with ketchup bottle and ashtray." Washes are kept to a minimum, as the painting emphasizes form over color, line over tonal patterns.

The broader appeal of watercolor, however, is not to be found in its capability of rendering meticulous detail. When the medium came into wide use during the sixteenth century, it was seen as having other, very different advantages. The fluidity of watercolor was conducive to rapid sketches and preparatory studies. Simple materials allowed for portability. Artists were able to cart their materials to any location, indoors or outdoors, and to register spontaneously their impressions of a host of subjects. Of course, watercolor is also used for paintings that stand as completed statements. Artists such as the German Expressionist Emil Nolde (Fig. **6-14**) were enticed by the transparency of tinted washes. Such washes permitted a delicate fusion of colors. As with the drawing medium of brush and wash, the effect is atmospheric. The edges of the forms are softened; they seem to diffuse into one another or the surrounding field. Nolde created his explosions of blossoms through delicately balanced patches of bold color and diaphanous washes. The composition is brightened by the white of the paper, which is brought forward to create forms as assertive as those in color.

Spray Paint

One can consider that spray painting has had a rather long history. The subtle coloration marking different species of animals on the walls of Paleolithic caves was probably achieved by blowing pigments onto a surface through hollowed-out reeds. Why are they there: decoration? ritual? history? Oddly enough, these questions can be asked of the contemporary graffiti artist and the

Painting is self-discovery. Every good artist paints what he is.

—JACKSON POLLOCK

6-15 CRASH (JOHN MATOS).
Arcadia Revisited (1988).
Spray paint on canvas. 96¼" × 68".
Courtesy of the artist

1 ft.

are more likely to call this defacing public property than creating works of art, but how do we describe the elaborate urban "landscapes" that might cover the outside of an entire subway car, filling the space with a masterful composition of shapes, lines, textures, and colors? On the street, they are called masterworks, and their artists are indeed legendary.

Some graffiti writers have "ascended" to the art **gallery** scene, exchanging their steel "canvases" for some of fabric and their high-speed exhibition spaces for highbrow gallery walls. One such artist, Crash (or John Matos), created a parody of his own subway style in a complex canvas work called *Arcadia Revisited* (Fig. **6-15**). All of the tools and techniques of his trade—commercial cans of spray paint, the Benday dots of comic-strip fame, the sharp lines of the tag writer's logos, the diffuse spray technique that adds dimensionality to an array of otherwise flat objects—are used to describe a violent clash of cultural icons that are fragmented, superimposed, and barely contained within the confines of the canvas.

MIXED MEDIA

Contemporary painters have in many cases combined traditional painting techniques with other materials, or they have painted on nontraditional supports, stretching the definition of what has usually been considered painting. For example, in *The Bed* (see Fig. 21-12), Pop artist Robert Rauschenberg splashed and brushed paint onto a quilt and pillow, which he then hung on a wall like a canvas work and labeled a "combine painting." The Synthetic Cubists of the early twentieth century, Picasso and Braque, were the first to incorporate pieces of newsprint, wallpaper, labels from wine bottles, and oilcloth into their paintings. These works were called *papiers collés* and have come to be called **collages**.

The base media for Howardena Pindell's *Autobiography: Water / Ancestors, Middle Passage / Family Ghosts* (Fig. **6-16**) are tempera and acrylic, but the work, on sewn canvas, also incorporates an array of techniques and substances—markers, oil stick, paper, photo-transfer, and vinyl tape. The detail achieved is quite remarkable. The artist seems to float in a shimmering pool of shallow water, while all

thousands upon thousands of writings that range in definition from "tags" to "masterworks." Why do they do it? Is it art? urban ritual? Will it speak in history to the trials of inner-city living?

Everyone has seen graffiti, but the complexity of the work and the social atmosphere from which it is derived may not be common knowledge. Stylized signatures, or "tags," can be seen everywhere; it seems as though no urban surface—interior or exterior—is immune. Some

around her images and objects of memory seem to enter and exit her consciousness. Included among them are the prominent white shape of an African slave ship, a reference to Pindell's African ancestry, and the whitened face of the artist's portrait that may have been influenced by Michael Jackson's "Thriller" makeup. The work resembles as much a weaving as a painting, further reflecting the tapestry-like nature of human recollection.

Miriam Schapiro is best known for her paint and fabric constructions, which she has labeled "femmage,"

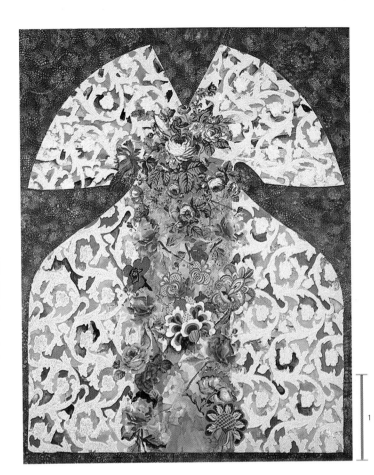

6-17 MIRIAM SCHAPIRO.
Maid of Honour (1984).
Acrylic and fabric on canvas. 60" × 50".
Collection of Lois Fichner-Rathus. ©2007 Miriam Schapiro and Flomenhaft Gallery

6-16 HOWARDENA PINDELL.
Autobiography: Water / Ancestors, Middle Passage / Family Ghosts (1988).
Acrylic, tempera, cattle markers, oil stick, paper, polymer photo-transfer, and vinyl tape on sewn canvas. 118" × 71".
Wadsworth Atheneum, Hartford, CT. Ellis Gallup Summer and Mary Catlin Sumner Collection

to express what she sees as their unification of feminine imagery and materials with the medium of collage. In *Maid of Honour* (Fig. **6-17**), Schapiro combines bits of intricately patterned fabric with acrylic pigments on a traditional canvas support to construct a highly decorative garment that is presented as a work of art. The painting is a celebration of women's experiences with sewing, quilting, needlework, and decoration.

The two-dimensional media we have discussed in Chapters 5 and 6, drawing and painting, create unique works whose availability to the general public is usually limited to photographic renditions in books such as this. Even the intrepid museumgoer usually visits only a small number of collections. So let us now turn our attention to the two-dimensional medium that has allowed millions of people to own original works by masters—printmaking.

7

PRINTMAKING

■

In comparison with painting and sculpture, engraving is a cosmopolitan art,
the immediate inter-relation of different countries being facilitated
by the portable nature of its creations.
—Arthur M. Hind

The value of drawings and paintings lies, in part, in their uniqueness. Hours, weeks, sometimes years are expended in the creation of these one-of-a-kind works. Printmaking permits the reproduction of these coveted works as well as the production of multiple copies of original prints. Printmaking is an important artistic medium for at least two reasons. First, it allows people to study great works of art from a distance. Second, because prints are less expensive than unique works by the same artist, they make it possible for the general public, not just the wealthy few, to own original works. With prints, art has become accessible. Like some drawings, however, prints not only serve a functional purpose but may also be considered works of art in themselves.

METHODS
OF PRINTMAKING

The printmaking process begins with a design or image made in or on a surface by hitting or pressing with a tool. The image is then transferred to paper or a similar material. The transferred image is called the **print**. The working surface, or **matrix**, varies according to the printmaking technique. Matrices include wood blocks, metal plates, stone slabs, and silkscreens. There are special tools for working with each kind of matrix, but the images in printmaking are usually rendered in ink.

Printmaking processes are divided into four major categories: relief, intaglio, lithography, and serigraphy (Fig. **7-1**). We shall examine a variety of techniques within each of these processes. Finally, we will consider the monotype and the combining of printmaking media with other media.

RELIEF

In **relief printing**, the matrix is carved with knives or gouges. Areas that are not meant to be printed are cut below the surface of the matrix (Fig. 7-1A), and areas that form the image and are meant to be printed are left raised. Ink is then applied to the raised surfaces, often from a roller. The matrix is pressed against a sheet of paper, and the image is transferred. The transferred image is the print. Relief printing includes woodcut and wood engraving.

Woodcut

Woodcut is the oldest form of printmaking. The ancient Chinese stamped patterns onto textiles and paper using carved wood blocks. The Romans used woodcuts to stamp symbols or letters on surfaces for purposes of identification. During the 1400s in Europe, woodcuts provided multiple copies of religious images for worshippers. After the invention of the printing press, woodcut assumed an important role in book illustration.

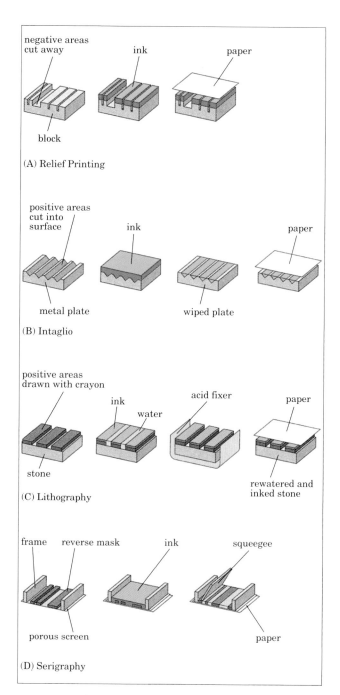

7-1 Printmaking technologies.

Woodcuts are made by cutting along the grain of the flat surface of a wooden board with a knife. Different types of wood and different gouging tools yield various effects.

Hiroshige's *Rain Shower on Ohashi Bridge* with Xiaomo's *Family by the Lotus Pond*

1 in.

7-2 ANDO HIROSHIGE.
Rain Shower on Ohashi Bridge (1857).
Color woodblock on paper. 13⅞" × 9⅛".
The Cleveland Museum of Art. Gift of J. J. Wade, 1921.318

ANDO HIROSHIGE, a nineteenth-century Japanese artist, achieved the finest detail in his works by choosing a close-grained wood and by tightly controlling the movement of his carving tools. Clean-cut, uniform lines define the steady rain and the individuals who tread huddled against the downpour across a wooden footbridge (Fig. **7-2**). These fine lines provide a delicate counterpoint to bold shapes and broad areas of color and create the illusion of a drawing.

The meticulous process by which Hiroshige achieved his sharply defined images is used to a very different effect in Zhao Xiaomo's *Family by the Lotus Pond* (Fig. **7-3**). This contemporary Chinese printmaker uses a range of woodblock techniques to create complex, energetic compositions that often simulate oil paintings. Inspired by Chinese peasant paintings, as they are not bound by "academic rules," Xiaomo creates mosaic-like surfaces with bold, two-dimensional patterns.

How does the visual impact of these two works differ? Consider the use of line, shape, and color. ∎

1 in.

7-3 ZHAO XIAOMO.
Family by the Lotus Pond (1998).
Multiblock woodcut printed with water-soluble ink.
42.7 cm × 41.7 cm.
Margaret Gentles Endowment, 2004.208, The Art Institute of Chicago.
Photography ©The Art Institute of Chicago.

1 ft.

7-4 CHEN XUHAI.
Golden Autumn (1998).
Woodcut, printed with oil-based ink. 64.2 cm × 61.1 cm.
Margaret Gentles Endowment, 2004.163, The Art Institute of Chicago.
Photography ©The Art Institute of Chicago.

Golden Autumn (Fig. **7-4**) by Chen Xuhai is a masterfully complex woodcut in which pockets of short lines of varying direction combine with long, velvet black crevices to create the signature landscape of an aging face.

Wood Engraving

The technique of **wood engraving** and its effects differ significantly from those of woodcuts. Whereas in woodcuts the flat surface of boards is used, in wood engraving many thin layers of wood are **laminated**. Then the ends of these sections are planed flat, yielding a hard, nondirectional surface. In contrast to the softer matrix used for the woodcut, the matrix for the wood engraving makes it relatively easy to work lines in varying directions. These lines are **incised** or engraved with tools such as a **burin** or **graver** (Fig. **7-5**), instead of being cut with knives and gouges. The lines can be extremely fine and are often used in close alignment to

give the illusion of tonal gradations. This process was used to illustrate newspapers, such as *Harper's Weekly*, during the nineteenth century.

The razor-sharp tips of engraving implements and the hardness of the end-grain blocks make possible the exacting precision found in wood engravings such as that by Paul Landacre (Fig. **7-6**), a well-known twentieth-century American printmaker. Tight, threadlike, parallel, and cross-hatched lines compose the tonal areas that define the form. The rhythmic, flowing lines of the seedling's unfurling leaves contrast dramatically with the fine, prickly lines that emanate like rays from the young corn plant. The print is a display of technical prowess in a most demanding and painstaking medium.

INTAGLIO

The popularity of relief printing declined with the introduction of the **intaglio** process. Intaglio prints are created by using metal plates into which lines have been incised. The plates are covered with ink, which is forced into the linear depressions, and then the surface is carefully wiped. The cut depressions retain the ink, whereas the flat surfaces are clean. Paper is laid atop the plate, and then paper and plate are passed through a printing press, forcing the paper into the incised lines to pick up the ink, thereby accepting the image. In a reversal of the relief process, then, intaglio prints are derived from designs or images that lie *below* the surface of the matrix (Fig. 7-1B).

Intaglio printing encompasses many different media, the most common of which are engraving, drypoint, etching, and mezzotint and aquatint. Some artists have used

7-5 Burin.

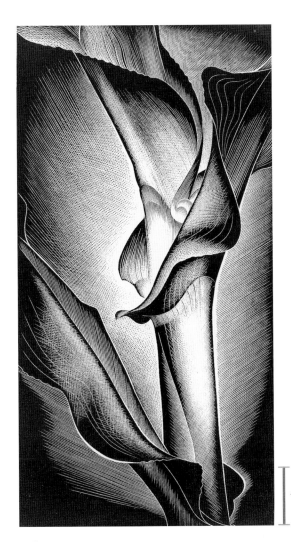

these techniques recently in interesting variations or combinations and have pioneered approaches using modern equipment such as the camera and computer.

Engraving

Although **engraving** has been used to decorate metal surfaces such as bronze mirrors or gold and silver drinking vessels since ancient times, the earliest engravings printed on paper did not appear until the fifteenth century. In engraving, the artist creates clean-cut lines on a plate of copper, zinc, or steel, forcing the sharpened point of a burin across the surface with the heel of the hand. Because the lines are transferred to paper under very high pressure, they not only reveal the ink from the grooves but have a ridgelike texture that can be felt by running a finger across the print.

An early, famous engraving came from the hand of the fifteenth-century Italian painter Antonio Pollaiuolo (Fig. **7-7**). Deep lines that hold a greater amount of ink define the contours of the ten fighting figures. As Landacre did, Pollaiuolo used parallel groupings of thinner and thus lighter lines to render the tonal gradations that define the exaggerated musculature. The detail of the print is described with the utmost precision, revealing the artist's painstaking mastery of the burin.

1 in.

7-6 PAUL LANDACRE.
Growing Corn (1940).
Wood engraving. 8½" × 4¼".
Library of Congress, Prints and
Photographs Division

7-7 ANTONIO POLLAIUOLO.
Battle of Ten Naked Men
(c. 1465–1470).
Engraving. 15½" × 23³⁄₁₆".
The Metropolitan Museum of Art,
New York. Purchase, Joseph Pulitzer
Bequest, 1917 (17.50.99). Image
©The Metropolitan Museum of Art

1 in.

1 in.

Drypoint

Drypoint is engraving with a simple twist. In drypoint, a needle is dragged across the surface, and a metal burr, or rough edge, is left in its wake to one side of the furrow. The burr retains particles of ink, creating a softened rather than crisp line when printed. The burr sits above the surface of the matrix and therefore is fragile. After many printings, it will break down, resulting in a line that simply looks engraved.

The characteristic velvety appearance of drypoint lines is seen in Rembrandt's *Christ Crucified between the Two Thieves* (Fig. **7-8**). The more distinct lines were rendered with a burin, whereas the softer lines were created with a drypoint needle. Rembrandt used the blurriness of the drypoint line to enhance the sense of chaos attending the Crucifixion and the darkness of the encroaching storm. Lines fall like black curtains enshrouding the crowd, and rays of bright light illuminate the figure of Jesus and splash down onto the spectators.

Etching

Although they are both intaglio processes, **etching** differs from engraving in the way the lines are cut into the matrix. With engraving, the depth of the line corresponds to the amount of force used to push or draw an implement over the surface. With etching, minimal pressure is exerted to determine the depth of line. A chemical process does the work. In etching, the metal plate is covered with a liquid, acid-resistant ground consisting of wax or resin. When the ground has hardened, the image is drawn upon it with a fine needle. Little pressure is exerted to expose the ground; the plate itself is not scratched. When the drawing is completed, the matrix is slipped into an acid bath, which immediately begins to eat away, or etch, the exposed areas of the plate. This etching process yields the sunken line that holds the ink. The artist leaves the plate in the acid solution just long enough to achieve the desired depth of line. If a variety of tones is desired, the artist may pull the plate out of the acid solution after a while, cover lines of sufficient depth with the acid-resistant ground, and replace the plate in the bath for further etching of the remaining exposed

1 in.

7-10 GIOVANNI DOMENICO TIEPOLO.
A Negro (1770).
Etching, 2nd state. 5⅝" × 4⁹⁄₁₆".
Museum of Fine Arts, Boston. George R. Nutter Fund, 54.974.
Photograph ©2009 Museum of Fine Arts, Boston

1 in.

7-9 HENRI MATISSE.
Loulou Distracted (1914).
Etching, printed in black. 7¹⁄₁₆" × 5".
Archives Matisse, France. ©2009
Succession H. Matisse, Paris/Artists Rights
Society (ARS), New York.

lines. The longer the plate remains in the acid solution, the deeper the etching. Deeper crevices hold more ink, and for this reason they print darker lines.

Etching is a versatile medium, capable of many types of lines and effects. The modern French painter Henri Matisse used but a few dozen uniformly etched lines to describe the essential features of a woman, *Loulou Distracted* (Fig. **7-9**). The extraordinarily simple yet complete image attests to the delicacy that can be achieved with etching.

Whereas Matisse's figure takes shape through the careful placement of line, the subject of the etching by Giovanni Domenico Tiepolo (who was the son of Giovanni Battista Tiepolo) exists by virtue of textural and tonal contrasts (Fig. **7-10**). This eighteenth-century Italian artist used a variety of wavy and curving lines to differentiate skin from cloth, fur from hair, figure from ground. Lines are spaced to provide a range of tones from the sharp white of the paper to the rich black of the man's clothing. The overall texture creates a hazy atmosphere that caresses the pensive figure.

Hung Liu: Chinese Traditions Unbound

IN MANY WAYS, HUNG LIU epitomizes the concerns and preoccupations of the Chinese artist whose life experiences during that country's Cultural Revolution have shaped their art—indeed their very existence. In 1984, Hung Liu arrived in the United States, in her words, with her "Five-thousand-year-old culture on my back. Late-twentieth-century world in my face. . . . My Alien number is 28333359." For four years in her home country, she was forced to work in the fields. In her chosen country, she is now a professor at Mills College and has had one-woman shows in New York, San Francisco, and Texas. Her art focuses on what she has called "the peculiar ironies which result when ancient Chinese images are 'reprocessed' within contemporary Western materials, processes, and modes of display."

Figure **7-11** shows an untitled mixed-media print, whose main image consists of a photo-etching onto which are affixed small rectangular wooden blocks—mahjong pieces—bearing the "high-fashion" portraits of Chinese women. The inspiration for this print, and full oil paintings on the same theme, came from a series of photographs of Chinese prostitutes from the early 1900s that

Hung Liu discovered on a recent return trip to China. When the Communist revolution took hold and all able-bodied individuals were forced into labor, these women were forced into prostitution because the traditions of oppression that led to the practice of binding their feet made them unfit for physical toil. They could barely walk.

Hung Liu feels the need to make known the pain, suffering, and degradation of generations of women before her:

> Although I do not have bound feet, the invisible spiritual burdens fall heavy on me. . . . I communicate with the characters in my paintings, prostitutes—these completely subjugated people—with reverence, sympathy, and awe. They had no real names. Probably no children. I want to make up stories for them. Who were they? Did they leave any trace in history?

In Hung Liu's work, we come to understand a piece of history. We are challenged to reflect, as she does, upon human rights and freedoms, spiritual and physical oppression, political expression, and silenced voices. ■

7-11 HUNG LIU.
Untitled (1992).
Photo-etching, mixed media.
33" × 22½".

Collection of Lois Fichner-Rathus. Photo courtesy of Bernice Steinbaum Gallery, Miami, FL.

1 ft.

Mezzotint and Aquatint

Engraving, drypoint, and etching are essentially linear media. With these techniques, designs or images are created by cutting lines into a plate. The illusion of tonal gradations is achieved by altering the number and concentration of lines. Sometime in the mid-seventeenth century, the Dutchman Ludwig von Siegen developed a technique whereby broad tonal areas could be achieved by nonlinear engraving, that is, engraving that does *not* depend on line. The medium was called **mezzotint**, from the Italian word meaning "half tint."

With mezzotint engraving, the entire metal plate is worked over with a curved, multitoothed implement called a **hatcher**. The hatcher is "rocked" back and forth over the surface, producing thousands of tiny pits that will hold ink. If printed at this point, the plate would yield an allover consistent, velvety black print. But the mezzotint engraver uses this evenly pitted surface as a point of departure. The artist creates an image by gradually scraping and burnishing the areas of the plate that are meant to be lighter. These areas will hold less ink and therefore will produce lighter tones. The more persistent the scraping, the shallower the pits and the lighter the tone. A broad range of tones is achieved as the artist works from the rich black of the rocked surface to the highly polished pitless areas that will yield bright whites. Mezzotint is a rarely used, painstaking, and time-consuming procedure.

The subtle tonal gradations achieved by the mezzotint process can be duplicated with a much easier and quicker etching technique called **aquatint**. In aquatint, a metal plate is evenly covered with a fine powder of acid-resistant resin. The plate is then heated, causing the resin to melt and adhere to the surface. As in line etching, the matrix is placed in an acid bath, where its uncovered surfaces are eaten away by the solution. The depth of tone is controlled by removing the plate from the acid and covering the pits that have been sufficiently etched.

Aquatint is often used in conjunction with line etching and is frequently manipulated to resemble tones produced by wash drawings. In *The Painter and His Model* (Fig. **7-12**), Pablo Picasso brought the forms out of void space

7-12 PABLO PICASSO. *The Painter and His Model* (1964). Etching and aquatint. 12⅝" × 18½".

Courtesy Museum of Fine Arts, Boston. Lee M. Friedman Fund, 65.937. Photograph ©2009 Museum of Fine Arts, Boston. ©2009 Estate of Pablo Picasso/Artists Rights Society (ARS), New York.

by defining their limits with dynamic patches of aquatint. These tonal areas resemble swaths of ink typical of wash drawings. Descriptive details of the figures are rendered in fine or ragged lines, etched to varying depths.

Other Etching Techniques

Different effects may also be achieved in etching by using grounds of different substances. **Soft-ground etching**, for example, employs a ground of softened wax and can be used to render the effects of crayon or pencil drawings. In a technique called **lift-ground**, the artist creates the illusion of a brush-and-ink drawing by actually brushing a solution of sugar and water onto a resin-coated plate. When the plate is slipped into the acid bath, the sugar dissolves, lifting the brushed image off the plate to expose the metal beneath. As in all etching media, these exposed areas accept the ink.

Given that the printing process implies the use of ink to produce an image, can we have prints without ink? The answer is yes—with the medium called **gauffrage**, or inkless intaglio. Josef Albers, a twentieth-century American abstract artist, created *Solo V*, the geometric image shown in Figure **7-13**, by etching the lines of his design to two

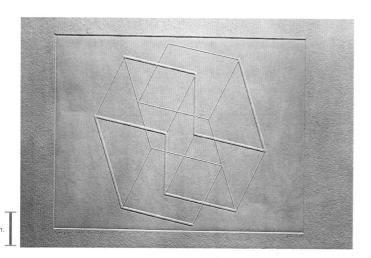

7-13 JOSEF ALBERS.
Solo V (1958).
Inkless intaglio. 6⅝" × 8⅝".
The Brooklyn Museum, Brooklyn, NY. Augustus A. Healy Fund.
©2009 The Josef and Anni Albers Foundation/Artists Rights Society (ARS), New York.

1 in.

different depths. Furrows in the plate appear as raised surfaces when printed. We seem to feel the image with our eyes, as light plays across the surface of the paper to enhance its legibility. Perceptual shifts occur as the viewer focuses now on the thick, now on the thin lines. In trying to puzzle out the logic of the form, the viewer soon discovers that Albers has offered a frustrating illustration of "impossible perspective."

LITHOGRAPHY

Lithography was invented at the dawn of the nineteenth century by the German playwright Aloys Senefelder. Unlike relief and intaglio printing, which rely on cuts in a matrix surface to produce an image, the lithography matrix is flat. Lithography is a surface or **planographic printing** process (Fig. 7-1C).

In lithography, the artist draws an image with a greasy crayon directly on a flat stone slab. Bavarian limestone is considered the best material for the slab. Sometimes a specially sensitized metal plate is used, but a metal surface will not produce the often-desired grainy appearance in the print. Small particles of crayon adhere to the granular texture of the stone matrix. After the design is complete, a solution of nitric acid is applied as a fixative. The entire surface of the matrix is then dampened with water. The untouched areas of the surface accept the water, but the waxy crayon marks repel it.

A roller is then used to cover the stone with an oily ink. This ink adheres to the crayon drawing but repels the water. When paper is pressed to the stone surface, the ink on the crayon is transferred to the paper, revealing the image. Different lithographic methods yield different results. Black crayon on grainy stone can look quite like the crayon drawing it is. On the other hand, lithographs with large blocks of colored ink can emphasize the commercial quality of the printmaking process.

Wang Guangyi's *Great Criticism: Coca-Cola* (Fig. **7-14**) reads like an anti-American propaganda poster, the kind that you could imagine seeing glued in multiples to plywood in an urban landscape. It features bold lines and a sharp definition of color and shape. The power of the image and its message are enhanced by the work's simplicity and directness, as well as our visual recognition of stereotypes—in this case the faces of Asian men, their standard laborer's overalls, and the Coca-Cola logo.

1 ft.

7-14 WANG GUANGYI.
Great Criticism: Coca-Cola (1990–1992).
Lithograph. 73 cm × 69 cm.
Image courtesy of Michael Berger Gallery, Pittsburgh, PA.

The impact of Käthe Kollwitz's lithograph *The Mothers* (Fig. **7-15**), which highlights the plight of lower-class German mothers left alone to fend for their children after World War I, could not be further removed from that of *Great Criticism: Coca-Cola*. The high contrast of the black and white and the coarse quality of the wax crayon yield a sense of desperation suggestive of a newspaper documentary photograph. All the imagery is thrust toward the picture plane, as in high relief. The harsh contours of protective shoulders, arms, and hands contrast with the more delicately rendered faces and heads of the children—all contributing to the poignancy of the work.

SERIGRAPHY

In **serigraphy**—also known as **silkscreen printing**—stencils are used to create the design or image. Unlike the case with other graphic processes, these images can be rendered in paint as well as ink.

One serigraphic process begins with a screen constructed of a piece of silk, nylon, or fine metal mesh stretched on a frame. A stencil with a cutout design is then affixed to the screen, and paper or canvas is placed beneath (Fig. 7-1D). The artist forces paint or ink through the open areas of the stencil with a flat, rubber-bladed implement called a **squeegee**, similar to those used in washing windows. The image on the support corresponds to the shape cut out of the stencil. Several stencils may be used to apply different colors to the same print.

1 in.

7-15 KÄTHE KOLLWITZ.
The Mothers (1919).
Lithograph. 17¾" × 23".
Philadelphia Museum of Art. Gift of Carl Zigrosser, 1945, acc. # 1946-79-1. ©2009 Artists Rights Society (ARS), New York/VG Bild-Kunst, Bonn

I think it was colors and weights and pushes and pulls and how to make a surface.

—ALEX KATZ, when asked what he learned from Matisse

1 ft.

7-16 ALEX KATZ.
Red Coat (1983).
Silkscreen, printed in color. 58" × 29".
The Museum of Modern Art, New York. John B. Turner Fund.
Digital Image ©The Museum of Modern Art/Licensed by SCALA/Art
Resource, NY. Art ©Alex Katz/Licensed by VAGA, New York, NY

Images can also be "painted" on a screen with use of a varnishlike substance that prevents paint or ink from passing through the mesh. This technique allows for more gestural images than cutout stencils would provide. Recently, a serigraphic process called **photo silkscreen** has been developed; it allows the artist to create photographic images on a screen covered with a light-sensitive gel.

Serigraphy was first developed as a commercial medium and is still used as such to create anything from posters to labels on cans of food. The American Pop artist Andy Warhol raised the commercial aspects of serigraphy to the level of fine art in many of his silkscreen prints of the 1960s, such as *Four Marilyns* (see Fig. 1-9). These faithful renditions of celebrities and everyday items satirize the mass media's bombardment of the consumer with advertising. They also have their amusing side.

Alex Katz defines his forms with razor-sharp edges, fixing his subjects in an exact time and place by the details of their clothing and hairstyles. At the same time, he transcends their temporal and spatial limits by simplifying and transforming their figures into something akin to icons. For example, the subject's intense red lips in his silkscreen *Red Coat* (Fig. **7-16**) serve as a symbol of contemporary glamour. *Red Coat* looks something like a photograph transported into another medium. The individual shapes seem carved into a single plane like sawed jigsaw puzzle pieces. As in a photo, the edges of the silkscreen crop off parts of the image. The woman looks like a supermodel, with her features exaggerated as they might be in a cover girl image.

MONOTYPE

Monotype is a printmaking process, but it overlaps the other two-dimensional media of drawing and painting. Like drawing and printmaking, monotype yields but a single image, and like them, therefore, it is a unique work of art.

7-17 EDGAR DEGAS.

The Ballet Master (c. 1874).

Monotype in black ink. 22" × 27½".

1 ft.

In monotype, drawing or painting is created with oil paint or watercolor on a nonabsorbent surface of any material. Brushes are used, but sometimes fine detail is rendered by scratching paint off the plate with sharp implements. A piece of paper is then laid on the surface, and the image is transferred by hand rubbing the back of the paper or passing the matrix and paper through a press. The result, as can be seen in a monotype by Edgar Degas (Fig. **7-17**), has all the spontaneity of a drawing and the lushness of a painting.

In Chapter 8, we conclude our discussion of two-dimensional media with an examination of imaging—photography, film, video, and digital arts. In Chapters 9 and 10, we turn our attention to sculpture and architecture. In drawing, painting, and printmaking, artists have frequently attempted to create the illusion of three-dimensionality. We shall see some of the opportunities and problems that attend actual artistic expression in three dimensions.

IMAGING: PHOTOGRAPHY, FILM, VIDEO, AND DIGITAL ARTS

Look at the things around you, the immediate world around you. If you are alive, it will mean something to you, and if you care enough about photography, and if you know how to use it, you will want to photograph that meaning.
—Edward Weston

Technology has revolutionized the visual arts. For thousands of years, one of the central goals of art was to imitate nature as exactly as possible. Today, any one of us can point a camera at a person or an object and capture a realistic image. Point-and-shoot cameras no longer even require that we place the subject in proper focus or that we regulate the amount of light so as not to overexpose or underexpose the subject. Technology can do all of these things for us.

Similarly, the art of the stage was once available only to those who lived in the great urban centers. Now and then a traveling troupe of actors might come by or local groups might put on a show of sorts, but most people had little or no idea of the ways in which drama, opera, dance, and other performing arts could affect their lives. The advent of motion pictures, or cinematography, suddenly brought a flood of new imagery into new local theaters, and a new form of communal activity was born. People from every station of life could flock to the movie theater on the weekend. Over time, cinematography evolved into an art form independent of its beginnings as a mirror of the stage.

More recently, television has brought this imagery into the home, where people can watch everything from the performing arts to sporting events in privacy and from the multiple vantage points that several cameras, rather than a single set of eyes, can provide. Fine artists have also appropriated television—or, more precisely, the technology that makes television possible—to produce **video art**. Technology has also given rise to the computer as a creative video-mediated tool. With the aid of artificial intelligence, we can instantly view models of objects from all sides. We can be led to feel as though we are sweeping in on our solar system from the black reaches of space, then flying down to the surface of our planet and landing where the programmer would set us down.

Millions of children spend hours playing video games, such as *Tetris*, which challenges them to rotate plummeting polygons to construct a solid wall, or *Tomb Raider*, which requires them to evade or blast a host of enemies before their computer-drawn heroes and heroines plunge into an abyss. Computer technology and computer-generated images have likewise been appropriated by fine artists in the creation of **digital art**. From illustrations of blue jeans that rocket through space, to snappy graphics that headline sporting events, to the web design that greets us every time we go online, computer-generated images punctuate our daily lives. DVDs, multimedia computers, and software that can blend or distort one shape or face into another are bringing a "virtual reality" into our lives that is in some ways more alluring than, well, "real reality."

In this chapter, we discuss photography, film (cinematography), video, and digital arts. These media have given rise to unique possibilities for artistic expression.

PHOTOGRAPHY

Photography is a science and an art. The word *photography* is derived from Greek roots meaning "to write with light." The scientific aspects of photography concern the ways in which images of objects are made on a **photosensitive** surface, such as film, by light that passes through a **lens**. Chemical changes occur in the film so that the images are recorded. This much of the process—the creation of an objective image of the light that has passed through the lens—is mechanical.

It would be grossly inaccurate, however, to think of the *art* of photography as mechanical. Photographers make artistic choices, from the most mundane to the most sophisticated. They decide which films and lenses to use, and which photographs they will retain or discard. They manipulate lighting conditions or printing processes to achieve dazzling or dreamy effects. Always, they are in search of subjects—ordinary, extraordinary, universal, personal.

Photography is truly an art of the hand, head, and heart. The photographer must understand films and grasp skills related to using the camera and, in most cases, to developing **prints**. The photographer must also have the intellect and the passion to search for and to see what is important in things—what is beautiful, harmonious, universal, and worth recording.

Photography is a matter of selection and interpretation. Similar subjects seen through the eyes of different photographers will yield wildly different results. In Ansel Adams's *Moon and Half Dome, Yosemite National Park, California* (Fig. **8-1**), majestic cliffs leap into a deep, cold sky.

8-1 ANSEL ADAMS.
Moon and Half Dome, Yosemite National Park, California (1960).
©Ansel Adams Publishing Rights Trust/CORBIS

8-2 NASA.
Earthrise (1969).
Photo courtesy of NASA

From our earthbound vantage point, the perfect order of the desolate, spherical moon contrasts with the coarseness of the living rock. Yet we know that its geometric polish is an illusion wrought by distance—the moon's surface is just as rough and chaotic. Adams's composition is as much about shape and texture as it is a photograph of a feature of the California landscape. Distance and scale come sharply into focus: This is a story of humans dwarfed by nature and nature dwarfed by the stars.

In the early nineteenth century, when photography was invented, the stuff of which *Earthrise* (Fig. **8-2**) is made would have been only fantasy. In this NASA photograph, taken during the first landing on the moon, the sharp lights and darks of the lunar landing module are silhouetted against the grays of the softly textured moon and balanced by the high-contrast values of black space and the arc of Earth above. The distance of the home planet lends it an abstract, geometric appearance. Out here, in space, the heavy landing module is very much closer and, despite its mechanical grotesqueness, it looks, frankly, much more like home.

Thus, the mood, stylistic inclinations, cultural biases, and technical preferences of the artist-photographer influence the nature of the creative product. As observers, we are as enriched by the diversity of this medium as by any other of the visual arts media.

Let us now consider two of the technical aspects of photography: cameras and films. Then we chronicle the history of photography.

Cameras

Cameras may look very different from one another and boast a variety of equipment, but they all possess certain basic features. As you can see in Figure **8-3**, the camera is similar to the human eye. In both cases, light enters a narrow opening and is projected onto a photosensitive surface.

The amount of light that enters the eye is determined by the size of the *pupil*, which is an opening in the muscle called the *iris*; the size of the pupil responds automatically to the amount of light that strikes the eye. The amount of light that enters a camera is determined by the size of the opening, or **aperture**, in the **shutter**. The aperture opening can be adjusted manually or, in advanced cameras, automatically. The size of the aperture, or opening, is the so-called **stop**. The smaller the f-stop, the larger the opening. The shutter can also be made to remain open to light for various amounts of time, ranging from a few thousandths of a second—in which case **candid** shots of fast action may be taken—to a second or more.

When the light enters the eye, the *lens* keeps it in focus by responding automatically to its distance from the object. The light is then projected onto the retina, which consists

retina (photosensitive surface)

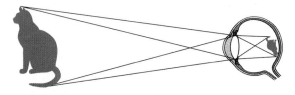

film (photosensitive surface)

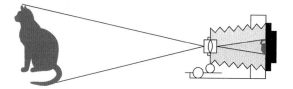

8-3 The camera and the human eye compared.

of cells that are sensitive to light and dark and to color. Nerves transmit visual sensations of objects from the retina to the brain.

In the same way, the camera lens focuses light onto a photosensitive surface such as **film**. A camera lens can be focused manually or automatically. Many photographers purposely take pictures that are out of focus, for their soft, blurred effects. **Telephoto lenses** magnify faraway objects and tend to collapse the spaces between distant objects that recede from us. **Wide-angle lenses** allow a broad view of objects within a confined area.

In their early days, cameras tended to be large and were placed on mounts. Today's cameras are usually small and held by hand. *The Steerage* (see Fig. 1-26) was shot with an early handheld camera. Many contemporary cameras contain angled mirrors that allow the photographer to see directly through the lens and thereby to be precisely aware of the image that is being projected onto the film.

Film

When an image is "shot," it is recorded on a device such as film or an electronic memory device such as a disk or memory stick. Contemporary black-and-white films are very thin, yet they contain several layers, most of which form a protective coating and backing for the photosensitive layer. The active layer contains an **emulsion** of small particles of a photosensitive silver salt (usually silver halide) suspended in gelatin.

After the film is exposed to light and treated chemically, it becomes a **negative**, in which metallic silver is formed from the crystals of silver halide. In this negative, areas of dark and light are reversed. Because the negatives are transparent, light passes through them to a print surface, which becomes the final photograph, or print. Here the areas of light and dark are reversed again, now matching the shading of the original subject. Prints are also usually made significantly larger than the negative.

Black-and-white films differ in color sensitivity (the ability to show colors like red and green as different shades), in contrast (the tendency to show gradations of gray as well as black and white), in graininess (the textural quality, as reflective of the size of the silver halide crystals), and in speed (the amount of exposure time necessary to record an image). Photographers select films that will heighten the effects they seek to portray.

Color film is more complex than black-and-white film, but similar in principle. Color film also contains several layers, some of which are protective and provide backing. There are two basic kinds of color film: **color reversal film** and **color negative film**. Both types of color film contain three light-sensitive layers.

Prints are made directly from *color reversal film*. Therefore, each of the photosensitive layers corresponds to one of the primary colors in additive color mixtures: blue, green, or red. When color reversal film is exposed to light and treated chemically, mixtures of the primary colors emerge, yielding a full-color image of the photographic subject.

Negatives are made from *color negative film*. Therefore, each photosensitive layer corresponds to the complement of the primary color it represents. (Additive color mixtures and primary and complementary colors are explained in Chapter 2.)

Color films, like black-and-white films, differ in color sensitivity, contrast, graininess, and speed. But color films also differ in their appropriateness for natural (daylight) or artificial (indoor) lighting conditions.

Digital Photography

Today, **digital photography** abounds. Digital cameras translate the visual images that pass through the lens into bits of digital information, which are recorded onto an electronic storage device such as a disk, not on film. High-quality (translation: extremely expensive) digital cameras take photos whose **resolution**—that is, sharpness—rivals that of images recorded on film. The stored information can then be displayed on a computer monitor. Rather than have several prints made, the photographer can "back up" the information repeatedly. It can also be sent over the Internet in digital form. Printed images can also be scanned, which coverts them into digital formats, and then stored on computer hard drives or sent over the Internet.

Digital photography has some advantages. One is that the photographer need not deal with film—loading and unloading it and having it developed. The images can be displayed immediately on a computer monitor or a screen built into the camera. Software then permits you to manipulate the images as desired. You can also print them out as you print out any other image or text.

The disadvantages are that (most) digital images do not have the sharpness of film images. They take up a tremendous amount of storage space (several megabytes each!) on your hard drive. Also, your printer may not print images that approach the quality of film images, even if you have stored enough information to do so. To get professional-quality prints, you may have to invest in professional equipment or take your disk elsewhere, just as you have to take film to a lab or processor to be developed. But the price of this equipment is falling steadily, and it may soon be that nearly anyone will be able to afford digital equipment that rivals the resolution of more traditional photography.

History of Photography

The cameras and films described previously are rather recent inventions. Photography has a long and fascinating history. Although true photography does not appear much before the mid-nineteenth century, some of its principles can be traced back another 300 years, to the camera obscura.

The Camera Obscura

The **camera obscura**—literally, the covered-over or darkened room—was used by Renaissance artists to help them accurately portray depth, or perspective, on two-dimensional surfaces. The camera obscura could be a box, as shown in Figure **8-4**, or an actual room with a small hole that admits light through one wall. The beam of light projects the outside

Fig. 434.

8-4 The camera obscura.
Heritage Image Partnership Ltd.

scene upside down on a surface within the box. The artist then simply traces the scene, as shown, to achieve a proper perspective—to truly imitate nature.

Development of Photosensitive Surfaces

The camera obscura could only temporarily focus an image on a surface while a person labored to copy it by tracing. The next developments in photography concerned the search for photosensitive surfaces that could permanently affix images. These developments came by bits and pieces.

In 1727, the German physicist Heinrich Schulze discovered that silver salts had light-sensitive qualities, but he never tried to record natural images. In 1802, Thomas Wedgwood, son of the well-known English potter, reported his discovery that paper soaked in silver nitrate did take on projected images as a chemical reaction to light. Unfortunately, the images were not permanent.

Heliography

In 1826, the Frenchman Joseph-Nicéphore Niepce invented **heliography**. **Bitumen**, or asphalt residue, was placed on a pewter plate to create a photosensitive surface. The bitumen was soluble in **lavender oil** if kept in the dark, but insoluble if struck by light. Niepce used a kind of camera obscura to expose the plate for several hours, and then he washed the plate in lavender oil. The pewter showed through where there had been little or no light, creating the image of the darker areas of the scene. The bitumen remained where the light had struck, however, leaving lighter values.

The Daguerreotype

The **daguerreotype** resulted from a partnership formed in 1829 between Niepce and another Frenchman, Louis-Jacques-Mandé Daguerre. The daguerreotype used a thin sheet of silver-plated copper. The plate was chemically treated, placed in a camera obscura, and exposed to a narrow beam of light. After exposure, the plate was treated chemically again.

Figure **8-5** shows the first successful daguerreotype, taken in 1837. Remarkably clear images could be recorded by this process. In this work, called *The Artist's Studio*, Daguerre, a landscape painter, sensitively assembled deeply textured objects and sculptures. The contrasting light and dark values help create an illusion of depth.

There were drawbacks to the daguerreotype. It had to be exposed from 5 to 40 minutes, requiring long sittings. The recorded image was reversed, left to right, and was

8-5 LOUIS-JACQUES-MANDÉ DAGUERRE.
The Artist's Studio (1837).
© Collection Société Française de Photographie, Paris.

so delicate that it had to be sealed behind glass to remain fixed. Also, the plate that was exposed to light became the actual daguerreotype. There was no negative, and consequently, copies could not be made. However, some refinements of the process did come rapidly. Within 10 years, the exposure time had been reduced to about 30 to 60 seconds, and the process had become so inexpensive that families could purchase two portraits for a quarter. Daguerreotype studios opened all across Europe and the United States, and families began to collect the rigid, stylized pictures that now seem to reflect days gone by.

The Negative

The negative was invented in 1839 by British scientist William Henry Fox Talbot. Talbot found that sensitized paper, coated with emulsions, could be substituted for the copper plate of the daguerreotype. He would place an object, such as a sprig of a plant, on the paper and expose the arrangement to light. The paper was darkened by the exposure in all areas except those covered by the object. Translucent areas, allowing some passage of light, resulted in a range of grays. Talbot's first so-called photogenic drawings (Fig. **8-6**), created by this process, seem eerie, though lyrically beautiful. The delicacy of the image underscores the impracticality of the process: How on earth would you "photograph" an elephant?

As with the daguerreotype, this process produced completed photographs in which the left and right of the image were reversed. In Talbot's photogenic drawings, the light and dark values of the image were also inverted. Talbot improved on his early experiments with his development of the **contact print**. He placed the negative in contact with a second sheet of sensitized paper and exposed them both to light. The resultant print was a "positive," with left and right, and light and dark, again as in the original subject. Many prints could be made from the negative. Unfortunately, the prints were not as sharp as daguerreotypes, because they incorporated the texture of the paper on which they were captured. Subsequent advances led to methods in which pictures with the clarity of daguerreotypes could be printed from black-and-white as well as color negatives.

Photography improved rapidly for the next 50 or 60 years—faster emulsions, glass-plate negatives, better camera lenses—and photographs became increasingly more available to the general public. The next major step in the history of photography came with the introduction by Louis Lumière of the autochrome color process in 1907. Autochromes were glass plates coated with three layers of dyed potato starch that served as color filters.

8-7 LOUIS LUMIÈRE.
Young Lady with an Umbrella (1906–1910).
Autochrome.
Institut Lumiere, Lyon, France

8-6 WILLIAM HENRY FOX TALBOT.
Botanical Specimen (1839).
Photogenic drawing.
©NMPFT/SSPL/The Image Works

A layer of silver bromide emulsion covered the starch. When the autochrome was developed, it yielded a positive color transparency. Lumière's autochrome photographs, such as *Young Lady with an Umbrella* (Fig. **8-7**), are akin to paintings by Postimpressionist artist Georges Seurat (see Fig. 19-25), an avid student of color theory, as well as to works by other photographers in the pictorial style. Autochrome technology was not replaced until 1932, when Kodak began to produce color film that applied the same principles to more advanced materials.

Portraits

By the 1850s, photographic technology and the demands of a growing middle class in the wake of the American and French revolutions came together to create a burgeoning business in portrait photography. Having a likeness of oneself was formerly reserved for the wealthy, who could afford to commission painters. Photography became the democratic equalizer. The rich, the famous, and average bourgeois citizens could now become memorable, could now make their presence known long after their flesh had rejoined the elements from which it was composed.

Photographic studios spread like wildfire, and many photographers, such as Julia Margaret Cameron and Gaspard Felix Tournachon—called "Nadar"—vied for famous clientele. Cameron's impressive portfolio included portraits

8-8 NADAR.
Sarah Bernhardt (1859).
Bibliothèque Nationale, Paris. Copyright Photos 12, Paris

of Charles Dickens; Alfred, Lord Tennyson; and Henry Wadsworth Longfellow. Figure **8-8** is Nadar's 1859 portrait of the actress Sarah Bernhardt. It was printed from a glass plate, which could be used several times to create sharp copies. Early portrait photographers such as Nadar imitated both nature and the arts, using costumes and props that recalled Romantic paintings or sculpted busts caressed by flowing drapery. The photograph is soft and smoothly textured, with middle-range values predominating; Bernhardt is sensitively portrayed—pensive and brooding, but not downcast.

Photojournalism

Prior to the nineteenth century, there were few illustrations in newspapers and magazines. Those that did appear were usually in the form of engravings or drawings. Photography revolutionized the capacity of the news media to bring realistic representations of important events before the eyes of the public. Pioneers such as Mathew Brady and

Alexander Gardner first used the camera to record major historical events such as the U.S. Civil War. The photographers and their crews trudged down the roads alongside the soldiers, horses drawing their equipment behind them in wagons referred to by the soldiers as "Whatsits."

Equipment available to Brady and Gardner did not allow them to capture candid scenes, so there is no direct record of the bloody to-and-fro of the battle lines, no photographic record of each lunge and parry. Instead, they brought home photographs of officers and of life in the camps along the lines. Although battle scenes would not hold still for Gardner's cameras, the litter of death and devastation caused by the war and pictured in Gardner's *Home of a Rebel Sharpshooter, Gettysburg* (Fig. **8-9**) most certainly did. Despite their novelty and their accuracy, not many works of such graphic nature were sold. There are at least three reasons for this tempered success. First, the state of the art of photography made the photographs high priced. Second, methods for reproducing photographs on newsprint were not invented until about 1900; therefore, the works of the photojournalists were usually rendered as drawings, and the drawings translated into woodcuts before they appeared in the papers. Third, the American public might not have been ready to face the brutal realities they portrayed. In a similar vein, social commentators have suggested that the will of many Americans to persist in the Vietnam War was sapped by the incessant barrage of televised war imagery.

During the Great Depression of the 1930s, the conscience of the nation was stirred by the work of many photographers hired by the Farm Security Administration. Dorothea Lange and Walker Evans, among others, portrayed the lifestyles of migrant farmworkers and sharecroppers. Lange's *Migrant Mother* (Fig. **8-10**) is a heartrending record of a 32-year-old woman who is out of work but cannot move on because the tires have been sold from the family car to purchase food for her seven children. The etching in her forehead is an eloquent expression of a mother's thoughts; the lines at the outer edges of her eyes tell the story of a woman who has aged beyond her years. Lange crops her photograph close to her subjects; they fill the print from edge to edge, forcing us to confront them rather than allowing us to seek comfort in a corner of the print not consigned to such an overt display of human misery. The migrant mother and her children, who turn away from the camera and heighten the futility of their plight, are as much constrained by the camera's viewfinder as they are by their circumstances.

Documentary photography records the social scene of our time. It mirrors the present and documents [it] for the future. Its focus is man in his relation to mankind. It records his customs at work, at war, at play. . . . It portrays his institutions. . . . It shows not merely their facades, but seeks to reveal the manner in which they function, absorb the life, hold the loyalty, and influence the behavior of human beings.

—DOROTHEA LANGE

In the very year that Lange photographed the migrant mother, Robert Capa's fearless coverage of the Spanish Civil War resulted in such incredible photographs as *Death of a Loyalist Soldier* (see Fig. 3-18). During the early 1940s, photographers such as Margaret Bourke-White carried their handheld cameras into combat and captured tragic images of the butchery in Europe and in the Pacific. In 1929, Bourke-White became a staff photographer for *Fortune*, a new magazine published by Henry Luce. When Luce founded *Life* in 1936, Bourke-White became one of its original staff photographers. Like Dorothea Lange, she recorded the poverty of the Great Depression, but in the 1940s, she traveled abroad to become one of the first female war photojournalists. As World War II was drawing to an end in Europe, Bourke-White arrived at the Nazi concentration camp of Buchenwald in time for its liberation by Gen. George S. Patton. Her photograph *The*

1 in.

8-10 DOROTHEA LANGE.
Migrant Mother, Nipomo, California (1936).
Gelatin silver print. 12½" × 9⅞".
Copyright The Dorothea Lange Collection. The Oakland Museum of Art. Gift of Paul S. Taylor

8-9 ALEXANDER GARDNER.
Home of a Rebel Sharpshooter, Gettysburg (July 1863).
Wet-plate photograph.
Chicago History Museum

8-11 MARGARET BOURKE-WHITE.
The Living Dead of Buchenwald, April 1945 (1945).
©Time and Life Pictures/Getty Images

8-12 RON BERARD.
Untitled (2001).
©Ron J. Berard

Living Dead of Buchenwald (Fig. **8-11**), published in *Life* in 1945, has become a classic image of the Holocaust, the Nazi effort to annihilate the Jewish people. The indifferent countenance of each survivor expresses, paradoxically, all that he has witnessed and endured. In her book *Dear Fatherland, Rest Quietly*, Bourke-White put into words her own reactions to Buchenwald. In doing so, she showed how artistic creation, an intensely emotional experience, can also have the effect of objectifying the subject of creation:

> I kept telling myself that I would believe the indescribably horrible sight in the courtyard before me only when I had a chance to look at my own photographs. Using the camera was almost a relief; it interposed a slight barrier between myself and the white horror in front of me . . . it made me ashamed to be a member of the human race.[1]

Dorothea Lange traveled rural America to photograph the effects of the Depression, and Margaret Bourke-White followed the U.S. troops abroad during World War II. As Bourke-White discovered, one of the keys to photojournalism is being in the right place at the right time—or in the wrong place at the wrong time. Photographer Ron Berard was also in the right—or wrong—place. He was living on an upper floor of an apartment building in Battery Park City, across a highway from the World Trade Center, on September 11, 2001, when Arab terrorists hijacked commercial aircraft and flew them into the twin towers, causing their collapse and the loss of nearly 3,000 lives. His photograph (Fig. **8-12**) captures the hellish quality of the destruction—the shard of the curtain wall that remained, the pile of rubble, the charred facade of a still-standing neighbor. The eerie smoke that rose from the pit would continue to rise for two months.

Another of Berard's photographs—an American flag flying, flapping, snapping against the grim background of the devastation of the World Trade Center site—was

---

1 Margaret Bourke-White, *Dear Fatherland, Rest Quietly* (New York: Simon and Schuster, 1946), 73.

picked up by *Time* magazine. Yet perhaps the best-known photo from the tragedy of September 11 is the one taken a day later by Thomas E. Franklin, a staff photographer for *The Record*, a local New Jersey newspaper. That image of firefighters raising the flag amidst the rubble—a symbol of survival, heroism, and pride—was made into a U.S. postage stamp. Its content, design, and emotional impact have been compared with the equally famous photograph of U.S. Marines raising the flag on the Pacific island of Iwo Jima during World War II.

Photography as an Art Form

Photographers became aware of the potential of their medium as an art form more than 100 years ago. Edward Weston, Paul Strand, Edward Steichen, and others argued that photographers must not attempt to imitate painting but must find modes of expression that are truer to their medium. Synergistically, painters were free to move toward abstraction because the obligation to faithfully record nature was now assumed by the photographer. Why, after all, do what a camera can do better? In 1902, Alfred Stieglitz founded the Photo-Secession, a group dedicated to advancing photography as a separate art form. Stieglitz enjoyed taking pictures under adverse weather conditions and at odd times of day to show the versatility of his medium and the diversity of his expression.

Edward Steichen's *The Flatiron Building—Evening* (Fig. **8-13**), photographed a century ago, is among the foremost early examples of the photograph as a work of art. It is an exquisitely sensitive nocturne of haunting shapes looming in a rain-soaked atmosphere. The branch in the foreground provides the viewer with a psychological vantage point as it cuts across the composition like a bolt of lightning or an artery pulsing with life. The values are predominantly middle grays, although here and there, beaconlike, street lamps sparkle in the distance. The infinite gradations of gray in the cast-iron skyscraper after which the picture is named, and in

the surrounding structures, yield an immeasurable softness. Although much is present that we cannot readily see, there is nothing gloomy or frightening about the scene. Rather, it seems pregnant with wonderful things that will happen as the rain stops and the twentieth century progresses.

It was not long before artists began to manipulate their medium so that they, too, could venture beyond mere imitation. The first steps were tentative, building on the familiar and the readily acceptable. Photographer James VanDerZee, known for his visual narrative of life in New York's Harlem, experimented with painted backgrounds and double-exposed images in otherwise traditional portraits.

8-13 EDWARD STEICHEN.
The Flatiron Building—Evening (1906).
Library of Congress, Prints and Photographs Division.
Reprinted with permission of Joanna T. Steichen.

8-14 JAMES VANDERZEE.
Future Expectations (1915).
Gelatin silver print.

Future Expectations (Fig. **8-14**) is both a visual record of a young couple on their wedding day and a symbol of their hopes and anticipations—a comfortable home with a blazing hearth, and beautiful children, secure in their love.

In the realm of photography and fantasy, we may take a quantum leap to the present day, when technology is such that the only impediment to the most innovative results is the artist's ability to fathom the unfathomable. In what sharp contrast to VanDerZee's interior stands Sandy Skoglund's *Radioactive Cats* (Fig. **8-15**)! Hopes and expectations for the good life fade into the dullness of gray, as a phlegmatic elderly couple live out their colorless lives. Yet sparks of life and humor permeate the deadly pallor of their environment—in the form of neon green cats. Skoglund sculpted the plaster cats herself and painted the room gray, controlling every aspect of the set before she shot the scene. Yet the photograph stands as the completed work of art.

From cats to dogs: artist-photographer William Wegman happened upon his most famous subject when his Weimaraner puppy virtually insisted on performing before his lights. Man Ray, named by Wegman after the Surrealist photographer, posed willingly in hundreds of staged sets that range from the credible to the farcical. *Blue Period* (Fig.

8-15 SANDY SKOGLUND.
Radioactive Cats (1980).
Cibachrome. 30" × 40".

1 ft.

8-16) is a spoof on Pablo Picasso's painting *The Old Guitar-ist* (see Fig. 20-5), enframed in a souvenir version in the left lower foreground. In both works, a guitar cuts diagonally across the composition, adding the only contrasting color to the otherwise monochromatic blue background. The heads of the old man and of Man Ray hang, melancholy, over the soulful instrument. As Picasso gave the old man's flesh a bluish cast, so did Wegman tint the Weimaraner's muzzle. In Wegman's photograph, however, we find the pièce de résistance—an object laden with profound mean-ing for the guitarist's stand-in: a blue rubber bone.

In contemporary photography, artists often use them-selves as subjects. Cindy Sherman adopts diverse personae for her photographs. She recalls a mundane, early inspira-tion for her approach: "I had all this makeup. I just wanted to see how transformed I could look. It was like painting

8-17 CINDY SHERMAN.
Untitled (1984).
Color photograph. 71" × 48½".
Courtesy of the Artist and Metro Pictures Gallery, New York

in a way."[2] Soon she set herself before elaborate backdrops, costumed in a limitless wardrobe. Dress designers began to ask her to use their haute couture in her photographs, and works such as *Untitled* (Fig. **8-17**) were actually shot as part of an advertising assignment for French *Vogue*. The result is less a sales device than a harsh view of the fashion industry. Sherman appears as a disheveled model with a troubling expression. Something here is very wrong. Regimented stripes go awry as the fabric of her dress is stretched taut across her thighs and knees. Her hands rest oddly in her lap, fingertips red with what seems to be blood. And then there is the smile—an unsettling leer implying madness.

1 in.

8-16 WILLIAM WEGMAN.
Blue Period (1981).
Color Polaroid photograph. 24" × 22".
©William Wegman.

2 Cindy Sherman, in Gerald Marzorati, "Imitation of Life," *Artnews 82* (September 1983): 84–85.

*I see my work as a pictorial excursus on the topic of feminism and contemporary Islam—
a discussion that puts certain myths and realities under the microscope and comes to the conclusion
that these are much more complex than many of us had thought.*

—SHIRIN NESHAT

8-18 DAVID HOCKNEY.
*Pearblossom Highway 11–18th
April 1986 (Second Version),* (1986).
Photographic collage. 71½" × 107".
Copyright ©David Hockney

1 ft.

8-19 SHIRIN NESHAT.
*Untitled (Women
of Allah)* (1994).
Gelatin silver print,
ink. 36 cm × 28 cm.
Courtesy of the artist and
Gladstone Gallery

1 in.

Skoglund, Wegman, and Sherman are photographers
who work, by their own admission, as painters. Painter
David Hockney has used photography to construct unified
compositions whose sum total of parts has a far greater
impact than the whole. In the process of photographing a
subject like *Pearblossom Highway 11–18th April 1986 #2* (Fig.
8-18), Hockney fragments the panorama, only to rebuild
it in his studio. It is almost as if he were reconstructing
the scene as most of us do from fragmented memories.
The result is a shimmering mosaic that elevates the commonplace to the level of fine art.

Iranian American photographer and video artist Shirin
Neshat came to the United States as a teenager, before
the shah was removed from power, and returned in 1990
to witness a nation transformed by the rule of Islamic
clergy. She was particularly concerned about how life had
changed for Iranian women, who now had limited opportunities outside the home and were veiled behind black
chadors. Figure **8-19** is one of a series called *Women of
Allah*, in which guns or flowers are frequently juxtaposed
with vulnerable though rebellious faces and hands that

emerge from beneath the veil. The exposed flesh is over-written with sensual or political texts by Iranian women in the native tongue of Farsi. To a non-Arabic-speaking Westerner, the calligraphic writing may first appear to be little more than a mélange of elegant and mysterious patterns and designs. Yet there is no mistaking its purpose as one of resistance. The photos are unlikely to be seen and "decoded" by the eyes of Iranians living in Iran, but the message of the artist to the world outside is clear.

Evolving technology has made it possible for photographers to achieve dazzling images such as the one in Harold Edgerton's *Fan and Flame Vortices* (Fig. **8-20**). Edgerton is an electrical engineer who invented the strobe light, a device that emits brief and brilliant flashes of light that seem to slow or stop the action of people or objects in motion. *Fan and Flame Vortices* is a high-speed photograph of a metal fan blade rotating at 3,600 revolutions per minute through the flame emitted by an alcohol burner. Changes in the density of the air and other gases are responsible for the fluctuating colors. Edgerton, like many other contemporary photographers, has used technological innovations to transform some of the mundane objects of the real world into vibrant abstract images.

Photographs have the capacity to stir us; because of their size, our relationship to them is intimate. At times they speak frankly to us; sometimes they leave much to the imagination. Because they are frozen moments in time, we can only wonder about what had gone before and what came after. This capacity to stir us is intensified, expanded, and altered in the art of cinematography. A large screen, movement, and—since the 1930s—sound capture the visual and auditory senses of the audience like no other medium.

8-20 HAROLD EDGERTON.
Fan and Flame Vortices (1973).
Dye transfer print. 13" × 11".
©1973 Kim Vandive & Harold Edgerton. Courtesy of Palm Press, Inc.

1 in.

FILM

The magic of **cinematography**—the art of making motion pictures—envelops our senses. Some members of the audience demand to be so encompassed that they sit in the front row, with the screen looming above them like a tidal wave. What associations does cinematography evoke for you? The big screen? The silver screen? The drive-in, with long lines for hot dogs and french fries? Speakers blasting from the walls? Popcorn? Ushers complaining about bringing drinks to the seats? Gum sticking to your shoe? Teenagers laughing, shouting, and necking? All of these images are part of Americana. Couples not only have their song; they often have their movie—what they saw on one of their first dates, what spoke to them deeply in their emotional vulnerability.

Varieties of Cinematographic Techniques

Despite their power to move us, motion pictures, or movies, do not really move. The illusion of movement is created by stroboscopic motion, which is the presentation of a rapid progression of images of stationary objects. The audience is shown 16 to 24 pictures or frames per second, like those shown in the series of Muybridge photographs

8-21 EADWEARD MUYBRIDGE.
Galloping Horse (1878).
Courtesy George Eastman House, International Museum of Photography, Rochester, NY

(Fig. **8-21**). Each picture or frame differs slightly from that preceding it. Showing them in rapid succession creates the illusion of movement. (Children similarly draw series of shapes or figures along the outer margins of books, then flip the pages to create the illusion of movement.)

At a rate of 22 or 24 frames per second, the motion in a film seems smooth and natural. At fewer than 16 or so frames per second, it is choppy. For that reason, **slow motion** is achieved by filming 100 or more frames per second. When the films are played back at 22 or 24 frames per second, movement appears to be very slow yet smooth and natural.

Eadweard Muybridge's *Galloping Horse* sequence was shot in 1878 by 24 cameras placed alongside a racetrack and was made possible by new fast-acting photosensitive plates. (If these plates had been developed 15 years earlier, Brady could have bequeathed us a photographic record of Civil War battle scenes.) Muybridge had been commissioned to settle a bet as to whether racehorses ever had all four hooves off the ground at once. He found that they did, but also that they never assumed the rocking-horse position in which the front and back legs are simultaneously extended.

Muybridge is generally credited with performing the first successful experiments in cinematography. He fashioned a device that could photograph a rapid sequence of images, and he invented the zoogyroscope, which projected these images onto a screen.

The motion-picture camera and projector were perfected by the inventor of the light bulb, Thomas Edison, toward the end of the nineteenth century. In 1893, the photographer Alexander Black made a motion picture of the president of the United States. In 1894, Thomas Edison's assistant Fred Ott was immortalized on film in the act of sneezing. Out of these inauspicious beginnings, a new medium for the visual arts was suddenly born.

Within a few short years, commercial movie houses sprang up across the nation, and motion-picture productions were distributed for public consumption. Sound was added to visual sensations by means of a sound track, and several silent film stars with noncompelling voices fell by the wayside.

Additional innovations have had a checkered history. There have been expansions to increasingly wider screens, including Cinemascope, Cinerama, Panavision, and films that are projected completely around the audience on a 360-degree strip wall or on the inner surface of a hemispherical dome. Stereophonic sound has been introduced. Three-dimensional (3-D) movies requiring special eyeglasses have been made. Today stereophonic sound, color, and reasonably wide screens remain in common use. But what photographers have noted about the role of photographic equipment seems also to apply to cinematography: the vision or creativity of the cinematographer is more important than technical advances.

Let us now consider several cinematographic techniques more closely: use of the fixed camera, the moving camera, editing, color, animation, and special effects.

Fixed Cameras and Staged Productions

With a stage play, the audience is fixed and must observe from a single vantage point. Similarly, many early motion pictures used a single camera that was more or less fixed in place. Actors came onstage and exited before them.

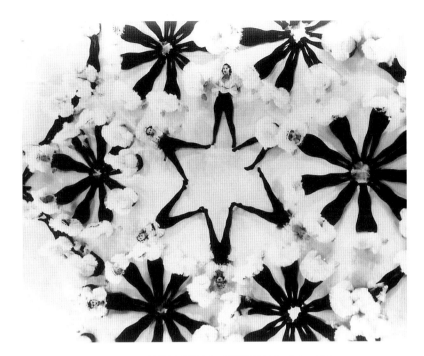

8-22 BUSBY BERKELEY.
Tutti Frutti number from Dames.
The Everett Collection

For the most part, the Busby Berkeley musicals of the 1930s (Fig. **8-22**) were shot on indoor stages that pretended to be nothing but stages. The motion picture had not yet broken free from the stage that had preceded it. Many directors used cinematography to bring the stages of the great urban centers to small cities and rural towns. We can note that the musicals of the 1930s were everything that the photographs of Dorothea Lange and the other Depression photographers were not: they were bubbly, frivolous, light, even saucy. Perhaps they helped Americans make it through these difficult times. Some musicals of the 1930s showed apple-cheeked kids getting their break on the Great White Way. Others portrayed the imaginary shenanigans of the wealthy few in an innocent era when Hollywood believed that they would offer amusement and inspiration to destitute audiences rather than stir feelings of social conflict through depiction of conspicuous consumption and frivolity.

The Mobile Camera

Film critics usually argue that motion pictures should tell their stories in ways that are inimitable through any other medium. One way is through the mobile camera. Film pioneer D. W. Griffith is credited with making the camera mobile. He attached motion-picture cameras to rapidly moving vehicles and used them to **pan** across expanses of scenery and action, as in the battle scenes in his *Birth of a Nation* (Fig. **8-23**). Today it is not unusual for cameras to be placed aboard rapidly moving vehicles and also to **zoom** in on and away from their targets.

8-23 D. W. GRIFFITH.
Scene from Birth of a Nation (1915).
Heritage Image Partnership Ltd.

Editing

Griffith is also credited with making many advances in film editing. **Editing** is the separating and assembling, sometimes called "patching and pasting," of sequences of film. Editing helps make stories coherent and heightens dramatic impact.

In **narrative editing**, multiple cameras are used during the progress of the same scene or story location. Then shots are selected from various vantage points and projected in sequence. Close-ups may be interspersed with **longshots**, providing the audience with abundant perspectives on the action while advancing the story. Close-ups usually better communicate the emotional responses of the actors, whereas longshots describe the setting, as in Alfred Hitchcock's thriller, *North by Northwest* (Fig. **8-24**).

In **parallel editing**, the story shifts back and forth from one event or scene to another. Scenes of one segment of a battlefield may be interspersed with events taking place at another location or back home, collapsing space. Time may also be collapsed through parallel editing, with the cinematographer shifting back and forth between past, present, and future.

In the **flashback**, one form of parallel editing, the story line is interrupted by the portrayal or narration of an earlier episode, often through the implied fantasies of a principal character. Orson Welles's *Citizen Kane* (Fig. **8-25**) innovated the use of the flashback, which usually gives current action more meaning. In the **flash-forward**, editing permits the

audience to see glimpses of the future. The flash-forward is frequently used at the beginning of dramatic television shows to capture the interest of the viewer who may be switching channels.

Motion pictures may proceed from one scene to another by means of **fading**. The current scene becomes gradually dimmer, or *fades out*. The subsequent scene then grows progressively brighter, or *fades in*. In the more rapid, current technique of the **dissolve**, the subsequent scene becomes brighter and the current scene fades out so that the first scene seems to dissolve into the second.

In **montage**, a sequence of abruptly alternating images or scenes conveys associated ideas or the passage of time. Images can suddenly flash into focus or whirl about for impact, as in a series of newspaper headlines meant to show the progress of the actors over time.

Color

Color came into use in the 1930s. One early color film, *The Wizard of Oz*, depicted the farm world of Kansas in black and white and the imaginary Oz in glorious, often expressionistic color. Madonna sort of reverses the pattern in *Truth or Dare*, where her stage performances (fantasy?) are in color and her (real?) backstage life is in black and white. Yet interestingly, this pattern is now frequently reversed in music videos, where fantasy is often portrayed in black and white and reality in (everyday, natural?) color.

The screen version of Margaret Mitchell's *Gone with the Wind* (Fig. **8-26**) was one of the first color epics, or "spectaculars." It remains one of the highest-grossing works of all film eras. In addition to the sweeping **panoramas**

8-27 BRAD BIRD.
Film still from *The Incredibles* (2004), a Walt Disney Production.
©Topham/The Image Works

of the Civil War battlefield wounded and the burning of Atlanta, *Gone with the Wind* included close-ups of the passion and fire communicated by Clark Gable as Rhett Butler and Vivien Leigh as Scarlett O'Hara.

Animation

Animation is the creation of a motion picture by photographing a series of drawings, each of which shows a stage of movement that differs slightly from the one preceding it. As a result, projecting the frames in rapid sequence creates the illusion of movement. The first cartoons were in black and white and employed a great deal of repetition.

During the 1930s, Walt Disney's studios began to produce full-color stories and images that have become part of our collective unconscious mind. Disney characters such as Mickey Mouse, Donald Duck, Bambi, Snow White, and Pinocchio are national treasures. In recent years, Disney has collaborated with Pixar Animation Studios to create a new generation of animated films, including *Toy Story; Finding Nemo; Monsters, Inc.;* and *The Incredibles* (Fig. **8-27**).

Special Effects

Over the years, filmmakers have raised the technical bar for special effects in their action movies. The industry has

8-26 VICTOR FLEMING.
"The Burning of Atlanta," a film still from *Gone with the Wind*.
©Selznick/MGM/The Kobal Collection

come a long way from tiny exploding capsules planted in the ground to simulate gunfire to the extravaganzas of effects in films such as *The Lord of the Rings, Star Wars,* or *The Dark Knight* (Fig. **8-28**). Complex motorized, remote-controlled models (the great white shark in *Jaws,* dinosaurs in *Jurassic Park,* starships and out-of-this-world inhabitants in *Star Wars,* prototype vehicles like the batmobile in *The Dark Knight*) and extensive computer graphics combine to create an extreme illusion of the director's reality.

Varieties of Cinematographic Experience

No discussion of cinematography can hope to recount adequately the richness of the motion-picture experience. Broadly speaking, motion pictures are visual experiences that entertain or move us. For example, as in novels, we identify with characters and become wrapped up in plots. Like other artists, cinematographers make us laugh (consider the great films of the Marx Brothers and Laurel and Hardy); create propaganda, satire, social commentary, fantasy, and symbolism; express artistic theories; and reflect artistic styles. Let us consider some of these more closely.

Propaganda

Although there are some early (and choppy) film records of World War I, cinematography was ready for World War II. In fact, while many American actors were embattled in Europe and the Pacific, former president Ronald Reagan was making films for the United States that depicted the valor of the Allied soldiers and the malevolence of the enemy.

Our adversaries were active as well. Before the war, in fact, German director Leni Riefenstahl made what is considered one of the greatest (though also most pernicious) propaganda films of all time, *Triumph of the Will* (Fig. **8-29**). Riefenstahl transformed the people and events of an historic event, the 1935 Nürnberg Congress, into abstract, symbolic patterns through the juxtaposition of longshots

8-29 LENI RIEFENSTAHL.

Film still from *Triumph of the Will* (1936).

Courtesy of the Museum of Modern Art, New York/Film Stills ©Leni Riefenstahl

Satire

Satire is the flip side of propaganda. Although Riefenstahl glorified national socialism in Germany, American filmmakers derided it. In one cartoon, for example, Daffy Duck clubs a realistic-looking, speechifying Adolf Hitler over the head with a mallet. Hitler dissolves into tears and calls for his mommy. British American filmmaker Charlie Chaplin added to the derision of the Führer in *The Great Dictator* (Fig. **8-30**). The film and television series *M*A*S*H* was set during the Korean War, but it satirized authoritarianism through the ages.

Social Commentary

Filmmakers, like documentary photographers, have made their social comments. *The Grapes of Wrath* (Fig. **8-31**), based on the John Steinbeck novel, depicts one family's struggle for survival during the Great Depression, when the banks failed and the Midwest farm basket of the United States turned into the Dust Bowl. Like a Dorothea Lange photograph, the camera comes in to record hopelessness and despair. Cinematographers have commented on everything from *Divorce, American Style* to *The Killing Fields* of Southeast Asia to the excesses of *Wall Street*.

and close-ups, and aerial and ground-level views. Her montage of people, monuments, and flag-bedecked buildings unified flesh and stone into a hymn to Nazism. The United States, England, Canada, and some other nations paid a backhanded compliment to the power of *Triumph of the Will* by banning it.

8-30 CHARLES CHAPLIN.

Film still from *The Great Dictator*.

The Everett Collection

8-31 JOHN FORD.

Film still from *The Grapes of Wrath*.

©20TH CENTURY FOX/THE KOBAL COLLECTION

I can make an audience laugh, scream with terror, smile, believe in legends, become indignant, take offense, become enthusiastic, lower itself or yawn with boredom. I am, then, either a deceiver or—when the audience is aware of the fraud—an illusionist. I am able to mystify, and I have at my disposal the most precious and the most astounding device [the motion-picture camera] that has ever, since history began, been put into the hands of the juggler.

—INGMAR BERGMAN

Fantasy

Fantasy and flights of fancy are not limited to paintings, drawings, and the written word. In the experimental films of Robert Wiene and Salvador Dalí and Luis Buñuel, events are not confined to the material world as it is; they occupy and express the innermost images of the cinematographer. The sets for Wiene's *The Cabinet of Dr. Caligari* (Fig. **8-32**) were created by three painters who employed Expressionist devices such as angular, distorted planes and sheer perspectives. The hallucinatory backdrop removes the protagonist, a carnival hypnotist who causes a sleepwalker to murder people who displease him, from the realm of reality. The muddy line between the authentic and the fantastic is further obscured by the film's ending, in which the hypnotist becomes a mental patient telling an imaginary tale. (It is

akin to the ravings of the mad Salieri, who, through flashbacks, recounts his actual and fantasized interactions with Mozart in the film *Amadeus*.)

Caligari has a story, albeit an unusual one, but Dalí and Buñuel's surrealistic *Un Chien Andalou* (Fig. **8-33**) has a script (if you can call it a script) without order or meaning in the traditional sense. In the shocking opening scene, normal vision is annulled by the slicing of an eyeball. The audience is then propelled through a series of disconnected, dreamlike scenes.

Symbolism

In writing about *Un Chien Andalou*, Buñuel claimed that his aims were to evoke instinctive reactions of attraction and repulsion in the audience, but that nothing in the film *sym-*

8-32 ROBERT WIENE.
Film still from *The Cabinet of Dr. Caligari* (1919).
©The Print Collector/Heritage-Images/The Image Works

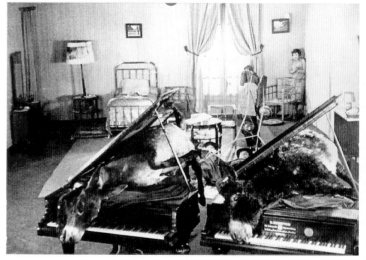

8-33 SALVADOR DALÍ AND LUIS BUÑUEL.
Film still from *Un Chien Andalou* (1928).
Image ©BUÑUEL-DALI/THE KOBAL COLLECTION. ©2009 Salvador Dalí, Gala-Salvador Dalí Foundation/Artists Rights Society (ARS)/New York.

bolized anything.[3] Fantastic cinematographers often portray their depths of mind literally. They create on the screen the images that dwell deep within their minds. Other cinematographers, such as Ingmar Bergman, do frequently express aspects of their inner world through symbols.

Since the 1950s, filmgoers have been struck by Bergman's mostly black-and-white films (Fig. **8-34**). As in so much other art, nature serves as counterpoint to the vicissitudes of the human spirit in Bergman's films. The Swedish summers are short and precious. The bleak winters seem, to Bergman, to be the enduring fact of life. Against their backdrop, he portrays modern alienation

from comforting religion and tradition. Bergman's films have ranged from jocular comedies to unrelieved dark dramas, and his bewitching screen images have brought together Nordic mythology and themes of love, death, and ultimate aloneness.

VIDEO

Video is used in television and in experimental video and mixed-media works that incorporate video monitors. The techniques of cinematography—methods of editing and so on—also apply to video.

Over a period of about 60 years, television has radically altered American life and placed the American lifestyle before the world. Commercial television broadcasts many of the images that reflect and create our common

---

3 Luis Buñuel, "Notes on the Making of *Un Chien Andalou*," in *Art in Cinema*, a symposium held at the San Francisco Museum of Art (repr., New York: Arno Press, 1968).

contemporary culture—from the pop world of Britney to the underworld of *The Sopranos*. Children spend as many hours in front of a TV set as they do in school. Congressional committees debate the impact of televised violence. For many people, television is an indispensable companion.

"Live" coverage enabled hundreds of millions of TV viewers to witness Neil Armstrong's first steps on the moon. Many millions watched in horror the live assassination of John F. Kennedy and the explosion of the *Challenger* space shuttle. Viewers who came to be called "gulf potatoes" seemed to be addicted to the televising of the Gulf War, the nation's first real video war—which began with CNN's live description of fighter-bombers over Baghdad in 1991. In 2001, viewers watched the destruction of the World Trade Center live—whether from the suburbs of New York or from Chicago or Los Angeles. We were a single community connected by wireless broadcasting and by cable.

The sights and sounds that are recorded by the television camera are transformed into electronic messages in the form of lengthy digital codes (a pattern of ones and zeroes). The digital information is transmitted wirelessly or by cable. The television set then reconstructs the digital information into visual images and sounds.

Commercial television is most often used to transmit news, sporting events, staged events, and films to viewers. Korean-born Nam June Paik and other fine artists, however, have appropriated video as their medium in the creation of works of art—video art. Video art is to be distinguished from the commercial efforts of the television establishment.

In *Three Mountains* (Fig. **8-35**), Japanese artist Shigeko Kubota incorporates video into a pyramidal sculptural piece, a combination intended to recreate the experience of the open western landscape. Video monitors are installed in a plywood base—the cutouts lined with mirrors. The mixed-media work confronts the viewer with multiple images of the Grand Canyon, as seen from a helicopter; a drive along Echo Cliff, Arizona; a Taos, New Mexico, sunset; and a Teton sunset. Kubota commented:

> My mountains exist in fractured and extended time and space. My vanishing point is reversed, located behind your brain. Then, distorted by mirrors and angles, it vanishes in many points at once. Lines of perspective stretch on and on, crossing at steep angles, sharp, like cold thin mountain air.[4]

---

4 Shigeko Kubota, *Video Sculptures* (Berlin: Daadgalerie; Essen: Museum Folkwang; Zurich: Kunsthaus, 1982), 37.

8-35 SHIGEKO KUBOTA.
Three Mountains (1976–1979).
Four-channel video installation with three mountains, constructed of plywood and plastic mirrors, containing seven monitors; Mountain I: 38" × 17" at top and 59" at base; Mountains II and III: 67" × 21" at top and 100" × 60" at base; four color videotapes, each 30 minutes.
Courtesy Electronic Arts Intermix (EAI), New York

8-36 DARA BIRNBAUM.

PM Magazine (1982).

Installation at San Francisco Museum of Modern Art, May 9–September 16, 1997; five-channel color video and sound installation. Installation panel 6' 8".

San Francisco Museum of Modern Art. Purchased through a gift of Rena Bransten and the Accessions Committee Fund. Gift of Collectors Forum, Doris and Donald G. Fisher, Evelyn and Walter Haas, Jr., Byron R. Meyer and Norah and Norman Stone. ©Dara Birnbaum

8-37 BILL VIOLA.

The Crossing (1996).

Two-channel color video and stereo-sound installation, continuous loop. 192" × 330" × 684" (487.7 cm × 838.2 cm × 1,737.4 cm).

Solomon R. Guggenheim Museum, New York. Gift of the Bohen Foundation 2000.61. Photograph by Sally Ritts. ©The Solomon R. Guggenheim Foundation, New York. Courtesy of the artist.

Dara Birnbaum's provocative videotapes and multimedia installations contribute to the contemporary discourse on art, television, and feminism. Her works appropriate and subvert the power of mass-media images to comment on the myths and stereotypes of our culture. Her installation *PM Magazine* (Fig. **8-36**) appropriated and modified footage from the former network magazine-format show to reveal how news and entertainment formats can exploit women. (How many older, unglamorous female TV news anchors and reporters do we see? How many "important" stories involve bizarre incidents of sex and violence?)

Bill Viola's *The Crossing* (Fig. **8-37**) is a video/sound installation that engulfs the senses and attempts to transport the viewer into a spiritual realm. In this piece, the artist simultaneously projects two video channels onto separate 16-foot-high screens or on the back and front of the same screen. In each video, a man enveloped in darkness appears and approaches until he fills the screen. On one channel, a fire breaks out at his feet and grows until the man is apparently consumed in flames (the content is not what we would call graphic or disturbing, however). On the other channel, the one shown here, drops of water fall onto the man's head, develop into rivulets, and then inundate him. The sound tracks accompany the screenings with audio of torrential rain and of a raging inferno. The dual videos wash over the viewer with their contrasts of cool and hot colors and their encompassing sound. Critics speak about the spiritual nature of Viola's work, but it is

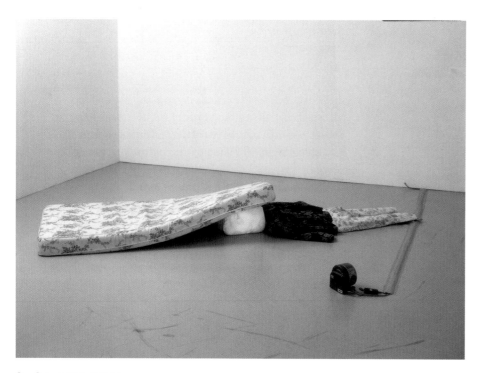

8-38 TONY OURSLER.

Getaway #2 (1994).

Mattress, cloth, LCD projector, VCR, videotape.

16" × 117½" × 86" overall.

Whitney Museum of American Art, New York. Purchased with funds from the Contemporary Painting and Sculpture Committee, 95.22. Courtesy of the artist and Metro Pictures.

also about the here-and-now reality of the sensory experiences created by his art form.

In *Getaway #2* (Fig. **8-38**), Tony Oursler projects a videotape with a sound track onto the cloth face of a life-size doll hiding adolescent-like beneath a mattress. A critic described his experiences as he and a companion observed another couple viewing the work in Williamstown, Massachusetts:

> We followed a couple into the gallery, and I saw one of them later taking great pains to get down on the ground to better see a piece consisting of a life-size doll whose head is underneath a mattress. The doll's projected face is yelling, "Hey, you! Get outta here!," plus various obscenities and epithets; and the aforementioned viewer, upon a heroic struggle to get

up again after that better look, exclaimed, "Whew! I almost became part of that piece!"[5]

I can empathize. I usually have to drag my youngest child through exhibitions, but when *Getaway #2* was "doing its thing" (that is, arguing with her and insulting her) at the Whitney Museum a couple of years back, she was spellbound and would not leave the gallery in which

5 Devon Damonte, "Vital Video in Williamstown: Personal Reflections on Some New Museum Exhibits in Western Mass," September 1999. www.newenglandfilm.com/news/archives/99september/museum .htm.

The role of the artist has to be different from what it was fifty or even twenty years ago. I am continually amazed at the number of artists who continue to work as if the camera were never invented, as if Andy Warhol never existed, as if airplanes, and computers, and videotape were never heard of.

—KEITH HARING

the piece was installed and uttering its R-rated phrases. It took weeks before we stopped hearing her parrotlike renditions of the doll's naughty verbal bits.

The message of many of Oursler's video works seems to be that people are unusually receptive to video images. They absorb them and then spout them. Television creates some of the most salient of the images we share in our culture—both video and audio—and as with any effort to define or describe the individual, we must wonder where the person's individuality leaves off and cultural influences begin. Perhaps they become so enmeshed that it is impossible to define the borders. Oursler seems to be saying that the border is porous.

the New York Institute of Technology. Haring's paintings are characterized by animated, mostly featureless figures bounded by thick, signature outlines, and his computer-generated image bears a close resemblance to his other work. Drawing on a computer screen must have seemed a natural segue for Haring. Haring was an experimenter by nature, an artist who challenged and pushed the limits, so his exploration of the possibilities of the computer as tool is not surprising. Yet when Haring created *Untitled* in 1983, he probably could only have imagined the directions that computer art would take in the coming decades.

Only within the last century have the horizons of artists been expanded by technological advances encompassing

DIGITAL ART

As we enter the new millennium in the arts, most readers undoubtedly have toyed with computer programs like Microsoft's *Paint* or *Paintbrush*. Software such as this, typically part of the computer manufacturer's standard package, enables the user—artistic or otherwise—to create illustrations by manipulating stock shapes, drawing "freehand," "spray painting" color fields, or enhancing the images with a variety of textural patterns—all of which are selected by directing the mouse to a menu of techniques and design elements. The resultant shapes or drawings can be flipped and rotated or stretched in any direction. Even word-processing programs such as Word and WordPerfect can be used to distort and otherwise play with images. The user-artist needn't have the talent to draw a straight line, simply the ability to point and click.

For most of us, the results are literally "child's play," but career artists who have sealed their reputations in other media have also been tempted by the computer as an artistic tool. Keith Haring, the infamous subway graffittist-turned-mainstream-artist, created *Untitled* (Fig. **8-39**) on the Images paint system of

8-39 KEITH HARING.
Untitled (1983).
35 mm slide of work created on the New York Institute of Technology's Images paint system.
©The Estate of Keith Haring

8-40 ROBERT LAZZARINI.

payphone (2001).

Mixed media. 108" × 84" × 48".

Hirshhorn Museum and Sculpture Garden, Smithsonian Institution, Washington, DC. Partial and promised gift of Robert and Pamela Goergen, 2007, 07.4, Photography by Lee Stalsworth. Courtesy of the artist.

1 ft.

8-41 YAEL KANAREK.

Copy: Potentially Endless A (2007).

Lambda print 44½" × 70". Edition of 3.

Courtesy of the artist and bitforms gallery nyc

anything and everything from the development of quick-drying acrylic paints to the advent of film and video. The computer has greatly expanded what can be achieved in these media and others. Today computer graphics software programs offer palettes of more than 16 million colors, which can be selected and produced on the monitor almost instantaneously. Compositions can be recolored in seconds. Effects of light and shade and simulated textured surfaces can be produced with the point and click of a mouse. Software programs enable artists to create three-dimensional representations with such astounding realism that they cannot be distinguished from photos or films of real objects in space. They can be viewed from any vantage point and in any perspective. Images can be saved or stored in any stage of their development, be brought back into the computer's memory at will, and modified as desired, without touching the original image. It is difficult to believe that these images are stored in computers as series of zeroes and ones, and not as pictures, but they are.

The herd of galloping dinosaurs in *Jurassic Park* was made possible by computer animation. Computer graphics is used to create environments as in video games (for example, the "tombs" raided by Lara Croft) or the virtual-reality world of the 1999 film *Matrix*.

Figure 8-39 is an example of *digital art*. Broadly speaking, digital art is the production of images by artists with the assistance of the computer. Just as artists have adapted the technical possibilities of photography, film, and video, so too have they appropriated the computer.

Digital artists can distort the commonplace according to meticulous mathematical formulas. Robert Lazzarini uses the computer to alter everyday objects, like the pay phones we find along the streets of cities (Fig. **8-40**), and then he builds sculptures based on the modified images. The sculptures are fabricated from the materials used in the actual objects. The viewer might try to get a visual handle on such works by viewing them from the "proper" angle, but no vantage point will "straighten out" these objects. The viewer is compelled to take a new look at the familiar, a goal of art for millennia.

Yael Kanarek's digital landscape in *Copy: Potentially Endless A* (Fig. **8-41**) is a screenshot of an interactive digital journal containing entries by a virtual character whose gender and ethnicity remain hidden to us. The viewer finds love letters and travel logs that have been written by the character in the course of an expedition to find treasure in a fantastic desert landscape. The work is constructed of networked interfaces featuring text, photography, sculpture, and performance.

Artists not only appropriate the technology of the day, but they also appropriate images that have special meaning within a culture. Lynn Hershman's *Digital Venus* (Fig. **8-42**) starts with Titian's well-known Renaissance painting *Venus of Urbino* (see Fig. 16-27) and substitutes digital imagery for the sumptuous glazes that defined the body. Many of Hershman's works comment on the voyeurism we find in the video medium, and *Digital Venus* is a way of showing

how frequently the images that affect us are composed of pixels—microscopically small bits of digital information that fool our senses into believing we are somehow connecting with a corporeal reality. And like the work of Dara Birnbaum, *Digital Venus* addresses feminist issues pertaining to the male gaze and the exploitation of women.

Artists are now only scratching the surface of digital art as a medium. Art courses in digital arts and interactive multimedia have never been more in demand. Just as photography was once termed a "democratizer" in the visual arts—enabling anyone with a camera to capture anything—so has the ubiquitousness of the digital camera and computer opened the door to limitless experimentation among artists and outsiders alike.

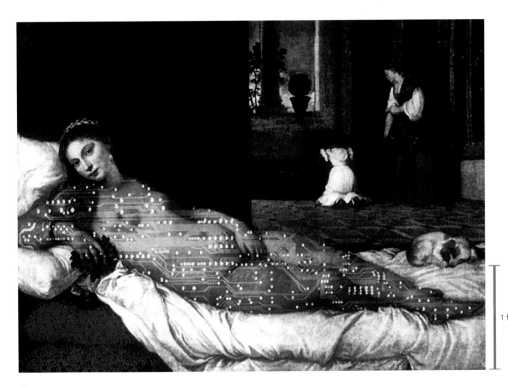

8-42 LYNN HERSHMAN.
Digital Venus (1996).
Iris print. 102 cm × 152 cm.
©Lynn Hershman Leeson, Hotwire Productions

9

SCULPTURE

■

A sculptor is a person obsessed with the form and shape of things, and it's not just the shape of one thing, but the shape of anything and everything: the hard, tense strength, although delicate form of a bone; the strong, solid fleshiness of a beech tree trunk.
—Henry Moore

What is a stone? To a farmer it is an obstacle to be dug and carted from the field. To a Roman warrior it was a powerful missile. To an architect it is a block, among many, to be assembled into a home or a bridge. But to a sculptor it is the repository of inner forms yearning for release. What is a steel girder? To an architect it is part of the skeleton of a skyscraper. To a sculptor it is the backbone of a fantastic animal or machine that never was, except in the imagination.

Stone, metal, wood, clay, plastics, light, and earth—these are some of the materials and elements that we have carved, modeled, assembled, and toyed with to create images of ourselves and to express our innermost fears and fantasies. Each of them affords the artist certain opportunities and limitations for self-expression. In this chapter and the next, we will see how these materials have been used in sculpture to grant three-dimensional reality to ideas. In Chapter 11, we will see how architects have used them to create aesthetic structures that protect us from the elements and provide settings for communal and intimate activities.

According to Greek myth, Pygmalion, the king of Cyprus, fell in love with the idealized statue of a woman. Aphrodite, goddess of love, heard his prayers and brought the statue to life. In one version of the myth, the statue becomes the goddess herself. In still another, Pygmalion was the sculptor who created the statue. In this myth, we find the elements of the human longing for perfection. We glimpse the emotionality that sculptors can pour into their works.

SIMON RODIA. Simon Rodia Towers in Watts (1921–1954). Cement with various objects. H: 98'. Cultural Affairs Department, Los Angeles. ©Sharon Hudson/Corbis.

SCULPTURE

Sculpture is the art of carving, casting, modeling, or assembling materials into three-dimensional figures or forms. Within this broad definition, architecture could be seen as a type of sculpture. But architecture serves the utilitarian purpose of providing housing and other structures for work and play, whereas sculptures need serve no practical purpose at all.

It could be argued that sculpture is more capable of grasping the senses than are the two-dimensional art forms of drawing, painting, and printmaking. We view two-dimensional works from vantage points to the front of the support. We might move closer or farther away, or squat or stand on tiptoe to gain new perspective, but the work itself, even if thickly laden with impasto, is essentially flat. **Relief sculptures** are similar to two-dimensional works in that their three-dimensional forms are raised from a flat background. In low relief, or **bas-relief**, especially, the forms project only slightly from the background; in **high relief**, figures project by at least half their natural depth.

But **freestanding sculptures** have fronts, sides, backs, and tops. They invite the viewer to walk around them. Sometimes viewers may climb on them, walk through them, or, as in the case of a Calder mobile, look up at them from beneath. As we move about a sculpture, we are impressed by new revelations. The spaces or voids in and around the work may take on as much meaning as the sculpted forms themselves.

Two-dimensional art forms are not meant to be touched, but much of the pleasure of appreciating a sculpture derives from imagining what it would be like to run one's hands over sensuous curving surfaces of cool marble or hand-rubbed walnut. In many cases, we may be prevented by ropes and guards—or by self-control—from touching sculptures, but many are made purposefully to be caressed. Some fool the eye, such as the "leather" jacket modeled from clay (see Fig. 12-2).

Recently developed forms of sculpture may interact with the viewer in other ways. The viewer may become involved in watching a kinetic sculpture run full cycle, or in trying to decipher just what the cycle is. Some kinetic sculptures and light sculptures may also literally be turned on and off, sometimes by the viewer.

Sculpture is a highly familiar medium. For thousands of years, we have used sculpture to portray our visions of the gods, saints, and devils. Religious people in earlier times—and some even now—believed that their gods actually dwell within the stone they chiseled or the wood they carved. We have carved and modeled the animals and plants of field and forest. We have exalted our heroes and leaders and commemorated our achievements and catastrophes in stone and other materials. The size of a sculpture has often been commensurate with the power ascribed to the hero or with the magnitude of the event. In addition to serving community and religious functions, sculptures are decorative. They adorn public buildings and parks. They sit on pedestals in walkways and stand in fountains, impervious to the spray, or perhaps contributing to the pool from the mouth or nether parts. Sculptures also serve as vehicles to express an artist's ideas and feelings.

In our discussion of sculpture, we will first distinguish between subtractive and additive sculpture and describe the techniques of each. Then we will examine the characteristics of several works that have been rendered in the traditional materials, such as stone, wood, clay, and metal. Finally, we will explore several modern materials and methods, ranging from new metals and found objects to kinetic sculpture and light sculpture.

SUBTRACTIVE AND ADDITIVE TYPES OF SCULPTURE

Sculptural processes are either subtractive or additive. In a **subtractive process**, such as carving, unwanted material is removed. In the **additive processes** of modeling, casting, and constructing, material is added, assembled, or built up to reach its final form.

Carving

In **carving**, the sculptor begins with a block of material and cuts portions of it away until the desired form is created. Carving could be considered the most demanding type of sculpture because the sculptor, like the fresco painter, must have a clear conception of the final product at the outset. The material chosen—stone, wood, ivory—strongly influences the mechanics of the carving process and determines the type of creation that will emerge.

Michelangelo believed that the sculptor liberated forms that already existed within blocks of stone. *The Cross-Legged Captive* (Fig. **9-1**) is one of a series of unfinished Michelangelo statues in which the figures remain partly embedded in marble. In its unfinished state, the tension and twisting in the torso almost cause us to experience the struggle of the slave to free himself fully from the marble and, symbolically,

*No painter ought to think less of sculpture than of painting
and no sculptor less of painting than of sculpture.*

—MICHELANGELO

9-1 MICHELANGELO. *The Cross-Legged Captive* (c. 1530–1534). Marble. H: 7′6½″. Galleria dell'Accademia, Florence. ©Scala/Art Resource, NY.

tools. Unlike carving, in which the artist must begin with a clear concept of the result, in modeling the artist may work and rework the material until pleasing forms begin to emerge.

Casting

The transition from modeling to casting can be easily seen in Louise Bourgeois's *Portrait of Robert* (Fig. **9-2**). Here the artist has expressionistically modeled a pliable material and converted the work to the more permanent bronze medium through a casting process. The white patina she has applied to finish the sculpture curiously subverts the material's

9-2 LOUISE BOURGEOIS. *Portrait of Robert* (1969). Cast bronze with white patina. 13″ × 12½″ × 10″. Courtesy Cheim & Read, New York. ©Louise Bourgeois/Licensed by VAGA, New York, NY.

from his masters. Despite the massiveness of the musculature, the roughness of the finish imparts a curious softness and humanity to the figure, which further increase our empathy. When we view this sculpture, it's as if we await the emergence of perfection from the imperfect—from the coarse and irregular block of stone. It is Michelangelo's genius that allows the figure to transcend its humble origins.

Modeling

In **modeling**, a pliable material such as clay or wax is shaped into a three-dimensional form. The artist may manipulate the material by hand and use a variety of

typical sheen and grants the work a claylike appearance—the very material with which the artist started.

In the **casting** process, a liquid material is poured into a mold. The liquid hardens into the shape of the **mold** and is then removed. In casting, an original model, made of a material such as wax, clay, or even Styrofoam, can be translated into a more durable material such as bronze. The mold is like a photographic negative, but one of form and not of color; the interior surfaces of the mold carry the reversed impressions of the model's exterior.

Any material that hardens can be used for casting. Bronze has been used most frequently because of its appealing surface and color characteristics, but concrete, plaster, liquid plastics, clay diluted with water, and other materials are also appropriate. Once the mold has been made, the casting may be duplicated.

The Lost-Wax Technique

Bronze casting is usually accomplished by means of the **lost-wax technique** (Fig. **9-3**), which has changed little over the centuries. In this technique, an original model is usually sculpted from clay, and a mold of it is made, usually from sectioned plaster or flexible gelatin. Molten wax is then brushed or poured into the mold to make a hollow wax model. If the wax has been brushed onto the inner surface of the mold, it will form a hollow shell. If the wax is to be poured, a solid core can first be placed into the mold and the liquid wax poured around the core. After the wax hardens, the mold is removed, and the wax model stands as a hollow replica of the clay. The hollow wax model is placed upside down in a container, and wax

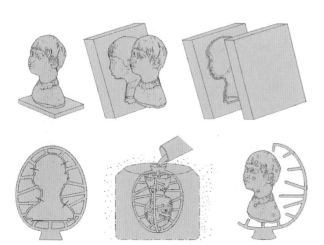

9-3 The lost-wax technique.

rods called gates are connected to it. Then a sandy mixture of silica, clay, and plaster is poured into and around the wax model, filling the shell and the container. The mixture hardens into a fire-resistant mold, or **investiture**. Thus, the process uses two models and two molds: models of clay and wax, and molds of plaster or gelatin and of the silica mixture.

The silica mold, or investiture, is turned over and placed in a **kiln**. As the investiture becomes heated, the wax turns molten once more and runs out. Hence the term *lost-wax technique*. The investiture is turned over again while it is still hot, and molten bronze is poured in. As the metal flows into the mold, air escapes through the gates so that no air pockets are left within. The bronze is given time to harden. Then the investiture and core are removed, leaving the bronze sculpture with strange projections where the molten metal had flowed up through the gates as it filled the mold. The projections are removed, and the surface of the bronze is **burnished** or treated chemically to take on the texture and color desired by the sculptor, as we shall see in the following bronze sculptures.

A statue by the French Impressionist Edgar Degas has an interesting history and metamorphosis from wax to bronze. As Degas grew blind, he turned to sculpture so that he could work out anatomical problems through the sense of touch. With one exception, his wax or clay experiments were left crumbling in his studio or discarded, although the intact figures were cast as a limited edition of bronze sculptures after his death. The exception was *The Little Dancer* (Fig. **9-4**), which he showed as a wax model at the 1881 Impressionist exhibition and later cast in bronze. This diminutive painted wax figure startled the public and critics alike with its innovative

9-4 EDGAR DEGAS.
The Little Dancer, 14 Years Old (1880–1881).
Bronze. H: 39".
Copyright Sterling and Francine Clark Art Institute, Williamstown, MA.

1 ft.

9-5 SHERRIE LEVINE.
Fountains after Duchamp (1991).
Bronze. Installation view at Sherrie Levine Exhibition
in the Zürich Kunsthalle (2.11.1991–3.1.1992),
Zürich, Switzerland.
Courtesy of the Jablonka Gallery, Köln, Germany.

sculptural realism: It sported real hair, a satin hair ribbon, a canvas bodice, and a tulle skirt. The styles of hair and clothing make the 14-year-old ballerina very much a product of her time and place.

Sherrie Levine's *Fountains after Duchamp* (Fig. **9-5**) consists of a series of bronze urinals, turned on their backs and displayed on pedestals as if to invite serious study and contemplation. The urinals pay homage to Marcel Duchamp's Dada masterpiece, *Fountain* (see Fig. 1-35), and in so doing, they represent what lies at the heart of Levine's artistic concept and strategy: the critical appropriation of objects and images that already exist in the visual lexicon of high art and mass culture. If Duchamp invested his readymades with a new *idea*—the reconsideration of ordinary objects in the artist's self-defined and self-imposed context of fine art—Levine's objects and reproductions are invested with a reconsideration of issues such as authorship and originality in relation to art making. Many contemporary artists come upon the art scene at a time when it seems that perhaps everything that can be done has been done. Some push to develop new styles, new subjects, new ways

of conceptualizing and defining art. Sherrie Levine, the foremost representative of "appropriation art," embraces what she believes to be the reality of working during a time when the major accomplishments in modernism have already been recorded as history. Her point of departure seems to be "There is nothing new under the sun. Now where does that take me?"

Casting of Human Models

Three Figures and Four Benches (Fig. **9-6**) by George Segal features intriguing variation on the casting process. Segal produced ghostlike replicas of human beings by means of plaster casts. Live models were covered in plaster-soaked cloth, which was molded and kneaded by the artist's hands. When the plaster was dry, the cast was removed in sections and then reassembled into whole figures. *Three Figures and Four Benches* was then cast in bronze, but the white surface of the original plaster cast was retained. Segal's figures are literally and figuratively shells. In unimaginable aloneness, his apparitions occupy an urban landscape of buses, gas stations, diners, and other settings, a kind of limbo of contemporary life. Although the figures are connected by virtue of their common medium, they do not seem to speak to one another or interact in any way. They are at once connected and disconnected, sharing a place and time and yet lost in their inner worlds.

9-6 GEORGE SEGAL.
Three Figures and Four Benches (1979).
Painted bronze. 52" × 144" × 58".
Theo Anderson, Allentown, PA.

Construction

In construction, or **constructed sculpture**, forms are built from materials such as wood, paper and string, sheet metal, and wire. As we shall see in works by Picasso, Louise Nevelson, and other artists, traditional carving, modeling, and casting are abandoned in favor of techniques such as pasting and welding.

TYPES OF MATERIALS

Sculptors have probably employed every known material in their works. Different materials tend to be worked in different ways, and they can also create very different effects. In this section, we will explore the varieties of ways in which sculptors have worked with the traditional materials of stone, wood, clay, and metal. In the section on modern and contemporary materials and methods, we shall see how sculptors have worked with nontraditional materials, such as plastic and light.

Stone

Stone is an extremely hard, durable material that may be carved, scraped, drilled, and polished. The durability that makes stone so appropriate for monuments and statues that are meant to communicate with future generations also makes working with stone a tedious process. The granite used by ancient Egyptians was extremely resistant to detailed carving, which is one reason that Egyptian stone figures were simplified and resemble the shape of the quarried blocks. The Greeks used their abundant white marble to embody the idealized human form in action and in repose. However, they painted their marble statues, suggesting that they valued the material more for its durability than for its color or texture.

The hand tools used with stone—such as the chisel, mallet, and **rasp**—have not changed much over the centuries.

But contemporary sculptors do not find working with stone to be quite so laborious because they can use power tools for chipping away large areas of unwanted material and for polishing the finished piece.

The Stone Age *Venus of Willendorf* (see Fig. 13-2) has endured for perhaps 25,000 years. The same stone that lent such durability to this rotund fertility figure apparently pressed the technological limits of the sculptor. There are clues that the artist found the stone medium arduous. As with ancient Egyptian sculpture, the shape of the figurine probably adheres closely to that of the block or large pebble from which it was carved. The rough finish further suggests the primitive nature of the artist's flint tools.

9-7 LOUISE BOURGEOIS.

Eyes (1982).

Marble. 74¾" × 54" × 45¾".

The Metropolitan Museum of Art, New York.
Anonymous gift (1986.397). Image ©The Metropolitan Museum of Art.
Art ©Louise Bourgeois/Licensed by VAGA, New York, NY.

1 ft.

It is a leap from the stone art of the Stone Age to the sculpture of, say, Michelangelo in *The Cross-Legged Captive* (Fig. 9-1) or the *David* (see Fig. 16-25). The *Captive*, like the *Venus*, does not stray far from the shape of the block or precariously extend its limbs. But except for the eternal nature of the *David*, the statue belies the nature of the material. The furrowed brow, the taut muscles, the veins in the hand all breathe life into the work.

The *Apollo and Daphne* (see Fig. 2-72) of the Italian Baroque sculptor and architect Gianlorenzo Bernini shows us yet more of the potential of marble. Marble can also capture the softness and sensuousness of flesh and the textures of hair, leaves, and bark. Observe the hundreds of slender projections, and imagine the intricacy of cutting away the obstinate stone to reveal them. In his *David* (see Fig. 16-26), Bernini portrays the moment in which the youth is twisting in preparation to fire the sling. David bites his marble lips; the muscles and veins of the left arm reflect the tightening of the hand; even his marble toes grip the rock beneath. When we view this sculpture, perhaps our own muscles tighten in empathy.

In *Eyes* (Fig. **9-7**), by Louise Bourgeois, two precisely tooled spheres are perched atop a marble cube, some of which has been chiseled to create hollows and other irregularities. The carved circular openings in the spheres suggest the penetrating pupils of eyes, a commonly used symbol among Surrealist artists (see Chapter 20). For Bourgeois, who often incorporated gender allusions in her work, the eyes may represent the female anatomy and the marble block, a house. The two strong shapes in contrast to each other may suggest a woman's relationship to her domestic role, a theme that Bourgeois revisited numerous times in her long career. Although Bourgeois's technique results in a finished work that remains close to the quarried marble block, the perfectly round eyes, the polish of the surfaces, and the carved interruptions create a striking contrast between a deliberate absence and an assertive presence of the artist's hand.

Wood

Wood, like stone, may be carved, scraped, drilled, and polished. But unlike stone, wood may also be permanently molded and bent. Under heat, in fact, plywood can be bent to take on any shape. Wood, like stone, varies in hardness and grain, but it is more readily carved than stone.

Although wooden objects may last for many hundreds of years, wood does not possess the durability of stone

9-8 Poro Secret Society mask (*Kaogle*). Liberian, Dan people. Wood. H: 9".
©Yale University Art Gallery/Art Resource, NY.

and tends to warp and crack. But wood appeals to sculptors because of its grain, color, and workability. Wood is warm to the touch, whereas stone is cold. When polished, wood is sensuous. Wood's **tensile strength** exceeds that of stone, so projecting wooden parts are less likely than their stone counterparts to break off. In recent years, wood has also become commonly used in assemblages.

The capacity of wood to yield beautiful, rough-hewn beauty is shown in the mask called *Kaogle* (Fig. **9-8**), by a sculptor of the African Dan people. The Dan of Sierra Leone, the Ivory Coast, and Liberia have carved masks for use in rituals and celebrations. Some Dan masks are polished and refined; others are intentionally crude. *Kaogle* is a powerful work of thrusting and receding planes. The abstracted, geometric voids are as commanding as the wooden form itself. Such a mask is believed to endow its wearer with the powers of the bush spirits and is an essential element in the garb of tribal law-enforcement officers.

British sculptor Barbara Hepworth's abstraction *Two Figures* (see Fig. 4-8) is carved from elm wood. Hepworth pierces solid masses to give contour to negative shapes.

The concavities, which are painted white, and the voids in her carved figures have as much "shape-meaning"—to use Henry Moore's term—as the solids. The viewer feels the urge to identify each form as male or female, but the sculptural "evidence" is too scant to allow such classification. At first glance, it might seem that a similar artistic effect could have been achieved by carving these figures from marble, but the wood grain imparts a warmth to the surface that would not have been attained in marble. Also, the painting of the concavities lends them a durability and hardness not found in the outer surface. Ironically, the voids attain more visual solidity than the outer surfaces.

9-9 PO SHUN LEONG.
Figure (1993).
Mahogany with hidden drawers. H: 50".
Courtesy of the artist.

There is an implied massiveness to both the *Kaogle* mask and Hepworth's *Two Figures*, but wood can also be used to create figures and forms of great complexity, delicacy, and intricacy. The rich mahogany surfaces of Po Shun Leong's *Figure* (Fig. **9-9**) have been polished, carved, striated, and gouged. There is a restlessness to the patterns, which, coupled with a host of hidden drawers punctuating the form—some open, some closed—creates a sense of constant motion.

Clay

Clay is more pliable than stone or wood. The modeling of clay is personal and direct; the fingerprints of the sculptor may be found in the material. Children, like sculptors, enjoy the feel and smell of clay.

Unfortunately, clay has little strength, and it is not usually considered a permanent material, even though an **armature** may be used to prevent clay figures from sagging. Because of its weakness, clay is frequently used to make three-dimensional sketches, or models, for sculptures that are to be executed in more durable materials. As was noted earlier, clay models may be translated into bronze figures. In ceramics, clay is fired in a kiln at high temperatures so that it becomes hardened and nonporous. Before firing, clay can also be coated, or glazed, with substances that provide the ceramic object with a glassy monochromatic or polychromatic surface.

Metal

Metal has been used by sculptors for thousands of years. Metals have been cast, **extruded**, **forged**, **stamped**, drilled, filed, and burnished. The process of producing cast bronze sculptures has changed little over the centuries. But in recent years, artists have also assembled **direct-metal sculptures** by welding, riveting, and soldering. Modern adhesives have also made it possible to glue sections of metal together into three-dimensional constructions.

Different metals have different properties. Bronze, an alloy of copper, has been the most popular casting material because of its surface and color characteristics. Bronze surfaces can be made dull or glossy. Chemical treatments can produce colors ranging from greenish blacks to golden or deep browns. Because of oxidation, bronze and copper surfaces age to form rich green or greenish blue **patinas**.

9-10 RICHARD SERRA.
Installation view, Guggenheim Museum, Bilbao, Spain.
©Vincent West/Reuters/Landov. ©2009 Richard Serra/Artists Rights Society
(ARS), New York.

For decades, Richard Serra has worked with steel, an alloy of iron, to create minimalist sculpture that expresses the physical properties and capabilities of his material. Like the installation at the Guggenheim Museum in Bilbao, Spain (Fig. **9-10**), many of his works have been monumental in size and site specific. Serra's steel surfaces grow more richly textured as time and oxidation work their effects upon them, serving as an apt metaphor for the effect on the visitor's memory that the experience of the installation might have. Serra's work is intended to be walked into, around, and through—intended to be experienced rather than viewed. The sheets of steel might enclose the visitor in a protected, almost private space or lead that same visitor, by way of an undulating path, to a more public, socially interactive space. Serra seems to have met his professed goal of "opening up the continuum of space." The mass is solid and the texture is tough, but the concept seems to reflect a nonmaterial realm—a gateway to something other within the real worlds we traverse every day.

MODERN AND CONTEMPORARY MATERIALS AND METHODS

Throughout history, sculptors have searched for new forms of expression. They have been quick to experiment with the new materials and approaches that have been made possible by advancing technology. During the past century, technological changes have overleaped themselves, giving rise to new materials, such as plastics and fluorescent lights, and to new ways of working traditional materials.

In this section, we will explore some new materials and approaches, including constructed sculpture, assemblage, readymades, mixed media, light sculpture, and kinetic sculpture. Although the search for novelty has been exhausting, this list is by no means exhaustive.

One starts to get young at the age of sixty and then it is too late.

—PABLO PICASSO

Constructed Sculpture

In constructed sculpture, the artist builds or constructs the sculpture from materials such as cardboard, celluloid, translucent plastic, sheet metal, or wire, frequently creating forms that are lighter than those made from carving stone, modeling clay, or casting metal. Picasso inspired a movement in this direction with works such as *Mandolin and Clarinet* (Fig. **9-11**). As critic Robert Hughes remarked, such works were "everything that statues had not been: not monolithic, but open, not cast or carved, but assembled from flat planes."[1] In spirit and style, reliefs from this era were very close to Picasso's paintings. But the unorthodox materials—wood, sheet metal, wire, found objects—challenged all traditions in art making. Sculpture would never be the same.

A Russian visitor to Picasso's Paris studio, Vladimir Tatlin, is credited with having realized the three-dimensional potential of constructed sculpture, which was then further developed in Russia by the brothers Antoine Pevsner and Naum Gabo. Naum Gabo's *Column* (see Fig. 20-16) epitomizes the ascendance of form and space over mass that is characteristic of many constructed sculptures. Gabo's translucent elements transform masses into planes that frame geometric voids. "Mass" is created in the mind of the viewer by the empty volumes.

Pop artist Claes Oldenburg's *Soft Toilet* (Fig. **9-12**) is constructed of vinyl, kapok, cloth, and Plexiglas. Our sensibilities are challenged in a lighthearted work: A familiar object that we know to be hard, cold, and unmovable is rendered soft, supple, and pliable—and certainly unusable.

---

1 Robert Hughes, "The Liberty of Thought Itself," *Time*, September 1, 1986, 87.

9-11 PABLO PICASSO.
Mandolin and Clarinet (1913).
Wood construction and paint.
Musée Picasso, Paris.
©Bridgeman-Giraudon/Art Resource, New York. ©2009 Estate of Pablo Picasso/Artists Rights Society (ARS), New York.

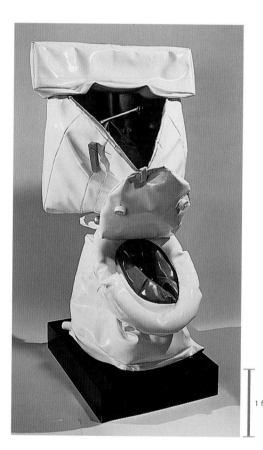

1 ft.

9-12 CLAES OLDENBURG.
Soft Toilet (1966).
Vinyl filled with kapok painted with Liquitex, and wood. 57¹⁄₁₆" × 27⅞" × 28¹⁄₁₆".
Collection Whitney Museum of American Art, New York.
50th anniversary gift of Mr. and Mrs. Victor W. Ganz, 79.83a–b.
Courtesy Oldenburg van Bruggen Foundation. ©2008 Glae Oldenburg.

I began using found objects. I had all this wood lying around and I began to move it around, I began to compose.

—LOUISE NEVELSON

9-13 LOUISE NEVELSON.
Royal Tide IV (1960).
Wood, with gold-spray technique.
323 cm × 446 cm × 55 cm.
Image ©Rheinisches Bildarchiv, Köln, Germany. ©2009 Estate of Louise Nevelson/Artists Rights Society (ARS), New York.

Assemblage

Assemblage is a form of constructed sculpture in which preexisting, or found, objects, recognizable in form, are integrated by the sculptor into novel combinations that take on a life and meaning of their own. American artist Louise Nevelson's *Royal Tide IV* (Fig. **9-13**), is a compartmentalized assemblage of rough-cut geometric shapes and lathed wooden objects with previous lives, such as finials. Similar assemblages include banal objects such as bowling pins, chair slats, and barrel staves and may be painted white or black, as well as gold.

Why walls? Nevelson explains:

> I attribute the walls to this: I had loads . . . and loads of creative energy. . . . So I began to stack my sculptures into an environment. . . . I think there is something in the consciousness of the creative person that adds up, and the multiple image that I give, say, in an enormous wall gives me so much satisfaction.[2]

The overall effect of Nevelson's collections is one of nostalgia and mystery. They suggest the pieces of the personal and collective past, of lonely introspective journeys among the cobwebs of Victorian attics—of childhoods that never were. Perhaps they are the very symbol of consciousness, for what is the function of intellect if not to impose order on the bits and pieces of experience?

Nature is the point of departure for Betye Saar's *Ancestral Spirit Chair* (Fig. **9-14**). In a work that was influenced

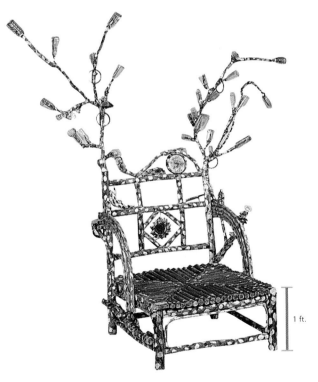

9-14 BETYE SAAR.
Ancestral Spirit Chair (1992).
Painted wood, bone, glass, plastic, metal, and vine. 60" × 46" × 32".
Smith College Museum of Art, Northampton, MA. Purchased with proceeds from the sale of a work donated by Mr. and Mrs. Alexander Rittmaster (Sylvian Goodkind, class of 1937) in 1958 and with funds realized from the sale of a work donated by Adeline Flint Wing, class of 1898, and Caroline Roberta Wing, class of 1896, in 1961, cs1992: 42a–c. Courtesy of Michael Rosenfeld Gallery, LLC, New York, NY.

---

2 Louise Nevelson, *Louise Nevelson: Atmospheres and Environments* (New York: C. N. Potter in association with the Whitney Museum of American Art, 1980), 77.

by Saar's African ancestry and tribal beliefs concerning ancestor worship, the artist combines remnants of nature and common objects of human existence. The chair is constructed of tree branches that have been sawed, shaped, or left in their natural state, reaching skyward like fingers on a hand. These "fingertips" are capped by a collection of glass saltshakers, and other found objects make their appearance here and there. The chair's surface is adorned with rhythmic white markings suggesting the body painting common to some African peoples. It is a curious piece—inviting, yet seeming to welcome only those who belong.

Perhaps the best-known assemblage is Picasso's *Bull's Head* (Fig. **9-15**). Consisting of the seat and handlebars of an old bicycle, the work possesses a rakish vitality. It is immediately and whimsically recognizable as animal—so much so that on first impression, its mundane origins are obscured.

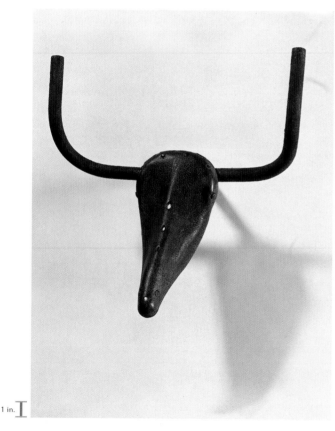

1 in.

9-15 PABLO PICASSO.
Bull's Head (1943).
Bronze cast of parts of a bicycle. H: 16⅛".
Image ©Réunion des Musées Nationaux/Art Resource, NY.
©2009 Estate of Pablo Picasso/Artists Rights Society (ARS), New York.

Readymades

The assemblages of Nevelson and Picasso are constructed from found objects. Early in the twentieth century, Marcel Duchamp declared that found objects, or readymades, such as bottle racks and urinals, could be literally elevated as works of art by being placed on pedestals—literally or figuratively. No assembly required. The urinal in Figure 1-35—appropriated some 80-plus years later by Sherrie Levine for her *Fountains after Duchamp* (Fig. 9-5)—was turned on its back, put into a new context, and given the title *Fountain*. These adjustments were said by the artist to invest the object with a new *idea*. Duchamp argued that the dimension of taste, good or bad, was irrelevant. The function of the readymade—not that it needed one—was to prompt the spectator to think, and to think again.

Duchamp recognized that artists could take advantage of the concept of the ready-made object and substitute cleverness for solid work should the "making" of readymades become a habit. For this reason, Duchamp advised that artists elevate common objects to the realm of art only a few times each year.

Mixed Media

In **mixed-media** constructions and assemblages, sculptors use materials and ready-made or found objects that are not normally the elements of a work of art. Contemporary painters also sometimes "mix" their media by attaching objects to their canvases. Robert Rauschenberg, discussed in Chapter 21, has attached ladders, chairs, and electric fans to his paintings and run paint over them as if they were continuations of the canvas. What do we call the result—painting or sculpture?

The sculptural environment known as the *Simon Rodia Towers in Watts* (Fig. **9-16**) was constructed by an Italian-born tile setter who immigrated to Watts, a poor neighborhood in Los Angeles. Rodia's whimsical towers are built sturdily enough—of cement on steel frames, the tallest one rising nearly 100 feet. As a mixed-media assemblage, the towers are coated with debris, such as mirror fragments, broken dishes, shards of glass and ceramic tile, and shells. The result is a lacy forest of spires that glisten with magical patterns of contrasting and harmonious colors. The towers took 33 years to erect and were built by Rodia's own hands. Rodia, by the way, knew nearly nothing of the world of art.

9-16 SIMON RODIA.
Simon Rodia Towers in Watts (1921–1954).
Cement with various objects. H: 98'.
Cultural Affairs Department, Los Angeles.
©Nik Wheeler/CORBIS.

Kinetic Sculpture

Sculptors have always been concerned with the portrayal of movement, but **kinetic sculptures** actually do move. Movement may be caused by the wind, magnetic fields, jets of water, electric motors, variations in the intensity of light, or the active manipulation of the observer. During the 1930s, the American sculptor Alexander Calder was one of the early pioneers of the first form of art that made motion as basic an element as shape or color—the mobile. As in his monumental mobile in the East Wing of the National

9-17 GEORGE RICKEY.
Cluster of Four Cubes (1992).
Stainless steel.
National Gallery of Art, Washington, DC. Gift of George Rickey and Patrons' Permanent Fund 1992, 1992.79.1. Art ©Estate of George Rickey/Licensed by VAGA, New York, NY.

Gallery of Art (see Fig. 2-70), carefully balanced weights are suspended on wires such that the gentlest current of air sets them moving in prescribed orbits.

George Rickey's welded, stainless steel cubes bear the mark of Calder's mobile constructions. Much of the work of both artists responds to the flow of currents of air. In Rickey's *Cluster of Four Cubes* (Fig. **9-17**), burnished steel "boxes" are attached by ball bearings to arms that branch from a trunklike post. The cubes are weighted and balanced to turn effortlessly in light breezes.

Light Sculpture

Natural light has always been an important element in defining sculpture, but only in the past century did sculptors begin to experiment with the use of artificial light in their compositions. Their concern has been with the physical and psychological effects of color and, at times, with the creation of visual illusions.

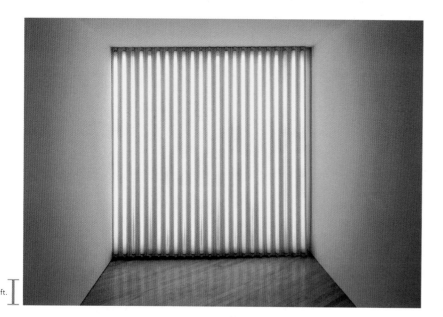

9-18 DAN FLAVIN.

Untitled (to Jan and Ron Greenberg) (1972–1973).
Installation view at the Dan Flavin Art Institute, Bridgehampton, NY.
Fluorescent light. 96" × 96".
Photo: Cathy Carver. Collection of Dia Art Foundation, New York.
©2009 Dan Flavin/Artists Rights Society (ARS), New York.

Dan Flavin is considered by many critics to have been the most revolutionary contemporary sculptor to have worked with light. Designing principally with fluorescent tubes, Flavin explored the resonance of color and its ability to define space. In his untitled piece seen in Figure **9-18**, a gallery dead-ends with a screen of yellow light placed back-to-back with a matching screen of green fluorescent tubes (which you cannot see from this side). Because the sculpture, when installed, blocked passage from one side of the room to another, only a glimpse of the light filling the room on the other side could be seen through the narrow spaces on either side between the walls and the light tubes. The result was an intriguing juxtaposition of regimented tubes of yellow and the unfettered glow of green light. The opposite effect was observed in viewing the work from the other side.

Other Materials

Sculpture today is where it has always been and where it has never been before. Materials have always been traditional and innovative; they have always been enduring and transient.

The figures in Kiki Smith's *Untitled* (Fig. **9-19**) were constructed of beeswax and microcrystalline wax. The artist's realism is, in a sense, more realistic than realism has ever been—even when compared to the Photorealism of artists such as Duane Hanson (see Fig. 21-26). The realism in Kiki Smith's couple is almost too painful to observe, too close to the realities of our own physical selves. Smith notes, "Most of the functions of the body are hidden . . . from society," and she thus has aimed to bring them out into the open. Smith has focused her eye on body parts and body by-products; one of her installations consisted of jars filled with bodily fluids from saliva to blood, reflecting her experience as an emergency medical service technician in New York City. In their state of deterioration, the effigies in Smith's untitled work have lost control over their bodily functions. The woman's figure is stained with, or drained of, milk that drips from her nipples. Semen drips down the man's leg. They are suspended in space, isolated in their loss of control, sharing the frailties of the human condition.

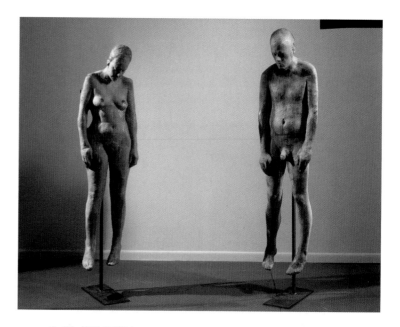

9-19 KIKI SMITH.

Untitled (1990).
Beeswax and microcrystalline wax figures on metal stands; female figure installed height 6' 1½"; male figure installed height 6' 4¹⁵⁄₁₆".
Collection Whitney Museum of American Art, New York. Purchased with funds from the Painting and Sculpture Committee, 91.13a–d. Photograph by Jerry L. Thompson.

Janine Antoni's *Gnaw* (Fig. **9-20**) may be overall reminiscent of a minimalist cube by an artist such as Donald Judd or Tony Smith, but it holds some sensory surprises: Antoni's medium is chocolate, and her sculptural tools consist of what nature has endowed her with—a good set of teeth. The surface texture of the piece records the process, for Antoni, the most important element of artmaking. The companion piece to *Gnaw* was an identical chunk of lard. The artist bit off pieces and then refashioned them into small objects such as lipstick tubes and chocolate boxes, which she then arranged in a mock version of a retail shop.

Sylvie Fleury's *Dog Toy 3 (Crazy Bird)* (Fig. **9-21**), like Antoni's *Chocolate Gnaw*, is a work in which the notion of permanence is insignificant. Chocolate will melt in your mouth or, with a bit of heat, into a nondescript and gooey pool. Neither does Styrofoam endure like the marble of "eternal" works; it can be dented with the point of a pencil, violated with the pressure of a thumb, bitten into to form a perfect impression. Fleury takes a

9-21 SYLVIE FLEURY.
Dog Toy 3 (Crazy Bird) (2000).
Styrofoam, paint. 260 cm × 210 cm × 180 cm.
Courtesy Galery Mehdi Chouakri

9-20 JANINE ANTONI.
Gnaw (1992).
Detail: (installation) 600 lbs. of lard, gnawed by the artist; 600 lbs. of collapsed lard, gnawed by the artist; 45 heart-shaped packages for chocolate made from chewed chocolate removed from the chocolate cube and 400 lipsticks made with pigment, beeswax, and chewed lard removed from the lard cube.
The Museum of Modern Art.
Digital Image ©The Museum of Modern Art/Licensed by SCALA/Art Resource, NY.
Courtesy of the artist and Luhring Augustine, New York.

familiar, nonthreatening, squeaky toy animal and raises it to the same nightmarish proportions that turned the smiling marshmallow man in the film *Ghostbusters* into a menacing monster crushing everything in his wake. Fleury invaded the art world in the 1990s with her series of *Shopping Bags*—installations of designer-labeled bags that appeared to have been left by visitors on the floors of galleries after a day of binge buying in upscale clothing stores. In the tradition of Andy Warhol and the Pop artists, Fleury elevated consumer products of a "disposable society" to the plane of gallery art.

In the next chapter, we will turn our attention to the shaping of materials into structures that house our work, our play, our family life, our worship, and our sleep—architecture.

Storm King Art Center

THE STORM KING ART CENTER in Mountainville, New York, is a sculpture garden located about one hour north of Manhattan. But this sculpture garden consists of 500 acres of landscaped lawns and fields, hills and woodlands, including views of the mountains of the lower Hudson Valley. There are permanent installations of works by sculptors including Isamu Noguchi, Alexander Calder, Henry Moore, Magdalena Abakanowicz, Mark di Suvero, Roy Lichtenstein, and Louise Nevelson. Works by Andy Goldsworthy and Richard Serra were commissioned for their sites. The Goldsworthy wall winds its way across more than 2,200 feet, dipping into ponds and climbing out. The four partially buried Serra shards of steel, *Shunnemunk Fork*, named after nearby Shunnemunk Mountain, occupy ten acres. Whereas the Goldsworthy and the Serra sculptures seem to have the permanence of the ages, huge

9-22

Left, top of hill:

ALEXANDER LIBERMAN.
Adam (1970).
Steel painted red-orange.
28' 6" × 24' × 29' 6".

Right, top of hill:

ALICE AYCOCK.
Three-Fold Manifestation II (1987; refabricated 2006).
Aluminum and stainless steel painted white.
29' 3" × 14' × 12'.

Center:

MENASHE KADISHMAN.
Suspended (1977).
Weathering steel.
276" × 396" × 48".

Storm King Art Center, Mountainville, New York. Photograph ©Spencer A. Rathus. All rights reserved. Courtesy Liberman Art Partners.

9-23 RICHARD SERRA.
Schunnemunk Fork (1990–1991).
Weathering steel.
(a) 96" × 589" × 2½";
(b) 96" × 421" × 2½";
(c) 96" × 460" × 2½";
(d) 96" × 652" × 2½".

Storm King Art Center, Mountainville, New York. Photograph ©Spencer A. Rathus. All rights reserved. ©2009 Richard Serra/Artists Rights Society (ARS), New York.

Among sculpture parks of the world, Storm King is King.

—J. CARTER BROWN

di Suvero sculptures, of steel but also airy, look as though they might without notice decide to pick themselves up and search out different prospects in the fields.

All this was founded by Ralph E. Ogden in 1960 as a museum for Hudson Valley painters. The landscape was wrecked from careless farming, and hundreds of truckloads of soil were brought in; grasses were planted. Fortunately, some woodlands with hills and boulders were in place. Ponds were dug and filled with water. A 1935 Normandy-style house was renovated, and it houses offices, temporary exhibitions, and a museum store. Early on works were acquired from the estate of the sculptor David Smith, and these alone became a magnet for visitors.

The place is like no other: Visit once and you are ensnared. Visit twice and you are mesmerized, because no two visits are alike. The times of the day cast their own shadows, changing patterns of cloud cover dim or brighten sunlight, and the changing seasons bring a distinctive palette to grasses and leaves. What lay in shade may suddenly gush into radiance with a burst of sunlight. There is no good weather or bad weather for this art—only different weather with variable, sometimes capricious, degrees of illumination. Come and observe the play of the sky across the fields, as did the artists of the Hudson River School two centuries ago. ■

9-24 MARK DI SUVERO.

Jambalaya (2002–2006).

Painted steel. 60' × 40' × 35'.

Storm King Art Center, Mountainville, New York. Photograph ©Spencer A. Rathus. All rights reserved. Courtesy of Mark di Suvero and Spacetime C. C.

9-25 ALEXANDER CALDER.

Five Swords (1976).

Sheet metal, bolts and paint. 213" × 264" × 348".

Storm King Art Center, Mountainville, New York. Photograph ©Spencer A. Rathus. All rights reserved. ©2009 Calder Foundation/Artists Rights Society (ARS), New York.

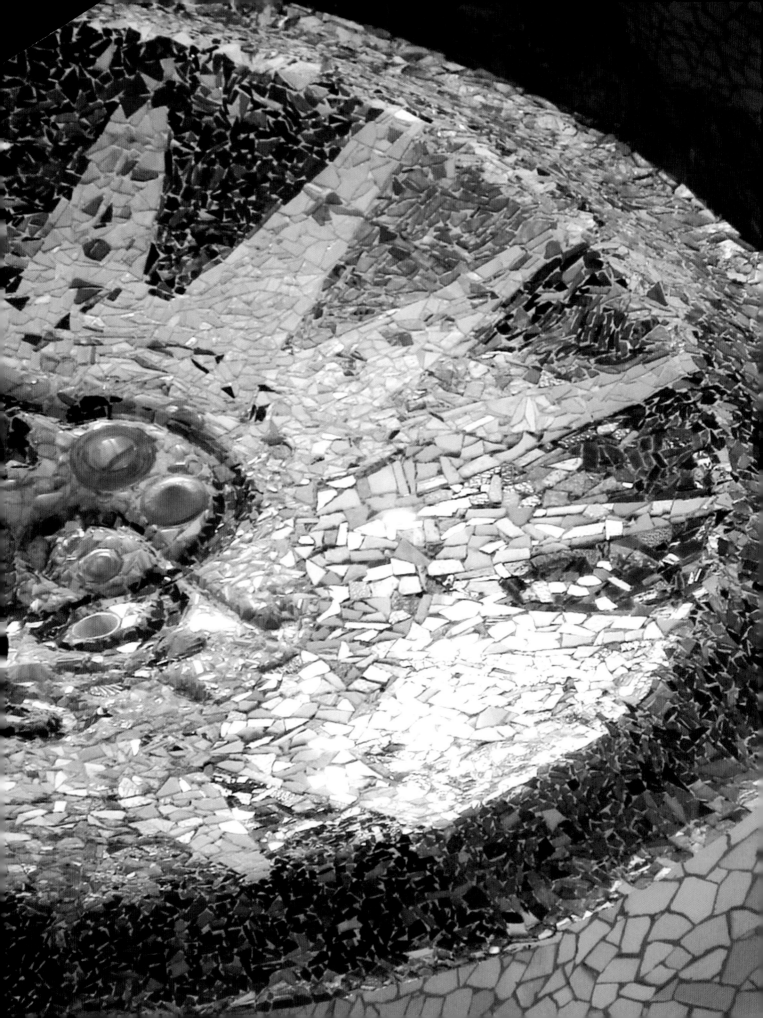

10

SITE-SPECIFIC ART

■
─

Give me a place to light and I will invent an installation that will bring it out.
—Dan Flavin

Everything is possible. You can do something great even in the smallest of contexts.
—Claude Simard

Site-specific works are distinguished from other artworks that are typically created in a studio with no particular spatial context in mind. Site-specific art is produced in or for one location and—in theory, at least—is not to be relocated. The work is in and of its site, and often the content and meaning of the work is inextricably bound to it. By this description, the history of art is full of examples of site-specific art, ranging from the sculptural decoration on the Parthenon (Fig. 14-10) and Michelangelo's Sistine Chapel ceiling (Figs. 16-21 to 16-22) to a mural by Orozco commissioned for Dartmouth College (Fig 1-36) or Kozloff's mosaic for a Philadelphia train station (Fig. 1-5). But the term *site-specific* came into use in the 1960s and 1970s as a blanket category for art that was created for or in a specific location. That location might be a museum or gallery, a public space, or a site in the natural landscape. Site-specific art consists of many types, goals, and styles, including land and environmental art, ephemeral art, public art, and monuments.

ANTONI GAUDÍ. Detail of mosaic sunburst in ceiling of hypostyle hall, *Parc Güell*, Barcelona, Spain (1900–1914).
Photograph ©Michael Miller.

10-1 ROBERT SMITHSON.
Spiral Jetty, Great Salt Lake,
Utah (1970).
Black rocks, salt, earth, water,
and algae. L: 1,500'; W: 15'.
Art ©Estate of Robert Smithson/
Licensed by VAGA, New York, NY

LAND ART

Land art is site-specific work that is created or marked by an artist within natural surroundings. Sometimes large amounts of earth or land are shaped into sculptural forms, as in the earthworks of the 1960s and 1970s. These works could be temporary or permanent and included great trenches and drawings in the desert, bulldozed configurations of earth and rock, and delicately constructed compositions of ice, twigs, and leaves. What such works have in common is the artist's use of local materials to create pieces that are unified with or contrapuntal to the landscape.

Robert Smithson's *Spiral Jetty* (Fig. **10-1**) is composed of basalt and earth bulldozed into a spiral formation in Utah's Great Salt Lake. The spiral shape of the jetty was inspired by a whirlpool, as well as the configuration of salt deposits that accumulate on rocks bordering the lake. After its creation, the jetty lay submerged underwater for many years. With a prolonged drought, the spiral began to reemerge in 1999 and, depending on the water levels of the lake, now "comes and goes."

The delicacy of many of Andy Goldsworthy's constructions stands in marked contrast with Smithson's bulldozed mounds of earth. They communicate, from another perspective, the fragility and changeability of nature. Goldsworthy works with materials he finds on site—leaves, sticks, stones, ice fragments—manipulating them with a soft, controlled touch or even, as with *Ice Star*, his breath (Fig. **10-2**). The following documentary narrative accompanied the piece:

> thick ends dipped in snow then water
> held until frozen together
> occasionally using forked sticks as
> support until stuck
> a tense moment when taking them
> away
> breathing on the stick first to release it

Goldsworthy explores both the transitory and the timeless in his varied works. *Storm King Wall* (Fig. **10-3**) incorporates the remains of a dilapidated farm fence found on the site of the Storm King Art Center into a 2,278-foot-long fieldstone wall. The work snakes through fields and around trees, at one point dipping into a pond and reappearing at the other side to continue its march along the landscape. As with many of Goldsworthy's pieces, the viewer experiences a quiet human presence—sometimes fleeting, sometimes enduring—in the midst of the natural world.

The more compelling artists today are concerned with "space" or "site."

— ROBERT SMITHSON

10-2 ANDY GOLDSWORTHY.
Ice Star (12 January 1987).
Cibachrome photograph. 76 cm × 76 cm.
Scaur water, Penpoint, Dumfriesshire, Scotland.

Copyright ©Andy Goldsworthy. Image ©Crown copyright:
UK Government Art Collection

10-3 ANDY GOLDSWORTHY.
Storm King Wall (1997–1998).
Field stone. 5' × 2,278' overall.
Photograph, Lois Ficher-Rathus.
©Andy Goldsworthy. Courtesy Galerie Lelong,
New York, and Storm King Art Center,
Mountainville, New York.

10-4 MARCO EVARISTTI.
The Ice Cube Project (2004).
Red dye and seawater,
Greenland coast.
©EPA/HO/Landov

10-5 ROBERT SMITHSON.

Yucatan Mirror Displacements (April 1969).
Color photographs. Nine parts, 27 cm × 27 cm each.
Collection: Solomon R. Guggenheim Museum,
New York.

Image courtesy James Cohan Gallery, New York.
Art ©Estate of Robert Smithson/Licensed
by VAGA, New York, NY

Isolation is the essence of Land Art.

— WALTER DE MARIA

Art that "makes marks" in nature is often temporary. In March 2004, Danish artist Marco Evaristti set sail in two icebreakers to find the perfect "frozen canvas" among the icebergs off the coast of Greenland. For two hours, a crew of 20 sprayed 780 gallons of red dye onto an almost 10,000-square-foot iceberg (Fig. **10-4**). The dye, diluted with seawater, was the same that is used for tinting meat. Evaristti's work can be found—for the time being, at least— near Ilullissat (which means "icebergs" in the Greenlandic language), a town of 4,000 that is popular among tourists for its spectacular and *artistic* scenery.

Another approach to land art can be seen in the works of Robert Smithson and Nancy Holt (see Fig. 2-25). Rather than creating works from natural materials present on the site, these artists interrupt the landscape with objects consisting of man-made materials. In so doing, the viewer is encouraged to consider the relationship between the environment and human activity. Holt's placement of gargantuan concrete cylinders on a desert floor is designed to enframe and focus the sun's light. In Smithson's *Yucatan Mirror Displacements* (Fig. **10-5**), topographic shifts, like vignettes, became the context for the placement of clusters of mirrors as the artist traveled through the landscape. The interactivity between nature and technology is clear. The mirrors transform the environment by interrupting the natural setting, and the environment in turn transforms them. The anonymity of the mirror surfaces is lost as they reflect the shapes, colors, and textures of their host environment. Smithson also explored the relationship between nature and man-made environments by moving gravel, sand, rock, and other materials indoors, into the gallery setting (Fig. **10-6**). Like *Mirror-Travel*, these works were temporary installations that exist today only in memory or documentary photographs.

One of the most spectacular examples of land art that combines nature and man-made materials is Walter de Maria's *The Lightning Field* (Fig. **10-7**). The field is constructed of 400 stainless steel poles (lightning rods)

10-6 ROBERT SMITHSON.
Chalk and Mirror Displacement (1969).
Chalk from quarry in Oxted, England, 16 mirrors, 25.5 cm × 150 cm each. H: 25 cm overall.
Image courtesy James Cohan Gallery, New York. Art ©Estate of Robert Smithson/ Licensed by VAGA, New York, NY.

10-7 WALTER DE MARIA.
The Lightning Field (1977).
400 polished stainless steel poles, each d. 5.1 (2) × h. 628.7 (247.5), total area 1 mile × 1 km. Quemado, New Mexico.
Photo: John Cliett. ©DIA Art Foundation.

Christo and Jeanne-Claude: *The Gates, Central Park, New York City, 1979–2005*

AS IF INTENTIONALLY TIMED TO SHAKE New York City out of its winter doldrums, 7,503 sensuous saffron panels were gradually released from the tops of 16-foot-tall gates along 23 miles of footpaths throughout Central Park. It was the morning of February 12, 2005—a date that marked the end of artists Christo and Jeanne-Claude's 26-year-long odyssey to bring a major project to their adopted city. For a brief 16 days, the billowy nylon fabric fluttered and snapped and obscured and enframed our favorite park perspectives (Fig. **10-8**). The park's majestic plan of ups and downs, of lazy loops and serpentine curves (as originally designed by Frederick Law Olmsted and Calvert Vaux), was being seen or reseen for the first time as we—the participants—wove our walks according to the patterns of the gates. The artists have said that "the temporary quality of their projects is an aesthetic decision," that it "endows the works of art with a feeling of urgency to be seen." For a brief 16 days, it was clear from the crowds in a winter park, from the constant cluster of buses at the 72nd Street entrance, and from the rubber-necking traffic on the streets and avenues bordering the park that the urgency of which Christo and Jeanne-Claude speak was very real.

As with all of Christo and Jeanne-Claude's works of environmental art, every aspect of *The Gates* project was financed and fought for by the artists. They developed the concept for *The Gates* in 1979, but their first proposal to the city in 1981 was rejected. Mayor Michael R. Bloomberg granted permission for the 2005 version of the project on January 22, 2003. The vital statistics of *The Gates, Central Park, New York City, 1979–2005* are staggering. Placed at 12- to 15-foot intervals, 7,503 vinyl gates, 16 feet high, varying in width from 5 feet 6 inches to 18 feet, covered 23 miles of footpaths (Fig. **10-9**). The free-hanging, saffron-colored fabric panels dropped from the top of each rectangular vinyl gate to 7 feet above the ground—just low enough for small children on their father's shoulders to sneak a touch. The project required more than 1 million square feet of vinyl and 5,300 tons of steel. Hundreds of paid volunteers assembled, installed, maintained, and removed the work, and most of the materials were to be recycled. The estimated cost of the project—borne by the artists alone—was $20 million.

The artists finance their environmental sculptures, which have included *Wrapped Reichstag, Berlin, 1971–95; Surrounded Islands, Biscayne Bay, Greater Miami, Florida, 1980–83; Running Fence, Sonoma and Marin Counties, California, 1972–76;* and others, by selling preparatory drawings and early works by Christo. Much of the funds thus accumulated have been used to cover the cost of

10-8 CHRISTO AND JEANNE CLAUDE. *The Gates, Central Park, New York City (1979–2005).*
©Andrew Gombert/EPA/Landov

10-9 Aerial view of *The Gates* in Central Park with Manhattan skyline.
©Andrea Mohlin/The New York Times/Redux

the materials used in the project, to pay workers, and, when necessary, for legal fees to combat suits brought by concerned environmentalists (as was the case with the *Running Fence* project).

The environmental art projects of artists Christo and Jeanne-Claude have been seen by millions, who have been enticed to experience their familiar surroundings with a heightened sensibility. Like the artists, I, too, live in New York City. I walked *The Gates* many times over 16 days, each time with a group of family members and friends who made the pilgrimage. When asked, Why was it so important to realize this work in Central Park? Christo responded, "When our son was a little boy, we used to take him to Central Park every day—he loved to climb the beautiful rocks. Central Park was a part of our life." I think of my own daughter, whose school held gym class on the park's Great Lawn. The Central Park that she will remember as a part of her life growing up in New York will forever include the 16 days when, in clear and in cold and a glorious snowfall, a "golden river" snaked through a barren winter scene, lighting the landscape with flashes of color. ■

10-10 Christo with your author in Central Park on the day after *The Gates* officially closed.
Photograph ©Spencer A. Rathus. All rights reserved.

anchored in a 1-by-.62-mile plot of earth. As with Holt's *Sun Tunnels*, nature's "behavior" in the grandest sense gives shape and meaning to the work. The enduring as well as transitory aspects of nature are woven into the varied experience of land art.

The intimate physical relationship between the individual artist and the environment forms the basis of the work of yet another group of land artists. Ana Mendieta's series of self-portraits (Fig. **10-11**) consisted of marking the presence of her body in the landscape using materials and methods that ranged from impressions in the snow

and mud to hollowed-out, body-shaped depressions filled with gunpowder and lit afire.

In a work that evokes the literary character Gulliver and his encounter with the tiny Lilliputians, Charles Simonds used his body as a building site for the miniature dwellings of an imagined civilization of Little People (Fig. **10-12**). The artist lay down on the earth and covered himself with clay, providing a convoluted landscape setting for the diminutive structures. Simonds's work can also be seen in an inconspicuous corner of a ledge in the stairwell of New York's Whitney Museum of American Art.

EPHEMERAL ART

Life is short, art endures. (Vita brevis, ars longa.)
—HIPPOCRATES (C. 460–400 BCE)

Hippocrates' oft-quoted words were intended to laud the significance of art, attributable in part to its longevity and survival across generations. Is its sentiment outdated? Consider much of the work we have discussed so far in this chapter, which did not last long beyond its creation. Goldsworthy's *Ice Piece* remained frozen just long enough for him to document it with his camera. Many artists work with ephemeral materials—in other words, materials that do not endure.

The term **ephemeral art** is used specifically to describe works that have a temporal immediacy or are built with the recognition that they will disintegrate. You see them one minute and the next they're gone. Most of this work is viewed only in photographs after the fact, unless one happens to be lucky enough to be present when the piece is crafted or performed. How does such work differ from land art? Sometimes it doesn't. Goldsworthy's *Ice Piece* comes under the category of land art that is ephemeral, but his *Storm King Wall* made of stone, is intended to endure.

Cai Guo Qiang's fireworks pieces (Fig. **10-13**) are classic examples of ephemeral art. *Transient Rainbow*, commissioned by the Museum of Modern Art (undergoing renovation at the time) was planned to coincide with the opening of its temporary space in Queens—across the East River from Manhattan. As Cai wrote:

> In my hometown every significant social occasion of any kind, good or bad—weddings, funerals, the birth of a baby, a new home—is marked by the explosion of fireworks. They even use fireworks when they elect Communist party officials, or after someone delivers a speech. Fireworks are like the town crier, announcing whatever's going on in town.

The project was a masterpiece of coordination in conception, creation, and documentation. After several iterations, shaped by the concerns of the New York City Fire Department, Transit Authority, Coast Guard, and Federal Air Administration, Qiang's piece came and went, in some 15 seconds, on June 29, 2002. The fireworks display consisted of 1,000 shells that were launched in sequence from the Manhattan side of the river, ascending and descending in an arc toward Queens, on the opposite side. The brilliant color palette unfolded so that, for a moment, a transient moment, the fireworks rainbow spanned the river.

Anyone who has tried to capture a fireworks display with a camera knows that it's a tough thing to do. The vibrancy and shimmer that sends "oooooos" through the crowd never seem to measure up in our photographic record. With a work that is literally there one minute and gone the next, its documentation becomes extremely important. Qiang hired 20 photographers in all—three of whom were specialized fireworks photographers from Japan—to capture *Transient Rainbow*. The video document and still photographs have become an essential part of the work: tangible records of an ephemeral art performance.

10-13 CAI GUO QIANG.
Transient Rainbow over East River, New York City (2002).

Heizer's *Rift* with Libeskind's *Jewish Museum*

IN 1967, MICHAEL HEIZER took to the bottom of a dry lakebed for *Rift* (Fig. **10-14**), one piece in his land art series called *Nine Nevada Depressions*. Almost three decades later, Daniel Libeskind used a startlingly similar shape for his extension of the Berlin Museum dedicated to the Holocaust and Jewish art and life (Fig. **10-15**). Libeskind's zigzag design was derived mathematically by plotting the Berlin addresses of Jewish writers, artists, and composers who were killed during the Holocaust. The building's jagged shape reads as a painful rift in the continuity of the neighborhood in which it stands; it is punctuated by voids that symbolize the absence of Jewish people and culture in Berlin.

Heizer's *Rift* consists of a displacement of local materials such that the normalcy of the landscape is interrupted. For Heizer, the process is perhaps less about symbolism than it is about artistic elements. His depressions play with the relative scale of humans and nature; he is as much interested in the disintegration of his piece by natural processes over time as he is with the initial creative act. Heizer's jagged "scar" on the earth faded over time and then disappeared. How did Libeskind use this shape to try to ensure that the story of the Jews of Berlin would not fade or disappear? Is there something inherent in these shapes in contrast to their surroundings that suggests a certain symbolism or elicits a certain emotional response? How much do content and context influence our analysis of works with such visual congruities? ∎

10-14 MICHAEL HEIZER.
Rift (deteriorated). First of Nine
Nevada Depressions (1968).
1.5 tonne displacement on the bottom
of a dry lake bed. 158 × 4.5 × 3 m.
Massacre Dry Lake, Nevada.
Courtesy of the artist

10-15 DANIEL LIBESKIND.
Extension of the Berlin Museum
(1989–1996).
©Studio Daniel Libeskind.

10-16 OLAFUR ELIASSON.
The New York City Waterfalls, Brooklyn Bridge (2008).

PUBLIC ART

The history of art is also full of works created for public spaces. Michelangelo's *David* (Fig. 16-25), even though it now has sanctuary in the Galleria dell'Accademia in Florence, was installed as a public work of art for the Piazza della Signoria, just outside the building that served as the political center of the city. A bit farther south, in Rome, one can see some of the most famous, most elaborate fountains in the world. They were created for the pleasure of the public (though often too for the glory of a pope). It is common also today for institutions (including the U.S. Federal Government) to allot a percentage of the overall cost of their building programs for works of art destined for the public spaces in and around buildings. You are probably familiar with works of public art in your own cities and towns, some dating back decades and some installed for a particular occasion or just for the season, as was Olafur Eliasson's *New York City Waterfalls* (Fig. **10-16**). Constructed under the Brooklyn Bridge in the summer of 2008, it was one of four sites featuring free-standing waterfalls funded by New York's Public Art Fund.

New York's Central Park forms the geographic and spiritual heart of that city and serves as the backdrop for one of its most beloved public sculptures. *Angel of the Waters* (Fig. **10-17**) (also known as Bethesda Fountain), by Emma Stebbins, towers above a circular brick plaza bordering a large lake. Warm weather brings sunbathers, break-dancers, newlyweds, and splashing dogs to this public gathering space that seems to sit protectively beneath the outspread wings of an angel.

10-17 EMMA STEBBINS.
Angel of the Waters (Bethesda Fountain) (1873).
Central Park, New York.

At the beginning of the twentieth century in Barcelona, one of its most famous native sons—Antoni Gaudí—was asked by his patron, Eusebi Güell, to create a gardenlike suburb for the very rich overlooking the city. The project was abandoned, but not before completion of what is now one of Barcelona's most treasured public sites, *Parc Güell*. A lively mosaic serpent (Fig. **10-18**) stands at the entrance of the park and has become one of the recognizable symbols of the city. Flights of steps lead to a variation on a hypostyle hall (Fig. **10-19**), with a forest of columns ornamented with lavish mosaic bases. The undulating ceiling is punctuated with mosaic discs called sunbursts (Fig. **10-20**). This space was originally intended to serve as a public market. Resting on top of the columned hall is an esplanade, the perimeter of which is lined with its serpentine, mosaic-clad stone bench (Fig. **10-21**). Gaudí was known for his playful, organic forms (see also his *Casa Mila*, Fig. 19-41) that helped define the Modernista style in Catalunya (or Catalonia), Spain.

Chicago's Millennium Park has its own very popular and very new gathering space, the focal point of which is Anish Kapoor's *Cloud Gate* (Fig. **10-22**). Nicknamed "the bean" because of its elliptical, beanlike shape, the work consists of highly polished, mirrorlike stainless steel plates that reflect the people, places, and things surrounding it, both permanent and transient. Kapoor has called his piece "a gate to Chicago, a poetic idea about the city it reflects." The work inspired a new jazz composition (*Fanfare for Cloud Gate*) by Orbert Davis, performed in Millennium Park on the occasion of the dedication of Kapoor's sculpture.

A bit of controversy surrounding *Cloud Gate* proves interesting with regard to the nature of land and environmental art, including commissioned public works of art. Kapoor owns the rights to the piece, and therefore photographs of it cannot be reproduced commercially (as in this book) without his permission. One particular photographer learned this the hard way, when he was not permitted to photograph "the bean" without a prepaid permit. The public response to limits on publishing

10-18 ANTONI GAUDÍ.
Serpent/Salamander (1900–1914).
Parc Güell, Barcelona, Spain.
©eddie linssen/ Alamy

10-19 ANTONI GAUDÍ.
Hypostyle Hall (1900–1914).
Parc Güell, Barcelona, Spain.
Photograph ©Jordan Spence Rathus.

10-20 ANTONI GAUDÍ.
Detail of mosaic sunburst in ceiling of hypostyle hall, *Parc Güell*, Barcelona, Spain (1900–1914).
Photograph ©Michael Miller.

10-21 ANTONI GAUDÍ.
Detail of mosaic serpentine bench, which sits in plaza above hypostyle hall. *Parc Güell*, Barcelona, Spain (1900–1914).
Photograph ©Michael Miller.

10-22 ANISH KAPOOR.
Cloud Gate (2004–2006).
Cloud Gate's exterior consists of 168 highly polished stainless steel plates. It is 33 feet by 66 feet by 42 feet (10m × 20m × 13m) tall, and weighs 110 short tons (99.8t/98.2 long tons). Millennium Park, Chicago.
©Ohad Shaha/Alamy

10-23 A woman in Copley Square passes one of about 100 painted cows that were to be found around Boston as part of "CowParade Boston 06," Saturday, June 10, 2006. Each cow is painted in its own unique design. Many of them are creations of local artists. The cows were on display throughout the summer. In September the cows were rounded up and auctioned off to raise money for charity.
AP Images/Michael Dwyer

Waga-Moo-Moo, one of the Dublin *Cow Parade*, fetched $148,000 for a good cause. The cow-craze has spawned many imitators, with different creatures popping up in cities everywhere.

MONUMENTS

The few examples of site-specific public art that we have looked at were designed or installed to enhance a particular open, public space. Their main purpose is or was aesthetic—to create beauty or to enhance the environment. Monuments comprise another category of site-specific public art. Their purpose is to preserve the memory of a person or an event.

The category of monuments is so broad that the few works we are able to concentrate on here represent an absurdly small percentage of what we live with in our communities. Equestrian monuments—men on horseback—seem almost ubiquitous in cities and towns, even though the identities of those memorialized are often forgotten. One of the purposes of monuments is to institutionalize memory. Monuments serve as expressions of the need or

personal photographs of this public work of art was strong; photographs began to appear all over the Internet (you can find them on Google Images or Flickr, a photo-sharing website). If public art is public (and sometimes supported in real dollars by the public), where, in your opinion, should the artist's rights end and the public's begin?

The Bethesda Fountain and *Cloud Gate* have become icons of their respective cities; there are permanent installations of comparable works of art in public spaces all over the globe. Public art can also be temporary, like the pandemic *Cow Parades*—installations of fiberglass cows painted in every conceivable style, on every imaginable theme, turning up in almost too many cities to mention: New York, Chicago, London, Brussels, Sydney, Stockholm, Athens, Sao Paolo, and Moscow to name some on the list (Fig. **10-23**). In all, it is estimated that Cow Parade has been seen by more than 100 million people worldwide. Some of the cows have been purchased after exhibition, raising money for charities.

10-24 The Field of Empty Chairs, Oklahoma City National Memorial and Museum.
AP Images/FILE/J. Pat Carter

10-25 Chair at the Oklahoma City National Memorial and Museum.

desire of a city, a country, or perhaps of a generation to "never forget."

The Oklahoma City National Memorial and Museum was created to remember the victims, survivors, and rescuers of the 1995 bombing of the Alfred P. Murrah Federal Building in that city. It is a multipart memorial site that incorporates various symbolic elements, the most arresting of which is the *Field of Empty Chairs* (Fig. **10-24**). One hundred sixty-eight chairs representing the individual victims were placed in nine rows corresponding to the office floors on which they worked. The chairs are crafted of stone and bronze on a glass base, each etched with a victim's name (Fig. **10-25**). The field of chairs overlooks a reflecting pool that is adjacent to a *Rescuer's Orchard* honoring those who risked their lives and rushed to the scene to help. The focal point of the orchard is the *Survivor Tree*, an elm that withstood the blast of the explosion and now honors the survivors of the attack. The memorial site, which occupies the footprint of the Murrah building, also includes a museum. The memorial was designed to touch everyone who experienced the event, reflecting the impact of the violence on the community. It is an interactive type of

monument, a place where one comes to witness history and to remember the dead and the living. The grief and the mourning are collective, but the relationship to the victims—through the symbol of the chair—is personal. The empty chair represents loss and literal absence—a father or mother or friend who is no longer at the table, no longer sharing in life's moments.

This sense of loss and absence is central to Peter Eisenman's Holocaust Memorial in Berlin (Fig. **10-26**), erected in memory of the European Jews murdered by the Nazis. Within view of the Brandenberg Gate and the Reichstag—two architectural monuments associated with Adolf Hitler and Nazism—Eisenman placed 2,711 gray, concrete **stelae** side by side in claustrophobic rows. The stelae are the same length and width but vary in height and are placed on slabs that are tilted in different directions. The paths between the slabs slope up and then down so that the journey among these stones shifts and changes. The concentration of stelae is greatest at the center of the monument, creating a disturbing sense of confinement. In sunlight, the shadows are sharp and harsh; shady areas that ought to provide welcome respite from the sun are, instead, menacing. On an overcast day, the relentless grayness of the stones and the

10-26 PETER EISENMAN.
Holocaust Memorial, Berlin (2004).

10-27 FRIEDRICH ST. FLORIAN.
National World War II Memorial (2004).
Washington, D.C.
Photograph United States Air Force.

sky is somber, ashen, and funereal. The site is also home to an exhibition space, underground beneath the stelae, that is dedicated to the historical background of the Holocaust. The feeling is cryptlike, but there are no bodies, no objects that belonged to the deceased, and therein lies a point of the memorial. The Nazis planned to annihilate the Jews of Europe and any memory of them.

As the competitions ensued for the commission of Berlin's Holocaust Memorial, questions were raised about the relevance of a modern, abstract design. Would it be understood? Would it have meaning? The same questions haunted Maya Lin's proposal for the *Vietnam Veterans Memorial* in Washington, D.C., decades earlier (see A Closer Look: The Vietnam Veterans Memorial—A Woman's Perspective).

The Oklahoma City Memorial, the Berlin Holocaust Memorial, and the Vietnam Veterans Memorial all have a very different feeling from traditional triumphal monuments. Rather than looking at stylized images of heroic figures, we are called upon to reflect quietly and intimately on acts of human courage in the face of death. Although an antitriumphal approach represents a significant trend in contemporary monument design, it is not by any means universal. The National World War II Memorial (Fig. **10-27**) in Washington, D.C., was dedicated in 2004, more than 50 years after the Allied victories in Europe and Japan. The design for the memorial, with its pavilions and pillars, stirred a different kind of controversy in that its traditional, classical forms were reminiscent, to one journalist, of the pompous style embraced by the Fascist regimes of the 1930s, the very regimes that the Allies fought to defeat. One critic went so far as to refer to the memorial as a "monument on steroids—vainglorious, demanding of attention and full of trite imagery."[1]

The reception of the National World War II Memorial was not all negative, although the controversy raises an interesting question about the ways in which people relate to memorials and critics evaluate them. Many contemporary artists have gravitated toward designs that are interactive, educational, and reflective. Artists working in a more traditional mode emphasize the larger-than-human, the heroic. Reactions to memorials are highly personal, and the way memory is institutionalized is a very sensitive topic. Critics can find themselves in a situation in which their criticism is viewed, at best, as politically incorrect or, at worst, as unpatriotic.

---

1 Thomas M. Keane Jr., *The Boston Herald,* 2004.

The Vietnam Veterans Memorial—A Woman's Perspective

WHEN WE VIEW THE EXPANSES of the Washington Mall, we are awed by the grand obelisk that is the Washington Monument. We are comforted by the stately columns and familiar shapes of the Lincoln and Jefferson memorials. But many of us do not know how to respond to the two 200-foot-long black granite walls that form a V as they recede into the ground. There is no label—only the names of 58,000 victims chiseled into the silent walls:

> As we descend along the path that hugs the harsh black granite, we enter the very earth that, in another place, has accepted the bodies of our sons and daughters. Each name is carved not only in the stone, but by virtue of its highly polished surface, in our own reflection, in our physical substance. We are not observers, we are participants. We touch, we write [letters to our loved ones], we leave parts of ourselves behind. This is a woman's vision—to commune, to interact, to collaborate with the piece to fulfill its expressive potential. . . .

> Maya Ying Lin has foregone the [format of the triumphal monument]. She has given us [the earth mother] Gaea, who, pierced by the ebony scar of suffering death, takes back her children, as she has done since the dawn of humanity.*

This is Maya Ying Lin's Vietnam Veterans Memorial (Fig. **10-28**), completed in 1982 on a two-acre site on the Mall. In order to read the names, we must descend gradually into the earth, and then just as gradually work our way back up. This progress is perhaps symbolic of the nation's involvement in Vietnam. The eloquently simple design of the memorial also stirs controversy, as did the war it commemorates.

This dignified understatement in stone has offended many who would have preferred a more traditional memorial. One conservative magazine branded the design a conspiracy to dishonor the dead. Architecture critic Paul Gapp of *The Chicago Tribune* argued, "The so-called memorial is bizarre . . . neither a building nor scultpture." One Vietnam veteran had called for a statue of an officer offering a fallen soldier to heaven. The public expects a certain heroic quality in its monuments to commemorate those fallen in battle. Lin's work is antiheroic and antitriumphal. Whereas most war monuments speak of giving up our loved ones to a cause, her monument speaks only of giving up our loved ones.

How did the Vietnam Memorial come to be so uniquely designed? It was chosen from 1,421 entries in a national competition. The designer, Maya Ying Lin, is a Chinese American woman who was all of 22 years old at the time she submitted her entry. A native of Ohio, Lin had just graduated from Yale University, where she majored in architecture. Lin recognized that a monumental sculpture or another grand building would have been intrusive in the heart of Washington. Her design meets the competition criteria of being "neither too commanding nor too deferential" and is yet another expression of the versatility of stone. ■

* Lois Fichner-Rathus, "A Woman's Vision of the War," *The New York Times*, August 18, 1991, H6.

It terrified me to have an idea that was solely mine to be no longer a part of my mind, but totally public.
—Maya Ying Lin, on her design for the Vietnam Veterans Memorial in Washington, D.C.

10-28 MAYA YING LIN.
Vietnam Veterans Memorial, Washington, D.C. (1982).
Polished black granite. L: 492'.
©Stock Connection Blue/Alamy

11

ARCHITECTURE

■
—

*The mother art is architecture. Without an architecture of our own
we have no soul of our own civilization.*
—Frank Lloyd Wright

Early humans found their shelters—the mouth of a yawning cave, the underside of a ledge, the boughs of an overspreading tree. But for thousands of years now we having been building shelters and fashioning them to our needs. Before we became capable of transporting bulky materials over vast distances, we had to rely on local possibilities. Native Americans constructed huts from sticks and bark and conical teepees from animal skins and wooden poles. They carved their way into the sides of cliffs. African villagers wove sticks and grass into walls and plastered them with mud; their geometrically pure cone roofs sat atop cylindrical bases. Desert peoples learned to dry clay in the sun in the form of bricks. From ice, the Inuit fashioned the dome-shaped igloo.

Architecture is the art and science of designing buildings, bridges, and other structures to help us meet our personal and communal needs. Of all the arts, architecture probably has the greatest impact on our daily lives. For most of us, architecture determines the quality of the environments in which we work, play, meditate, and rest.

Fortress of Machu Picchu, Urubamba Valley, Peru. Incan, 1490–1530. Detail of carved stone.
©Pablo Corral Vega/CORBIS.

Architecture is also a vehicle for artistic expression in three dimensions. More than any other art form, architecture is experienced from within as well as without, and at great length. If sculptures have fronts, backs, sides, tops, and bottoms, buildings have **facades**, foundations, roofs, and a variety of interior spaces that must be planned. If some sculptures are kinetic and some are composed of light sources, buildings may contain complex systems for heating, cooling, lighting, and inner transportation.

Architects, like sculptors, must work within the limits of their materials and the technology of the day. In addition to understanding enough of engineering to determine how materials may be used efficiently to span and enclose sometimes vast spaces, architects must work with other professionals and with contractors who design and install elements of the **service systems** of their buildings.

In a sense, the architect is not only an artist but also a mediator—a compromiser. The architect mediates between the needs of the client and the properties and aesthetic possibilities of the site. (Today's technology permits the erection of 20-story-high, 20-foot-wide "sliver skyscrapers" on expensive, narrow urban sites, but at what aesthetic cost to a neighborhood of row houses?) The architect balances aesthetics and the building codes of the community. (Since the 1930s, architects in New York City have had to comply with the so-called setback law and step back or contour their high-rises from the street in order to let the sun shine in on an environment that seemed in danger of devolving into a maze of blackened canyons.) Climate, site, materials, building codes, clients, contractors, service systems, and the amount of money available—these are just some of the variables that the architect must employ or contend with to create an aesthetically pleasing, functional structure.

In this section, we will explore traditional and modern ways in which architects have come to terms with these variables. We will survey the traditional materials and methods associated with building in stone and wood. Then we will examine some modern and contemporary architectural materials and methods, including those associated with cast-iron and steel-cage construction, use of reinforced concrete, and steel cable.

STONE ARCHITECTURE

As a building material, stone is massive and virtually indestructible. Contemporary wood-frame homes frequently sport stone fireplaces, perhaps as a symbol of permanence

11-1 Cliff Dwellings, Mesa Verde, Colorado. Native American, Pre-Columbian.
©Kent Meireis/The Image Works

Architecture completes nature.

—GIORGIO DE CHIRICO

and strength as well as of warmth. The Native American cliff dwellings at Mesa Verde, Colorado (Fig. **11-1**), could be considered something of an "earthwork high relief." The cliff itself becomes the back wall or "support" of more than 100 rectangular apartments. Circular, underground **kivas** served as community centers. Construction with stone, **adobe**, and timber creates a mixed-media functional fantasy. Early humans also assembled stone temples and memorials.

Post-and-Lintel Construction

The prehistoric Stonehenge (see Fig. 13-3) probably served religious or astronomical purposes. Its orientation toward the sun and its layout in concentric circles are suggestive of the amphitheaters and temples to follow. Stonehenge is an early example of **post-and-lintel construction** (Fig. **11-2A**). Two stones were set upright as supports, and a

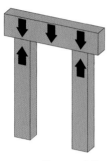

11-2A Post-and-lintel construction.

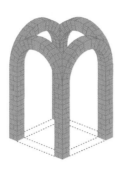

11-2B Rounded arches enclosing square bay.

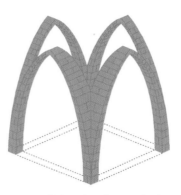

11-2C Pointed arches enclosing rectangular bay.

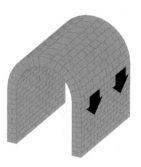

11-2D Tunnel or barrel vault.

11-2E Groin vault.

11-2F Groin vault showing ribs that carry greatest loads.

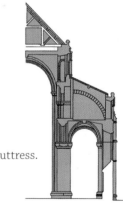

11-2G Flying buttress.

11-2H Dome.

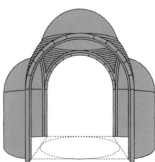

11-2I Pendentives.

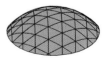

11-2J Geodesic dome.

11-3 Walls of Fortress of Machu Picchu, Urubamba Valley, Peru. Incan, 1490–1530.
©Topham/The Image Works

third was placed across them, creating an opening beneath. How the massive blocks of Stonehenge were transported and erected remains a mystery.

Early stone structures were erected without benefit of mortar. Their dry **masonry** relied on masterly carving of blocks, strategic placement, and sheer weight for durability. Consider the imposing ruin of the fortress of Machu Picchu, perched high above the Urubamba River in the Peruvian Andes. Its beautiful granite walls (Fig. **11-3**), constructed by the Incas, are pieced together so perfectly that not even a knife blade can pass between the blocks. The faces of the Great Pyramids of Egypt (see Fig. 13-12) are assembled as miraculously, perhaps even more so considering the greater mass of the blocks.

11-4 Temple of Amen-Re, Karnak. Egyptian, XVIII dynasty, 1570–1342 BCE.
©George Holton/Photo Researchers, Inc., New York.

An arch is two curves trying to fall.

— ANDY ROONEY

Stone became the favored material for the public buildings of the Egyptians and the Greeks. The Egyptian Temple of Amen-Re at Karnak (Fig. **11-4**) and the Parthenon (see Fig. 14-10) of the Classical period of Greece begin to speak of the elegance as well as the massiveness that can be fashioned from stone. The Temple of Amen-Re is of post-and-lintel construction, but the paintings, relief sculptures, and overall smoothness of the columns belie their function as bearers of stress (see Fig. 13-16). The virtual forest of columns was a structural necessity because of the weight of the massive stone lintels. The Parthenon is also of post-and-lintel construction. Consistent with the Greeks' emphasis on the functional purpose of columns, the surfaces of the marble shafts are free from ornamentation. The Parthenon, which may be the most studied and surveyed building in the world, is discussed at length in Chapter 14.

Arches

Architects of stone also use **arches** to span distances (Figs. **11-2B** and **11-2C**). Arches have many functions, including supporting other structures, such as roofs, and serving as actual and symbolic gateways. An Arch of Triumph, as in the city of Paris, provides a visual focus for the return of the conquering hero. Eero Saarinen's Gateway Arch (Fig. **11-5**), completed in St. Louis in 1966, stands 630 feet tall at the center and commemorates the westward push of the United States after the Louisiana Purchase of 1803. The Pont du Gard (see Fig. 14-22) near Nîmes, France, employs the arch in a bridge that is part of an aqueduct system. It is a marvel of Roman engineering. Early masonry arches were fashioned from **bricks**; each limestone block of the Pont du Gard weighs up to two tons, and they were assembled without benefit of mortar. The bridge stands and functions today, two millennia after its creation.

In most arches, wedge-shaped blocks of stone, called **voussoirs**, are gradually placed in position ascending a wooden scaffold called a **centering**. When the center, or **keystone**, is set in place, the weight of the blocks is all at once transmitted in an arc laterally and downward, and the centering can be removed. The pull of gravity on each block serves as "cement"; that is, the blocks fall into one another so that the very weight that had made their erection a marvel now prevents them from budging. The **compressive strength** of stone allows the builder to place additional weight above the arch. The Pont du Gard consists of three **tiers** of arches, 161 feet high.

11-5 **EERO SAARINEN.** Jefferson National Expansion Memorial, Gateway Arch, St. Louis, MO (1966).
©ChromoSohm Media/ The Image Works

Vaults

An extended arch is called a **vault**. A tunnel or **barrel vault** (Fig. **11-2D**) simply places arches behind one another until a desired depth is reached. In this way, impressive spaces may be roofed, and tunnels may be constructed. Unfortunately, the spaces enclosed by barrel vaults are dark, because piercing them to let in natural light would compromise their strength. The communication of stresses from one arch to another also requires that the centering for each arch be kept in place until the entire vault is completed.

Roman engineers are credited with the creation of the **groin vault**, which overcame limitations of the barrel vault, as early as the third century CE. Groin vaults are constructed by placing barrel vaults at right angles to cover a square space (Fig. **11-2E**). In this way the load of the intersecting vaults is transmitted to the corners, necessitating **buttressing** at these points but allowing the sides of the square to be open. The square space enclosed by the groin vault is called a **bay**. Architects could now construct huge buildings by assembling any number of bays. Because the stresses from one groin vault are not transmitted to a large degree to its neighbors, the centering used for one vault can be removed and reused while the building is under construction.

The greatest loads in the groin vault are thrust onto the four arches that compose the sides and the two arches that run diagonally across them. If the capacity of these diagonals is increased to carry a load, by means of **ribs** added to the vault (Fig. **11-2F**), then the remainder of the roof can be fashioned from stone **webbing** or other materials much lighter in weight. A true stone skeleton is created.

Note in Figure 11-2B that rounded arches can enclose only square bays. One could not use rounded arches in rectangular bays because the longer walls would have higher arches. Architects over the centuries solved the rectangular bay problem in several ingenious ways. The most important of these is found in **Gothic** architecture, discussed in Chapter 15, which uses ribbed vaults and **pointed arches**. Pointed arches can be constructed to uniform heights even when the sides of the enclosed space are unequal (Fig. 11-2C). Gothic architecture also employed the so-called flying buttress (Fig. **11-2G**), a masonry strut that transmits part of the load of a vault to a buttress positioned outside a building.

Most of the great cathedrals of Europe achieve their vast, open interiors through the use of vaults. Massive stone rests benignly above the heads of worshippers and tourists alike, transmitting its brute load laterally and downward. The **Ottonian** St. Michael's (see Fig. 15-11), built in Germany between 1001 and 1031 CE, uses barrel vaulting. Its bays are square, and its walls are blank and massive. The **Romanesque** St. Sernin (see Fig. 15-13), built in France between about 1080 and 1120, uses round arches and square bays. The walls are heavy and blunt, with the main masses subdivided by buttresses. St. Étienne (see Fig. 15-15), completed between 1115 and 1120, has high, rising vaults— some of the earliest to show true ribs— that permit light to enter through a **clerestory**. Stone became a fully elegant structural skeleton in the great Gothic cathedrals, such as those at Laon (see Figs. 15-20 and 15-21) and Chartres (see Fig. 15-23) and in the Notre-Dame of Paris (see Fig. 15-22). Lacy buttressing and ample **fenestration** lend these massive buildings an airy lightness that seems consonant with their mission of directing upward the focus of human awareness.

Domes

Domes are hemispherical forms that are rounded when viewed from beneath (see Figs. **11-2H** and **11-2J**). Like vaults, domes are extensions of the principle of the arch and are capable of enclosing vast reaches of space. (Buckminster Fuller, who designed the United States Pavilion [Fig. 11-22] for the 1967 World's Fair in Montreal, proposed that the center of Manhattan should be enclosed in a weather-controlled transparent dome two miles in diameter.) Stresses from the top of the dome are transmitted in all directions to the points at which the circular base meets the foundation, walls, or other structures beneath.

The dome of the Buddhist temple or Stupa of Sanchi, India, completed in the first century CE, rises 50 feet above the ground and causes the worshipper to contemplate the dwelling place of the gods (see Fig. 18-30). It was constructed from stones placed in gradually diminishing concentric circles. Visitors find the domed interior of the Pantheon of Rome (see Fig. 14-29), completed during the second century CE, breathtaking. Like the dome of the Stupa, the rounded inner surface of the Pantheon, 144 feet in diameter, symbolizes the heavens.

The dome of the vast Hagia Sophia (see Fig. 1-15) in Constantinople is 108 feet in diameter. Its architects, building during the sixth century CE, used four triangular surfaces called **pendentives** (Fig. **11-2I**) to support the dome on a square base. Pendentives transfer the load from the base of the dome to the **piers** at the corners of the square beneath.

Today, stone is rarely used as a structural material. It is expensive to quarry and transport, and it is too massive to handle readily at the site. Metals are lighter and have greater tensile strength, so they are suitable as the skeletons or reinforcers for most of today's larger structures. Still, buildings with steel skeletons are frequently dressed with thin facades, or **veneers**, of costly marble, limestone, and other types of stone. Many tract homes are granted decorative patches of stone across the front facade, and slabs of slate are frequently used to provide minimum-care surfaces for entry halls or patios in private homes.

WOOD ARCHITECTURE

Wood is as beautiful and versatile a material for building as it is for sculpture. It is an abundant and, as many advertisements have proclaimed, renewable resource. It is relatively light in weight and is capable of being worked on at the site with readily portable hand tools. Its variety of colors and grains, as well as its capacity to accept paint or to weather charmingly when left in its natural state, make wood a ubiquitous material. Wood, like stone, can be used as a structural element or as a facade. In many structures, it is used as both.

Wood also has its drawbacks. It warps and cracks. It rots. It is also highly flammable and stirs the appetite of termites and other devouring insects. However, modern technology has enhanced the stability and strength of wood as a building material. Chemical treatments decrease wood's vulnerability to rotting from moisture. **Plywood**, which is built up from sheets of wood glued together, is unlikely to warp and is frequently used as an under layer in the exterior walls of small buildings and homes. Laminated wood beams possess great strength and are also unlikely to become distorted in shape from exposure to changing temperatures and levels of humidity.

Architects, like artists and designers, use contrasting materials to create visual diversity and surface interest. They often reference textures found in nature in order to integrate a building with its site, or to create a dramatic counterpoint to it. The treehouses (Fig. **11-6**) designed by the German architects studio, baumraum, are extreme and playful examples of both. The designers refer to their endeavors as a blend of architecture, landscape design, and "arboriculture," aiming to integrate the structures into their forest surrounds and, at the same time, preserve the integrity of the host trees. In designing its lofty wood dwellings, bauraum—which literally means "tree space" in German—also takes into consideration factors such as the species of a tree, its distance off the ground, and the amount of clear building space available in order to successfully suspend the structures. The result is a study in contrast and connection between humans and their natural surroundings.

11-6 BAUMRAUM.
©Andreas Wenning

Post-and-Beam Construction

Post-and-beam construction (Fig. **11-7A**) is similar to post-and-lintel construction. Vertical and horizontal timbers are cut and pieced together with wooden pegs. The beams span openings for windows, doors, and interior spaces, and they can also support posts for another story or roof trusses.

Trusses

Trusses are lengths of wood, iron, or steel pieced together in triangular shapes of the sort shown in Figure **11-7B** in order to expand the abilities of these materials to span distances. Trusses acquire their strength from the fact that the sides of a triangle, once joined, cannot be forced out of shape. In many buildings, roof trusses are exposed and become elements of the design.

Balloon Framing

Balloon framing (Fig. **11-7C**), a product of the industrial revolution, dates back to the beginning of the twentieth century. In balloon framing, factory-cut studs, including the familiar two-by-four, are mass-produced and assembled at the site using thousands of factory-produced metal nails. Several light, easily handled pieces of wood replace the heavy timber of post-and-beam construction. Entire walls are framed in place or on their sides and then raised into place by a crew of carpenters. The multiple pieces and geometric patterns of balloon framing give it a sturdiness that rivals that of the post and beam, permitting the support of slate or tile roofs. However, the term *balloon* was originally a derisive term: inveterate users of post and beam were skeptical that the frail-looking wooden pieces could provide a rugged building.

Balloon framing has now been used on millions of smaller buildings, not only homes. Sidings for balloon-framed homes have ranged from **clapboard** to asbestos shingle, brick and stone veneer, and aluminum. Roofs have ranged from asphalt or cedar shingle to tile and slate. These materials vary in cost, and each has certain aesthetic possibilities and practical advantages. Aluminum, for example, is lightweight, durable, and maintenance-free. However, when aluminum siding is shaped like clapboard and given a bogus grain, the intended trompe l'oeil effect usually fails and can create something of an aesthetic embarrassment.

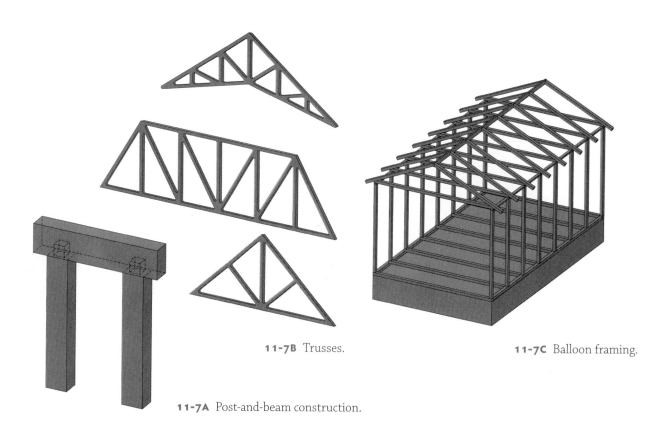

11-7B Trusses.

11-7C Balloon framing.

11-7A Post-and-beam construction.

11-8 RICHARD M. HUNT.
J. N. A. Griswold House,
Newport, RI (1862–1863).
©Roberto Schezen/ ESTO

Two other faces of wood are observable in American architect Richard Morris Hunt's J. N. A. Griswold House (Fig. **11-8**), built at Newport, Rhode Island, in 1862–1863 in the *Stick style,* and in the Cape Cod–style homes in Levittown, Long Island, a suburb of New York City (Fig. **11-9**). The Griswold House shows the fanciful possibilities in wood. The Stick style sports a skeletal treatment of exteriors that remind one of an assemblage of matchsticks, open interiors, and a curious interplay of voids and solids and horizontal and vertical lines. Shapes proliferate in this short-lived movement. Turrets and gables and dormers poke the roof in every direction. Trellised porches reinforce a certain wooden laciness. One cannot imagine the Griswold House constructed in any material but wood.

The house at Levittown is more than a home; it is a socioaesthetic comment on the need for mass suburban housing that impacted so many metropolitan regions during the marriage and baby boom that followed World War II. This house and 17,000 others almost exactly like it were built, with few exceptions, on 60-foot by 100-foot lots that had been carved out from potato fields. In what was to become neighborhood after neighborhood, bulldozers smoothed already flat terrain and concrete slabs were poured. Balloon frames were erected, sided, and roofed. Trees were planted; grass was sown. The houses had an eat-in kitchen, living room, two tiny bedrooms, one bath on the first floor, and an expansion attic. Despite the tedium of the repetition, the original Levittown house achieved a sort of architectural integrity, providing living space, the pride of ownership, and an inoffensive facade for a modest price. Driving through Levittown today, it seems that every occupant thrust random additions in random directions as the family grew, despite the limitations of the lots. The trees only partly obscure the results.

CAST-IRON ARCHITECTURE

Nineteenth-century industrialization also introduced **cast iron** as a building material. It was one of several structural materials that would change the face of architecture. Cast iron was a welcome alternative to stone and wood. Like stone, iron has great strength, is heavy, and has a certain brittleness, yet it was the first material to allow the erection

11-9 Cape Cod–style houses built by Levitt & Sons, Levittown, NY (c. 1947–1951).
©Hulton Archive/Getty Images

of tall buildings with relatively slender walls. Slender iron beams and bolted trusses are also capable of spanning vast interior spaces, freeing them from the forests of columns that are required in stone.

At the mid-nineteenth-century Great Exhibition held in Hyde Park, London, Sir Joseph Paxton's Crystal Palace (Fig. **11-10**) covered 17 acres. Like subsequent iron buildings, the Crystal Palace was **prefabricated**. Iron parts were cast at the factory, not the site. The new railroads facilitated their transportation, and it was a simple matter to bolt them together at the exhibition. It was also a relatively simple matter to dismantle the structure and reconstruct it at another site. The iron skeleton, with its myriad arches and trusses, was an integral part of the design. The huge plate-glass paneled walls bore no weight. Paxton asserted that "nature" had been his "engineer," explaining that he merely copied the system of longitudinal and transverse supports that one finds in a leaf. Earlier architects were also familiar with the structure of the leaf, but they did not have the structural materials at hand that would permit them to build, much less conceptualize, such an expression of natural design.

The Crystal Palace was moved after the exhibition, and until heavily damaged by fire, it served as a museum and concert hall. It was demolished in 1941 during World War II, after it was discovered that it was being used as a landmark by German pilots on bombing runs.

The Eiffel Tower (Fig. **11-11**) was built in Paris in 1889 for another industrial exhibition. At the time, Gustave Eiffel was castigated by critics for building an open structure lacking the standard masonry facade. Today the Parisian symbol is so familiar that one cannot visualize Paris without the tower's magnificent exposed iron trusses. The pieces of the 1,000-foot-tall tower were prefabricated, and the tower was assembled at the site in 17 months by only 150 workers.

Structures such as these encouraged **steel-cage construction** and the development of the skyscraper.

11-11 GUSTAVE EIFFEL.
Eiffel Tower, Paris (1889).
©Topham/The Image Works

11-10 Engraving of Sir Joseph Paxton's Crystal Palace, London (1851).
©The British Library/HIP/The Image Works

STEEL-CAGE ARCHITECTURE

Steel is a strong metal of iron alloyed with small amounts of carbon and a variety of other metals. Steel is harder than iron, and more rust and fire resistant. It is more expensive than other structural materials, but its great strength permits it to be used in relatively small quantities. Light, narrow, prefabricated I-beams have great tensile strength. They resist bending in any direction and are riveted or welded together into skeletal forms called **steel cages** at the site (Fig. **11-12**). Facades and inner walls are hung from the skeleton and frequently contribute more mass to the building than does the skeleton itself.

The Wainwright Building (Fig. **11-13**), erected in 1890, is an early example of steel-cage construction. Architect Louis Sullivan, one of the fathers of modern American

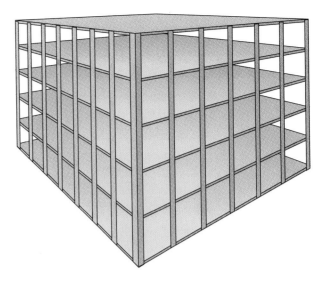

11-12 Steel-cage construction.

11-13 LOUIS SULLIVAN.
Wainwright Building, St. Louis, MO (1890).
Photography Bill Hedrich, Hedrich-Blessing/ Chicago History Museum

11-14 LE CORBUSIER.
Chapel of Notre-Dame-du-Haut,
Ronchamp, France (1950–1954).
©Spectrum Colour Library/Heritage-Images/The Image Works. ©2009 Artists
Rights Society (ARS), New York/ADAGP, Paris/FLC.

11-15 LE CORBUSIER.
Interior, south wall, Chapel of Notre-Dame-du-Haut.
©Kim Hart/Robert Harding. ©2009 Artists Rights Society (ARS), New York/
ADAGP, Paris/FLC.

architecture, emphasized the verticality of the structure by running **pilasters** between the windows through the upper stories. Many skyscrapers run pilasters up their entire facades. Sullivan also emphasized the horizontal features of the Wainwright Building. Ornamented horizontal bands separate most of the windows, and a severe decorated **cornice** crowns the structure. Sullivan's motto was "form follows function," and the rigid horizontal and vertical processions of the elements of the facade suggest the regularity of the rectangular spaces within. Sullivan's early "skyscraper"— in function, in structure, and in simplified form—was a precursor of the twentieth-century behemoths to follow.

REINFORCED CONCRETE ARCHITECTURE

Although cement was first produced in the early 1800s, the use of **reinforced concrete** is said to have begun with a French gardener, Jacques Monier, who proposed strengthening concrete flower pots with a wire mesh in the 1860s. In reinforced concrete, or **ferroconcrete**, steel rods and/or steel mesh are inserted at the points of greatest stress into concrete slabs before they harden. In the resultant slab, stresses are shared by the materials.

Ferroconcrete has many of the advantages of stone and steel, without some of the disadvantages. The steel rods increase the tensile strength of concrete, making it less susceptible to tearing or pulling apart at stress points. The concrete, in turn, prevents the steel from rusting. Reinforced concrete can span greater distances than stone, and it supports more weight than steel. Perhaps the most dramatic advantage of reinforced concrete is its capacity to take on natural curved shapes that would be unthinkable in steel or concrete alone. Curved slabs take on the forms of eggshells, bubbles, seashells, and other organic shapes that are naturally engineered for the even spreading of stress throughout their surfaces and are, hence, enduring.

Reinforced concrete, more than other materials, has allowed the architect to think freely and sculpturally. There are limits to what ferroconcrete can do, however; initial spatial concepts are frequently somewhat refined by computer-aided calculations of marginally more efficient shapes for distributing stress. Still, it would not be far from the mark to say that buildings of almost any shape and reasonable size are possible today, if one is willing to pay for them. The architects of ferroconcrete have achieved buildings that would have astounded the ancient stone builders—and perhaps Joseph Paxton as well.

Le Corbusier's chapel of Notre-Dame-du-Haut (Figs. **11-14** and **11-15**) is an example of what has been referred to as the "new brutalism," deriving from the French *brut*, meaning "rough, uncut, or raw." The steel web is spun, and the concrete is cast in place, leaving the marks of the wooden forms on its surface. The white walls, dark roof, and white towers are decorated only by the texture of the curving reinforced concrete slabs. In places the walls are incredibly thick. Windows of various shapes and sizes expand from small slits and rectangles to form mysterious light tunnels; they draw the observer outward more than they actually light the interior. The massive voids of the window apertures recall the huge stone blocks of prehistoric religious structures.

Frank Lloyd Wright's Kaufmann House (Fig. **11-16**), which has also become known as "Fallingwater," shows a very different application of reinforced concrete. Here cantilevered decks of reinforced concrete rush outward into the surrounding landscape from the building's central core, intersecting in strata that lie parallel to the natural rock formations. Wright's **naturalistic style** integrates his building with its site. In the Kaufmann House, reinforced concrete and stone walls complement the sturdy rock of the Pennsylvania countryside.

For Wright, modern materials did not warrant austerity; geometry did not preclude organic integration with the site. A small waterfall seems mysteriously to originate beneath the broad white planes of a deck. The irregularity of the structural components—concrete, cut stone, natural stone, and machine-planed surfaces—complements the irregularity of the wooded site.

Israeli architect Moshe Safdie's Habitat (Fig. **11-17**) is another expression of the versatility of concrete. Habitat was erected for Expo 67 in Montreal as one solution to the housing problems of the future. Rugged, prefabricated units were stacked like blocks about a common utility core at the site, so that the roof of one unit would provide a private

11-16 FRANK LLOYD WRIGHT.
Kaufmann House ("Fallingwater"), Bear Run, PA (1936).
©Scott Frances/ESTO. ©2009 Frank Lloyd Wright Foundation, Scottsdale, AZ/Artists Rights Society (ARS), New York.

11-17 MOSHE SAFDIE.
Habitat, Expo 67, Montreal (1967).
©Michael Freeman/CORBIS

> *Architecture is the first manifestation of man creating his own universe.*
>
> —LE CORBUSIER

> *Well, now that he's finished one building, he'll go write four books about it.*
>
> —FRANK LLOYD WRIGHT on Le Corbusier

deck for another. Only a couple of Safdie-style "apartment houses" have been erected since, one in Israel and one in Puerto Rico, so today Safdie's beautiful sculptural assemblage evokes more nostalgia than hope for the future. Its unique brand of rugged, blocky excitement is rarely found in mass housing, and this is our loss.

STEEL-CABLE ARCHITECTURE

The notion of suspending bridges from cables is not new. Wood-and-rope suspension bridges have been built in Asia for thousands of years. Iron suspension bridges, such as the Menai Strait Bridge in Wales and the Clifton Bridge near Bristol, England, were erected during the early part of the nineteenth century. But in the Brooklyn Bridge (Fig. **11-18**), completed in 1883, John Roebling exploited the great tensile strength of steel to span New York's East River with **steel cable**. In such a cable, many parallel wires share the stress. Steel cable is also flexible, allowing the roadway beneath to sway, within limits, in response to changing weather and traffic conditions.

Roebling used massive vaulted piers of stone masonry to support parabolic webs of steel, which are rendered lacy by the juxtaposition. In many more recent suspension bridges, steel cable spans more than a mile, and in bridges such as the Golden Gate, the George Washington, and the Verrazzano Narrows, the effect is aesthetically stirring.

11-18 JOHN A. ROEBLING.
Brooklyn Bridge, New York (1869–1883).
©Visions of America, LLC/Alamy

A doctor can bury his mistakes, but an architect can only advise his clients to plant vines.

—FRANK LLOYD WRIGHT

We may live without architecture, and worship without her, but we cannot remember without her.

—JOHN RUSKIN

There is another stirring aspect to the photograph of the Brooklyn Bridge. In the background you see the twin towers of the World Trade Center, which collapsed in the terrorist attack of September 11, 2001. Within months following September 11, dozens of architects and planners were submitting concepts to New York City for "Ground Zero," which included a memorial to those who had been killed in the attack and new buildings that might recapture the upward spirit of the city. At one point in the decision-making process, the commission was awarded to Studio Daniel Libeskind, whose original design for the World Trade Center site appears in Figure **11-19**. The twisting structures, about the same height of the original towers, were designed to reduce the dynamic effects of wind, much as the aerodynamic contours of an automobile do. They were to be significantly stronger; a combination of steel on the outside and concrete within would better resist the natural forces of wind and gravity, and the unnatural forces of a terrorist assault. Accompanying the lower buildings was a broadcast tower that would have been the tallest structure in the world. The elements of the plan would have seemed a perfect compromise, taking into account the sobering realities of doing business in a super high-rise skyscraper in a post-9/11 world and the desire of most Americans to build high and build proud. And although these tall structures would reassert the lower Manhattan skyline, which now dips mournfully into the harbor, the twisted planes of the building facades seem to bear some acknowledgment of vulnerability in the wake of the attack by foreign enemies on U.S. soil.

But Libeskind's integrated design would not survive the tangle of bureaucratic red tape that gripped (some say crippled) the process. What emerged was a compromise solution between two main architects—Libeskind and David Childs. The so-called Freedom Tower, which Libeskind designed to rise 1,776 feet, was an important symbolic aspect of the plan. According to the architect, that

11-19 STUDIO DANIEL LIBESKIND.
Computer-generated drawings of the design originally selected to rebuild the World Trade Center site, New York City.

AP Images/Lower Manhattan Development Corporation

number reflects "a date [America's year of independence from Britain] that speaks to the whole world." Although the tower will still top out at 1,776 feet, its original slender and graceful lines have been replaced by Childs with a

In Lights at Ground Zero, Steps toward Illumination*

FOR A MONTH IN THE SPRING OF 2002, twin towers of light at Ground Zero served as an architectural memorial to the twin towers of glass and steel that had been felled by terrorists, even if the medium could not be clutched by the hands. It was called *Tribute in Light* (Fig. **11-20**), and architectural critic Herbert Muschamp wrote about it in *The New York Times*:

"Tribute in Light" was a moving piece of urban spectacle. The project's impact surpassed even the dramatic digital renderings. In the renderings, the twin light towers appeared to be saying something. As realized, they seemed to be looking for something. More a question than a statement, the project set a rhetorical tone worthy of emulation by those who will be shaping the future of Lower Manhattan in days to come.

The project was conceived independently by two architects, John Bennett and Gustavo Bonevardi, and two artists, Paul Myoda and Julian LaVerdiere. On learning of each other's work, the two teams joined. Another architect, Richard Nash Gould, was later added. The lighting genius Paul Marantz executed the concept.

As realized, the concept gave the impression of an image revealed, rather than designed, as if two lustrous columns have been excavated by an archaeological team from the darkness of time. Like classical columns, the towers were fluted, an effect of the 44 individual high-power lamps used to create each one. Extra lamps at the corners reinforced the architectonic illusion. The effect was similar to that made by missiles thrusting off into space. Though stationary, the light towers appeared aimed for the arrival of signs from above. The eye wanted to follow, not just behold them.

Light, Marshall McLuhan reminded us, is a medium. Indeed, in his influential book *Understanding Media*, the Canadian thinker devoted his chapter on architecture to developing that idea. Light is a "pure" communication medium whose power to shape environments is independent of content. In artificial form, light reshaped the boundaries of buildings and entire cities. We encounter that form in its purest state at night, when gazing up at a skyline, or gazing down from an airplane window at suburban sprawl.

Ancient builders designed monuments to align sacred sites with the positions of sun and moon. The lightness of Gothic construction was inseparable from the biblical narratives inscribed in stained glass for the benefit of those who couldn't read.

But where have our two towers gone? "For the moment I can only cry out that I have lost my splendid mirage," F. Scott Fitzgerald wrote in 1945. "Come back, come back, O glittering and white!" ■

---

* Adapted from Herbert Muschamp, March 12, 2002. Copyright © 2002 by The New York Times Company. Reprinted by permission.

11-20 *Tribute in Light* (March–April, 2002).
©Rommel Pecson/The Image Works

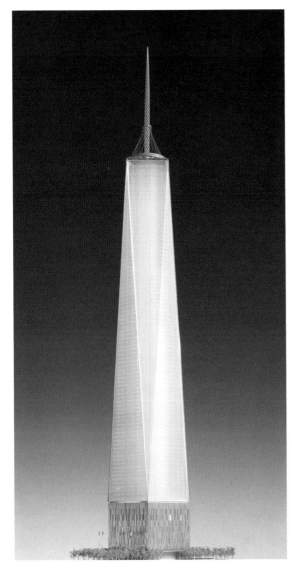

11-21 DAVID CHILDS IN COLLABORATION WITH DANIEL LIBESKIND.
Freedom Tower.
©Skidmore, Owings and Merrill/Landov

much more obviously fortified design (Fig. **11-21**) that speaks "safety first." Only the first 70 floors will be occupied by office space, and these sit on a base of concrete and steel about 200 feet high. A lattice structure filled with windmills at the top of the building will generate 20 percent of the building's energy. This part of the building is designed as a cable-suspension structure.

Daniel Libeskind's design was originally chosen from a distinguished group of finalists, including the firm of David Childs. The individual who owns the lease on the ill-fated twin towers appointed Childs as the lead architect, putting Childs and Libeskind into what the latter has called "a forced marriage." One critic described the result of the compromise a "Freedom Bunker" in place of Freedom Tower. As this book goes to press, city planners, businesspeople, politicians, architects, families of the victims, and other citizens continue to debate the proper uses of lower Manhattan—of Ground Zero and its adjoining areas and neighborhoods. Even though Childs's design appears to be the final vision for the moment, some believe that the process is not yet over. One can only hope for a solution that fits the spirit of the nation and also remains sensitive to the needs of the families of those who lost their lives.

SHELL ARCHITECTURE

Modern materials and methods of engineering have made it possible to enclose spaces with relatively inexpensive shell structures. Masonry domes have been replaced by lightweight shells, which are frequently flatter and certainly capable of spanning greater spaces. Shells have been constructed from reinforced concrete, wood, steel, aluminum, and even plastics and paper. The concept of shell architecture is as old as the canvas tent and as new as the geodesic dome (Fig. **11-22**), designed by Buckminster Fuller for the United States Pavilion at Expo 67 in Montreal. In many sports arenas, fabric roofs are held up by keeping the air pressure inside the building slightly greater than that outside. Like balloons, these roof structures are literally inflated.

11-22 BUCKMINSTER FULLER.
United States Pavilion, Expo 67, Montreal (1967).
©Lee Snider/The Image Works

Fuller's shell is an assemblage of lightweight metal trusses into a three-quarter sphere that is 250 feet in diameter. Looking more closely, one sees that the trusses compose six-sided units that give the organic impression of a honeycomb. Light floods the climate-controlled enclosure, creating an environment for any variety of human activity—and any form of additional construction—within. Such domes can be covered with many sorts of weatherproofing, from lightweight metals and fabric to translucent and transparent plastics and glass. Here the engineering requirements clearly create the architectural design.

NEW MATERIALS, NEW VISIONS

In architecture studios and schools, the saying goes, "Convention gets built; innovation gets published." But this adage is systematically being proven wrong as scientists and engineers have combined forces to turn architects' dreams into reality: "If you can think it, we can build it."

In 1997, Frank Gehry transformed architectural design with the use of titanium in the same way that reinforced concrete altered the look of the exterior "skin" of buildings in the 1950s and 1960s. His Guggenheim Museum in Bilbao, Spain (see Fig. 2-19), set a new artistic course for Gehry in terms of his own style and nurtured the adaptation of high-tech metals by architects worldwide. Gehry's Ray and Maria Stata Center (Fig. **11-23**), which opened in 2005 on the Massachusetts Institute of Technology campus, stands as a visual summation of his most recent designs, materials, and theories of spatial relationships. The 730,000-square-foot complex will be a hub for research in the fields of computer science, linguistics, and philosophy. The assertive clashing of shapes signifies the disparate disciplines that will be housed in the structure, while communal lounges and shared interior spaces encourage interaction, collaboration, and the cross-fertilization of ideas. Gehry said of the Stata Center: "It reflects the different groups, the collision of ideas, the energy of people and ideas. . . . That's what will lead to the breakthroughs and the positive results."

Architect Peter Testa's view is that there is a "need to rethink how we assemble buildings" and that it is time to design in collaboration with materials manufacturers and to explore the potential of nascent technologies. Testa and his partner, Devyn Weiser, have designed a high-rise tower out of composite materials (Fig. **11-24**). Their skyscraper would be held erect by a cross-hatched lattice made of carbon fiber—a material several times stronger than the traditional steel. The "woven building" would have an interior that is completely open (except for elevator shafts) and void of structural support.

The use and reuse of unorthodox materials by some contemporary architects is also worth noting. Shigeru Ban, a Tokyo architect who has designed public buildings on the principle that art should not be only for the privileged, uses paper tubes and plastic sheets among other materials typically associated with other circumstances. Some of his works include the Paper Refugee Shelter for the United Nations, the Paper Museum and Paper Church in Japan, and a paper-tube arch in the

11-23 FRANK GEHRY.
Ray and Maria Stata Center for Computer, Information, and Intelligence Sciences at MIT, Cambridge, MA (2005).
©Jeff Titcomb/Alamy

11-24 PETER TESTA AND DEVYN WEISER, TESTA ARCHITECTURE AND DESIGN.
Carbon Tower.
©2005 Testa Architecture/Design, Los Angeles.

11-25 SHIGERU BAN.
Nomadic Museum (2005).
©Tyler Hicks, The New York Times/Redux

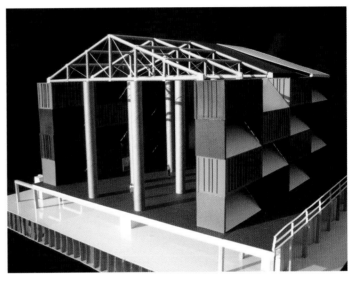

11-26 SHIGERU BAN.
Model of Nomadic Museum showing shipping containers, paper-tube columns, and roof trusses.
Shigeru Ban Architects

Museum of Modern Art, New York, sculpture garden. He also designed the 45,000-square-foot Nomadic Museum (Figs. **11-25** and **11-26**), a mobile structure whose walls are composed of 148 steel cargo containers; a roof and columns made of paper tubes; and a ceiling made of 1 million used, pressed, paper tea bags (tea leaves removed). The museum was constructed to display the work of Gregory Colbert, a Canadian-born artist whose photographs of elephants, whales, and human–animal relationships seem to have a visual and environmental affinity with the structure surrounding them. Sited at one point on Manhattan's historic Pier 54, the Nomadic Museum has an itinerary that includes Santa Monica Pier in California, as well as the Vatican in Rome. According to architect Ban, "It can be seen by more people all over the world if it moves. Maybe it remains in your memory if it's gone."

One hundred years ago, Will Rogers said, "Fort Worth is where the West begins and Dallas is where the East peters out." His description remains on the money even today. While the city of Dallas conveys a certain formality and self-conscious sophistication, Fort Worth revels in its "Cowtown" image.

Both cities can claim their skyscrapers, but the creation of an impressive Dallas-type skyline seems not to have been a temptation to the developers of Fort Worth. There things lie closer to the horizon, as shown in the downtown cobbled streets. It is as if the connection with the land wants to be emphasized, or will not be shaken. Dallas and Fort Worth, then, cannot be called twin cities, but one thing they have in common is that they have both lured world-class architects to grace their avenues and their vistas. Although they may be thousands of miles from the coasts and from classic civilizations, civilization has clearly found its way to the Southwest.

RENZO PIANO.
Nasher Sculpture Center, Dallas,
View of the Garden.
Photograph by Tom Jenkins, Courtesy Nasher Sculpture Center, Dallas, TX.

Dallas and Fort Worth lie only 33 miles apart. Along with their suburbs, they make up "the Metroplex." If you are visiting them, chances are you drove in on one of the interstates or flew into Dallas/Fort Worth (DFW) International Airport, which sits halfway between the two cities. Although the airport is one of the largest in the world and entertaining in and of itself, this is Texas, and "big" is where you start.

Downtown Dallas is easy to navigate by subway or on foot, unless you're braving the heat of summer. Most museums and cultural sites can be found within reasonable proximity to one another. I say, get a big-brimmed hat and a bottle of water and "cowboy it up"! You can walk from one end of downtown to the other in an hour.

The Dallas Arts District is 60 acres of museums, a performing arts center, and outdoor sculptures. Its centerpiece is the Dallas Museum of Art—a space that stretches more than 250,000 square feet. The museum's vastness stretches not only over its site but also across continents and eras. It features works from the Americas, Africa, Asia, the Pacific, and Europe. You will find paintings by Frida Kahlo and Frederic Edwin Church, and more Mondrians than in any other museum in the country. The famous Wendy and Emery Reves collection is installed in a setting that recreates the owner–donors' home on the French Riviera. Among the collection's stars are van Gogh, Monet, and Renoir.

Before you get too far, stroll in the Nasher Sculpture Garden (still have your hat on?) adjacent to the Dallas Art Museum. This 2.4-acre site was designed by Renzo Piano, architect of the famed Centre Pompidou in Paris (see the Paris Art Tour), and displays work by artists such as Alexander Calder, Willem de Kooning, Barbara Hepworth, Joan Miró, Richard Serra, and Auguste Rodin.

In the same neck of the woods, you'll find something very different—the Trammel Crow Museum. Once a private collection, it has grown into one of the largest collections of Asian art in the American Southwest. More than 300 objects and works of art from India, Japan, and China (including deities, shrines, scrolls, and vases) are amassed in a 12,000-square-foot space.

As you walk south toward the center of downtown Dallas—finally in dire need of a water break—you will happily come upon Fountain Palace. The fountain, one of Dallas's most popular sites, bears a famous signature; it was designed by I. M. Pei, who created the pyramidal entrance to the Louvre. More than a million gallons of water leap and dance in rhythm, while 172 bubbler fountains shoot water high into the air. Cool. Actually, very cool.

Elsewhere in Dallas, you'll find quirky and not-so-quirky museums, collections, and sites, including the American Museum of Miniature Arts (fantastic dollhouses, tiny toy soldiers, itty-bitty trains and cars); the African American Museum of Art, History, and Culture (the only one in the Southwest and the largest in the nation); the Meadows Museum (nicknamed "The Prado on the Prairie" with one of the major collections of Spanish art outside Spain); and the Women's Museum: An Institute for the Future (an exhibit that focuses on contributions of women throughout American history). Speaking of the very near future, Dallas will soon be home to the cubic Dee

I. M. PEI.
Fountain Palace, Dallas.
©Wes Thompson Photography/All residual rights reserved.

The Dee and Charles Wyly Theater.
Copyright REX/OMA, Office for Metropolitan Architecture

and Charles Wyly Theater designed by the pioneering Dutch architect Rem Koolhaas.

Pioneer Plaza—the setting for 70 six-foot tall, bronze longhorn steers being driven across a stream by a team of cowboys—is probably the largest bronze monument in the world. Speaking of longhorns, the Longhorn Trolley will steer you (pun intended) toward any of the three main districts that make up the metropolitan area of Fort Worth—the Cultural District, downtown/Sundance Square, and the Fort Worth Stockyards National Historic District.

Some of the country's best small museums are lined up like ducks in a row in Fort Worth's Cultural District—the Kimbell Art Museum, the Amon Carter Museum, and the Modern Art Museum. The Kimbell has, in fact, been called "America's best small museum." The initial funding was provided in the will of the industrialist Kay Kimbell, who called for a first-class museum in his name. In the 30 years since it opened its doors, the museum has amassed a diverse collection of art from antiquity to the modern, from Asia to Mesoamerica to Africa. It is best known, however,

LOUIS I. KAHN.
Kimbell Museum, Fort Worth.
©Kimbell Art Museum, Fort Worth, Texas/Art Resource, NY

for its stunning examples of European painting and sculpture from the Renaissance through the twentieth century. You will see works by Caravaggio, El Greco, Vigée-Lebrun, Delacroix, Monet, Renoir, Cézanne, Leger, Miró, and more—wrapped in the extraordinary architecture of Louis I. Kahn, one of the significant modern architects of the twentieth century.

The Amon Carter Museum opened in 1961 as a niche collection of Western art that belonged to the Fort Worth publisher and philanthropist Amon G. Carter. The original 400 paintings have grown to more than 300,000 works of art, and curators have cast a wide aesthetic net to include all styles of American paintings, drawings, prints, photographs, and sculptures. More recently, the Carter expanded (tripled!) its exhibition space to do what some museums cannot afford to do—bring their treasures out of storage and into public view.

The nearby Modern Art Museum of Fort Worth amplifies the city's modern and American collections with its mission of collecting and presenting post–World War II art. The roster of artists in its permanent collection reads like a who's who in

European and American art at midcentury and beyond: Pablo Picasso and Hans Hofmann; Jackson Pollock and Willem de Kooning; Agnes Martin and Dan Flavin; Andy Warhol and Jean-Michel Basquiat; Bill Viola and Tony Oursler; the list goes on and on—at least 2,800 objects in all. But the permanent collection represents only a part of what the museum has to offer. Its vast interior (150,000 square feet) also provides ample space for changing installations of contemporary work in all mediums.

The Fort Worth Stockyards and downtown Fort Worth offer two distinct clusters of tourist sites. As the name suggests, the Stockyards have a long and distinct history. If you are in the mood for a close-up, look at how "Cowtown" got its name—including Cattleman's Walk, the Fort Worth Livestock Exchange, and the Cowtown (rodeo) Coliseum—this is your destination.

If, on the other hand, the symphony or ballet or opera is your game, blaze your trail to downtown/Sundance Square and visit the Bass Performance Hall. Nancy Lee and Perry R. Bass donated the land for this remarkable space, and it was built by private donations to the tune of $67.5 million. Cowtown architecture it is not. The structure is modeled after the great opera houses of old Europe, complete with an 80-foot-diameter dome and two 48-foot angels flanking a bank of tall, arched windows on the facade. In a bow to pride and tradition, this neo–Beaux Arts design is rendered in homegrown Texas limestone.

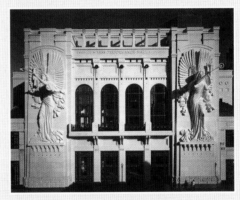

Bass Performance Hall, Fort Worth,
Showing the 48-Foot Angels.
Hedrich-Blessing Ltd. Courtesy Bass Performance Hall,
Fort Worth, TX.

Dallas and Fort Worth offer a study in contrasts, but they also share common ground. Both cities, their traditions and their cultural aspirations, aim to preserve their unique identities and balance those identities with awareness of the world and their place in the world—and, of course, in Texas.

To continue your tour and learn more about Dallas/Fort Worth, go to ArtExperience Online.

CRAFT AND DESIGN

■

I think art can exist within any craft tradition. Craft is just another way of saying means. I think it's a question of conscious intention, finally, and personal gifts, or giftedness. It seems that in art there is a primacy of idea over both means or craft, and function. Idea has to transcend both. I think this is probably why it's so difficult to make art out of something functional, or in a realm where craft has been nurtured for its own sake.
—Martin Puryear

An Attic vase, a Navajo rug, Tiffany glass, a Chippendale desk—which is art? Which is craft? Art critics and historians once had certain answers to these questions. Now, however, the perception of the relationship among functional objects, craft materials and techniques, and works of fine art has changed. Consider this story concerning one of the Metropolitan Museum of Art's most precious acquisitions, as retold by art critic Arthur C. Danto.[1] According to Thomas Hoving, the director of the museum at the time of the purchase, the vase in Figure **12-1** is "the single most perfect work of art I ever encountered . . . an object of total adoration." In his memoirs, Hoving further described his feelings upon his first encounter with the piece: "The first thought that came to mind was that I was gazing not at a vase, but at a painting." The director was obviously swept off his feet by this masterpiece of Greek art—a terra-cotta vessel painted with the scene of the *Dead Sarpedon Carried by Thanatos and Hypnos* and signed by both the potter and the painter. But why did Hoving diminish the significance of the potter's craft by essentially dismissing the pot as a mere support for an extraordinary painting? Danto suggests that Hoving's reaction is indicative of an art-world prejudice of sorts—one that attaches less importance to functional objects

1 Arthur C. Danto, "Fine Art and the Functional Object," *Glass*, no. 51 (Spring 1993): 24–29.

12-1 EUPHRONIOS AND EUXITHEOS.

Calyx Krater (1st quarter of 5th century BCE).
Ceramic. H: 18"; D: 21$^{11}/_{16}$".

The Metropolitan Museum of Art. Bequest of Joseph H. Durkee.
Gift of Darious Ogden Mills, and gift of C. Buxton Love. By exchange
(1972.11.10). Photograph ©1999 The Metropolitan Museum of Art,
New York. Courtesy Il Ministero per I Beni e la Attività Culturali
of Italy

and decoration of any kind. He warns that "the painting [on the vase] is there to decorate an object of conspicuous utility" and cannot be considered without reference to the vase itself. In fact, doing so precludes any real understanding of the work in the historical and artistic context in which it was created.

What purpose does this esoteric argument have for us who, as students, are trying to understand art? Simply this: The distinction between fine art and functional object is linked to the historical and cultural context in which a work was created. As Danto pointed out, the Greek philosophers praised craftspeople as somewhere between artists and philosophers, but held the view that no one was lower than the artist. Danto paraphrases Plato in *The Republic*: "The carpenter knows how to fashion in real life what the painter can merely imitate; therefore . . . artists have no real knowledge at all, trafficking only in the outward appearance of things."[2] More than two thousand years later, a French philosopher would declare, "Only what serves no purpose is truly beautiful."[3] Today, many

2 Ibid.
3 Théophile Gautier, Preface to his novel *Mademoiselle de Maupin*, 1835.

painters are turning their talent to utilitarian objects or creating paintings with techniques traditional to craft. Ceramic artists are creating works of sculpture, and sculptors are finding innovative ways to manipulate clay, wood, and metal. The glassmaker's art has reached new heights of experimentation while employing centuries-old techniques. For many artists, the distinction between art and craft is an artificial and limiting one. Any and all options should be exercised in pursuit of artistic expression. And the aesthetic and artistic merit of any creative work ought to be recognized.

In this chapter, we discuss a variety of media and categories of artistic expression. We consider the materials traditional to craft—clay, glass, fiber, metal, and wood—using historical and contemporary works as evidence of the broad technical and stylistic ranges of the media. We also examine graphic design, industrial design, web design, and urban design. In the realm of design, as with crafts, the distinction between art for art's sake and art for utility's sake is also sometimes blurred.

CERAMICS

Ceramics refers to the art or process of making objects out of baked clay. Ceramics includes many objects that range from the familiar pots and bowls of **pottery**, to clay sculptures, to building bricks and the extremely hard tiles that protect the surface of the space shuttles from the intense heat of atmospheric reentry.

Methods of Working with Clay

Ceramics is a venerable craft that was highly refined in the ancient lands of the Middle East and in China. For thousands of years, people have modeled, pinched, and patted various types of wet clay into useful vessels and allowed them to dry or bake in the sun, creating hard, durable containers. They have rolled clay into rope shapes, which they coiled around an open space. They have rolled out slabs of clay like dough, cut them into pieces, fastened them together, and smoothed them with simple tools, as Native Americans still do today. They discovered that if they allowed clay vessels to dry, then fired them in a type of oven called a kiln, or over coals, they became waterproof and more durable.

1 ft.

12-3 *The Hands of the Potter.*
Conrad Knowles forming a tray
and a bowl for his collection of
artful pottery.
©2005 Fritz Henle Estate.

Contemporary artist Cheryl Ann Thomas works almost exclusively with one of the oldest techniques in ceramics—coiling. For Thomas, creating the delicate ropes of clay through the rhythmic movements of her hands forges an intimate connection with her material. The individual coils retain their shape identity rather than being smoothed together. They are nestled next to one another and then folded and shaped into trompe l'oeil objects resembling woven cloth (Fig. **12-2**) . Thomas takes advantage of what she calls "the combined variables of climate, clay conditions and human attention/inattention [to yield] endless results."

The Potter's Wheel

The potter's wheel (Fig. **12-3**) was first used in the Middle East in about 4000 BCE and seems to have come into common use a thousand years later. A pot can be **thrown** quite rapidly and effortlessly on a wheel once the techniques have been mastered, in contrast to the more laborious and time-consuming process of building a pot by coiling. In **coiling**, ropes of clay are fashioned, then stacked upon one another. The walls of the pot are then scraped to a smooth finish and molded to the desired vessel shape. The walls of a wheel-thrown pot tend to be thinner and more uniform in thickness than coiled pots, and the outer and inner surfaces are smoother. This does not suggest, however, that coiled pots in the hands of some craftspeople do not approach wheel-thrown pots in their accomplishment. For example, Native Americans of the southwestern United States have never used the potter's wheel, yet their hand-built pots can be as thin walled and symmetrical as their wheel-thrown counterparts.

12-4 LUCY M. LEWIS.
Jar, Acoma Pueblo,
New Mexico (1983).
Earthenware. H: 9½"; W: 12".
National Museum of Women in the Arts, Washington, DC. Gift of Wallace and Wilhema Holladay.

1 in.

A wonderful example of coiling can be found in works by Lucy M. Lewis (Fig. **12-4**). Using techniques traditional among Native American potters, her works often simulate meticulously woven baskets in their surface decoration.

Anyone who has been a student in a ceramics class appreciates the difficulty experienced in mastering the potter's wheel. The body movement, rhythm of the wheel, placement, and force of the fingers must come together like a smoothly choreographed dance. The goal, generally, is to achieve perfect symmetry and a smooth contour. How ironic, then, are the works of James Makins (Fig. **12-5**), which, when seen alone, may look like the failed efforts of "frustrated student, Ceramics 101." These objects—vases? vessels? bottles?—are, in effect, records of variations in mental concentration, hand pressure, wheel speed, and glaze experimentation. Set on trays as they are, they suggest ritual or domestic objects or, to some, figures on a stage. The entire composition—incidentally an exceptional example of variety within unity—appears foremost as a sculpture, probably because these bottles seem far from utilitarian.

Glazing

Variation in color and texture is secured by the choice of clay and by glazing. The earliest-known glaze dates from about 3000 BCE and is found on tile from the tomb of the Egyptian king Menes. **Glazes**, which contain finely ground minerals, are used in liquid form. They are brushed, sprayed, or poured on ceramics after a preliminary **bisque firing** removes all water. During the second firing, the glaze becomes glasslike, or **vitrifies**, fusing with the clay. It gives the clay a glassy, **nonporous** surface coating that can be shiny or dull, depending on its composition. Glazing can create intricate, glossy patterns across otherwise uniform and dull surfaces.

Contrast the simple, pure form of the vase by Chester Nealie (Fig. **12-6**) with the unrefined forms of James Makins. The deep but mellow glaze of the Nealie "bottle" is modulated by light to impart a glowing intensity, in contrast to the opaque and uniform

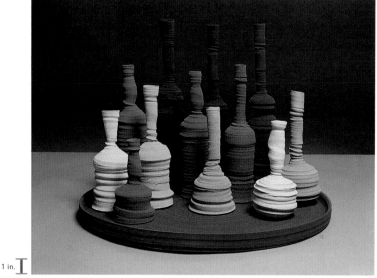

1 in.

12-5 JAMES MAKINS.
Junihitoe (1992).
Porcelain. 14½" × 20" × 20".
Museum Purchase. Everson Museum of Art, Syracuse. NY. 93.24 A-M

Every tool or finger mark, every emotion of making is left in the pot's form and surface to be read as a pathway to creation.

—GUY PETHERBRIDGE, about Chester Nealie's ceramics

glazes of Makins. In both groups, the glazes complement the potters' techniques. The graceful contours of the Nealie vase would lose their sensuality and delicacy with the bold colors and matte finish of the Makins piece. Similarly, the spontaneity, brusqueness, and uniqueness of those lilting bottles would be lost if they were to be enshrouded in a uniform, pearlescent glaze.

Robert Arneson's *Jackson Pollock* (Fig. **12-7**) provides a very different example of a glazed ceramic work and illustrates how blurred the line between craft and fine art can be. Arneson's figures are purposefully unrefined, intentionally

12-7 ROBERT ARNESON.

Jackson Pollock (1983).

Glazed ceramic. 23" × 13" × 7".

Collection of Dr. Paul and Stacy Polydoran.
Courtesy of George Adams Gallery, New York. Art ©Estate of Robert Arneson/
Licensed by VAGA, New York.

1 in.

12-6 CHESTER NEALIE.

Bottle (2000).

Celadon glaze. H: 30 cm.

Courtesy of the artist, Chester Nealie, woodfire potter.

1 in.

flawed, mirroring the ceramic artist's view of human nature as imperfect. The subject of the work, Jackson Pollock, was an Abstract Expressionist who became renowned for his drip paintings (see Chapter 21). Arneson's clay portrait unifies the artist and his works by providing the illusion of overall dripping and splattering on the bust.

Types of Ceramics

Ceramic objects and **wares** are classified according to the type of clay and the temperature at which they are fired.

12-8 Mangbetu Portrait Bottle, Zaire
(19th–20th centuries).
Terra-cotta. H: 11⅜".
The Metropolitan Museum of Art, New York.
The Michael C. Rockefeller Collection.
Bequest of Nelson Rockefeller, 1979. (1979. 206. 246).
Photograph ©1991 The Metropolitan Museum of Art.

1 in.

Earthenware derives its name from the fact that it is usually red or tan in color. It is made from coarse clay or shale clay and is usually fired at 1,000 to 2,000 degrees Fahrenheit. It is somewhat porous and is used for common bricks and coarse pottery. The Mangbetu bottle from Zaire (Fig. **12-8**) is made from terra-cotta, a heavy clay earthenware product fired at a higher temperature of about 2,070 to 2,320 degrees Fahrenheit. The head is an effigy or portrait of a Mangbetu citizen. Note that the textural decoration is reminiscent of a basket weave. It was probably fired in the open, on a bed of straw and twigs.

Stoneware is usually gray but may be tan or reddish. It is fired at about 2,300 to 2,700 degrees Fahrenheit. It is slightly porous or fully nonporous and is used for most dinnerware and much ceramic sculpture.

Claudi Casanovas's *Block #43* (Fig. **12-9**) is a cubic-form ceramic sculpture built around a hollow inner space. The work emphasizes the massive, angular forms inherent in hardened clay; the colors complement the natural earthen materials of the sculpture—black, brown, and beige, even a hint of gold—that we might find in the strata of the planet. The texture and fissures would have it seem that the work has been exposed to harsh elements from without and within. Yet it will endure. Casanovas, a visual artist and poet, wrote about his "blocks":

> Each piece is a silence
> If I were a poet, I would inscribe words there
> To bring us closer to the truth
> Which urges us on from within
> If I were a philosopher, or writer, I would
>   inscribe words so
> That the heart would overflow with knowledge
> And the meaning of clarity
> If I were a monk I would inscribe prayers in
>   which all spirit might find repose
> And glory in the same
> Being Only I am a simple mortal
> Surrounded by simple obscurity
> And unfailing silences
> Each piece is a silence
> That is filled with the sounds of your gaze.[4]

---

4 Translated from the Catalan by Marilyn McCull, in Miguel Jimenez, "Claudi Casanovas' Blocks," *Ceramics: Art and Perception*, no. 49 (2002): 45. Reprinted with permission.

> *Ceramic sculptural works are more specific than traditional sculpture with its expressive force coming from the surface of the body. The surface of the sculpture can be bare clay or clay with oxides and glazes; however, this surface tells us as much about the purpose of the sculpture as does the form itself.*
>
> —TANIA DE BRUKYNER

12-9 CLAUDI CASANOVAS.
Block #43 (2001).
30 cm × 30 cm × 26 cm.
©Claudi Casanovas.
Photo courtesy of Lois Fichner-Rathus.
Photo reproduced by kind permission
of Galerie Besson.

1 in.

Porcelain is hard, nonporous, and usually white or gray in color. It is made from fine, white kaolin clay and contains other minerals such as feldspar, quartz, and flint in various proportions. It is usually fired at 2,400 to 2,500 degrees Fahrenheit, and it is used for fine dinnerware. Chinese porcelain, or **china**, is white and fired at low temperatures. It is glasslike or vitreous and nonporous, and it may be translucent. It makes a characteristic ringing sound when struck with a fingernail. Porcelain has been used by various cultures for vases and dinnerware for thousands of years. Like other kinds of wares, it has also provided a vehicle for artistic expression.

Harumi Nakashima's *Porcelain Form* (Fig. **12-10**) illustrates how the smooth, sophisticated surfaces of fine porcelain stand in contrast to the rough-hewn, rocklike textures

1 ft.

12-10 HARUMI NAKASHIMA.
Porcelain Form (2001).
Porcelain. Inlaid decoration.
50 cm × 45 cm × 40 cm.
European Ceramic Work Centre, The Netherlands.
Photograph by Corné Bastiaansen.

often given center stage in earthenware. Here, the rounded surfaces have a biomorphic or organic quality. The repetition in the polka-dotted glaze complements the rhythms found in the budding protuberances. Whereas the colors of the Casanovas piece connect it with earth and reality, the unnatural blue of Nakashima's dots against the purity of the white surfaces disconnect the work from anything in our tangible experience.

One of the fascinating features of clay is its versatility. Clay can be used to form the refined vessels of Chester Nealie and the crude, slablike structures of both primitive and contemporary workers. It is said that one test of the integrity of a work is its trueness to its material. In the case of ceramics, however, one would be hard pressed to point to any one of the products of clay as representative of its "true" face.

GLASS

Glass, like ceramics, has had a long history and has been used to create fine art and functional objects. The Roman historian Pliny the Elder traced the beginnings of glassmaking (albeit accidental) to an account of Phoenician sailors preparing a meal on a beach. They set their pots on lumps of *natron*—an alkali they had on deck to embalm the dead—lit a fire, and when the hot natron mixed with the sand of the beach, molten glass flowed. In fact, glass predates the Phoenicians and the Romans, and the tale as recounted by Pliny probably has some gaps. But the truth is that the recipe for glass is quite simple; as researchers have found in trying to replay the sailor's experience, it could happen![5] The result may not have been that wondrous substance—transparent or translucent—that has the power to transform light into an ephemeral, jewel-like palette, but it was surely glass.

Techniques of Working Glass

Glass is generally made from molten sand, or **silica**, mixed with minerals such as lead, copper, cobalt, cadmium, lime,

soda, or potash. Certain combinations of minerals afford the glass a rich quality, as found in the stained-glass windows of the great cathedrals and in the more recent stained-glass works of Henri Matisse and Marc Chagall.

As Beethoven created his magnificent final symphony after he became deaf, Henri Matisse achieved something similar in scope in the visual works he created once he became bedridden with a serious illness. Rather than surrender to despair, Matisse found opportunity in disability and experimented with media that permitted him to express himself despite his physical limitations. Whereas he had been primarily known as a painter and sculptor, he turned to pasted paper cutouts, which he had previously used to plan large decorative compositions. Perhaps the incentive for these new works was found after Matisse moved to the Riviera town of Vence, where he was cared for by Dominican nuns while he was ill. To show his appreciation, Matisse designed for them a chapel complete with stained-glass windows, murals, and all the liturgical accoutrements—priests' vestments, an altar, candlesticks, and a crucifix. His stained-glass window, *The Tree of Life* (Fig. **12-11**), consists of twin elongated arches—shapes that are familiar in the tradition of stained glass in religious architecture—alive with what appear to be overlays of falling leaves. The luminosity of the color is such that the viewer is dazzled by the sense of growth and movement. Blues and greens "cool down" the light streaming through the window, whereas the brilliant yellow of the shapely oak leaves reinforces the feeling of warmth, of life.

Like ceramics, glass is versatile. Molten glass can be modeled, pressed, rolled, blown, and even spun into threads. **Fiberglass** is glass that has been spun into fine filaments. It can be woven into yarn for textiles, used in woolly masses for insulation, and pressed and molded into a plastic material that is tough enough to be used for the body of an automobile. About four thousand years ago, the Egyptians modeled small bottles and jars from molten glass. Contemporary machine-made glassware is usually pressed. Molten glass is poured into molds and then forced into shape by a plunger. The plate glass used for windows and mirrors is made by passing rollers over molten glass as it cools.

Just as the potter's wheel transformed the making of clay vessels both in terms of quality and quantity, so did the technique of **glassblowing** change the nature of glass production. This technique was developed by the Romans, who created pieces of all shapes, sizes, colors, and functions,

---

5 William S. Ellis, "Glass: Capturing the Dance of Light," *National Geographic* 184, no. 6 (December 1993): 37–69.

12-11 HENRI MATISSE.

Interior of the Chapel of the Rosary, Vence.

At left: *The Tree of Life*, stained glass.

making glass containers commonplace. In this method, a hollow tube or blowpipe is dipped into molten glass and then removed. Air is blown through the tube, causing the hot glass to form a spherical bubble whose contours are shaped through rolling and pulling with various tools. The process is usually quite rapid, but the glass can be reheated if it must be worked extensively. Once the desired shape has been achieved, the surface of the glass can be decorated by cutting or **engraving** planes that reflect light in certain patterns, by etching, or by printing.

The Chandeliers of Dale Chihuly

*They're going to think we're nuts over there, and of course
we are a little nuts, but we'll get this thing built.*

—DALE CHIHULY, about the Icicle Creek chandelier

12-12 DALE CHIHULY.
Rio delle Torreselle Chandelier (1996), Venice, Italy.
A chandelier installation in the Rio delle Torreselle,
part of the *Chihuly over Venice* project, Venezia Aperto Vetro.
Photo: Russell Johnson, courtesy Chihuly Studio.

"A LITTLE BIT NUTS." Artists, and even the rest of us, may have felt this way or been characterized this way at some point or another, especially when we were seeing things in an unconventional way. Glass artist Dale Chihuly has redefined the conventional definition and function of "chandelier" by designing works he describes by this name for public spaces from Venice to Jerusalem, from the world's great museums to the wilderness of the great outdoors. Although many chandeliers, in the traditional sense, are ornamental, they are also functional objects used, with candles or electricity, to illuminate an environment. But Chihuly's chandeliers are a different species. They do not emit light of their own. Rather, they reflect and transform ambient light—batteries not included.

Chihuly's extraordinary glassworks capture, amplify, and channel light. In their unusual stylistic juxtaposition with their surroundings, his chandeliers compel passersby to take another look at the context in which they are set—whether the Byzantine architecture and canals we find in Venice (Fig. **12-12**), the ancient ruins in Jerusalem, or in the wilderness, the literal natural state of affairs.

Chihuly designed the chandelier shown in Figure **12-13** for the Sleeping Lady mountain retreat at Icicle Creek in the state of Washington. He erected it on an ancient granite boulder among the grand pines of a primeval setting, surrounded by a river and a profusion of wildlife. The chandelier reflects and amplifies the frosted serenity of the site in winter. It enriches visitors' relationships with the area surrounding the retreat and with nature as a whole. The chandelier also adds Chihuly's—and humankind's—personal stamp to

Chihuly is a luminist. He uses glass as a literal and metaphorical prism through which he projects both ambient and intense theatrical light to produce sublime, luminous effects. This connects him to the long history of art in which light is cherished, "otherworldly," and implies divine presence.

—JACK COWART

a pristine wooded site. It also says something about the vision and the passion of the artist—unique in this case to Dale Chihuly, though made visual by a team of glassblowers and technicians. Does the work have deeper symbolic meanings—meanings that connect it with the history of art and civilization, meanings that connect it with contemporary technology and modes of expression? Much of the answer to that question lies in you. Perhaps you would like to consider these lines from Wallace Stevens's poem "Anecdote of the Jar":

I placed a jar in Tennessee,
And round it was, upon a hill.
It made the slovenly wilderness
Surround that hill.
The wilderness rose up to it,
And sprawled around, no longer wild.* ■

_____

* From *The Collected Poems of Wallace Stevens* by Wallace Stevens, © 1945 by Wallace Stevens and renewed 1982 by Holly Stevens. Used by permission of Alfred A. Knopf, a division of Random House, Inc.

12-13 DALE CHIHULY.
Icicle Creek Chandelier (1996).
Photo courtesy of the artist.

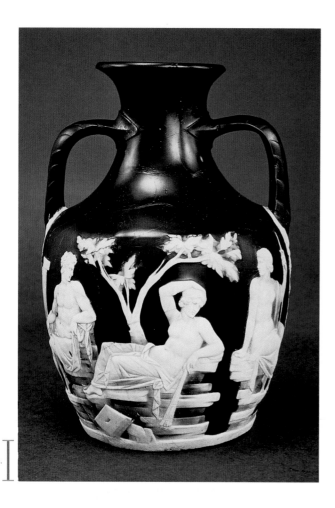

1 in.

12-14 Portland Vase (Roman, 3rd century).
Cameo-cut glass. H 24 cm, Diam. 17.7 cm
©Art Media/Heritage/The Image Works.

One of the earliest and best-known pieces of glass-ware is the Roman Portland Vase (Fig. **12-14**), which survives from the third century CE. The refinement of the piece testifies to the long tradition of glassmaking in Rome even before that time. The Portland Vase was created in three steps: The underlying form was blown from dark blue glass; a coating of semi-opaque white glass was added to the surface of the basic blue form; and the white glass was carved away to provide the bas-relief of figures and vegetation that circumscribe the vase. The relief consists of many subtle gradations. Where it is thinnest, the blue from beneath shows through to provide a shaded quality. Imagine the patience of the cameo cutter who meticulously chipped glass away from glass, leaving unscratched the brittle blue surface that serves as background for the figures. In various eras, different world centers became renowned for glassmaking. For example,

during the Middle Ages, Venetian glass became known for its lightness and delicacy.

Eighteenth-century Stiegel glass, made in Pennsylvania, became known for its use of flint (lead oxide) to achieve hardness and brightness. So-called **flint glass** is used for lenses of optical instruments and for crystal. Nineteenth-century Sandwich glass—from the town of Sandwich, Massachusetts—was pressed into molds to take on the appearance of a cut pattern. Ornamental Sandwich glass pieces in the shapes of cats, dogs, hens, and ducks became common home decorations.

During the second half of the nineteenth century, Louis Comfort Tiffany designed some of the most handsome **Art Nouveau** interiors. His glassware (Fig. **12-15**) attains a similar marriage of simplicity and exotic refinement. Graceful botanical forms swell and become attenuated. The translucent or iridescent glass is decorated by spiral shapes, swirling

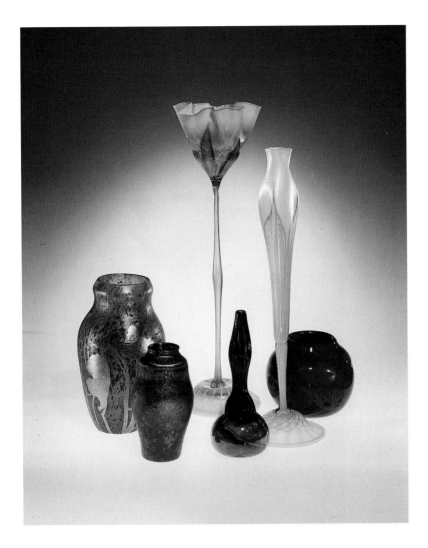

12-15 LOUIS COMFORT TIFFANY. Six pieces of glassware in Art Nouveau style made by the Tiffany Studio. Glass, favrile. Height, left to right: 8⁹⁄₁₆"; 5⅞"; 18¹¹⁄₁₆"; 7⅝"; 16 ¼"; 4½". The Metropolitan Museum of Art, New York (96.17.42; 41.121.9; 51.121.17–.18; 55.213.22; 55.213.28). Photograph copyright 1987 The Metropolitan Museum of Art, New York.

lines, and floating forms that seem to grow naturally out of the glassblowing process. They keep faith with the Art Nouveau creed that decoration should be a natural expression of the manufacturing process. Tiffany also fashioned many fine candlesticks, lamps, and lighting fixtures from bronze that show the same botanical whimsy he expressed in his glassware.

FIBER ARTS

Fibers are slender, threadlike structures that are derived from animals (for example, wool or silk), vegetable (cotton or linen), or synthetic (rayon, nylon, or fiberglass) sources.

The fiber arts refer to several disciplines in which fibers are combined to make functional or decorative objects or works of art. They include, but are not limited to, weaving, embroidery, crochet, and macramé.

Weaving

Weaving was known to the Egyptians, who placed patterned fabrics before the thrones of the pharaohs five thousand years ago. Only royalty could tread on certain fabrics. According to ancient Greek legend, King Agamemnon showed excessive pride by walking upon purple fabrics that were intended for the gods.

1 ft.

12-16 Arbadil carpet, probably Tabriz (1539–1540). Woolen pile. 34" × 17½".

©Victoria and Albert Museum, London/Art Resource, New York.

The **weaving** of fabric or cloth is accomplished by interfacing horizontal and vertical threads. The lengthwise fibers are called the **warp**, and the crosswise threads are called the **weft** or **woof**. The material and type of weave determine the weight and quality of the cloth. Wool, for example, makes soft, resilient cloth that is easy to dye. Nylon is strong, more durable than wool, mothproof, resistant to mildew and mold, nonallergenic, and easy to dye.

There are many types of weaves. The **plain** weave found in burlap, muslin, and cotton broadcloth is the strongest and simplest: the woof thread passes above one warp fiber and beneath the next. In the **satin weave**, woof threads pass above and beneath several warp threads. Warp and woof form broken diagonal patterns in the **twill weave**. In **pile weaving**, which is found in carpeting and in velvet, loops or knots are tied; when the knotting is done, the ends are cut or sheared to create an even surface. In sixteenth-century Persia, where carpet weaving reached an artistic peak, pile patterns often had as many as one thousand knots to the square inch.

The Persian rug shown in Figure **12-16** was woven in the sixteenth century. Like others of its kind, it portrays the old Islamic concept of Paradise as a garden. Here, a light-colored tree and an assortment of other plants grow on a claret red background. The date palm, the iris, a symbolic tree of life, hyacinths, and tulips were frequently depicted on such rugs.

Weaving is typically carried out by the hand **loom** or a power loom. The Alaskan Chilkat robe (Fig. **12-17**), however, was created by Native American weaver Dorica Jackson without a loom. Chilkat women traditionally achieved a very fine texture with a thread made from a core of a strand of cedar bark covered with the wool from a mountain goat. Clan members used robes such as these on important occasions to show off the family crest. Here a strikingly stylized, winged animal occupies the center of a field of eyes, heads, and mysterious symbols.

Traditional weaving techniques may surface in innovative ways in the hands of contemporary artists. Ed Rossbach's wall hanging (Fig. **12-18**), which, in overall shape, is not unlike the Chilkat robe, is worlds apart in its choice of materials and strong political message. Rossbach plaits construction paper in such a manner that his image emerges subtly from an overall mottled background.

The surfaces of fabrics can be enhanced by printing, embroidery, tie-dyeing, or batik. Hand printing has been known since ancient times, and Oriental traders brought the practice to Europe. A design was stamped on a fabric with a carved wooden block that had been inked. Contemporary machine printing uses inked rollers in the place of blocks, and fabrics can be printed at astonishingly rapid rates. In **embroidery**, the design is made by needlework.

Tie-dyeing and batik both involve dyeing fabrics. In **tie-dyeing**, designs are created by sewing or tying folds in the cloth to prevent the dye from coloring certain sections of fabric (Figs. 12-21 and 12-22). In **batik**, applications of wax prevent the dye from coloring sections of fabric that are to

12-17 DORICA JACKSON.
Chilkat robe (1976).
Cedar bark warp; sheep's wool wefts. W: 60".
Courtesy of the U.S. Department of the Interior. National Park Service.
Sitka National Historical Park, Sitka, AK.

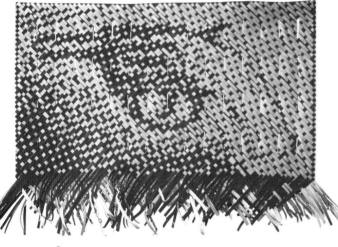

12-18 ED ROSSBACH.
Handgun (1975).
Plaited construction paper. 40" × 54".
The Collection of Craft Alliance.

be kept light or white. A series of dye baths and waxings can be used to create subtly deeper colors.

Basketry

In **basketry**, or basket weaving, fibers are also woven together in various patterns. The delightful Pomo gift basket (Fig. **12-19**) was woven from grass and glass beads. Triangles of warm primary red leap out from

12-19 Ceremonial feathered basket with bead and shell pendants.
Pomo, CA (American Indian, Pomo, 1900). H: 3½".
Phoebe A. Hearst Museum of Anthropology, University of California, Berkeley.

a backdrop of cool primary blue and pale straw. Native Americans from California made extremely fine basketry, with as many as 60 stitches to the inch. Barks, roots, and other fibers supplemented grass, and precious feathers and shells were sometimes used.

METALWORK AND JEWELRY

The refining and working of metals has been known for thousands of years. Iron and its alloys have been used to fashion horseshoes and arrowheads and, more recently, the skeletons of skyscrapers. **Stainless steel** is used in kitchen utensils and furniture. Lightweight aluminum is used in cookware and in aircraft. Bronze is the favorite metal of sculptors. **Brass** is seen everywhere from andirons to candlesticks to beds.

Silver and gold have been prized for millennia for their rarity and their appealing colors and textures. They are used in jewelry, fine tableware, ritual vessels, and sacred objects. In jewelry, these precious metals often serve as settings for equally precious gems or polished stones, or their surfaces can be **enameled** by melting powdered glass on them. These metals even find use as currency; in times of political chaos, gold and silver are sought even as the value of paper money drops off to nothing. Threads of gold and silver find their way onto precious china and into the garments and vestments of clergy and kings. Gold leaf adorns books, paintings, and picture frames.

Metals can be hammered into shape, **embossed** with raised designs, and cast according to procedures described

The Fiber Arts of Faith Ringgold

FAITH RINGGOLD WAS BORN in Harlem in 1930 and educated in the public schools of New York City. Raised with a social conscience, she painted murals and other works inspired by the civil rights movement in the 1960s and, a decade later, took to feminist themes after her exclusion from an all-male exhibition at New York's School of Visual Arts. Ringgold's mother, a fashion designer, was always sewing, the artist recalls, and at this time the artist turned to sewing and related techniques—needlepoint, beading, braided ribbon, and sewn fabric—to produce soft sculptures

1 ft.

such as those in *Mama Jones, Andrew, Barbara, and Faith* (Fig. **12-20**), from her series *The Family of Women*. African garments inspired the clothing of these family members, and the faces are reminiscent of African masks.

More recently, Ringgold is most well known for her narrative quilts, such as the highly acclaimed *Tar Beach* (see Fig. 1-27), which combine traditions common to African Americans and women—storytelling and quilting. *Matisse's Chapel* (Fig. **12-21**) is from Ringgold's *French Collection*, which inserts contemporary American artists, other colleagues, and family members into French settings. In one quilt, *Dancing at the Louvre*, friends, including the children of one, are shown in high spirits before the *Mona Lisa*. In *Picasso's Studio*, the famed Spanish artist (literally) draws inspiration for *Les Demoiselles d'Avignon* from a black model. In an ironic twist on Manet's *Luncheon on the Grass* (see Fig. 19-14), a nude Picasso sits on the grass in the company of clothed women. *Matisse's Chapel* places a wedding party composed of the artist's family in the chapel made famous by dint of Matisse's contributions, including *The Tree of Life* (Fig. 12-11).

Crown Heights Children's Story Quilt (Fig. **12-22**) is on permanent display at a Brooklyn public school. The quilt pictures 12 folktales of peoples who have contributed to the life of New York, including Jamaicans and West Africans (the top three on the left), the Dutch (upper right), two Native American peoples, Asians, Puerto Ricans, Italian Americans, and Jewish Americans. True to the genre of quilting, the artist uses her skills to patch together the myths and stories of different peoples in a nation composed of diverse ethnic groups. ∎

12-20 FAITH RINGGOLD.
Mama Jones, Andrew, Barbara, and Faith (1973).
Embroidery and sewn fabric. 74" × 69".
Copyright ©1973 Faith Ringgold. Artist's collection.

12-21 FAITH RINGGOLD.

Matisse's Chapel (1991).

Acrylic on canvas; tie-dyed, pieced fabric border. 74" × 79½".

From The French Collection series, Part I, #6. Private Collection

Copyright ©1991 Faith Ringgold.

1 ft.

12-22 FAITH RINGGOLD.

Crown Heights Children's Story Quilt (1994).

Painted and pieced fabric. 108" × 144".

Copyright ©1994 Faith Ringgold/ The New York City Board of Education PS90, Brooklyn, NY

1 ft.

12-23 Pectoral piece from Ordzhonikidze, Russia (4th century BCE).
Gold. D: 12".

Historical Museum, Kiev.
©Roman Beniaminson/Art Resource, NY

for bronze in Chapter 9. Each form of working metal has its own tradition and its advantages and disadvantages.

Ancient Greek goldsmiths wrought some of the finest gold jewelry. The pectoral piece shown in Figure **12-23** was meant to be worn across the breast of some nomadic chieftain from southern Russia and probably buried with him. Fortunately, it was not. People and animals are depicted with a realism that renders the fanciful **griffins** in the lower register as believable as the horses, dogs, and grasshoppers found elsewhere in the piece. The figures are balanced by the refined scrollwork in the central register, and all are contained by the magnificent coils.

The Renaissance sculptor and goldsmith Benvenuto Cellini created a gold and enamel saltcellar (Fig. **12-24**) for the French king Francis I that shows the refinement of his art. Its allegorical significance is merely an excuse for displaying the skill of Cellini's craft. Salt, drawn from the sea, is housed in a boat-shaped salt container and watched over by a figure of Neptune. The pepper, drawn from the earth, is contained in a miniature triumphal arch and guarded by a female personification of Earth. Figures on the base represent the seasons and the segments of the day—all on a piece 13 inches long. Unfortunately, the saltcellar is Cellini's sole major work in gold that survives.

12-24 BENVENUTO CELLINI.
Saltcellar of Francis I (1539–1543).
Gold and enamel. H: 10⅛"; L: 13¹/₁₆".

Kunsthistorisches Museum, Vienna.
©Erich Lessing/Art Resource, NY

12-25 Nose ornament, crayfish, Peru (Loma Negra, 3rd century CE).
Gold, silver, turquoise inlay. H: 4¾".
The Metropolitan Museum of Art, New York. The Michael C. Rockefeller Memorial Collection. Bequest of Nelson A. Rockefeller, 1979 (1979.206.1236). Photograph ©1998, The Metropolitan Museum of Art, New York.

12-26 KIFF SLEMMONS.
Transport (1990).
Sterling silver, aluminum, gauze, mesh, tape, tubing, pearls. 5" × 14" × 4½".
Courtesy of the artist. Photo by Rod Slemmons.

Kiff Slemmons's *Transport* (Fig. **12-26**) is a miniature sculpture that again bridges the supposed gulf between fine art and the functional object. It was constructed for the *Artworks for AIDS* exhibition that was held in Seattle in 1990. It is a miniature two-wheeled cart that refers to the history of mass deaths. Throughout the ages, such carts have been used in cities to truck away the victims of epidemics. The wheels of the cart are clocks with human hands, seeming to tick away as the number of deaths due to AIDS mounts. Hospital waste and a stylized "progress" chart with an alarming indicator of the rising toll of the epidemic complete the political message.

WOOD

Some relatively sophisticated technology is required to convert glass, metal, and clay into something of use. Wood, however, has only to be cut and carved to form a functional object. Two wood vases hint at the versatility of the medium. The soft, flowing contours of Melvyn Firmager's vase (Fig. **12-27**) highlight the swirling grain

Body ornament, ever growing in popularity to this day, spans history and geography. Consider the nose ornament from Peru in Figure **12-25**. The piece is fashioned of gold, silver, and turquoise inlay and is a characteristic example of the ancient Peruvian facility in handling complex metal techniques. Much of the jewelry available for us to see today has been unearthed from tombs of the very wealthy among Peruvian society. The images and their symbolism remain mostly undeciphered, but archeologists have nonetheless constructed a view of these people from such artifacts.

12-27 MELVYN FIRMAGER.
Untitled (1993).
Destroyed in 1994 Los Angeles earthquake.
Eucalyptus gunnii.
H: 13½"; D: 8".
Photo David Peters, courtesy of Del Mano Gallery, Los Angeles.

1 in.

12-28 DAVID ELLSWORTH.
Vessel (1992).
Norway maple burl. H: 4", D: 7".
Courtesy of the artist.

Industrial Design: The Object

Objects are three-dimensional products designed for consumer use by industrial designers, also known as product designers. They run the gamut from utilitarian designs (form follows function) to those in which aesthetics override usability (form over function). There are good and bad designs, and then there are objects for which the question "Good or bad?" seems moot. Consider the common houseware item—the citrus juicer—in Figures **12-29** to **12-31**. The first juicer seems to have been designed foremost with utility in mind. The user halves an orange, inverts it onto a conical plastic piece that has pronounced ribs or ridges,

patterns of the wood, which almost take on the character of glazing on a ceramic vase. The simple roundness, highly polished surface, and inherent grain patterns in David Ellsworth's vase (Fig. **12-28**) create the illusion of stone.

DESIGN

Design has a multiplicity of meanings. As a discipline or profession, it includes experts in industrial design (objects), fashion design (clothing), graphic design (communication), and web design (the Internet), to name a few. As a process, it involves the act of designing or creating a concept and product for consumption, communication, or interaction. We refer to the finished product as a design.

12-29 *Citrus Express.*
©Teubner/Getty Images

and twists it one way or another to release the juice from the orange. The juice flows down the cone between the ridges and into a plastic collection bowl in a quick and tidy fashion. The second juicer is also based on a thoughtful concept. The user presses the orange half onto a ridged cone, twists it back and forth, and the juice is collected in a flat bowl with a spout on one end for pouring. A row of plastic teeth is placed forward of the spout to hold back seeds and unwanted pulp. The only problem is that these teeth are placed exactly where the user's knuckles hit when twisting the orange to extract the juice—a great design in theory, but certainly not in practice. Now take a look at famed French designer Philippe Starck's citrus squeezer entitled *Juicy Salif*, purportedly conceived during a meal in which he was squeezing lemon over a squid. A clear example of "form over function," Starck's juicer has become an icon of 1990s

12-31 PHILIPPE STARCK.
Juicy Salif.
©2008 Photolibrary.com

12-30 *Juicer.*
©Foodcollection.com/Alamy

design, not because it works well, but because it looks great. In fact, *Juicy Salif*'s manufacturer, Alessi, recommends it for display and not for use.

Although few of us looking for a juicer would actually opt for Starck's product, consumers often make choices based as much on product design and cache as usability. Apple's iPod is a case in point. While there are many MP3 players on the market, a fair number of them more economically priced than the iPod, sales of the Apple product have swept the globe. In choosing an iPod MP3 player, the consumer is not only buying a product but also buying into a lifestyle.

Form and Function in Product Design

A great deal of contemporary product design embraces the philosophy of "form follows function" put forth by the architect Louis Sullivan, whose Wainwright Building we studied in Chapter 11 (see Fig. 11-13). Three of a multitude of examples come from the design collection of the Museum of Modern Art. Rody Graumans' *85 Lamps Lighting Fixture* (Fig. **12-32**) is an unadulterated cluster of naked lightbulbs and wiring that fans out into a more classic chandelier profile as a result of the spherical shapes of the touching bulbs. The "truth in art" that Sullivan sought through his philosophy seems also to have inspired Graumans' lighting fixture design: the whole truth and nothing but the truth, in fact.

The tiny *Moscardino Sporks* (Fig. **12-33**) by the Italian designers Guilio Iachetti and Matteo Ragni turn a common plastic utensil—the spoon-fork—into a well-designed, eco-friendly staple of picnics and meals on the go. Made of biodegradable corn-based plastic, the 3 1/2-inch-long sporks feature a bowl-shaped spoon on one end and a three-pronged fork on the other, and nest securely in sets of twenty-five. This is design at its most basic and most utilitarian, a form created with function foremost in mind.

Many objects of contemporary industrial design take **ergonomics**—the applied science of equipment design intended to minimize discomfort and therefore maximize performance of the user—into account. If your shoulders,

1 ft.

12-32 RODY GRAUMANS.

85 Lamps Lighting Fixture (1992).
Light bulbs, cords, and sockets. H: 39⅜" (100 cm); D: 39⅜" (100 cm).
Digital Image ©The Museum of Modern Art/Licensed by SCALA/Art Resource, NY.

12-33 GUILIOLACHETTI AND MATTEO RAGNI.

Moscardino Sporks.
Digital Image ©The Museum of Modern Art/
Licensed by SCALA/Art Resource, NY

12-35 Apple iPod Billboard.
©Richard Levine/Alamy.

neck, elbows, or wrists hurt from the physical stress of prolonged work at your computer, you can purchase an ergonomically designed keyboard that will keep your wrists at a proper angle and a mouse that will support the weight of your arm while mousing. These designs are based on the physiognomy of the human body and typical product use.

The *Aeron Chair* (Fig. **12-34**), ergonomically designed by Bill Stumpf and Don Chadwick, has emerged as the Porsche of office chairs and is also part of the design collection at the Museum of Modern Art. The metal-frame and mesh seat and back fully adjust to accommodate bodies of any shape, height, and weight. A tilt mechanism in the chair "floats" users with support no matter which position they are sitting in, and the mesh suspension system distributes weight equally. The quirky appearance of the Aeron Chair, a by-product of its adherence to ergonomic design, has achieved a sort of cult-status among trendy office workers. One television commercial advertisement even shows 20-something-year-olds playing office hockey while cruising in their Aeron Chairs.

The success of many product designs is linked to successful advertising campaigns. Returning to the iPod, we see one of today's most visually exciting, culturally attuned, and lucrative ad campaigns. From packaging and posters (Fig. **12-35**) to its distinctive logo—all part of its graphic design program—all of the elements interface with and enhance one another.

Graphic Design: Communication

Graphic design is an artistic process used to communicate information and ideas through writing, images, and symbols that are connected to contemporary human experience. Since the beginning of modern history, advances in technology—beginning with the printing press in the early 1400s—have enabled the global dissemination of graphic design products. Components of the graphic design include typography, page layout and book design, and corporate identity. Graphic design mediums include photography, printmaking, computer-aided design, and digital design. The history of graphic design can be traced back to marks made by humans on the walls of caves and the earliest forms of writing. In this section, we will consider contemporary examples of graphic design as it is the most ubiquitous of art forms, entering our consciousness and our lives in a steady stream on a daily basis.

Typography

Typography is the technical term for designing and composing letterforms. Until the digital age, printing was done with moveable pieces of metal (or wood) cast or carved with letters that are raised above the surface of the piece. These pieces were put together into strings of words and lines by typesetters. Today typesetting is done on computers, as is type design. Designers can choose from hundreds of typefaces and can manipulate things like scale, color, perspective, and the overlapping of letters and other images. A designer will use type to communicate with optimal clarity—a variant of form follows function—or with expressiveness. It is an eye-opener to realize that any and all type that we come into contact with as consumers originated with a graphic designer who was skilled in typography.

The clearest, most utilitarian form of typography is probably the pictogram, which is widely used in signage. From the simplified shapes of a woman in a dress and man in trousers, we can figure out which restroom is intended for whom, even if we find ourselves in a foreign country where we don't speak the language (Fig. **12-36**). So-called barrier-free communication is also seen in the now-familiar graphic design of a red circle with a line drawn through it signifying "NO!"—whatever *no* may apply to. The pictogram in Figure **12-37** consists of simple, easily understood symbols designating areas in which smoking is forbidden.

12-36 Signage for women's and men's restrooms.
©graficart.net/Alamy

12-37 Signage for nonsmoking and smoking areas.
AP Images/Fabian Bimmer

12-38 PAULA SCHER.

"Great Beginnings" spread for Koppel & Scher promotional booklet (1984).

Courtesy of Pentagram Design

Layout

A **layout** is a way of organizing the design elements in a printed work such as a poster, book, or magazine. Layouts typically consist of visual elements, including type and pictures, which may be drawings and photographs. The layout of children's books may also contain buttons to press, a variety of textures to feel, and speakers that make sounds.

The design of this book generally includes two columns of text which are "flush left" (vertically aligned on the left) and "ragged right" (ending in different lengths on the right side). Photographs and drawings are interspersed throughout in various locations in an effort to provide aesthetic appeal and to have works of art displayed on the same page on which they are discussed. "Running feet" display the page numbers, the chapter numbers, the names of the chapters (on the left) and the names of the sections (on the right). Major and minor heads are distinguished both by color and size. Boxed features, such as "A Closer Look" and "Compare + Contrast," are placed on what are called *screens* or *tint panels* to help set them apart from the main text. You are not expected to be thinking about all this as you read, but the layout is intended to be stimulating yet refined, to complement the subject matter, and to assist the reader in navigating the material.

Figure **12-38** shows the layout for a spread for a promotional booklet, "Great Beginnings," by Paula Scher. Because of a tight budget, she limited her palette to three colors:

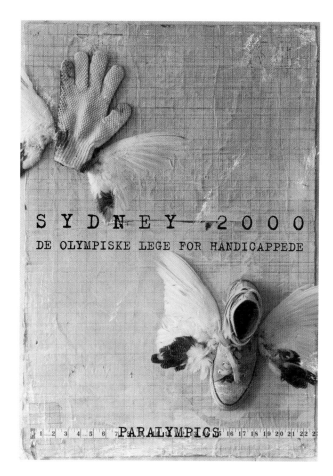

12-39 GITTE KATH.

Poster for the *Sydney 2000 Paralympics*.

Courtesy of the artist

there is only the suggestion of loss and caring. The colors are muted, the positioning of the objects and the graphics are balanced, and the allover grid and decay provide unity.

Henri de Toulouse-Lautrec, a late nineteenth-century French artist, is seen by some as the father of the color lithograph poster. Toulouse-Lautrec dwelled in nighttime Paris—its cafés, music halls, nightclubs, and brothels. The posters that he designed for concerts and other performances are among the most well known in the history of art. His designs (Fig. **12-40**) are successful because they capture, in a single image, the spirit and personality of the establishment and the performer. Areas of unmodulated color and high-contrast values in the poster design evoke theater lighting and costuming. The lyrical shapes

black, red, and a putty color. She turned to rarely used typefaces and to features of Art Deco and Russian Constructivism (see Chapters 19 and 20) three to four generations after their passing. Put more simply, her typefaces went from thick to thin, her colors like her subject alternated, she worked her key letters and numbers like columns, and her horizontal lines of text ramped uphill then down, but always left to right, requiring dizzying backward leaps. Even the red and the black work like shocking figures against the calming putty-colored background. The layout is all "metamorphosis," or change, as is the title of the work.

Gitte Kath's poster for the Sydney Paralympics (Fig. **12-39**) required her to collect materials such as the athletic shoe, glove, and feathers, post them on a worn, discolored wall in her home, paint and photograph them, then apply the graphics. The condition of the elements in the poster suggest the poignancy of the transitory nature of living things. There is nothing heroic about this poster;

12-40 HENRI DE TOULOUSE-LAUTREC.

Le Divan Japonais (1892).

Color lithograph. 31⅝" × 23⅞".

Musée Toulouse-Lautrec, Albi, France.
©Erich Lessing/Art Resource, NY.

and undulating lines, coupled with an oblique perspective and bold patterns influenced by Japanese prints, combine to catch the eye and draw the patron to the party.

Logos

A **logo** is an emblematic design used to identify and advertise a company or an organization. The most successful corporate identity designs are ones that will spring to mind immediately when you think of the entities they represent. The next time you are watching MTV (Fig. **12-41**), note the persistent logo in the corner of your screen. It is instantly recognizable. It also has its animated counterpart in a video version you see on TV. MTV's "M" pulsates and changes contours and colors. The logo for the Internet search engine Google (Fig. **12-42**) features broadly spaced letters of intense—mostly primary—colors. The simplicity of the design and the straightforwardness of the color scheme suggest an ease of use (even a child can do it) that the company would want to promote.

Logos are well conceived and deliberately designed symbols that are decided upon after much consideration and market research. When former Vice President and Nobel Prize recipient Al Gore sought to promote his nonprofit advocacy group for the prevention of global warming (Alliance for Climate Protection), he hired a well-known advertising firm to design an ad campaign, including a logo. The result was a simple green circle inscribed with white letters

12-42 The Google Logo.
http://www.google.com
Google Logo ©Google Inc. 2008, Reprinted with Permission.

12-43 Alliance for Climate Protection Logo.
Courtesy Alliance for Climate Protection

forming the word "we" (Fig. **12-43**). Answering questions about the concept, lead designer Brian Collins explained that the bright green color best expresses the idea of "green"—a word used to describe efforts to conserve and restore energy and the planet's environment and resources. The color is symbolic, but also uplifting and optimistic. The typeface used for the word "we," turned upside down, reads "me" backwards, and was created by typographer Chester Jenkins specifically for the Gore alliance's logo. The we-me inversion is intended to signify human cooperation to achieve a solution to the climate crisis. Finally, according to Collins, the circular shape of the logo symbolizes the Earth and draws attention to the fact that the climate crisis affects all of its inhabitants.

Web Design

Websites are an inextricable part of the information superhighway. Any of us cyberspace surfers can go online, access the website of a popular consumer magazine, and get the latest reviews on the new car we're drooling over. We can research without books, order books, book reservations, bid on a special

12-41 MTV Logo.
© Jane Butchofsky-Houser/Corbis.

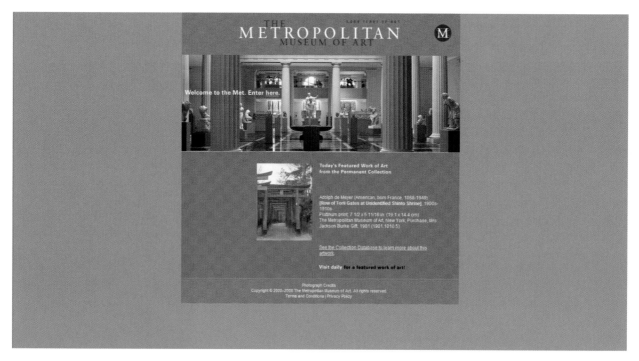

12-44 Website: Home page of the Metropolitan Museum of Art.
www.metmuseum.org. ©The Metropolitan Museum of Art.

reserve wine. And a big part of what keeps us attached to our PC's mouse at the end of an electronic umbilical cord is the visual feedback we get when we click. The better the design of the website, the more tantalizing the product or service—a clear fact not lost on the thousands upon thousands of businesses, organizations, agencies, and individuals for whom the website is the new face and first face to the consumer in the age of electronics.

We can think of web design as having two key tasks. One is technical and involves programming—how users click their way around a web page, how hot links to other pages and sites are established, and how to insert still images or animated clips and sound. The other task is an aesthetic one, encompassing art and design.

Art museums are among the untold numbers of organizations that can be accessed through websites. The home page of the website of the Metropolitan Museum of Art (Fig. **12-44**) (www.metmuseum.org) includes a photograph of the new Greek and Roman galleries. The website informs you of current exhibitions, allows you to view many of the

works in the collection, and includes links to pedagogical tools such as an invaluable timeline of art history. The more mundane but essential information about museum hours and current exhibits is reliably posted, but the functionality of the web design almost pales in comparison to its ability to transport virtual visitors to one of the world's great cultural centers from the comfort of their ergonomically designed computer chairs.

You can visit ArtMuseum.net (www.artmuseum.net) to view art exhibitions from various participating museums online. When you take your virtual tour of one of these sites, clicking on a "thumbnail" illustration of a work in the collection might enlarge it or display descriptive text. Some websites let you walk through a building or another environment and look in various directions as you do—something like "Super Mario Brothers Visit the Art Institute of Chicago," without the punching, flying, or shooting.

As you surf the web, you have no doubt been struck by the endless variety, quality, and quantity of web design—from sophisticated to tacky, from "high art" to "low art."

I, like you, come across interesting websites almost every day, so it was hard to settle for just one or two to highlight in this chapter among the wealth of riches and rags. Some current faves include the website for the Alvin Ailey American Dance Theater in New York City (known for its brilliant, mind-and-body-stretching choreography) (Fig. **12-45**). This and other websites feature hot spots that the user can click on to navigate the site for related web pages and information.

Web design is a big business, and many graphic designers set up shop in this realm. Students can now take web design in their college courses, whereas the rest of us can learn about it in how-to books such as *Web Design for Dummies*. Many individuals, like organizations, have websites on which they include text and uploaded photos and video clips. They serve as anything from electronic business cards

to ways for families to keep in touch. Cyberspace collapses the distance that separates us from the important people in our lives.

Fashion Design

It has become routine for me to enter a classroom on any given day to overhear a play-by-play analysis of a previous night's episode of the Bravo network's *Project Runway*. A reality TV program that pits established and up-and-coming fashion designers against one another in a series of challenges leading to a single winner, *Project Runway* has engendered a near cultlike following. So wide-ranging and popular is its appeal that, in the wake of an early 2008 season of the show, *Saturday Night Live* writers created a skit around

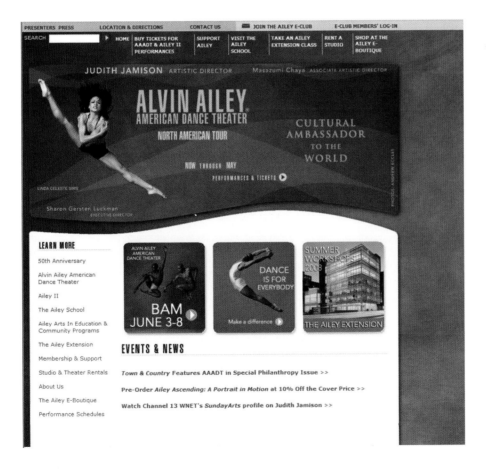

12-45 Website: Alvin Ailey American Dance Theater.
Courtesy of Alvin Ailey American Dance Theater.

the winning designer Christian Siriano (Fig. **12-46**), who, along with his skinny jeans and signature hair-sprayed coif, brought the words "fierce" and "hot mess" into contemporary parlance. *Project Runway* has raised the consciousness of the realities of the world of fashion design from initial design sketches through the construction of a garment to a completed piece. It has also introduced terms like *haute couture, ready-to-wear*, and *mass-market apparel*.

Haute couture is the French term for "high fashion." Haute couture designs are technically made-to-measure for individual customers from expensive materials combined with meticulous stitching, detail work, and finishing. Runway shows feature many haute couture designs that are impressive for their innovation and aesthetics as artforms (Fig. **12-47**).

On the opposite end of the spectrum from haute couture is mass-market apparel, designed for ordinary consumers to be more universal in style and more affordable in price. Fabrics are generally of a lesser grade in terms of quality, and detailed hand-stitching is replaced by machine work that both expedites the execution and thus makes large quantities of an item possible. Designs for mass-market fashion often follow in the footsteps of couture designs, and it is not uncommon to find high-end designers creating product lines that are more accessible to department store shoppers. Ready-to-wear is a fashion category that straddles haute couture and mass-market fashion. Fabrics used for ready-to-wear are of high quality, and the workmanship is careful and often complex. Because apparel is created in smaller quantities, price tags are high. Ready-to-wear lines of the couture industry appear in major European and American cities during Fashion Week runway exhibits.

Fashion design has always reflected the culture and society of its time as much as it has contributed toward contemporary taste. And fashion has been inspired by history

12-46 Christian Siriano, left, stands with a model on the runway during the Christian Siriano Fall 2008 Collection, part of Bravo Network's *Project Runway* final show during Mercedes-Benz Fall 2008 Fashion Week, in New York.

AP Images/Jennifer Graylock

12-47 Haute couture design, Christian Dior, Autumn/Winter 2007–2008.

©The Daily Telegraph/Stephen Lock

12-48 *Himation. Eirene, Daughter of Zeus and Themis.*
Roman copy of a Greek original of the 4th century B.C.

12-49 J MENDEL 2007.
Runway-MBFW Spring 08
NEW YORK UNITED STATES-SEPTEMBER 07: UK (OUT)
A model walks the runway during the J Mendel Spring 2008 Fashion Show at The Promenade in Bryant Park during the Mercedes-Benz Fashion Week Spring 2008 on September 7, 2007 in New York City.

as much as it has anticipated the look of the future. One particular style that has been characterized by a remarkable longevity is one inspired by ancient Greece. The *chiton* (a loose-fitting gown pinned at the shoulders), *himation* (a mantle that was draped over one shoulder and sometimes wrapped around the body; see Fig. **12-48**), and *peplos* (a gown pinned at the shoulders and cinched at the waist, see Fig. 14-8) have been mimicked and interpreted by costume and fashion designers stretching back to the Napoleonic era in France forward to today (Fig. **12-49**).

On the opposite end of the chronological and fashion spectrum, consider the "Hyper Space Couture Design Contest" held in Tokyo in 2006. Participating designers focused on a couture line of personal fashions for space travel and habitation (Fig. **12-50**).

12-50 A model wears futuristic makeup and clothing at the Hyper Space Couture Design Contest held at Tokyo University November 2, 2006.

Urban Design

Perhaps it is in urban design that our desire for order and harmony achieves its most majestic expression. Throughout history, most towns and cities have more or less sprung up. They have pushed back the countryside in all directions, as necessary, with little evidence of an overall guiding concept. As a result, the masses of great buildings sometimes press against other masses of great buildings, and transportation becomes a worrisome afterthought. The Rome of the early Republic, for example, was an impoverished seat of empire, little more than a disordered assemblage of seven villages on seven hills. Later, the downtown area was a jumble of narrow streets winding through mud-brick buildings. Not until the first century BCE were the major building programs undertaken by Sulla and then the Caesars.

The new towns of the Roman Empire were laid out largely on a rectangular grid. This pattern was common among centrist states, where bits of land were parceled out to the subjects of mighty rulers. The gridiron was also found to be a useful basis for design throughout history—from the ancient Greeks to the colonial Americans. Many cities of the Near and Middle East, such as Baghdad, have a circular tradition in urban design, which may reflect the belief that they were the hubs of the universe. The throne room of the palace in eighth-century Baghdad was at the center of the circle. The palace—including attendant buildings, a game preserve, and pavilions set in perfumed gardens—was more than a mile in diameter, and the remainder of the population occupied a relatively narrow ring around the palace.

Washington, D.C.

Few urban designs are as simple and rich as Pierre-Charles L'Enfant's plan for Washington, D.C. (Fig. **12-51**). The city is cradled between two branches of the Potomac River, yielding an uneven, overall diamond shape. Within the diamond, a rectangular grid of streets that run east-west and north-south was laid down. Near the center of the diamond, with its west edge at the river, an enormous Mall or green space was set aside. At the east end of the Mall is the Capitol Building. To the north, at its west end, is the president's house (which is now the White House). Broad boulevards radiate from the Capitol and from the White House, cutting across the gridiron. One radiating

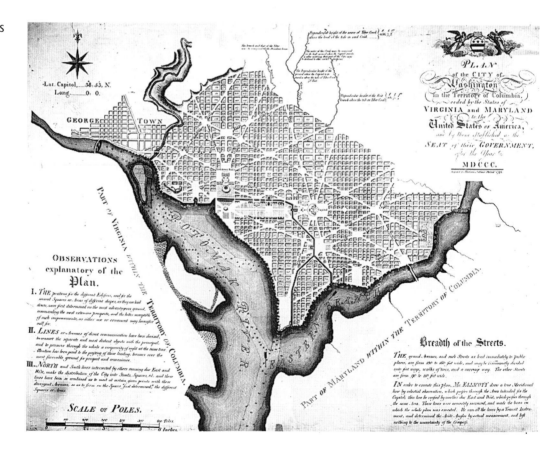

12-51 PIERRE-CHARLES L'ENFANT.
Plan for Washington, D.C. (1792).
Courtesy of the National Archives.

12-52 REM KOOLHAAS.
Design for Les Halles, Paris (2005).
Rem Koolhaas/OMA/photograph by Hans Werlemann.

boulevard runs directly between the Capitol and the White House, and other boulevards parallel it.

The design is a composition in which the masses of the Capitol Building and White House balance one another, and the rhythms of the gridiron pattern and intersecting diagonal boulevards create contrast and unity. The Mall provides an open central gathering place that is as much a part of American culture as it is respite from the congestion of the city. We see more of Washington, D.C. in the Art Tour at the end of the chapter.

Paris—Les Halles

L'Enfant's plan for Washington, D.C., was inspired by the art and architecture of Neoclassical France. Today, a visitor to both cities will note that avenues and grand boulevards culminate in monuments that punctuate the end of a long vista. Paris is often called the most beautiful city in the world, a title achieved after massive renovations to the city plan by Raoul Haussmann in the nineteenth century.

Then, as now, Paris was not without its pockets of urban problems requiring creative and politically sensitive solutions. The Parisian area of Les Halles has long been home to park and commercial spaces as well as a major transit hub. Architect Rem Koolhaas and his firm, OMA, submitted a design to bring together and make transparent to the surrounding neighborhood all the disparate parts of Les Halles (Fig. **12-52**). Shape and color dominate the plan, with circular gardens and luminous towers rising above the city's infrastructure. With this design, the dark, discontinuous, and chaotic environs of the old Les Halles would have been transformed through an innovative and practical urban design, into a signature city monument as innovative as the new glass pyramid in the courtyard of the Louvre. But like Daniel Liebeskind's design to replace the twin towers of the World Trade Center (see Chapter 11), which was actually "accepted" as winning the design competition to replace the towers, Koolhaas's design is also apparently destined to remain within the imagination of the architect.

On July 14, 1789, in what became the defining symbolic moment of the French Revolution, the Bastille prison was stormed by revolutionaries who freed a grand total of seven prisoners. Four years later, with the founding of a new Republic, the doors of the Louvre Museum (containing about 200 works that had belonged to the king) opened to the public.

The point to this story lies in its contrast with the next: In 1936, Andrew Mellon (an American statesman and financier) gave his art collection to the United States of America and built the National Gallery of Art in Washington, D.C., to house it. In subsequent years, other collectors followed suit until the "nation's collection" outgrew its space. Unlike many of the world's great art museums, such as the Louvre, the museums you will see in Washington, D.C., did not begin as private royal collections made accessible to the public only after revolution and democratization. The core of Washington's holdings came from entrepreneurs who willingly, even affectionately, gave their art to their fellow citizens. Much of what you will see in Washington, D.C., is yours by virtue of your U.S. citizenship. And seeing just about all of it costs you nothing.

Union Station.
©Bettman/CORBIS

If you're coming to Washington by train, come hungry. You will arrive, most likely, at Union Station—a fine example of the Beaux Arts architectural style. From the three main archways that define the entry (based on the Arch of Constantine in Rome!) to the magnificent gilded barrel-vaulted ceiling, Union Station is not simply a transit center to move through—linger and look. It opened in 1907, and for more than 50 years, this station was the largest in the world. After careful and costly restoration in 1988, this is now the second most visited site in Washington, D.C.

Union Station is home to one of the most fantastic food courts you will ever come upon, with selections to entice every palate. Take a spin around the stalls before you commit to that Maryland crab-cake sandwich.

Union Station is a well-situated starting point for your art tour of the capital. From there, a short stroll along Delaware or Louisiana Avenue will bring you to the U.S. Capitol and the Mall, the site of many museums and memorials. Here you will experience the *feeling* of the nation's capital—its Classical architecture (inspired, as was the new democratic government, by Greek and Roman ideals), expanses of tree-lined grassy lawn, reflecting pools, and marble and granite monuments. The Capitol Building (see Fig. 3-10) is at the "top"—or eastern end—of the Mall and has much to offer to the art seeker. The dome, designed by Thomas U. Walter, is one of the largest in the world. The rotunda (the large, circular space in the interior beneath the dome) contains many paintings and sculptures and is capped by Constantino Brumidi's mural depicting the *Apotheosis of Washington* (bring your binoculars and your sense of humor).

Outside the Capitol, the Mall is arrayed before the visitor, offering a perspective toward the Washington Monument on the west end and all that lies between. The Mall was designed by the French architect Pierre L'Enfant, who imported many of his elements of city planning (grand boulevards, elegant residences, well-situated monuments) from Paris. The first museum on your tour is the National Gallery of Art. The collection is

Entrance lobby of the National Gallery of Art, Washington, D.C., with sculpture of children holding hands.
© Bernard Annebicque/Corbis Sygma.

divided between two buildings—East and West. The West (Neoclassical) Building is the earlier museum—the one financed by Andrew Mellon and designed by John Russell Pope. Here the visitor will find Western art spanning the thirteenth through the nineteenth centuries, featuring stellar examples of works by such artists as Giotto, Botticelli, Leonardo da Vinci, Raphael (*The Alba Madonna*), Rembrandt, Rubens (*Daniel in the Lion's Den*), El Greco, Monet (*Woman with a Parasol—Mme Monet and Her Son*), Cassatt, Cézanne, Toulouse-Lautrec (*Quadrille at the Moulin Rouge*), Homer (*Breezing Up*), and Whistler (*Symphony in White, No. 1: The White Girl*), among many, many others of fame and note. And that's just the west wing. The entire East Building, designed by I. M. Pei and one of the few Modernist works of architecture in the city, houses the country's collection of twentieth-century art. A dramatic, soaring atrium, featuring an enormous mobile by Alexander Calder (see Fig. 2-70) and works by Henry Moore, Joan Miró, and Andrew Goldsworthy, is flanked by balconies and galleries in which one will find works from the permanent collection as well as traveling exhibitions. Both museums (connected underground) have wonderful restaurants and bookshops.

One of the highlights of the Mall is the Sculpture Garden of the National Gallery of Art, poised between the West Building and the National Museum of Natural History. Works of modern sculpture pepper the sections of lawn surrounding a refreshing fountain in summer and delightful skating rink in winter. Viewers can walk among and around pieces by Claes Oldenberg, Roy Lichtenstein, Louise Bourgeois, Joan Miró, and others. And from these fun-filled, art-filled surroundings, one can cross over a broad expanse of lawn to another collection of outdoor sculpture belonging to the Hirshhorn Museum, a private-turned-public collection displayed in a cylindrical building affectionately referred to as "the doughnut." Rodin's *The Burghers of Calais* (see Fig. 19-38) finds itself in equally prestigious company in this collection.

The Mall contains a staggering number of museums, galleries, and monuments. The old Smithsonian Castle, the building that once housed works that are now found in other sites along the Mall (don't miss wandering through its splendid gardens); the spectacular National Air and Space Museum; such small jewels as the Arthur M. Sackler Gallery of Asian Art, the National Museum of African Art, and the United States Holocaust Memorial Museum just beyond the Washington Monument merely scratch the surface of what one might discover on an art tour of the capital. And to these we must add artistic memorials such as the Vietnam Veterans Memorial, the Korean War Veterans Memorial, and the Franklin D. Roosevelt Memorial, all of which have altered the very concept of meaningful memorials for Washington, D.C., and the country.

MAYA YING LIN.
Vietnam Veterans Memorial. Names and Reflections on the Wall.

For many students in the United States, "the family trip to Washington" was viewed as essential to child rearing. For others, "the school trip to Washington" was the first independent trip away from home—traveling on a rowdy bus with one's peers to take in the sights and watch history come alive. Memories of these experiences traverse generations. We have always understood the importance of symbols to American history. Our own art tours of the nation's capital enable us to understand the importance of art to American people.

Smithsonian Castle.

 To continue your tour and learn more about Washington, D.C., go to ArtExperience Online.

THE ART OF THE ANCIENTS

*Art is exalted above religion and race. Not a single solitary soul these days believes
in the religion of the Assyrians, the Egyptians, or the Greeks. . . . Only their art,
whenever it was beautiful, stands proud and exalted, rising above all time.*
—Emil Nolde

The phrase "Stone Age" often conjures an image of men and women dressed
in skins, huddling before a fire in a cave, while the world around them—
the elements and the animals—threatens their survival. We do not generally
envision prehistoric humankind as intelligent and reflective, as having needs
beyond food, shelter, and reproduction, as performing religious rituals. or as
creating art objects. Yet these aspects of life were perhaps as essential to their
survival as warmth, nourishment, and progeny.

As the Stone Age progressed from the Paleolithic to the Neolithic periods,
humans began to lead more stable lives. They settled in villages and shifted
from hunting wild animals and gathering food to herding domesticated animals
and farming. They also fashioned tools of stone and bone and created pottery
and woven textiles. Most important for our purposes, they became image mak-
ers, capturing forms and figures on cave walls with the use of primitive artistic
implements.

Archeological exploration of Stone Age sites in France and Spain reveals the existence of shelters, tools, and an impressive array of sculptures and paintings in which humans and animals are represented. The sheer quantity of these art objects, although they are not works of art by the usual definition, would suggest a principal role for images and symbols in the struggle for human survival. As with much ancient art, we cannot know for certain what the reasons were for creating these works. But evidence suggests that Stone Age people forged links between religion and life, life and art, and art and religion. They faced intimidating and unknown forces in their confrontation with nature. Perhaps their "art" was an attempt to record and to control.

PREHISTORIC ART

Prehistoric art is divided into three phases that correspond to the periods of Stone Age culture: **Paleolithic** (the late years of the Old Stone Age), **Mesolithic** (Middle Stone Age), and **Neolithic** (New Stone Age). These periods span roughly the years 14,000 to 2000 BCE.

Works of art from the Stone Age include cave paintings, reliefs, and sculpture of stone, ivory, and bone. The subjects consist mainly of animals, although some abstract human figures have been found. There is no surviving architecture as such. Many Stone Age dwellings consisted of caves and rock shelters. Some impressive monuments such as Stonehenge exist, but their functions remain a mystery.

MAP 13-1 Prehistoric Europe.

Paleolithic Art

Paleolithic art is the art of the last Ice Age, during which time glaciers covered large areas of northern Europe and North America. As the climate got colder, people retreated into the protective warmth of caves, and it is here that we find their first attempts at artistic creation.

The great cave paintings of the Stone Age were discovered by accident in northern Spain and southwestern France. At Lascaux, France (Map **13-1**), two boys whose dog chased a ball into a hole followed the animal and discovered beautiful paintings of bison, horses, and cattle that are estimated to be more than 15,000 years old. At first, because of the crispness and realistic detail of the paintings, they were thought to be forgeries. But in time, geological methods proved their authenticity.

One of the most splendid examples of Stone Age painting, the so-called Hall of Bulls (Fig. **13-1**), is found in a cave at Lascaux. Here, superimposed upon one another, are realistic images of horses, bulls, and reindeer that appear to be stampeding in all directions. With one glance, we can understand the early skepticism concerning their authenticity. So fresh, lively, and purely sketched are the forms that they seem to have been rendered yesterday.

In their attempt at **naturalism**, the artists captured the images of the beasts by first confidently outlining the contours of their bodies. They then filled in these dark outlines with details and colored them with shades of ocher and red. The artists seem to have used a variety of techniques ranging from drawing with chunks of raw pigment to applying pigment with fingers and sticks. They also seem to have used an early "spray painting" technique in which dried, ground pigments were blown through a hollowed-out bone or reed. Although the tools were primitive, the techniques and results were not. They used **foreshortening** and contrasts of light and shadow to create the illusion of three-dimensional forms. They strove to achieve a most convincing likeness of the animal.

Why did prehistoric people sketch these forms? Did they create these murals out of a desire to delight the eye, or did they have other reasons? We cannot know for certain. However, it is unlikely that the paintings were merely ornamental, because they were confined to the deepest recesses of the cave, far from the areas that were inhabited, and were not easily reached. Also, new figures were painted over earlier ones with no apparent regard for composition. It is believed that successive artists added to the drawings, respecting the sacredness of the figures that already existed. It is further believed that the paintings

13-1 Hall of Bulls, Lascaux (Dordogne), France
(Upper Paleolithic, c. 15,000–10,000 BCE).
Jean Vertut

covered the walls and ceilings of a kind of inner sanctuary where religious rituals concerning the capture of prey were performed. Some have suggested that by "capturing" these animals in art, Stone Age hunters believed that they would be guaranteed success in capturing them in life. This theory, as others, is unproven.

The prehistoric artist also created sculptures, called **Venuses** by the archeologists who first found them. The most famous is the Venus of Willendorf (Fig. **13-2**), named after the site at which she was unearthed. The tiny figurine is carved of stone and is just over four inches high. As with all sculptures of this type, the female form is highly abstracted, and the emphasis is placed on the anatomical parts associated with fertility: the oversized breasts, round abdomen, and enlarged hips. Other parts of the body, like the thin arms resting on the breasts, are subordinated to

those related to reproduction. Does this suggest a concern for survival of the species? Or was this figure of a fertile woman created and carried around as a talisman for fertility of the earth itself—abundance in the food supply? In either or any other case, people created their images, and perhaps their religion, as a way of coping with these concerns.

13-2 Venus of Willendorf (Upper Paleolithic) (c. 25,000 BCE).
Stone. H: 4⅜".
Naturhistorisches Museum, Vienna.
©Erich Lessing/Art Resource, NY

1 in.

13-3 Stonehenge, Salisbury Plain, Wiltshire, England (Neolithic, c. 1800–1400 BCE).
Diameter of circle: 97'.
Height of stones aboveground: approx. 24'.
©Richard Nowtiz/National Geographic Image Collection

10 ft.

Neolithic Art

During the New Stone Age, life became more stable and predictable. People domesticated plants and animals, and food production took the place of food gathering. Toward the end of the Neolithic period in some areas, crops such as maize, squash, and beans were cultivated, metal implements were fashioned, and writing appeared. About 4000 BCE, significant architectural monuments were erected.

The most famous of these monuments is Stonehenge (Fig. **13-3**) in southern England. It consists of two concentric rings of stones surrounding others placed in a horseshoe shape. Some of these **megaliths** (from the Greek, meaning "large stones") weigh several tons. The purpose of Stonehenge remains a mystery. At one time it was believed to have been a druid temple, or the work of Merlin, King Arthur's magician. Lately, some astronomers have suggested that the monument served as a complex calendar that charted the movements of the sun and moon, as well as eclipses. Whatever the meaning or function, the fact that it was undertaken at all is perhaps its most fascinating aspect.

The Neolithic period probably began about 8000 BCE and spread throughout the world's major river valleys between 6000 and 2000 BCE—the Nile in Egypt, the Tigris and Euphrates in Mesopotamia, the Indus in India, and the Yellow in China. In the next section, we examine the birth of the great Mesopotamian civilizations.

ART OF THE ANCIENT NEAR EAST

Historic (as opposed to prehistoric) societies are marked by a written language, advanced social organization, and developments in the areas of government, science, and art. They are also often linked with the development of agriculture. Historic civilizations began toward the end of the Neolithic period. In this section, we will discuss the art of the Mesopotamian civilizations of Sumer, Akkad, Babylonia, Assyria, and Persia. We will begin with Sumer, which flourished in the river valley of the Tigris and Euphrates about 3000 BCE.

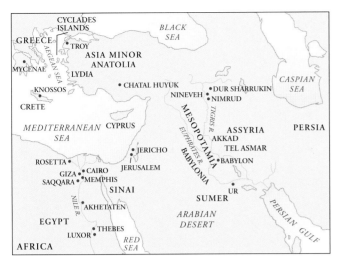

MAP 13-2 The Ancient Near East.

Sumer

The Tigris and Euphrates rivers flow through what is now Syria and Iraq, join in their southernmost section, and empty into the Persian Gulf (Map **13-2**). The major civilizations of ancient Mesopotamia lay along one or the other of these rivers, and the first to rise to prominence was Sumer.

Sumer was located in the Euphrates River valley in southern Mesopotamia. The origin of its people is unknown, although they may have come from Iran or India. The earliest Sumerian villages date back to prehistoric times. By about 3000 BCE, however, there was a thriving agricultural civilization in Sumer. The Sumerians constructed sophisticated irrigation systems, controlled river flooding, and worked with metals such as copper, silver, and gold. They had a government based on independently ruled city-states, and they developed a system of writing called **cuneiform**, from the Latin *cuneus*, meaning "wedge"; the characters in cuneiform writing are wedge shaped.

Excavations at major Sumerian cities have revealed sculpture, craft art, and monumental architecture that seems to have been created for worship. Thus, the Sumerian people may have been among the first to establish a formal religion.

One of the most impressive testimonies to the Sumerians' religion-based society is the **ziggurat**, a monumental platform for a temple also seen in the Babylonian and Assyrian civilizations of later years. The ziggurat was the focal point of the Sumerian city, towering high above the fields and dwellings. Typically, the ziggurat was a multilevel structure consisting of a core of sunbaked mud bricks faced with fired brick, sometimes of bright colors. Access to the **temple**, on the uppermost level of the ziggurat, was gained by stairs or a series of ramps leading from one level to the next, or in some instances, by a spiral ramp that rose continuously from ground to summit.

The White Temple at Uruk (Fig. **13-4A** and Fig. **13-4B**) and ziggurat, so called because of its white-washed walls, are among the earliest and best preserved in the region. The ziggurat, the corners of which are oriented toward the compass points, is some 40 feet high, but pales in comparison to the scale of later ziggurats. The ziggurat known to the Hebrews as the Tower of Babel, a symbol of mortal pride, was some 270 feet high.

The Sumerian gods were primarily deifications of nature. Anu was the god of the sky, Nannu the god of the moon, and Abu the god of vegetation. Votive sculptures found beneath the floor of a temple to Abu in Tell Asmar

13-4A White Temple at Uruk and Ziggurat (Sumerian, c. 3200–3000 BCE).
Sun-dried brick.
©Nik Wheeler/CORBIS

13-4B Reconstruction of White Temple and Ziggurat.
From E.S. Piggott, Ed., *The Dawn of Civilization*, London, Thames and Hudson, 1961, pg. 70.

Art of the Ancient Near East | **277**

13-5 Statues from Abu Temple, Tel Asmar (Sumerian, Early Dynasty period, c. 2900–2600 BCE).
Gypsum with shell and black limestone inlay. Height of tallest figures: 30".
Courtesy of The Oriental Institute Museum of the University of Chicago

1 ft.

(Fig. **13-5**) reinforce the essential role of religion in Sumerian society. These works functioned as stand-ins, as it were, for donor-worshippers who, in their absence, wished to continue to offer prayers to a specific deity. They range in height from under 12 to over 30 inches and are carved from gypsum with alert inlaid eyes of shell and black limestone. The figures are cylindrical and all stand erect with hands clasped at their chests around now-missing flasks. Distinctions are made between males and females. The men have long, stylized beards and hair and wear knee-length skirts decorated with incised lines describing fringe at the hem. The women wear dresses with one shoulder bared and the other draped with a shawl. These sculptures are gypsum, a soft mineral found in rock. The Sumerians, however, worked primarily in clay because of its abundance. They were expert ceramists and, as we have seen, were capable of building monumental structures with brick while their Egyptian contemporaries were using stone. It is believed that the Sumerians traded crops for metal, wood, and stone and used these materials to enlarge their repertory of art objects.

The Sumerian repertory of subjects included fantastic creatures such as music-making animals, bearded bulls, and composite man-beasts with bull heads or scorpion bodies. These were depicted in lavishly decorated objects of hammered gold inlaid with **lapis lazuli**. Found among the remains of Sumerian royal tombs, they are believed by some scholars to have been linked to funerary rituals.

For a long time, the Sumerians were the principal force in Mesopotamia, but they were not alone. Semitic peoples to the north became increasingly strong, and eventually they established an empire that ruled all of Mesopotamia and assimilated the Sumerian culture.

Akkad

Akkad, located north of Sumer, centered around the valley of the Tigris River. Its government, too, was based on independent city-states, which, along with those of Sumer, eventually came under the influence of the Akkadian ruler Sargon. Under Sargon and his successors, the civilization of Akkad flourished.

Akkadian art exhibits distinct differences from that of Sumer. It commemorates rulers and warriors instead of offering homage to the gods. It is an art of violence instead of prayer. Also, although artistic conventions are present, they are coupled with a naturalism that was absent from Sumerian art.

Of the little extant Akkadian art, the Stele of Naram Sin (Fig. **13-6**) shines as one of the most significant works. This relief sculpture commemorates the military exploits of Sargon's grandson and successor, Naram Sin. The king, represented somewhat larger in scale than the other figures, ascends a mountain, trampling his enemies underfoot. He is accompanied by a group of marching soldiers, spears erect, whose positions contrast strongly with those of the fallen enemy. One wrestles to pull a spear out of his neck, another pleads for mercy, and another falls headfirst off the mountain. The chaos on the right side of the composition is opposed by the rigid advancement on the left. All takes place under the watchful celestial bodies of Ishtar and Shamash, the gods of fertility and justice.

The king and his men are represented in a conceptual manner. That is, the artist rendered the human body in all of its parts as they are known to be, not as they appear at any given moment to the human eye. This method resulted in figures that are a combination of frontal and profile views. Naturalism was reserved for the enemy, whose figures fall in a variety of contorted positions. It may be that the convention of conceptual representation was maintained as a sign of respect. On the other hand, the conceptual manner complements the upright positions of the victorious, whereas the naturalism echoes the disintegration of the enemy camp.

The Akkadian Empire eventually declined, for reasons that are not clear. Historians have traditionally attributed its collapse to invading tribes. However, recent archeological research has led to the theory that it was not human violence that put an end to Akkadian supremacy but rather a severe and unrelenting drought that gripped the region for 300 years. With the end of the drought, the Sumerians regained power for a while with a Neo-Sumerian state ruled by the kings of Ur, but they, too, were eventually overtaken by fierce warring tribes. Mesopotamia remained in a state of chaos until the rise of Babylon under the great lawmaker and ruler, Hammurabi.

Babylonia

During the eighteenth century BCE, the Babylonian Empire, under Hammurabi, rose to power and dominated Mesopotamia. Hammurabi's major contribution to civilization was the codification of Mesopotamian laws. Laws had become cloudy and conflicting after the division of Mesopotamia into independent cities.

This code of law was inscribed on the Stele of Hammurabi (Fig. **13-7**), a relief sculpture of **basalt** over seven feet high. The lower portion of the stele is inscribed with the code itself, written in the Akkadian language with cuneiform characters. Above the code is a relief depicting Hammurabi and the sun-god Shamash. Hammurabi gestures in

13-6 Victory Stele of Naram Sin (Akkadian, c. 2300–2200 BCE). Stone. H: 6'6".
©Louvre, Paris, France/The Bridgeman Art Library.

13-7 Stele (upper portion) inscribed with the Law Code of Hammurabi, at Susa (Babylonian, c. 1760 BCE). Diorite. H: 7'4" (225 cm).
Louvre Museum, Paris.
©Erich Lessing/Art Resource, NY

respect and Shamash reciprocates by handing over to him a rod and ring, symbols of authority. The observer is led to believe, through this interaction, that Hammurabi's authority is god-given and thus, not to be challenged. The sculptor of the stele engaged in some conventions for representation, combining frontal and profile views as we have already seen in the Stele of Naram Sin. However, in the Hammurabi stele, there are some new attempts at naturalism. The artist has turned the figure of Shamash toward the viewer a bit and has rendered the lines in his beard as diagonals (rather than strict horizontals, as in the Sumerian votive figures), suggesting an experiment in foreshortening.

After the death of Hammurabi, Mesopotamia was torn apart by invasions. It eventually came under the influence of the Assyrians, a warring people to the north who had had their eyes on the region for hundreds of years.

Assyria

The ancient empire of Assyria developed along the upper Tigris River. For centuries, the Assyrians fought with their neighbors, earning a deserved reputation as a fierce, bloodthirsty people. They eventually overtook the Babylonians, and from about 900 to 600 BCE, they controlled all of Mesopotamia.

The Assyrians were influenced by Babylonian art, culture, and religion. But unlike Babylonia, Assyria was an empire built on military conquests and campaigns. Their obsession with war eventually depleted their resources, overtook their economy, and undermined their social structure. The Assyrian rulers ignored agricultural development, forcing the society to import most of its food. Their preoccupation with violence and power rather than stability and production eventually led to their demise.

Assyrian architecture consists of sprawling palaces and fortified citadels, and its extensive sculptural decoration—rendered in relief—reflects the power and might of the kings. The two most common subjects of these relief

sculptures are the king's military exploits and brutal hunts that were staged and tightly controlled to safely showcase the strength of the ruler. One of the most touching and sensitive works of ancient art records a scene from one of King Ashurbanipal's hunting expeditions. The Dying Lioness (Fig. **13-8**) is a limestone relief that depicts carnage for the sake of royal sport. A lioness, bleeding profusely from arrow wounds, seems to emit a pathetic, helpless roar as she drags her hindquarters, paralyzed in the assault. Her musculature is clearly defined, and the incised details are painfully realistic. The naturalism in this relief differs significantly from the way in which kings and members of their entourage were depicted. Artists adhered to rigid and stylized conventions for human forms.

13-8 The Dying Lioness, from Nineveh (Assyrian, 660 BCE).
Limestone. H: 13¾".
British Museum, London.
©Werner Forman/Topham/The Image Works

13-9 Processional Frieze (detail) from the royal audience hall, Persepolis. (Persian, c. 521–465 BCE). ©David Poole/Robert Harding Picture Library

Assyria waged almost constant warfare to protect its sovereignty in the area. Ashurbanipal's successors eventually lost control of the empire to Neo-Babylonian kings, the most famous of which was the biblical King Nebuchadnezzar. They remained in power until the conquest of the Persians.

Persia

As Persia, led by King Cyrus, marched toward empire, Babylon was but one on a growing list of casualties. By the sixth century BCE, the Persians had conquered Egypt and, less than a century later, were poised to subsume Greece into their far-reaching realm. The Persian Empire stretched from South Asia to northeastern Europe, and would have included southeastern Europe were the Greeks not victorious over the Persians in a decisive battle at Salamis in 480 BCE. Cyrus's successors grew the empire until the defeat of Darius II by Alexander the Great in 330 BCE.

The citadel at Persepolis, the capital of the ancient Persian Empire, was a sprawling complex of palatial dwellings, government buildings, grand stairways, and columned halls whose architectural surfaces were richly adorned with relief sculpture. A processional frieze from the royal audience hall (Fig. **13-9**) illustrates a technique that is notably different from Assyrian predecessors such as The Dying Lioness. The Persian relief is more deeply carved; that is, the figures stand out more against the background. They are fleshier,

more well-rounded. The artist has paid particular attention to detail, distinguishing the costumes of the participants who include Persian nobles and guards and visiting dignitaries from nations under Persian rule. Although the procession is regimented, some figures twist and turn in space, alleviating the visual monotony. Persian art is also characterized by fanciful animal forms and stylized floral decoration.

In 525 BCE, Persia conquered the kingdom of Egypt, but civilization in Egypt had begun some 3,000 years earlier.

EGYPTIAN ART

The lush land that lay between the Tigris and Euphrates rivers, providing sustenance for the Mesopotamian civilizations, is called the **Fertile Crescent**. Its counterpart in Egypt, called the **Fertile Ribbon**, hugs the banks of the Nile River, which flows north from Africa and empties into the Mediterranean Sea (Map 13-2). Like the rivers of the Fertile Crescent, the Nile was an indispensable part of Egyptian life. Without it, Egyptian life would not have existed. For this reason, it also had spiritual significance; the Nile was perceived as a god.

Like Sumerian art, Egyptian art was religious. There are three aspects of Egyptian art and life that stand as unique: their link to religion, their link to death, and their ongoing use of strict conventionalism in the arts that affords a sense of permanence.

The art and culture of Egypt are divided into three periods: The Old Kingdom dates from 2680 to 2258 BCE, the Middle Kingdom from 2000 to 1786 BCE, and the New Kingdom from 1570 to 1342 BCE. Art styles proceed from the Old to the New Kingdom with very few variations.

A break in this pattern occurred between 1372 and 1350 BCE, during the Amarna Revolution under the unorthodox leadership of the pharaoh Akhenaton. After his death, Egypt retreated to the old order.

Old Kingdom

Egyptian religion was bound closely to the afterlife. Happiness in the afterlife was believed to be ensured through the continuation of certain aspects of earthly life. Thus, tombs were decorated with everyday objects and scenes depicting common earthly activities. Sculptures of the deceased were placed in the tombs, along with likenesses of the people who surrounded them in life.

In the years prior to the dawn of the Old Kingdom, art consisted of funerary offerings of one type or another, including small, sculpted figures, ivory carvings, pottery, and slate palettes used to mix eye makeup. Toward the

end of this period, called the Predynastic period, Egyptian stonecutters began to create the large limestone works for which Egypt became famous.

Sculpture

Old Kingdom artists initiated a manner of representation that lasted thousands of years, a conceptual approach to the rendering of the human figure that we also encountered in Mesopotamian relief sculpture. In Egyptian reliefs, the head, pelvis, and legs are presented in profile, whereas the upper torso and eye are shown from a frontal view. The figures tend to be flat, and they are situated in a shallow space with no use of foreshortening. No attempt was made to give the illusion of forms that exist in three-dimensional space. Wall decoration was carved in very low relief with a great deal of **incised** detail. Sculpture in the round closely adhered to the block form. Color was applied at times but was not used widely because of the relative impermanence of the material. These basic characteristics were duplicated,

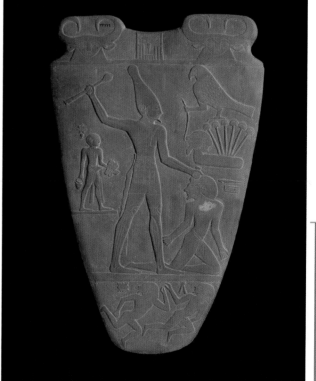

1 ft.

13-10 Narmer Palette (Egyptian, Old Kingdom, c. 3200 BCE). Front (left) and back (right) views. Slate. H: 25".

Egyptian Museum, Cairo.
©Erich Lessing/Art Resource, NY

with few exceptions, by artists during all periods of Egyptian art. There are instances in which a certain naturalism was sought, but the artist rarely strayed from the inherited stylistic conventions.

Art historian Erwin Panofsky stated that this Egyptian method of working clearly reflected their artistic intention, "directed not toward the variable, but toward the constant, not toward the symbolization of the vital present, but toward the realization of a timeless eternity." One of the most important sculptures from the Old Kingdom period, the Narmer Palette (Fig. **13-10**), illustrates these conventions. The Narmer Palette is an example of a type of **cosmetic palette** found in Egypt (Egyptians applied dark colors around their eyes to deflect the sun's glare as football players do today), but its symbolism supercedes its function. The Narmer Palette commemorates the unification of Upper Egypt and Lower Egypt, an event that Egyptians marked as the beginning of their civilization.

The back of the palette depicts King Narmer in the crown of Upper Egypt (a bowling pin shape) slaying an enemy. Beneath his feet, on the lowest part of the palette, lie two more dead enemy warriors. To the right, a falcon—the god Horus—is perched on a cluster of papyrus stalks that sprout from an object with a man's head. The papyrus is a symbol for Lower Egypt, and Horus's placement would appear to sanction Narmer's takeover of that territory. The top of the palette is sculpted on both sides with two bull-shaped heads with human features. They represent the goddess Hathor, who traditionally symbolized love and joy.

The king is rendered in the typical conventional manner. He is larger than the people surrounding him, symbolizing his royal status. His head, hips, and legs are carved in low relief and in profile, and his eye and upper torso are shown in full frontal view. The musculature is defined with incised lines that appear more as stylized patterns than realistic details. The artist has chosen convention over naturalism and, in the process, created a timeless image, at least as far as Egyptian history is concerned.

The front of the palette is divided into horizontal segments, or **registers**, that are crowded with figures. A hollowed-out well in the center of the palette held eye paint, and it is emphasized by the long, entwined necks of lionlike figures tamed by two men with leashes. The top register depicts King Narmer once again, reviewing the captured and deceased enemy. He is now shown wearing the crown of Lower Egypt and holding instruments that symbolize his power. To his right are stacks of decapitated bodies. This is not the first time that we have seen such a monument to a royal conquest, complete with gory details. We witnessed

1 ft.

13-11 Statue of Khafre, from Gizeh (Egyptian, Old Kingdom, c. 2500 BCE).
Diorite. H: 66".
Egyptian Museum, Cairo.
Hirmer Fotoarchiv, Munich

it in the Akkadian victory Stele of Naram Sin (Fig. 13-6). In both works, the kings are shown in commanding positions, larger than the surrounding figures, but in the Narmer Palette, the king is also depicted as a god. This concept of the ruler of Egypt, along with the strict conventions of his representation, would last some 3,000 years.

Egyptian tomb sculpture included large-scale figures carved in the round, usually from very hard materials that were likely to endure. Permanence was essential, as sculptures like Khafre (Fig. **13-11**) were created to house the ka, or soul, if the mummified remains of the deceased disintegrated. Ka sculptures were not portraits. The artists utilized stylistic conventions, including idealism. Regardless of the age of the deceased, the ka figure emblemized the individual in the prime of life. The statue of Khafre, an Old Kingdom pharaoh, is typical. Carved in diorite, a gray green rock, it shows the pharaoh seated on a throne ornamented with the lotus blossoms and papyrus that symbolize Upper and Lower Egypt. He sits rigidly, and his frontal gaze is reminiscent of the staring eyes of the Mesopotamian votive figures. Khafre is shown with the conventional attributes of the pharaoh: a finely pleated kilt, a linen headdress gracing the shoulders, and a long, thin beard (present on the carved faces of both male and female pharaohs), part of which has broken off.

The sun god **Horus**, represented again as a falcon, sits behind the pharoah's head and spreads his wings protectively around it. The artist confined his figure to the block of stone from which it was carved instead of allowing it to stand freely in space. The legs and torso appear molded to the throne, and the arms and fists are attached to the body. The sense of the solidity of the uncarved block is maintained and, with that, a certain confidence that the sculpture would remain intact. There were few, if any, pieces that were likely to break off. Khafre was rendered according to a specific **canon of proportions** relating different anatomical parts to one another. The forms rely on predetermined rules and not on optical fact. Naturalism was intermittent in Egyptian art, and more evident in the Middle Kingdom and the Amarna period.

Architecture

The most spectacular remains of Old Kingdom Egypt, and the most famous, are the Great Pyramids at Gizeh (Fig. **13-12**). Constructed as tombs, they provided a resting place for the pharaoh, underscored his status as a deity, and lived after him as a monument to his accomplishments. They stand today as haunting images of a civilization long gone, isolated as coarse jewels in an arid wasteland.

The pyramids are massive. The largest has a base that is about 775 feet on a side and is 450 feet high. It is constructed of 2,300,000 limestone blocks that weigh about 2.5 tons each. The stone for the pyramids was quarried from a nearby plateau and moved by workers to the site using wooden rollers and sled-like apparatuses. Stonecutters on the site carved the blocks more finely, after which they were stacked on top of one another in rows, using systems of ropes and pulleys. Artisans finished the surfaces of the pyramid with fine limestone, creating a flawless, smooth, and gleaming sheath.

The interiors of the pyramids consist of a network of chambers, galleries, and air shafts. Ostentatious and conspicuous as the pyramids were, thieves wasted no time in plundering them. During the Middle Kingdom, Egyptians designed less easily penetrated dwelling places for their spirits.

Middle Kingdom

The Middle Kingdom witnessed a change in the political hierarchy of Egypt, as the power of the pharaohs was threatened by powerful landowners. During the early years of the Middle Kingdom, the development of art was stunted by internal strife. Egypt was finally brought back on track, reorganized, and reunited under King Mentuhotep, and art flourished once again.

Middle Kingdom art carried the Old Kingdom style forward, although there was some experimentation outside the mainstream of strict conventionalism. We find this experimentation in sensitive portrait sculptures and freely drawn fresco paintings.

A striking aspect of Middle Kingdom architecture was the rock-cut tombs (Fig. **13-13**), which may have been designed to prevent robberies. They were carved out of the **living rock**, and their entranceways were marked by columned **porticoes** of post-and-lintel construction. These porticoes led to a columned entrance hall, followed by a chamber along the same axis. The walls of the hall and tomb chamber were richly decorated with relief sculpture and painting, much of which had a sense of liveliness not found in Old Kingdom art.

New Kingdom

The Middle Kingdom also collapsed, and Egypt fell under the rule of an Asiatic tribe called the Hyskos. They introduced Bronze Age weapons to Egypt, as well as the horse. Eventually, the Egyptians overthrew them, and the New Kingdom was launched. It proved to be one of the most vital periods in Egyptian history, marked by expansionism, increased wealth, and economic and political stability.

The art of the New Kingdom combined characteristics of the Old and Middle Kingdom periods. The monumental forms of the earliest centuries were coupled with the freedom of expression of the Middle Kingdom years. A certain vitality appeared in two-dimensional works like painting and relief sculpture, although sculpture in the round retained its concentration on solidity and permanence with few stylistic changes.

13-12 Great Pyramids at Gizeh (Egyptian, Old Kingdom, c. 2570–2500 BCE).
©Topham/The Image Works

13-13 Rock-cut tombs Beni Hasan, Egypt, c. 1950–1900 BCE .
©Foto Marburg/Art Resource, New York.

13-14 Mortuary Temple of Queen Hatshepsut, Thebes (Egyptian, New Kingdom, c. 1480 BCE).
©Andrew McConnell/Alamy

Egyptian society embraced a death cult, and some of its most significant monuments continued to be linked with death or worship of the dead. During the New Kingdom period, a new architectural form was created—the **mortuary temple**. Mortuary temples were carved out of the living rock, as were the rock-cut tombs of the Middle Kingdom, but their function was quite different. They did not house the mummified remains of the pharaohs, but rather served as their place for worship during life, and a place at which they could be worshipped after death.

One of the most impressive mortuary temples of the New Kingdom is that of a female pharaoh, Queen Hatshepsut (Fig. **13-14**). The temple backs into imposing cliffs and is divided into three terraces, which are approached by long ramps that rise from the floor of the valley to the top of pillared **colonnades**. Although the terraces are now as barren as the surrounding country, during Hatshepsut's time they were covered with exotic vegetation. The interior of the temple was just as lavishly decorated, with some 200 large sculptures as well as painted relief carvings.

As the civilization of Egypt became more advanced and powerful, there was a tendency to build and sculpt on a monumental scale. Statues and temples reached gigantic proportions. The delicacy and refinement of earlier Egyptian art fell by the wayside in favor of works that reflected the inflated Egyptian ego. Throughout the New Kingdom period, conventionalism was, for the most part, maintained. During the reign of Akhenaton, however, Egypt was offered a brief respite from stylistic rigidity.

The Amarna Revolution: The Reign of Akhenaton and Nefertiti

During the fourteenth century BCE, a king by the name of Amenhotep IV rose to power. His reign marked a revolution in both religion and the arts. Amenhotep IV, named for the god Amen, changed his name to Akhenaton in honor of the sun god, Aton, and he declared that Aton was the only god. In his monotheistic fury, Akhenaton spent his life tearing down monuments to the old gods and erecting new ones to Aton.

The art of Akhenaton's reign, or that of the Amarna period (so named because the pharaoh moved the capital of Egypt to Tell el-Amarna), was as revolutionary as his approach to religion. The wedge-shaped stylizations that stood as a rigid canon for the representations of the human body were replaced by curving lines and full-bodied forms.

King Tut: The Face That Launched a Thousand High-Res Images

THE VALLEY OF THE KINGS, Luxor, Egypt; January 5, 2005. Nearly 3,300 years after his death, the leathery mummy of the legendary boy-king was ever so delicately removed from its tomb and guided into a portable CT—computed tomography, or what we call "cat"—scanner. It was not the first time that modern technology was employed to feed the curiosity of scientists, archeologists, and museum officials over the mysteries surrounding the reign and death of Tut. More than three decades earlier, the mummy was X-rayed twice, in part to try to solve the mystery of the young pharaoh's death; Tutankhamen was crowned at the age of eight and died only 10 years later. These early X-rays revealed a hole at the base of Tut's cranium, leading to the suspicion that he was murdered. This time around, the focus—and the conclusions—changed. Dr. Zahi Hawass, secretary general of the Supreme Council of Antiquities in Cairo, said, "No one hit Tut on the back of the head." Scientists instead concluded that the damage noted in earlier X-rays was probably due to the rough removal of the golden burial mask by the tomb's discoverers. But they found something else: a puncture in Tut's skin over a severe break in the youth's left thigh. As it is known that this accident took place just days before his death, some experts on the scanning team conjectured that this break, and the puncture caused by it, may have led to a serious infection and Tut's consequent death. Otherwise, the young pharaoh was the picture of health—no signs of malnutrition or disease, with strong bones and teeth, and probably five and a half feet tall.

In all, scientists (including experts in anatomy, pathology, and radiology) spent two months analyzing more than 1,700 three-dimensional, high-resolution images taken with CT scans. Then artists and scholars took a turn. Three independent teams, one each from Egypt, France, and the United States, came up with their own versions of what Tut might very well have looked like in life: a bit of an elongated skull (normal, they say), large lips, a receding chin, and a pronounced overbite that seems to have run in the family (Fig. **13-15**). It was the first time—but certainly not the last—that CT scans would be used to reconstruct the faces of the Egyptian celebrity dead.

Although the price tag on this endeavor was most certainly steep, the Egyptian government stood to gain financially from the images. Their release was timed to coincide with the launch of the world-traveling exhibition Tutankhamen and the Golden Age of the Pharaohs.

Along with the scans and reconstruction images, the exhibit would feature King Tut's diamond crown and gold coffin, along with a total of almost 200 objects from his and various other noteworthy tombs. If history were any predictor of the insatiable thirst for things Egyptian, this, like the original exhibition of treasures from Tut's tomb, would attract millions of visitors. This time, however, it was hoped that the $10 million rental fee for each museum venue would bring in desperately needed funding for a museum being planned beside the pyramids in Gizeh. As in many parts of the world, antiquities are crumbling. "There are no free meals anymore," Hawass said. "We have a task. These monuments will be gone in 100 years if we don't raise the money to restore them." ∎

13-15 Reconstruction of face of King Tut.
©Kenneth Garrett/National Geographic Image Collection

The statue of Akhenaton (Fig. **13-16**) could not differ more from its precedents in the Old and Middle Kingdoms. The fluid contours of the body contrast strongly with those in earlier sculptures of pharaohs, as do the elongated jaw, thick lips, and thick-lidded eyes. These characteristics suggest that the artist was attempting to create a naturalistic likeness of the pharaoh, "warts and all," as the saying goes.

Aside from being at odds stylistically with other Egyptian sculptures, the very concept of the work is different.

13-16 Pillar statue of Akhenaton from Temple of Amen-Re, Karnak (Egyptian, New Kingdom, c. 1356 BCE).
Sandstone, painted.
Egyptian Museum, Cairo.
©Scala/Art Resource, NY

Throughout the previous centuries, adherence to a stylistic formality had been maintained, especially in the sculptures of revered pharaohs. If naturalism was present at all, it was reserved for lesser works depicting lesser figures. During the Amarna period, naturalism was used in monumental statues depicting members of the royal family as well.

One of the most beautiful works of art from this period is the bust of Akhenaton's wife, Queen Nefertiti (Fig. **13-17**). The classic profile reiterates the linear patterns found in the pharaoh's sculpture. An almost topheavy crowned head extends gracefully on a long and sensuous neck. The realism of the portrait is enhanced by the paint that is applied to the limestone.

The naturalism of the works of the Amarna period was short-lived. Subsequent pharaohs returned to the more rigid styles of the earlier dynasties. Just as Akhenaton destroyed the images and shrines of gods favored by earlier pharaohs, so did his successors destroy his temples to Aton. With Akhenaton's death came the death of monotheism—for the time being. Some have suggested that Akhenaton's loyalty to a single god may have set a monotheistic example for other religions.

Akhenaton's immediate successor was Tutankhamen—the famed King Tut. Called the boy-king, Tut died at about the age of 18. His tomb was not discovered until 1922, when British archeologists led by Howard Carter unearthed a treasure trove of gold artworks, many inlaid with semiprecious stones. By far, the most spectacular find was the young pharaoh's coffin (Fig. **13-18**), made of solid gold and weighing almost 250 pounds. Within this, the last of three nesting coffins, lay the body of the king, wrapped in linen, his face covered with an astounding gold mask. The lid of the coffin was fashioned out of sheet gold, with eyes of aragonite (a semihard mineral) and obsidian (black volcanic glass) and eyebrows inlaid with lapis lazuli. The hands of Tut's effigy cross over the chest and clutch the royal symbols of the crook and the flail, encrusted in deep blue faience—a signature Egytian opaque glazed earthenware.

Carter, upon viewing the revelation of the coffin, described the sense of marvel at the sight: "And as the last was removed a gasp of wonderment escaped our lips, so gorgeous was the sight that met our eye: a golden effigy of the young boy king, of most magnificent workmanship, filled the whole of the interior of the sarcophagus." Although Tut's coffin and mask are characteristically stylized, Carter observed an element of realism in the fashioning of the face. In fact, some residual stylistic effects of the Amarna period are evident in several works from Tut's reign—curvilinear forms not unlike those seen in the

A eulogy of Queen Nefertiti:

And the Heiress, Great in the Palace, Fair of Face, Adorned with the Double Plumes, Mistress of Happiness, Endowed with Favours, at hearing whose voice the King rejoices, the Chief Wife of the King, his beloved, the Lady of the Two Lands, Neferneferuaten-Nefertiti, May she live for Ever and Always.

— CYRIL ALDRED, in Akhenaton, King of Egypt

The-beautiful-one-is-come.

— Translation of the name Nefertiti

13-17 Bust of Queen Nefertiti (Egyptian, New Kingdom, c. 1344 BCE).
Limestone. H: approx. 20".
©Jean-Pierre Lescourret/CORBIS

13-18 Coffin of Tutankhamen (c. 1323 BCE).
Gold.
©Time & Life Pictures/Getty Images.

statue of Akhenaton, a certain naturalism and tenderness in representations of the boy and his queen.

After Akhenaton's death, Egypt returned to "normal." That is, the worship of Amen was resumed and art reverted to the rigid stylization of the earlier stages. The divergence that had taken place with Akhenaton and been carried forward briefly by his successor soon disappeared. Instead, the permanence that was so valued by this people endured for another 1,000 years virtually unchanged despite the kingdom's gradual decline.

AEGEAN ART

The Tigris and Euphrates valleys and the Nile River banks provided the climate and conditions for the survival of Mesopotamia and Egypt. Other ancient civilizations also flourished because of their geography. Those of the Aegean—Crete in particular—developed and thrived because of their island location. As maritime powers, they maintained contact with distant cultures with whom they traded, including those of Egypt and Asia Minor.

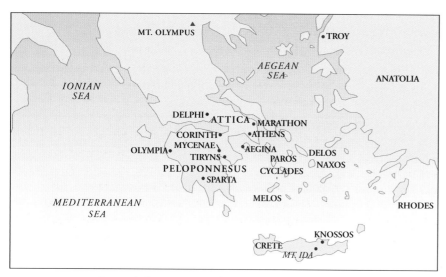

MAP 13-3 Greece (5th century BCE).

Until about 1870 CE, the Aegean civilizations that were sung by Greece's epic poet, Homer, in the *Iliad* and the *Odyssey*, were viewed as fancy rather than fact. But during the last decades of the nineteenth century, the German archeologist Heinrich Schliemann followed the very words of Homer and unearthed some of the ancient sites, including Mycenae, on the Greek mainland (Map **13-3**). Following in Schliemann's footsteps, Sir Arthur Evans excavated on the island of Crete and uncovered remains of the Minoan civilization also cited by Homer. The Bronze Age civilizations of **pre-Hellenic** Greece comprised these cultures and that of the Cyclades Islands.

The Cyclades

The Cyclades Islands are part of an archipelago in the Aegean Sea off the southeastern coast of mainland Greece. They are six in number and include Melos, the site where the famed Venus de Milo (see Fig. 14-17) was found; and Paros, one of the chief quarries for marble used in ancient Greece. The Cycladic culture flourished on

13-19 Cycladic idol, from Amorgos (c. 2500–1100 BCE).
Marble. H: 30".
Ashmolean Museum, Oxford, England.

1 in.

these six islands during the Early Bronze Age, from roughly 2500 to 2000 BCE.

The art that survives has been culled mostly from tombs and includes pottery and small marble figurines of women (Fig. **13-19**) and male musicians. It is not clear what purpose the small female figures served. Some say they represent goddesses, whereas others argue for a link to fertility. They are, in a way, pared-down, geometric versions of the Venus of Willendorf (Fig. 13-2); that is, the breasts, abdomen, and pubic area are more defined than the limbs and head. Because they were found in tombs, it would seem likely that they served a funerary function.

The figures range in height from a few inches to well over one foot, although some are life-size. They are essentially flat, with oval or wedge-shaped heads, squared torsos, and attenuated limbs. The smooth planes of the faces generally bear only one feature—a nose. Some traces of paint have been found. Male figures are typically seated and are playing stylized musical instruments. They were also found in tombs, and their function and identity are also open to speculation.

Crete

The civilization that developed on the island of Crete was one of the most remarkable in the ancient world, rich in painting, sculpture, and elaborate architecture. It also brought us names like King Minos (Crete's culture is known as Minoan, after the king) and creatures like the Minotaur. Homer spoke of youths sent to a Cretan labyrinth for sacrifice to the notorious man-beast, and of the hero Theseus, who slayed the Minotaur. Assuming that myths have some basis in fact, we might conclude that the extensive labyrinth that was part of the sprawling palace at Knossos—home to King Minos—inspired Homer's poetic narrative. Homeric descriptions of this island civilization were viewed as literary rather than historical. But as with Schliemann and Troy, the archeologist Sir Arthur Evan's excavations revealed Crete to have been an advanced and bustling civilization.

Evans divided the history of Minoan civilization into three parts: The Early Minoan period, known as the pre-Palace period, from which survive some small sculptures and pottery; the Middle Minoan period, or the period of the Old Palaces, which began around 2000 BCE and ended three centuries later with what was probably a devastating earthquake; and the Late Minoan period, when these palaces were reconstructed, which began during the sixteenth century BCE and ended probably in about 1400 BCE. At that time, the stronghold of Western civilization shifted from the Aegean to the Greek mainland.

During the Middle Minoan period, the great palaces, including the most famous one at Knossos, were constructed. A form of writing based on **pictographs**, called Linear A, was developed. Refined articles of ivory, metal, and pottery were also produced.

Unlike those of Mesopotamia and Egypt, Minoan architectural projects did not consist of tombs, mortuary temples, or shrines. Instead, the Minoans constructed lavish palaces for their kings and the royal entourage. Not much is known of the old palaces, except for those that were subsequently built on their ruins. Toward the end of the Middle Minoan period, the palace at Knossos was reduced to rubble either by an earthquake or by invaders. About a century after its destruction, however, it was rebuilt on a grander scale. Also during the Late Minoan period, a type of writing called Linear B was developed. This system, finally deciphered in 1953, turned out to be an early form of Greek. The script, found on clay tablets, perhaps indicates the presence of a Greek-speaking people—the Mycenaeans—on Crete during this period.

The most spectacular of the restored palaces on Crete is that at Knossos. It was so sprawling that one can easily understand how the myth of the Minotaur arose. The adjective labyrinthine certainly describes it. A variety of rooms were set off major corridors and arranged about a spacious central court. The rooms included the king's and queen's bedrooms, a throne room, reception rooms, servants' quarters, and many other spaces, including rows of **magazines**, or storage areas, where large vessels of grain and wine were embedded in the earth for safekeeping and natural cooling. The palace was three stories high, and the upper floors were reached by well-lit staircases. Beneath the palace were the makings of an impressive water-supply system of terra-cotta pipes that would have provided running water for bathrooms.

Some of the most interesting decorative aspects of the palace at Knossos—seen in the queen's bedroom (Fig. **13-20**)—are its unique columns and its vibrant fresco paintings. The columns, carved of stone, are narrower at the base than at the top. This proportion is the reverse of that of the standard columns found in Mesopotamia, Egypt, and later, in Greece. The columns are crowned by cushion-shaped capitals that loom large over the curious stem of the column shaft, often painted bright red or blue.

The rooms were also adorned with painted panels of plant and animal life. Stylized **rosettes** accent doorways, and delicately painted dolphins swim across the surface of the walls, giving one the impression of looking into a vast aquarium. This fascination with fish, sea mammals, and coastal plants in wall paintings and on pottery of the Late Minoan period reflects life on an island. The scale and complexity of the architecture reflects Crete as an impressive maritime power.

The palace at Knossos and all of the other palaces on Crete were again destroyed some time in the fifteenth century BCE. At this point, the Mycenaeans of the Greek mainland may have moved in and occupied the island. However, their stay was short-lived. Knossos, and the Minoan civilization, had been finally destroyed by the year 1200 BCE.

13-20 Queen's bedroom in Palace at Knossos (Late Minoan, c. 1500 BCE).
©Art Resource, NY

13-21 Lion Gate at Mycenae (c. 1300 BCE).
Height of sculpture above lintel: 9' 6½".
©Erich Lessing/Art Resource, NY

Mycenae

Although the origins of the Mycenaean people are uncertain, we know that they came to the Greek mainland as early as 2000 BCE. They were a Greek-speaking people, sophisticated in forging bronze weaponry as well as versatile in the arts of ceramics, metalwork, and architecture. The Minoans clearly influenced their art and culture, even though by about 1600 BCE Mycenae was by far the more powerful of the two civilizations. Mycenaeans occupied Crete after the palaces were destroyed. The peak of Mycenaean supremacy lasted about two centuries, from 1400 to 1200 BCE. At the end of that period, invaders from the north—the fierce and undaunted Dorians—gained control of mainland Greece. They intermingled with the Mycenaeans to form the beginnings of the peoples of ancient Greece.

Lacking the natural defense of a surrounding sea that was to Crete's advantage, the Mycenaeans were constantly facing threats from land invaders. They met these threats with strong fortifications, such as the citadels in the major cities of Mycenae and Tiryns. Much of the architecture and art of the Mycenaean civilization reflects the preoccupation with defense.

13-22 The Treasury of Atreus (Mycenaean, c. 1300–1250 BCE).
©Vanni/Art Resource, NY

Architecture

For the Mycenaeans, the need for impenetrable fortification did not preclude aesthetic solutions to architectural challenges. Even though the construction methods employed in palaces, tombs, and fortification walls are their most impressive attributes, citadels were embellished with frescoes and sculpture. One of the most famous carved pieces in Mycenae is the Lion Gate (Fig. **13-21**), one of the entranceways to the citadel of that city. The actual gateway consists of a heavy **lintel** that rests on two massive vertical pillars—another example of post-and-lintel construction. Additional large stones were piled in rows, or courses, above the lintel and **beveled** to form an open triangle. A relief sculpture of two lions flanking a Minoan-style column fills the space. The heads of the beasts, now gone, were carved of separate pieces of stone and fitted into place. Although the animal figures are not intact, their prominent and realistic musculature, carved in high relief, is an awesome sight, one that signified to intruders the strength of the army within the walls.

Another contribution of the Mycenaean architect was the **tholos**, or beehive tomb. During the early phases of the Mycenaean civilization, members of the royal family were buried in so-called **shaft graves**. These were no more than pits in the ground, lined with stones, and marked by a **stele**, or headstone, set above the entrance to the grave. As time went on, however, tombs for the wealthy became more ambitious.

The Treasury of Atreus (Fig. **13-22**), a tomb so named by Schliemann because he believed it to have been the tomb of the mythological ancient Greek king Atreus, is typical of such constructions. The Treasury consists of two parts: the *dromos*, or narrow passageway leading to the tomb proper; and the *tholos*, or beehive-shaped tomb chamber. The entire structure was covered by earth and has the appearance of a simple mound from the exterior. The interior walls were constructed of hundreds of stones laid on top of one another in concentric rings of diminishing size. The Treasury rose to a height of some 40 feet and enclosed a vast amount of space, an architectural feat not to be duplicated until the domed ceilings of ancient Rome were constructed.

Gold Work

Homer's epithet for Mycenae was "rich in gold." Archeologists came to uphold that description with the discovery of extraordinary quantities of finely wrought gold objects in graves throughout Mycenae, although the tholos tombs, like the pyramids before them in Egypt, were plundered well before the modern excavations. Thieves found their way into the Treasury of Atreus, like other tombs, soon after its construction. Nevertheless, Schliemann unearthed a wealth of treasures just inside the Lion Gate, which were buried in more inconspicuous graves. Archeologists refer to the mound as Grave Circle A. The most impressive find was a gold mask, which Schliemann believed was that of Agamemnon himself (Fig. **13-23**). Masks such as these were created from thin, hammered sheets of gold and placed over the faces of the deceased. Some aspects of the masks were stylized, such as the ears, eyebrows, and coffee-bean-shaped eyes, but the artists did endeavor to recreate specific characteristics that distinguished one portrait from another. Schliemann found other elaborate objects, including gold cups, bronze vessels, and daggers inlaid with silver and gold.

The Cyclopean walls of the Mycenaean citadels did not ward off enemies for long. After roughly 1200 BCE, the Mycenaean civilization collapsed from internal warfare, the onslaught of the better-equipped Dorian warriors, or both. The period following the Dorian invasions produced no significant art, architecture, or writing. But the people who emerged from this "Dark Age" would sow the seeds of one of the world's most influential civilizations and enduring artistic legacies—that of ancient Greece.

13-23 Funerary mask, from Grave Circle A, Mycenae, Greece (c. 1600–1500 BCE).
Beaten gold. H: 12". National Archaeological Museum, Athens.
©Nimitallah/Art Resource, NY

Jerusalem—a city set in history, a city beset by current events. Jerusalem—a city at once pluralistic and, more than once, intolerant. Jerusalem—spiritually, the home of three of the world's great religions and, emotionally, a house too often divided.

Over its 3,000-year history, Jerusalem and the Holy Land have been coveted territory. The ancient Egyptians battled the Canaanites in the coastal plains around the Dead Sea, bringing them under the rule of the pharaoh. And although the Hebrew tribes that coalesced into the entity known as Israel around 1200 to1000 BCE came to dominate the region, they met continual violent struggles with such peoples as the Philistines, Assyrians, and Babylonians (who captured Jerusalem in 586 BCE, destroyed Solomon's Temple, and drove the Jews into exile). When the Jews returned to Jerusalem from Babylonian captivity, they built a new temple on the site of the old, ushering in the period of the "Second Temple." Yet even during this era, they were not self-governed; the Persians remained dominant over the region until they were conquered by Alexander the Great.

From that point forward, the Jewish nation met a series of enemies. None were more formidable than ancient Rome, whose legions first took the city of Jerusalem in 63 BCE. For almost 100 years, clashes between the Jews and the Romans were constant, and this, according to the Christian Bible, was the state of affairs into which Jesus was born. Bloody skirmishes led to full-scale war in 66 CE. After four years, the Romans were finally victorious, capturing Jerusalem and destroying the city and the Second Temple. But the subjugation of the Jewish people did not occur until three years later, after a test of wills and military might at the fortress of Masada. It was a subjugation that would not last. A second war was fought from 132 to 135 CE, with Rome victorious once again. This time the Jews were driven from the city of Jerusalem, scattering in what is known as the Diaspora.

Other religions entered the region as watershed historical events took place. When the Roman emperor Constantine converted to Christianity and granted freedom of worship to early Christians in the year 313 CE, the doors to the Holy Land were opened to pilgrims of the new faith, who built churches on sites connected to events in the life of Christ. By the late fourth century, Christianity became the official religion of the Holy Land. A little more than three centuries later, Muslims—followers of Islam and its prophet, Muhammad—became the new rulers of the Holy Land. Muslims maintain, as do Jews and Christians, that Jerusalem is holy to their religion; they believe that Muhammad ascended into heaven from the same rock in Jerusalem on which, according to the Hebrew Bible, Abraham was about to sacrifice his son Isaac. The Dome of the Rock stands over this site, on which the Jews had originally built their temples. The coming

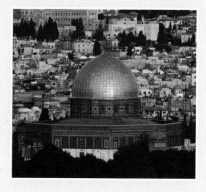

The Dome of the Rock.
©Alan Carey/CORBIS

and going of pilgrims to the Holy Land continued for some time, until Jerusalem fell to the Turks in 1071 and Christians were forbidden access to their religious sites. This event led to the Crusades, the military effort to take back the Holy City of Jerusalem and biblical sites.

It is against this historical backdrop that we can make sense of the present-day composition of the Old City of Jerusalem and the nature of its historic sites. Within the walls are four delineated sections: the Christian quarter, the Jewish quarter, the Muslim quarter, and the Armenian quarter. Just outside the fortress walls are the Mount of Olives (on which can be found the Garden of Gethsemane, where the apostle Judas was said to have betrayed Jesus to the Roman authorities) and Mount Zion (the place where it was believed the Last Supper took place.)

The Muslim quarter is the largest and most densely populated of the sections of the Old City and is physically dominated by one of the most extraordinary works of Islamic architecture in the world—the Dome of the Rock. Built in 688–691 CE, the mosque-shrine represents the epitome of Islamic architectural design, from the mathematical relationships of the individual

The Garden of Gethsemane.
©Richard T. Nowitz/CORBIS

parts to the building as a whole to the supremely ornamented tiles and mosaics of its interior.

Because the Islamic faith traditionally proscribed the rendering of the human figure, the walls and dome contain complex, decorative organic and abstract patterns, sometimes interlaced with Koranic verses and other inscriptions rendered in Arabic calligraphy. The Muslim quarter also includes the El-Aqsa Mosque, several well-known gates to the Old City (such as the Damascus Gate and Herod's Gate), a museum of Islamic art, and the Central Souk, a covered marketplace selling spices, clothes, and souvenirs. The Muslim quarter is also the site of the Via Dolorosa, venerated as the route taken by Jesus on the way to his Crucifixion.

The spiritual heart of the Jewish quarter of the Old City is the Western Wall—a section of the retaining wall of the Temple Mount that is the only part of the Second Temple complex that survives to this day. Since the sixteenth century, it has been Judaism's holiest site, having been reconstructed after Israeli troops gained control of the Jewish quarter during the 1967 war. Jewish pilgrims from all over the world (non-Jews are also allowed to approach the wall) come to what is also known as the Wailing Wall to lament the destruction of the temple and to pray. Many leave prayers inscribed on the smallest bits of paper, tucked into the cracks between the huge stone blocks that make up the wall.

The Western Wall with the Dome of the Rock above.
©Richard T. Nowitz/CORBIS

Today the Jewish quarter is a mixture of historic sites and contemporary places of business serving the local community as well as tourists. Here, as in the other quarters, souvenir shops abound. Several fascinating excavations have been undertaken in the Jewish quarter, including the Cardo—one of Jerusalem's oldest main thoroughfares. During the era of the Crusades, the Cardo became a covered marketplace; today it remains an exclusive shopping arcade, full of galleries and boutiques. The quarter has several synagogues and archeological museums, of which the Wohl Museum is perhaps best known. It is alive with bustling streets, such as Tiferet Yisrael Street, and squares that are the social centers of the contemporary Jewish quarter. Lovely homes built around courtyards are constructed—by decree of the British military governor in 1917—only of Jerusalem stone, a local material ranging from soft beige to pale rose in color.

Many of the common architectural elements and motifs of the three religious traditions are present even in these residential buildings, particularly the arch and the dome. The Christian quarter of Jerusalem took shape in the shadows of the domes of its most sacred site, the Church of the Holy Sepulchre. Within the walls of this vast structure are two of Christendom's most important monuments: Golgotha, or Calvary (the rock venerated as the site of Christ's Crucifixion), and Christ's tomb (a marble slab that covers the rock on which Jesus' body is believed to have been laid). Flanking the main entrance are a bell tower and many chapels that, together with many small churches, hospices, and souvenir shops, obscure the overall exterior plan of the church.

Over centuries, bitter disputes over who "owns" the church would arise until an Ottoman decree in 1852, known as the Status Quo, divided custody of the structure and its holy sites among the Roman Catholics, Copts, Armenians, Greeks, Ethiopians, and Syrians. Every day, a Muslim "key holder," a neutral intermediary, unlocks the doors of the church. Just within the walls of the Christian quarter, the Citadel of the Old City (most likely the place of Christ's trial and condemnation) now houses the Tower of David Museum of the History of Jerusalem. The museum contains specific routes that offer panoramic views of the city, a close look at archeological remains, and displays and dioramas focused on the three cultural-religious traditions of Jerusalem.

Interior of the Church of the Holy Sepulchre, showing Calvary.
©Carmen Redondo/CORBIS

The story of the Armenians in Jerusalem begins in the time of Constantine (the kingdom of Armenia was the first to declare Christianity as its state religion after the emperor's edict of 313) and continues through the early twentieth century, when a large number of Armenian citizens fled to Jerusalem to escape the genocide being committed by the Turks. Although their numbers have dwindled significantly over the decades, the Armenian Church still maintains jurisdiction over such sites as the Church of the Holy Sepulchre, the Mosque of the Ascension, and the Tomb of the Virgin on the Temple Mount. Armenian works of ceramic, mosaic, and manuscript illumination can be seen in the library of St. James Cathedral and in the Mardigian Museum in the Armenian quarter.

Modern Jerusalem is as bustling and magnificent a city as one will ever lay eyes on—fashionable hotels, ornate synagogues and mosques, gardens, fountains, upscale shopping districts, colorful markets, important museums. One of the most poignant aspects of this art tour is the recognition that, for many, because of the continuing unrest, instability, and violence that grip the city, it is only what lies on these pages that will bring them to Jerusalem.

 To continue your tour and learn more about Jerusalem, go to ArtExperience Online.

14

CLASSICAL ART: GREECE AND ROME

■

. . . the glory that was Greece
And the grandeur that was Rome.
—Edgar Allan Poe

No other culture has had as far-reaching or lasting an influence on art and civilization as that of ancient Greece. It has been said that "nothing moves in the world which is not Greek in origin." To this day, the Greek influence can be felt in science, mathematics, law, politics, and art. Unlike some cultures that flourished, declined, and left barely an imprint on the pages of history, that of Greece has asserted itself time and again over the 3,000 years since its birth. During the fifteenth century, there was a revival of Greek art and culture called the Renaissance, and on the eve of the French Revolution of 1789, artists of the Neoclassical period again turned to the style and subjects of ancient Greece. Our founders looked to Greek architectural styles for the buildings of our nation's capital, and nearly every small town in America has a bank, post office, or library constructed in the Greek Revival style.

Despite its cultural and artistic achievements, ancient Greece was conquered and absorbed by Rome—one of history's strongest and largest empires. Although Greece's political power waned, its influence as a culture did not. It was assimilated by the admiring Romans. The spirit of **Hellenism** lived on in the glorious days of the Roman Empire.

Colosseum, Rome (Early Empire, 80 CE). Concrete (originally faced with marble). H: 1609; D: 620' and 513'. Detail showing seating. ©Angelo Hornak/CORBIS.

> *To claim that we can get along without study of the antique and the classics is either madness or laziness.*
>
> —JEAN-AUGUSTE-DOMINIQUE INGRES

In contrast to the Greeks' intellectual and creative achievements, Rome's cultural contributions lay in the areas of building, city planning, government, and law. Although sometimes thought of as uncultured and crude, the Romans civilized much of the ancient world following military campaigns that are still studied in military academies.

Despite its awesome might, the Roman Empire also fell. It was replaced by a force whose ideals differed greatly and whose kingdom was not of this world—Christianity. In this chapter, we shall examine the artistic legacy of Greece and Rome. This legacy—called **Classical art**—has influenced almost all of Western art, from Early Christian mosaics to contemporary Manhattan skyscrapers.

GREECE

Humanity, reason, and nature were central preoccupations of the Greek mind, together formulating their attitude toward life. The Greeks considered human beings the center of the universe—the "measure of all things." This concept is called **humanism**. The value the Greeks placed on the individual led to the development of democracy as a system of government among independent city-states throughout Greece and defined the character of Greek art, literature, and philosophy. To reach one's full potential, to be both physically and mentally fit, was an individual imperative. Perfection for the Greeks was the balance between elements: mind and body, emotion and intellect. Their love of reason and admiration for intellectual pursuits led to the development of **rationalism**, a philosophy in which knowledge is assumed to come from reason alone, without input from the senses.

The Greeks also had a passion and respect for nature and viewed human beings as a reflection of its perfect order. **Naturalism**, or truth to reality based on a keen observation of nature, guided the representation of the human figure. When what nature dispensed fell short of the Greek concept of perfection, **idealism** (the representation of forms according to an accepted standard of beauty) held sway. Humanism, rationalism, naturalism, idealism— these are the elements of Greek art and architecture.

From ancient Greece come the names of the dramatists Aeschylus, Aristophanes, and Sophocles; the poets Homer and Hesiod; the philosophers Aristotle, Socrates, and Plato; scientists like Archimedes and mathematicians like Euclid; and the historian Herodotus. It has given us gods like Zeus and Apollo, Athena and Aphrodite, and heroic figures named Achilles and Odysseus and Penelope. Even more astonishing, although Greek culture spans almost 1,000 years, its Golden Age, or period of greatest achievement, lasted no more than 80 years. As with many civilizations, the development of Greece occurred over a cycle of birth, maturation, perfection, and decline. These points in

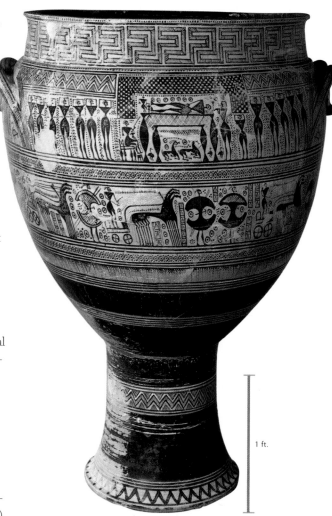

14-1 Dipylon Vase with funerary scene (Greek, 8th century BCE).
Terra-cotta. H: 42⅝".
The Metropolitan Museum of Art, New York. Rogers Fund, 1914 (14.130.14).
Image copyright ©The Metropolitan Museum of Art/Art Resource, NY

1 ft.

the cycle correspond to the four periods of Greek art that we will examine in this chapter: Geometric, Archaic, Classical, and Hellenistic.

Geometric Period

The **Geometric period** spanned approximately two centuries, from about 900 to 700 BCE. The period before is sometimes called the Dark Age of Greece because of a virtual collapse of civilization. Greece was gripped by chaos and poverty, the arts were lost, and its society was cut off from the outside world. During the eighth century, trade resumed, the economic situation improved, and with these, first steps were taken to regenerate the arts. The Geometric period is so called because of the predominance of geometric shapes and patterns in works of art. As in Egyptian art, the representation of the human figure was conceptual rather than optical, and usually reduced to a combination of geometric forms such as circles and triangles.

The Dipylon Vase (Fig. **14-1**), a large **krater** used as a grave marker and found in the Dipylon cemetery in Athens, is an early example of the Geometric style. Except for its base, most of the vessel is decorated with geometric motifs, some of which may have been inspired by the patterns of woven baskets. Two thicker bands around the body of the vase feature a funeral procession comprised of stylized, geometric figures. Distinctions are made between males and females, but overall, they march along with the same rigidity of the geometric patterns. The figures are a familiar combination of frontal, wedge-shaped torsos, profile legs and arms, and a profile head with a frontal eye. In the center of one of the bands, the deceased rests on a bier. Below, figures of warriors with apple core–shaped shields and teams of chariots are in attendance. The deceased was likely a Greek soldier. These geometric elements can also be seen in small bronze sculptures of the period, but the stylistic development is most evident in the art of vase painting.

Archaic Period

The **Archaic period** spanned roughly the years from 660 to 480 BCE, but the change from the Geometric style to the Archaic style in art was gradual. As Greece expanded its trade with Eastern countries, it was influenced by their art. Flowing forms and fantastic animals inspired

by Mesopotamian art appeared on Greek pottery. There was a growing emphasis on the human figure, which replaced Geometric motifs.

Vase Painting

During the Archaic period, Eastern patterns and forms gradually disappeared. During the Geometric period, the human figure was subordinated to decorative motifs, but in the Archaic period, it became the preferred subject. In the François Vase (Fig. **14-2**), for example, geometric patterns are restricted to a few areas. The entire body of the vessel, a **volute krater**, is divided into six wide bands, or registers, featuring the exploits of Greek heroes and legends, including Achilles and Theseus. Even though the drawing is somewhat stilted, the figures of men and animals have substance, and an attempt at naturalistic gestures has been made. Unlike the figures of the Dipylon Vase, those of the François Vase are not static. In fact, the movement of the battling humans and the prancing horses is quite lively. This energetic mood is echoed in the curling shapes of the volute handles.

The François Vase is a masterpiece of Archaic vase painting. No doubt, the potter and painter were proud of their

14-2 KLEITIAS.

François Vase. Attic volute krater (Greek, c. 570 BCE). Ceramic. H: 26".

Archaeological Museum, Florence.
©Scala/Art Resource, NY

The Women Weavers of Ancient Greece

NO WORKS OF ART BY GREEK WOMEN have survived, and only a scant number of names have been recorded. Yet there is plenty of evidence that women did have outlets for creative expression, including ceramics, basketry, and particularly, weaving. Noblewomen, commoners, and slaves wove as a pastime or to earn a living. Athena, the most important female god in the Greek pantheon, was best known as the goddess of war and wisdom, but she was also the patron goddess of potters and weavers.

Stories of women weaving come down to us from Homer in *The Iliad* and *The Odyssey*. In one scene in *The Iliad*, Helen of Sparta (now Helen of Troy) is visited by a goddess in disguise, who aims to rekindle her love for her abandoned husband, Menelaus:

She found Helen in her room,
weaving a large cloth, a double purple cloak,
creating pictures of the many battle scenes
between horse-taming Trojans and bronze-clad Achaeans,
wars they suffered for her sake at the hands of Ares.

In the *Odyssey*, Penelope, the wife of the wily (and missing-in-action) Odysseus, wards off suitors on the promise that she will choose one of them after she finishes weaving a funeral shroud for her father. Unbeknownst to them, Penelope spends her days weaving and her nights tearing out her work.

She set up a great loom in her palace, and set to weaving
a web of threads long and fine. Then she said to us:
'Young men, my suitors, now that great Odysseus has perished,
wait, though you are eager to marry me, until I finish
this web, so that my weaving will not be useless and wasted.
This is a shroud for the hero Laertes, for when the destructive
doom of death which lays men low shall take him, lest any
Achaian woman in this neighbourhood hold it against me
that a man of many conquests lies with no sheet to wind him.'
So she spoke, and the proud heart in us was persuaded.
Thereafter in the daytime she would weave at her great loom,
but in the night she would have torches set by, and undo it.

The importance of women weavers is suggested in the subject of a black-figure vase attributed to the Amasis Painter (Fig. **14-3**). Its large central panel features a scene of women working on looms and engaged in other aspects of cloth production. Some scholars have posited the even more widespread influence of women's weaving by connecting the patterns of geometric vase painting (Fig. 14-1) with those of Dorian wool fabrics.

The connection of women to weaving continues throughout the centuries. In the Middle Ages, for example, noblewomen, nuns, and commoners were all taught the skills of weaving and embroidery, and the great tapestries of this era were most certainly created by women. In our time, artists such as Faith Ringgold (see Fig. 1-27) and Miriam Schapiro (see Fig. 1-34) have explored the expressive possibilities of traditional needlework. ∎

1 in.

14-3 ATTRIBUTED TO THE AMASIS PAINTER,
ATTIC LEKYTHOS.
Women Working Wool on a Loom (Greek, c. 540 BCE).
Terra-cotta. H: 6¾". Said to have been found in Attica.
The Metropolitan Museum of Art, New York. Fletcher Fund, 1931 (31.11.10).
Image copyright ©The Metropolitan Museum of Art/Art Resource, NY

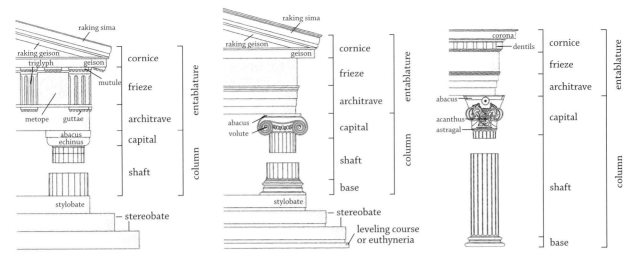

14-4 Left to right: Doric, Ionic, and Corinthian orders.

work, because the vessel is signed twice by each of them. The François Vase, named after the archeologist who found it, is an example of **black-figure painting**. The combination of black figures on a reddish background was achieved through a three-stage kiln-firing process. The figures were painted on a clay pot using a brush and a **slip**, a liquid of sifted clay, and then introduced to the kiln. The first stage of the firing process was called the **oxidizing phase**, because oxygen was allowed into the kiln. Firing under these conditions turned both the pot and the painted slip decoration red.

In the second phase of firing, called the **reducing phase**, oxygen was eliminated from the kiln, and the vase and the slip both turned black. In the third and final phase, called the **reoxidizing phase**, oxygen was again introduced into the kiln. The coarser material of the pot turned red, and the fine clay of the slip remained black. The result was a vase with black figures silhouetted against a red ground. The finer details of the figures were incised with sharp instruments that scraped away portions of the black to expose the red clay underneath or highlighted with touches of red and purple pigment. Although this technique was fairly versatile, the black figures were ultimately too visually heavy for Greek artists. Around 530 BCE, a reversal of the black-figure process was developed, enabling painters to create lighter, more realistic red figures on a black ground.

Architecture

Some of the greatest accomplishments of the Greeks are witnessed in their architecture. Although their personal dwellings were simple, the temples for their gods were fantastic monuments. During the Archaic period, an architectural format was developed that provided the basis for temple architecture throughout the history and territories of ancient Greece. It consisted of a central room (derived in shape from the Mycenaean **megaron**) surrounded by a single or double row of columns. This room, called the **cella**, usually housed the cult statue of the god or goddess to whom the temple was dedicated. The overall shape of the temple was rectangular, and it had a pitched roof.

There were three styles, or orders, in Greek architecture: the **Doric**, **Ionic**, and **Corinthian**. The Doric order, which originated on the Greek mainland, was the earliest, simplest, and most commonly used. The more ornate Ionic order was introduced by architects from Asia Minor and was generally reserved for smaller temples. The Corinthian order, differentiated from the Ionic by its intricate column capital, was not used widely in Greece but became a favorite design of Roman architects, who adopted it in the second century BCE. Figure **14-4** compares the Doric, Ionic, and Corinthian orders and illustrates the basic parts of the temple facade.

The major weight-bearing elements of the temple are cylindrical columns composed of drums stacked on top of one another and fitted with dowels. They sit on either a platform (**stylobate**) or a base and helped support the roof. The main vertical body, or shaft, of the column is crowned by a **capital** that marks a transition from the shaft to a horizontal member (the **entablature**) that directly bears the weight of the roof. In the Doric order, the capital is simple and cushionlike. In the Ionic order, it consists of a scroll or volute similar to those seen on the François Vase (Fig.

14-2). The Corinthian capital is by far the most elaborate, consisting of an all-around carving of overlapping acanthus leaves. The columns directly support the entablature, which is divided into three parts: the **architrave, frieze,** and **cornice.** The architrave of the Doric order is a solid, undecorated horizontal band, whereas those of the Ionic and Corinthian orders are subdivided into three narrower horizontal bands. The frieze, which sits directly above the architrave, is typically carved with relief sculpture.

The Doric frieze is divided into sections called **triglyphs** and **metopes.** The triglyphs are carved panels consisting of three vertical elements. These alternate with panels that were filled with figurative sculpture carved in relief. The Ionic and Corinthian friezes, by contrast, were carved with a continuous band of figures or—particularly in the Corinthian order—repetitive, stylized motifs.

The Ionic order liberated sculptors from the constraints of the square spaces that defined the Doric frieze, allowing the figures and the narrative to flow more freely. The topmost element of the entablature is called a **cornice** and, together with the diagonals of the **raking cornice,** it forms a frame for the **pediment.** The triangular spaces of the pediments, formed by the slope of the roof lines at the short ends of the temple, was also decorated with figurative sculpture.

The Doric order originated in the Archaic period, but it attained perfection in the buildings of the Classical period. In some buildings, like the Parthenon, the Doric and Ionic orders are combined. The Corinthian order, although developed by the Greeks, was used more universally by the Romans.

Sculpture

In the Archaic period, sculpture emerged as a principal art form. In addition to sculptural decoration for buildings, freestanding, life-size, and larger-than-life-size statues were created. Such monumental sculpture was probably inspired by Egyptian figures that Greek travelers would have seen during the early Archaic period.

In Greek temples, the nonstructural members of the building were often ornamented with sculpture. These

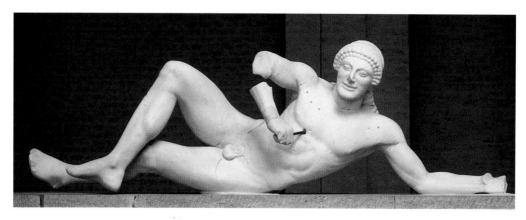

14-5 *Dying Warrior,* from the west pediment of the Temple of Aphaia at Aegina, Greece (500–490 BCE). Marble. Approx. 5' 2½" long.
Staatliche Anikensammlungen unde Glyptothek, Munich.
Courtesy of Saskia Ltd.
©Dr. Ron Wiedenhoeft

14-6 *Fallen Warrior,* from the east pediment of the Temple of Aphaia at Aegina, Greece (490–480 BCE). Marble. Approx. 6' 1" long.
Staatliche Anikensammlungen unde Glyptothek, Munich.
©CM Dixon/HIP/The Image Works

included the frieze and pediment. Because early Archaic sculptors were forced to work within relatively tight spaces, the figures from this period are often cramped and cumbersome. However, toward the end of the Archaic period, artists compensated for the irregularity of the spaces by arranging figures in poses that corresponded to the peculiarities of the architectural element. For example, the *Dying Warrior* (Fig. **14-5**) from the Temple of Aphaia at Aegina was positioned to fit into one of the angles of its west pediment. The figure is based somewhat on the observation of nature, although conventions dominate— the thick-lidded eyes and stylized hair, overly defined lips that purse in an artificial "smile," and linear patterns that define musculature.

Building projects like the Temple of Aphaia took years to complete, and the hands of artists of different styles were involved. Compare the warrior from the west pediment with one from the east pediment of the same building (Fig. **14-6**). This warrior's feet would have been wedged into the left corner of the pediment; his body fans out toward the shield, corresponding to the dimensions of the angle. Some conventions remain, like the thick-lidded eyes, subtle "smile," and unnaturally pointed beard. The body may not be wholly realistic, but the patterns that play over the surface of the warrior in the west pediment have been virtually eliminated as the artist aims for a convincing representation of muscles, bones, and tendons. The work reveals a marvelous attention to detail, both physical and psychological. It is, after all, a pitiful sight. The warrior, wounded in battle, crashes down upon the field with his shield in hand. He struggles to lift himself with his right arm, but to no avail. The hopelessness of the situation is echoed in the helplessness of the left arm, which remains trapped in the grasp of the cumbersome shield. It hangs there useless, the band of the shield restricting its flow of blood. It is an emotionally wrenching scene, although (or perhaps because) the trauma is not revealed in the face of the warrior. It remains masklike, bound to the restraining conventions of the Archaic style.

The *Fallen Warrior* from Aegina was created during the last years of the Archaic period and represents a stylistic transition to the Classical era. The history of Archaic Greek sculpture, however, began more than a century earlier, about 600 BCE, with large, freestanding figures. Some of the earliest of these are called **kouros figures**, devotional or funerary statues of young men. Figure **14-7** is typical of these figures. As in Egyptian sculptures, the arms lie close to the body, the fists are clenched, and one leg advances slightly. But the kouroi (plural) are different in a principal way: the

14-7 *Kouros figure* (Greek, Archaic, c. 600 BCE).
Marble. H: 6'4".
The Metropolitan Museum of Art, New York. Fletcher Fund, 1932 (32.11.10). Image copyright ©The Metropolitan Museum of Art/Art Resource, NY

1 ft.

stone was carved away from the body, releasing it from the block. These male figures are also depicted in the nude. The musculature is full and thick, and emphasized by harsh, patterned lines. The kneecaps, groin muscles, rib cage, and pectoral muscles are all flexed unrealistically. The head has also been treated according to the artistic conventions of the day. The hair is stylized and intricate in pattern. The eyes are thick-lidded and stare directly forward.

14-8 *Peplos Kore* (Greek, Archaic, c. 530 BCE).
Marble. H: 48".
Acropolis Museum, Athens.
©Nimitallah/Art Resource, NY

1 ft.

statement, "The Greeks made their gods into men and their men into gods."

The female counterpart to the kouros is the **kore**. Unlike the kouros, the kore is clothed and often embellished with intricate carved detail. The *Peplos Kore* (Fig. **14-8**)—so named because the garment the model wears is a **peplos**, or heavy woolen wrap—is one of the most enchanting images in Greek art, partly because touches of paint remain on the sculpture, giving it a lifelike gaze and sensitive expression. We tend to think of Greek architecture and sculpture as pristine and glistening in their pure white surfaces, but most sculpture was painted with subtle colors. Architectural sculpture was embellished with red, blue, yellow, green, black, and sometimes gold pigments. None of this painted decoration remains on temple sculpture. However, statues and wooden panels were painted with encaustic, a more durable and permanent medium combining pigment and wax.

The beauty of the *Peplos Kore* lies in its simplicity. The woman's body is composed of graceful columnar lines echoed in the delicate play of the long braids that grace her shoulders. As with kouroi, she remains close to, but not strictly bound to, the marble block from which she was carved. Her right arm is attached to her side at the wrist, but the left arm, now missing, extended outward and probably held a symbolic offering. Although the function of the kore figures is uncertain, they have been interpreted as votive sculptures because many have been found among the ruins of temples. These architectural and freestanding sculptures were all made of marble. Although expensive, it was readily available, and some of the finest marble in the world came from quarries near Athens.

The late Archaic period produced significant works of art and architecture against the backdrop of brutal war with the Persians. We encountered the might of the Persian empire in Chapter 13. By the late fifth century BCE, it appeared as if that empire would consume all of Greece. After horrible, violent losses, the Greeks defeated the Persians in a decisive battle on the plain of Marathon and captured a naval victory at Salamis. Greek pride surged and a Western identity was formed—one that stood in self-conscious opposition to the perceived barbarism of the Persians and their Asian civilization.

Early Classical Art

The change from the Archaic to the Classical period coincided with the Greek victory over the Persians at Salamis in 480 BCE. The Greek mood was elevated after this feat, and a

The youth has very high cheekbones and clearly defined lips that appear to curl upward in a smile. This facial expression, which we also saw on the warriors of the Temple of Aphaia, seems to have been an Archaic convention and thus is called an "Archaic smile." Kouroi were found in cemeteries, where they replaced large vases as grave markers. They were also used as votive sculptures (recall the votive figures of Tell Asmar, Fig. 13-5). In their stately repose and grand presence, these figures might impress us as gods rather than mortals. One is reminded of the oft-repeated

new sense of unity among the city-states prevailed, propelling the country into its "Golden Age." Athens, which was sacked by the Persians, became the center for all important postwar activity and the revival of the arts. The style of Early Classical art is marked by a power and austerity that reflected what were seen as Greek traits responsible for the defeat of the Persians. Although Early Classical sculpture developed beyond Archaic stylizations, some of the rigidity of the earlier period remains. The Early Classical style is therefore sometimes referred to as the Severe style.

Sculpture

The most significant development in Early Classical art was the introduction of implied movement in figurative sculpture. This went hand in hand with the artist's keener observation of nature. One of the most widely copied works of this period, which encompasses these new elements, is the *Diskobolos* (Fig. **14-9**), or Discus Thrower, by Myron. Like most Greek monumental sculpture, it survives only in a marble Roman copy after the bronze original. The life-size statue depicts an event from the Olympic Games—the discus throw. The athlete, a young man in his prime, is caught by the artist at the moment when the arm stops its swing backward and prepares to sling forward to release the discus. His muscles are tensed as he reaches for the strength to release the object. His torso intersects the arc of his extended arms, resembling an arrow pulled taut on a bow. It is an image of pent-up energy at the moment before release. As in most of Greek Classical art, there is a balance between motion and stability, between emotion and restraint.

Classical Art

Greek sculpture and architecture reached their height of perfection during the Classical period. Greece embarked upon a period of peace—albeit short-lived—and turned its attention to rebuilding its monuments and advancing art, drama, and music. The dominating force behind these accomplishments in Athens was the dynamic statesman Pericles. His reputation was recounted centuries after his death by the Greek historian Plutarch. On the one hand, Plutarch described the anger of the Greek city-states at Pericles' use of funds that had been set aside for mutual

14-9 MYRON.
Diskobolos (Discus Thrower) (c. 450 BCE).
Roman marble copy after bronze original. Life-size.
Palazzo Vecchio, Florence.
©Scala/Art Resource, NY

protection to pay for his ambitious Athenian building program. On the other hand, Plutarch wrote glowingly about postwar Athens: "in its beauty, each work was, even at that time, ancient, and yet, in its perfection, each looks even at the present time as if it were fresh and newly built. . . . It is as if some ever-flowering life and unaging spirit had been infused into the creation of these works."

Architecture

After the Persians destroyed the Acropolis, the Athenians refused to rebuild their shrines with the fallen stones that the enemy had desecrated. What followed was a massive building campaign under the direction of Pericles. Work

14-10 ICTINOS AND CALLICRATES.
The Parthenon on the Acropolis, Athens (448–432 BCE).
Studio Kontos

began first on the temple that was sacred to the goddess **Athena**, protector of Athens. This temple, the Parthenon (Fig. **14-10**), became one of the most influential buildings in the history of architecture.

Constructed by the architects Ictinos and Callicrates, the Parthenon stands as the most accomplished representative of the Doric order, although it does include some Ionic elements. A single row of Doric columns, now gracefully proportioned, surrounds a two-roomed cella that housed a treasury and a 40-foot-high statue of Athena made of ivory and gold. At first glance, the architecture appears austere, with its rigid progression of vertical elements crowned by the strong horizontal of its entablature. Yet few of the building's lines are strictly vertical or horizontal. For example, the stylobate, or top step of

the platform from which the columns rise, is not straight, but curves downward toward the ends. This convex shape is echoed in the entablature. The columns are not exactly vertical, but rather tilt inward. They are not evenly spaced; the intervals between the corner columns are narrower. The shafts of the columns also differ from one another. The corner columns have a wider diameter, for example. In addition, the shaft of each column swells in diameter as it rises from the base, narrowing once again before reaching the capital. This swelling is called **entasis**.

The reasons for these variations are not known for certain, although there have been several hypotheses. Some art historians have suggested that the change from straight to curved lines is functional. A convex stylobate, for example, might make drainage easier. Others have suggested that the variations are meant to compensate for perceptual distortions on the part of the viewer that would make straight lines look curved from a distance. Regardless of the actual motive, we can assume that the designers of the Parthenon sought an integrated and organic look to their building. The wide base and relatively narrower roof give the appearance of a structure that is anchored firmly to the ground yet growing dramatically from it. Although it has a grandeur based on a kind of austerity, it also has a lively plasticity. It appears as if the Greeks conceived their architecture as large, freestanding sculpture.

The subsequent history of the Parthenon is interesting and shocking. It was used as a Byzantine church, a Roman Catholic church, and a mosque. The Parthenon survived more or less intact, although altered by these successive functions, until the seventeenth century, when the Turks used it as an ammunition dump in their war against the Venetians. Venetian rockets hit the bull's eye, and the center portion of the temple was blown out in the explosion. The cella still lies in ruins, although fortunately the exterior columns and entablatures were not beyond repair.

Sculpture

The sculptor Phidias was commissioned by Pericles to oversee the entire sculptural program of the Parthenon. Although he concentrated his own efforts on creating the ivory and gold statue of Athena, his assistants followed his style closely. The Phidian style is characterized by a lightness of touch, attention to realistic detail, contrast of textures, and fluidity and spontaneity of line and movement.

As on other Doric temples, the sculpted surfaces of the Parthenon were confined to the friezes and the pediments. The subjects of the Doric frieze were battles between the Lapiths and the Centaurs, the Greeks and the Amazons, and the gods and the giants. In addition, the Parthenon had a continuous, inner Ionic frieze. This was carved with scenes from the Panathenaic procession, an event that took place every four years when the peplos of the statue of Athena was changed. The pediments depicted the birth of Athena and the contest between Athena and Poseidon for the city of Athens.

The *Three Goddesses* (Fig. **14-11**), a figural group from the corner of the east pediment, is typical of the Phidian style. The bodies of the goddesses are weighty and well-articulated, and their poses and gestures are naturalistic. The drapery falls over the bodies in realistic folds, and there is a marvelous contrast of textures between the heavier cloth that wraps around the legs and the more diaphanous fabric covering the upper torsos. The thinner drapery clings to the body as if wet, following the contours of the flesh. The intricate play of the linear folds renders a tactile quality not seen in art before this time. The lines both gently envelop the individual figures and integrate them in a dynamically flowing composition.

As mentioned previously, Greece had at one time come under Turkish rule. Some of the Parthenon sculptures were taken down by Lord Elgin between 1801 and 1803 while he was British ambassador to Constantinople. He sold them to the British government, who put them on display at the British Museum. Although there has been prolonged controversy concerning their return to Greece,

14-11 *The Three Goddesses*, from east pediment of the Parthenon (c. 438–431 BCE).
Marble. Height of center figure: 4′7″.
British Museum, London.
©Heritage-Images/The Image Works

1 ft.

there is no doubt that Lord Elgin saved the marbles from utter destruction.

Some of the greatest freestanding sculpture of the Classical period was created by a rival of Phidias named Polykleitos. His favorite medium was bronze, and his preferred subject was athletes. As with most Greek sculpture, we know his work primarily from marble Roman copies of the bronze originals. Polykleitos's work differed markedly from that of Phidias. Whereas the Parthenon sculptor emphasized the reality of appearances and aimed to delight the senses through textural contrasts, Polykleitos's statues were based on reason and intellect. Rather than mimic nature, he tried to perfect nature by developing a canon of proportions from which he would derive his "ideal" figures.

Polykleitos's most famous sculpture is the *Doryphoros* (Fig. **14-12**), or Spear Bearer. The artist has "idealized" the athletic figure—that is, made it more perfect and more beautiful—by imposing on it a set of laws relating part to part (for example, the entire body is equal in height to eight heads). Although some of Phidias's spontaneity is lost, the result is an almost godlike image of grandeur and strength. One of the most significant elements of Polykleitos's style is the **weight-shift principle**. The athlete rests his weight on the right leg, which is planted firmly on the ground. It forms a strong vertical that is echoed in the vertical of the relaxed arm. These are counterbalanced by a relaxed left leg bent at the knee and a tensed left arm bent at the elbow. Tension and relaxation of the limbs are balanced across the body *diagonally*. The relaxed arm opposes the relaxed leg, and the tensed arm is opposite the tensed, weight-bearing leg. The weight-shift principle lends naturalism to the figure. Rather than face forward in a rigid pose, as do the kouroi, the *Doryphoros* stands comfortably at rest. The ease and naturalism, however, were derived from a compulsive balancing of opposing parts.

Vase Painting

The weight-shift principle and the naturalistic use of implied movement can also be seen in Classical vase painting such as the Argonaut Krater (Fig. **14-13**), a red-figure vase by the so-called Niobid Painter. In the Dipylon krater and the François Vase, the human figures were confined to registers (see Figs. 14-1 and 14-2). On later vases, these registers were eliminated, making the broad field of the vase available for the portrayal of the human figure in a variety of positions. Until the Classical period, though, the figures were placed in a friezelike arrangement. That is, all of the heads were pretty much on one level, and depth was limited. The Niobid Painter, by contrast, attempted to create a sense of three-dimensional space by outlining a foreground, middle ground, and background. This was a noble attempt at realism, based on optical perception, but ultimately it fails because the artist did not shrink the sizes of the background figures to suggest distance. The ability to arrange figures in space convincingly came later with the development of perspective.

Vase painting was not the only two-dimensional art form in ancient Greece. There was also wall, or **mural painting**, none of which has survived. It is believed,

14-12 POLYKLEITOS.

Doryphoros (Spear Bearer) (c. 450–440 BCE).
Marble. Roman copy after Greek original. H: 6'6".
National Museum, Naples.
©Scala/Art Resource, NY

14-13 NIOBID PAINTER.
Argonaut Krater, Attic red-figure krater
(Greek, c. 460 BCE).
Ceramic. H: 24¼".
Louvre Museum, Paris.
©Giraudon/Art Resource, NY

however, that the Romans copied Greek wall painting, as they did sculpture, and it is thus possible to conjecture what Greek painting looked like by examining surviving Roman wall painting (Fig. 14-21).

14-14 PRAXITELES.
Hermes and Dionysos (c. 330–320 BCE).
Marble. H: 7'1".
Museum, Olympia.
©Scala/Art Resource, NY

Late Classical Art

Sculpture

The Late Classical period brought a more humanistic and naturalistic style, with emphasis on the expression of emotion. The stocky muscularity of the Polykleitan ideal was replaced by a more languid sensuality and graceful proportions. One of the major proponents of this new style was Praxiteles. His works show a lively spirit that was lacking in some of the more austere sculptures of the Classical period.

The *Hermes and Dionysos* of Praxiteles (Fig. **14-14**), interestingly, is the only undisputed original work we have by the Greek masters of the Classical era. Unlike most other sculptors who favored bronze, Praxiteles excelled in carving. His ability to translate harsh stone surfaces into subtly modeled flesh was unsurpassed. We need only compare his figural group with the *Doryphoros* to witness the changes that had taken place since the Classical period. Hermes is delicately carved, and his musculature is realistically depicted, suggesting the preference of nature as a model over adherence to a rigid, predefined canon. The messenger-god holds the infant Dionysos, the god of wine, in his left arm, which is propped up by a tree trunk covered with a drape. His right arm is broken above the elbow but reaches out in front of him. It has been suggested that Hermes once held a bunch of grapes toward which the infant was reaching.

Praxiteles' skill in depicting variations in texture was extraordinary. Note, for example, the differences between the solid, toned muscles of the man and the soft, cuddly flesh of the child; or rough, curly hair against the flawless, ivory skin; or the deeply carved, billowing drapery alongside the subtly modeled flesh. The easy grace of the sculpture comes from applying a double weight-shift principle. Hermes shifts his weight from the right leg to the left arm, resting it on the tree. This position causes a sway which is called an **S curve**, because the contours of the body form an S shape around an imaginary vertical axis.

Perhaps most remarkable is the emotional content of the sculpture. The aloof quality of Classical statuary is replaced with a touching scene between the two gods. Hermes' facial expression as he teases the child is one of pride and amusement. Dionysos, on the other hand, exhibits typical infant behavior—he is all hands and reaching impatiently for something to eat. There remains a certain restraint to the movement and to the expressiveness, but it is definitely on the wane. In the Hellenistic period, that classical balance will no longer pertain, and the emotion present in Praxiteles' sculpture will reach new peaks.

The most important and innovative sculptor to follow Praxiteles was Lysippos. He introduced a new canon of proportions that resulted in more slender and graceful figures, departing from the stockiness of Polykleitos and assuming the fluidity of Praxiteles. Most important, however, was his new concept of the motion of figure in space. All of the sculptures that we have seen so far have had a two-dimensional perspective. That is, the whole of the work can be viewed from a single point of view, standing in front of the sculpture. This is not the case in works such as the *Apoxyomenos* (Fig. **14-15**) by Lysippos. The figure's arms envelop the surrounding space. The athlete is scraping oil and grime from his body with a dull knifelike implement. This stance forces the viewer to walk around the sculpture to appreciate its details. Rather than adhere to a single plane, as even the S-curve figure of *Hermes* does, the *Apoxyomenos* seems to spiral around a vertical axis.

Lysippos's reputation was almost unsurpassed. In fact, his work was so widely admired that Alexander the Great, the Macedonian king who spread Greek culture throughout the Near East, chose him as his court sculptor. It is said that Lysippos was the only sculptor permitted to execute portraits of Alexander. Years after the *Apoxyomenos* was created, it was still seen as a magnificent work of art. Pliny, a Roman writer on the arts, recounted an amusing story about the sculpture:

Lysippos made more statues than any other artist, being, as we said, very prolific in the art; among them was a youth scraping himself with a strigil, which Marcus Agrippa dedicated in front

14-15 LYSIPPOS.

Apoxyomenos (c. 330 BCE).
Roman marble copy after a bronze original. H: 6' 6¾".
Vatican Museum, Rome.
©Scala/Art Resource, NY

1 ft.

of his baths and which the Emperor Tiberius was astonishingly fond of. [Tiberius] was, in fact, unable to restrain himself in this case and had it moved to his own bedroom, substituting another statue in its place. When, however, the indignation of the Roman people was so great that it demanded, by an uproar, that the Apoxyomenos be replaced, the Emperor, although he had fallen in love with it, put it back.[1]

Hellenistic Art

Greece entered the Hellenistic period under the reign of Alexander the Great. His father had conquered the democratic city-states, and Alexander had been raised amid the art and culture of Greece. When he ascended the throne, he conquered Persia, Egypt, and the entire Near East, bringing with him his beloved Greek culture, or Hellenism. With the vastness of Alexander's empire, the significance of the city of Athens as an artistic and cultural center waned.

Hellenistic art is characterized by excessive, almost theatrical emotion and the use of illusionistic effects to heighten realism. In three-dimensional art, the space surrounding the figures is treated as an extension of the viewer's space, at times narrowing the fine line between art and reality.

Sculpture

The Dying Gaul (Fig. **14-16**) illustrates the Hellenistic artist's preoccupation with high drama and unleashed passion. Unlike the *Fallen Warrior* (Fig. 14-6), in which the viewer has to extract the emotion by piecing together scattered realistic details that suggest a narrative, *The Dying Gaul* presents all of the elements that communicate the pathos of the work. Bleeding from a large wound in his side, the fallen "barbarian" attempts to sustain his weight on a weakened right arm. His head, rendered with coarse, disheveled hair, hangs down hopelessly. He has lost his battle and is now about to lose his life. Strength seems to drain out of his body and into the ground, even as we watch. Our perspective is that of a theatergoer; the Gaul seems to be sitting on a stage. Although the artist intended to evoke pity and emotion from the viewer, the figure's melodramatic pose and his placement on a stagelike platform detach the viewer from the event. We tend to see the scene as well-acted drama rather than cruel reality.

Hellenistic artists were often drawn to dramatic subjects. They did not focus on a balance between emotion and restraint but portrayed human excess. In the midst of this theatricality, however, there was another trend in Hellenistic art that reflected the simplicity and idealism of the Classical period. The harsh realism and passionate emotion of the Hellenistic artist could not be further in spirit from the serene and idealized form of the *Aphrodite*

---

1 J. J. Pollitt, *The Art of Greece 1400–31 BCE: Sources and Documents* (Englewood Cliffs, NJ: Prentice-Hall, 1965), 144.

14-16 *The Dying Gaul* (Hellenistic, c. 240–200 BCE). Roman marble copy after a bronze original. Life-size.
Capitoline Museum, Rome.
©Scala/Art Resource, NY

14-17 *Aphrodite of Melos (Venus de Milo)* (Hellenistic, 2nd century BCE).

Marble. Larger than life-size.

Louvre Museum, Paris.
©The Gallery Collection/CORBIS

In 146 BCE, the Romans sacked Corinth, a Greek city on the Peloponnesus, after which Greek power waned. Both the territory and the culture of Greece were assimilated by the powerful and growing Roman state. It has been said that "all roads lead to Rome," and so will this chapter. First, however, let us examine the art of the Etruscans, a civilization on the Italian peninsula that predated that of the Romans.

THE ETRUSCANS

The center of power of the Roman state was the peninsula of Italy, but the Romans did not gain supremacy over this area until the fourth century BCE, when they began to conquer the Etruscans. The Italian peninsula was inhabited by many peoples, but the Etruscan civilization was the most significant one before that of ancient Rome. The Etruscans had a long and interesting history, dating back to around 700 BCE, the period of transition from the Geometric to the Archaic period in Greece. They were not an indigenous peoples but are believed to have come from Asia Minor. This link may explain some similarities between Etruscan art and culture and that of Eastern countries.

Etruria and Greece had some things in common. Both were great sea powers. Both were divided into independent city-states. The Etruscans even borrowed motifs and styles from the art of Greece. There is one more similarity between the two civilizations: Etruria also fell prey to the Romans. They were no match for Roman organization, especially because neighboring city-states never came to one another's aid in a time of crisis. By 88 BCE, the Romans had vanquished the last of the Etruscans.

Architecture

Although the Etruscans constructed temples, none survive beyond their foundations because they were constructed of impermanent materials such as wood and mud brick. Yet in what almost seems a throwback to ancient Egypt, underground tombs, carved out of bedrock, suggest the lives and habits of the Etruscan people. The interiors were constructed to resemble those of domestic dwellings. The walls were covered with hundreds of everyday items carved in low relief, including such things as kitchen utensils and weapons. Like the Egyptians, and unlike the Greeks, the Etruscans apparently wanted to duplicate their earthly environments in their funerary monuments.

of Melos (Fig. **14-17**), often called the *Venus de Milo*. This contradictory style owes more to the artistic legacy of Praxiteles than to the contemporary illusionism of the sculptor of the *Dying Gaul*.

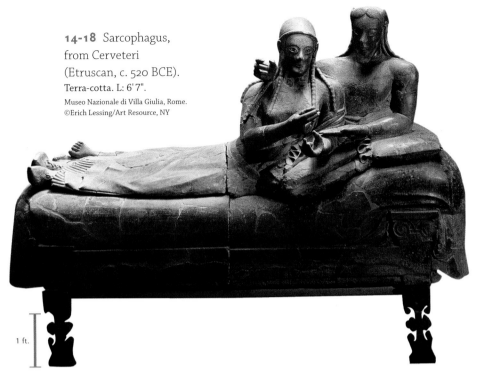

14-18 Sarcophagus, from Cerveteri (Etruscan, c. 520 BCE). Terra-cotta. L: 6′ 7″.
Museo Nazionale di Villa Giulia, Rome.
©Erich Lessing/Art Resource, NY

1 ft.

Sculpture

Much sculpture of bronze and clay has survived from these Etruscan tombs, and we have learned a great deal about the Etruscan people from these finds. For example, even though no architecture survives, we know what the exterior of domestic dwellings looked like from the clay models of homes that served as **cinerary urns**. We have also been able to gain insight into the personalities of the Etruscan people through their figurative sculpture, particularly that found on the lids of their **sarcophagi**.

The Sarcophagus from Cerveteri (Fig. **14-18**) is a translation into terra-cotta of the banquet scenes of which the Etruscans were so fond. A man and wife are represented reclining on a lounge and appear to be enjoying the dinner entertainment. Their gestures are animated and naturalistic, even though their facial features and hair are rigidly stylized. These stylizations, especially the thick-lidded eyes, resemble Greek sculpture of the Archaic period and were most likely influenced by it. However, the serenity and severity of Archaic Greek art are absent. The Etruscans appear to be as relaxed, happy, and fun loving in death as they were in life.

ROME

In about 500 BCE, the Roman Republic was established, and it would last some four centuries. The Roman arm of strength reached into northern Italy, conquering the Etruscans, and eventually stretched in all directions, gaining supremacy over Greece, western Europe, northern Africa, and parts of the Near East (Map **14-1**). No longer was this the republican city of Rome flexing its muscles—this was the Roman Empire.

Roman art combined native talent, needs, and styles with other artistic sources, particularly those of Greece. The art that followed the absorption of Greece into the Roman Empire is thus often called Greco-Roman. It was fashionable for Romans to own—or at the very least, have copies of—Greek works of art. This tendency gave the Romans a reputation as mere imitators of Greek art, a simplistic view laid waste by scholars of Roman art history. A marvelous, unabashed eclecticism pervaded much of Roman art, resulting in vigorous and sometimes unpredictable combinations of motifs. The Romans were also fond of a harsh, almost trompe l'oeil,

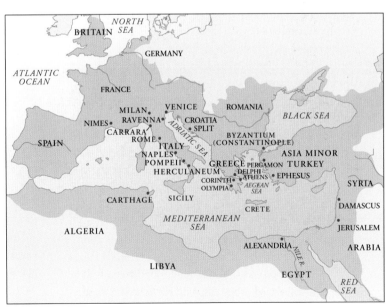

MAP 14-1 The Roman Empire (2nd century CE).

realism in their portrait sculpture, which had not been seen before their time. They were master builders (the inventors of concrete!), who created some of the grandest monuments in the history of architecture. Because of the vast expanse of the empire, these structures, or their remains, can be seen today almost everywhere.

The Republican Period

The ancient city of Rome was built on seven hills to the east of the Tiber River and served as the central Italian base from which the Romans would come to control most of the known world in the West. Their illustrious beginnings are traced to the **Republican period**, which followed upon the heels of their final victories over the Etruscans and lasted until the death of Julius Caesar in 44 BCE. The Roman system of government during this time was based on two parties, although the distribution of power was not equitable. The **patricians** ruled the country and could be likened to an aristocratic class. They came from important Roman families and later were characterized as nobility. The majority of the Roman population, however, belonged to the **plebeian class**. Members of this class were common folk and had less say in running the government. They were, however, permitted to elect their patrician representatives. During the Republican period, the famed Roman senate became the governing body of Rome. The rulings of the senate were responsible for the numerous Roman conquests that would expand its borders into a seemingly boundless empire.

By virtue of its construction, however, the republic was doomed to crumble. It was never a true democracy. The patricians became richer and more powerful as a result of the plundering of vanquished nations. The lower classes, on the other hand, demanded more and more privileges and resented the wealth and influence of the aristocracy.

After a series of successful military campaigns and the quelling of internal strife in the republic, Julius Caesar emerged as dictator of the Roman Empire. Under Caesar, important territories were accumulated, and Roman culture reached a peak of refinement. The language of Greece, its literature, and religion were adopted along with its artistic styles.

On March 15 (the ides of March) in 44 BCE, Julius Caesar was assassinated by members of the senate. With his death came the absolute end of the Roman Republic and the beginnings of the Roman Empire under his successor, Augustus.

Sculpture

Although much Roman art is derived in style from that of Greece, its portrait sculpture originated in a tradition that was wholly Italian. In this sculpture, we witness Rome's unique contribution to the arts—that of realism.

It was customary for Romans to make wax death masks of their loved ones and to keep them around the house, as we do photographs. At times, the wax masks were translated into a more permanent medium, such as

1 in.

14-19 *Head of a Roman* (Republican period, 1st century BCE).
Marble. H: 14⅜".
The Metropolitan Museum of Art, New York. Rogers Fund, 1912 (12.233).
Photograph ©2003 The Metropolitan Museum of Art

bronze or terra-cotta. The process of making a death mask produced intricately detailed images that recorded every ripple and crevice of the face. Because these sculptures were made from the actual faces and heads of the subjects, their realism is unsurpassed. The *Head of a Roman* (Fig. **14-19**) records the facial features of an old man, from his bald head and protruding ears to his furrowed brow and almost cavernous cheeks. No attempt has been made by the artist to idealize the figure. Nor does one get the sense, on the other hand, that the artist emphasized the hideousness of the character. Rather, it serves more as an unimpassioned and uninvolved record of the existence of one man.

Architecture

Rome's greatest contribution lay in architecture, although the most significant buildings, monuments, and civic structures were constructed during the Empire period. Architecture of the Republican period can be stylistically linked to both Greek and Etruscan precedents, as can be seen in the Temple of Fortuna Virilis (Fig. **14-20**). From the Greeks, the Romans adopted the Ionic order and post-and-lintel construction. From the Etruscans, they adopted the podium on which the temple stands, as well as the general plan of a wide cella extending to the side columns and a free portico in front. But there are Roman innovations as well. The column shafts, for example, are monolithic instead of being composed of drums stacked one on top of another. The columns along the sides of the temple are not freestanding but are engaged, or attached. Also, the frieze has no relief sculpture. The most marked difference between the temples of Greece and of Rome is the feeling that the Romans did not treat their buildings as sculpture. Instead, they designed them straightforwardly, emphasizing the relationship between form and function.

Painting

The walls of Roman domestic dwellings were profusely decorated with frescoes and mosaics, some of which have survived the ravages of time. These murals are significant in themselves, but they also provide a missing stylistic link in the artistic remains of Greece. That country, you will recall, was prolific in mural painting, but none of it has survived. Roman wall painting passed through several phases, beginning in about 200 BCE and ending with the destruction of Pompeii by the eruption of Mount Vesuvius in 79 CE. The phases have been divided into four overlapping styles.

14-20 Temple of Fortuna Virilis, Rome (Republican period, late 2nd century BCE).
Canali Photobank

14-21 *Ulysses in the Land of the Lestrygonians*, from a Roman patrician house (50–40 BCE). Fresco. H: 60".

Vatican Library, Rome.
©Scala/Art Resource, NY

Ulysses in the Land of the Lestrygonians (Fig. **14-21**) is an example of the **architectural style** in which the illusion of retreating space is achieved through various pictorial devices. It is as if the viewer were looking through a window and into the distance. In a loosely sketched and liberally painted landscape, the artist recounts a scene from *The Odyssey,* in which Ulysses' men were devoured by a race of giant cannibals. The figures rush through the landscape in a variety of poses and gestures, their forms defined by contrasts of light and shade. They are portrayed convincingly in three-dimensional space through the use of **herringbone perspective**, a system whereby **orthogonals** vanish to a specific point along a vertical line that divides the canvas. It is believed that Greek wall painting was similar to the Roman architectural style.

With the death of Julius Caesar, a dictator, Rome entered its **Empire period** under the rule of Octavian Caesar—later called Augustus. This period marks the beginning of the Roman Empire, Roman rule by emperor, and the Pax Romana, a 200-year period of peace.

The Early Empire

With the birth of the empire, there emerged a desire to glorify the power of Rome by erecting splendid buildings and civic monuments. It was believed that art should be created in the service of the state. Although Roman expansionism left a wake of death and destruction, it was responsible for the construction of cities and the provision of basic human services in the conquered areas.

To their subject peoples, the Roman conquerors brought the benefits of urban planning, including apartment buildings, roads, and bridges. They also provided police and fire protection, water systems, sanitation, and food. They even built recreation facilities for the inhabitants, including gymnasiums, public baths, and theaters. Thus, even in defeat, many peoples reaped benefits because of the Roman desire to glorify the empire through visible contributions.

Architecture

Although the Romans adopted structural systems and certain motifs from Greek architecture, they introduced several innovations in building design. The most significant of these was the arch, and after the second century, the use of concrete to replace cut stone. The combination of these two elements resulted in domed and vaulted structures that were not part of the Greek repertory.

One of the most outstanding Roman civic projects is the **aqueduct**, which carried water over long distances. The Pont du Gard (Fig. **14-22**) in southern France carried water more than 30 miles and furnished each recipient

The series of triumphal arches in Rome is a prototype of the billboard. . . . The triumphal arches in the Roman Forum were spatial markers channeling processional paths within a complex urban landscape. On Route 66 . . . the billboards perform a similar formal-spatial function.

—ROBERT VENTURI

14-22 Pont du Gard, Nîmes, France
(Early Empire, c. 14 CE).
L: 900'; H: 160'.

with some 100 gallons of water per day. Constructed of three levels of arches, the largest of which spans about 82 feet, the aqueduct is some 900 feet long and 160 feet high. It had to slope down gradually over the long distance in order for gravity to carry the flow of water from the source.

Although the aqueduct's reason for existence is purely functional, the Roman architect did not neglect design. The Pont du Gard has long been admired for both its simplicity and its grandeur. The two lower tiers of wide arches, for example, anchor the weighty structure to the earth, whereas the quickened pace of the smaller arches complements the rush of water along the top level. In works such as the Pont du Gard, form *follows* function.

One of the most impressive and famous monuments of ancient Rome is the Colosseum (see Fig. 14-24 in the "Compare + Contrast" feature). Dedicated in 80 CE, the structure consists of two back-to-back **amphitheaters** forming an oval arena, around which are tiers of marble bleachers.

Even in its present condition, having suffered years of pillaging and several earthquakes, the Colosseum is a spectacular sight. The structure is composed of three tiers of arches separated by engaged columns. (This combination of arch and column can also be seen in another type of Roman architectural monument—the triumphal arch (Fig. **14-23**). The Colosseum's lowest level, whose arches provided easy access and exit for the spectators, is punctuated by Doric columns. This order is the weightiest in appearance of the three architectural styles and thus visually anchors the structure to the ground. The second level features the Ionic order, and the third level the Corinthian. This combination produces a sense of lightness as one's eye moves from the bottom to the top tier. Thick entablatures rest on top of the rings of columns, firmly delineating the stories. The uppermost level is almost all solid masonry, except for a few regularly spaced rectangular openings. It is ornamented with Corinthian pilasters and crowned by a heavy cornice.

The exterior of the Colosseum was composed of masonry blocks held in place by metal dowels. These dowels were removed over the years when metal became scarce, and thus gravity keeps the structure intact.

14-23 Arch of Constantine, Rome (312–315 CE).

Stadium Designs: Thumbs-Up or Thumbs-Down?

THE SPORTS STADIUM HAS BECOME an inextricable part of our global landscape and our global culture. Just as diehard U.S. fans root for their football teams in the Louisiana Superdome, Olympic spectators half a world away cheer their country's athletes on to victory under a *super* dome likely erected just for the occasion. A city's bid for host of the Olympic Games can hinge entirely on the stadium it has to offer. These megastructures are not only functional—housing anticipated thousands—but they tend to become symbols of the cities, the teams, or now, the corporations who fund them. There's something about a space like this. The passion of friends and strangers and "fors and againsts" alike creates an odd sense of uniformity regardless of diversity. This observation has led some of history's political leaders to use—and abuse—the phenomenon of the stadium for their own propagandistic purposes.

The Colosseum (Fig. **14-24**) represented Rome at its best, but it also stood for Rome at its worst. A major feat of architectural engineering coupled with practical design, this vast stadium accommodated as many as 55,000 spectators who—thanks to 80 numbered entrances and stairways—could get from the street to their designated seats within 10 minutes. In rain or under blazing sun conditions, a gargantuan canvas could be hoisted from the arena up over the top of the stadium.

14-24 Colosseum, Rome (Early Empire, 80 CE).
Concrete (originally faced with marble).
H: 1609; D: 620' and 513'.
©UPPA/Topham/The Image Works

14-25 WERNER MARCH.
Olympic Stadium, Berlin (1936).
©Harf Zimmermann/Focus/Contact Press Images.

Although the Colosseum was built for entertainment and festivals, its most notorious events ranged from sadistic contests between animals and men and grueling battles to the death between pairs of gladiators. If one combatant emerged alive but badly wounded, survival might depend on whether the emperor (or the crowd) gave the "thumbs-up" or the "thumbs-down."

As in much architecture, form can follow function and reflect and create meaning. In 1936, Adolf Hitler commissioned Germany's Olympic Stadium in Berlin (Fig. **14-25**). Intended to showcase Aryan superiority (even though Jesse Owens, an African American, took four gold medals in track and field as Hitler watched), designer Werner March's stadium is the physical embodiment of Nazi ideals: order, authority, and the no-nonsense power of the state.

How different the message, noted critic Nicolai Ourussoff, when an architect uses design to cast off the shackles of "nationalist pretensions" and "notions of social conformity" in an effort to imbue the structure—and the country—with a sense of the future. Created in 1960 by Pier Luigi Nervi, the Palazzo dello Sport (Fig. **14-26**) in Rome symbolized an emerging internationalism in the wake of World War II. The unadorned and unforgiving pillars of March's Berlin stadium seem of a distant and rejected past. Nervi's innovative, interlacing concrete roof beams define delicacy and seem to defy gravity.

In 2008, China hosted the Olympic Games in the city of Beijing. A doughnut-shaped shell crisscrossed with lines of steel as if it were a precious package wrapped in string, the stadium (Fig. **14-27**) housed 100,000 spectators and came with a price tag in excess of $500 million. But beyond these staggering numbers, and like the Colosseum and the Berlin Stadium, it stands to symbolize the transformation of its city—and its country—into a major political and cultural force of its time. ∎

14-26 PIER LUIGI NERVI.
Palazzo dello Sport, Rome (1960).
©David Lees/CORBIS.

14-27 HERZOG AND DE MEURON.
Beijing Stadium for the 2008 Olympic Games (2005).
©Liu Jin/AFP/Getty Images

14-28 The Pantheon, Rome (Early Empire, 117–125 CE). Exterior view.
©allOver Photography/Alamy.

Roman engineering genius can be seen most clearly in the Pantheon (Figs. **14-28** and **14-29**), a brick and concrete structure originally erected to house sculptures of the Roman gods. Although the building no longer contains these statues, its function remains religious. Since the year 609 CE, it has been a Christian church.

The Pantheon's design combines the simple geometric elements of a circle and a rectangle. The entrance consists of a rectangular portico, complete with Corinthian columns and pediment. The main body of the building, to which the portico is attached, is circular. It is 144 feet in diameter and spanned by a dome equal in height to the diameter. Supporting the massive dome are 20-foot-thick walls pierced with deep niches, which in turn are vaulted in order to accept the downward thrust of the dome and distribute its weight to the solid wall. These deep niches alternate with shallow niches in which sculptures were placed.

The dome consists of a rather thin concrete shell that thickens toward the base. The interior of the dome is **coffered**, or carved with recessed squares that physically and visually lighten the structure. The ceiling was once painted blue, with a bronze rosette in the center of each square. The sole source of light in the Pantheon is the **oculus**, a circular opening in the top of the dome, 30 feet in diameter. The interior was lavishly decorated with marble slabs and granite columns that glistened in the spotlight of the sun as it filtered through the opening, moving its focus at different times of the day.

It has been said that Roman architecture differs from other ancient architecture in that it emphasizes space rather than form. In other words, rather than constructing buildings from the point of view of solid shapes, the Romans conceptualized a certain space and then proceeded to enframe it. Their methods of harnessing this space were unique in the ancient world and served as a vital precedent for future architecture.

Sculpture

During the Empire period, Roman sculpture took on a different flavor. The pure realism of the Republican period portrait busts was joined to Greek idealism. The result,

14-29 The Pantheon, Rome (Early Empire, 117–125 CE). Interior view.
©Paul Chesley/Stone/Getty Images

14-30 *Augustus of Primaporta* (Roman, c. 20 BCE).
Marble. H: 6' 8".
Vatican Museums, Rome.
©Scala/Art Resource, NY

14-12). Attired in military parade armor, he proclaims a diplomatic victory to the masses. His officer's cloak is draped about his hips, and his ceremonial armor is embellished with reliefs that portray both historic events and allegorical figures.

As the first emperor, Augustus was determined to construct monuments reflecting the glory, power, and influence of Rome on the Western world. One of the most famous of these monuments is the *Ara Pacis*, or Altar of Peace, created to celebrate the empire-wide peace that Augustus was able to achieve. The *Ara Pacis* is composed of four walls surrounding a sacrificial altar. These walls are adorned with relief sculptures of figures and delicately carved floral motifs.

Panels such as *The Imperial Procession* (Fig. **14-31**) exhibit, once again, a blend of Greek and Roman devices. The right-to-left procession of individuals, unified by the flowing lines of their drapery, clearly refers to the frieze sculptures of the Parthenon. Yet the sculpture differs from its Greek prototype in several respects: (1) the individuals are rendered in portrait likenesses; (2) the relief commemorates a specific event with specific persons present; and (3) these figures are set within a shallow, though very convincing, three-dimensional space. By working in high and low relief, the artist creates the sense of a crowd; fully three rows of people are compressed into this space. They actively turn, gesture, and seem to converse. Despite a noble grandness that gives the panel an idealistic cast, the participants in the procession look and act like real people.

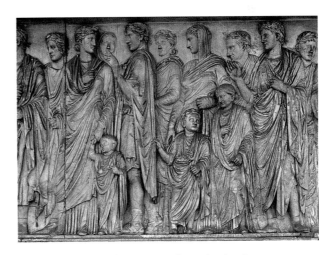

14-31 *The Imperial Procession*, from the *Ara Pacis Augustae*, Rome.
Marble relief.
Canali Photobank

evident in *Augustus of Primaporta* (Fig. **14-30**), was often a curious juxtaposition of individualized heads with idealized, anatomically perfect bodies in Classical poses. The head of Augustus is somewhat idealized and serene, but his unique facial features are recognizable as those that appeared on empire coins. Augustus adopts an authoritative pose not unlike that of Polykleitos's *Doryphoros* (Fig.

14-32 *Marcus Aurelius on Horseback*, Capitoline Hill, Rome (Early Empire, c. 165 CE).
Bronze. Larger than life-size.
Canali Photobank

adherence to Stoic philosophy. **Stoicism** advocated an indifference to emotion and things of this world, maintaining that virtue was the most important goal in life.

The equestrian portrait of Marcus Aurelius survives because of a case of mistaken identity. During the Middle Ages, objects of all kinds were melted down because of a severe shortage of metals, and ancient sculptures that portrayed pagan idols were not spared. This statue of Marcus Aurelius was saved because it was mistakenly believed to be a portrait of Constantine, the first Roman emperor to recognize Christianity. The death of Marcus Aurelius brings us to the last years of the Empire period, which were riddled with internal strife. The days of the great Roman Empire were numbered.

The Late Empire

During its late years, the Roman Empire was torn from within. A series of emperors seized the reins of power only to meet violent deaths, some at the hands of their own soldiers. By the end of the third century, the situation was so unwieldy that the empire was divided into eastern and western sections, with separate rulers for each. When Constantine ascended the throne, he returned to the one-ruler system, but the damage had already been done—the empire had become divided against itself. Constantine then dealt the empire its final blow by dividing

As time went on, the Roman desire to accurately record a person's features gave way to a more introspective portrayal of the personality of the sitter. Although portrait busts remained a favorite genre for Roman sculptors, their repertory also included relief sculpture, full-length statuary, and a new design—the **equestrian portrait**.

The bronze sculpture of Marcus Aurelius (Fig. **14-32**) depicts the emperor on a sprightly horse, as if caught in the action of gesturing to his troops or recognizing the applause of his people. The sculpture combines the Roman love of realism with the later concern for psychologically penetrating portraits. The commanding presence of the horse is rendered through pronounced musculature, a confident and lively stride, and a vivacious head with snarling mouth, flared nostrils, and protruding veins. In contrast to this image of brute strength is a rather serene image of imperial authority. Marcus Aurelius, clothed in flowing robes, sits erectly on his horse and gestures rather passively. His facial expression is calm and reserved, reflecting his

14-33 Basilica of Maxentius and Constantine, Rome (Late Empire, c. 310–320 CE).
300' × 215'.
Canali Photobank

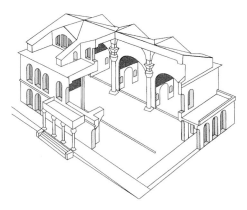

14-34 Reconstruction of Basilica of Maxentius and Constantine, Rome.

its territory among his sons and moving the capital to Constantinople (present-day Istanbul). Thus, imperial power was shifted to the eastern empire, leaving Rome and the western empire vulnerable. These were decisions from which the empire would never recover.

14-35 Head of Constantine the Great (Roman, Late Empire, early 4th century CE).

Capitoline Museum, Rome.
Photograph ©Spencer A. Rathus. All rights reserved.

Architecture

Although the empire was crumbling around him, Constantine continued to erect monuments to glorify it. Before moving to the East, he completed a basilica begun by his predecessor Maxentius (Fig. **14-33**) that bespoke the grandeur that had been Rome. In ancient Rome, basilicas were large public meeting halls that were usually built around or near the **forums**. The Basilica of Maxentius and Constantine was a huge structure, measuring some 300 by 215 feet. It was divided into three rectangular sections, or aisles, the center one reaching a height of 114 feet (Fig. **14-34**). The central aisle, called a nave, was covered by a groin vault, a ceiling structure that was very popular in buildings of such a vast scale. Little remains of the basilica today, but it survived long enough to set a precedent for Christian church architecture. It would serve as the basic plan for basilicas and cathedrals for centuries to come.

Sculpture

Some 300 years before Constantine's reign, a new force began to gnaw at the frayed edges of the Roman Empire—Christianity. The followers of Jesus of Nazareth were persecuted by the Romans for centuries after his death until the emperor Constantine proclaimed tolerance for the faith and accepted the mantle of Christianity himself. These events influenced artistic styles, as can be seen in the Head of Constantine the Great (Fig. **14-35**). The literalness and materialism of Roman art and life gave way to a new spirituality and otherworldliness in art. The Head of Constantine the Great was part of a mammoth sculpture of the emperor, consisting of a wooden torso covered with bronze and a head and limbs sculpted from marble. The head is over eight feet high and weighs more than eight tons. The realism and idealism that we witnessed in Roman sculpture were replaced by an almost archaic rendition of the emperor, complete with an austere expression and thick-lidded, wide-staring eyes. The artist elaborated the pensive, passive rigidity of form that we sensed in the portrait of Marcus Aurelius. Constantine's face seems both resigned to the fall of his empire and reflective of the Christian emphasis on a kingdom that is not of this world.

Everything about Rome is colossal—from the Colosseum (Rome's greatest amphitheater) (Fig. 14-24) to the colossal head of Constantine (Fig. 14-35), which is more than eight feet high. As the center of two of the great powers of the Western world—the Roman Empire and the Catholic Church—the city is rife with symbols that trumpeted their status in the times of their glory. A week of travel to Rome would barely do justice to this treasure trove of art and architecture.

It was said that "all roads lead to Rome," and, in truth, any road the visitor might take would lead to something wonderful. Starting with the Capitol, or the southern summit of Capitoline Hill, you will be in what has been called the symbolic center of the Roman world—its citadel as well as the location of three of its most important temples, including the Temple of Jupiter, where triumphal processions giving thanks for victory reached their climax. In the sixteenth century, Michelangelo, the Florentine artist otherwise famous for his sculpture of *David* (see Fig. 16-25) and murals for the ceiling of the Sistine Chapel (see Figs. 16-21 and 16-22), designed the geometric patterns of the elliptical plaza as well as the facades of the buildings that flank it on three sides. In the center stands a replica of the equestrian portrait of Emperor

Marcus Aurelius (Fig. 14-32); the real thing can be found just steps away in one of the Capitoline museums, along with an extensive collection of painting and sculpture, including Caravaggio's unusual Baroque portrayal of St. John the Baptist, the *Dying Gaul*, and the excessively large head and assorted limbs from the statue of Constantine.

If you duck around the back of the museums, you'll come to a wonderful view of the Roman forum below. It's good to linger here awhile to get the "lay of the land" before descending to wander among the ruins (miraculously "restored" by way of computer-generated imagery for the film *Gladiator*). The forum was the religious, political, and commercial center of the ancient city—the site of temples, courts of law, and the Senate house, along with food stores and brothels teeming with customers. For the contemporary visitor, even the summer tourist crowds might pale in comparison to the hubbub of the forum at the height of the empire. Of particular interest are the central courtyard of the House of the Vestal Virgins (girls from noble families who served as priestesses tending an eternal flame in the Temple of Vesta), the triumphal arches of the emperors Septimius Severus and Titus, and the monumental barrel vaults that remain from the Basilica of Constantine and Maxentius. One of the most curious, composite structures along the Via Sacra (or sacred way) is the ancient Temple of Antoninus and Faustina, now incorporated into a Catholic church, San Lorenzo in Miranda.

Down in the area of the forum, where cats creep and sleep among the ruins, the visitor will also come upon the Arch of Constantine (a popular backdrop for wedding photos) as well as the spectacular and notorious Colosseum. Built during the reign of Emperor Vespasian in 72 CE, the amphitheater was the site of deadly clashes between gladiators and wild beasts staged as sport and theater for the Roman citizenry by the emperors and upper classes. Stadium seating accommodated up to 55,000 spectators, who, on opening day, witnessed the slaughter of more than 9,000 wild animals in addition to a mock naval battle. The tiers of

The Temple of Antoninus and Faustina in the forum.

Tourists buying souvenirs in front of the Colosseum.

Hundreds of cats live in the Forum, the Colosseum, and other ancient sites. Women volunteers called *le gattare* feed and care for them.

the Colosseum, bearing columns in all three orders, or styles—Doric, Ionic, and Corinthian—served as inspiration for architects during the Renaissance. The artistic and architectural sources for the rebirth of Classicism in Italy were not, as it happened, so far from home.

You can ride the 81 bus from the Colosseum to witness the influence of Roman architecture on the grandest cathedral in Christendom, the Basilica of St. Peter's. Its rhythmic colonnades, imposing temple-front facade, and expansive hemispherical dome epitomize the Renaissance relationship to antiquity. St. Peter's (see Fig. 17-3) is the emblem of Roman Catholicism and the centerpiece of the Vatican, the world's smallest sovereign state, nestled within the city of Rome and ruled by the pope. The current, commanding building is constructed on the ruins of an earlier basilica erected by Constantine, who believed the site to be that in which the apostle Peter was buried. In another part of town, Michelangelo's *Moses*—part of the tomb of Pope Julius II—overlooks the shackles believed to have been used to imprison Peter before his execution.

Today St. Peter's is also the backdrop for magnificent works by Michelangelo (the *Pietà*—protected by glass since an attack on the sculpture in 1972—and the glorious dome over the main altar, the largest in the world) and by Gianlorenzo Bernini (the

Michelangelo, Moses.

Castle Sant'Angelo.

Baldacchino, or bronze canopy over the main altar, and several tombs and sculptures throughout the basilica, in addition to the design for the piazza and colonnades that grace the exterior). Visitors to St. Peter's should be aware that proper attire is required for entry to the cathedral; even in the oppressive heat of a Roman summer day, shorts and sleeveless shirts are forbidden.

The wealth of the popes is even more evident in the sublime collections and treasures of the Vatican Museums (the Hellenistic *Belvedere Torso* and *Laocoön* reside here) and the rooms of the Vatican Palace—including Michelangelo's paintings of the Sistine Chapel ceiling and Raphael's fresco for the Stanze della Segnatura (see Fig. 16-20) in the papal apartments. A grand boulevard—the Via della Conciliazone—leads the traveler from the steps of St. Peter's along the Tevere River toward the Castel Sant'Angelo. Constructed in 139 CE as a mausoleum for Emperor Hadrian, it went on to serve as a medieval citadel and prison, as well as a safe haven for popes (it was connected to the Vatican by an escape corridor). If you continue on foot along this broad avenue, you will eventually wind up in the area of the Roman Pantheon (Figs. 14-28 and 14-29), the great domed temple-turned-Christian-church, initially devoted to the gods and emperors of Rome. Raphael is buried here.

From its romantic fountains and lush gardens to its endless trattorias and pizzerias, museums and monuments, Rome is and has always been a cosmopolitan city on the go. It is a cacophonous mix of old and new (every youthful Roman seems to have a motor scooter and a cell phone), a vast city whose center is so small that a good map—and, even better, pair of running shoes—will take you everywhere.

 To continue your tour and learn more about Rome, go to ArtExperience Online.

16

THE RENAISSANCE

*The fundamental principle will be that all steps of learning should be sought from
Nature; the means of perfecting our art will be found
in diligence, study, and application.*
—Leon Battista Alberti

While Columbus brought his ships to the New World in 1492, a 17-year-old Michelangelo Buonarroti was perfecting his skill at rendering human features from blocks of marble. In 1564, the year that Shakespeare was born, Michelangelo died. These are two of the marker dates of the **Renaissance**. *Renaissance* is a French word meaning "rebirth," and the Renaissance in Europe was a period of significant historical, social, and economic events. The old feudal system that had organized Europe during the Middle Ages fell to a system of government based on independent city-states with powerful kings and princes at their helms. The economic face of Europe changed, aided by an expansion of trade and commerce with Eastern countries. The cultural base of Europe shifted from Gothic France to Italy. A plague wiped out the populations of entire cities in Europe and Asia. Speculation on the world beyond, which had so preoccupied the medieval mind, was counterbalanced by a scientific observation of the world at hand. Although Copernicus proclaimed that the sun, and not Earth, was at the center of the solar system, humanity, and not heaven, became the center of all things.

Interior View of the Dome of the Sagrestia Vecchia or Old Sacristy in the Basilica of San Lorenzo, Florence.
©Alinari Archives/CORBIS.

THE RENAISSANCE

The Renaissance spans roughly the fourteenth through the sixteenth centuries and is seen by some as the beginning of modern history. During this period, particularly in Italy, we witness a revival of Classical themes in art and literature, a return to the realistic depiction of nature through keen observation, and the revitalization of the Greek philosophy of humanism, in which human dignity, ideas, and capabilities are of central importance.

Changes, artistic and otherwise, took root all over Europe, but Italy and Flanders (present-day Belgium and the Netherlands) developed into world-class economic and cultural centers in the fifteenth century (see Map **16-1**). Given its Classical roots, Italy never quite succumbed to Gothicism and readily introduced elements of Greek and Roman art into its art and architecture. But Flanders was steeped in the medieval tradition of northern Europe and continued to concern itself with the spiritualism of the Gothic era, enriching it with a supreme realism. (It is worth noting that because the word *renaissance* generally refers to the artistic and cultural revival of Classical sources, some art historians no longer use it to describe northern art of this period.)

The difference in attitudes was summed up during the later Renaissance years by one of Italy's great artists, Michelangelo Buonarroti, not entirely without prejudice:

> Flemish painting will, generally speaking, please the devout better than any painting in Italy, which will never cause him to shed a tear, whereas that of Flanders will cause him to shed many. . . . In Flanders they paint with a view to external exactness or such things as may cheer you and of which you cannot speak ill, as for example saints and prophets. They paint stuffs and masonry, the green grass of the fields, the shadows of trees, and rivers and bridges.[1]

Thus, the subject matter of northern artists remained more consistently religious, although their manner of representation was that of an exact, trompe l'oeil rendition of things of this world. They used the "trick-the-eye" technique to portray mystical religious phenomena in a realistic manner. The exactness of representation of which Michelangelo spoke originated in **manuscript illumination**, where complicated imagery was reduced to a minute scale. Because this imagery illustrated texts, it was often laden with symbolic meaning. Symbolism was carried into **panel paintings**, where it was fused with a keen observation of nature.

FIFTEENTH-CENTURY NORTHERN PAINTING

Flemish Painting: From Page to Panel

A certain degree of naturalism appeared in the work of the northern book illustrator during the Gothic period. The manuscript illuminator *illuminated* literary passages with visual imagery. As the art of manuscript illumination

---

1 Robert Goldwater and Marco Treves, eds., *Artists on Art* (New York: Pantheon Books, 1972), 68.

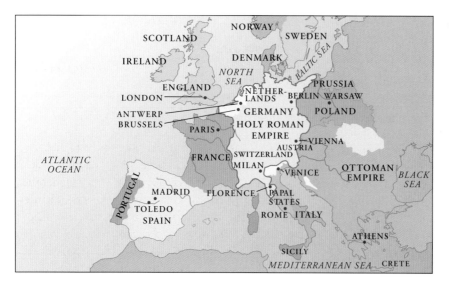

MAP 16-1 Renaissance Europe (c. 16th century).

progressed, these thumbnail sketches were enlarged to fill greater portions of the manuscript page, eventually covering it entirely. As the text pages became less able to contain this imagery, the northern Renaissance artist shifted to painting in tempera on wood panels.

The Limbourg Brothers

One of the most dazzling texts available to illustrate this transfer from minute to more substantial imagery is *Les Très Riches Heures du Duc de Berry*, a Book of Hours illustrated by the Limbourg brothers (born after 1385, died by 1416) during the opening decades of the fifteenth century. Books of Hours were used by nobility as prayer books and included psalms and litanies to a variety of saints. As did most Books of Hours, *Les Très Riches Heures* contained calendar pages that illustrated domestic tasks and social events of the 12 months of the year. In "May" (Fig. **16-1**), one of the calendar pages, we witness a parade of aristocratic gentlemen and ladies who have come in their bejeweled costumes of pastel hues to celebrate the first day of May. Complete with glittering regalia and festive song, the entourage romps through a woodland clearing on carousel-like horses. In the background looms a spectacular castle complex, the chateau of Riom.

The calendar pages of *Les Très Riches Heures* are rendered in the **International style**, a manner of painting common throughout Europe during the late fourteenth and early fifteenth centuries. This style is characterized by ornate costumes embellished with gold leaf and by subject matter literally fit for a king, including courtly scenes and splendid processions. The refinement of technique and attention to detail in these calendar pages recall earlier manuscript illumination. These qualities, and a keen observation of the human response to the environment—or in this case the merrymaking—bring to mind Michelangelo's assessment of northern painting as obsessed with representation of the real world through the painstaking rendition of its everyday objects and occurrences.

Although these calendar pages illustrated a holy book, the themes were secular. Fifteenth-century artists tried to reconcile religious subjects with scenes and objects from everyday life, and northern artists accomplished this by using symbolism. Artists would populate ordinary interiors with objects that might bear some spiritual significance.

1 in.

16-1 LIMBOURG BROTHERS.
"May" from *Les Très Riches Heures du Duc de Berry* (1416).
Illumination. 8⅞" × 5⅜".
Musée Conde, Chantilly, France.
©Réunion des Musées Nationaux/Art Resource, NY

Many, if not most, of the commonplace items might be invested with a special religious meaning. You might ask how you, the casual observer, are supposed to decipher the cryptic meaning lurking behind an ordinary kettle. Chances are that you would be unable to do so without a specialized background. Yet you can enjoy the warm feeling of being invited into someone's home when you look at a northern Renaissance interior and be all the more enriched by the knowledge that there really is something more there than meets the eye.

Robert Campin, the Master of Flémalle

Attention to detail and the use of commonplace settings were carried forward in the soberly realistic religious figures painted by Robert Campin, the Master of Flémalle (c. 1378–1444). His *Merode Altarpiece* (Fig. **16-2**) is a triptych whose three panels, from left to right, contain the kneeling donors of the altarpiece; an Annunciation scene with the Virgin Mary and the angel Gabriel; and Joseph, the foster father of Jesus, at work in his carpentry shop. The architectural setting is a typical contemporary Flemish dwelling. The donors kneel by the doorstep in a garden thick with grass and wildflowers, each of which has special symbolic significance regarding the Virgin Mary. Although the door is ajar, it is not clear whether they are witnessing

the event inside or whether Campin has used the open door as a compositional device to lead the spectator's eye into the central panel of the triptych.

In any event, we are visually and psychologically coaxed into viewing this most atypical Annunciation. Mary is depicted as a prim and proper middle-class Flemish woman surrounded by the trappings of a typical Flemish household, all rendered in exacting detail. Just as the closed outdoor garden symbolizes the holiness and purity of the Virgin Mary, the items within also possess symbolic meaning. For example, the bronze kettle hanging in the Gothic niche on the back wall symbolizes the Virgin's body—it will be the immaculate container of the redeemer of the Christian world. More obvious symbols of her purity include the spotless room and the vase of lilies on the table. In the upper left corner of the central panel, a small child can be seen, bearing a cross and riding streams of "divine light." The wooden

16-2 ROBERT CAMPIN.

Merode Altarpiece: The Annunciation with Donors and St. Joseph (c. 1425–1428).
Oil on wood. Center: 24¼" × 24⅞"; Wings: each 25⅜" × 10⅞".
The Metropolitan Museum of Art, The Cloisters, New York. Purchase, 1956 (56.70).
Image copyright ©The Metropolitan Museum of Art/Art Resource, NY

1 ft.

table situated between Mary and Gabriel and the room divider between Mary and Joseph guarantee that the light accomplished the deed. Typically, Joseph is shown as a man too old to have been the biological father of Jesus, although Campin's depiction does not quite follow this tradition. He is gray, but by no means ancient. Jesus' earthly father is busy preparing mousetraps—one on the table and one on the windowsill—commonplace objects that symbolize the belief that Christ was the bait with which Satan would be trapped.

The symbolism in the altarpiece presents a fascinating web for the observer to untangle and interpret. Yet it does not overpower the hard-core realism of the ordinary people and objects. With the exceptions of the slight inconsistency of size and the tilting of planes toward the viewer, Campin offers us a continuous realism that sweeps the three panels. There is no distinction between saintly and common folk; the facial types of the heavenly beings are as individual as the portraits of the donors. Although fifteenth-century viewers would have been aware of the symbolism and the sacredness of the event, they would have also been permitted to become "a part" of the scene, so to speak, and to react to it as if the people in the painting were their peers and just happened to find themselves in extraordinary circumstances.

Jan van Eyck

We might say that Campin "humanized" his Mary and Joseph in the *Merode Altarpiece*. As religious subjects became more secular in nature and the figures became rendered as "human," an interest in ordinary, secular subject matter sprang up. During the fifteenth century in northern Europe, we have the development of what is known as **genre painting**, painting that depicts ordinary people engaged in run-of-the-mill activities. These paintings make little or no reference to religion; they exist almost as art for art's sake. Yet they are no less devoid of symbolism.

Giovanni Arnolfini and His Bride (Fig. **16-3**) was executed by one of the most prominent and significant Flemish painters of the fifteenth century, Jan van Eyck (c. 1395–1441). This unique double portrait was commissioned by an Italian businessman working in Bruges to serve as a kind of marriage contract, or record of the couple's taking of marriage vows in the presence of two witnesses. The significance of such a document—in this case a visual one—is emphasized by the art historian Erwin Panofsky: According to Catholic dogma, the sacrament of matrimony is "immediately accomplished by the mutual consent of the persons to be married when this consent is expressed by words and actions" in the

16-3 JAN VAN EYCK.
Giovanni Arnolfini and His Bride (1434).
Oil on wood. 33" × 22½".
©National Gallery Collection; By kind permission of the Trustees of the National Gallery, London/CORBIS

presence of two or three witnesses. Records of the marriage were necessary to avoid lawsuits in which "the validity of the marriage could be neither proved nor disproved for want of reliable witnesses."[2]

Once again we see the northern artist's striking realism and fidelity to detail, offering us exact records of the facial features of the wedding couple. The figures of the two witnesses are reflected in the convex mirror behind the Arnolfinis. Believe it or not, they are Jan van Eyck and his wife, a fact corroborated by the inscription above the mirror: "Jan van Eyck was here." As in most Flemish paintings, the items scattered about are invested with symbolism relevant to the occasion. The furry dog in the foreground symbolizes fidelity, and the oranges on the windowsill may symbolize victory over death. Giovanni has kicked off his shoes out of respect for the holiness of the ground on which this sacrament takes place. Finally, the finial on the bedpost

---

2 Erwin Panofsky, "Jan van Eyck's 'Arnolfini' Portrait," *Burlington Magazine* 64 (1934): 117–27.

is an image of St. Margaret, the patroness of childbirth, and around her wooden waist is slung a small whisk broom, a symbol of domesticity. It would seem that Giovanni had his bride's career all mapped out. With Jan van Eyck, Flemish painting reached the height of symbolic realism in both religious and secular subject matter. No one ever quite followed in his footsteps.

German Art

Northern Renaissance painting is not confined to the region of Flanders, and some of the most emotionally striking work of this period was created by German artists. Their work contains less symbolism and less detail than that of Flemish artists, but their message is often more powerful.

Matthias Grünewald

These characteristics of German Renaissance art can clearly be seen in the *Isenheim Altarpiece* (Fig. **16-4**) by Matthias Grünewald (c. 1480–1528), painted more than three-quarters

16-4 MATTHIAS GRÜNEWALD.
The Crucifixion, center panel of *The Isenheim Altarpiece* (exterior) (completed 1515).
Oil on panel. 8'10" × 10'1".
©Musée d'Unterlinden, Colmar, France/The Bridgeman Art Library

of a century after Jan van Eyck's Arnolfini portrait. The central panel of the German altarpiece is occupied by a tormented representation of the Crucifixion, one of the most dramatic in the history of art. The dead Christ is flanked by his mother, Mary, the apostle John, and Mary Magdalene to the left, and John the Baptist and a sacrificial lamb to the right. These figures exhibit a bodily tension in their arched backs, clenched hands, and rigidly pointing fingers, creating a melodramatic, anxious tone. The crucified Christ is shown with a deadly pallor. His skin appears cancerous, and his chest is sunken with his last breath. His gnarled hands reach painfully upward, stretching for salvation from the blackened sky. We do not find such impassioned portrayals outside Germany during the Renaissance.

Albrecht Dürer

We appropriately close our discussion of northern Renaissance art with the Italianate master Albrecht Dürer (1471–1528). His passion for the Classical in art stimulated extensive travel in Italy, where he copied the works of the Italian masters, who were also enthralled with the Classical style. The development of the printing press made it possible for him to disseminate the works of the Italian masters throughout northern Europe.

Dürer's *Adam and Eve* (Fig. **16-5**) conveys his admiration for the Classical style. In contrast to other German and Flemish artists who rendered figures, Dürer emphasized the idealized beauty of the human body. His Adam and Eve are not everyday figures of the sort Campin depicted in his Virgin Mary. Instead, the images arise from Greek and Roman prototypes. Adam's young, muscular body could have been drawn from a live model or from Classical statuary. Eve represents a standard of beauty different from that of other northern artists. The familiar slight build and refined facial features have given way to a more substantial and well-rounded woman. She is reminiscent of a fifth-century BCE Venus in her features and her pose. The symbols associated with the event—the Tree of Knowledge and the Serpent (Satan)—play a secondary role. In *Adam and Eve*, Dürer has chosen to emphasize the profound beauty of the human body. Instead of focusing on the consequences of the event preceding the taking of the fruit as an admonition against sin, we delight in the couple's beauty for its own sake. Indeed, this notion is central to the art of Renaissance Italy.

*I hold that the more nearly and accurately a figure is made to resemble man,
so much better the work will be. If the best parts, chosen from many well-formed men,
are fitly united in one figure, it will be worthy of praise.*

—ALBRECHT DÜRER

16-5 ALBRECHT DÜRER.
Adam and Eve (1504).
Engraving, 4th state. 9⅞" × 7⅞".
The Metropolitan Museum of Art, New York. Fletcher Fund, 1919 (19.73.1).
Image copyright ©The Metropolitan Museum of Art/Art Resource, NY

1 in.

THE RENAISSANCE IN ITALY

The Early Renaissance

Not only was there a marked difference between northern and Italian Renaissance art, but there were notable differences in the art of various sections of Italy. Florence and Rome witnessed a resurgence of Classicism as

Roman ruins were excavated in ancient sites, hillsides, and people's backyards. In Siena, the International style lingered, and in Venice, a Byzantine influence remained strong. There may be several reasons for this diversity, but the most obvious is that of geography. For example, whereas the Roman artist's stylistic roads led to that ancient city, the trade routes in the northeast brought an Eastern influence to works of art and architecture. The Italian Renaissance took root and flourished most successfully in Florence. The development of this city's painting, sculpture, and architecture parallels that of the Renaissance in all of Italy. Throughout the Renaissance, as Florence went, so went the country.

Cimabue and Giotto

Some of the earliest changes from a medieval to a Classical style can be perceived in the painting of Florence during the late thirteenth and early fourteenth centuries, the prime exponents being Cimabue and Giotto. So significant were these artists that Dante Alighieri, the fourteenth-century poet, mentioned both of them in his *Purgatory* of *The Divine Comedy*:

O gifted men, vainglorious for first place,
how short a time the laurel crown stays green
unless the age that follows lacks all grace!
Once Cimabue thought to hold the field
in painting, and now Giotto has the cry
so that the other's fame, grown dim, must yield.[3]

Who were these artists? Apparently they were rivals, although Cimabue (c. 1240–c. 1302) was older than Giotto (c. 1276–c. 1337) and probably had a formative influence on the latter, who would ultimately steal the limelight.

---

3 From *The Divine Comedy* by Dante Alighieri, trans. John Ciardi. Copyright 1954, 1957, 1959, 1960, 1961, 1965, 1967, 1970 by the Ciardi Family Publishing Trust. Used by permission of W. W. Norton & Company, Inc.

1 ft.

16-6 CIMABUE.
Madonna Enthroned (c. 1280–1290).
Tempera on wood panel. 12' 7" × 7' 4".
Uffizi Gallery, Florence.
©Alinari/Art Resource, NY

1 ft.

16-7 GIOTTO.
Madonna Enthroned (c. 1310).
Tempera on wood panel. 10' 8" × 6' 8".
Uffizi Gallery, Florence.
©Scala/Art Resource, NY

The similarities and differences between the works of Cimabue and Giotto can be seen in two tempera paintings on wood panels depicting the Madonna and Child enthroned. A curious combination of Late Gothic and Early Renaissance styles betrays Cimabue's composition as a transitional work (Fig. **16-6**). The massive throne of the Madonna is Roman in inspiration, with column and arch forms embellished with **intarsia**. The Madonna has a corporeal presence that sets her apart from "floating" medieval figures, but the effect is compromised by the unsureness with which she is placed on the throne. She does not sit solidly; her limbs are not firmly planted. Rather, the legs resemble the hinged appendages of Romanesque figures.

This characteristic placement of the knees causes the drapery to fall in predictable folds—concentric arcs reminiscent of a more stylized technique. The angels supporting the throne rise parallel to it, their glances forming an abstract zigzag pattern. The resultant lyrical arabesque, the flickering color patterns of the wings, and the lineup of unobstructed heads recall the Byzantine tradition, particularly the Ravenna mosaics (see Fig. 15-5).

Giotto's rendition of the same theme offers some dramatic differences (Fig. **16-7**). The overall impression of the *Madonna Enthroned* is one of stability and corporeality instead of instability and weightlessness. Giotto's Madonna sits firmly on her throne, the outlines of her body and drapery forming a solid triangular shape. Although the throne is lighter in appearance than Cimabue's Roman throne—and is, in fact, Gothic, with pointed arches—it, too, seems more firmly planted on the earth. Giotto's genius is also evident in his conception of the forms in three-dimensional space. They not only have height and width, as do those of Cimabue, but they also have depth and mass. This is particularly noticeable in the treatment of the angels. Their location in space is from front to rear rather than atop one another as in Cimabue's composition. The halos of the foreground angels obscure the faces of the background attendants, because they have mass and occupy space.

The Renaissance Begins, and So Does the Competition

With Cimabue and Giotto, we witness strides toward an art that was very different from that of the Middle Ages. But artists, like all of us, must walk before they can run, and those strides that express such a stylistic advance from the "cutout dolls" of the Ravenna mosaics and the "hinged marionettes" of the Romanesque era will look primitive in another half century. Because the art of Cimabue and Giotto contains vestiges of Gothicism, their style is often termed proto-Renaissance. But at the dawn of the fifteenth century in Florence, the Early Renaissance began—with a competition.

Imagine workshops and artists abuzz with news of one of the hottest projects in memory up for grabs. Think of one of the most prestigious architectural sites in Florence. Savor the possibility of being known as *the* artist who had cast, in gleaming bronze, the massive doors of the Baptistery of Florence. This landmark competition was held in 1401. There were countless entries, but only two panels have come down to us. The artists had been given a scene from the Old Testament to translate into bronze—the sacrifice of Isaac by his father, Abraham. There were specifications, naturally, but the most obvious is the **quatrefoil** format. Within this space, a certain cast of characters was mandated, including Abraham, Isaac, an angel, and two "extras" who appear to have little or nothing to do with the scene. The event takes place out of doors, where God has commanded Abraham to take his only son and sacrifice him. When they arrive on the scene, Abraham, in loyalty to God, turns the blade to Isaac's throat. At this moment, God sends an angel to stop Abraham from completing the deed.

Filippo Brunelleschi and Lorenzo Ghiberti

The two extant panels were executed by Filippo Brunelleschi (c. 1377–1446) and Lorenzo Ghiberti (1378–1455). The obligatory characters, bushes, animals, and altar are present in both, but the placement of these elements, the artistic style, and the emotional energy within each work differ considerably. Brunelleschi's panel (Fig. **16-8**) is divided into sections by strong vertical and horizontal elements, each section filled with objects and figures. In contrast to the rigidity of the format, a ferocious energy bordering on violence pervades the composition. Isaac's neck and body are distorted by his father's grasping fist, and Abraham lunges viciously toward his son's throat with a knife. With similar passion, an angel flies in from the left to grasp Abraham's arm. But this intense drama and seemingly boundless energy are weakened by the introduction of ancillary figures that are given more prominence than the scene requires. The donkey, for example, detracts from Isaac's plight by being placed broadside and practically dead center. Also, one is struck by the staccato movement throughout. Although this choppiness complements the anxiety in the work, it compromises the successful flow of space and tires the eye.

In Lorenzo Ghiberti's panel (Fig. **16-9**), the space is divided along a diagonal rock formation that separates the main characters from the lesser ones. Space flows along this diagonal, exposing the figural group of Abraham and Isaac and embracing the shepherd boys and their donkey. The boys and donkey are appropriately subordinated to the main characters but not sidestepped stylistically. Abraham's lower body parallels the rock formation and then lunges expressively away from it in a dynamic counterthrust. Isaac, in turn, pulls firmly away from his father's forward motion. The forms move rhythmically together in a continuous flow of space. Although Ghiberti's emotion is not quite as intense as Brunelleschi's, and his portrayal of the sacrifice is not quite as graphic, the impact of Ghiberti's narrative is as strong.

It is interesting to note the inclusion of Classicizing elements in both panels. Brunelleschi, in one of his peasants, adapted the Classical sculpture of a boy removing a thorn from his foot, and Ghiberti rendered his Isaac in the manner of the fifth-century sculptor. Isaac's torso, in fact, may be the first nude in this style since Classical times.

Oh, yes—Ghiberti won the competition and Brunelleschi went home with his chisel. The latter never devoted himself to sculpture again but went on to become the first great Renaissance architect. Ghiberti was not particularly modest about his triumph:

16-8 FILIPPO BRUNELLESCHI.
Sacrifice of Isaac (1401–1402).
Gilt bronze. 21" × 17½".
Museo Nazionale del Bargello, Florence.
©Arte & Immagini srl/CORBIS

16-9 LORENZO GHIBERTI.
Sacrifice of Isaac (1401–1402).
Gilt bronze. 21" × 17½".
Museo Nazionale del Bargello, Florence.
©Arte & Immagini srl/CORBIS

To me was conceded the palm of victory by all the experts and by all . . . who had competed with me. To me the honor was conceded universally and with no exception. To all it seemed that I had at that time surpassed the others without exception, as was recognized by a great council and an investigation of learned men . . . highly skilled from the painters and sculptors of gold, silver, and marble.[4]

Donatello

If Brunelleschi and Ghiberti were among the last sculptors to harbor vestiges of the International style, Donatello (c. 1386–1466), the Florentine master, was surely among the first to create sculptures that combined Classicism with realism. In his *David* (Fig. **16-10**), the first life-size nude statue since Classical times, Donatello struck a balance between the two styles by presenting a very real image of an Italian peasant boy in the guise of a Classical nude figure. David, destined to be the second king of Israel, slew the Philistine giant Goliath with a stone and

a sling. Even though Donatello was inspired by Classical statuary, notice that he did not choose a Greek youth in his prime as a prototype for his David. Instead, he chose a barely developed adolescent boy, his hair still unclipped and his arms flaccid for lack of manly musculature. After decapitating Goliath, whose head lies at David's feet, his sword rests at his side—almost too heavy for him to handle. Can such a youth have accomplished such a forbidding task? Herein lies the power of Donatello's statement. We are amazed, from the appearance of this young boy, that he could have done such a deed, much as David seems incredulous as he glances down toward his body. What David lacks in stature he has made up in intellect, faith, and courage. His fate was in his own hands—one of the ideals of the Renaissance man.

Masaccio

The Early Renaissance painters shared most of the stylistic concerns of the sculptors. However, included in their attempts at realism was the added difficulty of projecting a naturalistic sense of three-dimensional space on a two-dimensional surface. In addition to copying from nature and Classical models, these painters developed rules of

4 E. G. Holt, ed., *Literary Sources of Art History* (Princeton, NJ: Princeton University Press, 1947), 87–88.

*The works made before [Masaccio's] day can be said to be painted,
while his are living, real, and natural.*

—GIORGIO VASARI

16-10 DONATELLO.
David (1408).
Bronze. H: 5'2".
Museo Nazionale del Bargello, Florence.
©Topham/The Image Works

1 ft.

1 ft.

16-11 MASACCIO.
Holy Trinity, Santa Maria Novella, Florence (c. 1428).
Fresco. 21' × 10'5".
©Erich Lessing/Art Resource, NY.

perspective to depict images in the round on flat walls, panels, and canvases. One of the pioneers in developing systematic laws of one-point linear perspective was Brunelleschi, of Baptistery doors near-fame.

Masaccio's *Holy Trinity* (Fig. **16-11**) uses these laws of perspective. In this chapel fresco, Masaccio (1401–1428) creates the illusion of an extension of the architectural space of the church by painting a barrel-vaulted "chapel" housing a variety of holy and common figures. God the Father supports the cross that bears his crucified son while the Virgin Mary and the apostle John attend. Outside the columns and pilasters of the realistic, Roman-inspired chapel kneel the donors, who are invited to observe the scene. Aside from the trompe l'oeil rendition of the architecture, the realism in the fresco is enhanced by the donors, who are given importance equal to that of the "principal" characters, similar to Campin's treatment of the donors in the *Merode Altarpiece* (Fig. 16-2). The architecture appears to extend our physical space, and the donors appear as extensions of ourselves.

Filippo Brunelleschi

The revival of Classicism was even more marked in the architecture of the Renaissance. Some 20 years after Brunelleschi's unsuccessful bid for the Baptistery doors project in Florence, he was commissioned to cover the crossing square of the cathedral of Florence with a dome.

Interestingly, Ghiberti worked with him at the outset but soon bowed out, and Brunelleschi was left to complete the work alone. It was quite an engineering feat, involving a double-shell dome constructed around 24 ribs (Fig. **16-12**). Eight of these ribs rise upward to a crowning lantern on the exterior of the dome. You might wonder why Brunelleschi, whose architectural models were essentially Classical, would have constructed a somewhat pointed dome reminiscent of the Middle Ages. The fact is that the architect might have preferred a more rounded or hemispherical structure, but the engineering problem required an ogival, or pointed, section, which is inherently more stable. The dome was a compromise between a somewhat Classical style and traditional Gothic building principles.

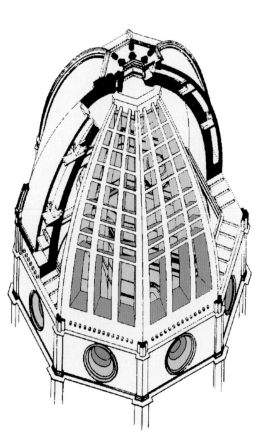

16-12 FILIPPO BRUNELLESCHI.
Construction of the cathedral dome, Florence (1420–1436).

16-13 ANDREA DEL VERROCCHIO.
David (c. 1470).
Bronze. H: 49⅝".
Museo Nazionale del Bargello, Florence.
©Erich Lessing/Art Resource, NY

1 ft.

Renaissance Art at Midcentury and Beyond

Andrea del Verrocchio

As we progress into the middle of the fifteenth century, the most important and innovative sculptor is Andrea del Verrocchio (1435–1488). An extremely versatile artist who was trained as a goldsmith, Verrocchio ran an active shop that attracted many young artists, including Leonardo da Vinci. We see in Verrocchio's bronze *David* (Fig. **16-13**), commissioned by the Medici family, a strong contrast to Donatello's handling of the same subject. The Medici also owned the Donatello *David*, and Verrocchio probably wanted to outshine his predecessor. Although both artists chose to represent David as an adolescent, Verrocchio's hero appears somewhat older and exudes pride and self-confidence rather than a dreamy gaze of disbelief. Whereas Donatello reconciled realistic elements with an almost idealized, Classically inspired torso, Verrocchio's goal was supreme realism in minute details, including orientalizing motifs on the boy's doublet that would have made him look like a Middle Easterner. The sculptures differ considerably also in terms of technique. Donatello's *David* is essentially a closed-form sculpture with objects and limbs centered around an **S-curve** stance; Verrocchio's sculpture is more open, as is evidenced by the bared sword and elbow jutting away from the central core. Donatello's graceful pose has been replaced, in the Verrocchio, by a jaunty **contrapposto** that enhances David's image of self-confidence.

Piero della Francesca

The artists of the Renaissance, along with the philosophers and scientists, tended to share the sense of the universe as an orderly place that was governed by natural law and capable of being expressed in mathematical and geometric terms. Piero della Francesca (c. 1420–1492) was trained in mathematics and geometry and is credited with writing the first theoretical treatise on the construction of systematic perspective in art. Piero's art, like his scientific thought, was based on an intensely rational construction of forms and space.

His *Resurrection* fresco (Fig. **16-14**) for the town hall of Borgo San Sepolcro reveals the artist's obsessions with order and geometry. Christ ascends vertical and triumphant, like a monumental column, above the "entablature" of his tomb, which serves visually as the pedestal of a statue. Christ and the other figures are constructed from the cones, cylinders,

16-14 PIERO DELLA FRANCESCA.
Resurrection (c. late 1450s).
Fresco. 7'5" ×6'6½".
Town Hall, Borgo San Sepolcro, Italy.
©Scala/Art Resource, NY

1 ft.

spheres, and rectangular solids that define the theoretical world of the artist. There is a tendency here toward the simplification of forms—not only of people, but also of natural features such as trees and hills. All of the figures in the painting are contained within a triangle—what would become a major compositional device in Renaissance painting—with Christ at the apex. The sleeping figures and the marble sarcophagus provide a strong and stable base for the upper two-thirds of the composition. Regimented trees rise in procession behind Christ, as they never do when nature asserts its random jests; Piero's trees are swept back by the rigid cultivation of scientific perspective. They crown, as ordered, just above the crests of rounded hills. The artist of the Renaissance was not only in awe of nature but also commanded it fully.

Sandro Botticelli

During the latter years of the fifteenth century, we come upon an artistic personality whose style is somewhat in opposition to the prevailing trends. Since the time of Giotto, painters had relied on chiaroscuro, or the contrast of light and shade to create a sense of roundness and mass in their figures and objects, in an effort to render a realistic impression of three-dimensional forms in space. Sandro Botticelli (c. 1444–1510), however, constructed his compositions with line instead of tonal contrasts. His art relied primarily on drawing. Yet when it came to subject matter, his heart lay with his Renaissance peers, for, above all else, he loved to paint mythological themes. Along with other artists and men of letters, his mania for these subjects was fed and perhaps cultivated by the Medici prince Lorenzo the Magnificent, who surrounded himself with Neoplatonists, or those who followed the philosophy of Plato.

One of Botticelli's most famous paintings is *The Birth of Venus* (Fig. **16-15**), or, as some art historians would have it, "Venus on the Half-Shell." The model for this Venus was Simonetta Vespucci, a cousin of Amerigo Vespucci, the navigator and explorer after whom America was named.

16-15 SANDRO BOTTICELLI.
The Birth of Venus (c. 1486).
Tempera on canvas. 5'8⅞" × 9'1⅞".
Uffizi Gallery, Florence.
©Summerfield Press/CORBIS

1 ft.

The composition presents Venus, born of the foam of the sea, floating to the shores of her sacred island on a large scallop shell, aided in its drifting by the sweet breaths of entwined zephyrs. The nymph Pomona awaits her with an ornate mantle and is herself dressed in a billowing, flowered gown. Botticelli's interest in Classicism is evident also in his choice of models for the Venus. She is a direct adaptation of an antique sculpture of this goddess in the collection of the Medici family. Notice how the graceful movement in the composition is evoked through a combination of different lines. A firm horizon line and regimented verticals in the trees contrast with the subtle curves and vigorous arabesques that caress the mythological figures. The line moves from image to image and then doubles back to lead your eye once again. Shading is confined to areas within the harsh, linear, sculptural contours of the figures. Botticelli's genius lay in his ability to utilize the differing qualities of line to his advantage; with this formal element, he created the most delicate of compositions.

Leon Battista Alberti

You could never accuse Leon Battista Alberti (1404–1472) of false modesty, or of any modesty at all. Like so many other artists of the Renaissance, including Ghiberti, Michelangelo, and Leonardo—and unlike the anonymous European artists of the Middle Ages—he sought fame with conscious conviction.

Some of the purest examples of Renaissance Classicism lie in the buildings Alberti designed. Alberti was among the first to study treatises written by Roman architects, the most famous of whom was Vitruvius, and he combined his Classical knowledge with innovative ideas in his grand opus, *Ten Books on Architecture*. One of his most visually satisfying buildings in the great Classical tradition is the Palazzo Rucellai (Fig. **16-16**) in Florence. The building is divided by prominent horizontal string courses into three stories, crowned by a heavy cornice. Within each story are apertures enframed by pilasters of different orders. The first-floor pilasters are of the Tuscan order, which resembles the Doric order in its simplicity; the second story uses a composite capital of volutes and acanthus leaves, seen in the Ionic and Corinthian orders, respectively; and the top-floor pilasters

16-16 LEON BATTISTA ALBERTI.
Palazzo Rucellai, Florence (1446–1451).
©Scala/Art Resource, NY.

are crowned by capitals of the Corinthian order. As in the Colosseum (see Fig. 14-24), this combination of orders gives an impression of increasing lightness as we rise from the lower to the upper stories. This effect is enhanced in Alberti's building by a variation in the masonry. Although the texture remains the same, the upper stories are faced with lighter-appearing smaller blocks in greater numbers. The palazzo's design, with its clear articulation of parts, overall balance of forms, and rhythmic placement of elements in horizontals across the facade, shows a clear understanding of Classical design adapted successfully to the contemporary nobleman's needs.

*I can make armored cars, safe and unassailable, which will enter the . . . ranks of the enemy
with their artillery, and there is no company of men at arms so great that they will not break it.
And behind these the infantry will be able to follow quite unharmed and without any
opposition. . . . If need shall arise, I can make cannon, mortars, and light ordnance,
of very beautiful and useful shapes, quite different from those in common use. . . .
Also I can execute sculpture in marble, bronze, and clay, and also painting, in which
my work will stand comparison with that of anyone else, who ever he may be.*

—LEONARDO DA VINCI (from a letter of application for a job)

The High Renaissance

The High Renaissance ushered in a new era for some artists—one of respect, influence, fame, and, most important, the power to shape their circumstances. Here is an example: Sometime in 1542, Julius II and Michelangelo Buonarroti were in conflict, and the artist was feeling the brunt of the pope's behavior. As if backing out of his tomb commission and refusing to pay for materials were not enough, the pope laid the last straw by having Michelangelo removed from the Vatican when the artist sought to redress his grievances. Michelangelo let his outrage be known:

> A man paints with his brains and not with his hands, and if he cannot have his brains clear he will come to grief. Therefore I shall be able to do nothing well until justice has been done me. . . . As soon as the Pope [carries] out his obligations towards me I (will) return, otherwise he need never expect to see me again.
>
> All the disagreements that arose between Pope Julius and myself were due to the jealousy of Bramante and of Raffaello da Urbino; it was because of them that he did not proceed with the tomb, . . . and they brought this about in order that I might thereby be ruined. Yet Raffaello was quite right to be jealous of me, for all he knew of art he learned from me.[5]

Although this is only one side of the story (Michelangelo might also have been somewhat jealous of Raphael), this passage offers us a good look at the personality of an artist of the High Renaissance. He was independent yet indispensable—arrogant, aggressive, and competitive.

From the second half of the fifteenth century onward, a refinement of the stylistic principles and techniques associated with the Renaissance can be observed. Most of this significant, progressive work was being done in

Florence, where the Medici family played an important role in supporting the arts. At the close of the decade, however, Rome was the place to be, as the popes began to assume the grand role of patron. The three artists who were in most demand—the great masters of the High Renaissance in Italy—were Leonardo da Vinci, a painter, scientist, inventor, and musician; Raphael, the Classical painter thought to have rivaled the works of the ancients; and Michelangelo, the painter, sculptor, architect, poet, and enfant terrible. Donato Bramante is deemed to have made the most significant architectural contributions of this period. These are the stars of the Renaissance, the artistic descendants of the Giottos, Donatellos, and Albertis, who, because of their earlier place in the historical sequence of artistic development, are sometimes portrayed as but stepping-stones to the greatness of the sixteenth-century artists rather than as masters in their own right.

Leonardo da Vinci

If the Italians of the High Renaissance could have nominated a counterpart to the Classical Greek's "four-square man," it most assuredly would have been Leonardo da Vinci (1452–1519). His capabilities in engineering, the natural sciences, music, and the arts seemed unlimited, as he excelled in everything from solving drainage problems (a project he undertook in France just before his death), to designing prototypes for airplanes and submarines, to creating some of the most memorable Renaissance paintings.

The Last Supper (Figs. **16-17**), a fresco painting executed for the dining hall of a Milan monastery, stands as one of Leonardo's greatest works. The condition of the work is poor, because of Leonardo's experimental fresco technique—although the steaming of pasta for centuries on the other side of the wall may also have played a role. Nonetheless, we can still observe the Renaissance ideals of

---

5 Robert Goldwater and Marco Treves, eds., *Artists on Art* (New York: Pantheon Books, 1972), 63.

16-17 LEONARDO DA VINCI.

The Last Supper (1495–1498).

Fresco (oil and tempera on plaster). 13' 9" × 29' 10".

Refectory, Santa Maria delle Grazie, Milan.

©Alinari/Art Resource, NY

Classicism, humanism, and technical perfection, now coming to full fruition. The composition is organized through the use of one-point linear perspective. Solid volumes are constructed from a masterful contrast of light and shadow. A hairline balance is struck between emotion and restraint.

The viewer is first attracted to the central triangular form of Jesus sitting among his apostles by orthogonals that converge at his head. His figure is silhouetted against a triple window that symbolizes the Holy Trinity and pierces the otherwise dark back wall. One's attention is held at this center point by the Christ-figure's isolation that results from the leaning away of the apostles. Leonardo has chosen to depict the moment when Jesus says, "One of you will betray me." The apostles fall back reflexively at this accusation; they gesture expressively,

deny personal responsibility, and ask, "Who can this be?" The guilty one, of course, is Judas, who is shown clutching a bag of silver pieces at Jesus' left, with his elbow on the table. The two groups of apostles, who sweep dramatically away from Jesus along a horizontal line, are subdivided into four smaller groups of three that tend to moderate the rush of the eye out from the center. The viewer's eye is wafted outward and then coaxed back inward through the "parenthetic" poses of the apostles at either end. Leonardo's use of strict rules of perspective and his graceful balance of motion and restraint underscore the artistic philosophy and style of the Renaissance.

Although Leonardo does not allow excessive emotion in his *Last Supper*, the reactions of the apostles seem genuinely human. This spirit is also captured in *Madonna of the Rocks*

(Fig. **16-18**). Mary is no longer portrayed as the queen of heaven, but as a mother. She is human; she is "real."

The soft, hazy atmosphere and dreamy landscape of *Madonna of the Rocks*, and the chiaroscuro that so realistically defines the form of the subtly smiling Virgin Mary, were still in Leonardo's pictorial repertory when he created what is arguably the most famous portrait in the history of art—the *Mona Lisa* (Fig. **16-19**). An air of mystery pervades the work—from her entrancing smile and intense gaze to her real identity and the location of the landscape behind her. With the *Mona Lisa*, Leonardo altered the nature of portrait painting for centuries, replacing the standard profile view of a sitter to one in which a visual dialogue could be established between the subject and the observer.

Raphael Sanzio

A younger artist who assimilated the lessons offered by Leonardo, especially on the humanistic portrayal of the Madonna, was Raphael Sanzio (1483–1520). As a matter of fact, Michelangelo was not far off base in his accusation that Raphael copied from him, for the younger artist freely adopted whatever suited his purposes. Raphael truly shone in his ability to combine the techniques of other masters with an almost instinctive feel for Classical art. He rendered countless canvases depicting the Madonna and Child along the lines of Leonardo's *Madonna of the Rocks*. Raphael was also sought after as a muralist. Some of his most impressive

1 ft.

16-18 LEONARDO DA VINCI.
Madonna of the Rocks (c. 1483).
Oil on panel, transferred to canvas. 78½" × 48".

1 in.

16-19 LEONARDO DA VINCI.
Mona Lisa (c. 1503–1505).
Oil on wood panel. 30¼" × 21".

Classical compositions, in fact, were executed for the papal apartments in the Vatican.

The commission came from Pope Julius, and to add fuel to Michelangelo's fire, was executed at the same time Michelangelo was at work on the Sistine Chapel ceiling. For the Stanza della Segnatura, the room in which the highest papal tribunal was held, Raphael painted *The School of Athens* (Fig. **16-20**), one of four frescoes designed within a semicircular frame. In what could be a textbook exercise of one-point linear perspective, Raphael crowded a veritable "who's who" of Classical Greece convening beneath a series of barrel-vaulted archways. The figures symbolize philosophy, one of the four subjects deemed most valuable for a pope's education. (The others were law, theology, and poetry.) The members of the gathering are divided into two camps representing opposing philosophies and are led, on the right, by Aristotle and on

the left, by his mentor, Plato. Corresponding to these leaders are the Platonists, whose concerns are the more lofty realm of Ideas (notice Plato pointing upward), and the Aristotelians, who are more in touch with matters of the Earth, such as natural science. Some of the figures have been identified: Diogenes, the Cynic philosopher, sprawls out on the steps, and Herakleitos, a founder of Greek metaphysics, sits pensively just left of center. Of more interest is the fact that Raphael included a portrait of himself, staring out toward the viewer, in the far right foreground. He is shown in a group surrounding the geometrician Euclid. Raphael clearly saw himself as important enough to be commemorated in a Vatican mural as an ally of the Aristotelian camp.

As in *The Last Supper* by Leonardo, our attention is drawn to the two main figures by **orthogonals** leading directly to where they are silhouetted against the sky breaking through the archways. The diagonals that lead toward a single horizon point are balanced by strong horizontals and verticals in the architecture and figural groupings, lending a feeling of Classical stability and predictability. Stylistically, as well as iconographically, Raphael has managed to balance opposites in a perfectly graceful and logical composition.

Michelangelo Buonarroti

Of the three great Renaissance masters, Michelangelo (1475–1564) is probably most familiar to us. During the 1964 World's Fair in New York City, hundreds of thousands of culture seekers and devout pilgrims were trucked along a conveyor belt for a brief glimpse of his *Pietà* at the Vatican Pavilion. A year later, actor Charlton Heston (who seems to bear a striking resemblance to the artist) reprised the tumultuous relationship between artist and patron and the traumatic physical experience surrounding the painting of the Sistine ceiling in the Hollywood film, *The Agony and the Ecstasy*. These two works stand as symbols of the breadth and depth of Michelangelo's talents as an artist.

That famed ceiling is the vault of the chapel of Pope Sixtus IV, known as the Sistine Chapel. The ceiling is some 5,800 square feet and is almost 70 feet above the floor. The decorative fresco cycle was commissioned by Pope Julius II, but the iconographic scheme was Michelangelo's. The artist had agreed to the project in order to pacify the temperamental Julius in the hope that the pontiff would eventually allow him to complete work on his mammoth tomb. For whatever reason, we are indeed fortunate to have this painted work from the sculptor's hand. After much anguish and early attempts to populate the vault with a variety of religious figures (eventually more than 300 in all), Michelangelo settled on a division of the ceiling into geometrical "frames" (Figs. **16-21**) housing biblical prophets, mythological soothsayers, and Old Testament scenes from Genesis to Noah's flood.

The most famous of these scenes is *The Creation of Adam* (Fig. **16-22**). As Leonardo had done in *The Last Supper*, Michelangelo chose to communicate the event's most dramatic moment. Adam lies on the Earth, listless for lack

16-21 MICHELANGELO.
The Sistine Chapel in the Vatican, Rome (1508–1512).
5,800 sq. ft. Vatican Museum, Rome.
Canali Photobank

The Creation of Adam (1508–1512). Detail from the ceiling of the Sistine Chapel in the Vatican, Rome.

Canali Photobank

of a soul, while God the Father rushes toward him amidst a host of angels, who enwrap him in a billowing cloak. The contrasting figures lean toward the left, separated by an illuminated diagonal that provides a backdrop for the Creation. Amidst an atmosphere of sheer electricity, the hand of God reaches out to spark spiritual life into Adam—but does not touch him! In some of the most dramatic negative space in the history of art, Michelangelo has left it to the spectator to complete the act. In terms of style, Michelangelo integrated chiaroscuro with Botticelli's extensive use of line. His figures are harshly drawn and muscular with almost marble-like flesh. In translating his sculptural techniques to a two-dimensional surface, the artist has conceived his figures in the round and has used the tightest, most expeditious line and modeling possible to render them in paint.

It is clear that Michelangelo saw himself more as a sculptor than as a painter. The "sculptural" drawing and modeling in *The Creation of Adam* attest to this. When Michelangelo painted the Sistine Chapel ceiling, he was all of 33 years old, but he began his career some 20 years earlier as an apprentice to the painter Domenico Ghirlandaio (1449–1494). His reputation as a sculptor, however, was established when, at the age of 27, he carved the 13 1/2-foot-high *David* (Fig. 16-25) from a single piece of almost unworkable marble.

Unlike the Davids of Donatello and Verrocchio, Michelangelo's hero is not shown after conquering his foe. Rather, David is portrayed as a most beautiful animal preparing to kill—not by savagery and brute force but by intellect and skill. Upon close inspection, the tensed muscles and the furrowed brow negate the first impression that this is a figure at rest. David's sling is cast over his shoulder, and the stone is grasped in the right hand, the veins prominent in anticipation of the fight.

Michelangelo's *David* is part of the Classical tradition of the "ideal youth" who has just reached manhood and is capable of great physical and intellectual feats. Like Donatello's *David*, Michelangelo's sculpture is closed in form. All of the elements move tightly around a central axis. Michelangelo has been said to have sculpted by first conceptualizing the mass of the work and then carefully extracting all of the marble that was not part of the image. Indeed, in the *David*, it appears that he worked from front to back instead of from all four sides of the marble block, allowing the figure, as it were, to "step out of" the stone. The identification of the figure with the marble block provides a dynamic tension in Michelangelo's work, as the forms try at once to free themselves from and succumb to the binding dimensions.

The "Davids" of Donatello, Verrocchio, Michelangelo, and Bernini

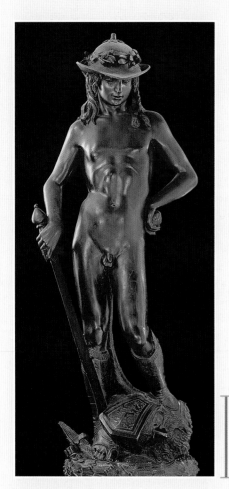

16-23 DONATELLO.
David (1408).
Bronze. H: 5'2".
Museo Nazionale del Bargello, Florence.
©Topham/The Image Works

SOMETIME SOON AFTER THE YEAR 1430, a bronze statue of *David* (Fig. **16-23**) stood in the courtyard of the house of the Medici. The work was commissioned of Donatello by Cosimo de' Medici himself, the founding father of the Republic of Florence. It was the first freestanding, life-size nude since Classical antiquity, poised in the same contrapposto stance as the victorious athletes of Greece and Rome. But soft, and somehow oddly unheroic. And the incongruity of the heads: David's boyish, expressionless face, framed by soft tendrils of hair and shaded by a laurel-crowned peasant's hat; Goliath's tragic, contorted

expression, made sharper by the pentagonal helmet and coarse, disheveled beard. Innocence and evil. The weak triumphing over the strong. The city of Florence triumphing over the aggressive dukes of Milan? "David" as a civic-public monument.

In the year 1469, Ser Piero from the Tuscan town of Vinci moved to Florence to become a notary. He rented a house on the Piazza San Firenze, not far from the Palazzo Vecchio. His son, who was a mere 17 years old upon their arrival, began an apprenticeship in the Florentine studio of the well-known artist Andrea del Verrocchio. At that time, Verrocchio was at work on a bronze sculpture of the young *David* (Fig. **16-24**). Might the head of this fine piece be a portrait of the young Leonardo da Vinci?

16-24 ANDREA DEL VERROCCHIO.
David (c. 1470).
Bronze. H: 49⅝".
Museo Nazionale del Bargello, Florence.
©Erich Lessing/Art Resource, NY

16-25 MICHELANGELO.
David (1501–1504).
Marble. H: 13½'.
Galleria dell 'Accademia, Florence.
©Scala/Art Resource, NY.

1 ft.

1 ft.

16-26 GIANLORENZO BERNINI.
David (1623).
Marble. H: 6' 7".
Borghese Gallery, Rome.
©Scala/Art Resource, NY.

For many years, a block of marble lay untouched, tossed aside as unusable, irretrievable evidence of a botched attempt to carve a human form. It was 18 feet high. A 26-year-old sculptor, riding high after the enormous success of his figure of the Virgin Mary holding the dead Christ, decided to ask for the piece. The wardens of the city in charge of such things let the artist have it. What did they have to lose? Getting anything out of it was better than nothing. So this young sculptor named Michelangelo measured and calculated. He made a wax model of David with a sling in his hand. And he worked on his *David* (Fig. **16-25**) continuously for some three years until, a man named Vasari tells us, he brought it to perfect completion. Without letting anyone see it.

A century later, a 25-year-old sculptor stares into a mirror at his steeled jaw and determined brow. A contemporary source tells us that on this day, perhaps, the mirror is being held by Cardinal Maffeo Barberini while Bernini transfers what he sees in himself to the face of his *David* (Fig. **16-26**). Gianlorenzo Bernini: sculptor and architect, painter, dramatist, composer. Bernini, who centuries later would be called the undisputed monarch of the Roman High Baroque, identifying with David, whose adversary is seen only by him.

The great transformation in style that occurred between the Early Renaissance and the Baroque can be followed in the evolution of David. Look at them: A boy of 12, perhaps, looking down incredulously at the physical self that felled an unconquerable enemy; a boy of 14 or 15, confident and reckless, with enough adrenaline pumping to take on an army; an adolescent on the brink of adulthood, captured at that moment when, the Greeks say, sound mind and sound body are one; and another full-grown youth at the threshold of his destiny as king. ■

High and Late Renaissance in Venice

The artists who lived and worked in the city of Venice were the first in Italy to perfect the medium of oil painting that we witnessed with van Eyck in Flanders. Perhaps influenced by the mosaics in St. Mark's Cathedral, perhaps intrigued by the dazzling colors of imports from Eastern countries into this maritime province, the Venetian artists sought the same clarity of hue and lushness of surface in their oil-on-canvas works. In the sixteenth century, Venice would come to figure as prominently in the arts as Florence had in the fifteenth.

Titian

Although he died in 1576, almost a quarter century before the birth of the Baroque era, the Venetian master Tiziano Vecellio (b. 1477)—called Titian—had more in common with the artists who would follow him than with his Renaissance

16-27 TITIAN.
Venus of Urbino (1538).
Oil on canvas. 47" × 65".
Uffizi Gallery, Florence.
©Scala/Art Resource, NY.

1 ft.

contemporaries in Florence and Rome. Titian's pictorial method differed from those of Leonardo, Raphael, and Michelangelo in that he was foremost a painter and colorist rather than a draftsman or sculptural artist. He constructed his compositions by means of colors and strokes of paint and layers of varnish rather than by line and chiaroscuro. A shift from painting on wood panels to painting on canvas occurred at this time, and with it a change from tempera to oil paint as the preferred medium. The versatility and lushness of oil painting served Titian well, with its vibrant, intense hues and its more subtle, semitransparent glazes.

Titian's *Venus of Urbino* (Fig. **16-27**) is one of the most beautiful examples of the glazing technique. The composition was painted for the duke of Urbino, from which its title derives. Titian adopted the figure of the reclining Venus from his teacher Giorgione, and it has served as a model for many compositions since that time. In the foreground, a nude **Venus pudica** rests on voluptuous pillows and sumptuous sheets spread over a red brocade couch. Her golden hair, complemented by the delicate flowers she grasps loosely in her right hand, falls gently over her shoulder. A partial drape hangs in the middle ground, providing a backdrop for her upper torso and revealing a view of her boudoir. The background of the composition includes two women looking into a trunk—presumably handmaidens—and a more distant view of a sunset through a columned veranda. Rich, soft tapestries contrast with the harsh Classicism of the stone columns and inlaid marble floor.

Titian appears to have been interested in the interaction of colors and the contrast of textures. The creamy white sheet complements the radiant golden tones of the body of Venus, built up through countless applications of glazes over flesh-toned pigment. Her sumptuous roundness is created by extremely subtle gradations of tones in these glazes rather than the harshly sculptural chiaroscuro that Leonardo or Raphael might have used. The forms evolve from applications of color instead of line or shadow. Titian's virtuoso brushwork allows him to define different textures: the firm yet silken flesh, the delicate folds of drapery, the servant's heavy cloth dress, the dog's soft fur. The pictorial dominance of these colors and textures sets the work apart from so many examples of Florentine and Roman painting. It appeals primarily to the senses rather than to the intellect.

Titian's use of color as a compositional device is significant. We have already noted the drape, whose dark color forces our attention on the most important part of the composition—Venus's face and upper torso. It also blocks out the left background, encouraging viewers to narrow their focus on the vista in the right background. The forceful diagonal formed by the looming body of Venus is balanced by three elements opposite her: the little dog at her feet and the two handmaidens in the distance. They do not detract from her because they are engaged in activities that do not concern her or the spectator. The diagonal of her body is also balanced by an intersecting diagonal that can be visualized by integrating the red areas in the lower left and upper right corners. Titian thus subtly balances the composition in his placement of objects and color areas.

Tintoretto

Perhaps no other Venetian artist anticipated the Baroque style so strongly as Jacopo Robusti, called Tintoretto, or "little dyer," after the profession of his father. Supposedly a pupil of Titian, Tintoretto (1518–1594) emulated the master's love of color, although he combined it with a more linear approach to constructing forms. This interest in draftsmanship was culled from Michelangelo, but the younger artist's compositional devices went far beyond those of the Florentine and Venetian masters. His dynamic structure and passionate application of pigment provide a sweeping, almost frantic, energy within compositions of huge dimensions.

Tintoretto's painting technique was unique. He arranged doll-like figures on small stages and hung his flying figures by wires in order to copy them in correct perspective on sheets of paper. He then used a grid to transcribe the figures onto much larger canvases. Tintoretto primed the entire canvas with dark colors. Then he quickly painted in the lighter sections. Thus, many of his paintings appear very dark, except for bright patches of radiant light. The artist painted extremely quickly, using broad areas of loosely swathed paint. John Ruskin, a nineteenth-century art critic, is said to have suggested that Tintoretto painted with a broom.[6] Although this is unlikely, Tintoretto had certainly come a long way from the sculptural, at times marble-like, figures of the High Renaissance and the painstaking finish of Titian's glazed *Venus of Urbino*. This loose brushwork and dramatic white spotlighting on a dark ground anticipate the Baroque style.

6 Frederick Hartt, *History of Italian Renaissance Art*, 2nd ed. (Englewood Cliffs, NJ: Prentice-Hall; New York: Harry N. Abrams, 1979), 615.

The Last Supper (1592–1594).
Oil on canvas. 12' × 18'8".
San Giorgio Maggiore, Venice.
©Cameraphoto/Art Resource, NY.

1 ft.

The Last Supper (Fig. **16-28**) seals his relationship to the later period. A comparison of this composition with Leonardo's *The Last Supper* (Fig. 16-17) will illustrate the dramatic changes that had taken place in both art and the concept of art over almost a century. The interests in motion, space, and time; the dramatic use of light; and the theatrical presentation of subject matter are all present in Tintoretto's *The Last Supper*. We are first impressed by the movement. Everything and everyone are set into motion: people lean, rise up out of their seats, stretch, and walk. Angels fly and animals dig for food. The space, sliced by a sharp, rushing diagonal that goes from lower left toward upper right, seems barely able to contain all of this commotion, but this cluttered effect enhances the energy of the event.

Leonardo's obsession with symmetry, along with his balance between emotion and restraint, yields a composition that appears static in comparison to the asymmetry and overpowering emotion in Tintoretto's canvas. Leonardo's apostles seem posed for the occasion when contrasted with Tintoretto's spontaneously gesturing figures. A particular moment is captured. We feel that if we were to look away for a fraction of a second, the figures would have changed position by the time we looked back! The timelessness of Leonardo's figural poses has given way to a seemingly temporary placement of characters. The moment that Tintoretto has chosen to depict also differs from Leonardo's. The Renaissance master chose the point at which Jesus announced that one of his apostles would betray him. Tintoretto, on the other hand, chose the moment when Jesus shared bread, which symbolized his body as the wine stood for his blood. This moment is commemorated to this day during the celebration of Mass in the Roman Catholic faith. Leonardo chose a moment signifying death, Tintoretto a moment signifying life, depicted within an atmosphere that is teeming with life.

HIGH AND LATE RENAISSANCE OUTSIDE ITALY

El Greco

The Late Renaissance outside Italy brought us many different styles, and Spain is no exception. Spanish art polarized into two stylistic groups of religious painting: the mystical and the realistic. One painter was able to pull these opposing trends together in a unique pictorial method. El Greco (1541–1614), born Domeniko Theotokopoulos in Crete, integrated many styles into his work. As a young man, he traveled to Italy, where he encountered the works of the Florentine and Roman masters, and he was for a time affiliated with Titian's workshop. The colors that El Greco incorporated into his paintings suggest a Venetian influence, and the distortion of his figures and use of an ambiguous space speak for his interest in Mannerism, which is discussed later.

These pictorial elements can clearly be seen in one of El Greco's most famous works, *The Burial of Count Orgaz* (Fig. **16-29**). In this single work, El Greco combines mysticism and realism. The canvas is divided into two halves by a horizontal line of white-collared heads, separating "heaven" and "earth." The figures in the lower half of the composition are somewhat elongated, but well within the bounds of realism. The heavenly figures, by contrast, are extremely attenuated and seem to move under the influence of a sweeping, dynamic atmosphere. It has been suggested that the distorted figures in El Greco's paintings might have been the result of astigmatism in the artist's eyes, but there is no convincing proof of this. For example, at times El Greco's figures appear no more distorted than those of other Mannerists. Heaven and earth are disconnected psychologically but joined convincingly in terms of composition. At the center of the rigid, horizontal row of heads that separates the two worlds, a man's upward glance creates a path for the viewer into the upper realm. This compositional device is complemented by a sweeping drape that rises into the upper half of the canvas from above his head, continuing to lead the eye between the two groups of

1 ft.

16-29 EL GRECO.
The Burial of Count Orgaz (1586).
Oil on canvas. 16' × 11'10".
Santo Tome, Toledo, Spain.
©The Gallery Collection/CORBIS

1 ft.

figures, left and right, up toward the image of the resurrected Christ. El Greco's color scheme also complements the worldly and celestial habitats. The colors used in the costumes of the earthly figures are realistic and vibrantly Venetian, but the colors of the upper half of the composition are of discordant hues, highlighting the otherworldly nature of the upper canvas. The emotion is high-pitched and exaggerated by the tumultuous atmosphere. This emphasis on emotionalism links El Greco to the onset of the Baroque era. His work contains a dramatic, theatrical flair, one of the hallmarks of the seventeenth century.

Pieter Bruegel the Elder

During the second half of the sixteenth century in the Netherlands, changes in the subject matter of painting were taking place that would affect the themes of artists working in northern Europe during the Baroque period. Scenes of everyday life involving ordinary people were becoming more popular. One of the masters of this genre painting was Pieter Bruegel the Elder (c. 1520–1569), whose compositions focused on human beings in relation to nature and the life and times of plain Netherlandish folk. *The Peasant Wedding* (Fig. **16-30**) is a good example of Bruegel's slice-of-life canvases. The painting transports us to a boisterous hall, where food and drink flow in abundance, and music

and merriment raise the rafters. The viewer's experience of this event relies on the degree to which the artist conveys the sense of noise, of laughter, of celebration. The circular rims of soup bowls are echoed in the spherical caps of the peasants and the mouths of the stacked, earthenware pitchers. In a sea of confusion, this simple repetitive element provides visual unity and guides the path of the eye. There is no hidden message here, no religious fervor, no battle between mythological giants. Human activities are presented as sincere and viable subject matter. There are few examples of such painting before this time, but genre painting will play a principal role in the works of Netherlandish artists during the Baroque period.

MANNERISM

During the Renaissance, the rule of the day was to observe and emulate nature. Toward the end of the Renaissance and before the beginning of the seventeenth century, this rule was suspended for a while, during a period of art that historians have named Mannerism. Mannerist artists abandoned copying directly from nature and copied art instead. Works thus became "secondhand" views of nature. Line, volume, and color no longer duplicated what the eye saw but were derived instead from what other artists had already seen. Several characteristics separate **Mannerist art** from the art of the Renaissance and the Baroque periods: distortion and elongation of figures; flattened, almost two-dimensional space; lack of a defined focal point; and the use of discordant pastel hues.

Jacopo Pontormo

A representative of early Mannerism, Jacopo Pontormo (1494–1557) used most of its stylistic principles. In *Entombment* (Fig. **16-31**), we witness a strong shift in direction from High Renaissance art, even though the painting was executed during Michelangelo's lifetime. The weighty sculptural figures of Michelangelo, Leonardo, and Raphael have given way to less substantial, almost weightless, forms that balance on thin toes and ankles. The limbs are long and slender in proportion to the torsos, and the heads are dwarfed by billowing robes. There is a certain innocent beauty in the arched eyebrows of the haunted faces and in the nervous glances that dart this way and that past the boundaries of the canvas. The figures are pressed against the picture plane, moving within a very limited space. Their weight seems to be thrust outward toward the edges of the composition and away from the almost void center. The figures' robes are composed of odd hues, departing drastically in their soft pastel tones from the vibrant primary colors of the Renaissance masters.

The weightlessness, distortion, and ambiguity of space create an almost otherworldly feeling in the composition, a world in which objects and people do not come under an earthly gravitational force. The artist accepts this "strangeness" and makes no apologies for it to the viewer. The ambiguities are taken in stride. For example, note that the character in a turban behind the head of the dead Jesus does not appear to have a body—there is really no room for it in the composition. And even though a squatting figure in the center foreground appears to be balancing Christ's torso on his shoulders after having taken him down from the cross a moment before, there is no cross in sight! Pontormo seems to have been most interested in elegantly rendering the high-pitched emotion of the scene. Iconographic details and logical figural stances are irrelevant.

The artists from the second half of the sixteenth century through the beginning of the seventeenth century all broke away from the Renaissance tradition in one way or another. Some were opposed to the stylistic characteristics

1 ft.

16-31 JACOPO PONTORMO.
Entombment (1525–1528).
Oil on panel. 10'3" × 6'4".
Capponi Chapel, Santa Felicitá, Florence.
©Scala/Art Resource, NY

of the Renaissance and turned them around in an original but ultimately uninfluential style called Mannerism. Others, such as Titian and Tintoretto, emphasized the painting *process*, constructing their compositions by means of stroke and color rather than line and shadow. Still others combined an implied movement and sense of time in their compositions, foreshadowing some of the concerns of the artist in the Baroque period. The High and Late Renaissance witnessed artists of intense originality who provide a fascinating transition between the grand Renaissance and the dynamic Baroque.

Leaf through the pages of the chapter on Renaissance Art and survey the figure captions accompanying the illustrations of Italian Renaissance art and architecture. Surprised at how many are in Florence? The fact is, Florence commanded Europe in the fourteenth and fifteenth centuries—in the worlds of finance, patronage, arts, and culture. Dante Alighieri (author of *The Divine Comedy*); Michelangelo Buonarroti (sculptor of the *David*, painter of the *Sistine Chapel*, architect of *St. Peter's Basilica*); Niccolo Machiavelli (political philosopher, advisor, and author of *The Prince*); Galileo Galilei (astronomer and mathematician, author of the heliocentric theory of the universe)—all were born in or lived in the city of Florence at this pivotal moment in history.

Florence began during Roman times when Julius Caesar passed a law providing land there for retired war veterans. The walls around the city were extended and fortified against the invasions of the Ostrogoths during the Byzantine era, but the territory was lost to the Lombards, along with all of Tuscany, by 570 CE. It was Charlemagne who "rescued" Florence from the "barbarians," incorporating the city into the Holy Roman Empire. From that point forward, it was ruled by princes and . . . the Medicis.

By far the dominant name associated with Renaissance Florence is Medici—a family renowned for their politics and patronage. Evidence of their money and taste seems ubiquitous in Florence, as every building they owned or were somehow connected to bears their coat of arms (a shield with round balls—pills—that signify the family's trade as apothecaries). Works of art and architecture that were commissioned by the Medici comprise the core of Florence's artistic legacy, bequeathed to the city by the last in the Medici family line—Anna Maria Luisa. The Galleria Degli Uffizi is home to many works from the Medici art collection, and the art institution that is a must-see for any traveler to Florence. (Make that *every* traveler to Florence.) Arrive early in the morning or a couple of hours before closing to avoid the outrageous lines, and start with this extraordinary monument to get a feel of the historic significance of the city.

Galleria Degli Uffizi with Palazzo Vecchio in the Background.
©Hubert Stadler/CORBIS

It stands on one side of a public square—the Piazza della Signoria—which was the political center of Florence and site of things glorious and inglorious (Michelangelo's *David* once stood

Piazza Della Signoria with the Palazzo Vecchio.
©Dennis Degnan/CORBIS

there; Savonarola, the would-be reformer-monk, was burned at the stake there). The piazza is also the site of the Palazzo Vecchio, which has served as Florence's Town Hall since the fourteenth century and has a spectacular interior. While you are in the square, check out Florence's best source for postcards—the Sorbi newspaper kiosk—and sample what many rank as the best gelato (Italian ice cream) place in Florence—Perché No! ("Why not!").

Florentine Gelato.
©Alantide Phototravel/CORBIS

Florence is an extremely walkable city, with an expansive pedestrian-only area that encompasses many of its highlights, including the Piazza della Signoria, the Duomo, the Ponte Vecchio, and Santa Croce.

If there is one symbol of Florence (like the Eiffel Tower in Paris or Big Ben in London), it is the Duomo. Literally the Italian word for "dome," the Duomo is the affectionate name for the cathedral of Santa Maria del Fiori. Looking at the skyline of the city, it is easy to understand its status as an icon. The dome, covered with reddish terracotta tiles and accented with eight white ribs, dominates its surroundings. It was constructed by Filippo Brunelleschi after he won a competition for the commission. Lorenzo Ghiberti, whose bronze reliefs for the doors of the nearby Baptistery are among Florence's greatest treasures, lost. Many tourists climb the 463 steps of the dome to the lantern on top to get an unsurpassed view of the city and surrounding hills. My advice is this: if you want to climb, go up into the cathedral's bell tower (the Campanile) instead. Not only do you get a great view of Florence, but the best view of the dome to boot. And

The Duomo and City of Florence as Seen from the Campanile.
©Free Agents Limited/ CORBIS

it's a mere 414 steps to the top. The cathedral, Baptistery, and bell tower are all faced with polychrome marble—white from Carrara, green from Prato, and pink from the Maremma area of southern Tuscany. The combination of light and dark marbles, in particular, characterize many of Florence's buildings, including the churches of Santa Maria Novella and Santa Croce.

Santa Croce lies to the east of the Piazza della Signoria and is the burial place of Florence's famous—including Michelangelo, Machiavelli, Galileo, and the composer Gioacchino Rossini (*The Barber of Seville*). There is also a memorial to Dante, although he isn't buried there. Santa Croce is filled with important frescoes by artists like Taddeo Gaddi and Giotto and a relief sculpture by Donatello. While there, look for the tide mark on the pillars and walls—evidence of a devastating flood that gripped the city in 1966.

While many of the art and architectural treasures of Florence were imperiled by the flood, the Old Bridge, or Ponte Vecchio, somehow survived the onslaught of water and silt when the river Arno rose over its banks. It was not the first time that floodwaters threatened the bridge; it had to be rebuilt in the fourteenth century after a flood. The Ponte Vecchio has a long history. At one time it was the only bridge across the river, and it was the only bridge that the Germans did not destroy during World War II. The Ponte Vecchio looks a bit odd, with shops lining both sides of a walkway across the bridge and a corridor on top of the buildings on one side. The Medici family built the corridor so they could walk across the bridge and not have to run into any *real* people. The bridge was always—dating back to the thirteenth century, at least—a place to shop, and since 1593, exclusive home to goldsmiths and jewelers. You can purchase Florentine gold on the Ponte Vecchio, although the prices can be significantly higher than in other shops around town. In addition to its gold (usually sold by weight), Florence is known for its leather goods, linens, ceramics, and marble-paper. You'll also find no shortage of plastic *Davids* and *Duomos*.

These highlights are clustered in the pedestrian area in the core of the city, but Florence has innumerable other sites within walking distance from one another: The Palazzos Pitti and Medici-Riccardi (Renaissance palaces that were at one time or another occupied by the Medici family); San Lorenzo (parish church and burial place of the Medici, and homage to their patronage of the arts); The Bargello (where all of the glorious sculpture is kept); the Galleria dell'Accademia (where Michelangelo's *David* now resides, along with the *Slaves* that the artist carved for the original design of the tomb of Pope Julius II); and the Boboli Gardens (an inner-city oasis of green behind the Palazzo Pitti to which travelers escape when they've had enough).

Church of Santa Croce.
©Tibor Bognar/CORBIS

The Ponte Vecchio.
©Alinari Archives/ CORBIS

The Renaissance in Italy was a tale of two cities: Florence and Rome. The fourteenth and fifteenth centuries belonged to Florence. No other city in Europe had her impact on art and culture. During the High Renaissance, as the money moved, so did the artists—to papal Rome. At 15 million visitors per year, though, the city of Florence has never lost its premier place in the history of art.

Boboli Gardens.
©Massimo Listri/CORBIS

To continue your tour and learn more about Florence, go to ArtExperience Online.

18

ART BEYOND THE WEST

◼
—

The map is open and connectable in all of its dimensions.
—Gilles Deleuze and Felix Guattari

The world is shrinking: The Global Village, The Global Stage, The Era of Globalization. As citizens of the world in the twenty-first century, we are connected to one another like never before. We travel to remote sites—across actual space (thanks to modern-day transportation) and cyberspace (thanks to the Internet). Money, goods, and services flow quickly from one part of the world to another. Information is more available to ordinary people, as access to modes of international communication has become the rule for the many rather than the exception for the few. Although *globalization* is a term most often linked to the current state of global business and politics, the concept has expanded to include historical and cultural studies. While investment bankers, corporate businesses, and entrepreneurs have developed mutually beneficial relationships with countries around the globe, which have only recently begun to tap into their rich economic potential, new groups of individuals—such as research academicians (sociologists, anthropologists, historians, political scientists)—have begun to investigate social, historical, cultural, and artistic phenomena of regions that are now within reach.

Sheik Lotfallah Mosque, Isfahan, Iran
©Michele Falzone/JAI/Corbis.

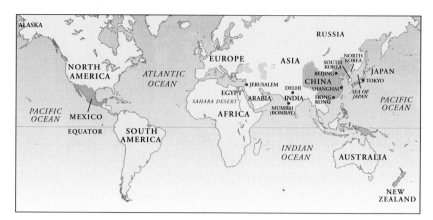

18-1 Art beyond the Western Tradition.

As citizens of the world, we also share an extensive and varied heritage. Western culture and the Western tradition in art—that which solidified in ancient Greece and developed in Western Europe and, later, the United States—may be more familiar to most of us than the art of other cultures and traditions that lie "beyond the West" (Map **18-1**). But those traditions are rich and varied and represent other ways of seeing and knowing that enable us to expand our understanding of ourselves in relation to the world.

Ancient African sculpture and the masquerade, intricately carved catamarans of the Oceanic islanders, colossal stone heads from pre-Columbian Mexico, the South American metropolises, Native American cliff palaces—these are but a handful of examples of art that embody ways of life that have developed along their own courses. They often reflect societal organizations based on the village or the tribe that are rural and self-sufficient and continue from generation to generation with little change. The art of such societies expresses the values and beliefs of a people and plays a pivotal role in the continuation of customs and traditions in societies that are dependent on oral rather than written history.

Europeans who colonized these territories between the sixteenth and twentieth centuries did not think much of the fetishes, idols, and other curiosities upon which they gazed. Today this art is avidly collected throughout the world, including the Western world. Islamic art or Chinese and Japanese art may be somewhat more familiar to the Western eye than the arts of Africa, Oceania, and Native America. As sacred spaces, the great mosques of the world of Islam, the cathedrals of Christian Europe, and synagogues around the world have some elements in common. Persian carpets are popular, and the Western eye need not be especially schooled to appreciate them. Some of the great works of the Indian subcontinent, such as the Taj Mahal, are also familiar, and the influence of China and Japan on Western

art has been felt since the explorations and beginnings of trade, for many hundreds of years. The refined ceramics of the Chinese, for example, were known to European potters, and the perspective techniques and delicacy of Japanese drawings and paintings influenced many modern artists of the nineteenth century.

In this chapter, we shall explore the world of art beyond the West. The breadth of the material precludes detailed discussion of the historical aspects of this work but need not preclude an appreciation for the widely diverse styles of these cultures and the significance of their art to their societies.

AFRICAN ART

African art is as varied as the cultures that have populated that continent. The earliest African art, like the earliest art of Europe and North America, consists of rock paintings and engravings that date to the Neolithic period. In tropical Africa—the central portion of the continent—the lost-wax technique was developed to cast small bronze sculptures as early as the ninth century.

The kingdom of Benin, which during the fourteenth through nineteenth centuries occupied what is now Nigeria, was rich in sculptures of many media, including iron, bronze, wood, ivory, and terra-cotta. Works such as the *Altar of the Hand* (Fig. **18-1**) illustrate the skill with which the Benin manipulated bronze, as well as the importance of symbolism to their art. The many figures that are cast in relief around the circumference of this small work are meant to venerate the king and glorify his divine office. The king is the central figure in both the relief and in the freestanding figures on top of the altar. He holds the staffs of his office in his hands, and his head is larger than those of his attendants. This purposeful distortion signifies the

> *One of the first principles of art . . . is truth to material. . . . Wood has a stringy, fibrous consistency and [the African sculptor could carve it] into thin forms without breaking [it]. Much [African] carving . . . has pathos, a static patience and resignation to unknown mysterious powers; it is religious and, in movement, upward and vertical like the tree it was made from, but in its heavy bent legs is rooted in the earth.*
>
> —HENRY MOORE

head as the center of being and source of intelligence and power. The king's importance is further underscored by his placement within a triangular frame of sorts, his head at the apex. The entire altar is cast with symbolic forms or incised with decorative motifs, all arranged in a symmetrical pattern. The monumentality that this altar achieves in its mere 17 inches or so is remarkable and impressive.

This penchant for ornament can also be seen in more recent tribal art from Nigeria, such as that of the Yoruba. The carved wooden doors in Figure **18-2** depict scenes of tribal life and ritual. The figures are angular and stylized; as in the *Altar of the Hand*, the king, who is seated on a throne, is shown larger than his attendants. The work reads rather like a comic strip, with parts of the narrative confined

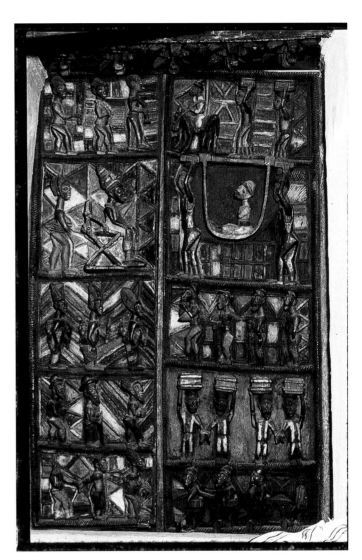

18-2 Door from Iderre, Nigeria (Yoruba, 1910–1914).
Wood. H: 6'.
British Museum, London.
©Werner Forman/Art Resource, NY.

1 in.

18-1 *Altar of the Hand*, Benin, Nigeria (17th–18th centuries).
Bronze. H: 17½".
©The British Museum/HiP/The Image Works.

African Art | **409**

down from generation to generation. In the ruler's costume, a veil composed of strands of beads covers the face, protecting onlookers from the power of the ruler's eyes. The height of the crown emphasizes the head as the center of power and often contains ritual medicines and potions to enhance that power.

Masks and headdresses are found in other regions of Africa as well, and their symbolism is as widely varied as their style. The simplest of these, such as the Etoumba mask (Fig. **18-5**), have facial features resolved into abstract geometric shapes. They are also sometimes punched and slashed with markings intended to represent body scarification. More intricate pieces, such as the mvoom helmet mask from the Kuba people of Zaire (Fig. **18-4**), might be embellished with brass, shells, beads, seeds, feathers, and furs. These contrasting textures, along with the protruding chin and prominent forehead, are symbols of royalty. The mask represents a primordial ancestor that oversees the passage of boys into adulthood.

18-3 The ruler of Orangun-Ila, Airowayoye I, with a beaded scepter, crown, veil, and footstool. Nigeria (Yoruba, 1977).
©John Pemberton III

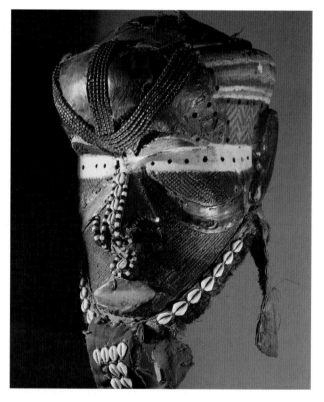

18-4 *Mvoom* helmet mask, Zaire (Kuba, 19th–20th centuries).
Wood, brass, cowrie shells, beads, seeds. H: 13".
Royal Museum for Central Africa, Tervuren, Belgium.
©Werner Forman/Art Resource, NY

to small compartments. In most sections, a geometric-patterned background adds a rich, tapestry-like quality to the work. These doors continue artistic traditions that were established in much older works.

The Yoruba are famous for their mix of the old and the modern in fanciful objects crafted for ceremonial or ritualistic purposes. Masks and headdresses are used in performances called masquerades. They incorporate music, dance, and elaborate costuming in a combination of theater and ritual that often involves social criticism. The beadwork evident in headdresses similar to the crown that is worn by the royal Yoruba ruler in Figure **18-3** is created by a guild of artisans who pass their techniques

Picasso's *Nude with Drapery* with an Etoumba Mask

IN THE EARLY YEARS OF THE TWENTIETH CENTURY, painter Pablo Picasso saw two large exhibitions in Paris. One was of ancient sculpture from his native Spain, carved by the Iberians before their conquest by the Romans; the other was of the native art of African peoples. Both would have a lasting impression on his art.

Compare the facial features of Picasso's painting (Fig. **18-6**) with those of an African mask like the ones he may have seen at the Musée de l'Homme in Paris (Fig. 18-5). What lines and shapes has Picasso adopted? What other conventions or stylizations of African art has he used? How has the painter captured the simplicity and strength of the traditional mask in his painting?

Picasso was enamored of the aesthetic of African art. But as he came to understand more fully the importance of the sacred and mystical powers of that art to its society, he began to see his own art and perhaps art in general as "a form of magic designed to be a mediator between this strange, hostile world and us, a way of seizing the power by giving form to our terrors as well as our desires." ■

18-6 PABLO PICASSO.

Nude with Drapery (1907).

Oil on canvas.

The State Hermitage Museum, St. Petersburg.
Image ©Erich Lessing/Art Resource, NY. ©2009 Estate of Pablo Picasso/
Artists Rights Society (ARS), New York.

1 in.

18-5 Mask, Etumbi region, Republic of Congo.
Wood. H: 35.5 cm

Copyright abm archives Barbier-Müller, Geneva. Photograph by
Pierre-Alain Ferrazzini.

18-7 Ancestral figure, Zaire (Kongo, 19th–20th centuries).
Wood and brass. H: 16".
Royal Museum for Central Africa, Tervuren, Belgium.
©Werner Forman/Art Resource, NY

18-8 *Nkisi nkondi* (hunter figure), Democratic Republic of Congo (collected before 1905).
Wood, nails, iron, fabric. H: 97 cm
Copyright abm archives Barbier-Müller, Geneva. Photograph by Pierre-Alain Ferrazzini.

1 in.

Other work from Zaire is more conventional in form. A so-called ancestral or power image from the Kongo peoples (Fig. **18-7**) is a delicate wood carving of a mother and child, most likely intended as a repository of the soul of a deceased noblewoman (recall the Ka figures of Old Kingdom Egypt). The function of the sculpture was probably to receive prayers for the woman's continuing guardianship and care of the community, but other such figures channeled ancestral powers from "medicines" placed within or on the sculptures to those in need—warriors in battle, farmers planting crops, or people trying to cure disease.

In many Western societies, Christians light votive candles to request favors from God, to seek the intervention of saints on their behalf, and to thank them for help. In many African societies, priests have hammered nails into carved, wooden **fetish figures** (Fig. **18-8**) to seek help

from the gods, to ward off evil, to vanquish enemies, or to solve problems in their villages. By driving nails into the figure, the villagers believe that wrongdoers will suffer pain. Once the social problem has been solved, the nails may be removed from the figure. Sometimes such fetish figures have human forms, but some are wild animals connected to ancestral spirits. In either case, these figures represent a vehicle for mediation between the living and the dead.

The seated primordial couple in Figure **18-9** are characteristic of another well-known style of African art—that of the Dogon people of Mali, in the western part of the continent. Although the Dogon artist often worked in a more naturalistic style, here the artist has opted for a highly stylized, rigid, and elongated figure, incised with overall geometric patterns. This treatment removes the subjects from contemporary reality. The group represents

18-9 Ancestral couple, Mali (Dogon).
Wood. H: 28¾".
The Metropolitan Museum of Art, New York. Gift of Lester Wunderman, 1977 (1977.394.15).
Image copyright ©The Metropolitan Museum of Art/Art Resource, NY

1 in.

the mythical ancestors of the human race, a kind of Adam and Eve of all of us.

Traders from North Africa brought Islam to Ghana in the eighth century CE, which, because of its wealth, became a vibrant center of Islamic culture. What emerged in terms of religious practice and art was a blend of both traditions. The plan of the Great Mosque at Djenne in Mali (Fig. **18-10**), like that of all early mosques, is based on the model of Muhammad's home in Medina. It has a walled courtyard in front of a wall that faces Mecca. Unlike the stone mosques of the Middle East, however, the mosque at Djenne is built of sun-dried bricks and puddled clay. Wooden poles jutting through the clay serve as a kind of scaffold support for workers who replaster the structure yearly to prevent complete erosion of the clay. They also provide a form of exterior ornamentation, an aspect of the highly decorative aesthetic of Muslim art and architecture.

OCEANIC ART

The peoples and art of Oceania are also varied. They span millions of square miles of ocean, ranging from the continent of Australia and large islands of New Guinea and New Zealand to small islands such as the Gilberts, Tahiti, and Easter Island. They are divided into the cultures of Polynesia, Melanesia, and Micronesia. We shall discuss works from Polynesia and Melanesia.

18-10 The Great Mosque, Djenne, Mali (14th century CE).
Puddled clay, adobe brick, and wooden poles.
©Sandro Vannini/CORBIS.

18-11 Great stone figures on Easter Island (Polynesian, 15th century CE). H: approx. 30'.
©George Holton/Photo Researchers, Inc.

Polynesia

The Polynesian artists are known for their figural sculptures, such as the huge stone images of Easter Island (Fig. **18-11**). More than 600 of these heads and half-length figures survive, some of them 60 feet tall. Polynesian art is also known for its massiveness and compactness. Carved between the fifth and seventeenth centuries CE, their jutting, monolithic forms have the abstracted quality of African masks and ancestor figures. Figure after figure has the same angular sweep of nose and chin, the severe pursed lips, and the overbearing brow.

Archeologists have determined that these figures symbolize the power that chieftains were thought to derive from the gods and to retain in death through their own deification. Political power in Polynesia was believed to be a reflection of spiritual power. The images of the gods were thought

to be combined with those of their descendants in the carvings and other artworks like those on Easter Island.

The Polynesian Maori of New Zealand are known for their wooden relief carvings. The plentiful nature of tough, durable pinewood allowed them to sculpt works with the curvilinear intricacy and vitality of the nearly six-foot-long canoe prow shown in Figure **18-12**. The figure at the front of the prow is intended to have an earthy phallic thrust.

The winding snake pattern on the mythic figure and scrollwork of the eighteenth-century canoe prow are like that found on the Maori's tattooed bodies. Body painting and tattooing are governed by tradition and are believed to link the individual to the spirits of ancestors. Ancestor figures are intended to appear menacing to outsiders, but they are perceived as benevolent within the group. Other Maori carvings are found on assembly houses, storehouses, and stockades.

Melanesia

Melanesian art is generally more colorful than that of Polynesia. The cloth masks of New Britain are woven with a certain flair, and the mixed-media ancestral poles of New Guinea (Fig. **18-13**) are painted in vivid hues. The intricate poles are carved from single pieces of wood and adorned with palm leaves and paint. Space flows around and through the ancestral poles as it could not pass through the figures

18-12 Canoe prow (Maori, pre-1935).
Wood. 70⅞" × 29½".

Musée d'Histoire Naturelle, Ethnographie et Prehistoire, Rouen, France.
©Réunion des Musées Nationaux/Art Resource, NY.

at Easter Island. The expressionistically elongated and attenuated bodies again represent ancestors. The open-work banners are phallic symbols, intended to give courage to community men in ceremonies before combat with other tribes. Practical, ceremonial, and decorative uses of art swept across the Pacific into the New World. Many historians and archeologists believe, in fact, that the Americas were first populated many thousands of years ago by migrations across the Pacific.

NATIVE ART OF THE AMERICAS

The art of the Americas was rich and varied before the arrival of European culture. We shall explore the native arts of North America and Peru.

Native Arts of Mexico

Some of the earliest, and certainly the most massive, art of the Americas was produced by the Olmecs in southern Mexico long before the Golden Age of Greece. In addition to huge heads such as that in Figure **18-14**, the Olmecs produced small stone carvings, including reliefs.

More than a dozen great heads up to 12 feet in height have been found at Olmec ceremonial centers. The hard basalt and jadeite from which they were carved had to be carted nearly 100 miles. The difficulty of working this material with primitive tools may to some degree account for the works' close adherence to the original monoliths. The

18-13 Ancestor poles, New Guinea (Melanesian, Amsat tribe, 1960).
Wood, paint, and fiber. Height of tallest pole: 17' 11".
The Metropolitan Museum of Art. The Michael C. Rockefeller Collection.
Image copyright ©The Metropolitan Museum of Art/Art Resource, NY

1 ft.

18-14 Colossal head, Villahermosa, Mexico (Olmec culture, c. 500 BCE–200 CE).
Basalt. H: 8'.
©2007 Westend61/Andreas M. Gross/Jupiter Images

1 in.

18-15 Effigy vessel, girl on swing, from Remojadas region, Veracruz, Mexico (300–900 CE).
Ceramic: 9¼".

The Metropolitan Museum of Art, New York. The Michael C. Rockefeller Memorial Collection. Bequest of Nelson A. Rockefeller, 1979 (1979.206.574). Copyright 1991 The Metropolitan Museum of Art, New York.

heads share the same tight-fitting helmets, broad noses, full lips, and wide cheeks. Whether these colossal heads represent gods or earthly rulers is unknown, but there can be no doubting the power they project.

Henry Moore stated that Mexican sculpture is known for its massiveness, but contrast the Olmec heads with the sprightliness of the kinetic sculpture of the swinging girl (Fig. **18-15**). This small piece is actually a whistle. The swinging girl was created many hundreds of years after the Olmec heads and was found in the same region of southern Mexico. We can find a continuity of tradition in the oversized head, but note the delicacy of the curved body. The entire length of the body is nothing but a spread-eagled, draped abstraction.

The Mayans, whose civilization reached its height in the Yucatán region of Mexico and the highlands of Guatemala from about 300 to 600 CE, built many huge limestone structures with **corbelled** vaults. Mayan temples were highly ornamented with figural relief carvings that represent rulers and gods and with commemorative and allegorical murals. The temple discovered at Bonampak in 1947 is decorated with murals of vivid hues, such as that in Figure **18-16**, in which prisoners are being presented for sacrifice.

The placement of the reasonably realistic figures along the receding steps symbolizes the social hierarchy. At the bottom are the common people. On the upper platform are noblemen and priests in richly embellished headdresses, as well as their personal attendants, and symbols of the heavens. The prisoners sit and kneel on various levels, visually without a home, whereas the Mayans are rigidly erect in their ascendance. There is no perspective; the figures on the upper registers are not smaller, even though they are farther away. The eye is drawn upward to the center of the composition by the pyramidal shape formed by the scattered prisoners. The figures face the center of the composition, providing symmetry, and the rhythm of the steps provides unity. The subject of human sacrifice is repugnant to us, and well it should be. The composition of the mural, however, shows a classical refinement.

18-16 Detail: Mural from Mayan temple at Bonampak, Mexico (c. 6th century CE).
Watercolor copy by Antonio Tejeda.
©Peabody Museum, Harvard University.

18-17 Temple of Quetzalcóatl, Teotihuacán, Mexico (300–700 CE).
©Erich Lessing/Art Resource, NY

1 ft.

18-18 Statue of Coatlicue (Aztec, Toltec culture, 15th century). Stone. H: 99".
National Museum of Anthropology, Mexico City.
©Gianni Dagli Orti/CORBIS

While the Mayans were reaching the height of their power in lower Mexico, the population of the agricultural civilization of Teotihuacán may have reached 100,000. The temples of Teotihuacán, harmoniously grouped in the fertile valley to the north of modern-day Mexico City, include the massive 250-foot-high Pyramid of the Sun and the smaller Temple of Quetzalcóatl (Fig. **18-17**). The god Quetzalcóatl was believed to be a feathered serpent. The high-relief head of Quetzalcóatl projects repeatedly from the terraced sculptural panels of the temple, alternating with the square-brimmed geometric abstractions of Tlaloc, the rain god. Bas-reliefs of abstracted serpent scales and feathers follow sinuous paths on the panels in between.

The warlike Aztecs were a small group of poor nomads until they established their capital, Tenochtitlán, in about 1325 CE on the site of modern-day Mexico City. Once established in Tenochtitlán, the Aztecs made great advances in art and architecture, as well as in mathematics and engineering,

but they also cruelly subjugated peoples from surrounding tribes. Prisoners of war were used for human sacrifice in order to compensate the sun god, who was believed to have sacrificed himself in the creation of the human race. It is not surprising that in the early part of the sixteenth century, the invading Spaniards found many neighbors of the Aztecs more than eager to help them in their conquest of Mexico. The Aztecs also helped seal their own fate by initially treating the Spaniards, who they believed were descended from Quetzalcóatl, with great hospitality. The Spaniards, needless to say, did not rush to disabuse their hosts of this notion and were thus able to creep into the hearts of the Aztecs within the Trojan horse of mistaken identity.

Coatlicue was the Aztec "Mother of Gods," associated with the Earth and the cycle of birth, death, and rebirth. The compact, monumental stone effigy in Figure **18-18** depicts the goddess as symbol of creation and destruction (the Earth gives but also takes away). She wears a skirt of

Cambios: The Clash of Cultures and the Artistic Fallout

IN THE YEAR 1492, the king and queen of Spain funded Columbus's trip to the New World. The day after he left Spain's shores, Jews were expelled from the country by decree. Some 27 years later, the Spaniard Hernán Cortez sailed to Mexico and conquered the Aztec Empire. His campaign was brilliant; the empire fell to only 500 Spanish soldiers. The Aztec capital was vanquished in a bloody siege, and much of the Native Mexican population eventually succumbed to smallpox, a virus that the Spaniards introduced and to which the Native Mexicans had not developed immunity. The picture of Spain in the sixteenth century is one of sharp contrasts. It was a country in its "Golden Age," marked by feats of exploration and cultural masterworks, and at the same time, marked by prejudice, savage domination, and the infliction of pain.

18-19 *Bargueño* (18th century).
Inlaid wood. 17¼" × 28" × 16¼".
Collection of Michael Haskell, Santa Barbara, CA.

The culture of Mexico survived, albeit in a transformed state. And the works of art that emerged during the Spanish Colonial period in Mexico, Central America, and South America bear evidence as well of artistic transformation. These works were the subject of a 1993 exhibition at the Santa Barbara Museum of Art in California: "Cambios: The Spirit of Transformation in Spanish Colonial Art." Cultural clash almost always leaves in its wake fascinating artistic imagery; perhaps in no other encounter of peoples has the interaction and reconciliation of disparate motifs been more well-defined than in the clash of the Spanish and Meso-American cultures.

The exhibition focused on how indigenous art forms, motifs, and techniques were integrated with European influences. In a review of the show in *Latin American Art*, Leslie Westbrook noted that the exhibit illustrated the great diversity of design influences as well as the willingness of artists to combine vocabularies from different cultures and contexts to create a "new world order" on the palette, so to speak.* Some examples of motifs include the Meso-American jaguar, flower-filled jars, leaf patterns,

and elaborate borders (Fig. **18-19**) reconciled with the lion image, a European formal symmetry, and Christian subject matter. Of special interest is a newly attributed work by Miguel Cabrera entitled *Castas (Depiction of Racial Mixtures)* (Fig. **18-20**). It represents the *mestizo*—the child born of the union of a European and a Native American. These children bear the physical characteristics of the two peoples, and as such symbolize the marriage of two cultures.

The "Cambios" exhibition brought together remnants of a sometimes cruel history, where, as the reviewer remarked, one civilization superseded and dominated another. Yet nothing directly spoke of the cruel and devastating effects of Spanish domination. Instead, a freewheeling creativity—one of absorption, reconciliation, and ancestral legacy—dominated the show, a testimony to the resilience of the human spirit. ∎

18-20 MIGUEL CABRERA.
Castas (Depiction of Racial Mixtures) (1763).
Oil on canvas. 52" × 40½".
Private collection.

---

* Leslie A. Westbrook, "Cambios: The Spirit of Transformation in Spanish Colonial Art," *Latin American Art* 5, no. 1: 54–57.

carved serpents, representing fertility, and a necklace of severed hands, hearts, and skulls. Scholars offer different interpretations of the uppermost part of the sculpture. Some read it as Coatilcue's head, composed of the heads of two facing snakes, whose eyes and fangs become her own. Others have said that the sculpture portrays a decapitated Coatlicue in which snakes coil out of her severed neck. This interpretation more directly references one of two myths, in which one of Coatlicue's 400 children called upon her siblings to kill their mother. The ferocity of the imagery, which is incised and carved in relief, while shocking, was typical of pre-Columbian societies.

Native Arts of Peru

The native arts of Peru include pyramid-shaped structures that form supports for temples, as in Mexico; stone carvings, mostly in the form of ornamental reliefs on ceremonial architecture; ceramic wares; and astounding feats of engineering.

The ceramic portrait jar shown in Figure **18-21** was created in about the fifth or sixth century CE by the Mochica culture along the Pacific coast of northern Peru. It has a typical flat bottom and stirrup-shaped spout. Other jars show entire human or animal figures, some of them caught in erotic poses.

Figure **18-22** shows the grand ruins of Machu Picchu, the fortress that straddled the Peruvian Andes. This structure, built by the Incas in about 1500 CE, shows an engineering genius that has been compared to the feats of the Romans. The tight fit of the dry masonry walls seems to reflect the tightness of the totalitarian fist with which the Incan nobility regulated the lives of their own masses and subjugated peoples from Ecuador and Chile. The conquering Spaniards were amazed by the great Incan "Royal Road of the Mountains." Thirty feet wide and walled for its entire 3,750 miles, it had no parallel in Europe.

Native Arts of the United States and Canada

Some native art objects in the United States and Canada date back nearly 12,000 years. As with African art, much of it is practical craft, much is ceremonial, and all is richly varied. Eskimo, or Inuit, sculpture exhibits a simplicity of form and elegant refinement in both its realistic and

18-21 Ceramic portrait jar from Peru (Mochica culture, c. 500 CE).
Terra-cotta with paint.
©Scala/Art Resource, NY

18-22 Fortress of Machu Picchu, Urubamba Valley, Peru (Incan, 1490–1530).
©Topfoto/The Image Works.

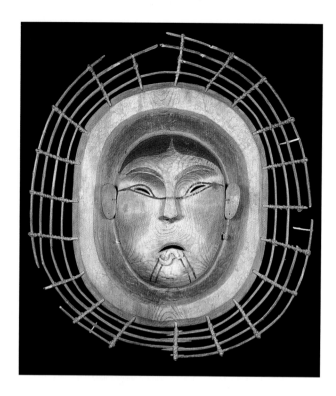

18-23 Eskimo mask representing a moon goddess (before 1900).
Phoebe A. Hearst Museum of Anthropology.
The University of California at Berkeley.

abstract designs. It can also be highly imaginative, as in a mask representing a moon goddess (Fig. **18-23**). Such masks, worn by shamans in ritual ceremonies, were carved of ivory or wood and often had movable parts that added to the drama and realism of the object.

Prehistoric sites in what is now the United States also have yielded many interesting works. One of the larger ceremonial sculptures to survive is an earthwork called the Serpent Mound, a snakelike form of molded earth that meanders some 1,440 feet in the Ohio countryside. Pyramidal temple platforms reminiscent of those of Mexico and South America have also been unearthed.

Among Native Americans, the Navajos of the Southwest are particularly noted for their fiber artistry and stylized sand paintings that portray the gods and mythic figures. Some of these works are believed to be empowered to heal.

Peoples of the Northwest Coast have produced masks used by shamans in healing rituals, totem poles not unlike the ancestor poles of Oceania, bowls, clothing, and canoes and houses that are embellished with carving and painted ornamentation. The wood and muslin of a four-foot-high Kwakiutl headdress from British Columbia (Fig. **18-24**) is vividly painted with abstracted human and animal forms. Like the Inuit moon goddess mask, it too has movable parts. When the string hanging from the inner mask is pulled, the two profiles to the sides are drawn together, forming another mask. The symbols represent the sun and other spirits. It is an extraordinary composition, balanced by the circular flow of fabric above the heads and by the bilateral symmetry in the placement of the shapes. As is often the case in ethnographic art, the embellishment of the work reflects traditional body decoration, such as painting, tattooing, or scarification.

The nomadic tribes of the Great Plains poured their artistic energies into embellishing portable items, such as garments and teepees. The muslin teepee lining of the Crow peoples of the Plains (Fig. **18-25**) is a multihued and fairly realistic portrayal of nineteenth-century warfare

1 ft.

18-24 Kwakiutl headdress from Vancouver Island, British Columbia, Canada (c. 1895–1900).
Wood and muslin. 52" × 46".
Courtesy, National Museum of the American Indian, Smithsonian Institution (T115235).
Photo by Carmelo Guadagno

What I know of Islam is that tolerance, compassion and love are at its very heart.

—SALMAN RUSHDIE

18-25 *Custer's Last Stand* (Plains culture, late 19th century).
Teepee lining. Painted muslin. 35" × 85".
National Museum of Natural History, Department of Anthropology, Smithsonian Institution, Washington, DC.

1 ft.

with the U.S. cavalry. In this symbolic collection of events, Crow warriors advance rhythmically from the right. Many chieftains sport splendid feather headdresses. The cavalry is largely unhorsed and apparently unable to stop the implied momentum of the charge, which is very much like the sequence of frames in a motion picture.

ISLAMIC ART

The era of Islam was founded in Arabia by Muhammad in 622 CE. Within a century, the Islamic—also known as Muslim—faith had been spread by conquering armies westward across North Africa to the Atlantic Ocean. It also spread to the east. So it is that many of the great monuments of Islamic art and architecture are found as far west as Spain and as far east as Agra in India. Muslims look upon the Old and New Testaments as well as the Koran as holy scriptures, and they number Abraham, Moses, and Jesus among their prophets.

The Great Mosque at Samarra, Iraq (Fig. **18-26**), was constructed between 848 and 852 CE. Once the largest mosque in the world of Islam, it now lies in ruins. Its most striking feature is the spiral minaret, from which a crier known as a **muezzin** called followers to prayer at

18-26 Great Mosque at Samarra, Iraq (Islamic, 848–852 CE).
©George Gerster/Photo Researchers, Inc.

18-27 Sanctuary of the Mosque at Córdoba, Spain (Islamic) (786–987 CE). Interior view.
©Adam Woolfitt/CORBIS.

18-28 Mihrab, Mosque at Isfahan, Iran (1617).
©Art Resource, NY

certain hours. Mosques avoid symbols, and early mosques in particular do not show ornamentation. Nor is there the clerical hierarchy in Islam that is found in many Christian religions. The leader of gatherings for worship, called the **imam**, stands on a pulpit in the mosque, near the wall that faces Mecca, the spiritual capital of Islam.

The mosque at Samarra was a simple building, 800 feet long and 520 feet wide, covered in part by a wooden roof, with a great open courtyard. The roof was supported by the **hypostyle** system of multiple rows of columns that could be expanded in any direction as the population of the congregation grew. By bowing toward Mecca in the same yard, worshipers were granted equal psychological access to Allah, the Islamic name of God.

The interior of the mosque at Córdoba, Spain (Fig. **18-27**) shows the system of arches that spans the distances between columns in the hypostyle system. A series of vaults, supported by heavier piers, overspreads the arches. There is no grand open space as in the Western cathedral; rather, air and light flow as through a forest of high-crowned trees. The interiors of mosques have traditionally been decorated with finely detailed mosaics, as seen in a mosque in Isfahan, Iran (Fig. **18-28**). Our photograph shows the **mihrab**, a niche in the wall facing Mecca that provides a focus of worship.

The Taj Mahal at Agra (Fig. **18-29**) is a mausoleum that was built by Shah Jahan in the seventeenth century in memory of his wife. In sharp contrast to the plainness of early Islamic architecture, tree-lined pools reflect a refined elegance. The three-quarters sphere of the dome is a stunning feat of engineering. Open archways, with their ever-changing play of light and shade,

18-29 Taj Mahal, Agra, India (Islamic, 1630–1648).
©Koch/Photo Researchers, Inc.

slender minarets, and spires give the marble structure a look of weightlessness. Creamy marble seems to melt in the perfect order.

INDIAN ART

Indian art, like that of the Americas, shows a history of thousands of years, and it too has been influenced by different cultures. Stone sculptures and **seals** that date to the second or third millennium BCE have been discovered. In low relief, the seals portray sensuous, rounded native animals and humanoid figures that presage the chief Hindu god, **Shiva**.

India once encompassed present-day Pakistan, Bangladesh, and the buffer states between modern India and China. Many religious traditions have conflicted and sometimes peacefully coexisted in India, among them the Vedic religion, Hinduism, Buddhism, and Islam. Today Islam is the dominant religion of Pakistan, and Hinduism predominates in India. Indian art, like Islamic art, is found in many parts of Asia where Indian cultural influence once reigned, as in Indochina.

Buddhism flowered from earlier Indian traditions in the sixth century BCE, largely as a result of the example set by a prince named Siddhartha. In his later years, Siddhartha renounced his birthright and earthly luxuries to become a Buddha, or enlightened being. Through meditation and self-denial, he is believed to have reached a comprehension of the universe that Buddhists call *nirvana*. After his death, Buddha's cremated remains were supposedly placed in *stupas* in eight different locations in India. These sites became places of worship and devotion for his followers. The Great Stupa at Sanchi (Fig. **18-30**) was completed in the first century CE. The stupa is crowned by a large dome that symbolizes the sky. The dome is visually separated from the base of the structure by a stone railing or fence—known as the *vedika*—echoing the separation of the heavenly and earthly spheres. Pilgrims circumnavigate the mound in a clockwise direction, as if tracing the path of the sun across the sky. The worshippers' relationship to the monument concentrates on the exterior rather than the interior as, for example, in the case of the Christian church.

The bracket figure (Fig. **18-31**) on a gateway to the Great Stupa is a *yakshia*, a pre-Buddhist goddess who was believed

18-31 *Yakshi* bracket figure from the east gate of the Great Stupa at Sanchi, India (Early Andhra period, 1st century BCE).
Stone. H: approx 60".
©Charles and Josette Lenars/CORBIS.

18-30 The Great Stupa, Sanchi, India (Shunga and Early Andhra periods, 3rd century BCE–early 1st century CE).
H: 65'.
©Adam Woolfitt/CORBIS.

1 ft.

18-32 *Buddha Calling on the Earth to Witness*, India
(Bengal Pala period, 9th century CE).
Black chlorite. H: 99 cm.
The Cleveland Museum of Art. Dudley P. Allen Fund, 1935.146

18-33 *Colossal Buddha*, Bamiyan, Afghanistan
(2nd–5th centuries CE). Destroyed in 2001.
Stone. H: 180'.
©Charles and Josette Lenars/CORBIS.

to embody the generative forces of nature. She appears to be nude, but a hemline reveals that she wears a diaphanous garment. Her ample breasts and sex organs symbolize the force of her productive powers. The voluptuousness of such figures stands in contrast to the often ascetic figures we find in Western religious art.

For many hundreds of years, there were no images of the Buddha, but sculptures and other representations began to appear in the second century CE. Some sculpted Buddhas show a Western influence that can be traced to the conquest of northwestern India by Alexander the Great in 327 BCE. Others have a sensuous, rounded look that recalls the ancient seals and is decidedly Indian. The slender chlorite Buddha (Fig. **18-32**) shows delicate fingers and gauzelike, revealing drapery. The face exhibits a pleasant cast that is as inscrutable as the expression of La Gioconda in Leonardo's *Mona Lisa* (see Fig. 16-19).

Let us briefly travel west of India to view the colossal Buddha carved out of living rock at Bamiyan, Afghanistan

(Fig. **18-33**). The statue portrays the eternal form of Buddha in the belief that his earthly form was purely transient. The concept of eternity is expressed in part through scale. This Buddha, 180 feet tall, and its somewhat smaller companion, 120 feet tall, commanded the surrounding landscape and was so well-known that tiny replicas were carved for visitors as souvenirs that they carried back to their home countries. Even though the photograph seems to suggest a rather rough-hewn rendering of Buddha, it is quite possible that it was gilded and had applications of plaster and pigment. The Taliban destroyed these figures in 2001 despite pleas by other nations, which offered to remove and preserve them at their own expense.

In the sixth and seventh centuries CE, Hinduism rose to prominence in India, perhaps because it permitted more paths for reaching nirvana, including the simple carrying out of one's daily duties. Another reason for the

1 ft.

18-34 *Nataraja: Shiva as King of Dance*, South India (Chola period, 11th century CE).
Bronze. H: 43⅞"; W: 40".
Copyright 2000 The Cleveland Museum of Art. Purchase from the J. H. Wade Fund 1930.331.

18-35 Kandariya Mahadeva Temple, Khajuraho, India (10th–11th centuries CE).
©George Holton/Photo Researchers, Inc.

popularity of Hinduism may be its frank appreciation of eroticism. Western religions impose a distinction between the body or flesh, on the one hand, and the soul or mind, on the other. As a consequence, sex is often seen as being at odds with religious purity. Hinduism considers sexual expression to be one legitimate path to virtue. Explicit sexual acts in high reliefs adorn temple walls and amaze Western visitors.

There are many Hindu gods, including Shiva, the Lord of Lords and god of creation and destruction, which, in Hindu philosophy, are one. Figure **18-34** shows Shiva as Nataraja, the King of Dance. With one foot on the Demon of Ignorance, this eleventh-century bronze figure dances within a symbolically splendid fiery aura. The limbs are sensuous, even erotic. The small figure to the right side of his head is Ganga, the river goddess. This periodic dance destroys the universe, which is then reborn. So, in Hindu belief, is the human spirit reborn after death, its new form reflecting the sum of the virtues of its previous existences.

Hindu temples are considered to be the dwelling places of the gods, not houses of worship. The proportions of the famous Kandariya Mahadeva Temple at Khajuraho (Fig. **18-35**) symbolize cosmic rhythms. The gradual unfolding of spaces within is highlighted by the sculptural procession of exterior forms. The organic, natural shapes of the multiple roofs are in most sections separated from the horizontal registers of the base by sweeping cornices. The main tower is an abstracted mountain peak, reached visually by ascending what appear to be architectural and natural hurdles. All of this can be seen as representing human paths to oneness with the universe. The registers of the base are populated by high reliefs of gods, allegorical scenes, and idealized men and women in erotic positions.

Other Hindu temples are even more intricate. Vast pyramidal bases contain forests of towers and spires, corniced at the edges as they ascend from level to fanciful level. They are thick with low and high reliefs. In the Buddhist temples of Indochina, the giant face of Buddha looms from the walls of imposing towers and gazes in many directions. Indian art, including Indian painting—of which little, sad to say, survives—teaches us again how different the content of the visual arts can be. Still, techniques such as that of stone carving and

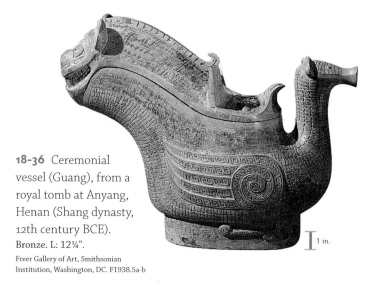

18-36 Ceremonial vessel (Guang), from a royal tomb at Anyang, Henan (Shang dynasty, 12th century BCE). Bronze. L: 12¼".
Freer Gallery of Art, Smithsonian Institution, Washington, DC. F1938.5a-b

1 in.

bronze casting, as well as elements of composition, seem to possess a universal validity.

CHINESE ART

China houses more than a billion people in a country not quite as large as the United States (compared to a U.S. population of approximately 300,000,000 as of 2007). Nearly 4,000 years ago, inhabitants of China were producing primitive crafts. Beautiful bronze vessels embellished with stylized animal imagery were cast during the second millennium BCE, such as the one shown in Figure **18-36**. During the feudal period of the Late Chou dynasty, which was contemporaneous with the Golden Age of Greece, royal metalworks were inlaid with gold, silver, and polished mirrors. Elegant carvings of fine jade were buried with their noble owners.

Confucianism ascended as the major Chinese way of life during the second century BCE. It is based on the moral principles of Confucius, which argue that social behavior must be derived from sympathy for one's fellows. Paintings and reliefs of this period show the **conceptual space** of Egyptian painting and create the illusion of depth by means of overlapping. Missionaries from India successfully introduced Buddhism to China during the second century CE, and many Chinese artists imitated Indian models for a few centuries afterward. But by the sixth century, Chinese art was again Chinese. Landscape paintings transported viewers to unfamiliar, magical realms. Many people believed that artist and work of art were united by a great moving spirit. Centuries after the introduction of

1 ft.

18-37 FAN K'UAN.
Travelers among Mountains and Streams (c. 1000 CE).
Hanging scroll, ink and colors on silk. H: 81¾".
Collection of the National Palace Museum, Taipei, Taiwan, Republic of China.

Buddhism, Confucianism again emerged. The present-day People's Republic of China is officially atheistic, but many Chinese still follow the precepts of Confucius.

Fan K'uan's *Travelers among Mountains and Streams* (Fig. **18-37**) was painted on a silk scroll during the early part of the eleventh century. Years of political turmoil had reinforced the artistic escape into imaginary landscapes. It is

A Chinese poem:
To what can our life on earth be likened?
To a flock of geese,
alighting on the snow.
Sometimes leaving a trace of their passage.

—SU DONGPO, 11th century CE

executed in the so-called Monumental style. Rocks in the foreground create a visual barrier that prevents the viewer from being drawn suddenly into the painting. Rounded forms rise in orderly, rhythmic fashion from foreground through background. Sharp brushstrokes clearly delineate conifers, deciduous trees, and small temples on the cliff in the middle ground. The waterfall down the high cliffs to the right is balanced by the cleft to the left. A high contrast in values picks out the waterfall from the cliffs. Distant mountains dwarf human figures. In contrast to the perspective typical of Western landscapes, there is no single vanishing point or set of vanishing points. The perspective shifts, offering the viewer a freer journey back across the many paths and bridges.

The blue-and-white porcelain vase from the Ming dynasty (Fig. **18-38**) speaks eloquently of the refinement of Chinese ceramics. The crafting of vases such as these was a hereditary art, passed on from father to son over many generations. Labor was also frequently divided so that one craftsman made the vase and others glazed and decorated it. The vase has a blue underglaze decoration—that is, a decoration molded or incised beneath rather than on top of the glaze. Transparent glazing increases the brilliance of the piece. In many instances, the incising or molding was so subtle that it amounted to "secret" decoration.

Li K'an's fourteenth-century ink painting, *Bamboo* (Fig. **18-39**), possesses an almost unbearable beauty. The entire composition consists of minor variations in line and tone.

18-38 Vase (Ming dynasty, 1368–1644 CE).
Porcelain.
Musée Guimet, Paris.
©Réunion des Musées Nationaux/
Art Resource, NY

18-39 LI K'AN.
Bamboo (1308 CE). Detail of 1st section.
Hand scroll. Ink on paper. 14¾" × 93½".
The Nelson-Atkins Museum of Art, Kansas City, MO. Purchase Nelson Trust, 48-16

1 in.

On one level, it is a realistic representation of bamboo leaves, with texture gradient providing a powerful illusion of depth. On another level, it is a nonobjective symphony of calligraphic brushstrokes. The mass of white paper showing in the background is a symbolic statement of purity, not a realistic rendering of natural elements such as haze.

In much of Chinese art, there is a non-Western type of reverence for nature in which people are seen as integral parts of the order of nature, neither its rulers nor its victims. In moments of enlightenment, we understand how we create and are of this order, very much in the way Li K'an must have felt that his spirit had both created and been derived from these leaves of bamboo and the natural order that they represent.

How can we hope to have spoken meaningfully about the depth and beauty of Chinese philosophies and Chinese arts in but a few sentences? Our words are mean strokes, but perhaps they point in the right direction.

JAPANESE ART

Japan is an island country off the eastern coast of Asia, holding more than 120 million people in an area not quite as large as California (which holds approximately 36.5 million people as of 2007). The islands were originally formed from porous volcanic rock, and thus they are devoid of hard stone suitable for sculpture and building. Therefore, Japan's sculpture tradition has focused on clay modeling and bronze casting, and its structures have been built from wood.

The Japanese tradition, like the Western tradition, has various periods and styles. In Japanese art, as in Western art, we find a developing technology, the effect of native materials, indigenous and foreign influences, a mix of religious traditions, and disagreement as to what art is intended to portray. Despite its vast differences from Western art, Japanese art shows similar meanings and functions. Japanese artists also use the same elements of art, in their own fashion, to shape brilliant compositions.

Ceramic figures and vessels date to the fourth millennium BCE. Over the past 2,000 years, Japanese art has been intermittently influenced by the arts of nearby China and Korea. In the fifth and sixth centuries CE, the Japanese produced **haniwa**, hollow ceramic figures with tubular limbs modeled from slabs of clay. Haniwa were placed around burial plots, but their function is unknown.

By the beginning of the seventh century, Buddhism had been exported from China and established as the state religion in Japan. Many sculptors produced wooden and bronze effigies of the Buddha, and Buddhist temples reflected the

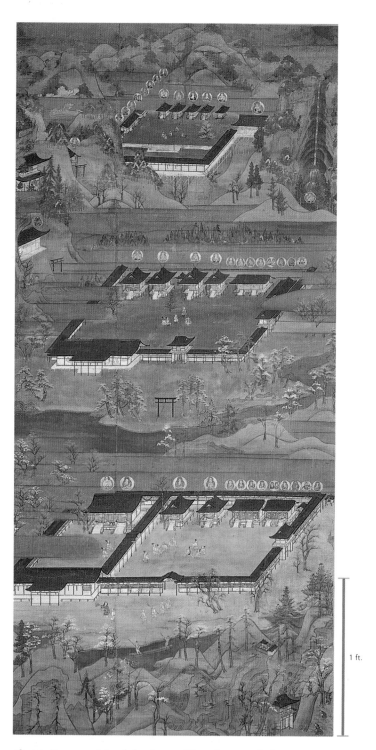

18-40 Kumano Mandala, Japan (Kamakura period, c. 1300 CE).
Hanging scroll. Color on silk. 53¾" × 24⅜".
The Cleveland Museum of Art. John L. Severance Fund, 1953.16

Chinese style. Shinto, the native religion of Japan, teaches love of nature and the existence of many beneficent gods, who are never symbolized in art or any other visual form.

A Japanese poem:
Temple bells die out.
The fragrant blossoms remain.
A perfect evening!

—MATSUŌ BASH, 17th century CE

For nearly 2,000 years, wooden Shinto shrines, such as those shown in Figure **18-40**, have been razed every 20 years and replaced by duplicates. The landscapes, portraits, and narrative scrolls produced by the Japanese during the Kamakura period, which spanned the late twelfth through the early fourteenth centuries CE, are highly original and Japanese in character. Some of them express the contemplative life of Buddhism, others express the active life of the warrior, and still others express the aesthetic life made possible by love of nature.

The Kumano Mandala (Fig. 18-40), a scroll executed at the beginning of the fourteenth century, represents three **Shinto** shrines. These are actually several miles apart in mountainous terrain, but the artist collapsed the space between them to permit the viewer an easier visual pilgrimage. The scroll pays homage to the unique Japanese landscape in its vivid color and rich detail. The several small figures of the seated Buddha portrayed within testify to the Japanese reconciliation of disparate spiritual influences. The repetition of forms within the shrines and the procession of the shrines afford the composition a wonderful rhythm and unity. A **mandala** is a religious symbol of the design of the universe. It seems as though the universe of the shrines of the Kumano Mandala must carry on forever, as, indeed, it did in the minds of the Japanese.

Some periods of Japanese art have given rise to an extraordinary realism, as in the thirteenth-century wood sculpture of *The Sage Kuya Invoking the Amida Buddha* (Fig. **18-41**). From the stance of the figure and the keen observation of every drapery fold, to the crystal used to create the illusion of actual eyes, this sculptor's effort to reproduce reality knew no bounds. The artist even went as far as to attempt to render speech: Six tiny images of Buddha come forth from the sage's mouth, representing the syllables of a prayer that repeats the name of Buddha. A remarkable balance between the earthly and the spiritual is achieved through the use of extreme realism to portray a subject that refers to religion.

1 ft.

18-41 *The Sage Kuya Invoking the Amida Buddha* (Kamakura period, 13th century CE).
Painted wood. H: approx. 46".
Rokuhara Mitsu-ji Temple, Kyoto.
©Pacific Press Services

Some three centuries later, Hasegawa Tohaku painted his masterful *Pine Wood* (Fig. **18-42**) on a pair of screens. It is reminiscent of Li K'an's study of bamboo in that the plant life stands alone. No rocks or figures occupy the foreground. No mountains press the skies in the background. Like *Bamboo*, it is also monochromatic. The illusion of depth—and the illusion of dreamy mists—is evoked by subtle gradations in tone and texture. Overlapping and relative size also play their roles in the provision of perspective. Without foreground and background, there is no point of reference from which we can infer the scale of the trees. Their monumentality is implied by the power of the artist's brushstrokes. The groupings of trees to the left have a soft sculptural quality and the overall form of delicate ceramic wares. The groupings of trees within each screen balance one another, and the overall composition suggests the infinite directional strivings of nature to find form and express itself.

We noted that Picasso was strongly influenced by the art of Africa. Many Western artists of the nineteenth century were influenced by the art of the East, particularly prints from Japan, which were being imported to Paris and other Western cultural centers. The French Impressionist

18-43 ANDO HIROSHIGE.
Rain Shower on Ohashi Bridge (1857).
Color woodblock on paper. 13⅞" × 9⅛".
The Cleveland Museum of Art. Gift of J. J. Wade, 1921.318

Edgar Degas, in fact, hung a print by Torii Kiyonaga in his bedroom. Modern artists were intrigued by the flatness of space, the decorative patterns, brilliant palette, and off-center compositions in Japanese woodcuts, such as Hiroshige's *Rain Shower on Ohashi Bridge* (Fig. **18-43**). Vincent van Gogh made an oil-on-canvas painting of this print, adding a decorative frame, complete with calligraphic patterns (Fig. **18-44**). The ordinariness of Japanese subjects also struck a chord among the Modernists, who were trying to escape the grip of mythological and historical painting.

The opening of trade between Japan and the West in the mid-nineteenth century revealed new artistic worlds to the painters in Western Europe. Van Gogh wasn't the only artist of his time to copy or reinterpret the masterworks of Japanese painters, printmakers, and porcelain artists. Copying, as we have seen, has always been a way to come

18-42 HASEGAWA TOHAKU.
Pine Wood (1539–1610 CE). Detail from a pair of sixfold screens.
Ink on paper. H: 61".
Tokyo National Museum/DNPArchives.com.

18-44 VINCENT VAN GOGH.
Bridge in the Rain, copy after Ando Hiroshige (1887).
Oil on canvas. 28¾" × 18¼".
Van Gogh Museum, Amsterdam.
©francis G. Mayer/CORBIS

18-45 SILVIA REINSTEIN.
Untitled.
Acrylic on paper with painted frame. 26" × 20".
Courtesy KS Art, New York.

to understand—and to know deeply—the process and the product of art. But according to art critic Lyle Rexer, for some self-taught, "outsider" artists (see Chapter 1), it has also been a way to experience times and places that would otherwise remain unreachable. Although never intended to hang anywhere nor appear in any compendium of art history, Silvia Reinstein's untitled acrylic work on paper, embellished by a painted gold frame (Fig. **18-45**), bears the same hallmark of inspiration by Japanese prints as the works of her "insider," Impressionist predecessors.

The ability to represent nature with exacting realism was a goal that united most Western artists through the ages. There were occasional deviations, as among the Christian artists of the Middle Ages, for whom representing the physicality of the figure was unimportant. Their choice was not based on an inability to mirror nature, but on the belief that the soul—and not the body—was a more relevant and intimate part of God's celestial plan. During the Renaissance, Western artists—including those who portrayed religious subjects—devised perspective to master the illusion of reality. As humanism took hold, the figure in sculpture and painting also appeared "more human."

Mimesis—imitation in representation—was never as much a goal for artists beyond the West, not because of lack of skill but because their artistic goals were not the same. Once art entered the modern era in the West, and artists had reached the height of their ability to represent nature with utmost accuracy, some continued in the realistic tradition, but others found it meaningless. After all, early enough in the nineteenth century, the camera would be able to do that for them. It was when art no longer needed to be consonant with realism that art beyond the West spoke most cogently to these artists. It was the exploration of art beyond the West that steered Western modernism on a different course.

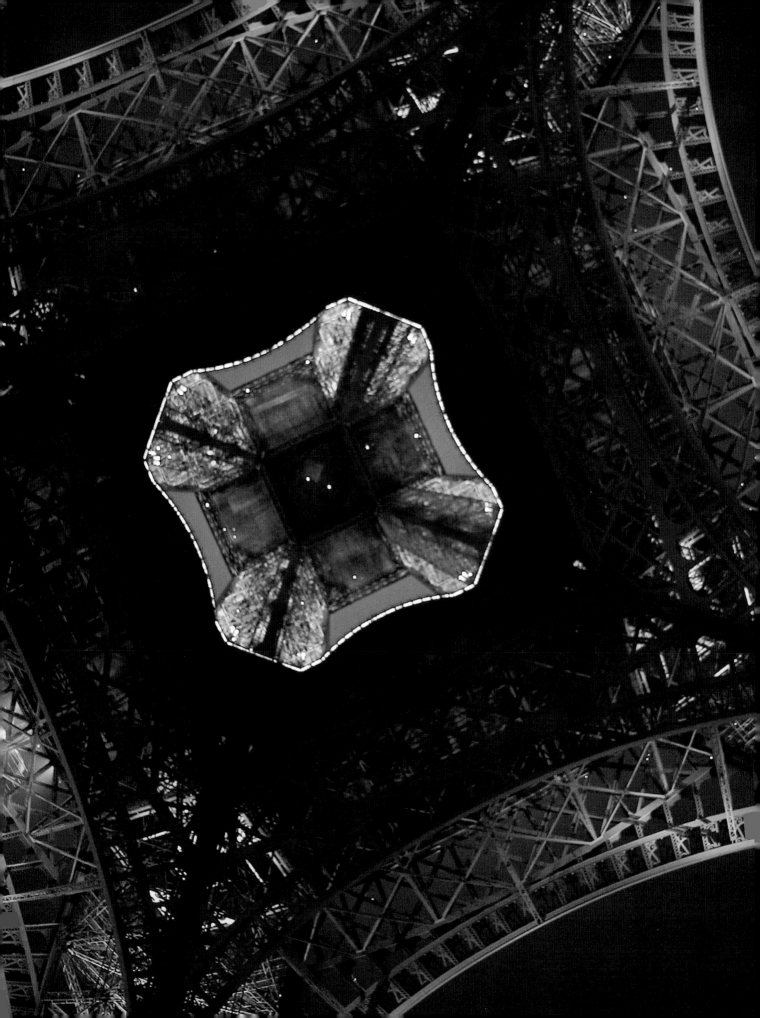

ART IN THE TWENTY-FIRST CENTURY: A GLOBAL PERSPECTIVE

■
▬

A few decades back, when the art world was smaller and easier to police,
and "international" meant Manhattan and Western Europe, New York more or less
dictated what kind of art would be looked at, what ideas would circulate, what would be cool.
But this is no longer so. The arena has expanded. Although economically powerful, New York is
increasingly just one of many art centers doing their local thing. Most work that turns up
in Manhattan galleries has little connection with, or pertinence to, what artists are doing
and thinking about in Africa or India or even in the Bronx.
—Holland Cotter[1]

GLOBALIZATION

When Holland Carter wrote these words for his introduction to an exhibition of Caribbean art at the Brooklyn Museum, he stated the facts as he observed them: that it seems no longer meaningful or even valid to be talking about a center of the art world, much less continuing to assign that center to the city of New York. Contemporary art has gone global—in venue, in subject, even in the raw economics of the art market—dovetailing with the phenomenon of globalization that characterizes spheres outside of the realm of culture.

---

1 Holland Carter, "Caribbean Visions of Tropical Paradise and Protest," *The New York Times*, August 31, 2007, F25, F27.

22-1 YVES TANGUY (PROBABLE ARTIST).
Surrealist Map of the World (1929).
From a special issue of Variétés, entitled Le Surréalisme, June, 1929.[p.183]

The word **globalization** has become ubiquitous in contemporary life, politics, economics, and art.

From this perspective, the 1929 Surrealist map of the world (Fig. **22-1**) seems almost prophetic. The 48 United States and Western Europe are all but invisible, whereas territories out of the stream of Western culture—Russia, Labrador, Easter Island, and Alaska—are assigned more significance by their exaggerated scale. Although the imaginary map asserts a radical surrealist political and cultural view at a moment in time—with a good dose of humor—it does capture a specific point for us; namely, that boundaries in the art world are culturally constructed, changeable, and permeable. The map also suggests that the era of dominance and exclusivity of the old bastions of culture has passed.

The phenomenon of globalization has created a world in which cultures are no longer distant from one another, and people and places are no longer separate. Television and the Internet create an immediacy

of communication of visual images as never before; a war around the globe finds its way into living rooms around the clock. "Distant" hurricanes, cyclones, and earthquakes happen everywhere at once. One stock market affects all stock markets. China's air pollution flows into California, and China's toys overflow in America's stockings at Christmastime. So too do visual images from various cultures invade the consciousness and the marketplace around the globe as never before. But familiarity and proximity do not necessarily beget understanding and tolerance. Much contemporary art on the global stage is directed toward awareness, understanding, and tolerance.

Art historians and critics have had to find new ways of analyzing and organizing material on the subject of multiculturalism and cross-culturalism in contemporary art. The traditional vocabulary is insufficient. As we consider works of art in the twenty-first century, we will add to our critical rubric concepts such as *hybridity, appropriation, high art and low culture*, and *postcolonialism*.

Hybridity

In the visual arts, one of the effects of globalization is **hybridity**, or the mixing of the traditions of different cultures to create new blends and new connections. As an example of the ways in which globalization has led to an intermingling of the world's cultural icons, Takashi Murakami (b. 1962) has been dubbed Japan's Andy

22-2 TAKASHI MURAKAMI.
Tan Tan Bo (2001).
Acrylic on canvas mounted on board.
141¾" × 212⅝" × 2⅝".

Collection of John A. Smith and Victoria Hughes.
Courtesy Tomio Koyama Gallery, Tokyo. ©2001 Takashi Murakami/Kaikai Kiki Co., Ltd. All rights reserved.

1 ft.

Warhol. Like the American Pop artist, Murakami draws on consumer culture for his imagery. And, like Warhol, Murakami is vigorously self-promotional, exhibiting his paintings and sculpture at major museums around the world while creating mass-market products ranging from T-shirts and key chains to mouse pads and upscale Louis Vuitton handbags.

As a boy, Murakami fantasized about illustrating Japanese graphic novels called *manga*, which are also hybrids. While illustrated manuscripts have as long and distinguished a history in Japanese art as they do in Western art, their modern form is heavily influenced by American comic books, which infiltrated Japanese culture soon after the end of World War II, when Japan was occupied by the United States and American culture became popular.

As a student, Murakami experimented with the large-eyed cartoon figures in the popular *anime* style (a style of animation developed in Japan), but he was also trained in classical Japanese painting techniques. Consequently, his work often aims to reconcile "high art" and "low culture." *Tan Tan Bo* (Fig. **22-2**) is filled with cartoon-like imagery rendered in simple, dark outlines filled in with bright colors. The overall shape may resemble a fierce Mickey Mouse, but the artist has dubbed his signature character "Mr. DOB" and identified it as a monkey. Murakami has created a multimedia sensation of Mr. DOB ranging from lithographs to inflatable balloons. In the tradition of "pure" pop, he makes no distinction between art and merchandise.

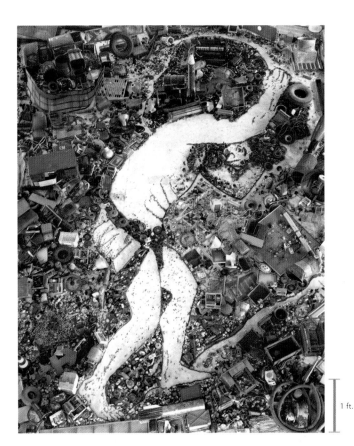

22-3 VIK MUNIZ.

Sisyphus, after Titian, from *Pictures of Junk* (2005).

C-print, composed on a hangar floor with truckloads of detritus. 229 cm × 183 cm.

Image courtesy of Sikkema Jenkins & Co. Art ©Vik Muniz/Licensed by VAGA, New York, NY.

Appropriation

Appropriation became part of the lexicon of contemporary art with the advent of postmodernism in the 1980s. The concept, however, was not a new one, stretching back to early-twentieth-century art movements such as Cubism and Dada. Appropriation consisted then of borrowed elements. Picasso and Braque, for example, incorporated materials and techniques from the nonart world—newspaper, wallpaper, and wine labels—into their collages; Duchamp used ordinary or familiar objects for his readymades, including a urinal and a bicycle wheel. Appropriation in the postmodern era became a more refined idea, specifically referring to the use of another artist's work as a basis for one's own. Sometimes the new work built upon or changed the one appropriated, but at other times, the original image was left unaltered.

Brazilian artist Vik Muniz (b. 1961) is known for using anything—beans, dirt, pepper, caviar, chocolate, and here,

junk. The artist collected literally tons of junk from a dangerous neighborhood in Rio de Janeiro for his photo series *Pictures of Junk*. As Muniz and his assistants rummaged around the area dubbed the Gaza Strip by locals, rival gang members were shooting at one another. The junk in his *Sisyphus, after Titian* (Fig. **22-3**) includes tons of wire, discarded sinks and tires, trash cans, fans, barrels, broken shelves, rusting appliances and countless chains, nuts, and bolts. The detritus was trucked to a dockside hangar, which the artist used as a makeshift studio. Muniz and his assistants meticulously arranged the junk, recreating Old Master paintings of mythological figures, such as Goya's *Saturn Devouring his Children* and Rubens's painting of Bacchus, and then photographing the results.

In the ancient myth, Sisyphus was condemned by the Greek gods to an eternity of frustration for having the audacity to consider himself as clever as they. His punishment—to roll a heavy rock up a hill only to have it roll back down just before he reached the top—was never-ending.

Muniz appropriated Titian's composition on the subject in which Sisyphus struggles uphill, head bent under the burden of an enormous rock. In Muniz's version, the rock and the thick, gray clouds of Titian's piece are replaced with a mosaic-like landscape of colorful pieces of junk, a terrain that Sisyphus traverses like an obstacle course. There is some commentary to be found in the futile task of eliminating society's waste, the nondegradable components of which are simply moved from one place to another.

High Art and Low Culture

High art and low culture were historically viewed as antithetical concepts. High art and high culture are associated with classical antiquity and perpetuated through the artistic traditions of the Renaissance. They include art of the Old Masters or compositions by Classical musicians or canonical works of literature, primarily from the West. These classics are associated with elitism; by contrast, low culture has been used derogatorily to describe popular or mass culture. Some contemporary art has focused particularly on the blurring of boundaries between high art and low culture, with artists appropriating images from low culture. Low art or low culture includes popular music, tattoo art, and *kitsch*—overly sentimental work that is viewed as tasteless decoration but that has its own sort of nostalgic charm.

Jeff Koons (b. 1955), like Andy Warhol, questions the separation of high art and low culture in his manipulation of ordinary, familiar (and cheaply produced) objects. Koons has arranged inflatable vinyl flowers and bunnies in mirrored, tabletop installations and created assemblages of pool toys juxtaposed with mundane objects like chairs and ladders. His mediums range from found objects to stainless steel sculpture and photorealist paintings, but the common denominator of his content is **kitsch**. Koons often further challenges

22-4 JEFF KOONS.
Elephant (2000–2004).
High chromium stainless steel, mirror polish finish with transparent color coating. 92.7 cm × 73.7 cm × 48.3 cm.
©Jeff Koons.

the boundaries between high art and low art—and between merchandising and the museum—by translating soft, vinyl objects into highly polished, perfectly wrought stainless steel sculptures as in *Elephant* (Fig. **22-4**). The meticulous craft of the gleaming surface and trompe l'oeil effect of inflatable mylar convey the art in what might otherwise be seen as an artless object.

Postcolonialism

Some aspects of globalization in the arts are a reaction to the retreat of the European empires that ruled much of the world throughout the middle of the twentieth century. The former colonies in the Americas, Africa, and Asia bear complex relationships with their former rulers—political, economic, ethnic, and, of course, cultural.

London-based artist Hew Locke was raised in Guyana on the Caribbean coast of South America. Like Canada, Australia, New Zealand, India, Pakistan, Egypt, and the original American colonies, Guyana was once part of the British Empire. England profited enormously from its Empire holdings, acquired by means of violence, colonization, and some diplomacy here and there. Locke's *El Dorado* (Fig. **22-5**) is a nine-and-a-half-feet-tall assemblage of plastic toys—bullets, lizards, flowers and feathers, and highly visible knives—all of which are arranged in the shape of a bust of a young Queen Elizabeth II as you might find it on a postage stamp. The title, *El Dorado,* refers to a hidden city of great wealth that lured the Spanish and other explorers to South America from the 1500s onward. Through the juxtaposition of the iconic profile of Elizabeth, the saturation of gold, and the cheap plastic toys that are often manufactured in third-world countries, Locke reflects on the enrichment of empire at the expense of native peoples. *El Dorado* seems a concrete symbol of Honoré de Balzac's statement that "Behind every great fortune lies a great crime."

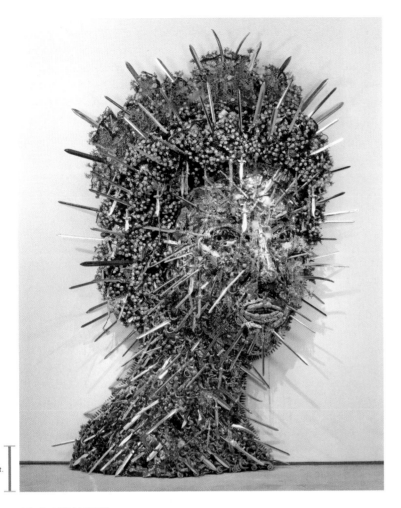

1 ft.

22-5 HEW LOCKE.
El Dorado (2005).
Mixed media. 114¼" × 68⅞" × 23⅝" (290 cm × 175 cm × 60 cm).
West Collection, Oaks, Philadelphia.
Image courtesy Hew Locke and Hales Gallery, photo by FXP Photography.
©Hew Locke/Artists Rights Society (ARS), New York/DACS, London.

Scholars have linked globalization to what they call the postcolonial condition:

> Many of the preoccupations and strategies of [post-colonial, global] art exhibit traces of continuity with earlier practice and theory exploring the legacy of European colonialism. . . . Many of the most intractable tensions between ethnicity, gender and class can be traced to [the change from] "classic" European imperialism to a post-colonial condition.[2]

Some of the art we will look at in the next part of the chapter will be rooted in European artistic traditions or self-consciously utilize those traditions to communicate content that is at odds with them. We also note the early-twenty-first-century exhibition at London's Tate Gallery of works by contemporary artists from diverse geographic locations called "Century City." This installation can be seen as an analogue for the process of globalization,[3] in that it focused on the avant-garde not only in art centers such as New York and Paris, but also in cities including Rio de Janeiro, Tokyo, and Mumbai. The rest of this chapter is organized along these lines—not around themes but around places.

LATIN AMERICA

The nations of the Caribbean and Latin America have a common history of colonialism, slavery, and interaction among racial and ethnic groups. Political instability and economic pressures have created migration northward to the United States and Canada, yet powerful cultural traditions and prejudices in new host countries have fostered unbreakable ties with Caribbean and Latin American homelands. Even as many natives attempt to leave, tourists from the north descend on the islands and the beaches of these southern paradises, especially in winter. Yet the tourist traps and resorts can be looked upon as "elaborate site-specific installations"[4] carved out of these postcolonial destinations. Tourists remain largely separated from native peoples during their visits, insulated from the harsh realties faced by most local people every day. The art produced by people of and from the Caribbean and Latin America tends to reflect these themes—the residue of colonialism, poverty, political conflict, the northward push, and what life means from day to day.

2 Niru Ratnam, "Art and Globalization," in Gill Perry and Paul Wood, eds., *Themes in Contemporary Art* (New Haven, CT: Yale University Press, 2004), 277–313.

3 Ibid.

4 Annie Paul, "Visualizing Art in the Caribbean," in Tumelo Mosaka, ed., *Infinite Island: Contemporary Caribbean Art* (NY: Brooklyn Museum in Association with Philip Wilson Publishers, 2007), 21–34.

1 ft.

22-6 ALEXANDRE ARRECHEA.
Elementos Arquitectronicos (2006).
Chromogenic print. 43" × 31" (109.2 cm × 78.7 cm).
Edition 2 of 4, 1AP.
Courtesy of Magnan Projects, New York.

constructed in a minimalist style, with sharp tonal contrasts and an overall starkness. The whitewashed faces of the bricks piled on top of one another in a strict vertical pile are reminiscent of Robert Ryman's white paintings. The artist's juxtaposition of a self-conscious modernity with the raw physicality of the laborer's life in a place that seems untouched by modernity raises questions about the relationships of art and life and social consciousness.

Haiti

Haitian artist Jean-Ulrick Désert has focused many of his projects on the relationship between immigrants and outsiders and their adopted or host countries, some of it growing out of his own experiences. *Negerhosen* is an ongoing work that began in 2000 after the artist was accosted in Berlin because of his race. It consists of a series of photographs documenting the artist's encounters with locals and tourists while dressed in the traditional German folk costume of *lederhosen*, or leather shorts and knee socks. Lederhosen is particularly associated with the Bavarian area of Germany,

Cuba

Much of Cuban artist Alexandre Arrechea's work is a commentary on the irony that while his country builds its new socialist society, its jewels—like the capital city of Havana—lie in disrepair. *Elementos Arquitectronicos* (Fig. **22-6**) is a stunning portrait of a laborer struggling to carry—or at least hold—a stack of whitewashed bricks that obscures his identity. Arrechea uses pictorial and symbolic devices—the hard fired clay of the brick against the man's flesh or the insinuation of the verdant plant life against the decaying stucco—to suggest the workers' struggle and chance at hope in a classless, collectivist society. Like Muniz's Sisyphus, the faceless man is locked into a task that seems to have no beginning or end; the image is one of quiet desperation.

There are also parallels to be found between Arrechea's work and the mid-nineteenth-century realists like Courbet (see Fig. 19-13), in which social issues were wrapped in the modernist aesthetic of the day. Arrechea's composition is

1 ft.

22-7 JEAN ULRICK DÉSERT.
*The Burqa Project: On the Borders of My Dreams
I Encountered My Double's Ghosts* (2001).
Flag-textiles, dye, lace. 63" × 118" (160 cm × 300 cm).
Installation at Infinite Island, Contemporary Caribbean Art, The Brooklyn Museum NY,
Courtesy of the artist.

where folk culture and national identity have been historically very strong. So the sight of a black man wearing this costume is not only an oddity, but it focuses attention on the degree to which Germany's racist Nazi past continues in the present. In this performance piece called *Negerhosen* (German for *black trousers*), Désert roams Germany, inviting Germans and others to walk with him and pose for photos. Many oblige with broad smiles, more engaged in the visual joke than aware of the artist's underlying message.

Cultural mixing and identity are also the concepts underlying *The Burqa Project* (Fig. **22-7**), in which Désert stitched national flags into burqas and draped them on mannequins. *Burqas* are garments that Muslim women in some countries choose or are forced to wear for the sake of modesty. The flags used in *The Burqa Project* represent the western countries of Germany, France, the United States, and the United Kingdom and seem to suggest the tensions between religious and national identity that occur when Western and non-Western cultures clash. Outward symbols of allegiance are often perceived as threatening to the homogeneity of nationalism and can lead to legislation (as it did in France) that forbids their use in state institutions (like a public school). The burqa-clad mannequins in Désert's piece offer a tangible resolution to the dilemma of allegiance.

Puerto Rico

Puerto Rican artist Miguel Luciano focuses much of his work on the cultural and economic relationship between the Caribbean island of Puerto Rico and the United States. Puerto Rico is a self-governing commonwealth that was ceded to the United States in a treaty with Spain that ended the Spanish-American war at the end of the nineteenth century. Historically, both the United States and Puerto Rico have had wavering feelings about their relationship. In the postwar years, the U.S. Congress was not unanimous in its support of annexation, and even today Puerto Ricans continue to debate the island's political status, between options of statehood, independence, or the commonwealth status-quo. Luciano's *Plántano Pride* (Fig. **22-8**) shows a Puerto Rican adolescent boy in a universal white T-shirt and culture-specific bling. Sugar, tobacco, and plantains—a banana-like fruit—were once the island's cash crops. The boy poses for the camera with a cocky expression, wearing with pride a symbol associated with his country's national identity, but also with American materialism and rap culture. Luciano's work addresses political, economic, and cultural subjugation.

1 ft.

22-8 MIGUEL LUCIANO.
Plántano Pride (2006).
Chromogenic print (platinum plantain). 40" × 30"
(101.6 cm × 76.2 cm).
Courtesy of the artist.

Mexico

Enrique Chagoya's (b. 1953) paintings and prints chronicle cultural change and exchange, often suggesting alternative histories that better explain the realities of contemporary politics and social conditions. Chagoya, who was born in Mexico City, is known for his juxtapositions of historical and cultural references with images of pop culture, especially from the world of Disney. A suite of small pencil drawings, for example, consists of portraits of world figures cast in the roles of *Snow White and the Seven Dwarfs*: Condoleeza Rice, U.S. Secretary of State under the George W. Bush administration, is portrayed as Snow White; Tony Blair, former British Prime Minister, is the Prince; Donald Rumsfeld, U.S. Secretary of Defense who led the invasion of Iraq, is Grumpy; President George W. Bush is Dopey; and Saddam Hussein is the Witch.

Chagoya most recently has turned his attention to immigration, a long-standing and unresolved issue between the United States and Mexico. His print entitled *Illegal Alien's Guide to Critical Theory* (Figs. **22-9** and **22-10**) is a satire on his own experience as an immigrant now leading an academic life at California's prestigious Stanford University. A detail of the work features Chagoya as a plucked chicken in a sombrero, peddling a bicycle as fast as he can while spouting a "critically correct" phrase torn from the pages of literary or artistic theory. Playing on the common cardboard placard graphic "Works for food," a talk-bubble next to the artist's head reads: "Works to suggest that the act finally distills into something dense and unknowable." Other details include visual references to pre-Columbian reliefs and wall paintings, particularly from the Mayan civilization (see Fig. 18-16). Chagoya says, "My artwork is a conceptual fusion of opposite cultural realities that I have experienced in my lifetime. I integrate diverse elements: from pre-Columbian mythology, western religious iconography, and American popular culture."

22-9 ENRIQUE CHAGOYA.
Illegal Alien's Guide to Critical Theory (2007).
Color lithograph. 24" × 40".
Courtesy of the artist and Shark's Ink, Lyons, Colorado.

22-10 ENRIQUE CHAGOYA.
Detail of *Illegal Alien's Guide to Critical Theory* (2007).
Color lithograph. 24" × 40".
Courtesy of the artist and Shark's Ink, Lyons, Colorado.

EUROPE

Europe was the center of the Western art world for many hundreds of years, and remained so throughout the first half of the twentieth century. As we saw in the previous chapter, the focus shifted to New York following World War II, but Europeans might not necessarily agree. As in the United States, European art today takes many directions and is expressed through many mediums.

The United Kingdom

Damien Hirst (b. 1965) established his reputation as one of the "yBa" generation (young British artists) making conceptual and installation art that aimed to challenge traditional aesthetics, ethics, morality, and to some, plain good taste. He is perhaps best known for his infamous installation of a dismembered shark suspended in formaldehyde (*The Physical Impossibility of Death in the Mind of Someone Living*, 1991).

Hirst's diamond-encrusted skull fits with the artist's penchant for anatomy and sensation. *For the Love of God* (Fig. **22-11**), as he entitled it after hearing his mother's response to his idea, is based on an eighteenth-century skull that Hirst found in a thrift shop. He commissioned London jewelers to copy the skull's proportions exactly in platinum and then cover it with 8,601 diamonds valued at more than $20 million. Hirst put it on the art auction block for $100 million. One critic noted that the result

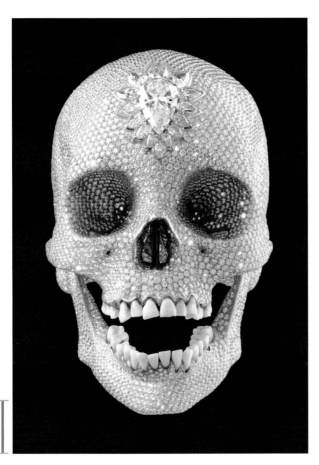

1 in.

22-11 DAMIEN HIRST.
For the Love of God (2007).
Platinum, diamonds, and human teeth. 6¾" × 5" × 7½"
(17.1 cm × 12.7 cm × 19.1 cm).
©Damien Hirst. DACS, London 2008. Photo: Prudence Cuming Associates Ltd.
Courtesy Jay Jopling/White Cube (London).

was the "most ambitious piece of British jewelry since the crown jewels."

The skull is laden with references. In Christian iconography, it is a symbol of mortality. Shakespeare's *Hamlet* recites one of his most well-known soliloquies—a meditation on death—with a skull in hand. And, in the history of art, *vanitas* paintings often contain images of skulls. *Vanitas* is a Latin word that means "emptiness," and it is often used to suggest the transitory nature of life and the ultimate uselessness of material things.

Much of British-born Sarah Lucas's (b. 1962) work comments on male–female relationships in life and in art. She has been profoundly interested in the political issues surrounding the male gaze and the woman as the stereotypical object of desire. One of her best-known works, *Au Naturel*, features an old mattress with a cucumber, pieces of fruit, and a bucket as stand-ins for male and female body parts. *The Fag Show* (Fig. **22-12**) was inspired by Lucas's conquest of her addiction to tobacco. (*Fag* is the slang word in Britain for cigarette.) The outer skins of the objects in the installation, including vacuum cleaners and Disneyesque dwarves, consist of swirling linear patterns of cigarettes. Much of Lucas's work focuses on blatant sexual imagery and the stuff of self-destruction and death.

Edward Steichen wrote, "Every other artist begins [with] a blank canvas, a piece of paper . . . the photographer begins with the finished product." Implicit in Steichen's statement is the reality of the planning and selection that permits the instantaneous creation of an image to be a "finished product." The contemporary images of Sam Taylor-Wood (b. 1967), who lives and works in England, are created with extensive forethought and with knowledge of, and reverence for, the history of art.

22-12 SARAH LUCAS.
The Fag Show (2000).
Installation view, Sadie Coles HQ, London.
Copyright Sarah Lucas. Courtesy Sadie Coles HQ, London.

22-13 SAM TAYLOR-WOOD.
Self-Pietà (2001).
35mm film/DVD
Duration: 1 minute 57 seconds
©The artist. Courtesy Jay Jopling/White Cube, London.

Taylor-Wood has become known for her room-encompassing video installations and 360-degree photographic panoramas, accompanied by sound tracks that depict people in the midst of personal dramas and fantasies. Although the actors in her dramas may be visually attractive, something about them is awkward and vulnerable, out of place. Even though some are involved in sexual activity, they appear to be emotionally isolated. Taylor-Wood's photographs are often structured like multipaneled Renaissance altarpieces, replete with art-historical references. In her *Soliloquy III*, for example, a reclining nude mimics the pose of Velázquez's *Rokeby Venus* (1650). Her grand-scale *Self-Pietà* (Fig. **22-13**) mimics Michelangelo's *Pietà*, in which the Virgin Mary holds her dead son in her lap. In Taylor-Wood's photo, the artist holds a motionless male—an icon, as it were, that threatens to slip from her hands.

Scottish photographer and sculptor Nathan Coley (b. 1967) explores the ways in which concepts of power authority are signified in objects and architecture. After witnessing the trial of terrorists accused of bombing a jetliner over Lockerbie, Scotland, he rebuilt the courtroom witness box to encourage viewers to reflect on the nature of truth. Coley has also built cardboard models of churches, synagogues, and mosques. *Camouflage Church* (Fig. **22-14**), placed in a public square at Spain's Santiago de Compostela (a famed pilgrimage destination in the Middle Ages), has the iconic shape of a church, but the colorful striped sheath of its exterior does anything but enable it to blend into its surroundings. In fact, it has the opposite effect. By disrupting the familiar, Coley draws attention to spaces and places that have become like wallpaper in our consciousness and perhaps also in our spiritual and emotional lives.

Germany

German artist Anselm Kiefer (b. 1945) became known in the 1970s and 1980s for his Neoexpressionist paintings (see Fig. 21-20) and lead sculptures that unearthed memories of the Holocaust and probed historic German myths. In more

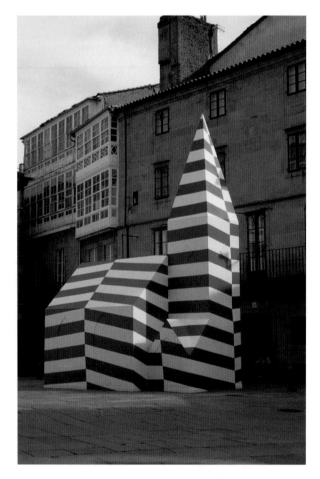

22-14 NATHAN COLEY.
Camouflage Church (2006).
Santiago de Compostela, Spain
Courtesy of the artist and doggerfisher.

22-15 ANSELM KIEFER.
Sonnenschiff (2007).
Concrete, earth, iron, lead, sunflowers.
AP Images/Michael Euler. Copyright ©Anselm Kiefer.

recent years, Kiefer has turned his attention to monumental sculpture, several examples of which he created to fill the vacuous space of Paris's Grand Palais for a solo exhibition. *Sonnenschiff (Sun Ship)* (Fig. **22-15**) comprises concrete, earth, iron and lead, and sunflowers—objects that frequently also find their ways in Kiefer's paintings. As in all of Kiefer's work, literary and historical references are woven throughout. Along with an enormity of scale, these references give the work a timeless, biblical quality. Kiefer has described himself as an individual who is in despair, who in order to survive creates illusions to escape melancholy and pessimism. Although he currently resides in rural France, his historical consciousness as a German continues to weigh heavily on him and his art.

The Netherlands

Kiefer's art is much about change—in his case from life to ruin to the process of rebuilding. Dutch photographer Rineke Dijkstra's (b. 1959) work also revolves around change, although on a much more personal scale. Her subjects, who have included a Bosnian girl in a home for refugees and young Israelis undertaking military service, are mostly adolescents who we observe at a transitional moment in their development. Dijkstra's large-format color photographs range from bust- to full-length portraits against backgrounds that range from specific to nondescript. Captured at a specific moment in time, the sitters communicate something of who they are now and what they have been in the past—through gestures, clothing, facial features and expressions—but their futures are really a blank slate. Dijkstra sometimes revisits her subjects to record the aging process or the effect that experience has had on the face and body. Her portrait of the ballet student, Stephanie (Fig. **22-16**), clad in a hooded Guess sweatshirt, simultaneously reveals the adolescent need for individuality and blending.

1 ft.

22-16 RINEKE DIJKSTRA.
Stephanie, Saint Joseph Ballet School, Santa Ana, CA, USA (2003, March 22).
C-print. 128 cm × 107 cm (framed).
Courtesy: Marian Goodman Gallery, New York.

Switzerland

Pipilotti Rist (b.1962) is a video-performance artist whose most common subject is her own nude body afloat in an endless sea (Fig. **22-17**). Her work has been projected in venues as diverse as New York's Times Square and the baroque ceiling of an Italian church (the Chiesa di San Stae) during the 2005 Venice Biennale, an international art exhibition. The first artist to adapt a music-video aesthetic, her videos are saturated with psychedelic color and play against a sound track of her own music (she created the all-women band, Les Reines Prochaines—The Next Queens). Using a jittery, handheld camera, the artist's vantage points shift unexpectedly, her images zoom in and out, and the pace changes from real time to slow motion and back, often against a field of kaleidoscopic effects. Rist's installations are sensuous and joyous, and according to one reviewer, the "walls liquefy and wash over the people like a psychic Jacuzzi, in order to set them afloat."[5]

---

5 Pipilotti Rist, in Uta Grosenick, ed., *Art Now* (Cologne, Germany: Taschen, 2005), 442.

22-17 PIPILOTTI RIST.
Frame from *Related Legs (Yokohama Dandelions)* (2001).
Video installation, Edition 3/3; 2 projections, 1 mirror scanner, 2 dvd/vhs players, 1 audio system, 1 computer device, steel cables, lace curtains, children's chairs, sound with Anders Guggisberg and Roland Widmer. Dimensions variable.
Collection of Adam Sender. Courtesy of the artist and Luhring Augustine, New York.

Spain

Spanish architect Santiago Calatrava is one of a few architects currently in demand all over the globe. He has designed the shell-like transportation hub under construction at Ground Zero in Manhattan and the Chicago Spire (Fig. **22-18**), which, with its broadcast antenna, will rise to 2,000 feet and make it, for now, the tallest structure in North America. The design is slender and graceful, with a glass facade that swirls downward in waves, cloaking the central core of the structure and yielding a

22-18 SANTIAGO CALATRAVA.
Chicago Spire, Chicago.
Courtesy: Shelbourne Development/Santiago Calatrava.

22-19 SHIRIN NESHAT.

Still from *Passage* (2001).
Color video installation with sound, 00:11:40.
Dimensions vary with installation. Edition 5 of 6.
Solomon R. Guggenheim Museum, New York. Purchased with funds contributed by
Dakis Joannou and the International Director's Council and Executive Committee
Members. 2001.70. Photograph courtesy of the artist and Gladstone Gallery.

feeling of movement. The spiraling—reminiscent of a smoke spiral and snail shell to Calatrava and a giant drill bit to Chicagoans—is also designed to reduce the effects of wind turbulence, which impacts all tall buildings. The tower's surface will shear off wind forces in multiple directions rather than allow them to build up in a single force. With this strategy, the structure need not fend off extremes of lateral forces. The design thus seems an updated embodiment of architect Louis Sullivan's maxim that "form follows function."

THE MIDDLE EAST

The Middle East is rich in tradition, rich in oil, and often drenched in conflict. As described in the Art Tour on Jerusalem (see Chapter 13), the Middle East is the birthplace of three great religions: Judaism, Christianity, and Islam. Contemporary art by artists in or from this region often reflects on the tensions between the secular and the religious within and among societies, particularly as these tensions are interwoven with politics.

Iran

Shirin Neshat (b. 1957) was born in Iran of parents who led Westernized lives before the Islamic revolution. She embraced feminism at an early age, encouraged by a father who insisted that his daughters have the same access as anyone else when it came to education, travel, and experiences. Neshat was in college in California when the revolution began, and she did not return to Iran until 1990. As a photographer, video-artist, and filmmaker, much of her work has been devoted to issues concerning gender roles in postrevolutionary Islamic society. Her renowned photowork series, *Women of Allah* (1993–1997), is a commentary

on the ways in which social and political changes in Iran directly affected the lives of women, particularly in terms of oppression by men. Neshat is often the sitter in these photographs, dressed in the traditional *chador*—a black garment that is pulled over the head and wrapped around the body, covering the hair, arms, and legs. Although wearing the chador is not required by law in Iran, many women choose to wear it, and many others are forced to wear it by men. The garment, like the burqa, has become both a symbol of female identity and oppression in the Muslim world.

Neshat's film *Passage* (Fig. **22-19**), commissioned by the world-renowned composer Philip Glass, follows the ritual of passage from this world to the next as men carry a shrouded body, women prepare a grave with their bare hands, and a little girl sets a fire that comes to circumscribe the scene. During one of the film's most abstract and intensely visual passages, Glass's pulsating score juxtaposed with a close-up of the women's thrumming chadors creates a sense of oil bubbling from the desert ground. The ingredients are natural and elemental—sticks, stones, fire, smoke, sand, and dust—and the repetitive movements, chanting, and music form a circle of life, death, and perhaps, rebirth.

Palestinian Territories

Emily Jacir was born (in 1970) in Saudi Arabia, and currently divides her time between the Palestinian territory of the West Bank and New York. She has engaged in numerous activities to bring to light the hardships of the Palestinian people, such as secretly filming Palestinian workers being delayed as they try to pass Israeli checkpoints in the West Bank or using her own U.S. passport and free-movement status to facilitate communication and grant requests among Palestinians living in occupied territory who are denied access to their families. Addressing the nature of life under occupation, the hardships, and the almost Darwinian approach to survival, Jacir has placed bogus personal ads in New York's *Village Voice* publication purportedly by Palestinian women in search of Israeli husbands in order to get residency permits. One of her most literal works is a tent stitched with the names of Palestinian villages (Fig. **22-20**) that have been depopulated by Israel over long years of conflict between the two peoples. Tents like these can be seen in refugee camps throughout Gaza.

Israel

Adi Nes (b. 1966) is best known for his hyperstaged photographs of young male actors posing as Israeli soldiers. The artist has said that, as a gay man, he is interested in issues of masculinity and male identity, particularly in a society that prizes—almost mythologizes—physical strength. His single most famous photograph recreates Leonardo da Vinci's fresco, *The Last Supper* (see Fig. 16-17), substituting soldiers at a table in a mess hall for apostles. Aside from the visual pun, Nes draws our attention to the concrete place (Israel) where so many events of the Bible (Hebrew and Christian) are said to have occurred and the links between the larger-than-life aspect of those events and the ordinary plight of individuals struggling to survive in his country today.

In Leonardo's version of *The Last Supper*, the apostles react to Jesus' announcement to them that one among them will betray him and that he will die. Despite the laughing and talking going on in Nes's version of the masterpiece, there is an implicit threat of danger and death embodied in the image of the soldier. In his *Abraham and Isaac* (Fig. **22-21**), a homeless man wheels his hapless son and his few belongings through the streets of Tel Aviv. The founder of the people of Israel—who was asked by God to sacrifice his son—is invoked to symbolize the sacrifices that people must make on a daily basis to survive. The lighting in the photo is intended to be reminiscent of the Baroque era, particularly the painting of Caravaggio. In his role of artist as social critic, some of Nes's work is intended to point out the discrepancy between the dream of Israel and certain social realities of contemporary Israel.

1 ft

22-20 EMILY JACIR.
Memorial to 418 Palestinian Villages Destroyed, Depopulated and Occupied by Israel in 1948 (2001).
Refugee tent, embroidery thread, daily log of names of people who worked on tent. 8' × 12' × 10'.
Collection: National Museum of Contemporary Art-EMST, Athens. No. 514/04.
Photo: courtesy of the artist.

1 ft

22-21 ADI NES.
Abraham and Isaac (2005).
Chromogenic print. 100 cm × 100 cm.
Courtesy of the artist and Jack Shainman Gallery, New York.

What she has achieved with her inimitable manipulation of walls, ground planes, and roofs, with those transparent, interwoven, and fluid spaces, are vivid proof that architecture as a fine art has not run out of steam and is hardly wanting in imagination.

—JUROR JORGE SILVETTI on Zaha Hadid's being the first woman to be awarded the Pritzker Prize in architecture

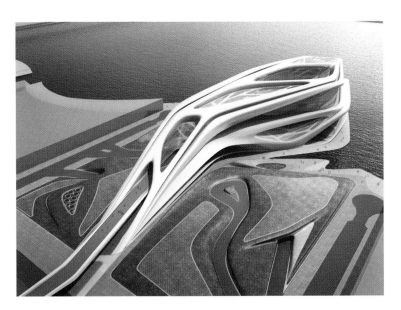

22-22 ZAHA HADID.
Performing Arts Centre, Abu Dhabi.
Courtesy Zaha Hadid Architects.

22-23 ZAHA HADID.
Dancing Towers, Dubai (2009).
Courtesy Zaha Hadid Architects.

Iraq

The realm of architecture has not been an easy one for women to crack. When one considers that situation, along with the fact that traditional Islamic societies in the Middle East often restrict the social and professional roles that women can play, Zaha Hadid's global position as an award-winning and highly-sought woman architect becomes especially notable. Hadid was born in Baghdad and educated in London, where she currently resides, but she has had several Middle Eastern commissions, including the Abu Dhabi Performing Arts Centre (Fig. **22-22**) and the Dancing Towers project in Dubai (Fig. **22-23**).

Hadid is a deconstructivist architect and, as such, works in the overall aesthetic of architects like Calatrava, Frank Ghery, Daniel Libeskind, and her teacher, Rem Koolhaas. Her design for the Abu Dhabi Performing Arts Centre (Fig. 22-22), described by Hadid as a "biological analogy," mimics the infrastructure of plant life in its stemlike linear elements, fibrous expanses of glass, and leafy shapes. She has likened the structure, with its many functional spaces, to fruits on a vine that crane toward the water, "a growing organism that sprouts a network of successive branches."[6]

If the performing arts center has organic undertones alluding to vegetation, the Dancing Towers resemble a choreographed interlacing of abstract torsos (Fig. 22-23). Three towers originate on a common base and then appear to "do their own thing," touching their companion towers here and there on certain levels where the functions of the individual towers overlap—offices, a hotel, residences, leisure facilities, and restaurants. The Dancing Towers evoke the fluidity of the oft-referenced image of the Three Graces in art history, in which a trio of beautiful women intertwine in dance, their collective positions combining to create a single, perfect form.

6 http://www.e-architect.co.uk/dubai/abu_dhabi_building.htm

ASIA

The phenomenon of globalization is perhaps nowhere more evident than in the Eastern nations of India, China, and Japan. Phone calls for tech support when our electronics go awry, or for customer service when our credit cards go missing, are often fielded by teams across the planet in places like Bangalore, India. Our basic life necessities—from T-shirts to pet food to the Nintendo Wii—are met, or at least supplemented, with products from China and Japan. As their economies and standard of living have boomed, so too have their art markets. Years ago, Japanese investors had little competition in auction houses when it came to high-ticket works of art; today, American investors, among others, are scrambling to own works of art from their part of the world. Our familiarity with the work of Indian, Chinese, and Japanese artists is attributed certainly to the decentralization of the art world, with artists of all countries exhibiting all over the world, but also is tied into the accessibility of popular culture and imagery over the Internet.

The art of these Eastern nations exhibits the same diversity of style that characterizes contemporary art in general around the globe. Although art from China, India, and Japan is often grounded in techniques that are traditional to these cultures, content often reflects global trends. Hybridity flourishes; many of their works combine contemporary subjects and traditional fashion, or express ancient ideas in novel ways.

India

Subodh Gupta (b. 1964) was born in one of the poorest and most violent provinces in India and lives today in New Delhi, a city of economic extremes. His work includes painting, sculpture, photography, installations, and video-art. It taps into sacred symbols and ancient cultural identity, but is connected to contemporary life realities through its found objects. A work like *Silk Route* (Fig. **22-24**) is an example. Just as India was once a key component of the Silk Route or Silk Road—a web of ancient trade routes that ran some 5,000 miles through the Indian subcontinent and connected China to the Mediterranean Sea—so is it in today's era of globalization an important economic conduit. Gupta's piece, composed

22-24 SUBODH GUPTA.
Silk Route (2007).
Stainless steel kitchen utensils.
BALTIC Centre for Contemporary Art.
Courtesy of the artist and Jack Shainman Gallery, New York ©Subodh Gupta. Photograph by Colin Davison.

1 ft.

22-25 PRAJAKTA PALAV AHER.
Ganpati Series Untitled I (2007).
Acrylic on canvas. 96" × 72".
Vadehra Art Gallery, New Delhi, India.

of simple, mundane kitchen utensils, is intended to illustrate the "current state of India's shifting society, migration, a sense of home and place, and the effects and frictions caused by a rapidly globalizing society."

Prajakta Palav Aher (b. 1979), who lives and works in Mumbai, is known for the photographic precision of her realist paintings. In the *Ganpati Series* (Fig. **22-25**), this realism lends a certain veracity to what otherwise appears to be a tall tale— a dressed-to-kill elephant riding on what appears to be a well-worn commuter train. In India, dreams of elephants are deemed messages of transformation and divine power— the emergence of one's Highest Self from the Collective Unconscious Mind. In Hinduism, the most widespread Indian religion, the deity, Ganesh (also known as Ganpati), has the head of an elephant and is seen as a remover of obstacles. Perhaps the artist is suggesting in her ironic portrait of the noble elephant aboard the train that something has happened to the myths, the symbols, and the spiritual life of India—or to Ganesh. The remover of obstacles is now, perhaps, more of a road warrior with a briefcase and a quota. Or perhaps—in a true manifestation of globalization—he handles phone calls from the United States and books airline reservations or troubleshoots software glitches on computers, removing obstacles for travelers or office workers.

China

Zhang Xiaogang's (b. 1958) *Big Family* (Fig. **22-26**) features a passage of bright red in a sea of monotonous beige and gray tones. For the artist, the uniformity of a drab palette reflects the appearance—indeed the lives—of what he calls a typical revolutionary family: "asexual, dressed in Mao suits, their gaze glassy and dismal. . . . They could be clones."[7] Red as a signifier of Chinese Communist culture creates points of narrative and visual emphasis, but there

---

7 M. Nuridsany, China *Art Now* (Paris: Flammarion, 2004), 114.

1 ft.

22-26 ZHANG XIAOGANG.
Big Family (2003).
Lithograph in an edition of 199. 27.5" × 32.5".
Image courtesy of Michael Berger Gallery, Pittsburgh, PA.

is more to the print than its design elements. The work addresses a fact of contemporary Chinese life: this "big" family is as big as a family is permitted to get in this overpopulated country, given its one-child policy. And because of sexism, abortion is not uncommon when an early sonogram reveals the fetus's sex to be female. Chinese social critics worry that the country seems to be headed toward a surplus of males and a resultant era of social instability.

Chinese painter Fang Lijun (b. 1963) is a proponent of the so-called Cynical Realist school, which sprang up in reaction to the 1989 demonstration in Tiananmen Square, in which the Communist government cracked down on protestors who were demanding more freedom. In that same year, the government closed an exhibition of Chinese avant-garde art, leaving the new generation of contemporary artists disenfranchised and disillusioned. Lijun's work from the 1990s featured what became one of the most famous images in contemporary Chinese art: a group of uniformly dressed, bald-headed men symbolizing the "mindless, manipulated masses." These early images had a desperation and despondency about them, but his newer work addresses some of the same social and political

1 ft.

22-27 FANG LIJUN.
30th Mary (2006).
Oil on canvas. 400 cm × 525 cm.
Courtesy of the Saatchi Gallery, London. ©Fang Lijun, 2008.

amidst the titanic forces of progress and modernization that are shaping the New China.

Shanghai artist Zhang Huan (b. 1965) grew up on a farm in rural China, but received an advanced degree in traditional painting techniques from the Beijing Central Academy of Fine Arts. Soon after graduation, he and fellow students, who found their art education too limiting for the expression of their own concerns and themes, formed the East Village group and focused on time-based pieces. Huan's performance art has since been seen in China and Western Europe; he also appeared at the 2002 Whitney Museum Biennial dressed in a fat suit fashioned from raw meat and, in a Buddhist gesture of compassion, released a flock of caged doves. Although China is officially atheist, Huan has maintained his interest in his childhood religion, Buddhism. Travel to Tibet brought him

concerns with a lighter hand. His painting *30th Mary* (Fig. **22-27**), for example, is a cynical adaptation of Western European baroque church ceilings wherein the ubiquitous cherubs are replaced by doll-like figures with Lijun portrait heads. The bald-headed figures, outfitted in pastel pinafores, seem to be sucked—smiling—into a cloud-lined vortex. The artist's commentary on disillusionment, individual identity, and government oppression may be intact, but it is delivered here with a dose of humor.

Wang Gongxin (b. 1960) is credited with being one of the first artists in China to transform video from a mere recording medium to an art medium. His works have largely focused on the anxieties experienced by ordinary Chinese people as their lives have been transformed by rapid industrialization—with its attendant pollution, relocations, and changes in traditional values. In recent years, China has experienced an unparalleled economic boom that has led to mushrooming growth of cities, mass migration from rural lands into these cities, and the projection of new economic and military power overseas.

Our Sky is Falling In! (Fig. **22-28**) portrays an everyday family scene that is suddenly disrupted when the ceiling begins to collapse. The video tells a personal story, but is also a commentary on the helplessness of the individual

22-28 WANG GONGXIN.
Our Sky is Falling in! (2007).
Video, The Tate Gallery, London.
Courtesy of the artist.

My decision to do performance art is directly related to my personal experience. I have always had troubles in my life, and these troubles often ended up in physical conflict. This frequent body contact made me realize the very fact that the body is the only direct way through which I come to know society and society comes to know me.

—ZHANG HUAN

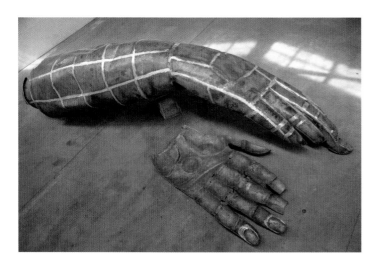

22-29 ZHANG HUAN.
Fresh Open Buddha Hand (2007).
Copper. 252" × 56" × 67"; 101" × 57" × 14".
Courtesy of Zhang Huan.

headquarters (Fig. **22-30**). While so many architects are building up (some 300 new towers are on the drawing table for the new Beijing Central Business District), Koolhaas has taken a different approach to his office space, designing an anti-skyscraper. He has been a vocal opponent of the sort of isolation that occurs in tall tower buildings, which he sees as collecting "their own little pathetic communities while breaking down the larger community around them." In an effort to prevent this at CCTV, Koolhaas designed a trapezoidal loop that puts everyone associated with the business (some 10,000 employees) under one roof—all using the same doors and elevators. The structure consists of two towers braced against one another and covered with a mesh

into contact with large, broken figures that he has emulated in recent works, such as the copper hands we see in Figure **22-29**. He has also made ashlike sculptures and paintings to reflect Buddhist religious rituals.

Chinese cities have become boomtowns for contemporary architecture, although—at least for the time being—the principal architects involved in the designs for these cities are not Chinese, but European and American. Zaha Hadid has called China "an incredibly empty canvas for innovation." Anthony Fieldman, of the Hong Kong office of architects Skidmore, Owings, and Merrill, has said that in China, "you're seeing things that no one in their right mind would build elsewhere." Between the buildup that occurred for the 2008 Beijing Summer Olympics and Shanghai's conglomerate Pudong skyline, it's no wonder that Wang Lu of Beijing-based *World Architecture* magazine has said, "Architecture in China has become like a kung fu film, with all of these giants trying to vanquish each other."

One of the Western giants of architecture building in China is Rem Koolhaas, who, with Ole Scheeren and Ove Arup, designed the new Central Chinese Television (CCTV)

22-30 REM KOOLHAAS AND OLE SCHEEREN.
Central Chinese Television (CCTV) Building, Beijing (c. 2009).
OMA/Ole Scheeren and Rem Koolhaas. Copyright OMA,
Office for Metropolitan Architecture.

sheath designed to withstand windstorms and earthquakes. Before Koolhaas got the go-ahead from China's political leaders, he had to convince them that the building would actually stand up. It reputedly took 75 engineers a full year to calculate the stress on every I-beam in the building.

A completely different approach is to be seen in the Shanghai World Financial Center (Fig. 22-31), designed by the international architectural firm, Kohn Pedersen Fox (KPF). Their 101-story structure is the tallest skyscraper in the financial district of Shanghai and will briefly be the tallest building in the world. The cutout near the building's apex is designed to alleviate wind pressure, as is the twisting of the elevations (the same principle is used in the Chicago Spire). The base of the cutout, at the 100th floor, is designed with an observation deck for the intrepid visitor.

Japan

Japanese artist Akira Yamaguchi (b. 1969) finds many of his sources in historic subject matter and styles, often mixing past and present, West and non-West. One work, painted on a traditional scroll, pairs ancient customers and contemporary sales clerks in a department store. His *Votive Tablet of a Horse* (Fig. 22-32) resembles wooden plaques with the image of a sacred white horse that were given as religious offerings to Japanese shrines and temples for many hundreds of years. The horses are believed to have symbolized purity, divine messages, and immortal poets. Yamaguchi

22-31 SHANGHAI KOHN PEDERSEN FOX ARCHITECTS.
Shanghai World Financial Center (2008).
Rendering courtesy Kohn Pederson Fox Associates, Architect.

22-32 AKIRA YAMAGUCHI.
Votive Tablet of a Horse (2001).
Oil, varnish on plywood. 182.5 cm × 183 cm.
Mizuma Art Gallery, Tokyo, Japan. Photo by Keizo Kioku.

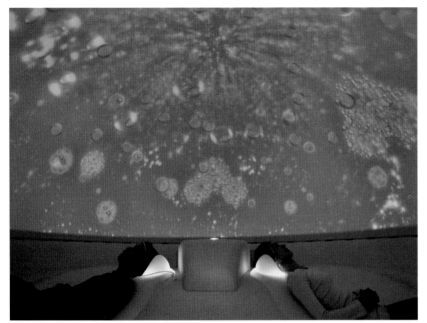

22-33 MARIKO MORI.
Wave UFO (2003).
Brainwave interface, vision dome, projector,
computer system, fiberglass, Technogel,
acrylic carbon fiber, aluminum, magnesium.
493 cm × 1134 cm × 528 cm.
Courtesy of Pinchuk Arts Center, Kiev, Ukraine and
Richard Leroyd, photographers.

replaces the horse's legs with a fantastical combination of motorcycle parts and robotics, as if to supercharge it into a more invincible machine. Yamaguchi's hybrid, alongside its sword-yielding samurai, raises the question: Would history have been different if its famed warriors had mounts like these?

Japanese photographer and video-artist Mariko Mori (b. 1967), a self-described "daughter of Warhol and granddaughter of Duchamp," has been labeled a "cyberchick" and "a cross between a geisha girl and a gidget." As descriptive as these images are, they only scratch the surface of what defines her. Channeling her experience as a former model and fashion design student, Mori has created computer-manipulated self-portraits in futuristic, cyber-couture. Her wide-eyed stare and plastic smile look a bit like a real-life version of Takashi Murakami's cartoon images.

Mori's *Wave UFO* (Fig. **22-33**) is a futuristic "vehicle" with a pop flair that mixes the mediums of sculpture, architecture, and video to create a transporting, sensory experience for the participant. We use the word "participant" instead of viewer because the imagery that appears on the screen within the eye-shaped capsule is determined by connecting a participant's brainwaves to an interactive biofeedback loop. Mori, who has begun to integrate references to Japanese religion and culture into her recent work, alludes to the Buddhist vision of nirvana in *Wave UFO*. She has said that the experience of the piece reveals that "human beings as collective living beings shall unify and transcend cultural differences and national borders through positive and creative evolution."[8]

THE UNITED STATES AND CANADA

New York may no longer be the one center of the art world, but much that is vital continues to happen in this and other North American cities today. There is still a certain cache in exhibiting in galleries in New York City, Los Angeles, Chicago, and Toronto, and architects still compete for major projects in these places.

Stephen Holden, the *New York Times* film critic, considers Matthew Barney (b. 1967) to be "the most important American artist of his generation." Contemporary artists continue to challenge the use of traditional mediums, and Barney is no exception, having fashioned dumbbells of

8 Bregrenz, Austria (March 23, 2003), "Wave UFO" by Mariko Mori in Kunsthaus Bregenz—A "Walk-in" Sculpture and Virtual Voyage in Space. (http://swissart.ch/e/news/index.php3?gl_cont=%2Fe%2Fnews%2Farchive-article.php3%3Fmyeditid%3D308%26langindex%3Den)

Norman Rockwell's *Freedom from Want* with John Currin's *Thanksgiving*

Thanksgiving conjures an image of warm gatherings, a time when people travel long distances to share home and hearth and celebrate their blessings. It's about as wholesome a symbol of family ties as we can imagine. But we also know that holidays are stressful times during which people often become intensely aware of the discrepancies between their lives as they actually are and as they think they ought to be, especially when they compare them with the images of idealized families depicted in the media.

Norman Rockwell, the famed illustrator of the *Saturday Evening Post,* has created many a "default image" in our minds of Americans and their holidays, including Thanksgiving. His *Freedom from Want* (Fig. **22-34**), painted in 1943, is one of the artist's series of "Four Freedoms," inspired by a speech on these freedoms—including *Freedom from Fear, Freedom to Worship,* and *Freedom of Speech*—delivered by President Franklin Delano Roosevelt to Congress two years earlier. Rockwell depicted a traditional Thanksgiving dinner in which an aproned matriarch brings her main-course masterpiece to a well-set table filled with gleeful, fresh-faced children and grandchildren. The patriarch stands at the head, looking proudly at his wife's accomplishment and, perhaps, nostalgically at his family. Rockwell, as always, captures a slice of life and instills it with his particular brand of ideology—this time family values.

What a perversion, then, of this ideal is John Currin's *Thanksgiving* (Fig. **22-35**). Gone is the squeaky-clean, Midwestern, all-American family with their freckled faces and upturned noses. In their place, Currin has given us an eccentric gaggle of pasty-faced women whose skin tones echo those of their undercooked turkey. In an age of abstraction and new media, John Currin (b. 1962) focuses on the figure, typically young women wearing off-kilter expressions that denote psychological beings distorted by the modern age. Dressed in sexless and timeless clothing, his Thanksgiving celebrants appear to mimic cheer among some classic props.

Both Thanksgiving paintings are meticulous in detail, suggesting a photographic veracity, yet both are contrived in their own way. How? And how does each artist use extreme realism to convey truth, despite the unlikelihood that these scenes describe most real-life experience? Happy Thanksgiving—are you convinced? ∎

22-34 NORMAN ROCKWELL.
Freedom from Want (1943).
The Saturday Evening Post, March 6, 1943 (story illustration).
Oil on canvas. 45¾" × 35½".

Norman Rockwell Art Collection Trust, Norman Rockwell Museum, Stockbridge, Massachusetts. Printed by permission of the Norman Rockwell Family Agency. Copyright ©1943 Norman Rockwell Family Entities.

22-35 JOHN CURRIN.
Thanksgiving (2003).
Oil on canvas. 172.7 cm × 132.1 cm.
©John Currin, courtesy of the Gagosian Gallery.

22-36 MATTHEW BARNEY.
Cremaster 2 (1999), from the *Cremaster* film series (1994–2002).
Silkscreened digital videodisc, tooled saddle leather, sterling silver, beeswax, polycarbonate honeycomb, acrylic, and nylon vitrine, with 35 mm print; digital video transferred to film with audio, 1:19:00, vitrine. 38⅜" × 40" × 46⅝". Edition of 10 + 2 APs.
Copyright Matthew Barney.
Photo by Michael James O'Brien. Courtesy Gladstone Gallery.

tapioca pudding and an exercise bench of petroleum jelly. But Barney is best known for his *Cremaster* series of five films. The characters in the films include androgynous nymphs, satyrs, and other legendary figures who are, or are not, what they seem to be. The narratives, enhanced with eclectic sound tracks, circle around various ritual masculine athletic challenges and a good deal of symbolic pagan pageantry. Much of *Cremaster 2* takes place in the wide-open spaces of the Wild West, accompanied by folk songs, the Mormon Tabernacle Choir, and other music. One scene transports the viewer to the 1893 Columbia International Exhibition, in which the novelist Norman Mailer impersonates the escape artist Harry Houdini (Fig. **22-36**), standing next to the artist in the guise of a bizarrely attired Gary Gilmore. Mailer's book *The*

Executioner's Song was about convicted murderer Gary Gilmore, who was executed by a firing squad in 1977. Gilmore, unlike Houdini, did not escape.

Historically, boundaries have existed between fine art and craft, but Betty Woodman (b. 1930) has challenged that segregation in her life's work. Described as one of the most important ceramic artists working today, Woodman has not only blurred the lines between art and craft, but has also conjoined cultural influences, East and West, in her vase painting. Woodman sees the vase as a cultural common denominator—all societies produce them—and one that connects her to history and art: "The centrality of the vase in my work is certainly a reference to a global perspective on art history and production." Woodman also produces monotypes, woodcuts, and lithographs based on her pottery, sometimes collaborating with printmaker Bud Shark. Works like *Aztec Vase #06-1* (Fig. **22-37**), while functional vases, are perhaps best thought of as ceramic

22-37 BETTY WOODMAN.
Aztec Vase #06-1 (2006).
Glazed earthenware, epoxy resin, lacquer, and paint. 62" × 42" × 9" (157.5 cm × 106.7 cm × 22.9 cm).
Photo by Eli Ping Weinberg. Image courtesy of the artist and Max Protetch Gallery, New York.

A CLOSER LOOK

Jacques-Louis David on a Brooklyn Tennis Court

JACQUES-LOUIS DAVID'S *Intervention of the Sabine Women* (Fig. **22-38**), in all of its Classical idealization, patriotism, and heroism, hangs among other prized examples of Neoclassicism in a quiet, stately gallery in the Louvre Museum in Paris. But on a raw, wintry day in 2005, the myth that gave birth to one of David's most symbolic works was revisited—reenacted—on a tennis court in Brooklyn, New York. Video artist Eve Sussman was once again exploring the "pictorial evolution of a masterpiece." In Sussman's version, the men wore suits (in David's painting, they are in their birthday suits). The women were not in chic retro Roman attire; they wore vintage 1960s couture.

We have already studied Nicolas Poussin's *The Rape of the Sabine Women* (see Fig. 17-21), which recounts the subject of the Romans' abduction of their neighbors' (the Sabines) women for the dubious purpose of growing their city's population. David's painting is, in effect, a follow-up to the story. Three years after the attack by Romulus (Rome's founder) and his men, the Sabine men

organized a counterattack to reclaim their women. When they arrive, the Sabine-turned-Roman women intervene! For the first time in David's career as a history painter, he placed a woman at the center of the action. She is Hersilia, daughter of the Sabine Tatius and wife of Romulus. And she's not going back. Hersilia and other now-Roman women stand between the warriors and their children and, through their gestures, appeal for a peaceful solution to the crisis. As in most examples of the Neoclassical style, there is balance between action and restraint. The flailing arms and emotional expressions of the women contrast with the firmly planted stances of the fighting men. The movement seems controlled, even frozen, despite the overall sense of violence and chaos.

Enter Eve Sussman. Lights . . . camera . . . smoke machine. "Just walk around," her choreographer told the actors. "Okay, now find somebody in the group and lock eyes with them, like they are a magnet pulling you together. Now lean your body against theirs." From these first tentative movements, a full-scale battle scene ensued

22-38 JACQUES-LOUIS DAVID.
The Intervention of the Sabine Women (1799).
Oil on canvas. 385 cm × 522 cm.
Louvre Museum, Paris.
©Réunion des Musées Nationaux/Art Resource

1 ft.

(Fig. **22-39**). Clothes were ripped off, people bumped, grinded, and fell over one another. The women screamed, cried, and desperately held children up in the air. Figures moved through the mist stepping over the carnage, surveying the destruction. Cut.

The scene thus shot may or may not be used in Sussman's video–opera project, *The Raptus of the Sabine Women*, a piece in progress that is based on the myth of the Sabine women (*raptus*, in ancient Rome, meant "carrying off by force" and was a crime of property theft). It follows a similar successful work based on Diego Velázquez's *Las Meninas* (see Fig. 17-15) called *89 Seconds at Alcázar* (Fig. **22-40**). The video and film stills visualize imagined moments before and after the scene that Velázquez chose to represent. Sussman said of her thought process in generating the idea for *89 Seconds at Alcázar*: "[The painting] has the feeling of a snapshot . . . as if the Enfanta could walk out and come back again. And you think, if this is a film still, then there is a still that came before, and one that came after."

Unlike *89 Seconds at Alcázar*, which involved sets and elaborate costumes replicating the interior backdrop of Velázquez's famous portrait, *Raptus* is far more loosely based on the David prototype. The artist admits to making it up as she and the actors go along. Working with a loose outline rather than a complete script, the collaborators are coming up with their own version of the myth, based on interpretation, interaction, and reaction. "We know we want a fight involving the Sabine women, and other than that we don't have a clue." ∎

22-39 EVE SUSSMAN.

Rehearsal footage for *The Raptus of the Sabine Women* (2005).
Performance video.

Image ©Michael Nagle/The New York Times/Redux.

22-40 EVE SUSSMAN.

Her Back to the Camera (2004)
Screen grab from *89 Seconds at Alcázar*.

Whitney Museum of American Art, New York. Partial and promised gift of Jeanne L. and Michael L. Klein (2005.86). Courtesy Eve Sussman & The Rufus Corporation.

We are all working so hard to change people's attitudes about race, but it's like handling a wet eel.

—KARA WALKER

sculptures showing a wide range of influences from the history of art and from Woodman's global voyages. The artist freely adopts shapes and colors from styles she is most drawn to, sometimes mixing and matching them on opposing sides of a vase. Her work is marked by an eclecticism and pluralism that energize her pieces, pay homage to a host of historical styles, and render her art relevant to the global arena.

Lorna Simpson's (b. 1960) stark black-and-white compositions are rooted in her early career as a documentary street photographer. This experience continues to inform her work stylistically and politically, providing the images that she often accompanies with provocative text. The artist has expanded her photography-based work—focused primarily on issues of race and discrimination—in different ways, printing on felt rather than glossy paper and incorporating the simple, arresting quality of stills into her video-art and films. One of Simpson's signature devices is fragmentation; she has used it to communicate what she sees as a fine line between individuality and anonymity. In her film *Easy to Remember* (Fig. **22-41**), a grid of 15 mouths stacked in rows of three hum along to saxophonist John Coltrane's version of the Rodgers and Hart song *Easy to Remember*. It's a piece of music that Simpson remembers from her childhood and with which she has a particular relationship. Yet our relationship to the people and the music is limited. All we see of them in these closely cropped frames is their lips; they do not sing, but hum in isolation and in unison. The words of the song go, "I know it's over, and yet it's easy to remember but so hard to forget." The poignant lyric speaks volumes about individual and collective memory in the African American experience.

As an African American woman, Kara Walker (b. 1969) has experienced much of her life in terms of black and white and now, like Lorna Simpson, produces much of her art in this dichotomous palette. She has worked in many mediums, but her life-size paper cutouts, which are used to silhouette her comments on the often brutal history of race relations in the United States, have captured the attention of the art world. Her figures are two-dimensional—often black figures pasted onto white gallery walls—and their flatness seems to echo the stereotyping that prevents people of one background from seeing people of other backgrounds in their full vitality and individualism.

Insurrection! (Our Tools Were Rudimentary, Yet We Pressed On) (Fig. **22-42**) recounts some grisly events taken from the history of slavery in the United States. A nude slave is propositioned by a plantation owner. A woman with a baby barely escapes being lynched. Elsewhere a group tortures a victim. The piece fills the walls of a large room, where additional shapes are projected onto the walls, and visitors find their own shadows projected among them. Viewers are thus integrated into the haunting works, as if they share in culpability or victimhood. Walker's installations are haunting in their disconnect between the lyrical shadow-puppet display and the dark content of the narrative.

Visitors to Architect Daniel Libeskind's (b. 1946) addition to the staid Royal Ontario Museum (Fig. **22-43**) enter an atrium of interlocking spatial volumes from which they can glimpse exhibitions that epitomize the museum's two themes: nature and culture. The entire ground level is made into a seamless space that unifies what Libeskind refers to as the "inherited architecture" and the new construction. The crystal-like "explosion" of the addition draws attention to the fortress-like older building, as if asking the passerby to reconsider what is housed within and to evaluate

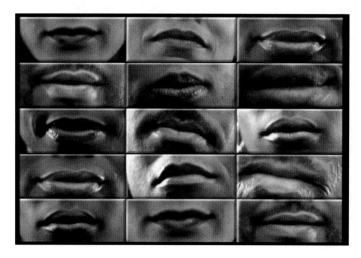

22-41 LORNA SIMPSON.
Still from *Easy to Remember* (2001).
16 mm film transferred to DVD, sound; 2½ minutes.
Courtesy of the artist. Used with permission 2006.

22-42 KARA WALKER.
Insurrection! (Our Tools Were Rudimentary, Yet We Pressed On) (2000). Installation view.
Cut-paper silhouettes and light projections, site-specific dimensions.

Solomon R. Guggenheim Museum of Art, New York. Purchased with funds contributed by the International Director's Council and Executive Committee Members. 2000.68. Photograph by Ellen Labenski ©The Solomon R. Guggenheim Foundation, New York. Courtesy of Sikkema Jenkins & Co.

it from a different perspective. The Royal Ontario Museum is just one of Libeskind's deconstructivist designs that marries traditional buildings with shockingly disparate additions.

Artists throughout the world are informed by their cultural and national traditions and by their artistic training. Today, more than ever, they are also influenced by their knowledge of what is happening in the political world at large, and by their awareness of the art world all around them—past and present. Globalization has struck the world of art as it has struck our political, social, and economic lives. Yet even as their worldview has expanded, their perspectives have widened, and their choices have become many, artists have held fast to their individual and local ideas and ideals.

22-43 DANIEL LIBESKIND.
Addition, Royal Ontario Museum, Queen's Park and Bloor Street, Toronto (2007).
Steel structure with aluminum cladding and glass facade.
©Studio Daniel Libeskind.

Cai Guo-Qiang—and the Twenty-First Century—on the Roof of the Met

DURING THE SUMMER OF 2006, thousands of tourists and native New Yorkers had the opportunity to photograph themselves alongside Saddam Hussein, Osama bin Laden, and Harry Potter—although not quite in the flesh. Along with other celebrities and political figures who drove events that are seared in our minds and sealed in history, these individuals were part of a monumental relief sculpture by Cai Guo-Qiang (b. 1957), a contemporary artist who was born in Quanzhou, China and now lives and works in New York.

Nontransparent Monument (Fig. **22-44**), a 32-foot-long by 9-foot-high relief, was one of the site-specific installations part of Cai's exhibition *Transparent Monument: Cai Guo-Qiang on the Roof*, an exhibition that represents the artist's reaction to issues of present-day concern. It chronicles the already momentous events of our still-young century, some of them horrific—like the attack on New York's World Trade Center, here accompanied by the faces of bin Laden and George W. Bush (Fig. **22-45**)—and others newsworthy or noteworthy—Harry Potter riding a broomstick, same-sex marriage, and the death of Pope John Paul II (Fig. **22-46**). *Nontransparent Monument* also includes references to illegal immigrants, Kim Jong Il of North Korea, Fidel Castro, a Chinese version of "American Idol," Severe Acute Respiratory Syndrome (SARS), the wars in Afghanistan and Iraq, breast implants, and Hurricane Katrina—to name a few. Good, bad, although probably not indifferent, these events read as a time capsule of our era—what affected us, what changed the way we live.

In opposition to the limestone relief, which reads like a cartoon-like scroll of current events, Cai placed another work: *Transparent Monument* (Fig. **22-47**), a large triple sheet of tempered glass with facsimiles of dead birds lying at its base (Fig. **22-48**). It is not difficult to imagine *Transparent Monument* as a window in a skyscraper, and the piece as a comment on the human impact on the environment.

22-44 CAI GUO-QIANG (B.1957, QUANZHOU CHINA; LIVES IN NEW YORK).

Nontransparent Monument (2006).
Green limestone. 274.3 cm × 970.3 cm (108" × 382").
Collection of the artist. Installation view at the Iris and B. Gerard Center Roof Garden, The Metropolitan Museum of Art, New York, 2006.

22-45 CAI GUO-QIANG.
Nontransparent Monument (detail, showing Osama bin Laden).

22-46 CAI GUO-QIANG.
Nontransparent Monument (detail, showing the death of Pope John Paul II, left; Harry Potter riding a broomstick, upper right; and same-sex marriage, center and lower right).

22-47 CAI GUO-QIANG (B.1957, QUANZHOU CHINA; LIVES IN NEW YORK).
Transparent Monument (2006).
Glass, papier-mâché, fiberglass, plastic, and feathers. 457.2 cm × 309.9 cm × 81.3 cm (180" × 122" × 32"). Collection of the artist. Installation view at the Iris and B. Gerard Center Roof Garden, The Metropolitan Museum of Art, New York, 2006.

22-49 CAI GUO-QIANG (B.1957, QUANZHOU CHINA; LIVES IN NEW YORK).
Move Along, Nothing to See Here (2006).
Painted resin with sharp objects confiscated at airport security checkpoints. Dimension variable. top: Crocodiles: 241.3 cm × 132.1 cm × 406.4 cm (95" × 52" × 160") and 228.6 cm × 116.8 cm × 426.7 cm (90" × 46" × 468"). Collection of the artist. Installation view at the Iris and B. Gerard Center Roof Garden, The Metropolitan Museum of Art, New York, 2006.

22-50 CAI GUO-QIANG.
Move Along, Nothing to See Here (detail showing knives, scissors, nail files, and other objects seized by security guards at airports following the destruction of the World Trade Center).

The rooftop installation also featured two life-size replicas of crocodiles, made of resin and pierced with knives, scissors, and other potential weapons (Fig. **22-49**) actually collected by security guards at airports after the destruction of the World Trade Center. According to Cai, *Move Along, Nothing to See Here* (Fig. **22-50**) represents a nation damaged from within as it has attempted to respond to external dangers.

One of the most dramatic elements of the installation was a time-based piece entitled *Clear Sky, Black Cloud* that appeared above the museum's roof garden at noon each day. Cai is known for his explosion events, examples of ephemeral art that have lit the sky in bursts of color. The sight and sound of *Clear Sky, Black Cloud*, on the other hand, were very stark and more psychologically related to the other works in the installation.

As wildly diverse as these images, mediums, and reflections on contemporary issues were, the progression from permanence to transience did perhaps suggest the ways in which humans memorialize events that are really just passing moments in the larger, cosmic framework of space and time. ■

GLOSSARY

Abstract art A form of art characterized by simplified (abstracted) or distorted rendering of an object that has the essential form or nature of that object; a form of *nonobjective art* in which the forms make no reference to visible reality.

Abstract Expressionism A style of painting and sculpture of the 1950s and 1960s in which artists expressionistically distorted abstract images with loose, gestural brushwork. Also see *expressionistic*.

Academic art A neoclassical, nonexperimental style promoted by the Royal French Academy during the eighteenth and nineteenth centuries.

Achromatic Without color.

Acquisition Purchase (of a work of art) for a museum or a formal collection.

Acropolis The fortified upper part of a Greek city; literally, "city on a hill."

Acrylic paint A paint in which pigments are combined with a synthetic plastic medium that is durable, water soluble, and quick drying.

Action painting A contemporary method of painting characterized by *implied motion* in the brushstroke and splattered and dripped paint on the canvas.

Actual balance Equal distribution of weight. Contrast with *pictorial balance*.

Actual line The path made by a moving point; a connected and continuous series of points. Contrast with *implied line*.

Actual mass The physical mass of an object as determined by its weight. Contrast with *implied mass*.

Actual motion The passage of a body or an object from one place to another. Contrast with *implied motion*.

Actual texture The texture of an object or picture, as determined by the sense of touch. Contrast with *visual texture*.

Additive process In sculpture, adding or assembling materials, as in modeling and constructing. Contrast with *subtractive process*.

Adobe Brick that has been dried in the sun rather than fired in a kiln.

Afterimage The lingering impression from a stimulus that has been removed. The afterimage of a color is its complement. Also see *complementary color*.

Allegory A narrative in which people and events have been given consistent symbolic meanings; extended metaphor.

Altar A raised platform or stand used for sacred ceremonial or ritual purposes.

Alternate a-b-a-b support system An architectural support system in which every other nave wall support sends up a supporting rib that crosses the vault as a transverse arch.

Alternate support system An architectural support system in which alternating structural elements bear the weight of the walls and the load of the ceiling.

Ambulatory In a church, a continuation of the side aisles of a *Latin cross plan* into a passageway that extends behind the choir and apse and allows traffic to flow to the chapels, which are often placed in this area (from *ambulare*, Latin for "to walk").

Amorphous Without clear shape or form.

Amphitheater A round or oval open-air theater with an arena surrounded by rising tiers of seats.

Analogous colors Colors that lie next to one another on the color wheel and share qualities of hue as a result of the mixture of adjacent hues; harmonious hues.

Analytic Cubism The early phase of Cubism (1909–1912) during which objects were dissected or analyzed in a visual information-gathering process and then reconstructed on the canvas.

Animation Creation of an animated cartoon; the photographing of a series of drawings, each of which shows a stage of movement that differs slightly from the previous one, so that figures appear to move when projected in rapid succession.

Annunciation The angel Gabriel's announcement to Mary that she would give birth to Jesus.

Aperture Opening.

Apocalypse The ultimate triumph of good over evil foretold in Judeo-Christian writings.

Appropriation (1) Borrowing elements from the non-art world such as newspapers and wine labels, as by Picasso and Braque. (2) The use of another artist's work as a basis for one's own.

Apse A semicircular or polygonal projection of a building with a semicircular dome, especially on the east end of a church.

Aquarelle A watercolor technique in which a transparent film of paint is applied to a white, absorbent surface.

Aquatint An etching technique in which a metal plate is colored with acid-resistant resin and heated, causing the resin to melt. Before printing, areas of the plate are exposed by a needle, and the plate receives an acid bath. Aquatinting can be manipulated to resemble washes.

Aqueduct A bridgelike structure that carries a canal or pipe of water across a river or valley (from Latin roots meaning "to carry water").

Arch A curved or pointed structure consisting of wedge-shaped blocks that span an open space and support the weight of material above by transferring the load outward and downward over two vertical supports, or piers.

Archaic period A period of Greek art dating roughly 660–480 BCE. The term *archaic* means "old" and refers to the art created before the Classical period.

Architectural style A style of Roman painting in which walls were given the illusion of opening onto a scene.

Architecture The art and science of designing aesthetic buildings, bridges, and other structures to help people meet their personal and communal needs.

Architrave In architecture, the lower part of an *entablature*, which may consist of one or more horizontal bands.

Archivolts In architecture, concentric moldings that repeat the shape of an arch.

Armature In sculpture, a framework for supporting plastic material.

Art Nouveau A highly ornamental style of the 1890s characterized by floral patterns, rich colors, whiplash curves, and vertical attenuation (French for "new art").

Assemblage A work of art that consists of three-dimensional objects assembled to create an image. Artists often manipulate preexisting objects in various ways and incorporate them with other media, such as painting or printmaking.

Asymmetrical balance Balance in which the right and left sides of a composition contain different shapes, colors, textures, or other elements and yet are arranged or "weighted" so that the overall impression is one of balance. Contrast with *symmetrical balance.*

Athena The Greek goddess of wisdom, skills, and war.

Atmospheric perspective An illusion of depth created through grades of texture and brightness, color saturation, and warm and cool colors. An indistinct or hazy effect produced by distance and the illusion of distance in visual art (the term derives from recognition that the atmosphere between the viewer and the distant objects would cause the effect).

Atrium A hall or entrance court.

Automatic writing Writing based on free association, practiced by Dadaists and Surrealists.

Automatist surrealism An outgrowth of automatic writing in which the artist attempts to derive the outlines of images from the unconscious through free association.

Avant-garde The leaders in new, unconventional movements; the vanguard (from French, "advance guard").

Balance The distribution of the weight, mass, or other elements of a work of art so as to achieve harmony.

Balloon framing In architecture, a wooden skeleton of a building constructed from prefabricated studs and nails.

Balustrade A railing held up by small posts, or balusters, as on a staircase.

Baroque A seventeenth-century European style characterized by ornamentation, curved lines, irregularity of form, dramatic lighting and color, and exaggerated gestures.

Barrel vault A roofed-over space or tunnel constructed as an elongated arch.

Basalt A dark, tough volcanic rock.

Basketry The craft of making baskets.

Bas-relief Sculpture that projects only slightly from its background (from *bas*, French for "low"). Contrast with *high relief.*

Batik The process of making designs in cloth by waxing fabric to prevent dye from coloring certain areas; a cloth or design made in this way.

Bay In architecture, the area or space spanned by a single unit of vaulting that may be marked off by piers or columns.

Bevel To cut at an angle.

Bilateral symmetry Mirror-type similarity between the sides of a composition. Also termed "pure" or "formal" symmetry.

Binder A material that binds substances together.

Biomorphic Having the form of a living organism.

Bisque firing In ceramics, a preliminary firing that hardens the body of a ware.

Bitumen Asphalt.

Black-figure painting A three-stage firing process that gives vases black figures on a reddish ground. In the first, oxidizing phase of firing, oxygen in the kiln turns the vase and slip red. In the second, reducing phase, oxygen is eliminated from the kiln and the vase and slip turn black. In the third, reoxidizing phase, oxygen is reintroduced into the kiln, turning the vase red once more.

Bohemian Literally, of Bohemia, a section of the Czech Republic. Because Gypsies, or Roma, in transit to Western Europe passed through Bohemia, the term has come to signify a nonconformist, unconventional style of life.

Brass A yellowish alloy of copper and zinc.

Brick A hard substance made from clay, fired in a kiln or baked in the sun, and used in construction.

Brightness gradient The relative degree of intensity in the rendering of nearby and distant objects, used to create an illusion of depth in a two-dimensional work.

Buddha An enlightened man.

Buon fresco True fresco, executed on damp lime plaster. Contrast with *fresco secco.*

Burin A pointed cutting tool used by engravers.

Burnish To make shiny by rubbing or polishing.

Buttress To support or prop up construction with a projecting structure, usually built of brick or stone; a massive masonry structure on the exterior wall of a building that presses inward and upward to hold the stone blocks of arches in place. Also see *flying buttress.*

Byzantine A style associated with Eastern Europe that arose after 300 CE, the year that Emperor Constantine moved the capital of his empire from Rome to Byzantium and renamed the city Constantinople (present-day Istanbul). The style was concurrent with the Early Christian style in Western Europe.

Calligraphy Beautiful handwriting; penmanship; ornamental writing with a pen or brush.

Camera obscura An early camera consisting of a large dark chamber with a lens opening through which an image is projected onto the opposite surface in its natural colors.

Candid In photography, unposed, informal.

Canon of proportions A set of rules governing the proportions of the human body as they are to be rendered by artists.

Capital In architecture, the area at the top of the shaft of a column that provides a solid base for the horizontal elements above. Capitals provide decorative transitions between the cylinder of the column and the rectilinear *architrave* above.

Caricature The gross exaggeration or distortion of natural features for the purpose of benign or malevolent satire.

Carolingian Referring to Charlemagne or his period. Charlemagne was emperor of the Holy Roman Empire from 800 to 814 CE.

Cartoon Originally, a preparatory drawing made for a fresco, usually on paper and drawn to scale; a drawing that caricatures or satirizes an event or person of topical interest. Also see *animation.*

Carving In sculpture, the process of cutting away material, such as wood.

Cast iron A hard alloy of iron containing silicon and carbon that is made by casting.

Casting The process of creating a form by pouring a liquid material into a mold, allowing it to harden, and then removing the mold.

Catacomb A vault or gallery in an underground burial place.

Cella The small inner room of a Greek temple, used to house the statue of the god or goddess to whom the temple is dedicated. Located behind solid masonry walls, the cella was accessible only to the temple priests.

Centering In architecture, a wooden scaffold used in the construction of an arch.

Central plan A design for a church or a chapel with a primary central space surrounded by symmetrical areas around each side. Contrast with *longitudinal plan*.

Ceramics The art of creating baked clay objects, such as pottery and earthenware.

Chalk A form of soft limestone that is easily pulverized and can be used as a drawing implement.

Charcoal A form of carbon produced by partially burning wood or other organic matter; it can be used as a drawing implement.

Chiaroscuro An artistic technique in which subtle gradations of value create the illusion of rounded three-dimensional forms in space; also termed *modeling* (from Italian for "light-dark").

China Whitish or grayish porcelain that rings when struck.

Cinematography The photographic art of creating motion pictures.

Cinerary urn A vessel used for keeping the ashes of the cremated dead.

Clapboard In architecture, siding composed of thin, narrow boards placed in horizontal, overlapping layers.

Classical Art Art of the Greek Classical period, spanning roughly 480–400 BCE; also known as Hellenic Art (from "Hellas," the Greek name for Greece).

Clerestory In a *Latin cross plan*, the area above the *triforium* in the elevation of the nave, which contains windows to provide direct lighting for the nave.

Close-up In cinematography or video, a "shot" made from very close range, providing intimate detail.

Coffer A decorative sunken panel.

Coiling A pottery technique in which lengths of clay are wound in a spiral fashion.

Collage An assemblage of two-dimensional objects to create an image; works of art in which materials such as paper, cloth, and wood are pasted to a two-dimensional surface, such as a wooden panel or canvas (from *coller*, French for "to paste").

Colonnade A series of columns placed side by side to support a roof or a series of arches.

Color negative film Film from which color negatives are made.

Color reversal film Film from which color prints ("positives") are made directly, without the intervening step of creating negatives.

Color-field painting Painting that uses visual elements and principles of design to suggest that areas of color stretch beyond the canvas to infinity; figure and ground are given equal emphasis.

Combine painting A contemporary style of painting that attaches other media, such as found objects, to the canvas.

Complementary color One of a specific pair of colors (e.g., red and green) that most enhance, or exaggerate, one another by virtue of their simultaneous contrast. Each pair of complementary colors contains one primary color plus the secondary color made by mixing the other two primaries. Because the complements do not share characteristics of hue and are as unlike as possible, the eye readily tells them apart. When complementary colors are placed next to one another, the effects are often jarring.

Composition The organization of the visual elements in a work of art.

Compound pier In Gothic style, a complexly shaped vertical support to which a number of colonnettes (thin half columns) are often attached.

Compressive strength The degree to which a material can withstand the pressure of being squeezed.

Computer art The production of images with the assistance of the computer. Artists can use the computer to create art for its own sake or as a design tool, as in architecture and graphic design.

Computer-assisted design (CAD) The use of the computer to assist artists and designers working in other media, such as architecture. CAD permits interior designers and architects to view their designs from various vantage points and to see how the modification of one element affects the entire design.

Conceptual Portrayed as a person or object is known or thought (conceptualized) to be; not copied from nature at any given moment. Conceptual figures tend to be stylized rather than realistic.

Conceptual art An anticommercial movement begun in the 1960s in which works of art are conceived and executed in the mind of the artist. The commercial or communal aspect of the "work" is often a set of instructions for what exists in the artist's mind.

Conceptual space Space that is depicted as conceptualized by the artist rather than in realistic perspective.

Conceptual unity Unity in a work that is achieved through the relationship between the meaning and function of the images.

Constructed sculpture Sculpture in which forms are built up from such materials as wood, paper, string, sheet metal, and wire.

Constructivism A sculptural outgrowth of Cubist collage in which artists attempt to use a minimum of mass to create volumes in space.

Contact print A photographic print that is made by placing a negative in contact with a sheet of photosensitive paper and exposing both to light so that the second sheet of paper acquires the image.

Conté crayon A wax crayon with a hard texture.

Content All that is contained in a work of art: the visual elements, subject matter, and underlying meaning or themes.

Contour line A perceived line that marks the edge of a figure as it curves back into space.

Contrapposto A position in which a figure is obliquely balanced around a central vertical axis. Also see *weight-shift principle*.

Cool color A color such as a blue, green, or violet that appears to be cool in temperature and tends to recede spatially behind warm colors.

Corbel A supportive, bracket-shaped piece of metal, stone, or wood.

Corinthian order The most ornate of the Greek architectural styles, characterized by slender, fluted columns and capitals with an acanthus leaf design.

Cornice In architecture, a horizontal molding that projects along the top of a wall or a building; the uppermost part of an *entablature*.

Cosmetic palette A palette for mixing cosmetics, such as eye makeup, with water.

Crayon A small stick of colored wax, chalk, or charcoal.

Cross-hatching Intersecting sets of parallel lines used to shade a drawing.

Crossing square In architecture, the area that defines the right-angle intersection of the vaults of the nave and the transept of a church.

Cubism A twentieth-century style developed by Picasso and Braque that emphasizes the two-dimensionality of the canvas, characterized by multiple views of an object and the reduction of form to cubelike essentials.

Cuneiform Wedge-shaped; descriptive of the characters used in ancient Akkadian, Assyrian, Babylonian, and Persian alphabets.

Curvilinear Consisting of a curved line or lines.

Dada A post–World War I movement that sought to use art to destroy art, thereby underscoring the paradoxes and absurdities of modern life.

Daguerreotype A photograph made from a silver-coated copper plate; named after Louis Daguerre, the innovator of the method.

Deconstructivist architecture A Postmodern approach to the design of buildings that disassembles and reassembles the basic elements of architecture. The focus is on the creation of forms that may appear abstract, disharmonious, and disconnected from the functions of the building. Deconstructivism challenges the view that there is one correct way to approach architecture.

Der Blaue Reiter (The Blue Rider) A twentieth-century German Expressionist movement that focused on the contrasts between, and combinations of, abstract form and pure color.

Design   The combination of the visual elements of art according to such principles as balance and unity.

De Stijl   An early twentieth-century movement that emphasized the use of basic forms, particularly cubes, horizontals, and verticals.

Diagonal rib   In architecture, a *rib* that connects the opposite corners of a groin vault.

Die Brücke (The Bridge)   A short-lived German Expressionist movement characterized by boldly colored landscapes and cityscapes and by violent portraits.

Digital art   Art that makes use of—or is developed with the assistance of—electronic instruments, such as computers, that store and manipulate information through the use of series of zeros and ones (digits); including but not limited to web design, *graphic design*, and *digital photography*.

Digital photography   Photography that stores visual information electronically rather than on film.

Direct-metal sculpture   Metal sculpture that is assembled by such techniques as welding and riveting rather than *casting*.

Dissolve   In cinematography and video, a fading technique in which the current scene grows dimmer as the subsequent scene grows brighter.

Dome   In architecture, a hemispherical structure that is round when viewed from beneath.

Doric order   The earliest and simplest of the Greek architectural styles, consisting of relatively short, squat columns, sometimes unfluted, and a simple, square-shaped capital. The Doric *frieze* is usually divided into *triglyphs* and *metopes*.

Drawing   The art of running an implement that leaves a mark over a surface; a work of art created in this manner.

Dry masonry   Brick or stone construction without use of mortar.

Dry media   Drawing materials that do not involve the application of water or other liquids. Contrast with *fluid media*.

Drypoint   A variation of engraving in which the surface of the matrix is cut with a needle to make rough edges. In printmaking, rough edges make soft rather than crisp lines.

Dynamism   The Futurist view that force or energy is the basic principle that underlies all events, including everything we see. Objects are depicted as if in constant motion, appearing and disappearing before our eyes.

Earthenware   Reddish tan, porous pottery fired at a relatively low temperature (below 2,000°F).

Earthwork   A work of art in which large amounts of earth or land are shaped into a sculpture.

Eastern Orthodox   A form of Christianity dominant in Eastern Europe, western Asia, and North Africa.

Editing   In cinematography and video, rearranging a film or video record to provide a more coherent or interesting narrative or presentation of the images.

Egg tempera   A painting medium in which ground pigments are bound with egg yolk.

Emboss   To decorate with designs that are raised above a surface.

Embroidery   The art of ornamenting fabric with needlework.

Emphasis   A design principle that focuses the viewer's attention on one or more parts of a composition by accentuating certain shapes, intensifying value or color, featuring directional lines, or strategically placing the objects and images.

Empire period   The Roman period from about 27 BCE to 395 CE, when the empire was divided.

Emulsion   A suspension of a salt of silver in gelatin or collodion used to coat film and photographic plates.

Enamel   To apply a hard, glossy coating to a surface; a coating of this type.

Encaustic   A method of painting in which the colors in a wax medium are burned into a surface with hot irons.

Engraving   Cutting; in printmaking, an *intaglio* process in which plates of copper, zinc, or steel are cut with a burin and the ink image is pressed onto paper.

Entablature   In architecture, a horizontal structure supported by columns, which, in turn, supports any other element, such as a pediment, that is placed above; from top to bottom, the entablature consists of a *cornice*, a *frieze*, and an *architrave*.

Entasis   In architecture, a slight convex curvature of a column used to provide the illusion of continuity of thickness as the column rises.

Ephemeral art   Works that have a temporary immediacy or are built with the recognition that they will disintegrate.

Equestrian portrait   A depiction of a figure on horseback.

Etching   In printmaking, an *intaglio* process in which the matrix is first covered with an acid-resistant ground. The ground is removed from certain areas with a needle, and the matrix is dipped in acid, which eats away at the areas exposed by the needle. These areas become grooves that are inked and printed.

Etruscan   From ancient Etruria, located along the northwestern shores of present-day Italy.

Existentialism   A literary and philosophical movement of the early twentieth century characterized by the belief that human beings are free and responsible for their behavior and actions. This freedom, according to proponents Søren Kierkegaard, Jean-Paul Sartre, and Martin Heidegger, leads to humanity's pain and anguish.

Expressionism   A modern school of art in which an emotional impact is achieved through agitated brushwork, intense coloration, and violent, hallucinatory imagery.

Expressionistic   Emphasizing the distortion of color and form to achieve an emotional impact.

Extreme unity   Unification of all elements in a composition.

Extrude   To force metal through a die or small holes to give it shape.

Facade   A French term for the face or front of a building.

Fading   In cinematography and video, the gradual dimming or brightening of a scene, used as a transition between scenes.

Fantastic art   The representation of fanciful images, sometimes joyful and whimsical, sometimes horrific and grotesque.

Fauvism   An early twentieth-century style of art characterized by the juxtaposition of areas of bright colors that are often unrelated to the objects they represent, and by distorted linear perspective (from French for "wild beast").

Fenestration   The arrangement of windows and doors in a structure, often used to create balance and rhythm as well as light, air, and access.

Ferroconcrete   Same as *reinforced concrete*.

Fertile Crescent   The arable land lying between the Tigris and Euphrates rivers in ancient Mesopotamia.

Fertile Ribbon   The arable land lying along the Nile River in Egypt.

Fetish figure   An object believed to have magical powers.

Fiber   A slender, threadlike structure or material that can be woven.

Fiberglass   Fine spun-glass filaments that can be woven into textiles.

Figurative art   Art that represents the likeness of human and other figures.

Figure–ground relationship   The relationship between the primary subject (figure) and other parts of the composition (ground or background).

Figure–ground reversal   A shift in a viewer's perception of a composition in which what at one moment appears to be the figure becomes the ground (or background), and vice versa.

Film   A thin sheet of cellulose material coated with a photosensitive substance.

Flashback   In cinematography and video, an interruption of the story line with the portrayal of an earlier event.

Flash-forward In cinematography and video, an interruption of the story line with the portrayal of a future event.

Flint glass A hard, bright glass containing lead oxide.

Fluid media Liquid-based drawing materials. Contrast with *dry media*.

Flying buttress A buttress that is exterior to a building but connected in a location that permits the buttress to support an interior vault.

Focal point A specific part of a work of art that seizes and holds the viewer's interest.

Foreshortening Diminishing the size of the parts of an object that are represented as farthest from the viewer. Specifically, rendering parts of an object as receding from the viewer at angles oblique to the picture plane so that they appear proportionately shorter than parts of the object that are parallel to the picture plane.

Forge To form or shape metal (usually heated) with blows from a hammer, press, or other implement or machine.

Form The totality of what the viewer sees in a work of art; a product of the composition of visual elements.

Formalist criticism An approach to art criticism that concentrates on the elements and design of works of art rather than on historical factors or the biography of the artist.

Forum An open public space, particularly in ancient Rome, used as a market and a gathering place.

Freestanding sculpture Sculpture that is carved or cast in the round, unconnected to a wall, and thereby capable of being viewed in its entirety by walking around it. Freestanding sculpture can also be designed for a niche, which limits the visible portion of the sculpture.

Fresco A type of painting in which pigments are applied to a fresh, wet plaster surface or wall and thereby become part of the surface or wall (from Italian for "fresh").

Fresco secco Dry fresco; painting executed on dry plaster. Contrast with *buon fresco*.

Frieze In architecture, a horizontal band between the *architrave* and the *cornice* that is often decorated with sculpture.

Futurism An early twentieth-century style that portrayed modern machines and the dynamic character of modern life and science.

Gate In the lost-wax technique of casting, one of a number of wax rods connected to the mold; as molten bronze flows into the mold, gates allow air to escape.

Gauffrage An inkless *intaglio* process.

Genre painting Simple human representations; realistic figure painting that focuses on themes taken from everyday life.

Geometric period A period of Greek art from about 900 to 700 BCE during which works of art emphasized geometric patterns.

Geometric shape A shape that is regular, easy to measure, and easy to describe, as distinguished from *organic* or *biomorphic shape*, which is irregular, difficult to measure, and difficult to describe.

Gesso Plaster of Paris that is applied to a wooden or canvas support and used as a surface for painting or as the material for sculpture (from Italian for "gypsum").

Gild To apply thin sheets of gold leaf or goldlike substance to a surface.

Glassblowing The art of shaping molten glass into glass objects by blowing air through a tube.

Glaze In painting, a semitransparent coating on a painted surface that provides a glassy or glossy finish. In ceramics, a hard, glossy coating formed by applying a liquid suspension of powdered material to the surface of a ware, which is then dried and fired at a temperature that causes the ingredients to melt together.

Globalization In general, the mutual influence of cultures, economies, marketplaces, and current events that were once distant and separate. In art, more specifically the world-wide invasion of visual images and the art marketplace from various cultures into people's consciousness; multiculturalism and cross-culturalism in contemporary art.

Golden mean The principle that a small part of a work should relate to a larger part of the work in proportion to the manner in which the larger part relates to the whole.

Golden rectangle A rectangle based on the *golden mean* and constructed so that its width is 1.618 times its height.

Golden section Developed in ancient Greece, a mathematical formula for determining the proportional relationship of the parts of a work to the whole.

Gothic A Western European style developed between the twelfth and sixteenth centuries CE, characterized in architecture by ribbed vaults, pointed arches, flying buttresses, and steep roofs.

Gouache Watercolor paint that is made opaque by mixing pigments with a particular gum binder.

Graphic design Design for advertising and industry that includes design elements such as typography and images for communication purposes.

Graphite A soft black form of carbon used as a drawing implement (from *graphein*, Greek for "to write").

Graver A cutting tool used by engravers and sculptors.

Greek cross plan A cross-shaped design, particularly of a church, in which the arms (nave and transept) are equal in length.

Griffin A mythical creature with the body and back legs of a lion, and the head, talons, and wings of an eagle.

Groin vault In architecture, a vault that is constructed by placing *barrel vaults* at right angles so that a square is covered.

Ground The surface on which a two-dimensional work of art is created; a coat of liquid material applied to a surface that serves as a base for drawing or painting. Also, the background in a composition. Also see *figure–ground relationship*.

Gum A sticky substance found in many plants, used to bind pigments as found, for example, in silverpoint, chalk, and pastel drawings.

Gum arabic A gum obtained from the African acacia plant.

Haniwa A hollow ceramic figure placed at ancient Japanese burial plots.

Hard-edge painting A contemporary style in which geometric forms are rendered with precision but with no distinction between foreground and background.

Hatcher An engraving instrument that produces thousands of tiny pits that will hold ink.

Hatching Fine parallel lines drawn or engraved to represent shading.

Heliography A photographic process in which bitumen is placed on a pewter plate to create a photosensitive surface that is exposed to the sun (from *helios*, Greek for "sun").

Hellenism The culture, thought, and ethical system of ancient Greece.

Herringbone perspective A portrayal of space in which *orthogonals* vanish to a specific point along a vertical line that divides a canvas.

Hierarchical scaling The use of relative size to indicate the comparative importance of the depicted objects or people.

High relief Sculpture that projects from its background by at least half its natural depth. Contrast with *bas relief*.

Horizon In linear perspective, the imaginary line (frequently, where the earth seems to meet the sky) along which converging lines meet. Also see *vanishing point*.

Horizontal balance Balance in which the elements on the left and right sides of the composition seem to be about equal in number or visual emphasis.

Horus The ancient Egyptian sun god.

Hudson River School A group of nineteenth-century American artists whose favorite subjects included the scenery of the Hudson River Valley and the Catskill Mountains of New York State.

Hue Color; the distinctive characteristics of a color that enable us to label it (as blue or green, for example) and to assign it a place in the visible spectrum.

Humanism A system of belief in which humankind is viewed as the standard by which all things are measured.

Hybridity In art, the mixing of the traditions of different cultures to create new blends and new connections.

Hypostyle In architecture, a structure with a roof supported by rows of piers or columns.

Ibex A wild goat.

Iconography A set of conventional meanings attached to images; as an artistic approach, representation or illustration that uses the visual conventions and symbols of a culture.

Iconology The study of visual symbols, which frequently have literary or religious origins.

Idealism The representation of forms according to a concept of perfection.

Illumination Illustration and decoration of a manuscript with pictures or designs.

Illusionistic surrealism A form of *surrealism* that renders the irrational content, absurd juxtapositions, and changing forms of dreams in a highly illusionistic manner that blurs the distinctions between the real and the imaginary.

Imam A prayer leader in a mosque; a religious and temporal ruler of a Muslim community or state.

Imbalance A characteristic of works of art in which the areas of the composition are unequal in *actual weight* or *pictorial weight*.

Impasto Application of a medium such as oil or acrylic paint so that an actual texture is built up on a surface.

Implied line A line that is completed by the viewer; a discontinuous line that the viewer perceives as being continuous; a line suggested by series of points or dots or by the nearby end-points of series of lines; or a line evoked by the movements and glances of the figures in a composition. Contrast with *actual line*.

Implied mass The apparent mass of a depicted object as determined, for example, by the use of forms or fields of color. Contrast with *actual mass*.

Implied motion An impression of movement created by the use of visual elements, composition, or content. Contrast with *actual motion*.

Implied time An impression of time's passage through the depiction of events that occur over a period of time.

Impressionism A late nineteenth-century style characterized by the attempt to capture the fleeting effects of light by painting in short strokes of pure color.

Incise To cut into with a sharp tool.

Industrial design The planning and artistic enhancement of industrial products.

Installation A work of art created for a specific gallery space or outdoor site.

Intaglio A printing process in which metal plates are incised, covered with ink, wiped, and pressed against paper. The print receives the image of the areas that are below the surface of the matrix.

Intarsia A style of decorative mosaic inlay.

International Gothic style A refined style of painting in late fourteenth-century and early fifteenth-century Europe characterized by splendid processions and courtly scenes, ornate embellishment, and attention to detail.

International style A post–World War I school of art and architecture that used modern materials and methods and expressed the view that form must follow function.

Investiture The fire-resistant mold used in metal casting.

Ionic order A moderately ornate Greek architectural style introduced from Asia Minor and characterized by spiral scrolls (*volutes*) on capitals and a continuous *frieze*.

Jamb In architecture, the side post of a doorway, window frame, fireplace, etc.

Jasper A kind of porcelain (also called jasperware) developed by Josiah Wedgwood that is characterized by a dull green or blue surface and raised white designs.

Ka figure According to ancient Egyptian belief, an image of a body in which the soul would dwell after death.

Keystone In architecture, the wedge-shaped stone placed in the top center of an arch to prevent the arch from falling inward.

Kiln An oven used for drying and firing ceramics.

Kinetic art Art that moves, such as the mobile.

Kinetic sculpture Sculpture that actually moves (as opposed to providing the illusion of movement).

Kitsch Overly sentimental work that is viewed as tasteless decoration but nevertheless has its own sort of nostalgic charm.

Kiva A circular, subterranean structure built by Native Americans of the Southwest for community and ceremonial functions.

Kore figure A clothed female figure of the Greek Archaic style, often adorned with intricate carved detail. A counterpart to the male kouros figure.

Kouros figure The male figure as represented in the sculpture of the geometric and Archaic styles (from Greek for "boy").

Labyrinth Maze.

Lamination The process of building up by layers.

Land art Site-specific work that is created or marked by an artist within natural surroundings.

Lapis lazuli An opaque blue, semiprecious stone.

Latin cross plan A cross-shaped church design in which the nave is longer than the transept.

Lavender oil An aromatic oil derived from plants of the mint family.

Lens A transparent substance with at least one curved surface that causes the convergence or divergence of light rays passing through it. In the eye and the camera, lenses are used to focus images onto photosensitive surfaces.

Lift-ground etching A technique in which a sugar solution is brushed onto a resin-coated plate, creating the illusion of a brush-and-ink drawing.

Light The segment of the spectrum of electromagnetic energy that stimulates the eyes and produces visual sensations.

Linear Determined or characterized by the use of line.

Linear perspective A system of organizing space in two-dimensional media in which lines that are in reality parallel and horizontal are represented as converging diagonals. The method is based on foreshortening, in which the space between the lines grows smaller until it disappears, just as objects appear to grow smaller as they become more distant.

Linear recession Depth as perceived through the convergence of lines at specific points in the composition, such as the horizon line.

Lintel In architecture, a horizontal member supported by posts.

Lithography A surface printing process in which an image is drawn onto a matrix with a greasy wax crayon. When dampened, the waxed areas repel water while the material of the matrix absorbs it. An oily ink is then applied, which adheres only to the waxed areas. When the matrix is pressed against paper, the paper receives the image of the crayon.

Living rock Natural rock formations, as on a mountainside.

Local color The hue of an object created by the colors its surface reflects under normal lighting conditions (contrast with *optical color*). Color that is natural rather than symbolic for the depicted objects.

Logo A distinctive company trademark or signature (short for "logogram" or "logotype").

Longitudinal plan A church design in which the nave is longer than the transept and in which parts are symmetrical against an axis. Contrast with *central plan*.

Longshot In cinematography and video, an image or sequence made from a great distance, providing an overview of a scene.

Loom A machine that weaves thread into yarn or cloth.

Lost-wax technique   A bronze-casting process in which an initial mold is made from a model (usually clay) and filled with molten wax. A second, fire-resistant mold is made from the wax, and molten bronze is cast in it.

Lunette   A crescent-shaped space or opening (French for "little moon").

Magazine   In architecture, a large supply chamber.

Mandala   In Hindu and Buddhist traditions, a circular design symbolizing wholeness or unity.

Mannerist art   A sixteenth-century, post-Renaissance style characterized by artificial poses and gestures, vivid—sometimes harsh—color, and distorted, elongated figures.

Manuscript illumination   Illustration or decoration of books and letters with pictures or designs.

Mass   In painting, a large area of one form or color; in three-dimensional art, the bulk of an object. Also see *implied mass* and *actual mass*.

Matrix   In printmaking, the working surface of the block, slab, or screen. In sculpture, a mold or hollow shape used to give form to a material that is inserted in a plastic or molten state.

Measure   Extent, dimensions, or capacity as determined by a standard.

Medium   The materials and methods used to create an image or object in drawing, painting, sculpture, and other arts (from Latin for "means").

Megalith   A huge stone, especially as used in prehistoric construction.

Megaron   A rectangular room with a two-columned porch.

Mesolithic   Of the Middle Stone Age.

Metope   In architecture, the panels containing *relief sculpture* that appear between the *triglyphs* of the *Doric frieze*.

Mezzotint   A nonlinear engraving process in which the *matrix* is pitted with a *hatcher*.

Middle Ages   The thousand-year span (400–1400 CE) from the end of Roman Classical Art to the rebirth of Classical traditions in the Renaissance. Although this period is sometimes referred to as the Dark Ages, it was actually a time of important contributions to economics, science, and the arts.

Mihrab   A niche in the wall of a mosque that faces Mecca and thus provides a focus of worship.

Mimesis   The practice of exact imitation in artistic representation.

Minaret   A tall, slender tower of a mosque from which Muslims are called to prayer.

Minimal art   Contemporary art that adheres to the Minimalist philosophy.

Minimalism   A twentieth-century style of *nonobjective art* in which a minimal number of visual elements are arranged in a simple fashion.

Mixed media   The use of two or more media to create a single image.

Mobile   A type of *kinetic* sculpture that moves in response to air currents.

Modeling   In two-dimensional works of art, the creation of the illusion of depth through the use of light and shade (*chiaroscuro*). In sculpture, the process of shaping a pliable material, such as clay or wax, into a three-dimensional form.

Modernism   A contemporary style of architecture that deemphasizes ornamentation and uses recently developed materials of high strength.

Mold   A pattern or matrix for giving form to molten or plastic material; a frame on which something is modeled.

Monochromatic   Literally, "one-colored"; descriptive of images that are executed in a single color or with so little color contrast as to appear uniform in hue.

Monolith   A single, large block of stone; in sculpture, monolithic refers to a work that retains much of the shape of the original block of stone.

Monotype   In printmaking, a technique in which paint is brushed onto a matrix that is pressed against a sheet of paper, yielding a single print.

Montage   In cinematography or video, the use of flashing, whirling, or abruptly alternating images to convey connected ideas, suggest the passage of time, or provide an emotional effect.

Monument   A type of site-specific public art that is intended to preserve the memory of a person or an event.

Mortuary temple   An Egyptian temple of the New Kingdom in which the pharaoh worshiped and was worshiped after death.

Mosaic   A medium in which the ground is wet plaster on an architectural element, such as a wall, into which small pieces (tesserae) of colored tile, stone, or glass are assembled to create an image.

Muezzin   Crier who calls Muslims to prayer five times a day from a *minaret*.

Mummification   A process by which a body is preserved, often by removing all moisture.

Mural   Image(s) painted directly on a wall or intended to cover a wall completely (from *muralis*, Latin for "of a wall").

Mural quality   A surface suitable for mural painting.

Narrative editing   In cinematography or video, selecting from multiple images of the same subject to advance a story.

Narthex   A church vestibule that leads to the nave, constructed for use by the catechumens (individuals preparing to be baptized).

Naturalism   Representation that strives to imitate nature rather than to express intellectual theory.

Naturalistic style   A style prevalent in Europe during the second half of the nineteenth century that depicted the details of ordinary life.

Nave   The central aisle of a church, constructed for use by the congregation at large.

Negative   In photography, an exposed and developed film or plate on which values—that is, light and dark—are the reverse of what they are in the actual scene and in the print, or *positive*.

Negative shape   Space that is empty or filled with imagery that is secondary to the main objects or figures depicted in the composition. Contrast with *positive shape*.

Neoclassical style   An eighteenth-century revival of Classical Greek and Roman art, characterized by simplicity and straight lines.

Neo-Expressionism   A violent, figurative style of the second half of the twentieth century that largely revived the German Expressionism of the early twentieth century.

Neolithic   Of the New Stone Age.

Neutrals   "Colors" (black, white, and gray) that do not contribute to the hue of other colors with which they are mixed.

New image painting   An art style of the second half of the twentieth century that sought to reconcile abstraction and representation through the use of simplified images to convey the grandeur of abstract shapes without dominating visual elements such as color and texture.

New Objectivity (Neue Sachlichkeit)   A post–World War I German art movement that rebelled against German Expressionism and focused on the detailed representation of objects and figures.

Nib   The point of a pen; the split and sharpened end of a quill pen.

Nirvana   In Buddhist belief, a state of perfect blessedness in which the individual soul is absorbed into the supreme spirit.

Nonobjective art   Art that does not portray figures or objects; art without real models or subject matter.

Nonporous   Not containing pores and thus not permitting the passage of fluids.

Nonrepresentational art   Art that does not represent figures or objects.

Ocher   A dark yellow color derived from an earthy clay.

Oculus   In architecture, a round window, particularly one placed at the apex of a dome (from Latin for "eye").

Offset lithography   A variation of *lithography* in which the image is hand drawn by the artist on Mylar.

Oil paint Paint in which pigments are combined with an oil medium.

One-point perspective Linear perspective in which a single vanishing point is placed on the horizon.

Op Art A style of art dating from the 1960s that creates the illusion of vibrations through afterimages, disorienting perspective, and the juxtaposition of contrasting colors. Also called "optical art" or "optical painting."

Optical Portrayal of objects as they are seen at the moment, especially depicting the play of light on surfaces. The painting of optical impressions is a hallmark of *Impressionism.*

Optical art See *Op Art.*

Optical color The perception of the color of an object, which may vary markedly according to atmospheric conditions. Contrast with *local color.*

Oran A praying figure.

Organic shape A shape characteristic of living things and thus appearing soft, curvilinear, and irregular. Contrast with *geometric shape.*

Orthogonal Composed of right angles.

Ottonian Of the period characterized by the consecutive reigns of German kings named Otto, beginning in 936 CE.

Oxidizing phase See *black-figure painting.*

Paint A mixture of a pigment with a vehicle or medium.

Painting The application of a pigment to a surface; a work of art created in this manner.

Palatine chapel A chapel that is part of a palace.

Palette A surface on which pigments are placed and prepared and from which the artist works; the artist's choice of colors as seen in a work of art.

Pan To move a motion picture or video camera from side to side to capture a comprehensive or continuous view of a subject.

Panel painting A painting, usually in tempera but sometimes in oil, whose ground is a wooden panel.

Panorama An unlimited view in all directions.

Papyrus A writing surface made from the papyrus plant.

Parallel editing In cinematography or video, shifting back and forth from one event or story line to another.

Pastel A drawing implement made by grinding coloring matter, mixing it with gum, and forming it into a crayon.

Pastoral Relating to idyllic rural life, especially of shepherds and dairymaids.

Patina A fine crust or film that forms on bronze or copper because of oxidation. It usually provides a desirable greenish or greenish blue tint to the metal.

Patrician A member of the noble class in ancient Rome.

Pattern painting A decorative contemporary style that uses evocative signs, symbols, and patterns.

Pediment In architecture, any triangular shape surrounded by *cornices,* especially one that surmounts the *entablature* of the *portico facade* of Greek temple. The Romans frequently placed pediments without support over windows and doorways.

Pencil A rod-shaped drawing instrument with an inner shaft that is usually made of *graphite.*

Pendentive In architecture, a spherical triangle that fills the wall space between the four arches of a *groin vault* in order to provide a circular base on which a dome may rest.

Peplos In Greek Classical Art, a heavy woolen wrap.

Photography The creation of images by exposure of a photosensitive surface to light.

Photorealism A movement dating from the 1960s in which subjects are rendered with hard, photographic precision.

Photosensitive Descriptive of a surface that is sensitive to light and therefore capable of recording images.

Photo silkscreen A variation of *serigraphy,* or *silkscreen printing,* that allows the artist to create photographic images on a screen covered with a light-sensitive gel.

Piazza An open public square or plaza.

Pictograph A simplified symbol of an object or action; for example, a schematized or abstract form of an ancestral image, animal, geometric form, anatomic part, or shape suggestive of a cosmic symbol or microscopic life.

Pictorial balance The distribution of the apparent or *visual weight* of elements in two-dimensional works of art. Contrast with *actual balance.*

Picture plane The flat, two-dimensional surface on which a picture is created. In much Western art, the picture plane is viewed as a window opening onto deep space.

Pier In architecture, a columnlike support with a rectilinear rather than cylindrical profile. Piers generally support arches.

Pigment Coloring matter that is usually mixed with water, oil, or other substances to make paint.

Pilaster In architecture, a decorative element that recalls the shape of a structural *pier.* Pilasters are attached to the wall plane and project very little. They may have all the visual elements of piers, including base, shaft, *capital,* and *entablature* above.

Pile weave A weave in which knots are tied, then cut, forming an even surface.

Plain weave A weave in which the woof thread passes above one warp fiber and below the next.

Planar recession Perspective in which the illusion of depth is created through parallel planes that appear to recede from the picture plane.

Planographic printing Any method of printing from a flat surface, such as *lithography.*

Plastic elements Those elements of a work of art, such as line, shape, color, and texture, that artists manipulate to achieve desired effects.

Plasticity Capacity of a material to be molded or shaped.

Plebeian class In ancient Rome, the common people.

Plywood Sheets of wood that resist warping because they are constructed of layers glued together with the grain oriented in different directions.

Pointed arch An arch that comes to a point rather than curves at the top.

Pointillism A systematic method of applying minute dots of unmixed pigment to the canvas; the dots are intended to be "mixed" by the eye when viewed. Also called "divisionism."

Pop Art An art style originating in the 1960s that uses commercial and popular images and themes as its subject matter.

Porcelain A hard, white, translucent, non-porous clay body. The *bisque* is fired at a relatively low temperature and the *glaze* at a high temperature.

Portico The entrance facade of a Greek temple, adapted for use with other buildings and consisting of a *colonnade, entablature,* and *pediment* (from Greek for "porch").

Positive shape The spatial form defined by the objects or figures represented in works of art. Contrast with *negative shape.*

Post-and-beam construction Construction in which vertical elements (posts) and horizontal timbers (beams) are pieced together with wooden pegs.

Post-and-lintel construction Construction in which vertical elements (posts) are used to support horizontal crosspieces (lintels). Also termed "trabeated structure."

Postimpressionism A late nineteenth-century style that relies on the gains made by Impressionists in terms of the use of color and spontaneous brushwork but that employs these elements as expressive devices. The Postimpressionists, however, rejected the essentially decorative aspects of Impressionist subject matter.

Postmodernism A contemporary style that arose as a reaction to Modernism and that returns to ornamentation drawn from Classical and historical sources.

Pottery Pots, bowls, dishes, and similar wares made of clay and hardened by heat; a shop at which such objects are made.

Poussiniste Those Neoclassical artists who took Nicolas Poussin as their model. Contrast with *Rubeniste*.

Prefabricate In architecture, to build beforehand at a factory rather than at the building site.

Pre-Hellenic Of ancient Greece before the eighth century BCE.

Primary color A hue—red, blue, or yellow—that is not obtained by mixing other hues; all other colors are derived from primary colors.

Print In printmaking, a picture or design made by pressing or hitting a surface with a plate or block; in photography, a photograph, especially one made from a negative.

Prism A transparent, polygonal body that breaks down white light into the colors of the visible spectrum.

Proportion The relationship of the size of the parts to the whole.

Propylaeum In architecture, a gateway building leading to an open court in front of a Greek or Roman temple; specifically, such a building on the Acropolis.

Psychic automatism A process of generating imagery through ideas received from the unconscious mind and expressed in an unrestrained manner.

Psychological line A connection between two points in a composition created by the action in a work, such as a figure pointing to an object or looking at another figure. Also referred to as *compositional line*.

Public art Works created for public spaces.

Quarry tile Reddish brown tile, similar to terra-cotta.

Quatrefoil In architecture, a design made up of four converging arcs that are similar in appearance to a flower with four petals.

Quill A pen made from a large, stiff feather.

Radial balance Balance in which the design elements radiate from a center point.

Radiating chapel An apse-shaped chapel, several of which generally radiate from the *ambulatory* in a *Latin cross plan*.

Rasp A rough file that has raised points instead of ridges.

Rationalism The belief that ethical conduct is determined by reason; in philosophy, the theory that knowledge is derived from the intellect, without the aid of the senses.

Readymade Found objects that are exhibited as works of art, frequently after being placed in a new context with a new title.

Realism A style characterized by accurate and truthful portrayal of subject matter; a nineteenth-century style that portrayed subject matter in this manner.

Rectangular bay system A church plan in which rectangular *bays* serve as the basis for the overall design. Contrast with *square schematism*.

Rectilinear Characterized by straight lines.

Reducing phase See *black-figure painting*.

Reformation A social and religious movement of sixteenth-century Europe in which various groups attempted to reform the Roman Catholic Church by establishing rival religions (Protestant sects).

Register A horizontal segment of a structure or work of art.

Regular repetition The systematic repetition of the visual elements in a work to create *rhythm*.

Reinforced concrete Concrete that is strengthened by steel rods or mesh. Same as *ferroconcrete*.

Relative size The size of an object or figure in relation to other objects or figures or the setting. See *scale*.

Relief printing Any printmaking technique in which the matrix is carved with knives so that the areas not meant to be printed (that is, not meant to leave an image) are below the surface of the matrix.

Relief sculpture Sculpture that is carved to ornament architecture or furniture, as opposed to *freestanding sculpture*. Also see *bas-relief* and *high relief*.

Renaissance A period spanning the fourteenth and fifteenth centuries CE in Europe. The Renaissance (French for "rebirth") rejected medieval art and philosophy; it first turned to Classical antiquity for inspiration and then developed patterns of art and philosophy that paved the way toward the modern world.

Reoxidizing phase See *black-figure painting*.

Representational art Art that presents natural objects in recognizable form.

Republican period The Roman period lasting from the victories over the Etruscans to the death of Julius Caesar (527–509 BCE).

Resolution In video and digital photography, the sharpness of a picture as determined by the number of lines or pixels composing the picture.

Rhythm The orderly repetition or progression of the visual elements in a work of art.

Rib In Gothic architecture, a structural member that reinforces the stress points of *groin vaults*.

Rococo An eighteenth-century style during the Baroque era that is characterized by lighter colors, greater wit, playfulness, occasional eroticism, and yet more ornate decoration.

Romanesque style A style of European architecture of the eleventh and twelfth centuries that is characterized by thick, massive walls, the *Latin cross plan*, the use of a *barrel vault* in the *nave*, round arches, and a twin-towered facade.

Romanticism A nineteenth-century movement that rebelled against academic Neoclassicism by seeking extremes of emotion as enhanced by virtuoso brushwork and a brilliant palette.

Root five rectangle A rectangle whose length is 2.236 (the square root of 5) times its width that can be constructed by rotating the diagonal of a half square left and right.

Rosette A painted or sculpted circular ornament with petals and leaves radiating from the center.

Rose window A large circular window in a Gothic church, assembled in segments that resemble the petals of a flower, usually adorned with stained glass and plantlike ornamental work.

Rubeniste Those Romantic artists who took Peter Paul Rubens as their model. Contrast with *Poussiniste*.

Salon An annual exhibition of the French Academy held in the spring during the eighteenth and nineteenth centuries.

Salon d'Automne An independent exhibition of experimental art held in the autumn of 1905; named the "Salon of Autumn" to distinguish it from the Academic salons that were usually held in the spring.

Sanguine Blood colored, ruddy; cheerful and confident (from Latin for "blood").

Sarcophagus A coffin or tomb, especially one made of limestone.

Satin weave A weave in which the woof passes above and below several warp threads at a time.

Saturation The degree of purity of hue measured by its intensity or brightness.

Scale The relative size of an object compared to other objects, the setting, or people.

Sculpture The art of carving, casting, modeling, or assembling materials into three-dimensional figures or forms; a work of art made in such a manner.

S curve Developed in the Classical style as a means of balancing the human form, consisting of the distribution of tensions so that tension and repose are passed back and forth from one side of the figure to the other, resulting in an S shape; *contrapposto*.

Seal A design or stamp placed on a document as a sign of authenticity.

Secondary color A color that is derived from mixing pigments of primary colors in equal amounts. The secondary colors are orange (obtained by mixing red and yellow), violet (red and blue), and green (blue and yellow).

Serigraphy A printmaking process in which stencils are applied to a screen of silk or similar material stretched on a frame. Paint or ink is forced through the open areas of the stencil onto paper beneath. Also termed *silkscreen printing*.

Service systems In architecture, mechanical systems that provide structures with transportation, heat, electricity, waste removal, and other services.

Shade The degree of darkness of a color determined by the extent of its mixture with black.

Shaft grave A vertical hole in the ground in which one or more bodies are buried.

Shape An area within a composition that has boundaries that separate it from its surroundings.

Shaped canvas A canvas that departs from the traditional rectangle and often extends the work into three-dimensional space, thus challenging the traditional orientation of a painting.

Shinto A major religion of Japan that emphasizes nature and ancestor worship.

Shiva The Hindu god of destruction and regeneration.

Shrine A repository for sacred relics and art objects intended to arouse feelings of religious devotion. A small structure or area intended for private religious devotion; a site or structure used in religious devotion.

Shutter In photography, a device for opening and closing the aperture of a lens so that the film is exposed to light.

Siding In architecture, a covering for an exterior wall.

Silica A hard, glossy mineral compound of silicon and oxygen.

Silkscreen printing A printmaking process in which stencils are applied to a screen of silk or similar material stretched on a frame. Paint or ink is forced through the open areas of the stencil onto paper beneath. Also termed *serigraphy*.

Silverpoint A drawing medium in which a silver-tipped instrument inscribes lines on a surface that has been coated with a *ground* or pigment.

Site-specific art Art that is produced in or for one location and is not intended to be relocated.

Slip In ceramics, clay that is thinned to the consistency of cream for use in casting, decorating, or cementing.

Slow motion A cinematographic process in which action is made to appear fluid but slower than actual motion by shooting a greater than usual number of frames per second and then projecting the film at the usual number of frames per second.

Soft-ground etching An etching technique in which a ground of softened wax yields effects similar to those of pencil or crayon drawings.

Sound track An area on the side of a strip of motion picture film that carries a record of the sound accompanying the visual information.

Square schematism A church plan in which the crossing square serves as the basis for determining the overall dimensions of the building. Contrast with *rectangular bay system*.

Squeegee A T-shaped tool with a rubber blade used to remove liquid from a surface.

Stainless steel Steel that has been alloyed with chromium or other metals to make it virtually immune to corrosion.

Stamp To impress or imprint with a mark or design.

Steel A hard, tough metal composed of iron, carbon, and other metals, such as nickel or chromium.

Steel cable A strong cable composed of multiple intertwined steel wires.

Steel-cage construction A method of building that capitalizes on the strength of steel by piecing together slender steel beams to form the skeleton of a structure.

Stele (or stela) An engraved stone slab or pillar that serves as a grave marker.

Stereoscopy An illusion of three-dimensionality created by simultaneously viewing two photographs of a scene taken from slightly different angles (as the scene would be seen by a pair of eyes).

Stippling Drawing or painting small dots or dabs to create shading or a dappled effect.

Stoicism The philosophy that the universe is governed by natural laws and that people should follow virtue, as determined by reason, and remain indifferent to passion or emotion.

Stoneware A ceramic that is fired at 2,300°F–2,700°F. The resulting object is usually gray but can be tan or reddish. Stoneware is nonporous or slightly porous and is used in dinnerware and ceramic sculpture.

Stop In photography, the aperture of a lens, which is typically adjustable; the "f-number."

Stopped time In photography, an image that captures action in midmovement by exposing the film very briefly.

Stroboscopic motion The creation of the illusion of movement by the presentation of a rapid progression of stationary images, such as the frames of a motion picture.

Stupa A dome-shaped Buddhist shrine.

Style A characteristic manner or mode of artistic expression or design.

Stylobate A continuous base or platform that supports a row of columns.

Stylus A pointed, needlelike tool used in drawing, printmaking, making impressions on electronic media, and so on.

Subtractive process In sculpture, the removal of material, as in carving. Contrast with *additive process*.

Subversive texture Texture that is chosen or created by artists to foil or undermine our ideas about the objects that they depict.

Support A surface on which a two-dimensional work of art is made.

Surrealism A twentieth-century art style whose imagery is believed to stem from unconscious, irrational sources and that therefore takes on *fantastic* forms. Although the imagery is fantastic, it is often rendered with extraordinary realism.

Symmetrical balance Balance in which imagery on one side of a composition is mirrored on the other side. Symmetrical balance can be pure, or it can be *approximate*, in which case the whole of the work has a symmetrical feeling but with slight variations that provide more visual interest than would a mirror image. Contrast with *asymmetrical balance*.

Symmetry Similarity of form or arrangement on both sides of a dividing line.

Synthetic Cubism The second phase of Cubism, which emphasized the form of the object and constructing rather than disintegrating that form.

Synthetism Gauguin's theory of art, which advocated the use of broad areas of unnatural color and primitive or symbolic subject matter.

Telephoto lens A lens that is shaped and distanced from the photosensitive surface so that it produces large images of distant objects.

Tempera A kind of painting in which pigments are mixed with casein, size, or egg—particularly egg yolk—to create a dull finish.

Tenebrism A style of painting in which the artist goes rapidly from highlighting to deep shadow, using very little modeling.

Tensile strength The degree to which a material can withstand being stretched.

Terra-cotta A hard, reddish brown earthenware used in sculpture and pottery; usually left unglazed.

Tertiary colors Colors derived from mixing pigments or primary colors and the secondary colors that adjoin them on the color wheel.

Texture The surface character of materials as experienced by the sense of touch.

Texture gradient The relative roughness of nearby and distant objects in two-dimensional media; nearby objects are usually rendered with more detailed and rougher surfaces than distant objects.

Tholos In architecture, a beehive-shaped tomb.

Throwing (a pot) In ceramics, the process of shaping that takes place on the potter's wheel.

Tie-dyeing Making designs by sewing or tying folds in cloth to prevent a dye from reaching certain areas.

Tier A row or rank.

Tint The lightness of a color as determined by the extent of its mixture with white.

Transept The "arms" of a *Latin cross plan*, used by pilgrims and other visitors for access to the area behind the crossing square.

Transverse rib In architecture, a rib that connects the midpoints of a *groin vault*.

Tribune gallery In architecture, the space between the *nave* arcade and the *clerestory* that is used for traffic above the side aisles on the second stage of the elevation.

Triforium In a church, a gallery or arcade in the wall above the arches of the *nave*, *transept*, or *choir*.

Triglyph In architecture, a panel incised with vertical grooves (usually three; hence, *triglyph*) that serve to divide the scenes in a *Doric frieze*.

Trompe l'oeil A painting or other art form that creates such a realistic image that the viewer may wonder whether it is real or an illusion (from French for "fool the eye").

Truss A rigid, triangular frame used for supporting structures such as roofs and bridges.

Twill weave A weave with broken diagonal patterns.

Two-point perspective Linear perspective in which two vanishing points are placed on the horizon line.

Tympanum Semicircular space above the doors of a cathedral.

Typography The art of designing, arranging, and setting type for printing.

Umber A kind of earth that has a yellowish or reddish brown color.

Unity The oneness or wholeness of a work of art.

Upper Paleolithic The later years of the Old Stone (Paleolithic) Age.

Value The lightness or darkness of a color.

Value contrast The degrees of difference between shades of gray.

Vanishing point In linear perspective, a point on the horizon where parallel lines appear to converge.

Vantage point The actual or apparent spot from which a viewer observes an object or picture.

Vault In architecture, any series of arches other than an *arcade* used to create space. See *barrel vault* and *groin vault*.

Vehicle A liquid such as water or oil with which pigments are mixed for painting.

Veneer In architecture, a thin layer of high-quality material used to enhance the appearance of the facade of a structure.

Venus The Roman goddess of beauty; a prehistoric fertility figure, such as the Venus of Willendorf.

Venus pudica A Venus with her hand held over her genitals for modesty.

Vertical balance Balance in which the elements in the top and bottom of the composition are in balance.

Video A catch-all term for several arts that use a video screen or monitor, including, but not limited to, commercial and public television, *video art*, and *computer graphics*.

Video art Works that use a video screen or an assemblage of screens or monitors; images shown on video monitors.

Visible light That segment of the spectrum of electromagnetic energy that excites the eyes and produces visual sensations.

Visitation In Roman Catholicism, the visit of the Virgin Mary to Elizabeth; a church feast commemorating the visit.

Visual elements Elements, such as line, shape, color, and texture, that are used by artists to create imagery. Also termed *plastic elements*.

Visual texture Simulated texture in a work of art; the use of line, color, and other visual elements to create the illusion of various textures in flat drawings and paintings. Contrast with *abstract texture*.

Visual unity The unity in a work of art as created by use of visual elements. Contrast with *conceptual unity*.

Vitrify To become hard, glassy, and nonporous.

Volume The mass or bulk of a three-dimensional work; the amount of space such a work contains.

Volute In architecture, a spiral scroll ornamenting an Ionic or Corinthian capital.

Volute krater A wide-mouthed vessel (krater) with scroll-shaped handles.

Voussoir A wedge-shaped stone block used in the construction of an arch.

Ware Pottery or porcelain; a good to be sold by a merchant.

Warm color Colors—reds, oranges, and yellows—that appear to be warm and to advance toward the viewer. Contrast with *cool colors*.

Warp In weaving, the threads that run lengthwise in a loom and are crossed by the weft or woof.

Wash A thin, watery film of paint, especially watercolor, applied with even, sweeping movements of the brush.

Watercolor A paint with a water medium. Watercolors are usually made by mixing pigments with a gum binder and thinning the mixture with water.

Weaving The making of fabrics by the interlacing of threads or fibers, as on a loom.

Webbing In architecture, a netlike structure that composes that part of a ribbed vault that lies between the ribs.

Weft In weaving, the yarns that are carried back and forth across the warp. Also called *woof*.

Weight-shift principle The situating of the human figure so that the legs and hips are turned in one direction and the chest and arms in another. This shifting of weight results in a diagonal balancing of tension and relaxation. See *contrapposto*.

Wide-angle lens A lens that covers a wider angle of view than an ordinary lens.

Woodcut Relief printing in which the grain of a wooden matrix is carved with a knife.

Wood engraving A type of relief printing in which a hard, laminated, nondirectional wood surface is used as the matrix.

Woof See *weft*.

Wordwork A contemporary work of art whose imagery consists of words.

Zen A Buddhist sect that seeks inner harmony through introspection and meditation.

Ziggurat A temple tower in the form of a terraced pyramid, built by ancient Assyrians and Babylonians.

Zoogyroscope An early motion-picture projector.

Zoom To use a zoom lens, which can be adjusted to provide long shots or close-ups while keeping the image in focus.

INDEX